A LIBRARY OF LITERARY CRITICISM

A Library
of Literary Criticism

MODERN MYSTERY, FANTASY AND SCIENCE FICTION WRITERS

Compiled and edited by
Bruce Cassiday

A Frederick Ungar Book
CONTINUUM • NEW YORK

1993

The Continuum Publishing Company
370 Lexington Avenue
New York, NY 10017

Printed in the United States of America

Library of Congress Cataloging-in-Publication Data

Modern mystery, fantasy and science fiction writers / compiled and
    edited by Bruce Cassiday.
        p.   cm. — (A Library of literary criticism)
    "A Frederick Ungar Book."
    Includes bibliographical references and index.
    ISBN 0-8264-0573-8
    1. Fiction—20th century—History and criticism.   2. Detective and
mystery stories—History and criticism.   3. Fantastic fiction—
    History and criticism.   4. Science fiction—History and criticism.
    I. Cassiday, Bruce. II. Series.
    PN3503.M526   1993
    809.3'87—dc20   92-33859
                                            CIP

CONTENTS

INTRODUCTION

Genre authors in the fields of mystery, fantasy, and science fiction have long been overlooked in reference works of modern criticism. Yet critiques in popular periodicals, scholarly journals, and books have been remarkably comprehensive.

Historically, the modern mystery had its origins in the American works of Edgar Allan Poe, was developed by the English writer Arthur Conan Doyle, and popularized by Agatha Christie and Dorothy L. Sayers in England, and Dashiell Hammett and Raymond Chandler in America. Representatives of today's modern practitioners are P. D. James, Sue Grafton, Sara Paretsky, Elmore Leonard, Ed McBain, and Robert B. Parker, to cite only a few. Science fiction and fantasy writing originated in France with the works of Jules Verne, was developed by H. G. Wells, H. P. Lovecraft, and others up through the durable works of Ray Bradbury, Ursula K. Le Guin, Stanislaw Lem, Margaret Atwood, and Stephen King.

Certain nineteenth-century authors are included in *Modern Mystery, Fantasy and Science Fiction Writers* to show roots and basic literary elements involved. But the bulk of the volume, like others in A Library of Literary Criticism, concentrates on twentieth-century writers prominently displayed in libraries and bookstores today. More than eighty-five authors are included in this survey.

Unlike others in the series, this volume represents a new dimension, inasmuch as it features genre works exclusively, deliberately departing from the traditional procedure of concentration on authors involved in mainstream literary efforts. One generally underestimated advantage of genre writing is the ability of its practitioners to reflect accurately and perceptively the moral values and attitudes of their contemporary world, since genre works tend to hold a true and unflawed mirror up to life as it is seen by the general reader.

All reviews and critiques have been carefully selected for readability and sense, with a majority reprinted verbatim, and others only slightly edited. When extensive segments have been omitted, ellipses are usually provided. The reader is enjoined to consult the original article or book for more detailed discussion. For that reason, sources of all reviews and critiques are clearly indicated in user-friendly terms for further study. (A handful of excerpts are written for reference works shortly scheduled for publication, and therefore appear here for the first time.)

Most of the excerpts in this volume are in chronological order within each section. I have sometimes deviated from this pattern, however, when an excerpt—often of fairly recent authorship—serves to introduce the reader in some important way to the career of the writer under consideration.

This volume is intended as a reference tool for school, library, or home—for the perusal of scholars and students, as well as browsers. A select bibliography is appended, listing the works mentioned in the accompanying critical excerpts. The reader is reminded, of course, that his or her understanding can only be accomplished when the work itself is considered in conjunction with its criticism.

In a few instances, important critical excerpts have been omitted because of problems in securing permission from copyright holders. Several other critiques are excerpted briefly because of publishers' wordage limitations. The editor and publisher wish to express their gratitude to the numerous publishers and copyright holders who made this book possible by granting permission to use quotations from their publications.

Sincere appreciation is in order for the staff of the Southwestern Connecticut Library Council, a cooperative organization of school, academic, public, and special libraries, and the High School Librarians of Fairfield County for their invaluable contribution in assessing the strengths and special qualities of contemporary writers in the mystery, fantasy, and science fiction genres. From them and others, a picture of the popularity of specific authors in the field of genre practitioners was obtained.

Access to the extensive resources of the Ferguson Library in Stamford is acknowledged with particular gratitude.

Thanks are due in a major way to my wife Doris, whose long association with Connecticut libraries and library organizations gave me important entree to the library community.

And finally, I would like to thank Evander Lomke, my editor at Continuum, who spearheaded this project from its inception through all its exhausting profundities to its eventual publication. Through all phases of publication he was there to lend a helping hand, to suggest an interesting nuance, to referee a difficult decision. The volume is, essentially, a tribute to his imagination, diligence, and editorial acumen.

                                                                B.C.

AUTHORS INCLUDED

Adams, Douglas
Ambler, Eric
Anderson, Poul
Anthony, Piers
Asimov, Isaac
Atwood, Margaret
Ballard, J.G.
Barnard, Robert
Bentley, E. C.
Block, Lawrence
Bradbury, Ray
Brett, Simon
Burgess, Anthony
Cain, James M.
Čapek, Karel
Carr, John Dickson
Chandler, Raymond
Chesterton, G. K.
Christie, Agatha
Clark, Mary Higgins
Clarke, Arthur C.
Collins, Wilkie
Crichton, Michael
Cross, Amanda
Davis, Dorothy Salisbury
Deighton, Len
Delany, Samuel R.
Doyle, Arthur Conan
Du Maurier, Daphne
Dürrenmatt, Friedrich
Francis, Dick
Gardner, Erle Stanley
Gilbert, Michael
Grafton, Sue
Greene, Graham
Hammett, Dashiell
Heinlein, Robert
Herbert, Frank

Hesse, Hermann
Highsmith, Patricia
Hillerman, Tony
Himes, Chester
Hoch, Edward D.
Huxley, Aldous
Innes, Michael
James, P. D.
Kafka, Franz
King, Stephen
le Carré, John
Le Guin, Ursula K.
Leiber, Fritz
Lem, Stanislaw
Leonard, Elmore
Lessing, Doris
Lewis, C. S.
Lovecraft, H. P.
McBain, Ed
McCaffrey, Anne
MacDonald, John D.
Macdonald, Ross
Marsh, Ngaio
Millar, Margaret
Muller, Marcia
Orwell, George
Paretsky, Sara
Parker, Robert B.
Poe, Edgar Allan
Pronzoni, Bill
Pynchon, Thomas
Queen, Ellery
Rendell, Ruth
Rinehart, Mary Roberts
Sayers, Dorothy L.
Simenon, Georges
Sjöwall and Wahlöö
Stout, Rex

Strugatsky, Arkadi and Boris
Sturgeon, Theodore
Tey, Josephine
Tolkien, J. R. R.
Twain, Mark
Van Dine, S. S.

Verne, Jules
Vonnegut, Kurt, Jr.
Waugh, Hillary
Wells, H. G.
Westlake, Donald E.
Whitney, Phyllis

ADAMS, DOUGLAS (1952–   )

In *The Hitchhiker's Guide*—a sardonically funny exercise in galactic globe-trotting—they hurtled through space. Here, they also speed through time—finally reaching Milliways, the fabled "Restaurant at the End of the Universe," an ultra-chic eatery boasting "lavatory facilities for all of fifty major life-forms" and laying on apocalypse as cabaret, since it is situated at the closing moments of the cosmos (for those who want to go to the opposite extreme, there is the Big Bang Burger Bar).

Not that Adams's characters spend much time eating. As usual, they are propelled through a series of interplanetary adventures. . . .

What makes this book, like its predecessor, almost impossible to put down is its surreal, comic creativity. Adams's galaxy blazes with spectacular phenomena like binary sunrises, and swarms with highly colored worlds—like Golgafrincham, a planet "rich in legend, red, and occasionally green with the blood of those who sought in days gone by to conquer her."

To fabricate it, he has taken hints from Lewis Carroll and Edward Lear: there are logical extensions of mad premises, grotesque creatures with crazily evocative names, chattering objects, moments of satiric farce, and picturesquely absurd landscapes. The tone, though—this is often wise-guy sci-fi—owes a lot to Raymond Chandler (one of Arthur's big regrets after the Earth's destruction was that all the Bogart movies had been wiped). In the previous book, the chunky Vogon ships "hung in the sky in much the same way that bricks don't." Here, there are snappy bouts of repartee: the droning robot is snubbed with the line, "Stay out of this, Marvin . . . this is organism talk."

Finally, the book comes down to earth—or, in any rate, to a replica of it being repopulated by detritus from another planet: ad-men, middle-management consultants and the like. It's not the best of maneuvres since it means that Adams's weakness—a sporadic tendency to Monty Pythonesque silliness—is given too much scope, while his genially weird inventiveness rather goes into abeyance. But for most of the book, the characters zoom exuberantly through other worlds.

Peter Kemp. *The Listener*. December 18 and 25,
1980, p. 866

Hot Black Desiato has made so much money out of ear-shattering plutonium rock music that he is having to spend a year dead for tax reasons. Gargravarr is a man whose mind and body have agreed to live apart on the grounds of incompatibility. And here again, bleep bleep hooray, is Marvin the Paranoid

Android robot, who manages to look permanently lugubrious, as far as it is possible for something with a totally metal face to show self-pity.

In short, and indeed in prolixity, chums, *The Restaurant at the End of the Universe* is the sequel to *The Hitchhiker's Guide to the Galaxy,* which has attracted a cult even among those normally impervious to the mechanical charms of science fiction. A summary of the plot would read like case notes of a nervous breakdown. Here be further adventures of Ford Prefect and his companions with odd numbers of heads in the highways and byways of the Universe. It is not *le silence eternel* of these infinite spaces that terrifies, but the incessant smart-aleck chatter of creatures like the nastier plastic things that come out of cornflake packets. Put your analyst on danger money, baby, before you read this.

It is a space *1066 and All That* crossed with *Alice in Wonderland* and *Gulliver's Travels,* best read after a Pan Galactic Gargle Blaster slug of the universal hooch, Jynnan Toenick. Jonathan Swift in *Gulliver's Travels* satirized contemporary politics. Adams has fun with the trendy manners of our time, from worship of the motor car to jogging, and from the pedantry of committee meetings, Point of Order Madam Chairperson, to religious enthusiasm and, engagingly, science fiction itself. All whimsy is the Beeblebrox; and the ark ship in space is full of deep-frozen middle management men sent to colonize another planet for their own planet's good. . . .

The Man who rules the Universe turns out to be a solipsist linguistic philosopher who believes in nobody else, except, thank heavens, his ginger cat. The travelers come to rest on a primitive planet that turns out to be prehistoric Earth, so becoming their own ancestors. Science fiction I can usually take, or preferably leave. But if this does not make you laugh, gee you guys are so unhip, it's a wonder your bums don't fall off.

Philip Howard. *London Times.* February 7, 1981,

p. 9

The hitchhikers in *The Restaurant at the End of the Universe* are searching for a perfect cup of tea and for a question, the answer of which is 42. They blunder onto one absurd situation after another, such as the Restaurant of the title, which is located in space and time at the very end of the universe. It is a nightclub that offers its guests the opportunity to watch the universe come to an end as floor-show entertainment every evening at the same time. Reminiscent of Stanislaw Lem's writing (without his underlying seriousness) and of Kurt Vonnegut's science fiction, it is both an entertaining, silly story and a successful satire of the worst of science fiction novels. As a sequel to *The Hitchhiker's Guide to the Galaxy,* it maintains the disrespectful, crazy tone and should be popular.

Claudia Morner. *School Library Journal.* April 15,

1982, p. 87

Humor is not that rare a quality in science fiction, but Douglas Adams's contribution to future mock must surely be unique: he violates science fiction taboos while at the same time and quite obviously regarding them with deep affection: you only hurt the genre you love. He is a treasure and science fictioneers should place a preservation order upon him.

Life, the Universe, and Everything, his latest guide to such spatial hitchhikers as everymanic Arthur Dent, the insufferable Ford Prefect, and guru Slartibartfast has them saving the Galaxy from the revived Krikkit robots and their kind. The game of flanneled fools, you will be interested to know, is a racial memory of a previous, horrendous galactic war. And that is the kind of joke—the combining of domestic detail with far-out concepts—that Mr. Adams makes with such skill; his anticlimaxes scatter our preconceptions like so many stumps.

There is a serious undertow to all this, of course, a Vonnegut-appreciation of the universe's futility which allows Mr. Adams to slip in some moments of sly terror so that the smile freezes on our face like ancient winter. But what with a talking mattress, a spaceship powered by Italian-bistro power and polluted time-streams, we are soon laughing again. Like a stricken Ford Prefect all it needs is ''a strong drink and a peer-group'' to bring us round.

Tom Hutchinson. London Times. September 9,
1982, p. 7

It is probable that no one will enjoy *Life, the Universe and Everything* as much as its predecessors. Once you expect the unexpected, it is no longer unexpected, and that which is startling and amusing only as long as it remains surprising cannot endure being spun out into trilogies. The books, in any case, cannot be as funny as the radio show: the dialogue of Marvin the paranoid android, for instance, is pretty dull in print but a real scream when rendered in a magnificently morose (and electronically distorted) voice. Then again, this third volume gives way more than the second (and much more than the first) to the inherent gloominess of Adams's temperament. His irony was always bitter, underlaid—and, indeed, fueled—by the supposition that things can and must not only go wrong, but go wrong in the most grotesque possible fashion, that being what you'd expect of our kind of universe. The answer to the riddle of life, the universe, and everything is 42, largely because by the time you get to that age (because you're as young as you feel, some people reach it much earlier than others, including Douglas Adams, who is only thirty) you know perfectly well that it doesn't matter a damn whether the riddle has an answer or not, or whether there's a riddle at all. Personally, I appreciate Adams's work, but can't really get all that enthusiastic about it because I've been ninety-two since I was fifteen and there's nothing he can tell me about the awful ways of the infinitely silly universe.

Brian Stableford. Science Fiction & Fantasy Book
Review. March 1983, pp. 19–20

AMBLER, ERIC (1909–   )

Eric Ambler's first novel, *The Dark Frontier,* was far from being one of his best books, but it marked a revolutionary, disillusioned approach to the spy story, particularly reflected in what one of the characters, Professor Bairstow, had to say: "It looked as if there would always be wars. What else could you expect from a balance of power adjusted in terms of land, of arms, of manpower and of materials: in terms, in other words, of Money? Wars were made by those who had the power to upset the balance, to tamper with international money and money's worth."

Ambler sounded the death-knell of the Hannays and the "Bulldog" Drummonds. He had begun to write in a period of intense depression for all thinking people who, in the 1930s, realized the hollowness of the politicians' pretense that the First World War was "the war to end all wars." Aggressive forces were on the march all over Europe and in the Balkans, democracy was being spelled out as a dirty word, and the private manufacture of arms was aiding the enemies of democracy rather more than the countries who actually produced the weapons. Ambler struck a note of neutralism in the spy story, sharply and astringently enlightening the reader that in espionage one side was really as bad as the other and that spies and spy-catchers were not only mainly unheroic, but very often of minor significance and unpleasant mien. In short, the agents and spies were not splendid patriots, but hired killers. Ambler was not a prophet in a didactic sense, but his stories of espionage revealed the truth and obliterated the romance. *The Uncommon Danger* had much the same message as *The Dark Frontier.*

With *Epitaph for a Spy* Ambler came into his own as a highly skilled, thoughtful, realistic, and meticulous writer of spy stories. He had done his homework on the spy story and was determined to modernize and improve the genre. Many years later, in his introduction to *To Catch a Spy,* he revealed that his research into the realms of spy fiction went back to Erskine Childers.

More recently, when commenting on a review in the *Times Literary Supplement* which said that all of Ambler's earlier books were influenced by the Ashenden ethos, he replied that they were indeed: "The breakthrough was entirely Mr. Maugham's. There is, after all, a lot of Simenon and a satisfactory quantity of W. R. Burnett, but only one *Ashenden.*"

Perhaps this is one reason why Ambler is a favorite writer of professional intelligence agents all over the world. While le Carré is the preferred reading of members of the British SIS and Len Deighton has his devotees in America, Ambler undoubtedly wins adherents in the "spook" community all over the world. He has the gift of making a commonplace incident seem dramatic and horrifying. What is even more important, Ambler is the most admirable exponent of the probable and the possible as against the improbable and the miraculous coincidence. It is one of the paradoxes of spy fiction that the "in writers"—i.e., those who have had inside knowledge of "the game"—tend to write about the improbable rather more than those authors who have never in any way been engaged in intelligence work. Ambler belongs to the latter category and it is surprisingly but nevertheless recognizably true that he has been far and away the most accurate of all modern spy fiction writers right down to the smallest detail. In all Ambler's books the chain of circumstances is rational and probable, his leading characters are ordinary, cautious people who find themselves caught up in disastrous situations. The detail is faultless, yet Ambler, as far as one knows, was never employed by the Secret Service or any similar organization.

In *Epitaph for a Spy* Ambler introduced a political element into his work. Even here he was being factual—and singularly prophetic, hinting at the possible emergence of defectors like Philby, someone such as Schimmler who is converted from being a moderate Social Democrat to a Communist. This is echoed again in *Cause for Alarm* and *Dimitrios,* in the latter of which there are objective and not unpleasant portraits of a Greek Communist and a Soviet agent. This would have been unheard of in the Buchan-"Sapper"-Le Queux era: had any author then described a Soviet agent as one who could spare the time to do a good turn to someone who had got into trouble through no fault of his own, he would undoubtedly have been dubbed as a fellow-traveler. But such was Ambler's skill and objectivity, his freedom from any hint of propaganda or prejudice and his talent for telling a lively story, that he was never challenged on this account, but only welcomed as a long-needed antidote to the old school of spy thriller writers.

Ambler also chose a different type of capital city for the setting for his books. Whereas hitherto such stories tended to be set in Paris, Berlin, Vienna, and Rome, or the smarter hotels of the Riviera, Ambler chose the seedier, but more topical and infinitely more fascinating cities of Istanbul, Belgrade, Sofia. *Dimitrios,* which in many respects is Ambler's masterpiece, opens with the discovery in a mortuary of the dead body of Dimitrios. With consummate craftsmanship, the author uses the lecturer and detective-writer, Latimer, to trace the life story of the mysterious Dimitrios. The minor characters are superbly drawn and full of interest in themselves.

After the war when the USSR and the Western Allies turned sour on one another and the Cold War began, Ambler's "neutral" approach to spy fiction became a little dated. Nevertheless, the quality of Ambler's work still compares well with anything that has been written since.

Donald McCormick and Katy Fletcher. *Spy Fiction: A Connoisseur's Guide* (New York: Facts on File, 1990), pp. 19, 20

Eric Ambler has not only given the spy-and-intrigue story new life in its own right in recent years; he has brought it close to a legitimate marriage with detection. "Streamlined" is an overworked word, but that is virtually what Ambler has done for the intrigue novel, replacing its stereotyped clichés

and slinky females in black velvet with skillful plot work and characterization and believable human beings. Furthermore, though there is ample physical action, cerebration is for once as important as shooting, and the two are
blended together with neatness and credibility. *Background to Danger* (1937)
was the first Ambler novel to be published in the United States (his first
English publication occurred a year earlier), but it was not until the memorable *Coffin for Dimitrios* (1939) that he really came into his own with the
discriminating readers who are now his devoted clientele. . . . The mood
of subtle understatement which he established seems already to have found
an echo in such superior works as Manning Coles's *Drink to Yesterday* and
Toast to Tomorrow and David Keith's *A Matter of Iodine,* as well as in the
sudden interest of so many of the erstwhile orthodox English fictional sleuths
in espionage. If Ambler's own work is still a little (but only a little) removed
from bona fide detection, it is not too much to think that he has opened up
a fresh avenue of development for the form proper. . . . Though he is still
a young man in his early thirties, Eric Ambler has already enjoyed a varied
and colorful career.

Howard Haycraft. *Murder for Pleasure: The Life
and Times of the Detective Story* (New York: Biblo
and Tannen, 1968), pp. 205–6

Not until Eric Ambler began writing in the late thirties did any degree of
sophistication about the powers of darkness enter the thriller. And even then
his perspective is, from our point of view, rhetorical and simplistic. It is in
Background to Danger that torture makes its delayed entrance into the spy
story. Ambler's books reflect the stages of contemporary conflict, from the
early days of Fascism and Nazism to the cold war.

In *Background to Danger* also Ambler displays for the first time in
thriller literature a critical attitude toward capitalism. . . . Earlier thriller
writers would have castigated Ambler's insistence that "at some point in the
business structure there is always dirty work to be done" [*Background to
Danger*]. "International business may conduct its operations with scraps of
paper, but the ink it uses is human blood" [*The Mask of Dimitrios*]. Ambler
himself was a little ashamed of such emotionalism. Nevertheless, Ambler's
antipathy toward Big Business was consistently expressed in novel after novel,
and he shared the view of young English intellectuals in the late thirties that
"political ideologies had very little to do with the ebb and flow of international relations. It was the power of business" [*Background to Danger*].

Ralph Harper. *The World Thriller* (The Press of
Case Western Reserve University, 1969),
pp. 32–34

A Coffin for Dimitrios contains two interwoven narratives, one devoted to a
quest and the other about the object of the quest, Dimitrios himself. The
quester is Charles Latimer, who becomes fascinated by Dimitrios after learn-

ing about him at the time of his apparent death in 1938. Latimer's informant in Istanbul is the head of the Turkish secret police, Colonel Haki, who outlines Dimitrios's life of crime and shows Latimer what is believed to be his corpse. Latimer then proceeds to pursue a wayward path around Asia Minor and Europe, virtually retracing Dimitrios's steps since the 1920s in order to piece together his extraordinary life story. This journey of discovery in 1938 is simultaneously a journey into the past, as Latimer consults old records in Smyrna and Athens, and interviews former colleagues and acquaintances of Dimitrios in Sofia, Geneva, and Paris.

Although Latimer is the central consciousness, Ambler's use of third-person narration puts a frame around him, so that the reader is partly distanced from him while also involved in his quest. It is important for Ambler's purpose to insist on Latimer's limited understanding of what is at stake, the difference between what he thinks he is doing and what he has inadvertently stumbled upon.

By making Latimer a successful writer of detective stories in the classical English mold, Ambler introduces another new dimension into his fiction. *A Coffin for Dimitrios* is partly a novel about a novelist. . . .

The nature of fiction is a pervasive theme from the opening, when Haki reveals himself to be a devotee of *romans policiers.*

In discussing Dimitrios, Haki emphasizes the distinction between the messiness of life and the highly formalized patterns of detective fiction ("Everything must be tidy, artistic") in order to undercut Latimer's desire to impose a logic and even a moral scheme on events so as to transform them into a conventional narrative. For Haki, the story of Dimitrios ("Incomplete. Inartistic. No detection, no suspects, no hidden motives, merely sordid") defies fictional treatment, like all real-life stories. Even at the outset of his quest Latimer accuses himself of "being a fool" for undertaking "this fantastic and slightly undignified wild goose chase."

The inadequacy of Latimer's viewpoint is most apparent in Ambler's ironic, even sardonic, ending, especially in comparison with Latimer's initial enthusiasm to conduct an investigation into Dimitrios's activities. The prospect of "an experiment in detection" to compile "the strangest of biographies" lures Latimer into the dark underside of contemporary Europe, but he finally retreats from the real world. . . . Latimer's concluding flight into the make-believe world of his fiction can be interpreted as Ambler's bitter comment on the naïveté and blindness of the English intelligentsia in the face of the fascist threat. The last sentence of the novel, "The train ran into a tunnel," is pertinent to Latimer's condition because what he possesses is tunnel vision. By burying his head in the sand, he is making his contribution to Europe's metaphorical rush into the darkness of a tunnel at the end of the 1930s. . . .

The distance Ambler puts between himself and the conventional thriller is most conspicuous in his replacement of an adventure plot with a narrative oscillating between past and present. Furthermore Ambler discards the usual mechanics of suspense by providing as early as the second chapter a résumé of Dimitrios's career from 1922 until his apparent death in 1938, as it is known to the Turkish authorities. Haki's dossier on Dimitrios covers most of the key events, so that Latimer's quest is not into unknown territory but into what has already been revealed in outline. What Latimer's travels add to the bare bones is the flesh covering them, the full story.

By eschewing the fast-moving, sequential action of the standard thriller, Ambler is able to concentrate much more on giving depth to his memorable assortment of characters: the minor ones as well as the three principals, Latimer, Dimitrios, and Peters.

Nevertheless Ambler does not totally dispense with the thriller ingredients of adventure, suspense, and melodrama. Latimer's quest is a kind of adventure, and the early hints in Smyrna and Athens that he is not the only person interested in Dimitrios's past add genuine thriller frissons, as does the subsequent revelation that Peters is pursuing Latimer because of what he may know about Dimitrios. The narrative shifts towards a thriller denouement when Latimer reaches Paris and realizes that the body he saw in Istanbul was not that of Dimitrios but of Visser, one of his drug-running associates. With his usual ingenuity Dimitrios has simultaneously disposed of the threat posed by Visser and made the murder look like his own death so as to protect his new identity by severing it completely from his past. Latimer immediately sees his quest in a new light, not as the gathering of facts about a fascinatingly evil man now safely dead, but as the inadvertent pursuit of a ruthless supercriminal very much "alive and in good health" as Peters puts it. . . .

Although Dimitrios's story emerges in fragmentary form, it gradually coheres into a portrait of the criminal as a successful capitalist. Beginning with an unspecified police record in Greece, Dimitrios has tried his hand at most illegal activities on a progressively larger scale: robbery and murder in Smyrna (for which another man was executed), blackmail and pimping in Sofia, attempted assassinations in various parts of Europe, espionage, international drug running, and the white slave trade on a global scale. A feature of his career has been his complete lack of qualms about double-crossing and betraying his associates. Of necessity Dimitrios has had to transform his identity frequently, discarding his own Greek surname of Makropoulos for Talat (Turkish and Moslem), Taladis (Greek and Christian), von Kiessling (German), Rougement (French), and C. K. (indeterminate European). A man of many masks, Dimitrios finally achieves his apotheosis as a wealthy, respectable businessman with a villa in an exclusive part of Cannes and a seat on the board of directors of a shadowy international bank based in Monaco, the Eurasian Credit Trust. . . .

Despite his failings Latimer is capable of insight, most conspicuously in his recognition that Dimitrios symbolizes the new brutality and counter-civilization unleashed by a fusion of monopolistic capitalism and fascist politics, and that Dimitrios and Hitler consequently belong in the same camp. . . .

Although Ambler does not [specifically] draw parallels between Dimitrios and Hitler and may not even have been conscious of them when writing the novel, they are too numerous to be coincidental. Both were born in 1889; both began to attract attention in the early 1920s; both were involved in political coups in 1923, the date of Hitler's attempted putsch in Munich; both achieved outward respectability and positions of power in the early 1930s in spite of their murky activities; and both interfered in the affairs of other countries in the later 1930s. In this sense Dimitrios is Hitler's shadow or doppelgänger. Hitler did not, of course, follow Dimitrios into a coffin in 1938 but survived for another seven years, during which the ''logic'' of *Mein Kampf* was catastrophically imposed on Europe.

Peter Lewis. Eric Ambler (New York: Ungar,
1990), pp. 63–73

In Ambler, values and loyalties are determined easily—by brutality and by responses to brutality. The kinds of brutality are varied but eventually lead to a common source, so that when we ask why a man becomes involved in espionage we find that economic pressure is one strong arm of a system whose other strong arm is physical brutality. The reaction away from brutality sets a character on the side of right and good. There is no ideology about it. These are political and economic novels but they are something else first. Before they are socialist realism they are democratic realism and before that they are romances.

In Ambler's third novel for example, *Cause for Alarm,* the forces of brutality trap the nonbrutal and helpless Marlow. Events are beyond his control. Determinism is a staple of the genre, and Ambler's people, the good and the bad both, are at the mercy of forces that push them about the European landscape like pawns in a game. Conflict comes from the protagonist's awareness of the push and his stubborn unwillingness to be pushed. Opposing force and violence is the individual will, strength, and integrity. The nearest tradition is the romance although Ambler's knight is often inept and is not even a professional knight. He becomes knightly through something like battlefield promotion, pushed into it unwillingly by circumstances. He is always the innocent bystander whose innate distaste and dislike for barbarism and bullies, violence, coercion, and inhuman weapons push him to opposition. Even this response is a force beyond his control, for what it turns out to be is the human spirit, desiring to be free and to allow others to be free, working through the good man and showing through as the element that makes him good. Put another way, man *is* free. And while he can not always control destiny the view is that each man plays his part in shaping the historical context. Reduced to its elements, the espionage and intrigue story is a contest of Good and Evil, with the Good winning out in its curious way: the more brutal the Evil, the more danger of provoking a crushing response from the Good. It is the pre-World War II morality play, and the protagonist is liberty against the antagonist fascism and tyranny.

Because force in Ambler's world is ultimately purely human, the real villains are not the strongarm operators like Mailler and Saridza in *Background to Danger* or the Italian Ovra hoods in *Cause for Alarm* but the avarice and social irresponsibility of the great banking houses and corporations seeking foreign trade concessions. Marlow and Kenton, the protagonists of *Background to Danger,* harried by the greed of others which has completely wiped them clean financially, do what they do to stay alive. There again is the spirit that works in them, that life force carrying with it a few simple (Conradian) notions of loyalty and fidelity, virtue, right.

After force has been applied, the free spirit reacts, recoils, and charges itself with reestablishing the fitness of things. It is a private sense of personal code, not so much of ethics as of propriety; of what can and can not be *done to* an individual rather than a code of what he can or can not do. It is always committed to in physical reaction to provocation, and never in analytic judgement, because it is due to outrages on the body. The heart tells the head. That puts us back in romance with its mistrust of intellect, reason, ideology, rules, all of these evils enlisting in the army of Greed; for, paradoxically, every reasoning moment leads to selfishness and gorging self-gratification. The heart has its reasons and the heart, always in the right place, is the place of liberty.

Ambler's philosophical drift is similar in each book. The criminal spies are all creatures whose code is expedience, and doing one's job because somebody has to do it, without looking into things, is evil. . . . Ambler reduces the world at war to an elemental, man to man level of battle. The moral clearly is: arise before it is too late to rise at all.

Robert Gillespie. Salmagundi. Summer 1970,
pp. 46–48

When Eric Ambler's most recent novel, *The Levanter,* appeared, I grumbled that nothing *happened* until page 80, a poor showing for a suspense story. It seems I missed Ambler's drift: in his new novel, *Dr. Frigo,* nothing happens until page 240. Ambler is going straight now (his publisher suggests that we start taking him seriously as a political novelist), and we all know that straight fiction doesn't require the lashings of fear and muscle that made Ambler's early stories famous. Talk and politics will do instead, with lashings of local color. . . .

Ambler is generous with authentic-sounding medical detail and precise observations of Caribbean islands, and it seems to me that if you can stand the boredom you may find much in this story that is skillfully performed.

The boredom will not inhibit *Doctor Frigo's* reception—most hugely popular novels are hugely boring—but it is fatal to the book's posture as serious political fiction. Political novels are difficult to write because political events, so fascinating in real life, are distracting in fiction except as catalysts of theme or character. (This is why some of the best have the narrowest focus: C. P. Snow's *The Masters,* set in a college, is a better political novel than is his *Corridors of Power,* which concerns the national government.) Political novels, until further notice, are stories about men who are unequal to occasions. Their true subjects are the effect of ambition on integrity and of power on process, of men subjected to stress that will make them squeal, of men confronted rudely by their own weakness and failure of vision. Ambler is not up to a real political novel; having written for nearly forty years suspenseful romances about men who prove less frail than first they seem, he lacks a vision of man's essential frailty.

Peter S. Prescott. *Newsweek.* October 14, 1974,

pp. 125–27

In the six novels he wrote before the outbreak of World War II, Eric Ambler . . . infused warmth and political color into the spy story by using it to express a Left Wing point of view. . . . The central character is an innocent figure mixed up in violent events who slowly comes to realize that the agents and spies working on both sides are for the most part unpleasant but not important men. They murder casually and without passion on behalf of some immense corporation or firm of armaments manufacturers whose interests are threatened. These, rather than any national group, are the enemy. *The Dark Frontier* (1936) is the least important of his books, but it contains one prophetic note in the detonation of the first atomic bomb. . . .

The political side of the books lies under the surface. Almost all the best thrillers are concerned, in one form or another, with the theme of the hunted man. Ambler was fascinated by European cities, and his hunts take place against a convincing background of places like Istanbul, Sofia, Belgrade, and Milan. He was interested also in the problems of frontiers and passports, so that the difficulty of moving from place to place plays a large part in the stories. And he showed from the beginning a high skill, which became mastery, in the construction of plot. His finest book of this period, a masterpiece of its kind, is *The Mask of Dimitrios* [in America, *A Coffin for Dimitrios*], in which flashback follows flashback in the attempt of the crime novelist Latimer to trace the career of the dead Dimitrios, and there is little direct action until three-quarters of the way through the book. To develop interest through a book composed in such a way is a mark of the highest technical skill. The story sparkles with incidents, like the interview with the retired spy, or the account of the white-slave traffic, that could be extracted as separate stories and yet continue to advance the plot. . . .

Ambler's later books are more like plain thrillers than spy stories. The best of them, *The Night Comers* (1956) [in America, *A State of Siege*], *The Light of Day* (1962), and *Dirty Story* (1967) are less sensational than some of the prewar novels, and they show the same mastery of construction. Something has been lost, however; a certain world-weariness has replaced enthusiasm and hope. They are detached from events rather than involved in them. There is much to admire and enjoy, but nothing to equal *The Mask of Dimitrios*.

> Julian Symons. *Mortal Consequences: A History—
> From the Detective Story to the Crime Novel* (New
> York: Harper & Row, 1972), pp. 238–39

Generally considered the inventor of the modern spy story, best-selling author Eric Ambler has in his twenty-second book, *The Care of Time*, delivered a cerebral tale involving a free-lance writer and a Persian Gulf sheikh who threatens world peace. Robert Halliday—a former World War II correspondent who was closely tied to the CIA—has been enlisted to serve as a negotiator between NATO and His Highness the Ruler. Readers accustomed to the fast pace of a Ludlum or a Follett may grow impatient with Ambler's more deliberate style, but *The Care of Time* is a convincing story, offering believable characters and a perceptive study of the ambiguities and dangers behind today's world order.

> Alan Moores. *Booklist*. July 1, 1981, p. 1369

Plot and counterplot have always been a part of Eric Ambler's arsenal; the surprise turn of events, the man or woman who is not at all what he or she seems, the reversal, the gradual unfolding of a conspiracy which turns our expectations around—all these Ambler has mastered from the first. But his world has never been as insidious as, say, that of the British agency in John le Carré's *The Looking Glass War* (or as riddled with insecurities and inefficiency). Despite the fact that Maas's employer has called him a psycho, that Michael Howell of *The Levanter* is a bloodless, amoral merchant egoist, that Dr. Frigo is, as his name implies, frozen meat—despite these explorations of Ambler's into more interesting characterization, he has not written about psychotics or such people as in *Black Sunday, The Wind Chill Factor, The Holcroft Covenant, The Chancellor Manuscript*, or *Marathon Man*. Man's darker side is ignored, while plot is foregrounded. Nor has Ambler been tempted by the more exquisite forms of torture his fellow writers seem to favor; very significantly, Stefan Saridza threatens Kenton with a dentist's drill when trying to intimidate him, to make him reveal the whereabouts of the papers, but it remains for William Goldman's Szell in *Marathon Man* (1974) to actually use it.

So, Ambler's postwar phase makes few concessions to the directions taken by other spy story writers. He lacks le Carré's deep questioning of clandestine agencies per se, or Len Deighton's glibness and fast-moving action. Ambler and Greene brought the spy novel a long way toward respectability. Ambler has disciplined himself in telling an engaging story of intrigue and suspense. And he has been getting better, now as he nears eighty. Greene has from the first seen the deeper implications raised by the existence of spies and their trade in an open society. He has explored the role of clandestinity in our world and has, perhaps deepest of all, scrutinized the values of loyalty and patriotism, obligation and commitment. More than any spy novelist (in his case especially, a writer who has written spy novels), Greene has returned the spy novel to the mainstream of contemporary fiction. It began as a story of adventure, moved to become a genre in its own right, and by the excellence of some of its most accomplished practitioners is moving back into the main currents of what is simply good fiction. Ambler may be, in the *San Francisco Chronicle*'s extravagant kudos, "the greatest spy novelist of all time." Greene, whose *Human Factor* revived talk of a Nobel prize (futilely), has surely given us, in the words of one reviewer, "the best espionage novel ever written." In the full context of Greene's achievement, this is modest praise.

John G. Cawelti and Bruce A. Rosenberg. *The Spy Story* (Chicago: University of Chicago Press, 1987), pp. 123–24

ANDERSON, POUL (1926–   )

Poul Anderson's beefy, beery, big-brained van Rijn, merchant adventurer extraordinary, stars in three long novelettes in *Trader to the Stars*—good ones—and proves for all time that when science fiction's sachem of swashbuckle sets out to write a story, he thinks first. He thinks clear across the spectrum . . . on micro- and macrocosmic terms. Add many a bloody fight and flight, a clear and sometimes edged view of human societies and motivations, and you have what's given Anderson his high status in the field. The long view—that is, considerations not on the biographical scale but on the historical and geological scales—is not only refreshing: it's vital. There is literally no other way in which humanity can be made to realize, and therefore made to prevent, the tragic repetition of its own errors.

Theodore Sturgeon. *National Review*. January 12, 1964, pp. 1074–75

In the five novelettes of *Operation Chaos* Poul Anderson posits an alternate Earth where magic works and is a part of everyday life, as well as of politics, warfare, medicine, the law, and, of course, religion. The hero and heroine have become the objects of special attention by the Adversary, though they seem only perfectly ordinary members of their society—he a werewolf, she a witch.

Poul's magic—his formal magic, that is—is borrowed eclectically from a good many different sources, and he has done a thorough job of making it seem an adjunct to, rather than a denial of, natural law.

In addition [to the speed of the action], the book is well populated and contains a great deal of humor; and—difficult though it is to imagine under these essentially playful circumstances—quite a lot of genuine emotion.

James Blish. *The Magazine of Fantasy and Science Fiction.* December 1971, p. 25

Poul Anderson's future in *The Enemy Stars* bears no resemblance to anything. This could be a less than admirable example of his work, for he is renowned among science fiction addicts. Although written with basic simplicity I found it very hard to understand. One is blinded by pseudoscience, then treated to rather eager statements about Man and God and the Universe.

Essentially it is the old, old story of four contrasting men trapped together in an unpromising situation. Danger lurks, escape is essential and, of course, character shows through. Anderson's trap is a vast space ship off course and magnetically fixed to a planet which is just a lump of iron.

The scientific mumbo jumbo is just not good enough to blind us to the fact that his characters are more than usually weak stereotypes—the golden youth, the cynical (but clever) older figure, the pilot who confesses himself frightened of space and so on. Were it dressed in anything but science fiction it would be naked.

Roger Baker. *Books and Bookmen.* August 1972, pp. xii–xiii

There is a basic attitude, I suppose, which underlies my writing—namely, that this is a wonderful universe in which to live, that it's great to be alive, and that all it takes is the willingness to give ourselves a chance to experience what life has to offer. If I preach at all, it's probably in the direction of individual liberty, which is a theme that looms large in my work.

But my main job is to entertain the reader and to hold his interest as best I can. I do this, primarily, by keeping the story moving. Since most stories have a basic content, though, I suppose they're bound to reflect certain philosophical overtones. And so, where I can, I try to say something that I feel is important, such as the need for additional scientific research and development.

Humor in my stories is very important. In fact, I've written several stories that were nothing more than comedy. Humor not only provides for relief, but is, after all, a significant aspect of human personality. In that sense, it's vital in most works of literature.

The idea behind my "puzzle" stories goes back to the basic format inherent in the old-fashioned mystery story, of which, incidentally, I've written a fair number. The idea is to set up the problem early on, plant a substantial number of good clues, and then let the reader have the fun of guessing the solution.

Politics is another important element in my books because it is an inherently fascinating thing in itself. It's also an integral part of life. One way or another, it's bound to show up in science fiction, particularly when you're dealing with alien societies. In the process of inventing new worlds, it's impossible not to touch on politics.

History is also very important. My whole future history series, which comprises a substantial percentage of my work, draws extensively on the past. I've used history in many of my stories. I don't see how anyone can make sense of the present, let alone construct an imaginary future that makes sense, without having some knowledge of the past.

It's conceivable that some critics are right in charging that my work reveals a blatantly chauvinistic attitude, although I certainly never intended to cast women in that light. Over the years, however, I've learned to handle characterization better, especially women characters. For a male writer, it's always more difficult to fashion female characters than it is members of his own sex. In earlier years, I tended to use comparatively few women characters, and usually not to give them leading roles in my stories. That grew out of my fear that I couldn't make then sufficiently plausible. I would like to point out, however, that in this same period, and, even earlier, I published a novel entitled, *Virgin Planet,* in which women were cast in almost heroic terms.

These days, I feel somewhat more comfortable with female characters. It's interesting, but some women have told me that my female characters tend to be so self-confident in recent works that it gives them an inferiority complex. For example, *The Dancer from Atlantis* is a novel about the kind of women I've met in recent years—strong, independent, proud. In that book, the leading character is absolutely indomitable, regardless of the situations which confront her. *The Winter of the World* depicts a society in which women assume positions of leadership and responsibility. I recently completed a novel, entitled *The Avatar,* in which two or three of the leading characters are women. In fact, one of the women is described as one of the leading intellects of her age.

Poul Anderson. Interview by Jeffrey M. Elliot.
Science Fiction Voices #2 (San Bernardino,
California: The Borgo Press, 1979), pp. 41–50

Poul Anderson deals with real issues quite often in his work, whether we agree with his conclusions or not. His first adult novel, *Brain Wave* (1954), a story of an Earth where all mammals experience increased IQ, brought Anderson early fame. He has won many Hugos and Nebulas since then, as a good writer with fannish orientation. A certain element of redskins among the stars marks Anderson's poorest work and he can seem quite inept at times: "It is Hloch of the Stormgate Choth who writes, on the peak of Mount Anrovil in the Weathermother. His Wyvan, Tariat, son of Lythran and Blawsa, has asked this. Weak though his grip upon the matter be, bloodpride requires he undertake the task." One cannot help but wish that Tariat hadn't bothered, bloodpride or not!

We may regard Anderson's attempt to sketch out a future history—from our century to the seventy-second century—as slightly futile. The future is certain to be anything but what we imagine it will be.

This aside, what is often overlooked in the welter of space operas produced by Anderson, is his ability to present a balanced argument about militarism. Among his best work is "No Truce with Kings" which counterpoints a Heinleinish bullishness—"I'd rather be dead than domesticated"—against a quite sensitive portrayal of a family ripped apart by civil war. Then there's also *Tau Zero* (1970), an enjoyable novel about the relativistic effects on the spaceship *Leonora Christine* and its crew as it approaches the speed of light and becomes as big as the universe, counterbalanced by an admittedly rather soppy love affair. The voyage through spacetime takes the ship beyond the dissolution of our universe.

Brian W. Aldiss. *Trillion Year Spree: The History
of Science Fiction* (New York: Atheneum, 1986),

p. 314

ANTHONY, PIERS (1934–   )

Anthony is at his best in *Thousandstar,* a rollicking examination of the age-old question: Is there anything more alien than the difference between male and female? Jessica of Cappela (humanoid) and Heem of Highfalls (giant alien jellyfish) discover that interspecies misunderstandings are inconsequential when compared with the cosmic differences between the sexes when, in order to be partners on a secret mission, Jessica's mind must share Heem's body. It is unthinkable, impossible, and accidental—an intersex alien mind transfer has never been accomplished before. . . . Once accomplished, it's too late to abort the mission . . . and they soon discover that their collective life hinges on the successful completion of an almost impossible task.

Anthony handles his subject with characteristic wit and aplomb, sending his hero/ines off on a series of misadventures which strip away their pretensions, expose their weaknesses, and make them more aware of and responsive to their innate cultural and sex role conflicts.

H. Sue Hurwitz. *Kliatt Young Adult Paperback
Guide*. September 1980, p. 12

Piers Anthony gave us a very nice belt in the funnybone early in his career, with *Prostho Plus*. Since then, he has moved into fairly mystical territory, telling us that intelligence, identity, and personality reside in Kirlian auras, which can be transmitted from one person to another across interstellar distances. It's a clap-trap premise, but it does allow some interesting situations—what is it like for a human to share an alien body? It also allows wide-ranging stories that duck the Einstein barrier, for . . . aural transmission is (of course) instantaneous.

And that is what we find in *Thousandstar,* a tale set in the Thousand-Star Cluster, where an artifact left behind by the mysterious Ancients has been found. Protocol demands that all interested species take part in a race to the artifact, winner to gain custody. The limits of Anthony's technology dictate that each species's specially trained representative must occupy the body of a local sapient, so that the human rep becomes a tenant of an ameboid energy-eater. However, the human, Jessica, is untrained. . . . Her host, Heem, is both a criminal and male, and the male-female pairing is supposed to be impossible. . . . Yet it happens, and Heem and Jessica find a unique *modus vivendi,* one that hinges on certain peculiarities of Jessica's aristocratic home culture, where she lacks a suitable marriage.

I've read several of Anthony's latest books, and I'm still not sure I like them. They don't grip, but they don't repel, either. What do they do? I confess perplexity. His plots are easy to summarize. . . . The complications are not, for he is given to baroquely ornamented personal histories and interactions that make his science fiction read more like fantasy. His creatures . . . and his science prove him fey. Perhaps I should simply say that, when I read him, I feel estranged. I witness the man's admittedly marvelous imagination as through a glass, darkly, with all participation in the story barred. Yet I wish for more, and I pick up each of his books in turn, hoping each time that now, finally, the glass will break. It hasn't so far, and I'm about ready to give up.

Tom Easton. *Analog Science Fiction/Science Fact.*
March 30, 1981, pp. 167–68

Juxtaposition, a work which combines both science fiction and fantasy, provides ample opportunity for Piers Anthony to demonstrate his skill in each field. . . .

This is the story of Stile, a rather diminutive but eminently resourceful individual, who as a serf on the planet Proton competes in the all-demanding Game, the ultimate prize being Citizenship with its considerable wealth. An unprovoked, mysterious attack transforms Stile's existence into a roller coaster ride of both highs and lows at breakneck speed. He then discovers a way to enter another frame of reality called Phaze, where magic is operative and the laws of physics are not. In Phaze his alternate self, a powerful image known as the Blue Adept, was murdered and Stile, though inheriting his double's mystic abilities, finds himself in mortal danger from his "own" slayers. . . .

As if he weren't busy enough, it is also swiftly approaching the time of Juxtaposition, an apocalyptic event for both worlds in which Stile is prophesied to play an essential role. At that point, the two frames are temporarily to fuse, only forever to separate—but Stile must first accomplish certain tasks to avert total disaster. Romance further complicates matters, for Stile is the beloved of a beautiful female robot, a shape-shifting unicorn/

woman, and of the magnificent Lady Blue, his own true love and the widow of his other self.

Although this all sounds too confusing, it somehow fits together and it's a lot of fun.

Paul Granahan. *Best Sellers*. July 1982,

p. 135

Piers Anthony undertakes several difficult tasks in *Viscous Circle*. First, he sets this novel against the complexity, energy, and wit of the earlier Cluster novels, *Cluster* (1978), *Chaining the Lady* (1978), *Kirlian Quest* (1978), and *Thousandstar* (1980). Second, the primary conflicts in the novel are emotional and spiritual rather than physical, resulting in extended static passages, such as an episode in which Ronald talks to himself for nearly twelve pages before dispatching a three-headed monster in three short, anticlimactic paragraphs. Third, Anthony creates an alien species, the Banda, who are almost quintessentially good—explicitly "angelic"—and have no conception of war, government, or selfishness. . . . And finally, Anthony concentrates on an essentially antihuman bias. It is one thing to show humans/ Solarians from alien perspectives, as he did in other Cluster novels; it is another, more dangerous, thing for the human to assume entirely the aliens' attitudes and commit conscious treason against his own species. . . . Utter misanthropy threatens to alienate reader from hero no matter how ideal the alternate society might be.

In addition, *Viscous Circle* seems tired. Anthony writes in an author's note that the book was "difficult when it should have been easy, and may lack that spark of wonder that is the essence of this type of writing." He is correct. The lushness of physical, verbal, and contextual invention that characterizes the first Cluster novels is here radically trimmed, chastened, muted. . . . Plot resolution is explained rather than presented. Compared with the climactic permutations in the final chapters of *Cluster* or *Chaining the Lady, Viscous Circle* seems . . . well, viscous.

Still, in spite of these barriers, the novel is a creditable job. It becomes engaging: and although Rondl/Ronald is far less interesting than Melody of Mintaka or Herald the Healer, he invites empathy. Anthony also continues the pattern of suggesting serious themes in his novels—in this case, he indicts human/Solarian greed and insensitivity. The novel opens slowly, with an amnesiac hero, but the second half is stronger and approaches more closely the intensity one associates with Anthony.

As an isolated novel *Viscous Circle* is interesting; as the latest in a long series of impressive novels . . . it seems tired. It lacks the sense of a richly embroidered tapestry, meticulously detailed and re-created, that lies at the heart of Anthony's appeal. The writing is smoother than is usual, with fewer verbal pyrotechnics, fewer ringings of variations on puns—but I think I prefer the old fire to fluidity.

Michael R. Collings. *Science Fiction & Fantasy*
Book Review. July–August 1982, pp. 17–18

Blue Adept can be read alone; but, it really would be better to read *Split Infinity* first as the author frequently refers to incidents and characters of the previous volume without enough explanation. Blue Adept in the frame of Phaze, a magical world, is Stile, a serf in the parallel frame of Proton, a world based on science. He shifts from one world to the other. As the Blue Adept he is the leading magician of Phaze suffering from unrequited love for the widow of the first Blue Adept who was the alternate self of Stile. (Clear?) There he seeks his enemy who has determined to kill him. . . . The author is a neat manipulator of words, as is evident in his choice of names and his skill in shifting from antiquated English to modern. Through-out the story he reveals his wide range of interests and expertise. Well worth reading for pleasure or rumination.

Sister Avila Lamb. *Kliatt Young Adult Paperback Book Guide*. September 1982, p. 17

The danger in writing speculative science fiction is that all too easily an author can sail off into a private universe and leave readers behind and bewildered. *Viscous Circle* nearly falls into that trap. A human agent's personality is projected into the body of a band, an alien sort of intelligent donut. . . . Rondl, the agent, turns sides in sympathy with the bands, whose society is an anarchist's utopia. The plot is rescued by a vision in which life after death is an imminent fact of existence. . . . Strangely, it is not the novel itself that makes *Viscous Circle* well worth reading, but the author's note at the end. Piers Anthony takes you on a guided tour of his life. . . . In 9 pages he has done what most novels don't in 300. That is to poke deep into the heart of one human being and find something to say. It's the kind of reading experience that will rescue you from the clutches of an overrated best-seller and leave you wishing for a full-length autobiography.

George M. A. Cumming, Jr. *School Library Journal*. September 1982, pp. 146–47

The world depicted in *On a Pale Horse* is a world very much like ours, except that magic has been systematized and is as influential as science. Satan's war against God is out in the open and abstractions like Time, War, Nature, and Fate are real people. No less a real person is Death, as Zane discovers when he kills him while attempting to commit suicide, thereby succeeding to the job himself. Zane slowly comes to understand the importance of his role, the mercy in ending hopeless pain. But he goes on strike when the woman he loves is threatened with an untimely death by Satan's plan for dominion over the Earth. Death, no longer a reluctant draftee, comes into his full powers as he confronts and defies the Devil. Anthony's prose is pedestrian, but his ideas are anything but. The author of the Xanth series has found a fascinating new direction for his fantasy.

Publishers Weekly. September 2, 1983, p. 72

Bio of a Space Tyrant is a five-volume, plodding white-wash biography edited by the tyrant's daughter. *Refugee,* the first volume, could be retitled "Wetbacks in Space." The story is of the poor but proud Hispanics' illegal flight from Callisto only to endure raid and rape on a regular basis from pirates. Hope Hubris manages to be responsible [for] murder, cannibalism, transvestism, theft, hijack, incest, prostitution of mother and sisters, and a host of stupid errors which he considers sacrificial deeds. If he were a better person, he concludes, he never would have survived. Who cares?

Mary S. Weinkauf. *Science Fiction & Fantasy*
Book Review, October 1983, p. 16

Dragon on a Pedestal exudes energy, humor, and delightful invention. Anthony seems to have set himself an impossible task in selecting a three-year-old heroine, and he compounds his trials with a zombie as the principle romantic interest, but the book is a success on many levels.

One of the first things to applaud is Anthony's sense of audience. He is aware of writing for a young reader, but he includes enough levels of action and meaning for open-minded adults as well. . . . This, like all the Xanth tales, is episodic in structure, and rich in classic mythic reference. Anthony is assembling, bit by bit, his own *Arabian Nights.*

The novel is entertaining, and it is literate. The puns which invade the book, as in others in the Xanth series, do fall flat upon occasion, but they succeed in communicating the vitality of language, the power of words. Language itself is one of the underlying values affirmed. This affirmation is particularly important for young readers who are being wooed away from books and the literary imagination into a nonverbal world of electronic color and sound.

In one sense, Xanth is a direct descendant of James Branch Cabell's Poictesme. Anthony shares Cabell's ironic humor without his intellectual arrogance. There is something Cabellian in Anthony's use of Florida as the locus for Xanth, and in the ironic play of such chapters as "Ivy League" (Ivy is the three-year-old heroine, daughter of King Dor and Queen Irene) or "Hugo Award" (Hugo is the somewhat retarded son of the Good Magician Humphrey). Some reviewers previously expressed disappointment that the Florida connection established by Chem Centaur's map of Xanth did not seem integral to the book, but this novel should dispel that criticism. The point for Anthony (as for Cabell) is that the fantastic begins in his own back yard. In *Dragon on a Pedestal* Florida figures centrally in the story, from its tropical climate which provides an ideal setting for Irene's plant-magic, to key plot elements like the Fountain of Youth. . . .

Three-year-old Ivy turns out to be a charming heroine, and Zora the Zombie is remarkably transformed into a suitable object for romance as bits of her flesh cease falling away and she begins to look almost lovely. Along the way Anthony includes parables of humane idealism which treat such themes as ecology, prejudice, healthy sexuality, and the power of positive thinking. The values, the invention, and the language of this book deserve applause. I have compared it to the *Arabian Nights* and works of Cabell because I think it, and the entire Xanth series, ranks with the best of American and classic fantasy literature.

Richard Mathews. *Fantasy Review*. March 1984,
pp. 24–25

ASIMOV, ISAAC [also known as PAUL FRENCH] (1920–1992)

There's no doubt that Isaac Asimov is the finest popular science writer working today, and in my opinion Ike is the finest who has ever written; prolific, encyclopedic, witty, with a gift for colorful and illuminating examples and explanations. What makes him unique is the fact that he's a bona fide scientist—associate professor of biochemistry at Boston University School of Medicine—and scientists are often rotten writers. . . . But our scientist professor, Asimov, is not only a great popular science author but an eminent science fiction author as well. He comes close to the ideal of the Renaissance Man.

Alfred Bester. *Publishers Weekly*. April 17, 1972,
pp. 18–19

Asimov has achieved a unique status, for not only is he admired and, by many, loved for his work in science fiction and for his engrossing regular science column in *The Magazine of Fantasy and Science Fiction*, but he is equally respected by professionals in some twenty-odd scientific disciplines. He has become the most perfect and the most inclusive interface between hard science (including math) and the layman, for he has a genius for bringing the obscure into the light. His writing career began in the so-called Golden Age of science fiction, under the aegis of the late John W. Campbell, Jr. . . .

The Early Asimov contains all his science fictions from 1940, when he was a teenage college student, through 1948; and they are fascinating to read. They are chronologically arranged, and the rubrics carry a wealth of anecdote, so that the development of this towering young mind becomes as engrossing as the stories themselves. Asimov came slowly to the fullness of the characterizations that marks his later fiction, but rapidly indeed to his knack of reordering facts and to his clear logic, even where logic led him to the wildest speculation.

Theodore Sturgeon. *The New York Times Book Review*. January 28, 1973, p. 10

The title story of Asimov's collection, *The Martian Way,* is surely one of the best science fiction novellas ever published. The story's taking-off point is simple: If no miracle fuels or propulsion systems come along, but Mars is to be colonized anyway, then it will have to be done with step rockets. A-B-C. All right, then what happens to the discarded steps—hundreds of thousands of tons of salvageable steel? Asimov's answer: they drift on out across the Martian orbit, until Scavengers in tiny two-man ships come out to get them.

The drama of *The Martian Way* is in those ships. Asimov, writing compactly and with enviable control, makes every phase of them intensely believable—the irritation that grows in the cramped quarters, the squabbling "Scavenger widows" at home, the monotony of waiting, the excitement— like hooking God's biggest fish—of a fat strike.

A lesser writer, fumbling for something to say, would have made these men little tin heroes, tight-lipped and glint-eyed, with shoulders from here to there. Asimov's characters are good-natured, human, unextraordinary, wonderful joes.

And a lesser writer, dealing with the long voyage to Saturn which turns this story from a vignette into an epic, would have marked time with muti- nies, sprung seams, mold in the hydroponics tanks, and Lord knows what all else. Asimov, instead, has rediscovered the mystic euphoria and beauty of space travel. Of those who have written about this imaginary journey, how many others have even tried to make Saturn glow in the reader's eyes like the monstrous jewel it is?

When you read this story, if you haven't already, you'll realize how much there is of heroics in run-of-the-mill science fiction, and how little true heroism. Asimov will make you feel the distances, the cold, the vast- ness, the courage of tiny human figures against that immense backdrop.

It's seldom that science fiction sticks as closely as this to its proper theme; if it happened more often, probably the respectable critics would have given in long ago.

Damon Knight. *In Search of Wonder* (Chicago:
Advent, 1967), pp. 93–94

Asimov's *The End of Eternity* is a curious patchwork, containing some mon- umentally good ideas and some startlingly uneven writing. In contrast to the intensely human pioneers of *The Martian Way,* Asimov's characters in this one are gadgeted and double-talked almost out of existence: Twissell, the most readily visible character in the book, is little more than a collection of mannerisms; Harlan, the hero, is not even that.

The book has one more serious handicap, for which Asimov is to blame as much or as little as the rest of us.

The background is extremely complex, involving a race of Eternals with a self-appointed mission to doctor reality all up and down the time- line—with a technology, mores, anxieties, a world-view, and a terminology to fit—none of which the reader has a fair chance to absorb before he is flung into the story proper.

This abrupt plunge into the action, though sanctioned by common practice, makes the first few chapters of the story perfectly unintelligible. What is all this blurred talk about Eternity and Time, Observers, Eternals, Reality Changes? Who is the girl with the funny name that the hero gets all tense about every now and then? The writer offers you no signposts; you have to pick your way as best you can, in the hope—justified, but after what effort!—that it will all become clear in time.

Once this barrier is passed, however, Asimov's story is a fascinating one. It has all the time-long sweep and mystery of Jack Williamson's creaky old "Legion of Time," plus an incisive logic that Williamson never had—and an occasional insight that's rare even in Asimov. Harlan's reaction when, by mistake, he all but meets himself, illuminates the doppelganger legend and the time-travel canon together, in one brilliant flash of subliminal understanding. Plot and counter-plot, in the best Williamson fashion, wind up spectacularly together, and there's a very acceptable happy ending.

This may be one of the last books of its kind. Science fiction is, pretty plainly, swinging away from its complex, cerebral, heavy-science-plus-action phase, toward a more balanced and easily digestible mixture of technology and human emotion. Only a writer trained in the days when science fiction was still a species of adventure pulp could write a novel like this one; and Asimov, whom I persist in thinking of as a rising young writer, is now one of the last of the Old Guard.

Damon Knight. In Search of Wonder (Chicago:
Advent, 1967), p. 94

Isaac Asimov is generally considered the father of modern science fiction, yet while others have invented supermen, supergods, and superbeasts, he has remained basically a conservative author. While they have prophesied he has speculated and as a practicing scientist has moved with caution, examining what is possible rather than what is fanciful. Yet still his Foundation trilogy is praised as being the cornerstone of that most fanciful craft, as being the point where it grew up. And if growing up means shedding one's belief in the utterly impossible, of losing innocence, then yes, he helped science fiction grow up.

One reason for Asimov's success lies in the fact that his characters are solid; he gives them a deeper history and knows more about them than he allows himself to divulge. If I speak of him as being a conservative writer, as being "safe," then it is not to complain: sometimes, particularly in his short stories, he gets near the craftsmanship of such mainstream giants as Somerset Maugham. His science fiction mystery stories are brilliant, could never have been solved by Holmes nor bettered by Doyle. His stories about robots are innovatory, and have laid waste once and for all the idea of robots as being tin-lizzies. His "Three Laws of Robotics" are considered so seriously by some American scientists that they might one day be lifted from the realm of fantasy and actually be applied. . . .

The most important of Asimov's achievements has been in the Foundation trilogy (*Foundation, Foundation and Empire, Second Foundation*) to inaugurate the convention of Mankind as already being on and controlling other planets. Before the Foundation books men were still (with a few important exceptions) journeying towards the stars. At the opening of the Foundation trilogy they have ruled the Galaxy for so long they are losing their hold, and Galactic civilization is crumbling.

Being a conservative writer Asimov decided that what would happen when men were in control of the Universe would be much the same as when they were in charge of a single planet: their main preoccupations would still be political intrigue, commercial opportunism, back scratching, revolution, and murder. Nor did new planets for Asimov necessarily mean a new kind of man. In the Foundation books some individual freaks, set apart from mankind, were allowed, but imagination was kept in check and man remained man, prone to all his usual disasters.

Since that trilogy in the early fifties and the Robot stories that appeared in book form shortly after, many newer writers have grown in confidence sufficiently to challenge Asimov's conception of the future, but none of his position as Master.

Brian Patten. Books and Bookmen. July 1973,
p. 104

Asimov is a highly circumstantial writer, sharing with Heinlein and with Norman L. Knight the ability to visualize his imagined world in great detail, so that it seems lived-in and perfectly believable. He does not, however, share Heinlein's lightness of touch; instead, he more closely resembles the elder Knight (no relation to Damon Knight) in writing everything with considerable weight and solidity, turning each sentence into a proposition, a sort of lawyer's prose which is clear without at any time becoming pellucid.

This kind of style is perfectly suited to a story which is primarily reflective in character, such as Asimov's recent robot yarns. It is also just what is required for a story in which history is the hero and the fate of empires is under debate.

William Atheling, Jr. The Issue at Hand (Chicago:
Advent, 1973), p. 28.

Isaac Asimov is often praised for the impressive quantity and variety of his work, and for his obvious and unusual intelligence. Certainly these are praiseworthy attributes, but such criticism obscures his most significant achievements.

Although Asimov has written more than two hundred books, including mysteries, biblical studies, histories, juveniles, and outstanding scientific works for the layperson, his thirty-four science fiction books are the ones that have made him famous.

Asimov began to write in the days when science fiction was published in periodicals such as *Astounding Science Fiction* and *Amazing Stories,* known as "pulps," descriptive of the cheap paper on which they were printed. The bulk of his science fiction, now collected as stories and novels in anthologies, was originally written for the pulp magazines. . . .

Asimov sold his first science fiction story, "Marooned Off Vesta," in 1938 at the age of eighteen. Twenty-eight years later his Foundation Trilogy was voted the World Science Fiction Convention's prestigious Hugo Award for the best all-time series, confirming his reputation as one of America's leading science fiction writers. He won a second Hugo, as well as the Nebula Award, for *The Gods Themselves,* published in 1972.

The leap from first story to Hugo and Nebula is a long one that spans many early rejections, innumerable revisions, and a great deal of hard work.

Although he always knew that he wanted to write, his expectations were rather modest. He had a college education to complete and a career in chemistry as a goal; writing was merely an amusement, and the most he felt he could hope for was to make some money that would help with his college tuition. . . .

In 1938 *Astounding Stories* became *Astounding Science Fiction,* and Asimov began to write letters to the magazine, letters that were actually published. . . . Then in 1938, he sold his first story—not to Campbell but to another magazine, *Amazing Stories.*

For eleven years he continued to sell science fiction to magazines, using the money to further his education—right up through a Ph.D in biochemistry. But he was not yet thinking of himself as primarily a writer. When in 1950 *Pebble in the Sky,* his first novel, was published, he was an associate professor at the Boston University School of Medicine and writing was still an avocation.

By the end of 1957 Asimov realized that writing was all he really wanted to do. He had begun to write books on straight science and could hardly consider "twoscore books in eight years a mere sideline. Especially since my writing income was now two and one-half times my school income."

In 1958 he abandoned teaching and began to devote himself entirely to writing. "And if I needed anything to tell me that I had made the right decision, it was the feeling of absolute delight that washed over me as I did so."

Since becoming a full-time writer, Asimov has had regrettably little time for science fiction. In the years between 1960 and 1981, despite a notoriously prodigious output, he has written only a few commissioned stories and one novel in the science fiction genre.

It is significant that virtually all of Asimov's science fiction is kept in print by his publishers, even stories written over thirty years ago when he was first attempting to find an outlet for his work. Despite his having written little science fiction since 1959, his stories and novels seem only to gain in popularity. Why does his work continue to attract readers when that of so many of his contemporaries has been supplanted by the work of a new generation of science fiction writers?

For us, the answer lies in his development from teenaged pulp magazine contributor to mature novelist. It would be a mistake, however, to equate strict chronological order with development, and in Asimov's case, it would be impossible, since he commonly worked on a number of stories at the same time, some quite minor and others that proved to be classics.

Jean Fiedler and Jim Mele. Isaac Asimov (New
York: Ungar, 1982), pp. 1–6

Foundation's Edge takes place several hundred years after the close of *Second Foundation.* . . . The First Foundation on Terminus and the Second Foundation on Trantor suspect each other of manipulating the Seldon Plan for the restoration of Galactic to its own advantage. Each sends out agents, and the adventures of these agents (including their search for Earth) make up the bulk of the novel. This is Asimov's longest novel and is distinctly uneven; the opening is positively sluggish and many settings and characters fail to come to life. On the other hand, a large part of the book is essentially a cross between science fiction and the detective story, where Asimov's skill is as great as ever. Asimov also appears to be planning future Foundation novels as part of a grand scheme to tie together into one future history his robot novels, the Foundation saga, and the Galactic Empire novels. A book in which the author's reach appears to have exceeded his grasp, but certainly destined for extreme popularity.

Roland Green. Booklist. September 15, 1982,
p. 73

In some respects *Foundation's Edge* is not simply a continuation of the earlier stories, but is a redirection. A certain amount of past history has had to be rewritten, notably the career of Asimov's famous Napoleonic character, the Mule. But more important is the shift of Asimov's own position toward the ideas in the stories. The previous stories, it is now clear in retrospect, emerged from the milieu of Hitler's Germany and World War II. The Foundations were a parable on Judaism: the sacred text and its rabbinical exegetes; xenophobia; persecution; existence under cover; chiliasm, and the double ghetto of the Foundations. These elements have now been minimized. The Seldon Plan is now revealed to be a fraud. The Second Foundationers, despite their paranormal abilities, are no longer pious saints but humans weighted somewhat on the down side. And the female Mayor of Terminus (chief magistrate of the Foundation Federation) is an arrogant horror. The walls, it is clear, are coming down. . . .

Foundation's Edge reveals many improvements over the earlier work. The ideas are better worked out; the plotting is better; the writing is superior;

and Asimov has outgrown his tendency to trick endings that didn't always work. Instead of good guys and bad guys, we now find credible motivations like arrogance, ambition, suspicion, and feelings of insecurity—all of which take form in manipulation. I could register a minor complaint, though, about some repetitiousness, and a stronger complaint about characterizations that sometimes do not gel. But suspense is high, and there is the usual Asimov clarity of expression. It will be an unusual reader who will put the book down unfinished.

E. F. Bleiler. *Washington Post Book World.*
September 26, 1982, p. 10

For Asimov the term science fiction is an appellation with two components—science and fiction. That he insisted on scientific accuracy may at times have kept him from fanciful conjecture, but at the same time it strengthened his fiction. Bound by his belief in and knowledge of science, he wrote about human characters and situations close to our own experience. The result is that futuristic hardware and exotic settings recede to the background. What shines through Asimov's work is the human quality that he is able to impart to aliens, semigaseous beings, even plants and machines.

Although Asimov admits to enjoying science fiction, he has been careful to point out that he takes it seriously—his work cannot be labeled escapist. In Asimov's fictional worlds, he has chosen themes that lose no validity when transferred to the future: artificial intelligence—its effects on society and society's effects on it; the uses and dangers of technology; the economic, political, religious forces behind the rise and fall of empires; the many manifestations of prejudice between races, species, men, and machines.

It is not mere coincidence that Asimov was writing at a time when science fiction outgrew its genre label and became a noteworthy component of contemporary fiction. Because his work is rooted in a recognizable reality, he is accessible to a wide and varied audience. The breadth of his appeal is still apparent today when even his earliest work not only remains in print but continues to attract new generations of readers.

In an age of specialization where the division between science and the arts is so sharply perceived, Asimov ignores the distinction by bringing the best of one to the other. To fiction he brings the rigorous investigations of science; to science he brings the unifying vision of fiction.

Jean Fiedler and Jim Mele. *Isaac Asimov* (New
York: Ungar, 1982), pp. 109–10

Asimov. What does one say in his praise that Asimov himself has not already said? ''Why, man, he doth bestride the narrow world like a Colossus,'' says Cassius of Shakespeare's Julius Caesar, and many Cassiuses have risen to pay similar homage to Asimov. . . .

He is a great producer. He enjoys enormous popularity. He has become monstrous. Yet there is still something sane, even likable, about many of his utterances. Asimov is the great sandworm of science fiction, tunneling under its arid places. And the critic's job remains that of a small termite, tunneling under Asimov.

Asimov employed the wide-angle lens for his view of life and it is a pity that his largest milestone, the *Foundation* trilogy, was written before science fiction authors were able to think of their books as books, not as short stories, or serials in cheap magazines (magazines that would have been ephemeral but for the dedication of fans). Conceived as an organic whole, the *Foundation* series might have risen to greater majesty. As it is, we must judge the original trilogy as it was conceived and presented to the readers of *Astounding* between May 1942 and January 1950.

The first part of the sequence, the novelette "Foundation," was written in August and September 1941. At once we are thrown into a situation where the Galactic Empire, a political unit involving tens of millions of inhabited planets, is in the first stages of collapse. A collapse brought about by indolence and complacency. The Foundation consists of a group of physical scientists established on the planet Terminus, on the galactic periphery. It is the outward manifestation of "psychohistory," an exact social science which deals with the statistically predictable actions of vast numbers of human beings. This highly mechanistic sociological reductionism—a kind of quantum physics applied to human beings—has been developed with one aim only: to prevent a ten-thousand-year Dark Age wherein the Galaxy might fall into technological barbarism. . . .

Most of the stories in the *Foundation* sequence depend upon individual action and appear thus to run counter to psychohistorical theory. Asimov's fiction is essentially of the puzzle-solving sort, detective novels of a very basic kind, set in a gimmick-ridden future not so very different from our own times in its psychology and social patternings. There is little genuine social or technological extrapolation. All is modeled on the past, the known. Few imaginative risks are taken.

The models for *Foundation* were Gibbon's *Decline and Fall of the Roman Empire* and a 1907 twenty-four-volume work, *The Historian's History of the World*. For Asimov's final two volumes, Arnold Toynbee's *Study of History* was a major influence. All in all, then, what Asimov presents us with is Rome in Space. . . .

Asimov recognizes his fictional limitations—and his immunity to twentieth-century literary influences, for instance—and his liberal views often emerge in his writings. . . . His most convincing work, however, is probably that which is nearest the detective format—with Conan Doyle's Sherlock Holmes as an obvious pattern. Two such science fiction detective novels appeared in the fifties, *The Caves of Steel* (1954) and *The Naked Sun* (1957). They are clever novels, extensions of his earlier robot stories—where Asimov created the "Three Laws of Robotics." They are murder mysteries involving logic, science, and elements of futuristic psychology; the last founded in the agoraphobia of the Earthmen, shut away in their underground cities.

The End of Eternity (1955) is a time-travel novel, depicting "a universe where Reality was something flexible and evanescent." As such it falls into that sub-category of time-travel books, the probability world tale. A group of humans outside of time, Eternals, act to ensure that mankind does not die out in the Galaxy. For much of the novel the pattern glimpsed in the *Foundation* series—of a steadily expanding *human*-settled galaxy—is denied. But by the end of the story the universe of *Foundation* has reasserted itself, thanks to the actions of the Eternals. There's also a love story—a Samson and Delilah story between Andrew Harlan and Noys Lambert—that culminates in a sexual relationship between them.

When returning to the genre in the late seventies, however, Asimov reverted to the patterns of the forties, and the complexity of *The End of Eternity* remains unique in his work. Asimov subsequently became one of the polymaths of our day, producing a stream of popularizations of various scientific and historical disciplines. The popularity of his novels continues. Like many another writer, Asimov began in a subversive vein, prophesying change and barbarism; but, generations later, such ideas lose their sting and become safe for a general public. Increasingly, one sees a solid conservative faith in technology in Asimov's novels. His short stories often err on the side of facetiousness.

Brian W. Aldiss. *Trillion Year Spree: The History of Science Fiction* (New York: Atheneum, 1986), pp. 264–67

Isaac Asimov came to science fiction via the fan movement, making his debut as an author in 1938 in *Amazing Stories*. He was immediately summoned to join *Astounding Stories*. Most of Asimov's books were written for the latter magazine. John W. Campbell, Jr., was the originator of the basic idea of "Nightfall" (a short story, 1941), which was voted the best science fiction story before 1965. Asimov's robot stories published during the 1940s brought him immense popularity, and these stories were gathered into a book in 1950 under the title *I, Robot,* which took the science fiction world by storm.

Asimov bases each story on a fundamental idea, which he uses to awaken suspense and interest in the opening section of the tale, working the idea through to produce his special effect in the closing pages. This close structure he took from Poe, one of his favorite short story authors. Thus, like Poe's detective Dupin, Asimov has his robot psychologist Susan Calvin (who is seventy-five in the stories, having been born in the year 1982) reach her astounding conclusions with the help of logic in most of the stories.

The special character in Asimov's work derives from the fact that the robots stand side by side with the humans. "There was a time when humanity faced the universe alone and without a friend. Now he has creatures to help him; stronger creatures than himself, more faithful, more useful, and absolutely devoted to him. Mankind is no longer alone. Have you ever thought of it in that way?''

In the early stories, Asimov's robots look like people; but later, Asimov moves away from this. In ''The Inevitable Conflict,'' the robots have become enormous thinking machines.

It was Asimov who, with the assistance of Campbell, postulated the famous three rules of robotics, which have been adopted by countless later authors. In later stories, conflicts arise from the fact that the robots ''overstep'' these rules. It is then necessary to reestablish the robot order as it was before. Asimov's three rules were most plainly expressed in his story ''Runaround,'' published in 1942:

''1—A robot may not injure a human being, or, through inaction allow a human being to come to harm; 2—A robot must obey the orders given it by human beings except where such orders would conflict with the First Law; and 3—A robot must protect its own existence as long as such protection does not conflict with the First or Second Laws.''

Apart from the robot stories, Asimov wrote many that were later republished in the volumes of the *Foundation* trilogy (*Foundation* [1951]; *Foundation and Empire* [1952]; *Second Foundation* [1953]). This cycle, despite its highly polished style, solid construction, and sense of humanist principle, was in fact little more than a space opera on a particularly large scale. Novels such as *The Stars, Like Dust* (1951) and *The Currents of Space,* are not exactly sequels but are nonetheless firmly based in the huge empire of the *Foundation* trilogy.

Asimov experimented with his emphatic style in stories and novels that fall rather into the category of a halfway stage between science fiction and the detective story. These include *The Caves of Steel* (1953) and *The Naked Sun* (1957), and also the short stories in the collection published as *Asimov's Mysteries.*

After World War II, Asimov wrote *C-Chute* (1951), in which he condemned the Korean War. In 1952 he wrote a damning indictment of McCarthyism in his book *The Martian Way,* and in *Silly Asses* (1957) he registered a protest against the manufacture of the hydrogen bomb.

Essentially, Asimov has remained true to his humanist conception of technologically based fantasy, even when forced to make concessions to public taste.

Dieter Wuckel and Bruce Cassiday. The Illustrated
History of Science Fiction (New York: Ungar,
1986, 1989), pp. 117–18

ATWOOD, MARGARET (1939–   )

Recently the Canadian poet and novelist Margaret Atwood was asked to describe her religious views for her listing in *Contemporary Authors.* ''God is everywhere, but losing,'' was her answer. In *The Handmaid's Tale,* her fifth and most powerful novel, she looks into the clouded glass of the future and, fully attuned to some of the negative signals in the present, envisions startling but by no means illogical consequences. In opening her imagination to what we might find some years down the road, Atwood joins the company of Doris Lessing, J. G. Ballard, and Anthony Burgess, literary writers of future shock fiction—a genre whose pioneers include H. G. Wells, Aldous Huxley, and George Orwell.

In a period when the novel of bourgeois life increasingly suffers from a poverty of subject—when we read over and over again about the attenuated sufferings of those in comfortable circumstances who should be a little happier than they are—the novel of the disastrous future offers the writer of fiction rejuvenated possibilities. Characters are placed in extremis, calling upon all their resources of courage and ingenuity in order to survive. Rebels defy the rules of society, risking everything to retain their humanity. If the world Atwood depicts is chilling, if ''God is losing,'' the only hope for optimism is a vision that includes the inevitability of human struggle against the prevailing order.

Just as the world of Orwell's *1984* gripped our imaginations, so will the world of Atwood's handmaid. She has succeeded in finding a voice for her heroine that is direct, artless, utterly convincing. It is the voice of a woman we might know, of someone very close to us. In fact, it is Offred's poignant sense of time that gives this novel its peculiar power. The immense changes in her life have come so fast that she is still in a state of shock and disbelief as she relates to us what she sees around her. Her present reality is constantly invaded by painful memories of what she has lost—everyday life as we ourselves know it. Vestiges of the recent past take her by surprise.

In Atwood's Gilead, even the male leaders are not immune to longings for the illicit pleasure of the past, to ''an appreciation of the old things,'' although Offred's elderly commander points out to her that men used to suffer because sex used to be too easily come by. ''Anybody could just buy it. There was nothing to work for, nothing to fight for.'' The double standard still prevails, however. Offred's commander takes it upon himself to break the rules, summoning her to visit him alone in his private study. She goes to the assignation expecting, as the reader does, whips and chains, sexual perversion. Instead there is a marvelously comic turn. What he wants is to play a game of Scrabble with her, and he wants to be kissed as if she means it. In return, she asks for a bottle of hand lotion to use on her face and—because women have been deprived of knowledge—she makes a classic demand for something even more valuable and forbidden: ''I want to know,'' she says. ''Whatever there is to know. What's going on.''

The Handmaid's Tale is a novel that brilliantly illuminates some of the darker interconnections of politics and sex, and it will no doubt be labeled a ''feminist *1984.*'' Yet it is Atwood's achievement to have produced a political novel that avoids the pitfall of doctrinaire writing. Offred lives and breathes. She is defiant in her own way, but no Superwoman. She resembles neither her mother, a militant feminist leader of drives against pornography, nor her friend Moira, a gay activist who refuses to become a handmaid and briefly manages to join the underground. She is simply a warm, intelligent, ordinary woman who had taken for granted the freedoms she was to lose— the freedom to love, the freedom to work, the freedom to have access to knowledge. Gilead threatens those who break its rules with extinction. Yet for Offred, the price of obedience is even higher—the death of the senses, the death of the spirit. She catches herself in the absurd contradiction of smearing butter on her face to preserve her complexion and simultaneously contemplating hanging herself from a hook in her closet. Overwhelming loneliness and boredom afflict her even more than oppression. "Nobody dies from lack of sex," she discovers. "It's a lack of love we die from. There's nobody here I can love, all the people I could love are dead or elsewhere. Who knows where they are or what their names are now? They might as well be nowhere, as I am for them. I too am a missing person."

Offred's plight is always human as well as ideological, and so is her inevitable assertion of her needs. Her tale, in Atwood's masterful hands, is extraordinarily satisfying, disturbing, and compelling.

Joyce Johnson. *Washington Post Book World.*
February 2, 1986, pp. 1–2

America in Atwood's bleak, unnerving novel is the theocracy of Gilead, established by religious fanatics who have dismantled the republic, liquidated the opposition and replaced our present political system with a quasi-military infrastructure. The northeastern United States has been transformed into Gilead with terrifying swiftness and remarkably little resistance, the transition eased by a lingering Puritan tradition fortified by neo-fundamentalism. The overriding concern of this regime is human reproduction; the time is the foreseeable future, when a devastating combination of chemical pollution, radiation, and epidemic venereal disease has caused the national birthrate to fall below replacement level. For an assortment of good, bad, and indifferent reasons, too few children have been born in the preceding decades to keep America from extinction. Arthur Campbell, a demographer quoted in the January 13 issue of *Newsweek,* believes that more than a fifth of the women born in the 1950s may never have a child. By the time *The Handmaid's Tale* begins, he has been proved right and reforms long advocated by radical elements of the Moral Majority have become law.

Unlike science fiction, which is sharply fanciful, this sort of speculative literature merely extrapolates from past and present experience to a future firmly based upon actuality, beginning with events that have already taken place and extending them a bit beyond the inevitable conclusions. *The Handmaid's Tale* does not depend upon hypothetical scenarios, omens, or straws in the wind, but upon documented occurrences and public pronouncements; all matters of record. For contemporary American women, *The Handmaid's Tale* could be the ultimate Doomsday Book; a man's reaction may well be ambivalent. In Gilead, such distinctions between the sexes have been revived and emphasized with a vengeance.

The narrator of the tale is Offred; the literary mode a diary of her circumscribed existence. Offred's young daughter has been kidnaped, her husband apparently shot while trying to cross the border into Canada; her mother and a close friend, both outspoken feminists, have vanished without a trace. Offred herself is living on borrowed time. Each handmaid has three years in which to produce a healthy child for a Commander. Should she fail to become pregnant in that time, she too will disappear, either to "The Colonies," where infertile women are used to clean up toxic waste, or if she is more fortunate, to forced labor on a farm. The third option is a secret bordello set up to stimulate the Commanders' lagging interest in sex, which tends to wane under the circumstances. Because the birthrate has not yet been raised by these Draconian measures, even more heroic tactics may soon be required. As it stands, life in Gilead exceeds the grim primitive reality described by Hobbes in *Leviathan,* "no arts, no letters, no society, and which is worst of all, continual fear and danger of violent death." The university system has been demolished, public executions are frequent, the economy is faltering, secret police are everywhere, and virtually all civil rights gained by women and minorities during the last century have been rescinded.

Given conducive circumstances, every one of the atavistic changes in this novel could be implemented virtually overnight, smoothly and efficiently. The legislative machinery is already in place, the communications networks established; vast sums of money available to the advocates of such a system. As a Harvard educated Canadian with a particular interest in Puritan history, Atwood can observe these changes from a privileged vantage point; close enough for involvement, sufficiently removed for perspective. In a recent CBC interview she said, "Canada's role in this novel is the role Canada has always taken in bad times in the United States . . . so Canada's position would be to do what she always does: to remain neutral without antagonizing the superpower to the South."

Atwood has created a spirited and engaging narrator and surrounded her with an array of active and passive supporting characters, each of whom represents a type familiar in America today. She has rounded off her icy cautionary tale with a desperately needed and hilarious spoof of an academic convention in the year 2195, at which time Gilead is a defunct society, regarded by all as a trivial aberration in cultural history, but despite this full complement of literary virtues, the power of the book comes not from Atwood's inspired flights of fancy or felicities of style but from her deliberate subjugation of imagination to demonstrable fact. Only the form of *The Handmaid's Tale* is fiction, as the form of *Mein Kampf* was autobiography.

Elaine Kendall. *Los Angeles Times Book Review.*
February 9, 1986, pp. 1, 12

Surely the essential element of a cautionary tale is recognition. Surprised recognition, even, enough to administer a shock. We are warned, by seeing our present selves in a distorting mirror, of what we may be turning into if current trends are allowed to continue. That was the effect of *Nineteen Eighty-Four,* with its scary dating, not forty years ahead, maybe also of *Brave New World* and, to some extent, of *A Clockwork Orange.*

It is an effect, for me, almost strikingly missing from Margaret Atwood's very readable book *The Handmaid's Tale,* offered by the publisher as a "forecast" of what we may have in store for us in the quite near future. A standoff will have been achieved vis-à-vis the Russians, and our own country will be ruled by right-wingers and religious fundamentalists, with males restored to the traditional role of warriors and us females to our "place"—which, however, will have undergone subdivision into separate sectors, of wives, breeders, servants, and so forth, each clothed in the appropriate uniform. A fresh postfeminist approach to future shock, you might say. Yet the book just does not tell me what there is in our present mores that I ought to watch out for unless I want the United States of America to become a slave state something like the Republic of Gilead whose outlines are here sketched out. . . .

The new world of *The Handmaid's Tale* is a woman's world, even though governed, seemingly, and policed by men. Its ethos is entirely domestic, its female population is divided into classes based on household functions, each class clad in a separate color that instantly identifies the wearer—dull green for the Marthas (houseworkers); blue for the Wives; red, blue, and green stripes for the Econowives (working class); red for the Handmaids (whose function is to bear children to the head of the household, like Bilhah, Rachel's handmaid in Genesis, but who also, in their long red gowns and white wimple-like headgear, have something of the aura of a temple harlot); brown for the Aunts (a thought-control force, part-governess, part-reform-school matron). . . .

Infertility is the big problem of the new world and the reason for many of its institutions. A dramatically lowered birth rate, which brought on the fall of the old order, had a plurality of causes, we are told. "The air got too full, once, of chemicals, rays, radiation, the water swarmed with toxic molecules." During an earthquake, atomic power plants exploded ("nobody's fault"). A mutant strain of syphilis appeared, and of course AIDS. Then there were women who refused to breed, as an antinuclear protest, and had their tubes tied up. Anyway, infertility, despite the radical measures of the new regime, has not yet been overcome. Not only are there barren women (mostly shipped to the colonies) but a worrying sterility in men, especially among the powerful who ought to be reproducing themselves. The amusing suggestion is made, late in the book at a symposium (June 25, 2195) of Gileadean historical studies, that sterility among the Commanders may have been the result of an earlier gene-splicing experiment with mumps that produced a virus intended for insertion into the supply of caviar used by top officials in Moscow.

The Handmaid's Tale contains several such touches of deft sardonic humor—for example, the television news program showing clouds of smoke over what was formerly the city of Detroit: we hear the anchorman explain that resettlement of the children of Ham in National Homeland One (the wilds of North Dakota) is continuing on schedule—three thousand have arrived that week. And yet what is lacking, I think—what constitutes a fundamental disappointment after a promising start—is the destructive force of satire. *Nineteen Eighty-Four* had it, *A Clockwork Orange* had it, even *Brave New World* had it, though Huxley was rather short on savagery. If *The Handmaid's Tale* doesn't scare one, doesn't wake one up, it must be because it has no satiric bite.

The author has carefully drawn her projections from current trends. As she has said elsewhere, there is nothing here that has not been anticipated in the United States of America that we already know. Perhaps that is the trouble: the projections are too neatly penciled in. The details, including a Wall (as in Berlin, but also, as in the Middle Ages, a place where executed malefactors are displayed), all raise their hands announcing themselves present. At the same time, the Republic of Gilead itself, whatever in it that is not a projection, is insufficiently imagined. The Aunts are a good invention, though I cannot picture them as belonging to any future; unlike Big Brother, they are more part of the past—our schoolteachers.

But the most conspicuous lack, in comparison with the classics of the fearsome-future genre, is the inability to imagine a language to match the changed face of common life. No newspeak. And nothing like the linguistic tour de force of *A Clockwork Orange*—the brutal melting-down of current English and Slavic words that in itself tells the story of the dread new breed. The writing of *The Handmaid's Tale* is undistinguished in a double sense, ordinary if not glaringly so, but also indistinguishable from what one supposes would be Margaret Atwood's normal way of expressing herself in the circumstances. This is a serious defect, unpardonable maybe for the genre: a future that has no language invented for it lacks a personality. That must be why, collectively, it is powerless to scare.

One could argue that the very tameness of the narrator-heroine's style is intended as characterization. It is true that a leading trait of Offred (we are never told her own, real name in so many words, but my textual detective work says it is June) has always been an unwillingness to stick her neck out, and perhaps we are meant to conclude that such unwillingness, multiplied, may be fatal to a free society. After the takeover, she tells us, there were some protests and demonstrations. "I didn't go on any of the marches. Luke (her husband) said it would be futile, and I had to think about them, my family, him and her (their little girl)." Famous last words. But, though this may characterize an attitude—fairly widespread—it does not constitute a particular kind of speech. And there are many poetical passages, for example (chosen at random): "All things white and circular. I wait for the day to unroll, for the earth to turn, according to the round face of the implacable clock." Which is surely oldspeak, wouldn't you say?

Mary McCarthy. *The New York Times Book Review*. February 9, 1986, pp. 1, 35

At the end of *Lady Oracle* (1976) Margaret Atwood's author/narrator declares, "I won't write any more Costume Gothics. . . . But maybe I'll try some science fiction." In *The Handmaid's Tale* (1985) Atwood makes good that promise in what one might call "political-science fiction" but what she calls "speculative fiction." This boldly political and darkly comic novel illustrates Atwood's grasp of the cultural, historical, philosophical, and literary facets of Western tradition, and the role of woman within that frame. Atwood demonstrates the absurdity of Western patriarchal teleology that views woman's biology as destiny and exposes the complicity of women in perpetuating that view. She also ridicules the mental gymnastics of academics, specifically those bent on establishing "the text." Instead of a modest proposal, her Swiftean seriocomic vision comprises an ironic indictment of a society that treats a woman's body as a pawn and her life as an academic question. Ultimately, Atwood, with a bow to *écriture féminine,* suggests that even in such a context an imaginative woman willing to improvise and take risks can beat the system and savor a measure of joy in the process.

Although more overtly political than her previous work, *The Handmaid's Tale* is no departure from Atwood's system. As Sherrill E. Grace has pointed out, Atwood's vision has not essentially changed, but has expanded and deepened. The political component in her poetry and prose, respectively, from *The Circle Game* (1966) and *The Edible Woman* (1969) onward, intensified in their counterparts, *Power Politics* (1971) and *Bodily Harm* (1982). In *The Handmaid's Tale* the context is essentially political, and, as the protagonist remarks, "Context is all."

In a 1985 interview, several months before *The Handmaid's Tale* appeared, Atwood addressed the matter directly: "the political to me is a part of life. It's part of everybody's life." "What we mean [by political]," she continued, "is how people relate to a power structure and vice versa. And this is really all we mean by it. We may mean also some idea of participating in the structure or changing it. But the first thing we mean is how is this individual in society? How do the forces of society interact with this person?" The protagonist Offred in *The Handmaid's Tale,* struggling against oppressive structures, embodies Atwood's definition. Moreover, Offred promises to come off a winner: "I intend to last," she says.

Set within this political context, Atwood's novel deconstructs Western phallocentrism and explores those aspects of French feminist theory that offer women a measure of hope.

Lucy M. Freibert. In Judith McCombs, ed.,
Critical Essays on Margaret Atwood (Boston:
G. K. Hall, 1988), pp. 280–89

BALLARD, J. G. (1930–   )

The young English science fiction writer J. G. Ballard is preoccupied with time, and his novels and stories give us a new slant on it. For Ballard time assumes grotesque, dreamlike forms. Human consciousness alters the conventional notion of chronology. The paintings of Francis Bacon—whom Ballard admires—provide a visual sense of the author's preoccupation with the psychic states that may be more "real" than any objective notion of time or history.

Ballard seems to have found his way into the depths of the great collective unconscious, only to remain stuck there, trapped among the primordial images, sitting, unable to take the next step. And if there is a suggestion here of escape into the ahistorical vision of an Eastern philosophy, the setting remains nevertheless unalterably Western.

In spite of our criticisms of his visions, Ballard remains for us one of the most powerful voices of contemporary science fiction. Indeed, there is real validity in symbolically stopping time so that we can momentarily cease our seemingly headlong rush into the future and take a good long look at where we are right now.

Lois and Stephen Rose. *The Shattered Ring:*
Science Fiction and the Quest for Meaning (n.p.:
John Knox Press, 1970), pp. 100–104

Terminal Beach is a much better collection than we have any right to expect in this wicked world. Not only have the stories virtue in their own right; they show Ballard developing in a way that did not seem likely from his earlier writing.

Ballard's first (English) volume, *Four Dimensional Nightmare,* showed him limited as to subject. There were too many stories about time, more particularly about the stoppage of time. In the new volume, he remains limited as regards theme, but the limitation represents an absorbed concentration and the theme pours forth its rewards. And that in fact is his theme: that limits whether voluntary or imposed bring ample compensation by deflecting attention to occurrences and states of mind not available to the "normal" world-possessed man.

Some of the best stories in the *Terminal Beach* collection hover—as all good science fiction should—on the verge of being something other than science fiction. "The Drowned Giant," for instance, is an apparently straightforward eyewitness account of the dismemberment of a gigantic, though otherwise human, body cast up on an unspecified shore. The manner of telling recalls such stories of Kafka's as "Metamorphosis" or "The Giant Mole." It begins with this sentence: "On the morning after the storm the body of a drowned giant was washed ashore on the beach five miles to the north-west of the city." The important thing, the narrator tells us, is to remember where the giant appeared, not the fact that he was a giant; to be amazed would be impolite. And by describing the dismemberment of the giant corpse, Ballard weans us of our desire to know where he came from. He concentrates on the important things, and by so doing makes the ends pursued by most science fiction seem trivial ones. In the hands of the first fifty science fiction writers you care to name, this story would end with other giants coming down from Akkapulko XIV to rescue him, and the shooting beginning. By eschewing sensationalism, Ballard makes us realize how much science fiction is given over to sensationalism.

Ballard replaces sensationalism with wit. The critics have not noticed how witty Ballard is, yet a unifying wit is his dominant characteristic. Fandom seems to have decided he is the prophet of despondence and let it go at that. Ballard is seldom discussed in fanzines (nor for that matter is anyone but Heinlein), but the occasional reference tends to be disparaging. Thus a correspondent in *Vector* calls Ballard a "melancholy johnnie."

Ballard's wit lies chiefly in imagery that, like the imagery of such metaphysical poets as Carew or Donne, can surprise and delight by its juxtaposition of hitherto separate ideas. . . .

Ballard's attitude is such that we are often reminded of science fiction by the very things he is ostentatiously not doing. Ballard likes to regard himself as something of an outcast among the science fiction fraternity. He avoids most other authors, he believes—in sharp distinction to adulation expressed by other writers—that "H. G. Wells" has had a disastrous influence on the subsequent course of science fiction, he seems to regard William Burroughs as the greatest of science fiction writers, and of course he is the apostle of "Inner Space.". . .

Despite his care to keep within the science fiction framework, Ballard is often careless with his facts. Or perhaps it is more accurate to say that he is rather lordly about his material, just as he is about his readers. At the beginning of "The Drowned World," the identity of the submerged city is left vague: "Had it once been Berlin, Paris, or London? Kerans asked himself." Ballard seems to put his own thought into Kerans's head when he says, a few pages later, "despite the potent magic of the lagoon worlds and the drowned cities, he had never felt any interest in their contents, and never bothered to identify in which of the cities he was stationed." But you'd think someone would know; the navigator, perhaps. . . .

His witty and nervous worlds, littered with twitching nerves and crashed space stations, carry their own conviction that will eventually win him popular support. For his characters, the worst blow is always over, they are past their nemesis and consequently free. One can only hope that for Ballard too the worst misunderstanding is over, so that he will be free to create in a more intelligent atmosphere. Despite some shortcomings, his stories represent one of the few stimulating forces in contemporary science fiction.

Brian Aldiss. In Thomas D. Clareson, ed., *SF: The Other Side of Realism—Essays on Modern Fantasy and Science Fiction* (Bowling Green, Ohio: Popular Press, 1971), pp. 116–29

Love & Napalm is not a masterpiece in the way that, say, *The Great Gatsby* and *Miss Lonelyhearts* are masterpieces, but it is a brilliant and useful book. Like the fictions of Jorge Luis Borges, which it resembles in some of its concerns and in the mock erudition and dryness of its prose, it might well be considered a long poem on metaphysical themes. That is the difficult part; the horrifying part is that this philosophic investigation is conducted in terms of violent death and perverse sexuality.

After the nine stories that chronicle Dr. Travers's despairing search for new kinds of union, there are six pieces less closely related to one another also concerned with sexuality and violent death. Several of these read like abstracts of the results of market research intended to design a nightmare. Ballard's fiction has always been described as gloomy, and he regrets that nobody seems to notice the irony that runs through the book; he uses the language of behavioral science for ironic effect as Borges uses the language of literary erudition.

In various interviews Ballard has said he is not much of a reader, at least in the sense of keeping up with contemporary writing, and he told me he feels closer to the visual arts than to most modern literature. There is little dialogue in *Love & Napalm,* and the nine sections concerned with Dr. Travers are heavily weighted toward visual description.

The events of the story include exhibitions of paintings and sculpture, conceptual art, and intermedia works. At one point Ed Kienholz's construction "Dodge '38" appears on a road near London. Max Ernst's name is mentioned continually. Dali, Bellmer, and Tanguy also pop up. Dali is quoted as having said that mind is a state of landscape, and this idea is one of the keys to understanding Ballard.

Jerome Tarshis. *Evergreen Review.* Spring 1973, pp. 137–48

J. G. Ballard, along with Kurt Vonnegut, Jr., and younger Americans like Thomas Disch, once seemed capable of rescuing the genre [of science fiction] from the mountain of fifth-rate hackwork it had become. In the earlier part of his career Ballard produced a well-written, dissonant series of novels and stories chiefly built about a single theme: the slow, terrible drift of the earth toward an apocalypse of inanition. Everything slowed and stilled and froze solid: it was a slender column to support a stack of books, but the nerviness of the language and the density of the imagination creating the disasters made the early Ballard novels readable and engrossing beyond the tight, fanatical world of the adepts. Then Ballard changed his manner and became altogether more inventive and modernist.

In *Vermilion Sands,* however, he is back in the old harness, and for all his attempts to make these nine stories widely significant, they fail even to come up to his early novels—again, he is coasting along on the strength of one idea, twisting all his material into one repetitive pattern, and the slickness and indulgence of the stories make them difficult to remember an hour after the book's been closed. The writing is creamy and precise, almost always delightful, but it cannot carry its load of inconsequential and lazy plot. . . .

What Ballard attempts in these stories is the creation of an original and grotesque world, to be revealed in an unspectacular, offhand way. But the conventional analogy between short stories and poetry contains a good deal of truth; any false step or slackness becomes cruelly evident. The limpness of the stories in *Vermilion Sands* is that of a poet going lax and complacent.

Peter Straub. *New Statesman.* December 7, 1973,
pp. 874–75

J. G. Ballard is one of England's best and most imaginative science fiction writers, and he has created some masterly tales and novels. He is also one of the few contemporary science fiction authors I've come across whose work rises above comicbook fantasy and style. But for several years now he has been producing pretentious futuristic pieces and, because of their inventive, experimental appearance, winning acceptance in "serious" literary circles. His admirers can't seem to realize that although he is an accomplished technician and dreamer, he doesn't have any terribly new or significant observations concerning the future. His "serious" work is filled with stunning but pointless effects. *Crash,* which his American publisher foolishly compares [to] *A Clockwork Orange,* is all effect, a superficial nightmare vision of a car-and-sex-oriented society. The narrator and his acquaintances are adult car crash freaks who explore, with maniacal seriousness, the eroticism of destruction. When they are not creating havoc on the highways or smacking their lips over mutilations, then they are grasping for chrome and genitalia. What they would have done in, to, and with, our Edsel, simply staggers the imagination. If the fantasies in *Crash* reflect Ballard's state of mind when he's behind the wheel, then his driver's license should be revoked immediately. The man is a potential menace.

Gerald Weales. *The Hudson Review.* Winter 1973–
74, pp. 782–83

Ballard's early novels are ostensibly cataclysmic science fiction stories in the routine Wyndham mode; gradually, though, as the texture of the prose thickens and Ballard's stare hardens on the bizarre landscape he has precipitated, the cataclysm ceases to be of much importance. In *The Crystal World,* for instance, the opulent refractions of the imagery become virtually self-generating, causing the end of the world to seem a rather footling affair by comparison. Although all these novels incorporate their own theoretical time schemes—which are very complicated and (between ourselves) not very interesting—they are, broadly speaking, speculative and futuristic. More recently, Ballard has applied the imaginative habits of a lush, numinous fantasist to the present day, imposing an over-conceptualized, over-poeticized vision on the metal and concrete furniture of a technologized society. In the jangling, piecemeal *Atrocity Exhibition,* Ballard sets himself up as the apologist of deviance, breakdown and psychopathology. Its successor, *Crash,* a novel born of quite immeasurable perversity, posits an "alternative sexuality," a sexuality emotionless, stylized, and unerotic which is offered as the appropriate response to a dehumanizing technocracy. . . . While one is inevitably sickened and appalled by Ballard's glib whimsicality, *Crash* remains a mournful and hypnotic tour de force, possibly the most extreme example in modern fiction of how beautifully and lovingly someone can write 70,000 words of vicious nonsense.

For Ballard is the rarest kind of writer—an unselfconscious stylist: it is the measure of his creative narcissism that he has his eye on no audience. Equally, Ballard's characterization is hardly more than a gesture—his men are morose and fixated, his women spectral nonentities, his minor figures perfunctory grotesques. He has nothing coherent to "say," and his plots are merely the gateways to exotic locales. *Concrete Island* is by far his most realistic novel to date and, patently, a writer with little nous, wit, or concern for individuals has no business being realistic; the book is slight not because the obsession fails to engage us but because it demonstrably fails to engage Ballard. His *raison,* after all, is his awesome visual imagination and the complementary verbal intensity with which to realize it. Ballard's vision is, simply, too occult for the observable world; it needs some grand perversity to give it the altitude which good writing alone can sustain.

Martin Amis. *The New Review.* May 1974, p. 92

J. G. Ballard has concerned himself in much of his work with problems of time and identity, and in *Concrete Island,* a modern *Robinson Crusoe,* he shows the effect of one upon the other, the ways in which we think we control time and know ourselves and the sudden crumbling away of that power and knowledge when we are confronted with a situation in which a true understanding of time and identity is the only tool for survival. . . .

Ballard's talent, as a novelist writing in the last third of the twentieth century, is to show us what we refuse to see—the extraordinary mixture of old ideas and modern architecture, the self-contradictory expectation of "human" responses in a landscape constructed to submerge all traces of iden-

tity—and to prove that it is only by knowing ourselves that we can understand the technology we have created. . . .

It's often said that the modern urban landscape lacks identity. But maybe
that's because we lack knowledge of our own. If we complain about the
speed of change and an architecture which seems to allow us little individuality, it is into ourselves that we must look for the reasons. Ballard, psy-
choanalyst of the high-rise and prophet of the six-lane, proves in this brilliant novel that although "to know what one knows is frightening," it is
not, in the end, as frightening as not knowing can be.

Emma Tennant. New Statesman. May 10, 1974,
p. 699

Ballard's latest novel *Hello America* in many respects is a return to his
earlier science fiction mode. Set towards the end of the twenty-first century,
the novel follows the course of an exploratory expedition to the USA, now,
as a result of a series of ecological disasters, an unpopulated wasteland. As
the small band of explorers moves across the continent, they encounter, in
various strange and hybrid forms, the remnants of the American Dream, its
icons, totems, and myths exposed in the harsher glare of the country's dys-
topic isolation.

Ballard's reevaluation of the role America has played in our consciousness, and the pervasive nature of its influence on the twentieth century, is
fascinating. However harsh and satirical he might be at times, on the whole
Ballard's attitude is approving. The properties of American life can provide
marvelous opportunities for the imagination, and it's in this area in particular that *Hello America* excels as the novelist indulges in some superb—and
quintessentially Ballardian-set-pieces. Ballard's unique style functions at full
power in this novel, practically every page provides a compelling example.

William Boyd. London Magazine. November 1981,
pp. 83–85

Empire of the Sun is a curious contribution to the literature of survival, and
an important addition to the Ballard canon. His first novel that doesn't resemble science fiction, it serves as a kind of portrait of the artist as a young
entropist. It is as well crafted and chilly as anything he has written.

Ballard casts few veils over his own history in this autobiographical
novel. The most obvious departure he makes from what really happened is
in editing out his parents. Playing it as straight as he can, he limits his urge
to make the story taller but allows himself the liberty of bizarre similes to
express the strangeness of the experience: "The rotting coffins projected
from the loose earth like a chest of drawers."

It may be true that schoolboys of Jim's age and background don't think
about their parents much and inhabit violent dream worlds, but it is amazing
and perversely intriguing that an author should take as harrowing an experience as this and present it with such stylized impersonality. In his first

venture beyond genre fiction, Ballard wears his pacemaker squarely on his sleeve.

Edward Fox. *The Nation*. January 26, 1985,
pp. 89–90

Ballard's short stories and some of his novels have succeeded in attracting readers through their rich style and sharp inventiveness of language and form. Ballard's work shows a movement away from traditional science fiction toward what may be termed "inner space," the exploration of the psychic events in the progress of mankind. This is especially true of his short stories dating from the middle of the 1960s, but is also observable in his two novels *The Drowned World* (1962) and *The Crystal World* (1966). He himself has called his type of writing "fiction of psychological fulfillment." Generally recognized as his best works, these two books involve individual reactions to doomsday catastrophes that have overtaken humankind. In *The Drowned World,* for example, the hero winds up traveling south toward the Sun—and toward certain death. Nevertheless, Ballard points out that this move is "a sensible course of action that will result in absolute psychological fulfillment" for the hero. *Crash* (1973) is a departure from his earlier books, set as they are in distant landscapes. It takes place in the world of today, and is an ugly and neurotic story, almost in the horror genre. Two years later *High-Rise* appeared—equally contemporary, but certainly more fun to read. The *Unlimited Dream Company* (1979) is a fantasy of life fulfillment, loaded with surreal images and odd-ball events.

As to writing technique, Ballard uses all the well-established and traditional literary devices familiar to mainstream literature at the beginning of the twentieth century: present-tense narration, interior monologue, abandonment of linear description of events in time sequence, and stream-of-consciousness. Ballard says that science fiction, primarily a prospective literary genre dealing with the immediate present in terms of the future rather than of the past, demands narrative techniques that reflect its themes. Until now, he argues, all authors (not excepting himself) have ignored this because they have failed to realize that the foremost narrative technique of retrospective prose—namely the relating of a tale in a continuous, orderly development recording a predetermined complex of events—is wholly unsuitable to the creation of pictures of a future that has not yet arrived. *The Best Science Fiction of J. G. Ballard* (1977) serves as a good introduction to his works in the short-story form, including brief forewords by the author to elucidate each piece. He considers his novels "condensed novels" rather than simply novellas. He claims that the length of the ideal science fiction novel should be closer to 40,000 words than 60,000, the accepted conventional wordage. He seems most comfortable writing in this truncated length.

Such a lifting of the aesthetic quality and adoption of the narrative techniques of modern "genuine" literature should in turn have led to a renewal of subject matter and content and the rejection of the old clichéd ideas. This demanding program was however only partially achieved in practice. Most science fiction literature remained immune to the new theory, or those writers who tried harder tended to be met with blank stares and were commercial failures.

Dieter Wuckel and Bruce Cassiday. *The Illustrated
History of Science Fiction* (New York: Ungar,
1986, 1989), pp. 198–99

J. G. Ballard's works represent a major locus in determining the psychologies and hermeneutics of late-twentieth-century signification, the "wisdom of light" that we await along with the new millennium that arrives less than a decade hence. Reconstructing ourselves, we organize anew the constructive metaphors by/through which a tentative seizure of significance coheres. Ballard's voice echoes today as an important sounding-forth, heedful of the past, yet oriented toward what is only beginning to come into view (perhaps at Cape Canaveral?). Our gentility of style repeatedly inhibits such collocations of meaning that dare new seizures of significance. Resisting such conservatism, Ballard's hermeneutical temporalizations may be as much as we may anticipate reasonably, given the existential dearth of revelatory diction in our era: "Not myths which will one day *replace* the classical legends of ancient Greece, but *predictive mythologies;* those which in a sense provide an operating formula by which we can deal with our passage through consciousness—our movements through time and space."

What if our spiritualities reflected not the established, but the projective? What if notions of the divine included on-the-edge thinking instead of merely the received/traditional? Ballard is one of the access points; there are others. Who knew in the second century that later generations would need to revise, reestablish, stipulate originaries as strongly as they did? Plastic palmtrees (in Ballard's office) and those automobile-accident detrita that will come to dramatistic sophistication in *Concrete Island* spiritualities dare not remain in the bounds/bonds of a previous generation, lest they invite only passing snickers at the matinee devoted to religious curiosities of the previous generation.

"Deep assignments run through all our lives; there are no coincidences" *(The Atrocity Exhibition)*: just what I think when I pass the emptied swimming pool on my morning exercise-walk. And when I ask yet again: why? What was all this for, if not to change, to advance, to determine less the securities of the past than the adventurous revisionings of that generation I'll just begin to glimpse as I carry out the disciplines in which I was trained, the generation I've jostled toward innovations that can replace or inscribe our own revisions (Gerhard Ebeling, in a seminar at Drew when I was a graduate student, noted that one's students are always one's pallbearers also). Why, I wonder repeatedly, do traditional religiosities insist upon repeating endlessly what everyone already knows (Heidegger's "gossip," dictionary-frozen language)? When there are, yes, Ballardian fictions and reimaginings and revisionings and so many yet to be heard voices waiting their venue, their own influences: Ballard's spirituality has no privilege against the traditional except that, as I've tried to show, it articulates not so much anything we've been accustomed to as what we've yet to imagine, must imagine if we're to survive.

William G. Doty. "J. G. Ballard: Contemporary
Apocalyptic Spirituality." *Continuum*, vol. 2,
no. 1. March 1992, pp. 41–42

BARNARD, ROBERT (1936–   )

In *A Talent to Deceive,* Robert Barnard produced the finest critical study extant of Agatha Christie, and in many ways his own books fit right in with the cozy and comfortable school of British detective fiction she best exemplified. His crimes usually take place in incongruously respectable settings and involve a closed circle of suspects. The emphasis is on verbal jousting rather than violent physical action. Fairness to the reader is scrupulously observed. But Barnard's biting wit and darkly satirical world-view set him apart from the hard-core cozies.

A Little Local Murder gives an indication of what is to come. The English village of Twytching (a name that rather sets the tone) is to be immortalized in a radio broadcast to be produced for airing in the American city of Twytching, Wisconsin, and the local citizens hilariously jockey for position on the program. As in later books, the grim and shocking ending is all the more effective for its contrast with the comedic tone of the rest of the novel.

In *Death of an Old Goat,* the setting is an Australian university, where an elderly visiting professor from Oxford gets not quite the reception he expected. *Blood Brotherhood,* set in an Anglican community in Yorkshire where a symposium on the role of the Church is being held, turns a jaundiced eye on religion and depicts an amusing variety of clerical types. *Unruly Son* and *Posthumous Papers,* the latter including a wicked caricature of an American scholar, do a neat job on the book world.

Death in a Cold Climate, concerning the murder of an Englishman in Tromsø, Norway, gives a strong impression on how somber and depressing a Scandanavian winter can be, while providing the customary well-constructed plot and incisive social observations. It may be his best book to date.

Barnard introduces a fresh [detective] character in each of his early novels, but not until Perry Trethowan, the Scotland Yard sleuth of *Death by Sheer Torture,* does Barnard introduce a detective he would choose to return to. In his first case, Trethowan must investigate a murder in his own rather embarrassing family, a clan of crazy British eccentrics. His father has been found dead, wearing spangled tights in a medieval torture machine called a strappado. Perry becomes a royal bodyguard in *Death and the Princess,* a relatively weak Barnard entry from a plot standpoint but one with much telling satire on the institution of royalty.

Little Victims, centering on a hopelessly mediocre English prep school, introduces one of the great schoolboy villains in Hilary Frome and over-comes a disappointingly predictable stunt ending with bitterly ironic obser-vations on the failures of education, not just in Britain.

One of the best practitioners of the classical mystery to make a debut in the 1970s, Barnard seems a safe bet for long-lasting fame in the field.

Jon L. Breen. In John M. Reilly, ed., *Twentieth-Century Crime and Mystery Writers* (New York: St. Martin's Press, 1985), p. 55

Robert Barnard's first detective story was *Death of an Old Goat . . .* which came out in 1974. It takes place at Drummondale University, in Australia, where a doddering old goat of an English professor is murdered, and its hilarious doings are wonderfully satirical, with a marvelous set of the most unpleasant characters in a down-under setting you'll never find in travel books. In addition to his devastating sense of humor, Barnard shows to beautiful advantage his deep knowledge of English literature, his feeling for language, and his background of Australia from his six years of teaching there. Once you've read this book by Barnard, you'll be hooked on him, as I was.

In 1976, he became Professor of English Literature at the University of Tromsø in Norway and head of its English Department. The institution has the distinction of being Europe's most northerly university. He remained there, with his wife, Mary Louise Tabor, a librarian, until 1983, when he returned to Leeds, England, where he now lives and writes full-time.

In *Death of an Old Goat* you get an absolutely murderous picture of small-town college life in Australia from someone who could say, like Huck Finn, "I been there before." The very same thing can be said about the British town with the delicious name of Twytching in *A Little Local Murder.* As for this novel, read what Newgate Callendar has to say in his May 8, 1983 *New York Times Review:* "It is the writing that counts here. Mr. Bar-nard goes about it with a quietly malicious sense of humor and has given us a comedy of manners that looks back to Jane Austen and Trollope. He knows his Thackeray too. The murder of the lady is written almost as an aside, in much the same way that George Osborne's death is tossed off in *Vanity Fair,* with much the same kind of shock." High praise indeed.

In *Death on the High C's,* you feel as if you're not just sitting in the audience watching a murder at the opera but you're backstage with the sing-ers and stage hands taking part in what's going on. In *Death and the Prin-cess,* you are similarly brought inside the royal palace and other high places where Royalty comes and goes; and while it is easy to understand how Barnard knows so much about academic life—as seen in *Death of an Old Goat* and *Death in a Cold Climate* (set in a Norwegian college town)—it is striking how much he tells us about opera in *Death on the High C's* and about royalty in *Death and the Princess*. This, plus writing style and wit and humor, is what sets Barnard apart from other mystery writers.

Among the accolades to come Barnard's way have been four nominations for Edgar Awards and—which I find more interesting—no fewer than six of his books have been selected by G. K. Hall & Co., the Boston publisher, for inclusion in its Large Print Editions and the Nightingale Series for the partially sighted. These came out between 1980 and 1983, and all of them are still in print.

Praise from reviewers usually reserved for writing of a more serious nature than the usual mystery/detective story has also come to Barnard: the reviewer for *Publishers Weekly* calls *Death by Sheer Torture* (entitled *Sheer Torture* in England) "witty, intelligent and a joy to read," and says, "behind the writing there is obviously a civilized mind that is rather amused at the foibles of humanity." T. J. Binyon writes in *The Times Literary Supplement* that *Death on the High C's* is "as bright and lively a detective story as one is likely to meet this year [1977]: good characters, good detail, a lot of music . . . and a lot of humor."

William White. The Armchair Detective. Summer
1984, pp. 296–97

Unlike the circumstances of most deaths, the fiction of death reveals in advance just when the end will occur. The cleverer yet weaker writers, recognizing the nature of the artifact held in the hand, fall prey to the temptation to heap sensation upon sensation in the final pages, following double with triple and Maltese crosses, to the point of losing all touch with the logic that has shaped their discourse before. (There are exceptions, certainly, as in . . . some of the best work of Robert Barnard. . . .) The highest praise is, for such writers, to have kept the reader guessing "to the last page." This, being false to life, often makes for poor fiction, though not invariably.

Robin W. Winks. Modus Operandi: An Excursion
into Detective Fiction (Boston: David R. Godine,
1982), p. 83

Robert Barnard's output reminds us of Michael Innes's and not only quantitatively. The full-time writer is of course expected to turn out his products at a rapid rate. But to teach at a university, with all the ancillary duties filling one's "free" time, well—one can only gasp and admire. Of course, the feat is remarkable only if quality is maintained, and this Mr. Barnard has achieved so far. *Death of a Mystery Writer* (1979), *Death of a Literary Widow* (1979), *Death of a Perfect Mother* (1980), and the present book have followed hard on the heels of *Death on the High C's* and *Blood Brotherhood*

(1977) and two others are now in press. It must be that the practice of writing essays at the English university (Balliol College in Mr. Barnard's case) gives an unfaltering facility with the pen. After a stint at the Fabian Society, Mr. Barnard went to New South Wales as lecturer in English for six years (University of New England!), next to Bergen for ten years, and now he is full professor at Tromsø, north of the Arctic Circle, which is the setting for *Death in a Cold Climate.*

The competent Norwegian Inspector of Police Fagermo is faced with the murder of a young Englishman, the reason for whose presence in the town is, to say the least, ambiguous. Though Fagermo has to make journeys to Trondheim and to England, there is great unity in the plot, as well as convincing local color supplied by an author who knows not only the place, but its denizens of all ages, and from all over. Detection is rather slow-moving but not static, and the Inspector finally builds up a convincing case against his chief suspect. Something a little frigid may be observed in the telling of the sundry insertions of sex and may even cause the reader to feel sympathy with the nicely portrayed criminal; but after all, Tromsø is always freezing (or nearly so) and narrative chilblains are not inappropriate.

> Jacques Barzun and Wendell Hertig Taylor. *The Armchair Detective.* Winter 1982, p. 76

Superintendent Peregrine Trethowan of Scotland Yard makes his second appearance for Robert Barnard in *Death and the Princess.* . . .

Dorothy L. Sayers makes her investigations such a joy that the solution almost doesn't matter. Agatha Christie makes the solution such a triumph that her sometimes tedious investigations are more than worth the effort. Barnard/Perry's investigation is long and tedious; the solution, though a bit surprising, does not make up for what has not come before.

Barnard does have his moments. His description of Edwin Frere is priceless: "he was tall, fretful, handsome, with a lock of hair falling over cold blue eyes; he had a ski-slope nose and petulant mouth, and he looked at the [gambling] tables with a yearning, hungry expression, as if he had arrived at the gates of Paradise five minutes after closing time." And I must confess that Perry gets better with every outing. He is almost human (or at least interesting) in *The Case of the Missing Brontë,* Barnard's third book starring this Scotland Yard Superintendent.

But *Death and the Princess,* though a "nice little murder," is definitely forgettable.

> Mattie Gustafson. *The Armchair Detective.* Fall 1987, p. 96

BENTLEY, E. C. (1875–1956)

Edmund Clerihew Bentley, imagining that it would be good fun to write a detective story, found the labor of actually writing so exhausting that "he meant never to attempt a detective novel again,'' and therefore decided to call it *Philip Gasket's Last Case*. The original publishers, the Century Company of New York, suggested changing the hero's name to Trent and the title to *The Woman in Black*, and with these alterations it was published in America in 1912. In March of the following year it was issued in England, by Nelson's, with the title that it has borne ever since, *Trent's Last Case*.

Mr. Bentley, a distinguished journalist, at one time on the staff of the *Daily News* and later with the *Daily Telegraph*, has set down in detail how this remarkable first novel came to be written. From boyhood he had delighted in Sherlock Holmes, but came to dislike his eccentricities and his ''extreme seriousness.'' He disliked even more the seriousness of Holmes's imitators, and thought it ought to be possible to create a detective who was a human being, ''not quite so much the 'heavy' sleuth.'' Accordingly, he drew up a list of ''things absolutely necessary to an up-to-date detective story,'' added ''a crew of regulation suspects,'' and decided to introduce two original features, a love interest and the idea of ''making the hero's hard-won and obviously correct solution of the mystery turn out to be completely wrong.'' Having worked out the plan in his mind, he wrote the last chapter first, thus following, perhaps unconsciously, the method used by many of his notable predecessors.

Trent's Last Case, unlike most detective fiction of the period, gave an important place to character drawing, the creation of credible portraits of human beings with their changing thoughts and emotions. The detective himself is a cultured man of leisure, a successful painter with an analytical habit of mind, who once solved a murder mystery simply by studying newspaper reports of the case, just as Poe had done in the matter of Mary Rogers. When the great financier, Sigsbee Manderson, is found murdered, Trent is called in, unofficially, to find out what he can of the circumstances.

His deductions are at first based upon his observation of detail—footprints in the garden, clothing, and other personal possessions of the dead man and his associates—on ''Serendipity,'' in fact, with nothing more scientific than a fingerprint or two. He gains further information from studying the individual characteristics of his suspects, their background, hobbies, casual conversation, even the habitual expression of their features. Intuition, which served Father Brown so well, does nothing to help Trent reach his conclusions. It does, however, restrain him from making those conclusions public. Although his perceptive and logical brain has built up what seems a completely water-tight proof, he feels there is something wrong somewhere, as indeed there is. E. C. Bentley had planned *Trent's Last Case* to be ''not so much a detective story as an exposure of detective stories,'' and the same note is struck in the closing lines of the novel itself:—

> The Manderson affair shall be Philip Trent's last case. His high-blown pride at length breaks under him. I could have borne everything but that last revelation of the impotence of human reason.

But this attempt at "exposure" did no disservice to detective fiction. What Bentley had, in fact, done was to devise a new method of presenting a detective story. He had broken the convention inherited from Poe, that such a tale must move in ordered sequence like a proposition in Euclid, from "Given" and "Required to Prove," to the logical steps that end with Q.E.D. In *Trent's Last Case* the detective's soundly argued conclusions, which normally form the end of such a story, are given when the tale is little more than half told. What he has proved is true, but not the whole truth. He has discovered facts with great cleverness, but is wrong in the construction he places on those facts. Thereafter, veil after veil is lifted by other hands, still leaving veil after veil behind, until the complete surprise that explains the crux of the mystery is sprung on Trent, and on the reader, in the final pages.

Trent's Last Case, a novel written at a period when the short detective story was still the most popular form of the genre, brought to fiction of this kind a more spacious atmosphere, time to consider and reconsider the implications of the evidence, and a new literary excellence. It is that rare thing, a detective story that can be read with pleasure even when the secret is known, for the skill with which the puzzle is devised and concealed, and for qualities that are less frequently found in detective fiction, its sensitive study of character and its delightful prose.

> A. E. Murch. *The Development of the Detective Novel* (New York: Philosophical Library, 1958), pp. 202–4

The plot of *Trent's Last Case* is at once unorthodox and cunningly contrived. To outline it here would be superfluous for those who have read the masterpiece and unfair to those who still have that abounding pleasure ahead of them. The style is adept, light, and entertaining. . . . The detection is of a highly superior brand—but the detective's conclusions are happily far from the truth. To complicate matters still further (and this is where the greatest unorthodoxy enters) the detective breaks all the rules by humanly falling in love with the supposed culprit. The eventual revelation of the murderer is almost as startling as in Agatha Christie's *Roger Ackroyd* but is accomplished without resort to debatable devices. The character drawing is the subtlest in the form since *The Moonstone.* The whole performance, in fact, is pervaded by an indescribable flavor of literacy and naturalness that can be conveyed only by first-hand acquaintance.

Yet a word of caution is advisable. *Trent's Last Case,* like every epochal work, must be regarded in its own historical spectrum to be fully appreciated. Compared to the highly developed product of today, it is competent, literate, and ingenious enough—but in no sense of the word pyrotechnic. Its deceptive *un*-remarkableness, in fact, is the chief reason for its uniqueness in an era in which flamboyance and overwriting were the hallmarks of the crime novel. Contrasted with the turgid narratives of its own period, its civilized effortlessness and engaging humor are as twin beacons in a fog, and its real worth becomes apparent. Judged by this, the only fair standard, *Trent's Last Case* stands truly first among modern examples of the genre. It is one of the great cornerstones of the detective story, and if any contemporary writer is heir to the mantle of Wilkie Collins, the honor could not fall on worthier shoulders than those of E. C. Bentley.

Howard Haycraft. Murder for Pleasure: The Life and Times of the Detective Story (New York: Biblo and Tannen, 1968), pp. 118–19

Trent's Last Case is in every way admirable, though it seems . . . a flaw and not a merit that the final twist should have three and not two turns: the motive is weakened, the surprise has been overstretched. Still, the outcome does not take away from the masterly development of the problem and the brilliant conduct of the detection.

[The novel] is gripping and its solution good solid work. If only Bentley's generation of English writers had not strongly believed that all things mysterious and titillating must happen in France, the tale would be nearly as perfect as its predecessor.

Jacques Barzun and Wendell Hertig Taylor. A Catalogue of Crime (New York: Harper & Row, 1971), pp. 51, 52

That the line between the comic and the serious in the detective story is a fine one is shown by *Trent's Last Case* (1913). Its author, Edmund Clerihew Bentley, made his living as a journalist, and was for more than twenty years chief leader writer on the *Daily Telegraph*. Bentley had a talent for light humorous writing, and invented the tart little four-line verse known as the *clerihew*. In 1910, he thought that "it would be a good idea to write a detective story of a new sort." The book would be light-hearted, because Bentley disliked both the egotism and the seriousness of Holmes. The detective also was to be treated lightly, and perhaps for this reason was originally called Philip Gasket. In tune with this was the "most pleasing notion of making the hero's hard-won and obviously correct solution of the mystery turn out to be completely wrong," so that the whole thing would be "not so much a detective story as an exposure of detective stories." Bentley started with the last chapter, in which Gasket is staggered by the revelation of what really happened, and worked backward from this, revising the plot several times while walking from his Hampstead home to his Fleet Street office. The final result seemed to him poor, and when John Buchan, who was at that time reader for Nelson's, accepted the book, Bentley thought that he was offering far too much money. With Gasket changed to Trent, it was published in England and in America under the title *The Woman in Black*. Its success was immediate, not as an "exposure" of detective stories, but as light entertainment.

Writing elsewhere about *Trent's Last Case,* I have said that it is difficult now to understand the high regard in which the book was held, and that "the writing seems stiff and characterless, the movement from one surprise to another, and the final shock of revelation, rather artificial." Perhaps it is a sign of the benevolence of age that this judgment now seems too severe. I think it remains true, though, that the book falls into two parts which are not very well connected. It was dedicated to G. K. Chesterton, and Bentley shared at this time Chesterton's radical dislike of the rich, and particularly of rich speculators. The opening treats the death of the millionaire Sigsbee Manderson with an almost savage irony, stressing that "to all mankind save a million or two of half-crazed gamblers, blind to all reality, the death of Manderson meant nothing." His epitaph is provided by the editor of the newspaper, who looks at the large broadsheet announcing "Murder of Sigsbee Manderson" and says: "It makes a good bill."

This ironic note recurs occasionally but is not maintained, and Manderson after being introduced with such a flourish becomes more shadowy as the story proceeds. The major part of the book deals with Trent's investigation and his (as it proves erroneous) discovery of what really happened. Much of this is ingenious, although it depends upon some actions that seem very unlikely, like an innocent man's removal of a denture from the dead Manderson's mouth. Of more importance is the fact that the detection wavers uneasily between a desire to treat the whole thing as a joke and Bentley's impulsion to write seriously about the fact that Trent falls in love with the woman whom he supposes to be involved in the murder. There is a similar uncertainty in the treatment of Trent, who, as Bentley said, "is apt to give way to frivolity and the throwing about of absurd quotations from the poets at almost any moment" and yet, since he is the hero, cannot be regarded as a figure of fun. But perhaps this is still pressing too hard on a book that was acclaimed everywhere as something new in detective stories. The other works in which Trent appears, published more than twenty years later, showed only that Bentley was not able to adapt himself to the further development of the form.

Julian Symons. *Mortal Consequences: A History—
From the Detective Story to the Crime Novel* (New
York: Harper & Row, 1972), pp. 93–95

I suppose everybody has at least heard of *Trent's Last Case.* It holds a very special place in the history of detective fiction. If you were so lucky as to read it today for the first time, you would recognize it at once as a tale of unusual brilliance and charm, but you could have no idea how startlingly original it seemed when it first appeared. It shook the little world of the mystery novel like a revolution, and nothing was ever quite the same again. Every detective writer of today owes something, consciously or unconsciously, to its liberating and inspiring influence. . . .

The book crept quietly into the world at a cheap price, and without any of the heralding of blare and blurb which a present-day publisher would lavish on a work so brilliantly unconventional. The public welcomed it eagerly, and it ran through four editions in five months. After twenty years, it reads as freshly as the day it was written and has lost nothing of its prestige or popularity, and it will always take rank with *The Moonstone* and *Sherlock Holmes* as a classic of detective fiction.

What are the virtues that have placed it so high? It has, of course, a good plot—slight, it is true, by the Freeman Wills Crofts standard, but sound, logical, and scrupulously fair. And this bony framework, without which no detective story can survive, is surrounded with a living structure of real flesh and blood. There was the amazing, the enthralling novelty.

The old stock characters were gone, in their place were real people— Trent the journalist, Marlowe, Bunner, old Cupples and (still more astonishingly) Mrs. Manderson the heroine—all breathing and moving with abounding vitality. Most vital of all, perhaps, is the murdered millionaire who is never seen alive, but whose personality dominates the book from that first splendid chapter, which shows the financial world rocking under the blow of his death down to the final pages which lay bare the inner chambers of his wicked soul. When we think of the countless millionaires who have died in first chapters without leaving a trace on the imagination, we realize how remarkable this particular achievement is. And even the love story, so often a weak sister, is, in this masterly book, made moving, credible, and integral to the plot.

But when all is said, it is by the writing that every work of literature must in the long run stand or fall, and *Trent's Last Case* is supremely well written without ever straying too far from the plot, or getting out of key with the general tone of the book; the style ranges from a vividly colored rhetoric to a delicate and ironical literary fancy. Now touching on the greater issues of human life, now breaking into a ripple of comment on arts and letters, running into little sidestreams of wit and humor, or spreading into crystal pools of beauty and tender feeling, *Trent's Last Case* welled up in the desiccated desert of mystery fiction like a spring of living water. No other writer had ever handled that kind of theme with so light and sure a hand. . . .

Undramatic? Too fanciful? Too literary? Possibly. But to lose things like that is to lose the whole savor of the thing, and if any such mayhem is committed on *Trent's Last Case* there will be another murder done.

Dorothy Sayers. Introduction to *Trent's Last Case*,
by E. C. Bentley (New York: Harper & Row,
1978), pp. x–xiii

BLOCK, LAWRENCE (1938–   )

Lawrence Block, in creating a series figure, Matt Scudder (and then apparently abandoning him for a verbose, and singularly silly, burglar-turned-detective, Bernie Rhodenbarr), apparently proved too tough for his readers, who did not materialize. Even so, on my short list of underappreciated writers, I would place Block high for three of the most effective transfers of the [Raymond] Chandler method into the milieu of New York City: *The Sins of the Father, In the Midst of Death,* and *Time to Murder and Create.*

Robin W. Winks. *Modus Operandi: An Excursion into Detective Fiction* (Boston: David R. Godine, 1982), pp. 100–101

Lawrence Block's Matt Scudder is far and away the gloomiest and most guilt-ridden of all the private eyes. While many of his colleagues experience periodic bouts of depression and disillusionment—often at the end of a case when their work is over and they must return to the solitude of their lonely lives to wait until the next case comes along—Scudder is unremittingly glum. Dashiell Hammett, employing a terse, hard-boiled style, managed to produce a kind of poetry of violence; Block has instead aimed at creating in the Scudder books a kind of poetry of despair.

Scudder owes his melancholic disposition to a single tragic incident in his life. A New York City policeman for fifteen years, he was enjoying an off-duty drink in a bar one evening when two young punks entered, held up the place and killed the bartender on their way out. Scudder chased after the pair and shot them both, killing one and crippling the other. But one of his bullets went astray, ricocheted off something and struck a seven-year-old girl named Estrellita Rivera in the eye, killing her instantly. Exonerated of blame in the incident and even awarded a department commendation for his actions in apprehending the killers, Scudder's life has nevertheless been irrevocably altered by the incident. He decided he no longer wanted to be a policeman, or a husband and father for that matter. He resigned from the force, left his wife and two sons in Syosset, Long Island, and moved into a hotel on 57th Street in Manhattan, where he nurses his guilt and sorrow in lonely isolation.

Scudder is not officially a private eye. Put off by thoughts of an examination and of all the paperwork involved in keeping records and filing income tax returns, he never applied for a license. He simply does favors for people, for money. One advantage of this arrangement is that since he is never actually hired, he can never be fired. His needs are few, so he works as infrequently as he can, and the cases he agrees to take, he does so without enthusiasm. He also has an unorthodox way of deciding on his fee, usually settling on a figure on the spot: in *Time to Murder and Create* (1977), for example, he charges a man $320 because that is the exact amount the man had paid for the suit he is wearing.

Once he receives his fee—which he demands in advance—he routinely does two things with it: he purchases a money order and sends as much as he can spare to his ex-wife and sons on Long Island; and he stuffs ten percent of the total amount into the poor box of the nearest church as a tithe. Scudder isn't a religious man, though he does have a keen sense of sin and guilt. He confesses that if he didn't consider suicide a sin, he would have killed himself years ago. He spends a great deal of his time just sitting in churches. He claims to have no clear idea why he does this.

The most important house of worship Scudder frequents, however, is not a church at all but a place called Armstrong's, a bar located on Ninth Avenue right around the corner from his hotel. Scudder is an alcoholic. Ever since the incident that has disrupted his life, he has come to rely more and more heavily on what he calls "maintenance drinking," usually coffee laced with bourbon. That way, he explains, "You still get drunk eventually. But you don't get tired out en route."

Scudder's drinking has become an increasingly serious problem. In *Time to Murder and Create,* he woke up after one of his binges in a strange hotel room and had to check his wallet to see if he had spent the night with a prostitute. Lately, however, he has twice awakened from his blackouts to find himself lying in a hospital bed. One doctor even gives him an ultimatum: stop drinking or die. And so he begins dropping into neighborhood AA meetings, though he behaves there in much the same way as when he visits churches—as a detached observer rather than an active participant. *Eight Million Ways to Die* (1982) depicts the struggle between Scudder's desire to get off the booze and his failure to understand why "anyone would think it a good idea to stay sober in this city."

Scudder's decision to assume the role if not the actual profession of private eye was not, as is the case with many of his predecessors, prompted by disillusionment with the practices or policies of the official law enforcement agencies. Detecting is simply all he knows and all he ever did "insofar as I did anything."

But he is not without a code, albeit a simple one: "It's bad for society when murders remain unpunished." Scudder is no Galahad off on a crusade to save the world nor committed to rescuing damsels in distress. He walks right past a man beating a woman during an argument in *Eight Million Ways to Die,* determined not to get involved. But he cannot tolerate an unsolved murder, even one, as in *A Stab in the Dark,* that occurred nine years earlier. The thought of someone not paying for his sins nettles him, perhaps because of the high price he paid for killing Estrellita Rivera.

It isn't enough that he merely track the killer down, either; Scudder has his own personal standards of justice. In *The Sins of the Father,* for instance, after discovering that the murderer is a minister, he confronts the man and offers him a choice: either kill himself within the next forty-eight hours—he even provides the bottle of Seconal tablets—or he will go to the police with the evidence he has of the man's guilt. The minister chooses suicide.

Scudder's tales are narrated in a tough, unsentimental prose with precious little levity in it, wisecracks being inappropriate for a somber man like himself. Given his bleak outlook, it's a wonder the books don't collapse under the weight of all the gloom. Block, however, does an excellent job of keeping Scudder's self-pity to a bare minimum and, especially in *Eight Million Ways to Die,* of balancing the many instances of urban horror with an equal number of hopeful tales told by the participants at the AA meetings Scudder drops in on. There are also few colorful similes or lyrical flourishes in the novels, the laconic prose perfectly suited to a man whose life has been stripped of most everything save guilt. Raymond Chandler used a rich, evocative prose to bathe Philip Marlowe in the romantic glow of the Arthurian knight errant. Block employs a much sparer style in order to present Scudder in a harsher, less flattering light, exposing all the warts and blemishes. It isn't the dashing knight on his white charger that interests Block but rather the dark night of the soul that haunts his hero.

Block uses the private-eye genre as a vehicle for examining the evil and corruption of modern society, but his primary interest is in laying bare the tortured soul of his hero. It is a tribute to his skill that he has made the morose Scudder such a compelling figure, for though he depicts him without sentimentality, he views him with compassion. Perhaps because he seems more in need of help than those who seek his assistance, we find ourselves caring about him, rooting for him to make it, especially during his struggle to climb out of the bottle. Scudder may not be the most likable or most engaging private eye ever to have been created, but in his troubled ordeal he is one of the most human.

David Geherin. *The American Private Eye* (New
York: Ungar, 1985), pp. 190–95

BRADBURY, RAY (1920–   )

A Medicine for Melancholy comprises twenty-two tales, most of them very brief, which range over time and our earth as well as the universe. Many of them pack a chuckle whereby the author is laughing not at his ability to confound the reader (though undoubtedly he often does just that) but with the reader at the endless variety of human wants and hopes and tastes and drives. Reading these wholly unusual tales will reward those who can bring to them some of the zest and nimbleness of imagination that has gone into the writing.

Mary Ross. *New York Herald Tribune Book
Review.* March 29, 1959, p. 10

Something about Mr. Bradbury's style—its terseness, its simplicity, or its flashes of imagery—invites a serious approach and arouses an eager expectancy of fresh insight into the human condition.

Although his modern parables do not always convey clear-cut meanings, their imaginative approach, suggestive of overtones of significance, keep the reader hunting for a message or moral. . . .

Readers should be warned that Mr. Bradbury's unorthodoxy, particularly in earth-bound episodes, leads occasionally to distasteful and morbid conclusions.

But when the author puts these themes aside, he is capable of storytelling flavored with humor, sentiment, suspense, and awe in a wide variety of settings.

Frederick H. Guidry. The Christian Science
Monitor. June 4, 1959, p. 11

Despite Bradbury's regrettable tendency to dime-a-dozen sensitivity, he is a good writer, wider in range than any of his colleagues, capable of seeing life on another planet as something extraordinary instead of just challenging or horrific, ready to combine this with strongly held convictions. . . . The suppression of fantasy, or of all books, is an aspect of the conformist society often mentioned by other writers, but with Bradbury it is a specialty.

There is about Bradbury, as about those I might call the nonfiction holders of his point of view, a certain triumphant lugubriousness, a kind of proleptic *schadenfreude* (world copyright reserved), a relish not always distinguishable here from satisfaction in urging a case, but different from it, and recalling the relish with which are recounted the horrors of *1984* and a famous passage that prefigures it in *Coming Up for Air.* Jeremiah has never had much success in pretending he doesn't thoroughly enjoy his job, and whereas I agree with him, on the whole, in his dislike of those who reach for their revolver when they hear the word "culture," I myself am getting to the point where I reach for my ear plugs on hearing the phrase "decline of our culture." But in this respect Bradbury sins no more grievously than his non-fiction colleagues, whom he certainly surpasses in immediacy, for *Fahrenheit 451* is a fast and scaring narrative. . . . The book emerges quite creditably from a comparison with *1984* as inferior in power, but superior in conciseness and objectivity.

Bradbury's is the most skillfully drawn of all science fiction's conformist hells. One invariable feature of them is that however activist they may be, however convinced that the individual can, and will, assert himself, their program is always to resist or undo harmful change, not to promote useful change.

Kingsley Amis. New Maps of Hell: A Survey of
Science Fiction (New York: Harcourt, 1960),
pp. 106–10

Why is Ray Bradbury so good? It is not—the conventional science fiction criterion—that his ideas are so striking. They tend to be no better than average; indeed many of these stories, as usual, are not science fiction at all and don't claim to be. It is partly a remarkable economy and delicacy of style; there aren't many people writing today who can say so easily exactly what they want to say. It is partly pure sentiment, that dogrose and cornflower sweetness common to so many American writers. This can be unspeakable corn, or not: Mr. Bradbury sometimes teeters toward the borderline.

Stephen Hugh-Jones. New Statesman. September
18, 1964, p. 406

Much of the bulk of Ray Bradbury's fiction has been concerned with a single theme—the loss of human values to the machine. Now Bradbury has brought his message to a new medium, the theater, and, typically, he has mustered all the resources of imagination, talent, and ingenuity available to make the stage speak for him with the effectiveness of the printed page. . . .

The World of Ray Bradbury, an evening of three one-act plays, represents more than dabbling in a new literary form for Bradbury. It is a full commitment to put time, energy, and money into the theater. . . .

Bradbury buffs will recognize the plots of these plays because all three appeared originally as short stories. There is, of course, nothing new about adapting narrative material to the stage, but in the case of science fiction it presents several difficult problems. As a genre, science fiction combines the plot and moral tone of melodrama with the fantasy of romance, a combination which is a genuine literary novelty. The methods of melodrama are easily accommodated on the stage, but successful fantasy occurs more naturally in narrative fiction where the imagination can create worlds that never were. When fantasy is dramatized, it is usually combined with music, dance, and comedy. . . . Film is much more congenial to science fiction than the stage because special-effects technicians are able to take the most fantastic imaginings of the writer and actually construct them from plastic or plasterboard. In a movie we don't have to use our imagination—the Martian landscape is there before our eyes.

How is a playwright to place science fiction on the stage? Will a bare stage and an appeal to the audience's imaginative powers be adequate for a play like *The Veldt?* Can we believe in such a machine without some hint of what it looks or sounds like? Bradbury's solution to these problems has been the same as the filmmaker's: turn it over to the technician. We are presented with a stunning array of futuristic projections and costumes, control panels with blinking lights, and a persistent sound track that bleeps and hums like a satellite orbiting around the balcony.

Many of the defects of the three plays can be attributed to the difficulties a playwright is bound to encounter when he creates a theater for his own work. . . . Taking into account inexperience, it is not too surprising that the theatrical balance, which one would expect to be weighted toward action and dialogue in a playwright's theater, was instead shifted noisily in the direction of stagecraft.

When asked recently whether he would do it the same way again, Bradbury refused to make excuses. "The final decisions were mine and I take full responsibility for what appears on the stage," he said. He did admit, however, that if he had learned anything from his first attempt to stage his own work it was "to trust the word." "You've got to believe in your own language," he said. But he is not defensive about his new theater. "I don't think much of most of the theater I see today," he said. "I'm not interested in writing an Albee play or a Baldwin play because it's the fashionable thing to do. I'm interested in experimenting with something different and in having fun doing it."

John J. McLaughlin. *The Nation.* January 25, 1965, pp. 92–94

Although Bradbury has a large following among science fiction readers, there is at least an equally large contingent of people who cannot stomach his work at all; they say he has no respect for the medium; that he does not even trouble to make his scientific double-talk convincing; that—worst crime of all—he fears and distrusts science. . . .

All of which is true, and—for our present purposes, anyhow—irrelevant. The purists are right in saying that he does not write science fiction, and never has. . . .

People who talk about Bradbury's imagination miss the point. His imagination is mediocre; he borrows nearly all his backgrounds and props, and distorts them badly; wherever he is required to invent anything—a planet, a Martian, a machine—the image is flat and unconvincing. Bradbury's Mars, where it is not as bare as a Chinese stage setting, is a mass of inconsistency; his spaceships are a joke; his people have no faces. The vivid images in his work are not imagined; they are remembered. . . .

There is so much to say about Bradbury's meaning that perhaps too little has been said about his technique. . . . His imagery is luminous and penetrating, continually lighting up familiar corners with unexpected words. He never lets an idea go until he has squeezed it dry, and never wastes one. I well remember my own popeyed admiration when I read his story about a woman who gave birth to a small blue pyramid; this is exactly the sort of thing that might occur to any imaginative writer in a manic or drunken moment; but Bradbury wrote it and sold it. . . .

Learned opinion to the contrary, Bradbury is not the heir of Poe, Irving, or Hawthorne; his voice is the voice (a little shriller) of Christopher Morley and Robert Nathan and J. D. Salinger. As his talent expands, some of his stories become pointed social commentary; some are surprisingly effective religious tracts, disguised as science fiction; others still are nostalgic vignettes; but under it all is still Bradbury the poet of twentieth-century neurosis, Bradbury the isolated spark of consciousness, awake and alone at midnight; Bradbury the grown-up child who still remembers, still believes. . . .

Childhood is Bradbury's one subject, but you will not find real childhood here, Bradbury's least of all. What he has had to say about it has always been expressed obliquely, in symbol and allusion, and always with the tension of the outsider—the ex-child, the lonely one. In giving up this tension, in diving with arms spread into the glutinous pool of sentimentality that has always been waiting for him, Bradbury has renounced the one thing that made him worth reading.

> Damon Knight. *In Search of Wonder: Critical*
> *Essays on Science Fiction* (Chicago: Advent,
> 1967), pp. 108–13

Ray Bradbury's stories cannot be half read. They compel the reader without pause to the final shock revelation, the neat twist, or the poetically just conclusion. Bradbury wraps fantasy in minuscule details of reality, so that the reader believes all and is ready for anything. Even in macabre tales such as "Pillar of Fire," his rhythmic, word-savoring style makes poetry out of a dead man's emergence from the grave. These sixteen stories of science fiction and fantasy [in *S Is for Space*] offer proof of the range of Bradbury's art form from the Messianic theme of "The Man" to the mounting horror of "Come into My Cellar," and the clear, sharp warning against conformity in "The Pedestrian." Bradbury suggests that Jules Verne was his father; H. G. Wells, his uncle; and Flash Gordon, one of his friends. No doubt about it!

> Jane Manthorne. *The Horn Book Magazine.*
> February 1967, p. 70

Ray Bradbury has drawn the sword against the dreary and corrupting materialism of this century; against society as producer-and-consumer equation, against the hideousness in modern life, against mindless power, against sexual obsession, against sham intellectuality, against the perversion of right reason into the mentality of the television viewer. His Martians, specters, and witches are not diverting entertainment only: they become, in their eerie manner, the defenders of truth and beauty.

Bradbury thinks it probable that man may spoil everything, in this planet and in others, by the misapplication of science to avaricious ends—the Baconian and Hobbesian employment of science as power. And Bradbury's interior world is fertile, illuminated by love for the permanent things, warm with generous impulse. . . .

Bradbury knows of modern technology, in the phrase of Henry Adams, that we are "monkeys monkeying with a loaded shell." He is interested not in the precise mechanism of rockets, but in the mentality and the morals of fallible human beings who make and use rockets. He is a man of fable and parable.

Bradbury is not writing about the gadgets of conquest; his real concerns are the soul and the moral imagination. When the boy hero of *Dandelion Wine,* in an abrupt mystical experience, is seized almost bodily by the glowing consciousness that he is really *alive,* we glimpse that mystery: the soul. When, in *Something Wicked This Way Comes,* the lightning-rod salesman is reduced magically to an idiot dwarf because all his life he had fled from perilous responsibility, we know the moral imagination.

"Soul," a word much out of fashion nowadays, signifies a man's animating entity. That flaming spark—the soul—is the real space-traveler of Bradbury's stories. "I'm alive!"—that exclamation is heard from Waukegan to Mars and beyond, in Bradbury's fables. Life is its own end—if one has a soul to tell him so.

The moral imagination, which shows us what we ought to be, primarily is what distinguishes Bradbury's tales from the futurism of Wells's fancy. For Bradbury, the meaning of life is here and now, in our every action; we live amidst immortality; it is here, not in some future domination like that of Wells's *The Sleeper Awakens,* that we must find our happiness.

What gives *The Martian Chronicles* their cunning is their realism set in the fantastic: that is, their portrayal of human nature, in all its baseness and all its promise, against an exquisite stage set. We are shown normality, the permanent things in human nature, by the light of another world; and what we forget about ourselves in the ordinariness of our routine of existence suddenly bursts upon us as fresh revelation.

In Bradbury's fables of Mars and of the carnival in *Something Wicked This Way Comes,* fantasy has become what it was in the beginning: the enlightening moral imagination, transcending simple rationality.

The trappings of science fiction may have attracted young people to Bradbury, but he has led them on to something much older and better: mythopoeic literature, normative truth acquired through wonder. Bradbury's stories are not an escape from reality; they are windows looking upon enduring reality.

Russell Kirk. *Enemies of the Permanent Things:*
Observations of Abnormity in Literature and
Politics rpt. Peru, Illinois: Sherwood Sugden &
Company [1969], 1988 pp. 116–20, 120–24

Science fiction fans complain that snooty literary reviewers are ignoring a vital genre by failing to review science fiction. Well, no science fiction writer is more lauded than Ray Bradbury. His new volume of stories *[I Sing the Body Electric!]* comes with an amazing list of devotees—Graham Greene, Bertrand Russell, Christopher Isherwood, Bernard Berenson, Thornton Wilder, Ingmar Bergman, Nelson Algren, and Gilbert Highet. I think, really, they must read Bradbury as great men were once said to relax with detective stories. Bradbury is pretentious, and in this collection gives full vent to his aspirations. There are stories here definitely aimed at being writing with a capital R. In some he almost brings it off. ''The Inspired Chicken Motel'' re-creates the nomadic life of the Great Depression seen through an ordinary family, rather than through the Okies of Steinbeck, or Agee's *Let Us Now Praise Famous Men*. There is a genuine warmth and humanity about the story, but Bradbury ruins it, carrying the story a paragraph too far with a last sentimental belaboring of the point. This sentimentality runs amok in most of the tales, showing that under the still sparkling surface the treacle runs deep.

Stanley Reynolds. New Statesman. March 27,
1970, pp. 451–52

Ray Bradbury is a conventional writer: that is, for the most part he adheres to literary conventions and, even if he did propose some of them himself, among those his often overweening and more than occasionally vertiginous lyricism, by now the reader can normally know what to expect out of a Bradburian piece. But not in this instance. And immediately I should warn you that less than half of the twenty-two stories [in *Long after Midnight*] are even horror tales, let alone science fiction; and I should also warn you that only five of the twenty-two are any good at all. They happen to be superb.

Of those five, two in particular are tours-de-force. ''The Better Part of Wisdom,'' the most sensitive, most restrained, most graceful treatment of homosexuality I've ever read, ought to be required reading for all gay writers. ''Have I Got a Chocolate Bar for You!'' deals very subtly with a very subtle relationship between a priest and a penitent. Neither of them relies in the least on genre devices. Both of them, when they wax lyrical, do so only in the most disciplined and appropriate ways. The other three are each well planned, carefully written, and substantial in the points they make. ''The October Game,'' for the satisfaction of Bradbury aficionados, is a horror story of exquisite structure. But the other seventeen pieces. . . .

Many of them ought not to have been published in their present form; they are so lax as to be nearly aimless. Some of them ought never to have been published at all; they are not only pointless but, alone, could never possibly be brought to any point. And those few which might be considered technically publishable are so literarily audacious as to be embarrassing to even the most ill-read. Bradbury dares to write, not like, but as George Bernard Shaw; he dares to write as Thomas Wolfe. He can't. It's painful. But, worse, ''Getting through Sunday Somehow'' is a most unsubtle James Joyce ripoff, set in Dublin, replete with pub scene and harp. And even worse than that, ''Interval in Sunlight'' transcends the ripoff: it actually appears to be a fictionalization of parts of Douglas Day's biography of Malcolm Lowry.

Ralph A. Sperry. Best Sellers. December 1976,
p. 275

Bradbury looks askance at the younger generation's belief in pseudo-sciences, political fanaticism, or hero worship of one sort or another, but sees it as inevitable in the light of the century's relative religious vacuum. He has suggested, however, that present scientific aspirations can fill that void. "As the years went by," he explains, "I found myself getting more and more interested in just the whole universe—you know, who we are, what we're doing here, where we're going, what our plans are for the next billion years. That's a long time and space is one of our ways of planning. The more we get into space, the more religious we've got to become. We're going to be meeting more mysteries." It is no surprise then that Bradbury described his following the first satellite across the night sky as "an absolutely religious experience." For more than ever before science has put man closer to the heavens he had formerly considered the territory of the gods. Since man's ascension into space has clearly brought the dreams of a god-like flight to fruition, Bradbury predictably places man at the center of the universe in the romantic and Renaissance tradition.

Steven Dimeo. Journal of Popular Culture. Spring
1972, pp. 970–78

Elements of what may be called "fantasy" were present in Ray Bradbury's works from the beginning of his writing career. His own recent remark distinguishing science fiction from fantasy in literature is that "science fiction could happen." This implies, of course, that fantasy could not happen. But in today's world, where change occurs at such rapid rate, nobody would venture to state dogmatically that any idea is incapable of realization. Therefore, whether or not a work of literature is fantasy becomes more a matter of the author's intention rather than a matter measurable by objective criteria. This is especially true of an author such as Bradbury, who by his own admission writes both science fiction and fantasy.

Bradbury's own brand of fantasy apparently came to birth in the world of the carnival. His imagination was nurtured with carnival imagery. . . . Whenever a traveling circus or carnival came through Waukegan in the 1920s and early 1930s, Bradbury and his younger brother were always present. . . . [The] carnival became for him a sort of subconscious touchstone for a whole system of moods and images which emerged later in his writings. As a result, the carnival world can be thought of as a clearinghouse for Bradbury's imagination—the place where he goes for his symbols when he is writing a tale of horror, nostalgia, fantasy, or some combination of the three. . . .

But of Bradbury's tales [during the 1940s] more were horror than fantasy. Perhaps he would regard an attempt to distinguish between horror and fantasy in his works as mere semantic quibbling. The difference, it seems to me, can almost be described as a matter of levity. In the horror tales, he was completely serious and trying his best to achieve a shock effect upon his readers. In the best of these, he probably succeeded because he also achieved, in the writing process, a shock effect upon himself. He was trying to exorcise something in himself as he wrote. Thus his horror tales were not written to enable his readers to escape, but rather to cause them to suffer so that they might be cleansed. . . . The fantasy stories, on the other hand, allow the readers' spirits to expand rather than to contract, as is the effect in the horror tales. The thrust of his effort seems to lie in the creation of a mood, and, lost in this mood, the readers can escape to a Secondary World. . . .

[This] idea, or moral, if that is a better word, . . . seems to be at least implicit in the majority of Bradbury's stories from the late 1950s until the present. He did not cease to be a teacher when he stopped writing science fiction, but he did place a moratorium upon the more evangelistic kind of moralizing which he was practicing in the late 1940s and early 1950s. Now, at last, his own sense of values seems to have become completely at one with his art.

Anita T. Sullivan. English Journal. December
1972, pp. 1309–14

Ray Bradbury is a writer with a particular skill at committing his dreams to paper and, in so doing, making them live for others. He dreams dreams of magic and transformation, good and evil, small-town America, and the canals of Mars. His dreams are not only popular—they are durable. The great body of his work consists of short stories, which are notoriously difficult to publish and keep before the public eye. Yet his stories have stayed in print, in some cases for nearly three decades.

The subjects that engage Bradbury's pen are many: magic, horror, and monsters; rockets, robots, time, and space travel; growing up in a midwestern town in the 1920s, and growing old in an abandoned earth colony on another planet. Despite their varied themes, Bradbury's stories contain a sense of wonder, often a sense of joy, and a lyrical and rhythmic touch that sets his work apart.

Using an analytical approach to such stories is to do a kind of violence to them, but between the dream and the finished story is a considerable amount of craftsmanship. The illustration of that craftsmanship, along with some elucidation of the writer's themes, hopefully will enrich the reader's understanding and appreciation of one of the major artists in his field.

The approach here is thematic: the various collections of Bradbury's stories have been "taken apart," and the stories regrouped and compared with one another in terms of elements and common themes.

Generally speaking, Bradbury's handling of a given theme in an early story as compared to a later story is essentially the same. That is, his themes do not display a growth in emotional depth or logical complexity as time goes on. Instead, Bradbury treats his themes in what might be called a Baroque manner—changing the ornamentation, emotional tone, or relative prominence of the theme from story to story. In a way, this is like the variations on a theme in music. For example, "The Next in Line" and "The Life Work of Juan Diaz" both center around the mummies in the cemetery at Guanajuato in Mexico. The former is a horror story as well as a psychological study of a marital relationship. The latter describes a very different marital relationship and concludes on a note of whimsical irony.

I have referred above to Bradbury as being one of the major artists in his field. It should be understood at the outset that there is a considerable amount of confusion as to just what this field is. The demands of the commercial marketplace and the need to confine a popular writer and his work within an easily recognizable image have resulted in Bradbury's being jammed uncomfortably into the box labeled "Science Fiction." No definition of science fiction exists that pleases everybody, and even if it did, to apply it casually to the work of Ray Bradbury would be inaccurate and unfair. H. G. Wells, whom many regard as a classic science fiction writer, had this to say about his own novels: "They are all fantasies; they do not aim to project a serious possibility; they aim indeed only at the same amount of conviction as one gets in a good gripping dream. They have to hold the reader to the end by art and illusion and not by proof and argument, and the moment he closes the cover and reflects he wakes up to their impossibility." Wells here is contrasting his stories with those of Jules Verne, which he calls "anticipatory inventions." Viewed this way, virtually all of Bradbury's stories are fantasies, with Wells's concept of the "good gripping dream" coming closest to describing their effect.

Bradbury's first publishing successes were in the pages of the horror, detective, and science fiction pulp magazines of the 1940s. As a result, his work has suffered from a certain amount of guilt by association with these forms of popular literature. When in the 1950s Bradbury began to publish regularly in major "slick" magazines, he was often referred to as having broken out of the limited field of science fiction. But this was not due so much to a change on Bradbury's part as to a recognition of the quality of his writing by a larger audience. Even today, Bradbury's place in literature is far from clear. On one hand, Harlan Ellison cites him as an example of how good science fiction can be: "Every time we try to hype some nonbeliever into accepting science fiction and fantasy as legitimate *literature,* we refer him or her to the words of Ray Bradbury. . . . We whirl them over to the meager science fiction racks in most bookstores and we may find no Delany, no Lafferty, no Knight or Disch or Dickson, but by God, we always find *The Martian Chronicles.*" On the other hand, Clifton Fadiman, in his prefatory note to the 1954 Bantam edition of *The Martian Chronicles,* seems a bit condescending in noting that the book ". . . has lifted itself easily out of the ruck of its competitors," and in calling Bradbury a "moralist." True as these assertions may be, they reflect common attempts to reassure the insecure reader that Bradbury's writing is somehow worthwhile, and therefore all right to take seriously—reassurances which Bradbury neither seeks nor requires. Bradbury regards himself as an entertainer, more specifically a magician, and his stories are written primarily to amuse. Perhaps the passage of time will alleviate the problem of which niche Bradbury is to occupy—or better still, subvert the tendency to pigeonhole him altogether. Few today would insist on labeling Rudyard Kipling an ''Indian'' writer, or feel it necessary to apologize for enjoying the entertainments of Saki (H. H. Munro). In a somewhat similar fashion, Bradbury's literary family goes beyond the Arthur C. Clarkes and the Isaac Asimovs, to include such recorders of small-town America as Sinclair Lewis and Sherwood Anderson, and such contemporary fantasists as Roald Dahl and John Collier.

Wayne L. Johnson. Ray Bradbury (New York:
Ungar, 1980), pp. ix–xiii

Ray Bradbury began his life with science fiction in the fan movement, publishing his first attempts in *Futuria Fantasia,* a magazine he edited himself and for which he wrote almost all the contents. In the 1940s he produced a number of stories set on Mars. These were brought together in 1951 in book form under the title *The Martian Chronicles,* . . . one of the classics of science fiction literature. The stories are set in the years between the ''rocket summer'' of January 1999, and the ''eternal picnic'' of October 2026, and together tell the history of the colonization of Mars. The first three expeditions from Earth fail because Mars is trying to protect itself against a threatening cultural collapse and barbarism. Delightful humor informs the portraits of the Earth men, as they are shown expecting to be welcomed with open arms by thousands of Martians. What they encounter is complete indifference; everyone is occupied with their workaday duties. Then they land in a lunatic asylum, where they are greeted with the expected jubilation. But . . . when the fourth expedition lands, the whole population of Mars has fallen victim to an epidemic of chickenpox, against which they have no protection. Rocket after rocket can now land freely. For Bradbury, the ancient Martian culture and its relics, including buildings and books, pottery, and so on, obviously humanist in character, is destroyed by the besieging ''pioneers.'' He repeatedly suggests parallels between the events of his story and the colonization methods used by nations; the glorification of the first settlers, which lies at the core of the western, is subject to special scrutiny. Instead of the old harmony grown up on Mars over millions of years, there now comes to that planet what Bradbury particularly was critical of in American society: greed for money, struggles for power, and a social order of rigid hierarchy.

Bradbury makes reference to many literary motifs and themes, weaves them into new variations and uses them to highlight his own interpretations. In ''Usher II,'' for instance, he looks back at Poe's famous tale of ''The Fall of the House of Usher.'' A symbol of the modern pseudocivilization is Sam Parkhill's Hot Dog Restaurant in *The Martian Chronicles,* the glass of which has been broken from the old Martian buildings in the hills. In No-

vember 2005, the settlers of Mars experience from their great distance fiery
explosions on Earth, receiving the message flashing by Morse code that:

AUSTRALIAN CONTINENT ATOMIZED IN PREMATURE EXPLOSION OF ATOMIC
STOCKPILE. LOS ANGELES, LONDON BOMBED. WAR. COME HOME. COME HOME.
COME HOME. COME HOME.

Most of the settlers on Mars leave and return to Earth to play their part in
an atomic war, and are lost in the general destruction. In the twentieth year
after the war, Mars is a dead planet, and Earth is also dead. A small handful
of people use the last rocket to fly to Mars, in order to make a fresh start
there. "Life on Earth never settled down to doing anything very good. Science ran too far ahead of us too quickly, and the people got lost in a mechanical wilderness. . . . Wars got bigger and bigger and finally killed Earth.
. . . Now we're alone. We and a handful of others who'll land in a few
days. Enough to start over. Enough to turn away from all that back on Earth
and strike out on a new line."

This is at once Bradbury's humanist message and his warning. This
aspect of his work is even more pointedly marked in his dystopia *Fahrenheit
451*. When this novel was first published in 1953, McCarthyism in the U.S.
was reaching its climax. The anticommunist hysteria had affected almost
every area of American society. Anxiety shut the mouths of many writers,
including some science fiction writers. Ray Bradbury found a successful
way of tackling the problem through fantasy. In the social system depicted
in *Fahrenheit 451*, it is not difficult to see the relation it bears to a country
terrorized by a type of McCarthyism or Hitlerism. The title hints at the
central symbol of Bradbury's theme: "Fahrenheit 451: the temperature at
which book-paper catches fire and burns." The book burning is a symbol of
the rooting out of any remaining humanity in this inhuman social system, a
symbol that of course refers to much more than simply McCarthyism. The
society is blessed with much luxury and technology, but there exists an
absolute prohibition against the reading of books. The main character, Guy
Montag, works in the fire service, which has meanwhile totally reversed its
functions, with Montag's duty to oversee not the saving but the burning of
books. The rationale for this is given by Beatty, the fire captain: "A book
is a loaded gun in the house next door."

The first part of the novel, "It Was a Pleasure to Burn," tells of Guy
trying to hide books away despite the fact that punishment for this is imprisonment. At last he and his wife begin to read the twenty or so books
they have collected. The second part of the book shows the first effects of
his new experience ("The Sieve and the Sand"): Guy makes contact with a
Professor Faber. He develops a plan to print books secretly and smuggle
them into the houses of the firemen, with the aim of striking a death blow
to those in power—a kind of partisan scheme to preserve culture. But then

the unexpected happens: the fire engine stops before his own house, led there by information given by Guy's wife, Mildred.

The third part of the book, "Burning Bright," sees Guy forced to burn down his own house. He kills the captain, two fire officers, and destroys the "mechanical hound" that terrorizes them all. Now Guy must flee. Eventually he reaches a group of "outsiders," former intellectuals who preserve the great books of world literature in their memories for posterity. These people are Bradbury's hope for the future. The television screens show someone referred to as "Guy Montag" captured and killed. It is a fake news report. The powers that be think they have avenged Guy's crime. But there are in fact thousands of outsiders: looking no more than tramps they are in fact a library of culture. After the war, they will each commit the book they carry in their memories to paper, and the volumes will then be printed and circulated. They already see the airplanes coming and the city razed in seconds. They start their journey back to the totally flattened world, to bring the spirit back into it.

Bradbury's vision is a warning of the possible future of any country upon which McCarthyism or any similar book-burning terror is unleashed. The vision derives some of its detail from the book burnings experienced during the Nazi regime and during World War II. Bradbury also demonstrates how such a society contains within it the seeds of war. Thus he makes his contribution to the preservation of peace.

Dieter Wuckel. *The Illustrated History of Science Fiction* (New York: Ungar, 1989), pp. 123–25

BRETT, SIMON (1945–   )

Simon Brett's first mystery novels are set in the British theatrical system, and star Charles Paris, an aging actor, no detective—amateur or professional—but a man who *does* manage to help unravel mysteries and crimes that take place in the peculiar show-biz world about him. Brett's style is studded with marvelously cynical observations about that world—comments that could indeed as easily pertain to the world the rest of us inhabit.

The Charles Paris series began with *Cast, in Order of Disappearance* in 1975 (U.S., 1976). In 1987, Brett temporarily departed from Charles Paris and produced *A Shock to the System,* an ironic crime novel following the convoluted machinations of a man thrust into the role of killer by his own unique psychological makeup. That same year Brett made a further departure from his original speciality and initiated a series of mysteries allied to the Agatha Christie-type format in *A Nice Class of Corpse*—following the adventures of Melita Pargeter, "Mrs. Pargeter," the widow of a shadowy master criminal whose colleagues rally around her to help solve puzzling murders that seem to pop up around her presence in sometimes exotic locales. The crime novels and the third series allow Brett an even greater latitude to entertain his readers with his delightful tongue-in-cheek observations on modern life.

Waltraud Woeller and Bruce Cassiday. *The Literature of Crime and Detection* (New York: Ungar, 1988), p. 168

Ian Compton, a young advertising copywriter, is trendiness personified:

> He was wearing a double-breasted gangster-striped suit over a pale blue T-shirt. Around his neck hung a selection of leather thongs, one for a biro, one for a packet of Gauloise, one for a Cricket lighter, and others whose function was not immediately apparent. His lapels bristled with badges, gollies, teddy bears, a spilling tomato ketchup bottle and similar trendy kitsch. . . .

Since 1975 Simon Brett has written yearly a novel featuring actor-detective Charles Paris, and those novels have made Brett one of the principal younger writers of detective fiction in Great Britain. On more than one occasion he has made some variation on the statement his novels are intended as entertainment. They are indeed that, for they are a continuation of that long tradition of the seemingly easy—but treacherously difficult—sophisticated, comic British detective novel. Using his own experience and knowledge of the theater, radio, and television, Brett has also added, with much more expertise than most, to that large and popular subgenre: the theatrical murder mystery. Whereas earlier writers in that subgenre, most notably Dame Ngaio Marsh, presented the theatrical murder as comedy of manners, Brett surrounds it with social satire. In fact, it is as a social satirist that Brett shows his greatest distinctiveness as a mystery writer. He is not just a satirist of the theater and the media; rather, the satire provided by Charles Paris's acting jobs and the resultant murder cases is of contemporary British life with British show business serving as a microcosm of the problems, frustrations, stupidities, dislocations, and antagonisms present in that larger world outside the theater or studio. In both his adherence to the conventions of British detective fiction—even when breaking those conventions—and his contemporaneity of attitude, Simon Brett is most significantly the detective novelist as satirist of his society. . . .

Charles Paris comes in contact with all sorts of people in the novels. Some are presented in a sort of comic-pathetic way, particularly old people, such as the studio audiences and the unbalanced radio fan, Mrs. Moxon, of *The Dead Side of the Mike.* But the major type of person satirized is the member of the middle class who is either too trendy or too conventional; both are present in *An Amateur Corpse.*

How far Brett will take Charles Paris, theatrical murder, and satire of contemporary Britain is unknown. Already he has shown that he ranks among the most innovative of recent mystery writers. His insider's knowledge of the British entertainment world and his sharply focused observations of people, institutions, and manners have been employed within the framework of the detective novel to satirize, with the full range of comedy, both implicitly and explicitly life in contemporary Britain. As a social satirist in the detective genre, he has fulfilled his expressed purpose of entertaining and, in doing so, has produced a distinctive body of work which is a reflection of and comment on his time. Finally, there is Charles Paris. He may not be a star as an actor, some might even say he is not a star as a great detective, but he is a star as a fictional character for whose appearances readers eagerly await, and with just eight novels his creator rightly deserves a place with his predecessors among these dozen Englishmen of mystery.

Earl F. Bargainnier. *Twelve Englishmen of Mystery*
(Bowling Green, Ohio: Popular Press, 1984),
pp. 304–25

Simon Brett's new mystery, *Not Dead, Only Resting,* can be best compared to the majority of episodes of the television series *Murder, She Wrote.* It is diverting, sometimes fun or thrilling, and it moves along fairly well, yet, in the end, it hasn't done much beyond what was expected.

The ''resting'' of the title is the term used by the English acting profession as the time between acting jobs. Professional actor/amateur detective Charles Paris finds himself in one of these periods and takes up with a fellow actor to do a redecorating job in order to make ends meet. The flat they are to do is owned by two homosexual men who own and operate the restaurant below. They have closed it up and gone for a month-long holiday in France. When Charles and friend show up, they find one of the men murdered and the other missing.

It is hard to say much more about the plot without giving away too much because there is not a great deal of substance until all the loose ends are tied up toward the end. A large portion of the book is concerned with setting up all the supposedly unrelated elements of the mystery. Though they are not boring, they are not quite interesting enough to stop the reader from thinking, ''Where is all this leading?''

There are a few elements from the *Murder, She Wrote* school of plot structuring that make the book less than believable. One is the obvious red herring suspect. You know, the prime suspect who has been given the most obvious motive and opportunity so that the audience will not miss it, but, because it is so blatant, he couldn't have done it. If he had, there would be no mystery. Another is the ''big coincidence.'' There is a coincidence in *Not Dead, Only Resting* on which most of the solution hinges, yet there seems to be little or no reason for it to happen the way it did, except to serve the plot.

In the way of characters, the book is lacking. Much of what it is trying to say is that we should be more tolerant of homosexuals, yet it portrays them as stereotypes. As for Charles Paris, he seems constantly downtrodden and depressed. He is separated from his wife, he drinks too much, and he has an agent who will barely lift a finger for him. None of this is recent—it has been happening for years. Paris just does not seem to have enough nerve to do anything about it. He does not seem to have much character, good or bad, to command the reader's interest.

All in all, *Not Dead, Only Resting* has little to offer except a mildly diverting read, which does not make it bad, just okay.

John Kovaleski. The Armchair Detective. Fall
1987, pp. 94–95

Charles Paris is back in his twelfth mystery, *What Bloody Man Is That?*, by Simon Brett. This time, he is investigating murder Shakespeare-style.

Having been out of work for quite a while, Charles accepts the role of the Drunken Porter and the Bleeding Sergeant in Gavin Scholes's repertory production of *Macbeth*. Whenever he takes on a new job, he also takes on murder. The murder victim this time is Warnock Belvedere, a loud, boisterous man playing the part of Duncan. Unfortunately for Charles, the police suspect him of the murder.

Simon Brett is one of the most engaging English mystery writers working today. He introduces some fascinating and delightfully eccentric characters such as Felicia Chatterton, who plays a young Lady Macbeth to the much older Macbeth acted by comedy actor George Birkitt. Using the theater world as his setting enables Brett to introduce an intriguing puzzle and to limit the suspects. *What Bloody Man Is That?* is a whodunit sprinkled with comedy, and it makes entertaining reading.

Actors sometimes play a game with walnuts. During the performance, they try to pass it into the next actor's hand. At the end of the play, the one with the walnut is the loser. Charles Paris plays the game by trying to find the real murderer and pass police suspicions on to someone else.

When the walnuts fall into place, all the questions are neatly and plausibly answered.

Carl A. Melton. The Armchair Detective. Summer
1988, pp. 297–98

BURGESS, ANTHONY (1917–   )

The book that made Anthony Burgess's reputation in the United States is *A Clockwork Orange,* which is his own particular vision of horrors yet to come. It is probably not as good a book as *1984,* it is certainly not as chilling as *Brave New World* where the slaves do not even know they are slaves and the miserable have lost the power to recognize or name their misery, but it is quite good enough, and it serves well as an introduction to the Burgess canon. Set in England some time in the future, written only partly in English and partly in a language devised by Burgess for the occasion, it is the story of a young thief-rapist-murderer who is betrayed to the police by one of his comrades, jailed, treated by doctors, and cured at once of his criminal tendencies and of all his humanity. The effect of the book is made no less dour by the ending that restores Alex to his old, vicious, music-loving self. He is set loose to kill again, to mug old men for the fun of it, except now he will be sheltered by the government because the matter of his chemical brain washing has become a political cause célèbre. We leave him listening to Beethoven, speaking his own curious lingo, thinking his salacious thoughts.

At the other end of Burgess's range is his first written—though not first published—novel, and not one of his strongest, *A Vision of Battlements*. This is a mundane story of a soldier's life in the relatively safe precincts of Gibraltar. The book is, as one might expect, generally and in some way specifically autobiographical. The hero, Richard Ennis, is a composer—as is Burgess—and Burgess tells us in a preface to the American edition that he spent three years of his own army service on Gibraltar, and that the writing of *Battlements* was in part an effort to exorcise the pain and loneliness that he suffered there. The lines along which the narrative develops are of no consequence: there is a little sex, a little violence, a good deal of satirical writing about army life and army types. But the book does display, in at least a rudimentary form, Burgess's gloomy, tolerant, and comic view of the human condition, his love of words and his gift for them, his extravagant sense of image and of plot. Thus, as different as the two books are, in their basic technical achievements, and their primary philosophical thrusts, *Battlements* and *Clockwork Orange* fit the same mold.

It is easy to get the feeling, reading his fiction, that prolific as Burgess is, his creative life is a hand to mouth affair. For him, there may really be a Muse, and one can imagine him sitting down to work in the morning having no notion of where he is going, sublimely content to follow in any direction that his mind might lead. Usually, his mind leads well, and even in moments of weak motivation and flawed structure, Burgess can rely on his wit and his extraordinary sense of language to see him through.

Walter Sullivan. *The Hollins Critic*. April 1969,
pp. 1–3

In his proleptic nightmare, *The Wanting Seed,* Burgess presents a horrifying, though richly comic, picture of life in a world freed of the scourge of war but overpopulated beyond Malthus's most fearful imaginings. An awareness of Malthus's demographic theories is essential to a full appreciation of the comedy and satire, but this is surely not too much to expect of the average twentieth-century reader, and it is astonishing that *The Wanting Seed,* like *A Clockwork Orange,* has been so completely misunderstood by some critics. All of Malthus's positive and preventive "checks"—through "misery," "vice," and "moral restraint"—are brought into play and it becomes apparent that even in England circumstances could make them much less distinguishable from one another than Malthus assumed.

In addition to splendid multipronged satire, *The Wanting Seed* contains a complete statement and illustration of a cyclical theory of history which Burgess had partially formulated in his first novel, *A Vision of Battlements*. In that novel an American officer describes how the Pelagian denial of Original Sin had spawned "the two big modern heresies—material progress as a sacred goal; the State as God Almighty." The former has produced "Americanism" and the latter, "the Socialist process." In *The Wanting Seed* all government history is seen to be an oscillation between two "phases," a Pelagian phase and an Augustinian. When a government is functioning in its Pelagian phase, or "Pelphase," it is socialistic and committed to a Wellsian liberal belief in the goodness of man and his ability to achieve perfection through his own efforts. Inevitably man fails to fulfill the liberal expectation and the ensuing "disappointment" causes a chaotic "Interphase," during which terrorist police strive to maintain order by force and brutality. Finally, the government, appalled by its own excesses, lessens the brutality but continues to enforce its will on the citizenry on the assumption that man is an inherently sinful creature from whom no good may be expected. This pessimistic phase is appropriately named for the saint whose preoccupation with the problems of evil led him, like Burgess, into Manichaeism. During "Gusphase" there is a capitalist economy but very little real freedom for the individual.

[*The Wanting Seed*] is a magnificent black comedy, in many ways Burgess's best. He encompasses far more than either Orwell or Huxley do in their famous dystopias, and he is far more entertaining. The novel's only significant flaw proceeds from Burgess's tendency to be too entertaining and too witty. It is full of playful references to his fellow-novelists and other literary figures. There is, for example, the description of the bearded giant atop the Government Building which is identified from time to time with various figures of cultural and political importance, including "Eliot (a long-dead singer of infertility)." And the reports of cannibalism during the Interphase include the account of how "a man called Amis suffered savage amputation of an arm off Kingsway," and "S. R. Coke, journalist, was boiled in an old copper near Shepherd's Bush; Miss Joan Waine, a teacher, was fried in segments." In themselves, these allusions and fantasies are delightful, but they combine with occasional flippancies of tone to deprive the book of some of its potential impact. As with *Dr. Strangelove,* the hilarity of presentation occasionally tends to make it difficult to bear in mind the seriousness of the themes.

Geoffrey Aggeler. *Arizona Quarterly.* Vol. 25,
No. 3. 1969, pp. 243–46

A late bloomer, Anthony Burgess did not devote himself entirely to writing until he left the British colonial service in his forties, but in the following two decades he has made up for lost time. His twenty-odd volumes of fiction range over vast immensities of time and space, and are full of flashy erudition and restless experiments with language and form. . . .

Where Joyce sought to compress the whole of European civilization into a single moment of historical time, Burgess deployed his erudite fascination with language in a futuristic morality tale. *A Clockwork Orange* is Burgess's masterpiece, a savage prophecy of a future socialist England in which teenage gangs called Nadsats roam the streets in an ecstasy of mindless violence. . . .

In his account of the Pavlovian conditioning which the state employs to transform the vicious Alex into a docile citizen, Burgess sought to press home his certainty that man, however depraved, must be free to make a moral choice between good and evil. Deeply suspicious, as he once remarked, of "any political ideology which rejects original sin and believes in moral progress," Burgess in *A Clockwork Orange* turned the liberal piety of the welfare state on its head, repudiating the simpleminded faith of our age in rehabilitation and social conditioning. More recently Burgess spelled out the point once again in *1985,* a rather cranky attempt to bring Orwell's dystopia up to date: "I recognize that the desire to cherish man's unregenerate nature, to deny the possibility of progress and reject the engines of enforced improvement, is very reactionary, but, in the absence of a new philosophy of man, I must cling to whatever I already have."

What Burgess is saying—that moral reform cannot be induced—is presumably indisputable. Yet his implication that the evil of violence, freely chosen, is preferable to the brainwashed passivity of "reconditioned" sinners shrinks the actual human alternatives with ludicrous severity. Any absolute principle, no matter how uncompromisingly it declares itself for moral freedom, becomes twisted in its absolute application. And the lesson of the last thirty years, the lesson that makes a tragedy of the Enlightenment, is that even when virtues are positive they may prove to be irreconcilable. As a thinker Burgess is considerably less persuasive than as a virtuoso of language.

Pearl K. Bell. *Commentary*. February 1981,
pp. 71–72

When the artist, the mythmaker, the poet, and the word-player become the focus of a novel—when love and language become inseparable—Burgess's art triumphs. His best characters are men like himself—Enderby, the poet, and even Alex, the droog, who in a brutal futuristic world, still likes to "shine artistic." Even some of the lesser characters, such as Denis Hillier and J. W. Denham and Kenneth Toomey, share his delight in language and concern about moral values in the contemporary world. When the single dogged consciousness of the artist occupies Burgess's energies in a novel, the vision of restorative, redemptive powers of art and language blossom fully, no matter how brutal the world which surrounds it continues to be.

In the portrayal of each of these characters, Burgess does not bypass human frailty, disease, and guilt; in each, he confronts these fully, suggesting the very real possibility of redemption and fulfillment—especially in art and in his own Manichean "faith"—that may grow out of the very human soil in which they are planted. This is his triumph. In playing serious but comic games, in devising new myths or replaying old ones, in constantly celebrating the continuous display of man's imagination and creativity through word and deed, Burgess views the artist as a man capable of constructing his own salvation. It doesn't always work. In his best novels, however, he convinces us it can.

Samuel Coale. *Anthony Burgess* (New York:
Ungar, 1981), pp. 195–99

CAIN, JAMES M. (1892–1977)

The Postman Always Rings Twice is a brutal story of adultery and murder whose appropriate setting is a wayside filling station in California. Up to a certain point it rings horribly true: the bungled attempt at murder, the unsuccessful crime, the maggots of mutual suspicion that begin to prey on the guilty partners. But then Mr. Cain begins to make things up. He has almost succeeded in showing two triumphantly evil people—the reader is uncomfortable but can't let the story drop—when his intention falters: he converts his two villains into another Paolo and Francesca and rings down the curtain on a Hollywood-tragic ending. *The Postman Always Rings Twice* is a short, meretricious but exciting book; it does not pretend to tell the whole story, but it does pretend to tell nothing but the truth.

T. S. Matthews. The New Republic. February 28,
1934, p. 80

The hero of the typical Cain novel is a good-looking down-and-outer, who leads the life of a vagrant and a rogue. He invariably falls under the domination—usually to his ruin—of a vulgar and determined woman from whom he finds it impossible to escape. . . . Cain's heroes are capable of extraordinary exploits, but they are always treading the edge of a precipice; and they are doomed, like the heroes of Hemingway, for they will eventually fall off the precipice. But whereas in Hemingway's stories it is simply that these brave and decent men have had a dirty deal from life, the hero of a novel by Cain is an individual of mixed unstable character, who carries his precipice with him like Pascal.

His fate is thus forecast from the beginning; but in the meantime he has fabulous adventures—samples, as it were, from a *Thousand and One Nights* of the screwy Pacific Coast: you have jungle lust in roadside lunchrooms, family motor trips that end in murder, careers catastrophically broken by the vagaries of bisexual personality, the fracas created by a Mexican Indian introduced among the phonies of Hollywood.

Cain is particularly ingenious in tracing from their first beginnings the tangles that gradually tighten around the necks of the people involved in those bizarre and brutal crimes that figure in the American papers; and is capable even of tackling—in *Serenade,* at any rate—the larger tangles of social interest from which these deadly little knots derive. Such a subject might provide a great novel: in *An American Tragedy,* such a subject did. But as we follow, in a novel by Mr. Cain, the development of one of his plots, we find ourselves more and more disconcerted at knocking up—to the destruction of illusion—against the blank and hard planes and angles of something we know all too well: the wooden old conventions of Hollywood. Here is the Hollywood gag: the echo of the murdered man's voice reverberating from the mountains when the man himself is dead, and the party in *Serenade,* in which the heroine stabs the villain under cover of acting out a bullfight; the punctual Hollywood coincidence: the popping-up of the music-loving sea captain, who is the *deus ex machina* of *Serenade;* the Hollywood reversal of fortune: the singer who loses his voice and then gets it back again, becoming famous and rich in a sequence that lasts about three minutes.

Mr. Cain is actually a writer for the studios. . . . These novels are produced in his off-time; and they are a kind of Devil's parody of the movies. Mr. Cain is the *âme damnée* of Hollywood. All the things that have been excluded by the Catholic censorship: sex, debauchery, unpunished crime, sacrilege against the Church—Mr. Cain has let them loose in these stories with a gusto as of pent-up ferocity that the reader cannot but share. What a pity that it is impossible for such a writer to create and produce his own pictures!

In the meantime, *Serenade* is a definite improvement on *The Postman.* It, too, has its trashy aspect, its movie foreshortenings and its too-well oiled action; but it establishes a surer illusion. *The Postman* was always in danger of becoming unintentionally funny. Yet even there brilliant moments of insight redeemed the unconscious burlesque; and there is enough of the real poet in Cain—both in writing and in imagination—to make one hope for something better than either.

Edmund Wilson. The New Republic, November 11,
1940, pp. 20–22

Cain deals with ciphers, picturesque cardboard characters whom he cuts into attractive designs. He has certain specific knowledges that he draws on in all his novels: the workings of the law, the inside of the restaurant business, and the world of music. He has a few favorite themes: fate, the relationship of art and sex, and particularly the relationship of sex and violence. All his books give the sense of having been pieced together skillfully out of these shiny bits of glass, having no organic existence or internal necessity.

Stanley Edgar Hyman. The New Republic. October
16, 1941, p. 442

In James M. Cain's work there is clearly a difference between sensationalism for its own sake and the effects sought by a writer obviously concerned with style and technique, even when the basic premise is violence. And it is truly an astonishing style, rippling and easy in a nervous sort of way, the people talking as such people would talk, the writing vivid and direct. For when Mr. Cain's faults have all been pointed out—and the principal one is that character doesn't matter much in his writing—the pertinent fact remains: when he is at the top of his form it is all but impossible to put down the story he is telling.

John K. Hutchins. *New York Herald Tribune Book Review*. April 18, 1943, p. 7

James M. Cain's novel, *Mildred Pierce,* wantonly squanders what could have been a very good and representative American story; it could even have been a great one.

One of the striking and promising features in the early portions of this novel is that the two main characters are presented with reference to objects and to conventional conceptions. They possess little of the individuality of many merely literary characters. The style of the book is objective, even a little flat in places; it records movements, performances, the handling of things, such as Bert bracing the trees, Mildred cooking, and the ingredients which go into the making of something she will sell. Thus there is presented a life in which things, commodities, have almost become the protagonists.

Mildred Pierce has been developed in terms of Hollywood simplicities but does not indicate the character of the opportunity Cain has squandered. Cain's stories are swift moving, punctuated by shocks and violence. His novels are written as a kind of literary movie. But since greater latitude is permitted the novelist than the scenarist, novels like *Mildred Pierce* have the appearance of greater reality than do most films. Unrestrained by a production code, a Cain story can follow the patterns of real life more closely than can a motion picture. In *Mildred Pierce,* Cain began with a real problem, one relatively untouched in contemporary writing. *Mildred Pierce* could have been a poignant account of the middle-class housewife. The fictional character, Mildred, could have been representative of hundreds of thousands of such women. At times there are suggestions of this. The opening portions of the book are promising. But then we see where James M. Cain has learned his literary lessons. Story values take the place of Mildred's problems. Plot involvements, relationships based on plot and story, falsify what was begun as a story about people.

Cain writes of people who are cruel, violent, self-centered, and who have a minimum of awareness. In his world there is neither good nor bad and there is little love. The values of these people are very crude, and they are described in such a way that no concept of experience worthy of the name can be implied to the author. People commit adultery and the wicked are not always punished. If the wicked are punished it is purely fortuitous: punishment is the result of the needs of the story and not of the stern hand of Providence or of the pitiless forging of a chain of necessities. This, plus the element of violence, frequently unmotivated, deceives careless readers: they consider Cain to be a serious writer.

Writers like Cain stand between the work of a serious and tragic character which has been fathered in America by such men as Dreiser and the work derived from the more-or-less-forgotten writings of Robert W. Chambers, Gene Stratton-Porter, or Harold Bell Wright. And in this in-between, neither-fish-nor-fowl literary medium, James M. Cain has become the master. He is a literary thrill producer who profits by the reaction against the sentimentality of other years and, at the same time, gains from the prestige of more serious and exploratory writing. Thus James M. Cain is not an insignificant or unimportant American literary phenomenon. He has helped to perfect a form which can properly be termed movietone realism.

One of the major virtues of serious realism is that it describes the pitiless force of circumstance and the equally pitiless drive of human emotions which often play so central a role in causing the tragic destruction of human beings. But in this pseudorealistic type of novel . . . the pitiless force of circumstance and of human impulse is replaced by the fortuitousness of automobile accidents and the like and by a melodramatically simplified conception of good girls and bad girls.

James T. Farrell. *Literature and Morality* (New York: Vanguard Press, 1947), pp. 79–89

A world immense with freedom, women hellish and infantile by turns, money, power, the tantalizing promise of adventure—these are the common elements of James M. Cain's novels. His reputation is by this time a vague one, grown generalized and perhaps sentimentally overrated (along with the reputations of Dashiell Hammett and Raymond Chandler) since he is no longer "read." We have Camus, we have the films of Jean-Luc Godard, we have any number of cryptic realists who can give us Cain's pace and excitement without Cain's flaws—*and* in the form of art. Though he deals constantly with the Artistic, Cain, it will be said, never manages to become an artist; there is always something sleazy, something eerily vulgar and disappointing in his work. Let us abandon all claims for Cain's "place in American literature" if it is literature only that is significant, and let us concentrate instead on the relationship between Cain's work and his hypothetical audience, America of the thirties and forties, and the archetypal rhythms of his works whether the works themselves ultimately satisfy as art. . . .

Cain's world is by no means "realistic": coming to him from the great psychological realists, Joyce and Mann, one understands how barren, how stripped and bizarre this Western landscape has become. It is as if the world extends no farther than the radius of one's desire. Within this small circle (necessarily small because his heroes are usually ignorant), accidental encounters have the force of destiny behind them. . . .

Cain's heroes have an aura of doom about them, suggested to us by the flatness of their narration, their evident hurry to get it said. They follow the same archetypal route, obeying without consciousness the urges that lead them (and their tragic ancestors) to disaster. . . . And what happens finally is always repentance, for the Cain hero is no more metaphysically inclined than he is morally substantial. . . .

Cain's heroes fight a losing battle with the forces of the unconscious (which they may describe in a number of ways). But, since they go beyond the point of self-control, a vigorous and all-powerful social unit awaits them and will protect us from them. The social instruments by which justice is granted may be no more moral than the victims who are punished, but if so, this is one more element of the tabloid poetry that pleases a popular audience: the sadism of Cain's heroes will always be turned against them, and the phenomenon of an audience both identifying with and rejecting a victim is not surprising. It is the very ordinariness of Cain's heroes that make them fit victims for "justice." If they were wiser, more clever, more audacious or evil, they might escape, but then they would be monsters and valueless to a reading public, which demands characters with whom one can identify. But the fact that they are nonheroic heroes, animalistic, or even mechanical in their responses, even (in the case of John Howard Sharp) masculine only by effort and luck, and somehow losers in the economic struggle of America, will necessitate their total failure. . . .

It is not Cain's writing so much as the success of that writing which is interesting. His works may be discussed as mirrors of the society that gave birth to them, and rewarded their creator handsomely for them, but the ambiguities and paradoxes of the works bear analysis. Money is important, but it is important secondarily. Of first importance is the doomed straining toward a permanent relationship—an emotional unit which the male both desires and fears. Whether love or sex, it is certainly dominated by unconscious motives, a complex of impulses which shuttle between violence and tenderness. Thus the innocent victim of *The Butterfly* becomes a moonshiner and, rather abruptly, a brutal murderer because of his confused feelings toward his "daughter"; and once his power is relinquished to her, his doom is certain. To love and therefore to relinquish one's power are tantamount to being destroyed. One must remain solitary and invulnerable, yet one cannot—and so the death sentence is earned. Mildred Pierce, masculine in her determination for economic success and possession of her daughter, survives only because in her novel, Cain attempts to write a realistic story, without the structural contrivance of murder and retribution. Mildred is "destroyed" in a thematic sense, but in the suspense-novel genre she would have been killed.

Cain's parable, which is perhaps America's parable, may be something like this: the passion that rises in us is both an inescapable part of our lives and an enemy to our lives, to our egoistic control of ourselves. Once unleashed it cannot be quieted. Giving oneself to anyone, even temporarily, will result in entrapment and death; the violence lovers do to one another is no more than a reflection of the proposed violence society holds back to keep the individual passions in check. . . . Just as the soap operas and the American movies not only of the thirties and forties but of the present have played back again and again certain infantile obsessions to the great American public, so Cain's novels serve up, in the guise of moral tracts, the lesson of the child who dares too much and must be punished. And there is satisfaction in knowing he will be punished—if not for one crime, then for another; if not by the law, then by himself or by an accomplice. In any case the "postman," whatever symbol of fate or death or order in the form of a uniformed and familiar person, will "ring twice"; there is no escape.

There is perhaps no writer more faithful to the mythologies of America than Cain, for he writes of its ideals and hatreds without obscuring them in the difficulties of art.

Joyce Carol Oates. In David Madden, ed., *Tough Guy Writers of the Thirties* (Carbondale, Illinois: Southern Illinois University Press, 1968), pp. 110–28

Beating at the heart of every Cain novel are basic, simple, universal elements, presented baldly in bold action: sex, love, evil, religion, food, money, violence, the lure of the forbidden, among others. One of the most obvious elements in Cain's simple, melodramatic, terse fables of sex, murder, and money is violence. It takes many forms: sexual, physical, verbal, violence of nature, and even, we might say, violence of literary technique, perpetrated upon the reader. He satisfies the average American's inexhaustible craving for details of crime and punishment. Cain's characters commit robbery, embezzlement, graft, bribery, assault, fraud, perjury, treason, and other crimes. Many men wish to commit a crime, if they can get away with it; his characters do, for a while, and we live their success. The typical rhythm of violence in Cain is from crime climax to sex climax to the fall of one or both of the lovers. Cain's works reflect a vision of popular culture, based on assumptions which his observations of society have encouraged. Without deliberately attempting to depict the world of his times, Cain does evoke it. Though he may criticize it and his own tastes may turn elsewhere, it is out of *this* culture that Cain writes and to this culture that his novels belong. That American readers have blessed his novels with their approval is in itself a comment on society. Even in his less violent novels, Cain depicts a world produced by violent conditions, revealing a vision that sees "American tragedy colored by American farce."

It is easy to understand his appeal to the average reader; for, when Cain is at his best, there is little difference between author and reader. His characters are not far removed in status or aspiration from the average reader Cain envisions. Thus, his knowledge of what his reader wants is phenomenal. But it is fallacious to call his work "popular" in the negative sense. Part of his ability lies in the way he mingles serious and popular fictive elements. Even the serious reader becomes so involved that he is unaware, until after finishing a Cain novel, of ways in which the author's achievement may be examined technically as literature. Sophisticated literary elements operate in Cain, but so "naturally" that they neither tax the popular reader's patience nor, at first, impress the sophisticated reader.

Certainly Cain's art, more than anything else, moves even the serious reader to almost complete emotional commitment to the traumatic experiences Cain renders; and this artistic control convinces me that without his finest novels—*The Postman, Serenade, Mildred Pierce,* and *The Butterfly*—the cream of our twentieth-century fiction would be thinner. Straddling realism and expressionism, he often gives us a vivid account of life on the American scene as he has observed and experienced it; and, in his best moments, he provides the finer vibrations afforded by the aesthetic experience. Cain the entertainer may fail to say anything truly important about life, but he takes us through experiences whose special quality is found in no other writer's work.

David Madden. *James M. Cain* (Boston: Twayne, 1970), pp. 17–19, 21–22, 59, 66, 75–91, 120, 138–39, 164, 175–76

In the Twain-Crane-Dreiser-Hemingway tradition, Cain successfully made the leap from journalism to fiction although he never abandoned magazine writing. Journalism not only provided him with some knowledge of a number of career fields but, more significantly for his craft, helped him achieve the compression, tautness, and detached objectivity which, coupled with his sensational and brutal subject matter, characterize his writing and link him with other "tough guy" writers of the period.

Cain's L.A. novels, drawing on this tradition, express the collective and destructive fantasies of the depression decade and turn these fantasies into nightmares. All of his heroes and heroines are self-destructively driven by sexual passion, a too-consuming love, or an overpowering desire for material possessions. Such hunger is always the force driving them to desperate acts. Cain's pattern is to give his protagonists the temporary illusion of victory and then to take everything away from them.

What defeats Cain's heroes is not what defeats Fitzgerald's: the truth that the dream, once realized, can neither be preserved nor recaptured. For Cain the characters are defeated because their dreams are in direct conflict with those of others. Each character is yoked to, and set against, another—Frank and Cora, Mildred and Veda, Walter and Phyllis—and destroyed because the other is more ruthless, more clever or simply more determined. The pairs are suicidally tied to each other by passion, greed and jealousy. There is never a chance they will get away with anything.

For Cain, who arrived in Los Angeles soon after the Crash and remained through the Depression, the city came to represent the betrayed dreams of the whole nation. In the boom years hundreds of thousands had come seeking their fresh starts and new beginnings—a detached house, open space, mobility, good climate, renewed health, and a piece of the wealth. The dream seemed within grasp. Fortunes, real and rumored, were being made in real estate, restaurants, oil, and movies. Where the dream was most fervently believed and seemed closest to fulfillment, the collapse was more painful. Cain gave us a sense of what it was like to live, work, and dream in Los Angeles in the thirties. His restless, driven, and self-destructive heroes and heroines remind us of the hunger and the desperation that were a part of that not-so-distant past.

David M. Fine. American Scholar. Spring 1979,
pp. 27–29, 33–34

Cain's ideal reader is suggested by a story he loved to retell about director Billy Wilder's secretary, who "snuck off" to the washroom with a copy of *Double Indemnity* Cain's agent had sent hoping to interest Wilder in the novel. When she finally returned, she had the novel "pressed to her bosom— she'd just finished it and had this ga-ga look on her face." Submerged in Cain's tale, this woman undergoes as a reader just the kind of inescapable enchantment that overcomes Cain's protagonists at their moment of passionate awakening.

It is this ability of Cain's to invest his figures with symbolic significance that helps us both forgive and learn from the transgressions of Cain's heroes and heroines—that allows us to see them as victims at least as much as victimizers. Cain's personal insecurities and obsessions made him an ideally suited spokesman for the vulnerabilities of a class of men and women in the 1930s who had been denied selfhood. His best novels of that time detail the consequences of desire—the objectifications and fantasy projections it engenders, the self-doubt from which it emerges, the sexual narrowness that is proscribed for it by social values and imposed limits to possible fulfillment. His confessional frame not only signifies the protagonist's failure to satisfy his longings, but his isolation as well—a dominating loneliness that is perhaps Cain's most chilling insight into American individualism and the assumptions of self-actualization and self-fulfillment that our national myths encourage.

Cain's artistry was compelled by the paradoxes inherent in our yearning to be other—to be more—than we are: our fear of impotence, our sense of failure, our despair at a seemingly exitless existence. Detailing his characters' doomed attempts to transcend their fates, Cain surreptitiously revealed the terms of his own lifelong struggles for self-contentment and satisfaction, and managed to tap into the melodrama of a nation, the entrapped longings and frustrations dominating the souls of millions of readers. A character's efforts to circumvent and overcome such conditions result usually in failure and in the curious form of confession—an effort to find forgiveness for defeated and destructive desires. Like his characters, Cain struggled between a dream of life independent of social constraints, and one bound by conventional moral codes; his writing allowed him to experience something of both.

It is just as Cain transcribes the inarticulate yearnings beneath the headlines, gives substance to the immoral actions that fascinate and compel us all as voyeuristic readers who prey on the venom of our fellow citizens, that he deserves our admiration, respect, and thanks. With a touch of the poet, and never completely free of the habits of the hack, Cain will continue to draw readers to his only partially satisfying but singularly fascinating works. Like his version of Pandora, as artist Cain is a bit of a seducer, a bit of a pimp, a bit of a genius, a bit of a beggar and parasite, whose magic narratives open to delight and horrify us, and to whom we give the respect of our time and attention, hidden desires and eager identification.

Paul Skenazy. James M. Cain (New York:
Continuum, 1989), pp. 176–78

ČAPEK, KAREL (1890–1938)

The strength of Karel Čapek's *R.U.R.* lies even more in its hour than in its subject. The mechanical figures made by men in their own image are bound sooner or later to usurp world dominion and exterminate their masters. We foresee the development of the ''Robots'' from industrious automata into creatures with whims and passions, moods and frenzies, a heart and a soul. We even foresee dimly the day when the last surviving man, a white-bearded scientist, will seek in his laboratory the lost formula for manufacturing inhabitants of this earth. If there be no more men, let there at least be Robots.

A dead planet cries for life. One step farther and we foresee the Adam and Eve of the Robot family in the earliest stage of courtship, ready to repeople the earth with a race that shall be no longer mechanical, but human and humane. In their garden lurks as yet no serpent. There is little originality in the idea. You may piece it together, bit by bit, from all the classical and modern tales of men who made beings like themselves. The motive is always recurring in literature, like the motive of the heavenly visitor who is taken for a man. The last man in a plague-stricken world, driven to the woods by hordes of wild creatures that invade his empty cities, lies on a bough and watches eagerly the anthropoid apes who fumble with bits of wood and stone. This year perhaps they will carve a weapon; next year maybe a tool; next decade a dwelling; and in centuries or ages a cathedral. The watcher will die, but the race will go on. It is a subject for ''fantastic melodrama,'' as this play is well called.

Fortunately, there is something more in it than the sensational power of the old tale. That something is Čapek's instinct for feeling the response of his audience at every given moment—an instinct sincere but unerring. The play is not a piece of dramatic literature; it is scarcely even a deep or thoughtful work. It is a piece of brilliant journalism of the stage, a work of temperamental power that ''carries,'' as actors say, because the author believes in it, and believes in his audience, and is interested in their reaction to what he has to say. But Čapek goes farther than belief. He has a natural understanding of crowds and crowd psychology. Europe of today is his stage and the world his audience, not because we feel his plays to be immortal, but because we feel them to be inevitable. They are as inevitable as the leading article on the morrow of the Budget—good journalism, well phrased, well presented, and, above all, well timed.

Ashley Dukes. *The Youngest Drama: Studies of Fifty Dramatists* (London: Ernest Benn, Ltd., 1923), pp. 107–40

Karel Čapek is best known as the author of *R.U.R.,* that drama on "the mechanization of the proletariat," which gave to English as well as to other languages the word *robot.* His plays are implicit sermons, disguised by the dramatic adroitness of the born playwright.

Stanley J. Kunitz and Howard Haycraft. *Twentieth Century Authors* (New York: H. W. Wilson, 1942), pp. 246–47

One of science fiction's few genuine classics, out of print in this country since 1937, is Karel Čapek's wonderful *War with the Newts.* . . . This is a satire, one of the great ones. It has enormous charm, human warmth, gaiety, wit—and all the time, gently, patiently, it is flaying human society by inches.

The Newts (a giant species hitherto known only as a fossil) were discovered on the shore of Tanah Masa by gloomy old Captain J. van Toch, who took a paternal liking to them. ("What's the use, you ought to be honest even with animals.") At first they brought up pearl shells, in exchange for tools to build their dams and breakwaters, and weapons to fight sharks. Later, when it was discovered that they could talk, it was natural for more and more people to seek other uses for them.

With great ingenuity, and in spite of the most disheartening obstacles, people succeeded.

> The flesh of the Newts has also been taken to be unfit for human consumption and even poisonous; if eaten raw, it causes acute pains, vomiting, and mental hallucinations. Dr. Pinkel ascertained after many experiments performed on himself that these harmful effects disappear if the chopped meat is scalded with hot water (as with some toadstools), and after washing thoroughly it is pickled for twenty-four hours in a weak solution of permanganate of potash. Then it can be cooked or stewed, and tastes like inferior beef. In this way we ate a Newt called Hans; he was an able and intelligent animal with a special bent for scientific work; he was employed in Dr. Pinkel's department as his assistant, and even refined chemical analysis could be entrusted to him. We used to have long conversations with him in the evenings, amusing ourselves with his insatiable thirst for knowledge. With deep regret we had to put Hans to death, because my experiments on trepanning had made him blind.

Fed, protected, dissected, exploited, armed by every nation against every other, the Newts continued to grow in numbers as well as in knowledge. Not so many years after old Captain van Toch passed away, there were already twenty billion worker and warrior Newts in the world, or about ten times more Newts than people.

> The young Newts apparently stood for progress without any reservations or restrictions, and declared that below the water they ought to assimilate all land culture of every kind, not omitting even football, fascism, and sexual perversions.

Then one day the world awakened to find an earthquake had sunk three hundred square miles of Louisiana under shallow water. A strange croaking radio voice came out of the sea:

> Hello, you people! Don't get excited . . . There are too many of us. There is not space enough for us on your coasts any longer. Therefore we must break down your continents.

Only out of a landlocked and tired little nation could have come such raw despair, so incredibly blended with gentle, calm affection. "The Newts," says Egon Hostovsky in his Note on the Author, "are, of course, symbols of nazis and communists." So they are, fleetingly, at the end of the book, which trails off into a nightmare much as Mark Twain's *A Connecticut Yankee* does; but most of the time, I think, the Newts are ourselves as Čapek saw us—gentle, long-suffering, mute; the natural prey of businessmen, politicians, experimenters, militarists, and all other sharks of the land.

Damon Knight. In Search of Wonder (Chicago:
Advent, 1967), pp. 11–12

The Makropulos Secret was first played in the National Theater of Prague in November of 1922, and it was then that Karel Čapek wrote to his audience:

"The idea of this new comedy first occurred to me about three or four years ago, before writing *R.U.R.* It seemed then to be an ideal subject for a novel, but that is a form of writing I do not care for. The idea itself came from the theory of Professor Mecnik, that age is caused by an auto-intoxicating organism.

"I make these statements because Bernard Shaw's new play, *Back to Methuselah,* which I have seen in synopsis only, appeared this winter. In actual measure, it is very impressive. It, too, has the motif of longevity. This likeness in theme is entirely accidental, and, it seems to me from the synopsis, that while Bernard Shaw comes to the same conclusion as I do, it is in quite the opposite manner. Mr. Shaw believes that it is possible for an ideal community of people to live several hundred years in a sort of paradise. As the playgoer perceives, long life in my play is treated quite differently; I think that such a condition is neither ideal nor desirable. Both ideas are purely hypothetical since neither has the proof of experience. Yet perhaps I may say this much: Mr. Shaw's play is a classic example of optimism, and my own—a hopeless instance of pessimism.

"Whether I am called an optimist or a pessimist will make me neither happier nor sadder; yet, 'to be a pessimist' implies, it would seem, a silent rebuke from the world for bad behavior. In this comedy I have striven to present something delightful and optimistic. Does the optimist believe that it is bad to live sixty years but good to live three hundred? I merely think that when I proclaim a life of the ordinary span of sixty years as good enough in this world, I am not guilty of criminal pessimism. If we say that, at some future time, there will be no disease, misery, or poverty—that certainly is optimism. If we say that this daily life of ours, full of deprivation and sorrow, is not really so irreconcilable, but has in it something of immense value—is that pessimism? I think not. One turns from bad to higher things: the other searches for something better and higher in ordinary existence. The one looks for paradise—there is not a loftier vision for the human soul—the other strives for recompense in life itself. Is this pessimism?"

The technician and the layman sit alike in admiration before a playwright who can arrest attention and kindle interest in the very first speeches of his play; who can coordinate the introduction of the personages into the progress of the narrative; who from the interaction of both can quicken premises into curiosity aroused and suspense set a-vibrating. Of such a Čapek is the first act of *The Makropulos Secret*. Before it is done we are engrossed in the suit of Gregor against Prus—a hundred years old; in Emilia Marty, singing woman, mysterious intervener and informer; in the spell she lays with nearly every contact; in the fulfillment forthwith of her sayings. Prus, Gregor, Vitek, Kolonaty have all come, as well, into individual human and theatric being. . . .

Such work of the theater stirs the pride, quickens the zest of those who still love it. Yet Čapek and *The Makropulos Secret* would not so prevail unless they carried freight of matter to engage the mind, quicken the imagination, stir the spirit—matter, moreover, intrinsically human in content and implication, by the playwright and the stage vitalized. *The Makropulos Secret* is the secret of life unending. The mystery of Emilia Marty, born Elena Makropulos, is the mystery of endless existence dovetailing into the daily lives of men and women that are mortal. Her spell is the spell of a woman persisting and all-knowing, case-hardened in the virtue and vice, the experience and the sensation, of a life that has ceased to begin and wax, to waver and decline—a life that is perpetual.

Matter of fantasy, it is true, but matter that weaves these imaginings into the actualities of human experience. Matter of the theater, it is also true, but matter impregnated with human content and choice, speculation and even philosophy. Matter indeed of substance and vitality for the mind, the imagination and the spirit.

H. T. Parker. In Randal C. Burrell, ed., *The Makropulos Secret*, by Karel Čapek (New York: John W. Luce & Co., 1925), pp. 5–6, vii–xi

War with the Newts presents a more terrifying fantasy world than either *Brave New World* or *1984,* and in any case complements these works by encompassing the economic sphere of life, an area of little concern for either Huxley or Orwell.

The reasons for the present neglect of Čapek's satire are not difficult to establish. Although Čapek is one of the three Czech writers of the twentieth century with international reputations (Kafka and Hasek are the others) it is for the play *R.U.R.* that Čapek is best known. *War with the Newts* suffered mixed or indifferent reviews and inevitable comparison with *Brave New World* when translations appeared in England and America. None of the major studies of satire in the last ten years has acknowledged its existence.

Even as satire, *War with the Newts* is unconventional. Episodic in extreme, without a central hero, a grab bag of satiric techniques, Čapek's work will not satisfy readers and critics who come to the book with conventional novelistic expectations. To call it episodic is in fact generous. A major portion of the novel is really a mock-historical narrative interspersed with various kinds of documents exhibited in mock-scholarly style. Although *War with the Newts* has several richly realized characters, the scope of Čapek's satire would have been undesirably restricted by the convention of a novelistic hero. . . .

If Čapek fails (or chooses not) to provide his readers with a conventional novellike book, he amply compensates for these features, especially for the reader attuned to the techniques and devices of satire. Moreover Čapek's satiric commentary, while grounded in conditions and events of the thirties, has the merit of still seeming prophetic while describing reality more accurately with each passing day.

The Newts are, at the simplest level, Čapek's convenient animal metaphor for man and his culture, for from the first time that van Toch comes upon these writhing, grotesque beasts in their protected backwater habitat, they dominate this Menippean satire despite their being submerged throughout.

Actually the Newts' metaphorical function is far richer than this account suggests. van Toch, their ''liberator,'' exemplifies a paternalistic racism, despite his generally humane attitude.

In developing the concept of the Newts as a new labor force to be exploited, Čapek builds in significant parallels with the slave trade of the eighteenth and nineteenth centuries. Later Čapek mocks do-gooders who seek to make over educationally and culturally in their own image the emerging Newt population. As a symbol for the nonwhite races, Čapek uses the Newts to comment on racism as it manifests itself in exploitation and in attempts to integrate nonwhite races into Western society.

But the Newts also symbolize what sociologists have come to call ''the mass man.'' The Newts have a deleterious influence on language. Art and music hold no interests for them. The worship of Moloch is the only religion that takes any extensive hold on the Newts. But above all the Newts are consumers and producers without parallel.

The Newts come ultimately to stand for society itself. Economic development, technological changes, and universal armament are forces set in motion by man's greed and thirst for power. Čapek pictures these forces as irreversible and self-destructive. Like all the great satirists, Čapek is attacking man's pride, man's failure to impose reasonable limitations on what is and is not proper, man's refusal to come to terms with the limitations imposed by his nature and his environment. He seems to suggest that man can find happiness within these limitations, unhappiness and frustration outside them. To try to be more than a man is to transgress an unchangeable rule of nature at one's own peril. . . .

It may be that Čapek's success as a satirist in *War with the Newts* is the most damaging statement one can make about him. Unlike Huxley and Orwell whose fantasies are projected into the future where man and his institutions have changed, Čapek takes the world before World War II and injects a device of fantasy, the Newts. Neither time, place nor characters have to be changed. In fact Čapek uses real places and the names of actual people. The introduction of the Newts is a simple device, but one that makes Čapek's book even more terrifying, ultimately, than Orwell's. For in both *1984* and *Brave New World* the future is given, the reader must willingly suspend his disbelief. Čapek's device forces the reader to participate in the coming of the future.

As a satiric writer Čapek combines the rich comic inventiveness of Huxley with the unnerving desire to see the thing as it really is of Orwell. This is only to say that Čapek is an effective satirist. But unlike either of them, Čapek does not fraction his view of man so completely as they seem to.

Literary history is filled with examples of neglected works that posterity has raised to the status of classics, and conversely with overvalued works that have sunk into oblivion with the years. Čapek's *The War with the Newts* was not overvalued when it was first published; it would be foolhardy to proclaim it as a future classic. It is safe to claim however that it is an undeservedly neglected modern satire and compares more favorably with Orwell's and Huxley's classics than its present reputation would indicate.

George A. Test. *Studies in Contemporary Satire.*
Spring 1974, pp. 1–10

A Czech novelist, dramatist, and miscellaneous writer, Karel Čapek is the most internationally known, though not the best, of all modern Czech writers: the typical and anxious product of the First Czechoslovakian Republic, the betrayal of which killed him. His plays—notably *R.U.R.* (1920; tr. 1923) and *Ze života hmyzu* (1921; tr. *The Insect Play,* 1923), both with his brother the painter and author Josef Čapek (1887–1945)—gave him his world reputation; but, as critics agree, his fiction is more important. He was essentially an intelligent and skillful popular author whose approach is often superficial but totally honest; his response to the Czech situation between the wars was genuinely anguished but was decent rather than profound. He is, though, a thoroughly worthy writer. He saw the coming crisis, and warned against it; but a soft-centered romanticism vitiated his awareness of it; this tends to weaken his work. Early books are candidly Wellsian: *Továrna na absolutnu* (1922; tr. *The Absolute at Large,* 1927), *Krakatit* (1924; tr. 1925). His chief work, in which he partly rises above himself, is the trilogy of novels *Hordubal* (1933; tr. 1943), *Povětroň* (1934; tr. *Meteor,* 1935), and *Obyčejný život* (1935; tr. *An Ordinary Life,* 1936). Here crisis forces him inwards, to examine the conflict between a cerebral determinism and a rather fuzzy faith in democracy. The balance is resolved in favor of the former but the nature of the inner resources by which the individual may attain peace is not clearly outlined.

Martin Seymour-Smith. *Who's Who in Twentieth Century Literature* (New York: Holt, Rinehart and Winston, 1976), p. 70

Strong and convincing humanism is especially pervasive in *The War with the Newts,* one of the masterworks of science fiction. A sea captain makes an unusual discovery on an island near Sumatra—a special kind of salamander that can be trained to fish for pearls, build dams, and so on. Businessmen form a "Salamander Syndicate" and begin to publicize and sell these "slaves." The mass media laps up the story of this wonderful species, which can even be taught to speak. Very soon England, France, and Italy are employing large numbers of this cheap labor; they also establish a standing army of salamanders against the possibility of war. Germany—and here the satire is especially sharp—demands living space for her "aristocratic" salamanders, which have the elongated Nordic skull and are of special "Prussian" discipline. Very soon the salamander population has grown so large and powerful that it turns against man. These newcomers remove portions of land and create new coastlines, in the quest for new space (*lebensraum*) for themselves. This is "the end for us," sighs a character at the end of the story.

The fantastical story of the salamanders is an amusing and at the same time a most meaningful satire on the ramifications of both the colonial system and the barbarism of fascism. Above all the novel is an appeal to the powers of humanism the world over to continue the struggle against the abuse of power.

Dieter Wuckel and Bruce Cassiday. *The Illustrated History of Science Fiction* (New York: Ungar, 1989), pp. 129–32

CARR, JOHN DICKSON [also known as CARTER DICKSON and CARR DICKSON] (1906–1977)

John Dickson Carr is one of today's most notable writers of detective fiction. Under his own name or as "Carter Dickson," sometimes as "Carr Dickson," he has, during the last quarter of a century, written a great number of novels and short stories as remarkable for the craftsmanship of their plot and their well-sustained interest, as for their literary quality and their atmosphere of effortless ease. His stature as a writer has steadily improved through the years, but even his first novel, *It Walks by Night* (1930), deserves to be remembered. In it, Carr introduced one of the best-known French detectives in contemporary English fiction, Bercolin, and experimented with a technique which he employed in later novels with even better effect, the trick of building up suspense by implying that the mystery must be due to supernatural agency. There is nothing supernatural about the eventual explanation, however, and Carr has a talent for making the ingenious mechanism of his solutions seem entirely credible as presented, whether actually feasible or not.

In Carr's hands, even that well-worn theme, murder in a "sealed room," entered upon a new lease of life, notably in *The Hollow Man* (1935), in which that massive [detective] figure, Doctor Gideon Fell, foreshadowed the success he gained later in such novels as *The Arabian Nights Murder* (1936), and *The Problem of the Wire Cage* (1939).

As "Carter Dickson," Carr created yet a third memorable detective in Sir Henry Merrivale, better known as "H.M.," or "the old man," in *The Plague Court Murders* (1934). Character drawing in Carr's work is well defined and convincing, his grasp of psychology sound, and his settings, whether in London, Chartres, Scotland, or the New Forest, aboard the liner *Queen Victoria,* or deep in the old Waxworks Museum in Paris, all have the atmosphere of reality.

Besides producing excellent examples of traditional detective stories, Dickson Carr has struck out upon new lines. In *The Reader Is Warned* (1939), he brings a new interpretation to the "fair play" convention, giving the reader footnote "warnings" which still do not help him to escape bewilderment, so subtle is the misdirection. A contemporary setting has long been customary in detective fiction, but several times in recent years Carr has given his work a historical background. *The Bride of Newgate* (1950) recreates London in the 1800s; *The Devil in Velvet* (1951) takes us back to the days of Charles II; his recent novel, *Fire Burn!* (1957) is set in the Regency period; and his clever short story, "The Gentleman From Paris," brings to life the New York waterfront in 1849, and conjures up an imaginary incident in the life of Edgar Allan Poe so realistically that it seems actually true.

In addition to his own fictional works, John Dickson Carr has compiled with sympathetic insight a biography of the creator of Sherlock Holmes, *The Life of Sir Arthur Conan Doyle,* and has collaborated with that distinguished author's son, Adrian Conan Doyle, to produce an apocryphal, nostalgic group of short stories, *The Exploits of Sherlock Holmes* (1954).

A. E. Murch. *The Development of the Detective Novel* (New York: Philosophical Library, 1958), pp. 234–35

This book *The Blind Barber,* by John Dickson Carr, is a farce about murder.

I feel I should give you fair warning, because this sort of thing hasn't been common lately. But if your instant reaction is shocked withdrawal, please pause a moment and hear me out.

If I have one major complaint about the 300-odd mysteries that I read each year as a reviewer, it is that none of them is funny. Oh, I admit Richard S. Prather or Carter Brown can be amusing, but only in the trimmings: it's the writing that's funny, rather than the story.

And I long for the days of Craig Rice and Alice Tilton and Richard Shattuck and Jonathan Latimer when there was a wild cockeyed preposterousness in the events surrounding murder and even in murder itself—and not just in the style of the narrator.

I suppose this longing dates me. It's a 1930ish attitude. There was a fine film late in the Depression, starring Carole Lombard and written by Ben Hecht, called *Nothing Sacred.* It was a rowdy comedy about a (supposed) cancer victim. The "nothing-sacred" approach seems out of place today; now we take things more seriously, especially death.

But death and laughter are old friends. The medieval *Totentanz* is comic; and the macabre poet Thomas Lovell Beddoes christened his major tragedy *Death's Jest Book.* As Duncan sinks in his gore, the drunken porter rises with merry and improper quips. And the murders of real life seldom lack their element of comedy. One of the most terrible days in the annals of American murder opened on a scorching morning with a man named John Vinnicum Morse eating warmed-over mutton soup for breakfast. . . .

There's a strong comic element in many of Carr's books. It's most prevalent in the cases of Sir Henry Merrivale, by "Carter Dickson" (and I realize with a sudden shock that it's almost ten years since H.M. has appeared in a new book); but it turns up frequently in Dr. Gideon Fell's cases, too—as in the noble drinking sequences in *The Case of the Constant Suicides.*

But these are intrusions, like the porter. Just once did Carr set himself to write an all-out farce (with murder as the intrusion). And, being the incomparable technician that he is, he produced something unique.

Wisely, he kept Dr. Fell out of the merry maelstrom and made him act, for once, as a pure armchair detective, in the manner of the Baroness

Orczy's Old Man in the Corner. Then he threaded through his fantastic plot a careful set of clues for a faultless formal problem in detection.

Unlike almost all other comedies of terrors, *The Blind Barber* is a detective story, in the strictest sense. But never was a reader more bedeviled with distractions from detection. Who observes clues while he's wiping his laughter-streaming eyes?

I hope you enjoy the challenge . . . and the fun.

Anthony Boucher. Introduction, *The Blind Barber*,
by John Dickson Carr (New York: Collier Books,
1962), n.p.

John Dickson Carr is the present day "undisputed master" of the locked room tale. An essay on the treatment accorded the locked room puzzle at the hands of Mr. Carr (oftentimes imperfectly concealed behind the pseudonym of Carter Dickson) would occupy many, many pages and, come to think of it, would probably result in a completely fascinating monograph.

It is enough to say here that Carr-Dickson specializes in making the seemingly impossible possible; and that he solves many a knotty fictional problem by doing so. He delights in having a victim walk out into the middle of a tennis court, leaving distinct footprints, and there vanish into thin air. He takes similar enjoyment from having a man dive into an ordinary back-yard swimming pool and disappear from sight. But his favorite and most entertaining pastime is creating and solving one locked room puzzle after another. His methods are infinite and varied, for it is apparent that he has given more than offhand attention to the problem and the possibilities it offers.

Donald A. Yates. *The Armchair Detective*. Winter
1970, n.p.

John Dickson Carr . . . is unique among crime writers in his unswerving devotion to one form or another of the locked-room mystery. . . .

In *The Hollow Man* (1935) [in America, *The Three Coffins*], Carr offers in one chapter, through his detective Dr. Gideon Fell, a splendidly lively and learned discussion of locked-room murders and their possible solutions under seven different classifications, with some subdivisions relating to methods of tampering with doors. In his dozens of books, Carr/Dickson has rung the changes on the possibilities with astonishing skill. Often his postulates are improbable, but the reader rarely feels them to be impossible, and the deception is built up, sustained with teasing hints that can be interpreted in half a dozen different ways, and at last revealed, with staggering skill. The best Carr/Dickson is the most ingenious, and my vote would go to *The Hollow Man* itself, one of the books which, as Dr. Fell says, "derives its problem from illusion and impersonation." (The kind of improbable postulate I mean, which doesn't affect enjoyment at the time but may do so afterward, is shown here by the evidence of three witnesses, all of whom accept the inaccurate time shown by a street clock. Did nobody possess a wristwatch?) The conjurer's illusion is marvelously clever. But almost every one of the early books has its passionate admirers. Among those most praised by most people are *The Arabian Nights Murder* (1936), *The Burning Court* (1937), *The Black Spectacles* (1939) [in America, *The Problem of the Green Capsule*], and the Carter Dickson *The Judas Window* (1938). To these I would add two favorites of my own, one Carter Dickson called *The Ten Teacups* (1937) [in America, *The Peacock Feather Murders*], and one John Dickson Carr, *The Emperor's Snuff Box* (1942). For almost twenty years, Carr's fertility seemed endless. He wrote an average of two or more books a year, every one of them playing a fresh variation on the locked-room theme. Perhaps because there is after all a limit to such variations, perhaps because the formula itself is now badly worn, his recent books are much inferior to the early ones.

The trouble with exploiting such a formula is that everything else becomes subservient to it, or at least that is what has happened with Carr. He was strongly influenced by Poe and Chesterton. (Dr. Fell with his great bulk, his cane, his eyeglasses on a black ribbon, flowing cloak, and rumpled hair is a very Chestertonian figure.) His books are full of reference to macabre events and possibilities, and of Chestertonian paradox, but in the later work especially these are mere stage trappings. There is genuine feeling in some of Chesterton's short stories, but very little in any of Carr's writing after his first half-dozen books. Since the whole story is built round the puzzle, there is no room for characterization, and the limitation of these clever stories is clearly expressed in the fact that what one remembers about them is never any of the people, but simply the puzzle.

Julian Symons. *Mortal Consequences: A History—
From the Detective Story to the Crime Novel*
(Harper & Row, 1972), pp. 119–21

Magic plays a major role on almost every level of John Dickson Carr's novels. There are allusions to Houdini and Maskelyne in several books. More important is the fact that Carr peppers every one of his books with the terms "conjuring" and "sleight of hand," and his favorite way of describing the business in the books is to call it "hocus pocus." Several of the novels contain characters who are professional magicians.

In fact, Carr is pretty clear about the relationship between magic and murder from his first novel. Jeff, in *It Walks by Night,* quotes a section of the murdered Edouard Vautrelle's play which makes the connection between magic and murder:

> The art of murder, my dear Maurot, is the same as the art of the magician. And the art of the magician does not lie in any such nonsense as "the hand is quicker than the eye," but consists simply in directing your attention to the wrong place. He will cause you to be watching one hand while with the other hand, unseen though in full view, he produces his effect.

Not a bad description of puzzle writing either, since the detective writer, like the magician, gives clues but distracts the readers' attention so that they will not see them. Magic is, thus, central to Carr's detective writing; it is the reason that stage setting is so important in the novels. Not only stage setting, but also accomplices. When a magician saws a woman in two there is an accomplice hidden in the box to provide the legs for the illusion. Not only stage setting and accomplices come into the books from magic, but so too do most of the devices which make the plots work.

There is yet one more step to Carr's magic formula. The murderers in Carr's books act as the conjuror setting the stage, making illusions, creating props, and forming an atmosphere of terror and horror against which to work their tricks. In the middle ages this sort of thing would have been called black magic—the illegitimate manipulation of nature for illicit or satanic ends. Carr frequently connects the villains with this background. The detective acts, much in the mold of Maskelyne or Houdini, in a double fashion: as the unmasker of phony, evil illusionists, and as the entertainer. All of Carr's detectives unmask illusionists, they make the impossible happen by explaining inexplicable events, and they entertain the readers with their patter. Behind them stands Carr the magician practicing his sleight of hand with the narrative.

LeRoy Lad Panek. *Watteau's Shepherds: The Detective Novel in Britain 1914–1940* (Bowling Green, Ohio: Popular Press, 1979) pp. 175–77

The detective story permits us to move up close to sins that we could not, for ourselves, contemplate. Perhaps this is why the detective story so often is said to be therapeutic: it provides the nightmares of morality that we cannot otherwise meet directly. While spy fiction is, at base, all action—even when mixed with deceit, landscape, and intelligent dialogue, movement is the key to the thriller—the mystery novel, though a puzzle, is primarily an investigation of character in relation to crime as society defines it. While the fears we entertain are worn water-smooth in our dreams, the written word brings those fears to the surface, externalizes them, and best of all, in the end gives them a plausible, even rational, explanation. Perhaps one reason John Dickson Carr and Carter Dickson, one and the same, are intolerable upon rereading is that they are utterly abstracted from any reality one might imagine: the reality of the street, of the boudoir, of the police cell, of the nightmare. They produced puzzles written at length, wherein character is not only allowed scant play, character is virtually never the explanation of the mystery itself. Yet, in any genuine mystery, of fiction or of fact, the answer arises from character.

Robin W. Winks. *Modus Operandi: An Excursion into Detective Fiction* (Boston: David R. Godine, 1982), p. 80

CHANDLER, RAYMOND (1888–1959)

The Big Sleep should stir up a lot of valuable discussion. It can boast of an admirable hard-boiled manner, it contains several characters who will scare you with their extraordinary brands of wickedness, and the nightmare atmosphere is the real thing in spots. In our opinion, though, Mr. Chandler has almost spoiled it with a top-heavy cargo of lurid underworld incident, and he should therefore be stood in a corner and lectured upon the nature and suitable use of his talents. . . . Phil Marlowe is a slick sleuth in the Hammett tradition. It's a much better than average tough item; we're only saying that it might have been better with less high-pressure plot—but, then, it would have been another story. Moreover, Mr. Chandler deserves a medal for his handling of some wicked scenes; we shudder to think what some of our bad young bafflers would have done with them.

Will Cuppy. *New York Herald Tribune Book Review*. February 5, 1939, p. 12.

The Big Sleep is very unequally written. There are scenes that are all right, but there are other scenes still much too pulpy. Insofar as I am able I want to develop the objective method—but slowly—to the point where I can carry an audience over into a genuine dramatic, even melodramatic, novel, written in a very vivid and pungent style, but not slangy or overly vernacular. I realize that this must be done cautiously and little by little, but I think it can be done. To acquire delicacy without losing power, that's the problem.

Raymond Chandler. Letter to Alfred A. Knopf, February 19, 1939. In Dorothy Gardiner and Kathrine Sorley Walker, eds., *Raymond Chandler Speaking* (New York: Houghton Mifflin, 1977), pp. 209–10

Chandler writes not out of habit and not with synthetic materials, as do so many mystery writers, but with an artistry of craftsmanship and a realism that can rank him with many a famous novelist. In his hands, words do become beautiful and wonderful things, operating with economy and precision. What a delight it is to come upon a writer who tosses off a good image on almost every page.

Chandler is prodigal in his imagery. If they seem more wisecracks than high-flown literary similes, I will point out that Chandler writes the characteristic American speech and uses characteristic American humor. In doing this he comes closer to literature than other writers who disdain the native brand of thought and language.

There are descriptive passages that a poet might envy; and phrases that have a beauty which shows that Chandler cannot be pigeonholed merely as an expert in tough language.

There is more of the tough language in Chandler's works than of the other kind, but this is because he writes of a world and order of society in which there is little beauty or serenity.

He believes, and rightly I think, that most murder stories no longer have any relation to real life—that they have become a literary form and convention remote from realism. If we were to judge from most murder stories, murders are most prevalent among the middle and upper classes and as often as not are solved, not by the police, but by private individuals possessed of bulging brains and a vast assortment of strange knowledges. It is manifestly ridiculous. Chandler in his works has returned to that world where murder is a commonplace: the world of racketeers in drugs and liquor, in gambling and prostitution; a world in which police and racketeers and politicians are often mixed up in sub-surface alliances. It is not a bad thing that we should be told about the murky depths of our civilization, that this realism should be Chandler's subject, for, as we well know, this is indeed the area of American society in which murder is most frequent.

It is strange to meet a murder-novel writer who attacks his work with the earnest attention and serious social thought which are supposed to be the prerogative of eminent novelists. This is what Chandler does; and, so doing, he has removed his work from the realm of merely conventional entertainment to the point where it becomes a serious study of a certain kind of American society. This quality, and a grim sense of humor allied with an even grimmer sense of realism—for example, his description of the seedy Fulwider Building in *The Big Sleep*—plus a superb writing ability, have produced five novels which are worth the attention of more readers than just those alone who are interested in the literature of murder.

Mr. Chandler has done his vigorous best to explode the empty convention behind ordinary murder stories, but he ought not to set up a convention for himself. We who read three or four shockers a week can't stand monotony in murder.

D. C. Russell. *The Atlantic Monthly.* March 1945,
pp. 123–24

Mr. Raymond Chandler has written that he intends to take the body out of the vicarage garden and give murder back to those who are good at it. If he wishes to write detective stories, i.e., stories where the reader's principal interest is to learn who did it, he could not be more mistaken; for in a society of professional criminals, the only possible motives for desiring to identify the murderer are blackmail or revenge, which both apply to individuals, not to the group as a whole, and can equally well inspire murder. Actually, whatever he may say, I think Mr. Chandler is interested in writing, not detective stories, but serious studies of a criminal milieu, the Great

Wrong Place, and his powerful but extremely depressing books should be read and judged, not as escape literature, but as works of art.

W. H. Auden. *Harper's*. May 1948, pp. 406–12

To be caught with a Raymond Chandler whodunit in hand is a fate no high-brow reader need dread. When *The Big Sleep*, his first, was published, it not only wowed the choosiest mystery reviewers; it also won him a large audience in which even the most determined intellectual could feel at home. Chandler proved in his next three books that the cheers were justified. They had everything a good detective story needs: ingenuity, suspense, pace, credibility. But they had a lot more. Their private-eye hero, Philip Marlowe, was just tough enough, just sentimental enough to move like a born natural through the neon-nylon wilderness of a Los Angeles world that the movies never made until Chandler showed them how. Chandler's tense situations mushroomed naturally with almost no trace of fabrication. Best of all, he wrote fresh, crackling prose and it was peppered with newly minted similes.

Chandler is at his best in conveying the special flavor of depressing police-station offices, the even more depressing outlook of cynical police-men, and cheap-hotel dicks. He makes Marlowe good, but not too good to make mistakes, human enough to feel resentment and despair.

Time. October 3, 1949, pp. 82–83

Mr. Chandler has emphasized his own dislike for plot construction. The realistic method, he says, has freed him from "an exhausting concatenation of insignificant clues," and he can now let the characters work out the story for themselves.

Here we see the main weakness in Mr. Chandler's novels. From the first page he goes whooping along at high speed, magnificently if somewhat confusedly, until he reaches the last chapter. There he takes one sweet spill into a net. He thrashes wildly, but he can't get out; he can't explain why his characters acted as they did, and he can't even talk intelligibly. This, presumably, is realism.

Mr. Chandler is a serious-minded man, and it would be unjust not to take him seriously. He can write a scene with an almost suffocating vivid-ness and sense of danger—if he does not add three words too many and make it funny. His virtues are all there. If, to some restraint, he could add the fatigue of construction and clues (the writer he most admires, Mr. Ham-mett, has never disdained clues and has always given them fairly)—then one day he may write a good novel.

I say nothing of new ideas or plot twists, because Mr. Chandler does not have them. He will never disturb the laurels of Mr. Queen or Mr. Gardner or Mr. Stout. Perhaps it is best to let him alone, and offer no suggestions.

When he forgets he cannot write a true detective story, when he forgets to torture words, the muddle resolves and the action whips along like a numbered racing-car.

Mr. Chandler will do even better when he discovers that you cannot create an American language merely by butchering the English language.

John Dickson Carr. The New York Times Book Review. September 24, 1950, p. 36

It seems to me a fantastic misrepresentation to say that the average detective novel is an example of good storytelling. The gift for telling stories is uncommon, like other artistic gifts, and the only one of this group of writers—the writers my correspondents have praised—who seems to me to possess it to any degree is Mr. Raymond Chandler. His *Farewell, My Lovely* is the only one of these books that I have read all of and read with enjoyment. But Chandler, though in his recent article he seems to claim Hammett as his master, does not really belong to this school of the old-fashioned detective novel. What he writes is a novel of adventure which has less in common with Hammett than with Alfred Hitchcock and Graham Greene—the modern spy story which has substituted the jitters of the Gestapo and the G.P.U. for the luxury world of E. Phillips Oppenheim. It is not simply a question here of a puzzle which has been put together but of a malaise conveyed to the reader, the horror of a hidden conspiracy that is continually turning up in the most varied and unlikely forms. To write such a novel successfully you must be able to invent character and incident and to generate atmosphere, and all this Mr. Chandler can do, though he is a long way below Graham Greene. It was only when I got to the end that I felt my old crime-story depression descending upon me again—because here again, as is so often the case, the explanation of the mysteries, when it comes, is neither interesting nor plausible enough. It fails to justify the excitement produced by the elaborate build-up of picturesque and sinister happenings, and one cannot help feeling cheated.

Edmund Wilson. "Who Cares Who Killed Roger Ackroyd?" Classics and Commercials: A Literary Chronicle of the Forties (New York: Farrar, Straus & Giroux, 1950), pp. 262–63

I pulled his leg about his plots, which always seem to me to go wildly astray. What holds the books together and makes them so compulsively readable, even to alpha minds who would not normally think of reading a thriller, is the dialogue. There is a throwaway, downbeat quality about Chandler's dialogue, whether wisecracking or not, that takes one happily through chapter after chapter in which there is no more action than Philip Marlowe driving his car and talking to his girl, or a rich old woman consulting her lawyer on the sun porch. His aphorisms were always his own.

Ian Fleming. London. December 1959, p. 50

Whether Chandler will ever be elected into literary history is another question. The odd thing is that he is known and enjoyed by those who have the power to vote him in—critics, writers, scholars, literary historians—and even so it begins to look as though his nomination for membership may not be seconded. To be sure, any comprehensive literary chronicle of the age will certainly list him along with Dashiell Hammett and Mickey Spillane as one of the chief practitioners of the "tough-guy mystery"; but this is indiscriminate and flattening.

I would bet a good deal that right now (1) most of the literary folk of the country have read some of Chandler's best work with pleasure and profit but, ashamed of their pleasure, would deny it any literary value; and (2) these same people have read of Wallace Stevens's poems few more than the often-anthologized pieces, and those without anything like full comprehension or pleasure, and yet would grant high value to the body of his poetry. Well, I do not mean to suggest that I think Stevens is less than excellent or that Chandler is more than pretty good. But I do suggest that it is time we publicly honor Chandler (and Hammett, his master).

There is no use pretending that the detective story has much to recommend it as a form. In fact, I should imagine that no novel written within its conventions could be first-rate, just as no opera written within the conventions of the Broadway musical could be first-rate. The detective story damagingly interferes in what is of the very essence of a novel; it manipulates the motives and relationships of its characters for an artificial and trivial end. Even in those rare detective stories where the motives are credible enough and the relationships are reasonably subtle and valid, the reader is kept from apprehending them in a way that is really serious. Knowledge of motive and relationship is parceled out to him for reasons of plot excitement—a matter of some, but low, value—and this very excitement works against a profound or thoughtful or complexly moving appreciation of the characters' essential natures.

Chandler's novels are a good deal more successful as thrillers than as detective stories, and a thriller, as demonstrated by the example of Graham Greene (he's respectable), need not distort motive or relationship very much. It forbids that contemplation which is essential to reading great fiction, the movement of which is most of the time quite slow. But a thriller can do a good many things of literary value, and some of these things Chandler does admirably.

The obvious accomplishment of his thrillers is to generate a sort of nervous tension, which is the literary analogue to the tension generated just by being an American citizen. Tension alone is not so much: one can induce it by chain-smoking a couple of packs of cigarettes and slugging down a fair amount of liquor, driving eighty miles an hour to a juke box joint where one drinks black coffee and plays a slot machine, then driving home again chortling every so often, "We sure had a good time, didn't we?" In fact this sort of tension making is an unexceptional way to spend the evening in

Southern California, and if Philip Marlowe did not do things like it we would not believe in him. . . .

If you want the feel and aspect of Los Angeles and vicinity during the thirties, forties, and early fifties, you could hardly do better than to read his fictions. There is a considerable change in this fictional world between *The Big Sleep* and *The Long Goodbye;* part of this change was a deepening in Chandler as a writer and part of it was, no doubt, a result of his greater acquaintance with the region; but part of it too took place in Southern California itself. As it has grown in population, wealth, and importance, its appearance has become less macabre and its vileness has turned inward, hidden behind solider false fronts.

Chandler saw his region not just as it saw itself but in his own way too. And his version of it was so congenial and so strong that it affected his readers' versions. Chandler's fictions are one of the reasons Southern California now is seen as it is seen.

If you object that in the long view this is not so much for a writer to do, I cannot disagree. What I would maintain, though, is that he did as much as the J. F. Coopers of our literature ever did and that his novels are, for the time being, a lot more fun to read.

> George P. Elliott. *The Nation.* April 23, 1960,
> pp. 354–56, 358–60

Chandler's hero is the all-American boy with whom the reader easily identifies himself, the rough man of action who would never harm a fly but would stamp out injustice with a vigorous passion. Thematically, Chandler's work is in one of the mainstreams of American literature, not the nineteenth-century New England one of concern for the brooding thoughts of the introvert, but the broad stream of frontier literature that moved from Georgia of the 1830s to the California of the 1950s—enveloping as it traveled westward the simple problems of the extrovert who, by knowing right from wrong, had only to exert a courageous amount of rugged individualism in order to end up a hardened but virtuous hero. This mainstream of American literature contributed thousands of modern morality plays, of which Chandler's are excellently written examples.

T. S. Eliot discovered his poetic home in England; Eugene O'Neill rarely strayed from the Atlantic or its seaboard; Raymond Chandler found Los Angeles to be the natural milieu for his hero's efforts to untangle the messy web into which the American man had naively wandered.

> Philip Durham. *Down These Mean Streets a Man
> Must Go: Raymond Chandler's Knight* (Chapel
> Hill: University of North Carolina Press, 1963),
> pp. 5–6

In reading *Raymond Chandler Speaking,* a collection of the late mystery writer's letters and literary fragments, one gets a sense of the peculiar loneliness of the writer of integrity who works in a popular genre that attracts few writers like himself and that the American literary culture tends to dismiss with easy, contemptuous generalizations. Chandler was a talented and devoted craftsman, one who spent his life either in spurts of hard work on his novels or in long periods of lying fallow and brooding about the lack of serious understanding and appreciation with which his work was received.

At the same time, this feeling of being left out, of working at a vocation in which one's best and most conscientious efforts were underrated and misunderstood, can also be seen to have informed Chandler's fiction.

His great theme was not crime and punishment, though his letters reveal him to have had a sound technical knowledge of criminal history, psychology, and technique. His theme was, rather, an exploration of the belief that the moral man, who refuses to play the game of life in a conventionally immoral or amoral way, is doomed to the kind of loneliness Chandler himself suffered.

This understanding of Chandler and his theme provides, in turn, for speculation about the decline of a once promising figure in popular mythology, the private eye. As created by Dashiell Hammett and developed by Chandler, the private eye offered a unique perspective on loneliness as a central condition of modern urban existence. Philip Marlowe, Chandler's detective, masked his feeling of emptiness behind a protective set of tough-guy mannerisms, and it is because Chandler's legion of imitators borrowed them, but not Marlowe's inner spirit, that the hard school is no longer very interesting. The books are sometimes amusing as puzzles, but nothing about them catches in the mind. Marlowe did.

The atmosphere of cheap furnished apartments, of second-rate bars where one can always find a conversation and sometimes a woman, the very feel of an empty city street to the man who has just killed the evening alone in a second-run movie house, are done with wonderful rightness. So are the psychic defenses of the lonely man. Marlowe plays endless games of chess with himself, carefully setting up the classic problems, then spending the evening trying to solve them, sipping at a bourbon highball. He is persnickety, in an old-maidish way, about small things like coffee. The careful construction of an ideal cup of it occupies a lovingly written paragraph in almost every Marlowe novel. In fact, popular misapprehension to the contrary, Marlowe is more interested in good coffee than he is in booze, good or otherwise. Nor is Marlowe much of a boudoir athlete. He is rather offhand about women, perhaps a little defensive. Physically, of course, he needs them, but emotionally he knows they pose a threat to his independence. Consequently, he is wary, though gallant, in his treatment of them.

The two great private detectives of the hard school, Marlowe and Hammett's Sam Spade, were both code heroes, like those of Hemingway (whose style also had its influence on that school). Consciously or unconsciously, the classic private eye represents an attempt to transfer the man with a code from the lost Eden of the nineteenth-century American West to the modern Jungle of the Cities.

Marlowe was a class figure. He was most believable when there were distinct differences between the styles of the rich, or at least upper middle class, and lower middle class. He began to seem a little out of place in the prosperous fifties, when even college professors were being cut in on the wealthiest society in human history. His stubborn refusal to join up with the rest of society seemed more eccentric than heroic, more adolescent than mature. Marlowe had begun to suffer from cultural lag.

Chandler, in his concern with the real psychological issues of his time, and in his ability to focus these issues by his excellent anti-hero, was at least the equal of a middle rank "serious" novelist—perhaps the equal, on occasion, of a first-rate one.

Richard Schickel. Commentary. February 1963,
pp. 158–61

Chandler's achievements are impressive: he mastered the American style— a combination (as he defined it) of idiom, slang, wisecrack, hyperbole, and tough talk that in the hands of a man of genius can be made to do anything; he had a view of the world more serious and more valid than a good many craftsmen working in a more respected genre; he invented a hero, Philip Marlowe, who has been called a "great creation"; he expressed his vision with wit and vigor, though occasionally with sentimentality; he is indisputably the best writer about urban California, and he wrote the best novel about Hollywood. But all these achievements seem somehow not enough to overcome the fact that he realized them while working in the mystery genre. This fact has kept him out of any serious literary discussion, a silence which even some honorable exceptions (Richard Schickel, George P. Elliott, Auden, Maugham) have not broken. . . .

Chandler's hero does not think, he has character, and he responds to character in others. He knows and understands character; he makes distinctions between people; he responds to their moral qualities and is himself moral; he believes in truth, and justice, and honesty, and fidelity, and he will go to any length to protect those in whom he sees these qualities, usually the aged (with some important exceptions). Just so, he responds to the qualities of the city; and just so, Chandler gives a richness and fullness to his style. There are all gradations of class and milieu and speech and diction in Chandler's novels. For these reasons, Chandler, through Marlowe, succeeds as no one else has succeeded in portraying Los Angeles, including Hollywood, and it seems at times that it is neither the violence nor the solution of the mystery Chandler is interested in as it is the city and the people, through the whole range of which, in the solution of the crime, Marlowe moves.

Yet Marlowe, though heroic, tough, and wise, is a sad character. For all the personal life he has and the people he can trust, he might as well be

in the wilderness. He is a lonely figure, a man without personal life. . . .
This is the farthest that Chandler had gotten with the character of Marlowe,
as opposed to his catalytic function, until, in the unfinished *The Poodle
Springs Story* he was to treat him as character in domestic conflict with
wealth and in public conflict with unlawful power, with some suggestion
that this conversion of convention into character would undermine the legit-
imacy of the convention. Marlowe as character would destroy Marlowe as
function. With Marlowe's function destroyed, the mystery novel could indeed not go beyond Chandler.

Herbert Ruhm. In David Madden, ed., *Tough Guy
Writers of the Thirties* (Carbondale: Southern
Illinois University Press, 1968), pp. 171–85

Raymond Chandler came late to the writing of crime stories. He was in his
forties when, after the ruin in the Depression of the small oil companies
with which he was associated, he began to read pulp magazines and "decided that this might be a good way to try to learn to write fiction and get
paid a small amount of money at the same time." His early short stories are
almost indistinguishable from much of the other material in *Black Mask,*
although a good deal is made of them now. His reputation, like Hammett's,
rests on his novels. There were seven, beginning with *The Big Sleep* (1939),
published when he was fifty years old.

Chandler had a fine feeling for the sound and value of words, and he
added to it a very sharp eye for places, things, people, and the wisecracks
(this out-of-date word seems still the right one) that in their tone and timing
are almost always perfect. "Did I hurt your head much?" Philip Marlowe
asks a blonde in *The Big Sleep* after he has hit her with his gun. She replies:
"You and every other man I ever met." It is impossible to convey in a
single quotation Chandler's almost perfect ear for dialogue, but it comes
through in all the later books whether the people talking are film stars or
publicity agents, rich men, gangsters, or policemen. To this is joined a generous indignation roused in him by meanness and corruption, and a basic
seriousness about his violent entertainments.

The actual plotting of the books improved greatly as he became more
sure of himself. In the first two or three stories, that joke about solving plot
problems by having a man come in the door with a gun is not too far away
from the truth, but the plots of *The Little Sister* (1949) and *The Long Goodbye* (1953) are as smoothly dovetailed as a piece of Chippendale. Yet plotting was never something he really enjoyed. Nothing could better indicate
the difference between Chandler and a typical Golden Age writer than the
fact that for the Golden Age writer the plot is everything and the writing
might often be done by computer, whereas Chandler thought that "plotting
may be a bore even if you are good at it" but "a writer who hates the actual
writing to me is simply not a writer at all." And we do read Chandler first
of all for the writing, and afterward for the California background, the jokes,

the social observation, the character of Marlowe. The plots are firm and adequate, but they are not what we take away from the books.

Julian Symons. *Mortal Consequences: A History—From the Detective Story to the Crime Novel* (New York: Harper & Row, 1972), pp. 142–43

The Big Sleep, and the six other novels by Chandler, are in the tradition of a negative romanticism which is perhaps the dominant mode of American literature from Hawthorne to our contemporary black humorists—that power of darkness which Hawthorne, Poe, and Melville explored, which Mark Twain could not laugh away, and which created a mythical landscape in Faulkner. Poe's "The Fall of the House of Usher" can be regarded as the rehearsal for the saga of the Sartoris-Compson-Sutpen families in Yoknapatawpha County. And the predecessor of Chandler's Californian nightmare had his hero Dupin "be enamored of the night for her own sake." But where Poe brought inductive light to moral darkness, Chandler refuses to cheat his vision in like manner. When Marlowe has solved a dilemma, he has not explained the enigma. All of Chandler's books end on a note of dissatisfaction. The purported solution does not tidy things up since there is no end to a waking nightmare.

This dark vision has lost none of its power today. The excess of violence of which Chandler has been needlessly accused is now hardly noticeable, nor was it lovingly attended to for shock effect, but rather described because life is simply that cheap in this truly egalitarian society: literally, a matter of fact. And so Chandler does not laud death with the lyrical mesmerism of Hemingway, nor does he play metaphysical games with it in Sartrean ingenuity. A death is a waste of life.

E. M. Beekman. *Massachusetts Review.* Winter 1973, p. 164

As he grew older, Chandler felt himself becoming more interested in "moral dilemmas" than in who killed whom. He even wondered whether he shouldn't "retire and leave the field to younger and more simple men." The feeling dates from the time that he finished the first draft of *The Long Goodbye,* begun in 1950 and published at the end of 1953. While working on the longest and most ambitious novel of his career, Chandler also woke in the middle of the night "with dreadful thoughts," terrified at a prospect of loss and solitude, for his wife had developed the fibrosis of the lungs that was slowly weakening and killing her.

He had intended to write a novel with only one murder, but ended up with two, still far below his usual average. The result is his purest example of a mystery based on character exposition, and once more the dominant character remains largely an off-stage presence. Terry Lennox, whom Marlowe meets in the opening scene, is reported to have committed suicide in Mexico forty pages later. He doesn't reappear until the last few pages, yet controls all the intervening action, since the mystery hinges on whether he killed his rich wife or whether his confessional suicide note was a fake.

In spite of its complex and perfectly organized mystery, *The Long Goodbye* is first of all a study of Chandler's private eye as he reaches the end of his emotional tether. He not only feels a sudden desire for friendship but considers an involvement with a married woman in her late thirties, the sister of Lennox's wife. Linda Loring decides to divorce her husband and wants to marry Marlowe. In a lonely hearts scene before she leaves for Europe, she asks to be loved as well as made love to. Marlowe agrees to the second but not to the first, partly because she's too rich, partly because he's still not ready to give up the habit of independence. By the end of the novel he has said two goodbyes.

The Long Goodbye is equally concerned with the trap of wealth, its impact on an outsider, its connections with violence, the wreckage of promising lives. Marlowe's good-bye to Lennox, disguised as a Mexican after plastic surgery, is touched with a powerful disillusion: "You had nice ways and nice qualities, but there was something wrong. . . . You were just as happy with mugs or hoodlums as with honest men. Provided the hoodlums spoke fairly good English and had fairly acceptable table manners." Since Lennox formerly used the name of Paul Marston, Chandler's story implies a curious subterranean link between the two men. The shared initials suggest an alter ego that reflects Marlowe's, and perhaps everybody's, potential for corruption. Throughout the novel they often echo each other, as if to show the hairbreadth separating lives of honesty and fraud.

Lennox tells Marlowe that the rich have no real fun but don't recognize it because "they never had any," Later, Marlowe listens open-mouthed to Lennox's father-in-law, a newspaper magnate, deliver an angry monologue on his need to buy privacy. The old man denounces the public world, newspapers included, as a huge disgusting swindle that specializes in beautifully packaged junk. "You've got a hundred million dollars," is Marlowe's reaction, "and all it has brought you is a pain in the neck." Soon after they meet, Marlowe warns Lennox that he doesn't like hoodlums, and Lennox answers: "That's just a word. . . . We have that kind of world." Near the end of the novel, Marlowe echoes him again:

> We're a big, rough, rich, wild people and crime is the price we pay for it, and organized crime is the price we pay for organization. . . . Organized crime is just the dirty side of the sharp dollar.
> "What's the clean side?"
> "I never saw it. . . ."

The real murderer is again a woman, but a total departure from the greedy ambitious creatures of Chandler's previous work. In the past, Eileen Wade has been briefly and violently in love with Lennox. She meets him again years later, when she's unhappily married to a successful alcoholic novelist, and he seems broken and cynical. She withdraws into a frustrated romantic fantasy of a lost and perfect love, and in an eerie psychotic moment, heightened by moonlight and sleeping pills, she even confuses Marlowe with Lennox: "I always knew you would come back. . . . All these years I have kept myself for you."

Classifying the various types of killers he's encountered, Marlowe sees her as the killer in love with the idea of death, "to whom murder is a remote kind of suicide." In *The Long Goodbye* almost everyone is haunted by the idea of some kind of suicide. Its narrative excitement and wit contain an overview of aching maladjusted lives. The power-obsessed millionaire has a lonely sour intelligence. The novelist is adrift in self-pity. "I always find what I want," Linda Loring says. "But when I find it, I don't want it any more." And Lennox finally confesses to Marlowe:

> "An act is all there is. There isn't anything else. In here"—he tapped his chest with the lighter—"there isn't anything. I've had it, Marlowe. I had it long ago."

Only cops and hoodlums remain pitiless and unpitied.

Gavin Lambert. The Dangerous Edge (New York:
Grossman, 1976), pp. 229–31

Raymond Chandler's loneliness at the end of his life was painful to see and revives equally distressing memories of that of Auden at the end of his life. Although Auden was a far closer and more long-standing friend, and we had beliefs in common, sitting over luncheon at Carlton Hill was quite like sitting over tea in our kitchen in Loudoun Road with Auden, discussing "LIFE." Though their achievements were of a totally different order, in history they were not unlike; both devoted to memories of "saintly" mothers and both always searching to be mothered, both concerned with the discipline aspect of writing and justly proud of their craftsmanship, both in old age nervy and demanding, both childless, both drinking, and both craving only companionship and a gentle round of domestic chores—nothing more. But where Raymond in work and life was sentimental, a fantasist, and self-deluding (his drinking had a long life history), even self-pitying, Auden was absolutely nonfantasist, controlled, and stoic, his daily litany being a counting of his blessings. In Raymond it is possible that childlessness explained his skirmishes against both Christianity and psychoanalysis, for both creeds recognize the primacy, vulnerability, and sacredness of childhood. Auden's Christianity originated in his relationship to a loving mother; his compassion was easily accommodated in both creeds. Raymond on occasions found it hard to keep in touch with his. Raymond was proud to think of himself as a "passionate moralist," which sounds comparatively merciless towards himself and others; Auden believed benevolently in redemption and forgiveness, and was a "compassionate moralist."

Natasha Spender. The New Republic. June 27,
1976, pp. 15–28

Chandler was a naturally gifted and fluent writer, but for nearly fifty years he was unable to find a medium that suited him. He endured continuing disappointments and frustrations and, already sensitive, he became withdrawn and introverted. When at last he began to write stories for the pulps and published his own novels, he pulled together the opposed aspects of his nature and created something extraordinarily vital and original. Chandler tended to deprecate his own importance as a writer, but he had a clear idea of what he had achieved, and he knew that his writing held him together.

His double vision—half-English, half-American—enabled him to see the world he lived in with exceptional insight. His vision of America has become increasingly fulfilled, although twenty-five years ago few people could have imagined the relevance of his work today. He was a prophet of modern America; out of the European literary tradition he wrote about a world that both repelled and delighted him. He did not generalize or theorize. Rather, he trusted his impulses, and like Chaucer or Dickens he wrote about the people, places, and things he saw with scorn and also with love. This has made him one of the most important writers of his time, as well as one of the most delightful.

Frank MacShane. *The Life of Raymond Chandler*
(New York: Dutton, 1976), pp. 268–69

An American crime writer who began, at the time of the Depression, to write hard-boiled short stories for pulps and for *Black Mask* (from 1933), Raymond Chandler had previously been a journalist and businessman. Rather too much is now made of Chandler as artist but, after Dashiell Hammett, his acknowledged master, he was the best crime writer of his time. As a critic wrote, Chandler's prose is "image-laden," "raw-colored," Hammett's "all-bone." The early stories (some in *Killer in the Rain,* 1964 and *The Smell of Fear,* 1965) are not distinguished, but with his first novel it became clear that Chandler was more than an entertainer. His detective Philip Marlowe is not a convincing character—he is a masochist projection of Chandler himself—but he acts as a perfect vehicle for his creator's wit, acutely critical sociological viewpoint, and ear for dialogue. Of the seven novels the first four (*The Big Sleep,* 1939; *Farewell My Lovely,* 1940; *The High Window,* 1942; *The Lady in the Lake,* 1943) are badly plotted, but they are superior to the last three—*The Little Sister* (1949), *The Long Goodbye* (1954), *Playback* (1958)—which are cleverly constructed but more sentimental and less deeply felt.

Martin Seymour-Smith. *Who's Who in Twentieth
Century Literature* (New York: Holt, Rinehart and
Winston, 1976), p. 79

Now if in comparing the tender and the tough conventions one is looking for "real life" in the verifiable sense, one must conclude that although the first kind of story will not bear skeptical examination, the second is—as

Shakespeare says apropos of two liars—"an even more wonderful song than the other." Nor is this all that Raymond Chandler's essay ["The Simple Art of Murder"] brings to mind. The tender school aims at producing a denouement having the force of necessity, as in Greek tragedy. All the facts (clues, words, motives) must converge to give the mystery one solution and one only. That by itself is a good reason for making the crime occur in a law-abiding circle, where the habits of the dramatis personae are by hypothesis regular and reasonable. In such a setting the violence of murder is the more striking, and stronger also the desire to manacle the offender. Murder among thugs and drug addicts is hardly unexpected, and the feeling that in this milieu anything can happen does not increase but rather lessens the interest. Hence the artistic need for the tough writer to involve some innocent, whose ways *are* peaceable, and to put steadily in peril the detective-defender of that lump of virtue. In short, in murder à la Chandler, murder is not enough to keep us going—and neither is detection, since it is never a feature of the foreground.

Chandler as artist is so aware of these lacks that he reinforces the damsel-in-distress motive with what is nothing less than a political motive. He makes it clear in his essay that the hero of the new and improved genre is fighting society. Except for the favored victim, he alone is pure in heart, a C-green incorruptible. The rich are all crooked or "phonies," and cowards in the end. Since the police, the mayor, the whole Establishment are soon shown as a conspiracy to pervert justice and kill off troublemakers, we naturally share the detective's smothered indignation and are powerfully driven, like him, to see the right vindicated.

Jacques Barzun. In Miriam Gross, ed., *The World
of Raymond Chandler* (Reading, Mass.: Addison &
Wesley, 1977), pp. 161–62

Chandler remained by temperament a romantic aesthete. His feebly literary early essays and poems are full of either/ors like science and poetry, romance and realism. Are we to be saved "by the science or by the poetry of life"? That, he said, "is the typical question of the age," and he came down on the side of poetry as opposed to science and of romance against realism. Or rather, of realism seen romantically, so that "any man who has walked down a commonplace city street at twilight, just as the lamps are lit" would see that a true view of it must be idealistic, for it would "exalt the sordid to a vision of magic, and create pure beauty out of plaster and vile dust." The phrases echo Chesterton, and also look forward to the famous peroration of "The Simple Art of Murder" which runs: "Down these mean streets a man must go." . . . It was Chandler's strength, and his weakness, that he brought this basically sentimental aestheticism to the crime stories, so that they had increasingly to be about a romantic hero whose activities gave the novels at least "a quality of redemption" so that he could think of them as art. That was the weakness. The strength lay in the fact that by treating seriously everything he did Chandler achieved even in his early stories for the pulps more than his fellow practitioners. . . .

If we read the stories today it is for occasional flashes of observation that got by the blue pencil, and for the use of language. Chandler's ear for the rhythms of speech was good from the beginning, but it developed with astonishing speed. The stories written in the later 1930s, like "Killer in the Rain," "The Curtain," "Try the Girl," and "Mandarin's Jade" are often as well written as the novels, where the early tales are full of clichés. "Smart-Aleck Kill" . . . has eyes that get small and tight, eyes with hot lights in them, eyes that show sharp lights of pain. There are cold smiles playing around the corners of mouths, and mirthless laughter. But within a very few years these have almost all disappeared, and we recognize the sharp cleverness of the novels when we are told that the garage of a modernistic new house is "as easy to drive into as an olive bottle" or that a smart car in a dingy neighborhood "sticks out like spats at an Iowa picnic."

It was these later and better stories that Chandler cannibalized, to use his own word, to make three of the novels. This was an extraordinary process. Other writers have incorporated early material in a later work, but nobody else has done it in quite this way. Most writers who adapt their earlier work take from it a particular theme or character and jettison the rest. Chandler, however, carved out great chunks of the stories, expanded them, and fitted them into an enlarged plot. Where gaps existed, like spaces in a jigsaw, he made pieces to fit them. It meant, as Philip Durham has said, adapting, fusing, and adding characters, blending themes from different stories, combining plots. Much of his first novel, *The Big Sleep,* was taken from two stories, "Killer in the Rain" and "The Curtain," plus fragments from two other stories. About a quarter of the book was new material, but the passages from the two principal stories used were much enlarged. There could be no better proof of the limitation Chandler felt in being forced to work within the pulp magazine formula.

The pulp magazines had shaped him, but once he had learned the trade they were a restriction. The novels enabled him to burst the bonds and to express the essential Raymond Chandler: a romantic aesthete and a self-conscious artist, an introvert with the power of catching the form, the tone, the rhythm, of American speech supremely well on paper. In its kind Chandler's mature dialogue is perfect. One cannot see how it could be better done. The stories are not much in themselves, but without them perhaps we should never have had the novels.

Julian Symons. In Miriam Gross, ed., *An Aesthete Discovers the Pulps* (New York: Addison & Wesley, 1978), pp. 19–30

Chandler's uniqueness—and the source of his popularity—is the product of a wide variety of personal traits and talents, circumstances, and coincidences. He brought to his work a European sensibility and education supported by a bedrock of childhood experiences in the American Great Plains of the late nineteenth century. He arrived in California while the pioneering spirit still thrived and witnessed the rise of the movie studios and the attendant exploitation of glamour and illusion. He barely survived the First World War and was just achieving the peak of his writing career as Western civilization threatened to fall apart in the Second.

Given his far-ranging experience, it is perhaps remarkable that he maintained the conviction throughout it all that "the best way to comment on large things is to comment on small things." The "small things" that preoccupied him were character and language. By concentrating on the motives of individual characters, he approaches such larger themes as the unpredictability of human emotion under pressure and the manner in which changing times appear to alter one's ethical possibilities. He illuminates the way in which characters are alternately responsible for the world in which they live, and trapped by that world. As Dostoyevsky reminded us in *Crime and Punishment,* "this damnable psychology cuts both ways." The reactions of Chandler's characters to their psychic binds imply the pervasive instability at the core of modern society. And the language by which these characters reveal themselves allows the author to convey a sense of the delicate web by which we are all bound together.

The most significant "small things" that occupy Chandler are the mind and actions of his detective, Philip Marlowe. Marlowe is a microcosm of both Chandler's concern for character and his concern for the language by which that character is expressed. It is Marlowe's voice, of course, that is the constant ground of Chandler's stories. It is the detached, ironic, frequently alienated tone of that voice that holds our attention and provides an interpretive framework for the tales.

But while we may feel we know Marlowe's voice almost instinctively, a close examination of the novels reveals very little of a "factual" nature about the detective. We know a few details about his surroundings, almost nothing about his past, and very little about his personal motives. We almost never see his mind working, except as that mental activity is translated into dramatic action. And yet, we identify with him.

Understanding that identification may be as close as we can come to appreciating Chandler's power and uniqueness as a writer. And comprehending what Chandler called his "objective method" is essential to that appreciation.

Jerry Speir. *Raymond Chandler* (New York:
Ungar, 1981), pp. vii–viii

It seems worthwhile casting a glance at the role of brutality in the typical private-eye story. Big-city life in reality was tough, and was presented as such in U.S. crime fiction. A murder is a murder; it is and remains a horrible crime. In the P.I. novel, crime is not escapism, a flight from reality. In his essay, "The Simple Art of Murder" (1950), Chandler distanced himself from classic English crime writing in which, he maintained, villains, made of papier mâché, were unmasked by detectives of incredibly aristocratic stupidity. Chandler takes his place in a development alongside Hammett and Hemingway, writers who present an unpleasant world in a realistic fashion. They write about the world in which they live. Hammett portrays people who murder for logical reasons, not simply to produce a body for a novel's beginning. In committing murders these people use everyday means, not handmade duelling pistols, South American poisons, or tropical fish. They are real people and Hammett makes them talk and think in the language they use every day. Chandler describes the readers of the classic detective story as excited old aunts—male, female, or even neuter—and of any age. They like their murder cases magnolia-scented, never wishing to be reminded of the truth—namely that murder is something quite awful.

By 1954 Chandler softened his harsh verdict on classic crime fiction. In an essay he admitted some literary value to novels and tales that had succeeded in creating character and atmosphere well enough to last for several decades.

Because Hammett and Chandler experienced and presented hard and dangerous conditions in their stories, they were driven to adopt a hard style of writing. Inhumanity and cruelty being crimes, both authors took this as a starting point for their worldview. Tough statements were made in tough style. This kind of writing goes well beyond the limits of entertainment, that, by and large, had been the function of crime fiction. Yet Hammett's and Chandler's books are not read by the intelligentsia alone; they do entertain, if on a higher level. In condemning cruelty and inhumanity, they represent an important strand of American literary realism.

Waltraud Woeller. The Literature of Crime and
Detection (New York: Ungar, 1988), pp. 135–37

See also under ERLE STANLEY GARDNER: Paul Hofrichter, *Bookman's Weekly,* May 3, 1982, p. xx.

CHESTERTON, G. K. (1874–1936)

Each story in the Father Brown Saga presents a mystery, proposes explanations of a demoniacal or magical sort, and then replaces them at the end with solutions of this world. Skill is not the only virtue of those brief bits of fiction; I believe I can perceive in them an abbreviation of Chesterton's life, a symbol or reflection of Chesterton. The repetition of his formula through the years and through the books (*The Man Who Knew too Much, The Poet and the Lunatic, The Paradoxes of Mr. Pond*) seems to confirm that this is an essential form, not a rhetorical artifice.

Chesterton was a Catholic, he believed in the Middle Ages of the Pre-Raphaelites ("Of London, small and white, and clean"). Like Whitman, Chesterton thought that the mere fact of existing is so prodigious that no misfortune should exempt us from a kind of cosmic gratitude. That may be a just belief, but it arouses only limited interest; to suppose that it is all Chesterton offers is to forget that a creed is the underlying factor in a series of mental and emotional processes and that a man is the whole series. In Argentina, Catholics exalt Chesterton, freethinkers reject him. Like every writer who professes a creed, Chesterton is judged by it, is condemned or acclaimed because of it. His case is not unlike that of Kipling, who is always judged with reference to the English Empire.

Poe and Baudelaire proposed the creation of a world of terror, as did Blake's tormented Urizen; it is natural for their work to teem with the forms of horror. In my opinion, Chesterton would not have tolerated the imputation of being a contriver of nightmares, a *monstrorum artifex . . .* , but he tends inevitably to revert to atrocious observations.

Chesterton restrained himself from being Edgar Allan Poe or Franz Kafka, but something in the makeup of his personality leaned toward the nightmarish, something secret, and blind, and central. Not in vain did he dedicate his first works to the justification of two great gothic craftsmen, Browning and Dickens; not in vain did he repeat that the best book to come out of Germany was *Grimm's Fairy Tales*. He reviled Ibsen and defended Rostand (perhaps indefensibly), but the Trolls and the creator of *Peer Gynt* were the stuff his dreams were made of. That discord, that precarious subjection of a demoniacal will, defines Chesterton's nature. For me, the emblems of that struggle are the adventures of Father Brown, each of which undertakes to explain an inexplicable event by reason alone. ["Most writers of detective stories usually undertake to explain the obscure rather than the inexplicable."] That is why I said, in the first paragraph of this essay, that those stories were the key to Chesterton, the symbols and reflections of Chesterton. That is all, except that the "reason" to which Chesterton subjected his imaginings was not precisely reason but the Catholic faith or rather a collection of Hebrew imaginings that had been subjected to Plato and Aristotle.

I remember two opposing parables. The first one is from the first volume of Kafka's works. It is the story of the man who asks to be admitted to the law. The guardian of the first door says that there are many other doors within, and that every room is under the watchful eye of a guardian, each of whom is stronger than the one before. The man sits down to wait. Days and years go by, and the man dies. In his agony he asks, "Is it possible that during the years I have been waiting, no one has wanted to enter but me?" The guardian answers, "No one has wanted to enter this door because it was destined for you alone. Now I shall close it." . . . The other parable is in Bunyan's *Pilgrim's Progress*. People gaze enviously at a castle guarded by many warriors; a guardian at the door holds a book in which he will write the name of the one who is worthy of entering. An intrepid man approaches the guardian and says, "Write my name, sir." Then he takes out his sword and lunges at the warriors; there is an exchange of bloody blows; he forces his way through the tumult and enters the castle.

Chesterton devoted his life to the writing of the second parable, but something within him always tended to write the first.

Jorge Luis Borges. *Other Inquisitions: 1937–1952*
(Austin, Texas: University of Texas Press, 1964),
pp. 82–85

A high-spirited, combative, opinionated man, G. K. Chesterton impressed on everything that he wrote a strong, whimsical, humorous personality which marked him out as a genuine man of letters—credited for his wit, his broad humanity, his personal kindliness, love of liberty, and gift of prose.

Stanley J. Kunitz and Howard Haycraft. *Twentieth
Century Authors* (New York: H. W. Wilson,
1942), pp. 275–76

When you take to writing detective stories, the measure of your success depends on the amount of personality you can build up round your favorite detective. Whether because Sherlock Holmes has set the standard for all time, or because the public does not like to see plots unraveled by a mere thinking machine, it is personality that counts. It is because he drops his parcels and cannot roll his umbrella, because he blinks at us and has fits of absent-mindedness, that Father Brown is such a good publisher's detective. He is a Daniel come to judgment.

The real secret of Father Brown is that there is nothing of the mystic about him. When he falls into a reverie the other people in the story think that he must be having an ecstasy, because he is a Catholic priest, and will proceed to solve the mystery by some kind of heaven-sent intuition. And the reader, if he is not careful, will get carried away by the same miscalculation; here, surely, is Chesterton preparing to show the Protestants where they get off. Unconsciously, this adds to the feeling of suspense.

Father Brown began life as short stories in the *Saturday Evening Post,* and short stories he remained; for an author so fertile in ideas, perhaps it was the simplest arrangement. But it must be confessed that this enforced brevity produces a rather breathless atmosphere; the more so, because Chesterton was an artist before he became an author, and occupies a good deal of his space with scene painting. And the scene painting takes up room— valuable room, the pedantic reader would tell us. . . .

For Chesterton (as for Father Brown) the characters were the really important thing. The little priest could see, not as a psychologist, but as a moralist, into the dark places of the human heart; could guess, therefore, at what point envy, or fear, or resentment, would pass the bounds of the normal, and the cords of convention would snap, so that a man was hurried into crime. Into crime, not necessarily into murder; the Father Brown stories are not bloodthirsty, as detective stories go; a full third of them deal neither with murder nor with attempted murder, which is an unusual average nowadays; most readers demand a corpse. The motives which made it necessary for Hypatia Hard to elope with her husband, the motives which induced the Master of the Mountain to pretend that he had stolen the ruby when he hadn't—the reader may find them unimpressive, because there is no black cap and no drop at the end of them. But, unless he is a man of unusual perspicacity, he will have to admit that he also found them unexpected. . . .

If we are to judge the Father Brown cycle by the canons of its own art, we shall not be disposed to complain that these are something less than detective stories; rather, that they are something more. Like everything else Chesterton wrote, they are a Chestertonian manifesto. And it may be reasonably maintained that the detective story is meant to be read in bed, by way of courting sleep; it ought not to make us think—or rather, it ought to be a kind of *catharsis,* taking our minds off the ethical, political, theological problems which exercise our waking hours by giving us artificial problems to solve instead. If this is so, have we not good reason to complain of an author who smuggles into our minds, under the disguise of a police mystery, the very solicitudes he was under contract to banish?

I am inclined to think that the complaint, for what it is worth, lies against a good many of the Father Brown stories, but not all, and perhaps not the best. Where the moral which Chesterton introduces is vital to the narrative, belongs to the very stuff of the problem, the author has a right, if he will, to mystify us on this higher level. In the over-civilized world we live in, there are certain anomalies which we take for granted; and he may be excused if he gently mocks at us for being unable, because we took them for granted, to read his riddle. There is something artificial in a convention which allows us to say that nobody has entered a house when in fact a postman has entered it, as if the postman, being a State official, were not a man. But it must be confessed that in some of the stories, especially the later ones, the didactic purpose tends to overshadow, and even to crowd out, the defective interest; such stories as "The Arrow of Heaven," and "The Chief Mourner of Marne." If we read these with intent, it is not because they are good detective stories, but because they are good Chesterton.

> Ronald Knox. Introduction, in *Father Brown:*
> *Selected Stories,* by G. K. Chesterton, ed. by
> Ronald Knox (Oxford: Oxford University Press,
> 1955), vii–xvii

Chesterton had a genius for the shape of wickedness; that is to say, he had an allegorical imagination. All of *The Man Who Was Thursday* is a dark conceit, and so is *Manalive* and *The Ball and the Cross* and *The Napoleon of Notting Hill.* Even the Father Brown stories have something in them of allegory or parable: each offers an inscrutable, irrational, often obscurely unnatural event, and then explains it, through Father Brown's understanding, as an aspect of the intelligible order of existence. At the end of each story the sanity of the world has been defended against the stark anarchies, and we are reassured.

It is in his uses of his allegorical imagination that Chesterton seems most "modern," for nightmare is the allegorical form for our time, an allegory of the unconscious by which our deepest anxieties and fears are revealed. It is not surprising that a parabolical writer like Jorge Luis Borges should admire Chesterton, or that he should have written the best short appreciation of Chesterton's imagination.

The sense of the world as a moral battlefield is at the center of Chesterton's thought: it underlies his allegorical fiction, and it informs his criticism. It made it possible for him to live in a world of anarchies and negations and yet preserve that moral energy that he called optimism. "This world can be made beautiful again," he wrote in his *Charles Dickens*, "by beholding it as a battlefield. When we have defined and isolated the evil thing, the colors come back into everything else. When evil things have become evil, good things, in a blazing apocalypse, become good."

It is in part because he saw the world in this way that he was so excellent a critic of the Victorian period; for he understood the importance of religious struggle for the age, and emphasized it even at the peril, as he put it, of making the spiritual landscape too large for the figures. He was born into that landscape, and he sympathized with the Victorians in their High Seriousness. But he was also an Edwardian, removed enough from the past age so that he could see it whole, and thus become the first Victorianist.

Samuel Hynes. *Edwardian Occasions: Essays on*
English Writing in the Early Twentieth Century
(Oxford: Oxford University Press, 1972),
pp. 84–85

Chesterton's interest in dialogue as against monologue comes out strongly in the third novel, *The Ball and the Cross* (1909), an undervalued and, I find, largely overlooked work. Just what sort of novel it is is once more not easy to tie down. It opens like a kind of science fiction, in the marvelous flying machine of Professor Lucifer; its middle and main part is a blend or alternation of Polemicist material and a simple but vigorous action story. Atheist and Christian—the one is made as attractive a character as the other—fight it out in words and, when not prevented by officious interveners, notably policemen, with swords as well. The physical duel is inconclusive; the metaphysical comes out predictably but acceptably.

The final section is as fantastic as its counterpart in *The Man Who Was Thursday,* but this is more overtly theological: Lucifer lives up to his name in the role of superintendent of a gigantic lunatic asylum in which, were he to triumph, the mass of mankind would end up incarcerated. Chesterton's interest in madmen, which pervades his fiction, is at more than first sight surprising in so sane a writer and human being. Some of it serves his love of paradox, furnishing the man whose devotion to rationalism deprives him of his reason, the man whose devotion to reason makes him appear insane in the eyes of the illogical or the incurious. This is not the whole story, the rest of which I confess I cannot for the moment discover. But it must be stressed that Chesterton is not anticipating, would on the contrary have found devilish, current trendy notions that sanity is a relativist or quasi-political label, that there are insane societies but no insane individuals, etc.

By the time of *Manalive* (1912), the novels are in sad case. The hero, Innocent Smith—a name, like the title, that bodes no good—spends his inexhaustible leisure on projects like dropping his wife off at boardinghouses or places of business in order to reencounter and rewoo her. As a long lecture near the close informs us flatly, this is his way of demonstrating (to whom?) his belief in the perpetual freshness of marriage. The author has to keep telling us that Smith is irrepressible and a harlequin, that "he filled everyone with his own half-lunatic life." These assertions are never demonstrated; Chesterton could not create comic incident or write funny dialogue.

Kingsley Amis. In John Sullivan, ed., *G. K.
Chesterton: A Centenary Appraisal* (New York:
Barnes & Noble, 1974), pp. 36–37

Chesterton himself did not attach great importance to the Father Brown stories. Ordered in batches by magazine editors and publishers, they were written hurriedly for the primary purpose of helping to finance his Distributist paper, *G. K.'s Weekly*. And though they have proved to be the most popular of Chesterton's writings, critical attention to them has been casual. This is partly because they are detective stories; and the detective story is commonly dismissed, without argument, as a very low form of art. That it is also a very difficult and demanding form, in which many clever writers have failed, is not regarded as relevant. Nor is there much respect for the innovators in this genre, or much comment on their remarkable rarity. If there were, Chesterton's reputation would stand very high; for his detective stories, while they may not be the best ever written, are without doubt the most ingenious. But to show ingenuity and originality in the detective story is for the superior critic merely to have a knack for a particular sort of commercial fiction. It is not the sort of thing he takes seriously. And Chesterton himself, it seems, would have agreed with him.

What is Chesterton saying in the Father Brown stories? Their meaning must be understood in terms of their genre. . . . Chesterton, like all detective story writers, derives from Poe. Indeed, it might be said that he derives from a single story of Poe: many of the Father Brown stories can be regarded as ingenious variations on the theme of "The Purloined Letter." . . . There are no chemical analyses or careful checking of alibis in these stories. Nor is there the dry intellectuality of Dupin. . . . [Between] Poe and Chesterton comes Conan Doyle.

Every imaginative writer must choose his genre, and every genre has limitations. Those of the detective tale are obvious, and the most serious is this: no character can have depth, no character can be done from the inside, because any must be a potential suspect. It is Chesterton's triumph that he turned this limitation of the genre into an illumination of the universal human potentiality of guilt and sin. No character in the stories matters except Father Brown. But this is not a fault, because Father Brown, being a man, epitomizes all their potentialities within himself. "Are you a devil?" the exposed criminal wildly asks. "I am a man," replies Father Brown, "and therefore have all devils in my heart."

This ability to identify himself with the murderer is the "secret" of Father Brown's method. Some readers have misunderstood Chesterton's intention here. They suppose that Father Brown is credited with special spiritual powers, pertaining to his rôle as a priest. They see him as a thaumaturgic Sherlock Holmes. . . . But it is made quite clear that Father Brown owes his success not to supernatural insight but to the usual five senses. He is simply more observant, less clouded by conventional anticipations and prejudices, than the average man.

But Father Brown's ordinariness is ordinariness à la Chesterton. He shares his creator's aesthetic sense. Indeed, his detective powers are closely connected with his aesthetic sense. . . .

We might say that Father Brown is imagined by Chesterton as a child whose vision is undistorted. The psychological critic will no doubt see in the contrasting distortions of perspective, the "wrong shapes," the murderous yet strangely unheated fantasies of the stories, some relationship to the child's bizarre notions of the behavior of adults. For reasons of temperament, period, and literary mode, Chesterton avoids overtly sexual themes in the Father Brown stories. Yet it was presumably the real Father Brown's knowledge of sexual depravities that shocked Chesterton. And in "The Secret of Father Brown" the priest confides to his interlocutor that he "acted out" in his imagination all the crimes that he had investigated. What renders Father Brown invulnerable is precisely this anterior playacting.

The main critical problem posed by these stories, as by Chesterton's work as a whole, is how to distinguish between the childlike and the childish.

W. W. Robson. In John Sullivan, ed., *G. K. Chesterton: A Centenary Appraisal* (New York: Barnes & Noble, 1974), pp. 58–72

The common view of Chesterton's social philosophy is that is expresses a longing for a literal return to medieval times. A careful study of the novels indicates the falsity of such a view. The shortest summary of what they have to say about the restoration of a medieval social order is that it is a dangerous political dream. In *The Napoleon of Notting Hill,* Adam Wayne's neo-medievalism brings back poetry and pageantry to modern life, but it also creates a neo-Imperialism which is as oppressive as the Imperialism it was supposed to replace. In *The Ball and the Cross,* MacIan's dream of a medieval theocracy turns out to be a nightmare of authoritarian terror and oppression. Even in a later novel such as *Tales of the Long Bow,* which corresponds most closely to the popular view of his medievalism, surprisingly little is said about a return to a medieval past: what is achieved by the successful Distributist revolution is the protection of a newly created and broadly based agrarian society.

But the most subtle and ironic treatment of medievalism is found in the novel which was serialized in *G. K.'s Weekly,* at a time when Chesterton was simultaneously director of the Distributist League and editor of the paper which was its organ. *The Return of Don Quixote* is perhaps the best example of the way in which the best fiction is at once sophisticated and well-balanced propaganda for a political philosophy and extraordinarily effective literature. The medieval experiment which the hero introduces does little to alter the political realities of modern life, except to the extent that it distracts the people from the existence of the real social problems which it leaves unaltered. The restoration of pageantry and color to political life which delights Herne and his followers is also a means of deceiving them. It might be argued that the Distributist criticism of State Socialism and Capitalism is now turned against Distribution itself. Certainly nothing that Chesterton's critics have written about the folly of romantic medievalism in politics hits as shrewdly as his own criticism of it in what is ostensibly his most flamboyantly medieval novel.

> Ian Boyd. *The Novels of G. K. Chesterton: A
> Study in Art and Propaganda* (London: Paul Elek,
> 1975), pp. 192–93

G. K. Chesterton was a prolific literary professional; his Catholic onesidedness has possibly robbed him of some of the serious consideration he deserves, though he has never lost his popular appeal. His poetry is attractive but never (as T. S. Eliot said of the best of Monro) "the real right thing." His criticism is uneven and inaccurate but often contains more than enough insight to make it valuable, especially to the as yet uninitiated. As a purveyor of paradox and in some fiction, however, he displayed genius. The novel *The Man Who Was Thursday* (1908) is rather more than "excellent light entertainment" (a standard judgment) and so are the best of the Father Brown stories (*The Father Brown Omnibus,* 1947; the collection of the same title, USA only, 1951, adds one more story): they are the best of a writer who could never develop—but who has all the promise of genius. Chesterton was unreliable and dogmatic, but wisdom and compassion slip through, and one of his own remarks serves him well as an epitaph: "If a job's worth doing it's worth doing badly." *Collected Poems* (1933); *Chesterton* (1970) is Auden's selection from the nonfictional prose; *Chesterton Reprint Series* (1960–) collect most of the fiction except the Father Brown stories.

Martin Seymour-Smith. *Who's Who in Twentieth Century Literature* (New York: Holt, Rinehart and Winston, 1976), pp. 81–82

One reason why Chesterton exasperated many fastidious souls relates to what I am going to illustrate as his concern with formal causality. He was vividly aware of his public and of its needs both to be cheered and to be straightened out. So pervasive is this feature in Chesterton that it scarcely matters at what page one opens in order to illustrate it.

The formal cause, or the public itself is in perpetual flux and always in need of clarification and refocusing of its problems. Style itself, whether in poetry or painting or music, is a way of seeing and knowing, which is otherwise unattainable. . . . The style is the response of the artist to his audience and its needs. Chesterton's style was playful in an age that was very earnest and his perceptions and thoughts were paradoxical or multifaceted in a time that was full of intense specialism in politics and economics and religion.

Perhaps, before moving on, I should pause to indicate why Western philosophers and scholars may have shirked consideration of formal causality in the study of the arts and science. Since scarcely anybody has studied the audience of any writer from Plato to the present, there must surely be both a profound and a simple reason for so vast and consistent an omission. I suggest that this reason is to be found in the visual bias of Western man. Visual man is typically concerned with the lineal and the connected and the logical. Visual order has regard to *figure* and not to *ground*. The audience is always the hidden *ground* rather than the *figure* of any discourse. The *ground* is discontinuous, murky and dynamic, whereas the *figure* tends to be clear and distinct and static. However, without the interplay of *figure* and *ground,* no art or knowledge is possible. It might even be argued that the abrupt and bumpy and grotesquely sprockety contours of Chesterton's prose are very much a response of his sensitivity to a perverse and misbegotten public that he earnestly but good-naturedly was determined to redeem from its banalities.

In the everyday order, formal causality reveals itself by its *effects*. There is a strange paradox in this, because since the effects come from the hidden *ground* of situations, the effects usually appear before their causes. When a Darwin or an Einstein appears, we say "the time was ripe" and that the *figure* appeared in its natural *ground*. Chesterton was almost Oriental in his sensitivity to effects, his capacity for noting the consequences embedded in innovations and special attitudes or situations. In fact, Chesterton was always aware of "the law of the situation." This phrase was much used by Mary Parker Follett, the inventor of modern management studies. She was always concerned with discovering the question rather than the answer. It was she who began to ask managers: "what business do you think you are in?" They would point to the *figure* in their enterprise, and she would give the *ground,* or the *effects* of the *figure.* She would point out to a window-blind manufacturer that he was really in the business of environmental light control. . . . Chesterton's awareness of the *figure/ground* consequences pervades his studies of history and human thought in general. It made it easy for him to enter the field of detective fiction, since the detective story is written backwards, starting with the effects, and discovering the cause later, and, as it were, incidentally. The history of detective fiction, at least since Edgar Poe, relates to the law of the situation very intimately.

Poe is perhaps best known for his account of the composition of "The Raven." He explained that, seeking in the first place to achieve an effect of maximal melancholy and gloom, he set about discovering the means to *get* this effect, noting that art must always start with the *effect.* This is another way of saying that art must start with formal cause, and with concern with the audience. Sherlock Holmes frequently explained to Watson (who was typical of the unenlightened public) that the detective must put himself in the place of the criminal. The criminal is the person who is entirely concerned with *effects.* He considers the entire situation as one to be manipulated, both *figure* and *ground,* in order to achieve a very special effect. The criminal, like the artist, takes into account both the *figure* and the *ground,* that is, the work to be done in order that the effect may be achieved. It is this interplay between *figure* and *ground,* and the confronting of the latter in the situation, which gives to the detective story so much of the poetic character. Chesterton's *Father Brown* is always sensitive to the hidden laws of the situation that are so easily obscured by the ordinary concern with *figure* and points of view: for it is of the essence of formal causality that it is not a point of view, but, rather, a statement of a situation.

It was the "rhetorical" interplay between philosophy and its public which was eliminated by Descartes in the seventeenth century with the result that formal cause was transferred from the public to the subjective life of the individual philosopher or student of philosophy. The further consequence was that the "content" of philosophy and the arts became relegated to efficient causality. Formal causality simply ceased to have any *conscious* role in the arts and sciences from then until our own day. Chesterton was part of the *avant-garde* in rediscovering formal causality in his multileveled grasp of his public and his themes.

Marshall McLuhan. *The Chesterton Review.*
Spring-summer 1976, pp. 253–59

Unlike the Holmes cycle the Father Brown stories never develop into a cohesive work. Instead of a deepening exploration of life, they show a gradual imaginative decline. The first two collections, written before 1914, contain most of the best tales. "The Wisdom," written shortly after Chesterton's conversion to Rome, contains the rest. The final volumes read like formula stuff, turned out for quick money. Throughout his life, Chesterton's uneasy prolific mind yields brilliant ideas that bore him after a while. A rhapsodic writer, the longer forms elude him. Themes somehow emerge from the wealth of improvisation. But after writing "The Blue Cross" he shows no interest in creating a frame for the Father Brown material.

The first story introduces the priest-detective, Flambeau the master-criminal, and the coldly sceptical Vallentin, head of the Paris police and "the most famous investigator in the world." In "The Secret Garden," which follows, Father Brown exposes the chief of police as a murderer and he kills himself. In the next story the priest encounters Flambeau again, and in the next persuades him to abandon his life of crime. Flambeau then sets up on his own as a private investigator. He and Father Brown work together as a detective team with undertones of Holmes and Watson. Each seems to be the other's only close friend, yet their relationship has little detail or intimacy. By the end of the first collection Chesterton has really shot his bolt. . . .

From the time that he first locked himself into an embrace with the church, the momentum of his work as a whole began to falter. He originally discussed conversion to Rome with Father O'Connor in 1911. After many hesitations on the brink he was received, swordstick in hand, in 1922. The church publicized the event as a surprise ceremony, but Chesterton and Rome were really like lovers who decide at last to get married. They'd already had several children, of which *The Innocence of Father Brown* was the first.

Gavin Lambert. The Dangerous Edge (New York: Grossman, 1976), pp. 68–75

CHRISTIE, AGATHA (1891–1976)

The Murder of Roger Ackroyd really turns a new trick in detective fiction, surely a difficult enough achievement "with the competition so strong." Most writers of detective stories develop their own special detectives, following the lead of the famous. Agatha Christie's pet detective is Hercule Poirot.

Poirot is merely one factor in a tale so ingeniously constructed, so dextrously plotted as to warrant our complete admiration. It is unfortunate for us that we may not indicate here the most original element in Miss Christie's planning of the story. But that would be treachery to the author, and the reader has no right to be too well informed in advance.

Suffice it to say that Miss Christie's dedication of the book is to one "who likes an orthodox detective story, murder, inquest, and suspicion falling on every one in turn!" So she set herself to write such an orthodox story, with the strange result that she has succeeded in producing one of the few notable for originality.

For those who prefer certain backgrounds to others for their mystery tales we may say that Miss Christie's are always English in setting. To those who hate "loose ends" we may remark that this author ties all her knots neatly and bites off the thread. Her characterization is sharp in outline, her motivation is sound, complications of the plot never "get away from her." Everything in the puzzle falls neatly into place, and the complete picture leaves upon us an ineradicable impression. There are no inexplicable and glossed-over details. It is all an almost mathematical demonstration so far as the fundamental brainwork goes. Yet that it is no mere clever intellectual exercise, witness the fact that the reader is left with the strongest emotions of pity and wonder over the disastrous coil the weak and erring weave. There are indications, in fact, of an even deeper psychological insight than can be actively exercised in a book of this kind. For a detective story must move. The author cannot pause to philosophize. But one is rather closer in touch, in this tale, with the mad logic of actual criminality, with the criminal as a mainly average human being with one tragic twist, than is at all usual.

We do not overpraise this story, we believe, when we say that it should go on the shelf with the books of first rank in its field. The detective story pure and simple has as definite limitations of form as the sonnet in poetry. Within these limitations, with admirable structural art, Miss Christie has genuinely achieved.

William Rose Benét. Saturday Review. July 24, 1926, p. 951

The puzzle mystery, I was assured, had been brought to a high pitch of ingenuity in the stories of Agatha Christie. So I read the new Agatha Christie, *Death Comes as the End,* and I confess that I have been had by Mrs. Christie. I did not guess who the murderer was, I was incited to keep on and find out, and when I did finally find out, I was surprised. Yet I did not care for Agatha Christie and I hope never to read another of her books. I ought, perhaps, to discount the fact that *Death Comes as the End* is supposed to take place in Egypt two thousand years before Christ, so that the book has a flavor of Lloyd C. Douglas not, I understand, quite typical of the author. ("No more Khay in this world to sail on the Nile and catch fish and laugh up into the sun whilst she, stretched out in the boat with little Teti on her lap, laughed back at him"); but her writing is of a mawkishness and banality which seem to me literally impossible to read. You cannot *read* such a book, you run through it to see the problem worked out; and you cannot become interested in the characters, because they never can be allowed an existence of their own even in a flat two dimensions but have always to be contrived so that they can seem either reliable or sinister, depending on which quarter, at the moment, is to be baited for the reader's suspicion. . . . It is all like a sleight-of-hand trick, in which the magician diverts your attention from the awkward or irrelevant movements that conceal the manipulation of the cards, and it may mildly entertain and astonish you, as such a sleight-of-hand performance may. But in a performance like *Death Comes as the End*, the patter is a constant bore and the properties lack the elegance of playing cards.

Edmund Wilson. "Why Do People Read Detective
Stories?" *Classics and Commercials: A Literary
Chronicle of the Forties* (New York: Farrar, Straus
and Giroux, 1950), pp. 234–35

What makes all Agatha Christie's work commendable, on stage or between covers, is its total incapacity for offending, despite its burden of rage, hate, and offensive weapons. Characters murder and are murdered, and not in jest either, but everything is cleansed and purified and raised to a level of calm speculation and cool logic. There's no gratuitous poring over horror: the camera eye doesn't dwell on flies drinking the blood of the victim. The corpse is an item in an argument. We end up admiring the shape of this argument, not shuddering at the distortions of the criminal mind. . . .

Agatha Christie has been entertaining us so long and so relentlessly that she has soared above the level of the entertainer. There are scholars who are prepared to take her art, the skill of devising fresh and insoluble puzzles, with the seriousness proper to a Joyce or James or Lawrence. T. S. Eliot once planned a great tome on the detective novel, with a whole swath devoted to her books.

Anthony Burgess. *Life*. December 1, 1967, p. 8

Of the impressive list of Mrs. Christie's volumes, mostly about Poirot, the best known and most widely discussed is the brilliant *The Murder of Roger Ackroyd*. At the present late date it is betraying no secret to say that this remarkable story, a tour de force in every sense of the word and one of the true classics of the literature, turns on the ultimate revelation of the narrator as the criminal. This device (or trick, as the reader may prefer) provoked the most violent debate in detective story history. Scarcely had the ink dried on the pages before representatives of one school of thought were crying, "Foul play!" Other readers and critics rallied as ardently to Mrs. Christie's defense, chanting the dictum: "It is the reader's business to suspect *every one*." The question remains unsettled today, and the inconclusive argument will probably continue as long as detective stories are read and discussed.

Happily, Poirot richly merited the attention he has received. For when he is at the top of his form few fictional sleuths can surpass the amazing little Belgian—with his waxed mustaches and egg-shaped head, his inflated confidence in the infallibility of his "little gray cells," his murderous attacks on the English language—either for individuality or ingenuity. His methods, as the mention of the seldom-forgotten "cells" implies, are imaginative rather than routine. Not for Poirot the fingerprint or the cigar ash. His picturesque refusal to go to Holmes-like on all fours in pursuit of clues is classic in the literature. (But his inventor does not scorn to employ one of the tritest of the Conanical devices almost ad nauseam, in the person of Captain Hastings, easily the stupidest of all modern Watsons.) Not quite an armchair detective, Poirot nevertheless spurns the aid of science. He is the champion of theory over matter. What this postulate may lack in verisimilitude it gains in dramatic possibilities, which the author knows well how to exploit to advantage.

The only really serious grounds for criticism of the stories, in fact, is Mrs. Christie's too great reliance on, and not always scrupulous use of, the least-likely-person motif.

Mrs. Christie occasionally turns her hand, for diversion, presumably, to stories in which other detectives appear; but none of these secondary creations has ever seriously rivaled the mustachioed Belgian. His own investigations, one regrets to report, have begun to reveal now and then symptoms of ennui, so that the publication of "a new Christie" is not always now the item of interest to the discriminating reader that it once was.

Nevertheless, few sleuths have been more rewarding than Poirot at the height of his powers. He still comes closer to symbolizing his profession in the popular mind than any storybook detective since Holmes whose methods he professes to deplore—but with whose essential histrionism he has so much in common. The hypercritical may feel that Mrs. Christie sometimes allows her hero to lean too heavily on intuition, and that her own art could be improved by a little greater variety in method and closer attention to the probabilities and the canons of fair play. But none can gainsay that at her frequent best Agatha Christie is easily one of the half-dozen most accomplished and entertaining writers in the modern field.

Howard Haycraft. *Murder for Pleasure: The Life
and Times of the Detective Story* (New York:
Biblio and Tannen, 1971), pp. 130–33

Compared, not only with Sherlock Holmes and Father Brown, but with Nero Wolfe or Dr. Fell or Lord Peter Wimsey, Poirot is a distinctly cardboard character, an obvious artifact. Agatha Christie herself prefers Miss Marple, and her new book, *Passenger to Frankfurt,* contains neither of them.

The fact remains, however, that Poirot, like a survivor from an almost extinct race of giants, is one of the last of the Great Detectives: and the mention of his name should be enough to remind us how much pleasure Agatha Christie has given millions of people over the past fifty years.

So what is it, this quality which Agatha Christie possesses and so many imitators have lacked?

The secret does lie partly in her plots. *The Murder of Roger Ackroyd, Murder on the Orient Express, The A.B.C. Murders,* and her other classic tours de force deserve their fame. If they seem hackneyed or contrived now or even too easily guessable, that is precisely because they left so permanent an impression on the detective story genre. These books are famous because each of them turns on a piece of misdirection and a solution which, in their day, were startlingly innovatory: but there are many others—*Crooked House, Cards on the Table, Death on the Nile, Mrs. McGinty's Dead, 4.50 from Paddington*—which, in their overall construction, the ingenuity of their clues, and the satisfactory smoothness with which their unexpected solutions fall into place, are just as good and perhaps better. It would be silly to pretend that Mrs. Christie has never written a bad book. She has—several: but, compared with the size of her output, amazingly few. Almost always, skilled professional that she is, she can outplot her readers, tripping them up with an extra twist in the tail of the story.

But this isn't all. The real secret of Agatha Christie is subtler. It lies not in the carpentering of her plots, excellent though that is, but in the texture of her writing; a texture smooth and homely as cream. Her books are the easiest of reading. They "go down a treat," as the saying is.

In a literary sense she doesn't write particularly well. But there is another sense, which for a writer of fiction is perhaps even more important. The ability to buttonhole a reader, to make (as Raymond Chandler put it) "each page throw the hook for the next," is a separate and by no means common art.

She has one other key quality—the quality of coziness. There are no nightmares in her books, nothing nasty, nothing horrid, as Jane Austen would say. . . . This is an important attribute of the true detective story. Its secure and restful formality is part of the pleasure; we don't really have to weep for the victim or for the villain; we ought not to be harrowed, any more than we are by the loss of pieces in a game of chess.

This type of book—and therefore this type of pleasure—has become rare. One reason, the main one probably, is that every new detective story, unlike other kinds of fiction, needs an at least marginally new idea—a new way of committing a murder, or of concealing a murderer's identity, or of solving a murder: and, in the nature of things, finding such new devices gets harder all the time.

Mrs. Christie herself has sometimes ventured a little outside the classic field; *Passenger to Frankfurt,* as it happens, is an example. But she belongs fairly and squarely in the old tradition.

The Great Detectives were—and, in Mrs. Christie's hands, thank goodness, still are—engaged on a great business. They move, untouched, incorruptible, undefeated, among the mysteries of life and death, teaching us in a parable that there is a reason for everything, that puzzles were made to be solved, that what seems like chaos may be only the observed effects of unknown causes; in short, that the world, instead of being as meaningless as a modern novel, may be like a good detective story, in which the truth and a happy ending are kept for the final chapter.

Anthony Lejeune. *The Spectator.* September 19, 1970, p. 294

Agatha Christie's career moved in a steady but unspectacular way until 1926, when *The Murder of Roger Ackroyd* appeared. . . . The setting is a village deep in the English countryside; Roger Ackroyd dies in his study; there is a butler who behaves suspiciously but whom we never really suspect, and for good servant measure a housekeeper, a parlormaid, two housemaids, a kitchenmaid, and a cook. We are offered two of the maps that had by now become obligatory, one of the house and grounds, the other of the study. So far so conventional, but we notice at once the amused observant eye which makes something interesting out of the standard material. It is a mark of the best Golden Age writers that they were unable to stick to those injunctions about subduing the characters. The narrator's sister Caroline, good-natured but intensely inquisitive, a retailer of one ridiculous rumor after another, is a genuine comic character done with affectionate ridicule. The detective is Poirot, who in the best Holmesian style asks obscure questions that turn out to be meaningful, like his concern here with the color of a suspect's boots.

During the thirties, Agatha Christie produced, year after year, puzzle stories of varied ingenuity and constant liveliness. Her skill was not in the tight construction of plot, nor in the locked-room mystery, nor did she often make assumptions about the scientific and medical knowledge of readers. The deception in these Christie stories is much more like the conjurer's sleight of hand. She shows us the ace of spades face up. Then she turns it over, but we still know where it is, so how has it been transformed into the five of diamonds? It is on her work during this decade, plus half a dozen of her earlier and later books, that her reputation chiefly rests, perhaps most specifically upon *Peril at End House* (1932), *Lord Edgware Dies* (1933) [in America, *Thirteen at Dinner*], *Why Didn't They Ask Evans?* (1934) [in America, *The Boomerang Clue*], *The A.B.C. Murders* (1936), and *Ten Little Niggers* (1939) [in America, *And Then There Were None*]. There were some mis-hits in her very considerable output at this time, but she succeeded wonderfully often in her two objectives of telling an interesting story about reasonably plausible characters and of creating a baffling mystery. Her work stayed at its peak until roughly the end of World War II. Since then it has shown a slow decline, although she is alone among Golden Age writers in remaining as readable as ever and in her capacity sometimes still to bring off a staggering conjuring trick.

Julian Symons. *Mortal Consequences: A History—
From the Detective Story to the Crime Novel* (New
York: Harper & Row, 1972), pp. 129–30

When Edmund Wilson asked, forty years ago, "Who Cares Who Killed Roger Ackroyd?" his answer—"Not I, nor any other intelligent reader"— helped to hurl the mystery-novel form into the nearest dustbin, dismissed as trash. Wilson fashioned a comfortable logic for literary tastemakers—that mysteries are trash, that the Great Unwashed find it easy and likable to read trash, that mysteries are therefore popular. Appropriate, perhaps, for Erle Stanley Gardner or Ellery Queen or Mickey Spillane. For Agatha Christie, however, the simplistic toss into the spittoon just won't suffice. Only Shakespeare and the Bible can compete with the Christie canon for total sales or, more significantly, for variety of foreign-language translations. It is a relatively easy matter to create profitable trash for a readership in one place at one time, catering to trends and hot topics and current lowest common denominators. But, for fifty-five years, Agatha Christie has commanded vast audiences from all cultures with novels that, as it happens, reflect the decade-by-decade changes in social mores perhaps less than those of any noticeable, long-lived writer. *The Mysterious Affair at Styles,* vintage 1920, never goes out of print. Something timeless is going on here.

Possible explanations. A great storyteller? Yes. Sometimes. A dozen, perhaps twenty, of the eighty Christie volumes provide object lessons in crafting a tale of suspense. A few (*The Hollow* or *At Bertram's Hotel,* for example) are even well written by novelistic standards. But *Curtain* is not well written or well told by any standards, and it will be read and reread, just as *Nemesis* and *The Big Four,* equally weak as narratives, have taken their places in the always-in-stock library. Agatha Christie surely deserves her reputation as a genius of pacing and plotting, but, even when those qualities are reported missing, something else remains. That "something else" certainly has little to do with the illumination of character. Christie's detectives, Hercule Poirot, Miss Marple, and the occasional Superintendent Battle or Mrs. Oliver, have their oft-repeated physical and behavioral trademarks, but reality never intrudes upon their stagy personae. Albert Finney embodied the ideal cinematic Hercule Poirot in *Murder on the Orient Express* precisely because his was so obviously a larger-than-life, layers-of-make-up performance. Similarly, actress Margaret Rutherford chose simply to ignore the Miss Marple of the novels and gave us, joyfully, Margaret Rutherford undiluted, demonstrating how small a role character plays in the vitality of a Christie story. (Imagine, by way of contrast, an actor bypassing Conan Doyle's portrait while impersonating Sherlock Holmes.) Moreover, supporting characters in the Christie world often seem to be refugees from Gothic romances, Noel Coward comedies, or turn-of-the-century melodramas. Doddering colonels, addled dowagers, headstrong heiresses, sensual Latins, family retainers, prodigal sons, loyal spinsters, absent-minded ministers. Without self-consciousness and with occasional ulterior motivation, Agatha Christie most often uses a palette of clichés to paint in her cast of characters.

One reads Conan Doyle for the Baker Street household and for the intellectual intricacies of the Holmesian deductions. One reads Dorothy Sayers for Lord Peter's life-style, for the baroque curves in the language and the landscapes. One reads Raymond Chandler for the Marlovian outlook on life, Rex Stout for Nero Wolfe and Archie and the orchids. One reads Agatha Christie—and only Agatha Christie (Edgar Allan Poe to one side)—for the murders themselves.

Who cares who killed Roger Ackroyd? Virtually everyone who's read the book. (Edmund Wilson who proclaimed that no one *cared* who killed Ackroyd admitted to having sampled only one Christie—*Death Comes as the End.* A loser. Agreed.) For the sake of the last five pages of a Christie mystery, readers will forgive the stereotypes, the caricatures, the forced comedy, and the narrative lapses. Unlike virtually all other detective fiction, the Christie library is read for substance, not form or style. It truly *does* matter who-done-it; it matters enough for unnerved readers to lose sleep, to reread in disbelief, to come back for more.

"The truth is that one doesn't really know anything about anybody. Not even the people who are nearest to you." So says a character in *A Caribbean Mystery;* so says Agatha Christie in everything she's written. "The least likely person," which serves other dispensers of suspense merely as a device for the bamboozling of readers, comes from Christie as a thematic imperative, a warning, a keening. And, for a world in a century of growing paranoia—personal, national, planetary—the Christie mysteries offer a working out, an acting out of the fears that we must deal with in silence or be called mad.

Evil is real, Agatha Christie reminds us again and again, and not merely a literary convention developed to make detective stories possible. As if she were doing penance for making light of evil by using it to entertain, Christie attempts to convey a sense of danger beyond the confines of paper and ink. Comforting clichés of character and situation are arranged artistically, only to be brutally knocked apart when the perception of evil's reality and pervasiveness displaces the falsely mirrored picture. Agatha Christie may not have been the first writer to toy with the notion of the seemingly mad being the sanest of us all, but she is certainly the only mystery writer to incorporate that theme into a genre otherwise weak in the philosophy department.

If the essence of the Christie magic is indeed its illumination of paranoid fantasies, the source of that distrust of the world may be the author's unconscious sense of her own capacity for evil—projected upon those around her. The false identities, the costumes and makeup, the sexual confusion, the paradox of victims and villains, of sanity and madness, the doubts about the people one loves and trusts—all point to the realization that Agatha Christie deals with the individual's suspicions and unsureness of his or her own identity. Who are we and what acts are we capable of? Add a clever plot, Hercule Poirot, and the English countryside, and it's no wonder Agatha Christie is giving Shakespeare and the Bible a run for the money.

Josh Rubins. *Harvard Magazine.* October 1975,
pp. 51–55

Most Christie readers will willingly suspend disbelief as long as that blissful ritual of murder among "nice" people unfolds according to the dictates, not of actuality, but of convention (the butler never does it unless he is a gentleman in disguise). Readers of the hard-boiled school or of police procedurals can take heavy doses of reality, but Christie fans hear a cozier, more muffled drummer. They want, all in one go, both violence and its denial. This is the fix that Mrs. Christie and the other so-called "teacake ladies" promise their addicts.

The Soviet critic who in the late fifties said Mrs. Christie "reflects the poisoned air which exists in bourgeois society" may have been on to something. When we open her books, we are enclosed in a claustrophobic setting peopled by suspects and victims, along with servants (usually portrayed by Mrs. Christie as dolts), mulish policemen, and the detective, sometimes accompanied by a thickheaded friend. (Poirot's crony Captain Hastings makes Holmes's Watson seem a giant of intellect.)

Her sleight of hand is to reveal and render harmless the death and hostility that haunt us—no matter how hard we pretend they do not—by incorporating them into a game. We never mourn her victims, and their deaths never seem agonizing (although she did make a mistake in her first book, *The Mysterious Affair at Styles,* by going on too long about a woman in the throes of arsenic poisoning). When a corpse is discovered, speculation immediately begins about where this character or that one was standing when the drink was tampered with, leaving little time for any response but curiosity.

She further distances death by bringing it about in an upper-middle-class milieu of consummate orderliness, where a housemaid will always answer the bellpull—unless she has been strangled after unwisely burbling to the cook that she saw something funny from her window under the eaves. Nobody neglects meals just because two or three of the other guests have been killed. There is a kind of marvelous aplomb at work here, of the sort associated with the British at war. There is also a suggestion of snobbery in this constricted view, and certainly the question arises as to whether the society Mrs. Christie depicts ever existed in England—even forty years ago. If it did not, one suspects Mrs. Christie would have invented it just the same. . . . Interestingly, she has made a point of saying she avoids the sordid, as though the deaths for gain or revenge she describes have nothing sordid about them.

The highest card in her artful trumping of death is the sleuth, essentially an "armchair detective" (such a snug term), who orders the chaos of events into a satisfactory pattern, transforming the visceral into the cerebral. Both Poirot and Miss Marple are made a little bit absurd, so that we do not begrudge them their astuteness. Encountered in book after book, they become well-loved, gift-bearing uncles and aunts. They will set things to rights and uncover the murderer—who is always unlikely, but rarely, thank God, likable. Emotional dissonances seldom intrude upon her codas.

Ralph Tyler. *Saturday Review.* October 4, 1975,
pp. 24–27

In a fifty-five-year period a writer's style is bound to change, but although Christie's language has altered from using Victorian terms like "hark" for "listen" and "tantalus" for "bottle" in her books of the twenties, and even though her plots have evolved in line with the world's intrigues and wars, her basic genius of palming the ace in the best tradition of legerdemain has never varied.

Certainly her best mysteries include *Murder on the Orient Express, The A.B.C. Murders, And Then There Were None,* and, of course, *The Murder of Roger Ackroyd,* but I have two favorites of my own that I would like to mention: *Towards Zero,* while Poirot-less, has Superintendent Battle of Scotland Yard who uses cool British logic to solve the crime in much the same way that Poirot uses Gallic reasoning. This complex mystery is built on an unsuspected murder committed by a child who has grown into a guilt-ridden, psychopathic adult. Another favorite is *Death Comes as the End,* one of the mystery novels that comes from Christie's experiences on archae-ological digs. This mystery takes place in ancient Egypt, where human na-ture and motivation are shown to be strikingly similar to today's.

Through the years I have continued to check out the latest Christie thriller at the library, and I enjoyed every one. I did, however, consider that enjoyment as a sort of throwback to childhood—like a taste for Crackerjack. It wasn't until I was packing for a year's stay in Central Africa that I real-ized that my logic had been arguing with my taste. I could take just so many pounds of books with me, and since there was no other kind of entertain-ment where I was going, I had to consider what sort of fiction I wanted to have with me for pure relaxation and enjoyment. There was no question about what I wanted to read by a kerosene lamp; Agatha Christie mysteries won by a landslide.

Betty Jochmans. *Prairie Schooner.* Summer 1976,
pp. 184–85

It was a glorious moment in Conan Doyle's *The Final Problem* when Sher-lock Holmes and the archvillain Moriarity tumbled to their deaths at Rei-chenbach Falls, their bodies locked together in a wrestling embrace. It had all the elements of an inevitable end, the great detective concluding his life work by destroying his own mirror image.

The death of Hercule Poirot in Agatha Christie's *Curtain* has similar elements. Like Holmes, Poirot is facing the archantagonist of his career, a villain who sits at the center of a web of seemingly unconnected murders, who will strike again, but who cannot be caught because there is no proof of crime. Like Holmes, Poirot faces a criminal whose powers are a twisted version of his own. And like Holmes too, Poirot goes down with his enemy, leaving behind a letter that will explain the final events to a bewildered assistant.

But here the similarities end. Poirot's death is much less dramatic. The aged, arthritic Belgian detective and his older but no wiser Watson, Captain Hastings, return to Styles, the country estate of Christie's first book which introduced the pair fifty-six years ago. The setting can hardly match Swit-zerland's rapids, Poirot is but a dim reflection of Holmes, and his antagonist is nowhere near so terrifying as the evil professor. For all the earnest straining after legend here, it does not quite work.

Curtain is not a triumph. Though written many years ago, it is already permeated by that weariness and solemnity which would become more evident in Christie's works as she grew older. One of her earlier virtues was a refusal to take herself too seriously. She enjoyed the game—laying out the false clues, the countless motives, the innumerable threads of coincidence and threats of murder, in a seemingly hopeless tangle, wasting no time on unnecessary description or character development, except as these might serve as clues for the detective, or red herrings for the reader. These early books claim no motive other than entertainment—some even had ''Casts of Characters'' in front which read like advertisements for the movies they might go on to become. But *Curtain,* though written at a time when Christie could still turn out an engaging story, has little of this lightness and playfulness. Already there are hints of that bombastic and moralizing side of Agatha Christie—the one given to railing at the ''younger generation'' and such things—which would become more and more apparent as she aged.

In *Curtain* there is little respite from Christie's earnestness and ''insights''; the book is all but buried under them. Worst of all, the puzzle and its solution—usually the centerpiece of Christie's mysteries and the part she executed best—simply do not come off. Her most memorable books are memorable chiefly for that final unraveling when, most often, the suspects are gathered together to witness the unveiling of the murderer. The reader too witnesses an almost magical transformation of the events of the book through a paradigmatic act of understanding. But in *Curtain* this transformation fails to occur because the design of the book violates the rules of the genre. For one thing, the puzzle itself is a fraud, involving as it does a partial deception by Poirot of both Hastings and the reader. Secondly, the criminal's methods are absurd, even in the permissive context of mystery fiction. Thirdly, and most important, the criminal acts themselves are performed out of motives which are irrational and hence inaccessible to the reader. In mystery stories the introduction of unpredictable, irrational elements is inexcusable—one cannot play chess when one's opponent overturns the board.

Christie's crimes have a curious regularity to them. These are ''class'' murders, crimes which arise out of demanding another's place and not knowing one's own, or out of a desire to preserve an illusion hitherto sustained by deceit. The setting and the characters are usually British and sufficiently affluent to warrant the presence of a ''butler.'' Poirot, on the other hand, is an outsider to the system, and thus in a perfect position to rectify the misdeeds of the criminal—another outsider, but one who is disguised. The denouement of these stories always involves the restoration of order, the return of things and people to their proper places in the hierarchy via a ritual exorcising of the disguised criminal.

Beyond the comforting, indeed the primal, regularity of these stories, however, there is something which also recalls the earlier, religious meaning of the word mystery: "truth that man can know by revelation alone," as Webster puts it. The unmasking of the deceiver must come as a complete surprise, as revelation; the traitor may be anyone, but he is never what he seems, and he must be subtle, crafty, and clever, a diabolical opponent. The detective for his part has the conviction of the prophet doing God's will on earth. As the criminal works from below, so does the detective work from above; he sees through the masks of men's souls and finds the one among them who is dissembling virtue. With the purging of the criminal from the community, the random collection of former suspects is bound together for a moment and transfigured into a society bearing witness to revealed truth. Like the religious rites of ancient times, the solution of the mystery imparts "enduring bliss to the initiate." Poirot departs, leaving behind a better world; the victim, having played his necessary part in the drama, is all but forgotten.

Stretching a point perhaps, one could say that the skeleton of Christie's plots is in fact similar to that of the mystery-passion plays of the Middle Ages, with their ritualized tale of vengeance upon evil and the triumphant reversal of Christ's death. In this similarity, perhaps, lies one reason for the persistence in the contemporary detective novel (almost alone among literary genres) of overt prejudice against Jews and other outsiders.

Curtain attempts to universalize the myth of the dark outsider by moving the criminal into every individual and thereby, so to speak, internalizing the Levantine. But the attempt is simply beyond the author's reach; *Curtain* is a mere gesture, a slight wave of an arthritic hand. Still, it will serve as a finish to Poirot. His death is no great loss. "I have a bourgeois attitude toward murder," he once remarked. "I disapprove of it." But though Poirot destroyed many villains before his own demise, he did not destroy the fear of these villains—the foreigners, traitors, climbers, and imposters, hiding among us, and plotting against us. It was this fear that was at the heart of Agatha Christie's darkness, and possibly of her popularity as well.

Edward Rothstein. Commentary. June 1976,
pp. 80–84

Christie's characters are neither interesting in themselves nor particularly indicative of any class or country, but the parade of the suspects can leave someone not paying much attention to believe that the carefully timed appearances of each is a sign of carefully ordered lives, lived, in spite of the overwhelming evidence, better than their own.

What animates Christie's tireless completion of her appointed rounds is her imperious innocence. Not only is someone "guilty," but in order for people to be suspects at all they must have done something to be guilty about. But these motives are only squiggles, passions for which Christie only knows the words. The murderer, when exposed and if male, may say "damn," but otherwise no one is distinguishable from anyone else. All suspects get equal time, and seem guilty of nothing more than being dull. In this way Christie does what is called playing fair. Readers of mysteries want a book that stays resolutely a book, walled off from life, and there may not be so much as a whimper of humanity in all eighty-five books.

What in other writers or in life one might call sexism, snobbery, or racism is in Christie only a passion for keeping the squiggles in place. What in other writers might be an image of hell, paradise, or both—an isolated group on a train or a boat, in a country house or a village—is in Christie only a backdrop for the dance of words. At some moments in some of the books one suspects she is being shrewd or observant about a character. Perhaps she is, too, but soon that potentially interesting character, or situation, is ordered back into the lockstep of the dance, because we must get on with it.

Roger Sale. The New York Review of Books. April
29, 1976, pp. 37–38

The Christie output was torrential: eighty-three books, including a half-dozen romances written under the name Mary Westmacott; seventeen plays, nine volumes of short stories, and *Come, Tell Me How You Live,* in which she described her field explorations with her second husband, British Archaeologist Sir Max Mallowan. The number of printed copies of her books is conservatively put at three hundred million. New Guinea cargo cultists have even venerated a paperback cover of her *Evil under the Sun*—quite possibly confusing the name Christie with Christ.

Her own characters were much less exotic: doctors, lawyers, army officers, clergymen. Her stalking grounds were usually genteel English houses, and she rarely strayed. "I could never manage miners talking in pubs," she once said, "because I don't know what miners talk about in pubs."

In a Christie murder mystery, neatness not only counts, it is everything. As the genre's undisputed queen of the maze, she laid her tantalizing plots so precisely and dropped her false leads so cunningly that few—if any—readers could guess the identity of the villain. The reader surrenders to an enigma in which the foul act of murder seems less a sin against man or God than a breach of etiquette. Yet, as W. H. Auden observed, the British murder mystery, with its accent on clever detection rather than violence, seems to provide an escape back into the Garden of Eden. There innocence and order are restored, and readers "may know love as love and not as the law." The Great Restorer is the godlike genius detective. Christie's own genius resided in a mind of intimidating clarity. She never allowed emotion or philosophical doubt to cloud her devious conceptions or hinder the icy logic of their untanglings.

Time. January 26, 1976, p. 75

As a prose stylist Christie is hardly distinguished. From the beginning she wrote in a neutral, simple fashion using short sentences and brief paragraphs which do not tax the reader. Occasionally, however, she uses her lack of a prose style to spring traps on the readers: this is the case with the intrusion of figurative description in *And Then There Were None,* as well as the irritatingly simple-minded style adopted for *Easy to Kill.* If Christie has any particular claim to literary originality, though, it is because of her use of point of view. The important lesson which she learned early and well was that detective stories work chiefly because of the way in which they are told. Using Hastings as the narrator in *The Mysterious Affair at Styles* shows that from the beginning she liked Conan Doyle's method of hiding the obvious from the reader by using an obtuse narrator. She also realized, in the early twenties, that this technique was old hat and she started to poke about for alternate styles of narration which would obscure the facts which needed to be withheld until the conclusion. In *The Man in the Brown Suit* she mixed straight narration with extracts from two diaries, covering the facts by switching the point of view. This mixture of points of view, although it is not always so obvious, appears in most of the non-Hastings novels—and in *The A.B.C. Murders* which Hastings narrates—written subsequently. The point of view of a typical Christie novel of the period usually shifts among (1) straight third person narration describing people and events from the outside, (2) third person narration over the shoulder of a particular character following him or her around, (3) selectively omniscient narration which probes some of the characters' minds, and (4) dramatic presentation of dialogue with little more than speech tags supplied. By switching from one point of view to another, Christie manipulates her readers in several ways. First, she gives the readers the false confidence that they can sympathize with and trust the judgments of the character whom the narrative follows. Almost equally important is the impression which the readers receive from the omniscient passages: they falsely believe that they receive insight into all of the characters' thoughts, while this never happens. By tossing together these different points of view, Christie can keep her important facts back and fool her readers almost every time.

LeRoy Lad Panek. *Watteau's Shepherds: The Detective Novel in Britain 1914–1940* (Bowling Green, Ohio: Popular Press, 1979), pp. 62–63

Certain it is that Agatha Christie's durability is already astonishing, and shows no sign of waning. Roger Ackroyd was murdered more than fifty years ago, yet there are still as many people as ever who care who killed him. The irritation one felt at the garrulity and the slackened grip of those last Christie novels cannot alter the fact that Christmas has not felt the same these last few years without her offering. Already the signs are that she will not suffer seriously from the slump in reputation that most writers experience after their death. So already we are beginning to get the idea that as well as spanning age, intelligence and class barriers she will jump the gap that separates her era from succeeding ones.

Why? She created a timeless, changeless world, peopled by cardboard characters who somehow manage to maintain our interest in that dazzling conjuring trick that is to be performed on page 190. She nourished our instinctive hopes that in the end right and truth will triumph over the evil and the obscure. And she brought murder into the home, where it belonged, seeing the murderous glint in the eye of the self-effacing bank clerk, the homicidal madness in the flutterings of the genteel lady companion. Chandler saw evil in the social organisms of which we are part; Christie saw it in our wives, our friends, the quiet circle of which we are a part. And perhaps thereby she made us sense it in ourselves.

Robert Barnard. A Talent to Deceive: An
Appreciation of Agatha Christie (New York: Dodd,
Mead, 1980), p. 126

How important a writer was Agatha Christie? By quantitative measures—sales of books and box office demand for her plays, she may prove the best-selling writer in English in the twentieth century. Her books have outsold any other writer's, and *The Mousetrap* and *Witness for the Prosecution* have become transatlantic dramatic institutions. Agatha Christie has found a prodigious reading and play-going audience.

Measuring Agatha Christie qualitatively is more difficult. Despite her popular success, some of her writing is clearly trivial and some, after only half a century, seems extremely dated. No one, for instance, could take Christie seriously as a poet, and not all her prose merits close attention. Her romance thrillers seem either excessively arch or simply silly today, and her spy thrillers tend to be either preachy or absurd. For both kinds of thrillers, she contrived loose and incredible plots and settled for unconvincing, slang-filled dialogue. . . .

The Christie achievement must be measured by her whodunits. She dominated twentieth-century classic British detective fiction in all three of its forms: the short story, the novel, the play. As a mystery writer, she outproduced her rivals, even as she maintained an extraordinary level of workmanship for over half a century.

Her detective fiction is outstanding, both for the variety she achieved within the form's rigorous rules for plot development, and for her invention of entertaining, if stylized, characters. Such fiction allows only one basic kind of resolution. The detective must discover who committed the crime and must explain away the puzzlement and misunderstanding the criminal managed to generate. With a Christie whodunit, a reader confidently anticipates an ending that will satisfy expectations, but he can count on being surprised by the manipulation of details that lead to that ending.

Agatha Christie's remarkable success in creating many plots of this type clearly depended on her ingenuity with mutations and permutations of basic patterns. She constantly reused situations, characters, clusters of characters, and settings. But she made her tales seem fresh by varying at least one basic narrative element from work to work. If she reused a situation, she modified characters. If she reused characters, she put them in new settings. When she expanded a short story into a novel or adapted a story or novel for the stage, she often changed her original ending. No other writer of this century has so fully understood the craft of combining and recombining, to give readers a familiar, yet new, imaginative experience.

In short, she perfected the art of plotting, while her "serious" contemporaries shied away from plot as an oversimplification of the complexities of experience.

Further, as other twentieth-century writers began to avoid highly typed, externalized characters, Agatha Christie polished the art of creating them. Though others subscribed, perhaps hastily, to E. M. Forster's dicta about round characters and flat characters, and generally accepted the view that flat characters lack interest and significance, Christie specialized in creating figures readily identifiable by their manners and their social or personal quirks, figures belonging to the grand tradition of eighteenth- and nineteenth-century British fiction, the tradition of Fielding, Smollett, Austen, and Dickens. Christie peopled her mystery tales with figures whose manners, dress, and speech invited readers to label them according to their social identities and personal quirks. These characters rarely, perhaps never, reveal new dimensions of human nature. Instead they suggest that an understanding of individuals, whatever social microcosms they occupy, is merely a matter of recognizing what types of people they are.

This comedy-of-manners approach to characterization in Agatha Christie's mystery tales sets up a comedy-of-manners approach to social history, one that focuses on little details of life-style. Christie may have seen the folkways of the British upper-middle-class more nostalgically than most of her contemporaries did, but she obviously drew her settings from observed places and people. And with her specificity about manners, Christie entices willing suspension of disbelief in the kinds of characters and the kinds of situations she invents. She also recorded a time and a place convincingly. Conceivably, future generations may use her works as a source of social history, as twentieth-century social historians now use the writings of Smollett and Trollope.

Finally, the fact that the distinguishing techniques of Agatha Christie's whodunits are out of step with current practices may, paradoxically, represent the most significant aspect of her career. The extraordinary popularity of her works suggests that there are still readers drawn to plot and to typed characters, as well as to the recording of social history. Her works demonstrate the fact that the traditional elements of fiction have vitality in them yet. Because she imbued her mystery making with this vitality, Agatha Christie, who modestly saw herself as a literary sausage maker, may claim a more important place in literary history than she seemed ever to expect. In her subgenera, she kept alive elements of the grand tradition in British novel writing.

Mary S. Wagoner. <i>Agatha Christie</i> (Boston:
Twayne, 1986), pp. 141–43

CLARK, MARY HIGGINS (1929–   )

Mary Higgins Clark's romantic thrillers are tougher and scarier than most traditional Gothics. She does not depend on an old house, a moldering residence, or an ancient castle for her backgrounds. She sets her stories in the everyday world with which her readers are well acquainted.

It is important to realize that the romantic thriller in the hands of Mary Higgins Clark is in no way a detective novel. Only the protagonist—never a police officer and never an amateur detective—is at the center of the action. There are no clues of the type a policeman searches for in order to establish leads or to make deductions. The members of the police force who may be about are present for reasons not usually involving the heroine's problem per se.

In a Clark story, terror is always lurking very close to the surface of one's everyday experiences in life. Her characters are ordinary people, but unlike them, her protagonist is caught up quite suddenly and frighteningly in a situation fraught with evil—on a bus ride, in a crowded store, while vacuuming the livingroom rug, or in another situation known to everybody. The familiar world about her suddenly takes on a sinister cast that quite soon becomes menacing, dangerous, and finally, life-threatening. Clark uses the elements of the mystery novel in the same way the English writer June Thomson uses them in her stories of the English countryside.

For example, the protagonist of *The Cradle Will Fall* inadvertently sees an unknown man placing what appears to be the body of a dead woman in the trunk of a car. Later on the heroine learns that her sister's neighbor—a pregnant housewife—has been murdered. The protagonist then learns the identity of the man with the body: he is a world-famous obstetrician known for his work with women unable to conceive. The fact that the heroine *knows* this world-famous obstetrician to be a killer means nothing. She has no proof, nor can she convince anyone that what she has seen is real. When the obstetrician finds out she knows, she is in deep trouble. From that moment on, it is a matter of survival by the moment.

From the beginning of a Clark book the salient facts are known, much in the manner of a Ruth Rendell non-Wexford novel. In spite of the fact that there are no secrets to spring at the end of the story, Clark manages to propel the reader through the pages of mounting suspense in the same manner that Rendell does. How can the heroine protect herself from this mad killer doctor? How can she bring him to justice? More to the point, how can she survive?

One trick Clark has mastered in her treatment of this type of novel is the one the father of the suspense film—Alfred Hitchcock—understood instinctively from the beginning. So too, in fact, did the Greeks. That trick is to set a story or a narrative incident within a strict time frame. Hitchcock's bomb is going to go off in twenty minutes. The audience knows it; the hero or heroine does not. Or perhaps the hero or heroine *does* know it, which only increases the suspense and the dread.

Where Are the Children? takes place within the time frame of one day, *A Stranger Is Watching* in three days. The plots of these stories are carefully constructed so that by the time the story reaches its conclusion the suspense has become almost unbearable. The terror building in the reader is the dread of knowing that *something is going to happen* to the protagonist; will she discover the truth in time to do something about it?

Clark tries to establish a true sense of values in her work that will create a rapport between herself and her readers; she tries to delineate strong people who are able to confront the forces of evil surfacing to destroy them; she tries to show how individuals who are good can actually vanquish the multiple evils seeking to do them in.

For a Clark character, fate never intervenes; it is up to the individual to fight her own battle for survival. In this manner, she manages a social commentary on the world about her, holding up a mirror to society, showing people how they *can* react to the wildly fictional situations she improvises for their amusement and occasional frisson.

Bruce Cassiday. *The Literature of Crime and Detection* (New York: Ungar, 1988), pp. 165–66

What if . . . someone such as Alice Crimmins (the New York cocktail waitress who was convicted of killing her small son) went to prison, served her time, was released, remarried, had other children . . . *and it all happened again?* That's the sort of "what ifs" Mary Higgins Clark asks herself, and the answers produce some kind of today's most electrifying suspense novels.

That "what if" was the basis of the plot of Clark's first suspense novel, *Where Are the Children?* The fact that readers can almost—but not quite—identify a behind-the-headlines element in her books may account partially for their success. The menace of innocents is a recurring theme for Clark—a theme that has gripped readers since the days of Hansel and Gretel. . . .

Clark is a master storyteller who builds her taut suspense stories in a limited time frame. *Where Are the Children?* begins at 9 A.M. and ends at 7 P.M. the same day. Only three days elapse in *A Stranger Is Watching.* . . .

"I like to write about very nice people who are confronted by the forces of evil and who, through their own intelligence, work their way through to deliverance," Clark says.

Her stories are of the quiet terror lurking beneath the surface of an ordinary life. "I write about people not looking for trouble. They find evil in their own car, their home, their everyday life."

Even though the spark of the idea for *Where Are the Children?* came from the Alice Crimmins case, the novel does not parallel the case.

"I just thought of a mother of children who had been murdered who is then tried for their murders," she says, "and took the next step to the possible."

Elaine Budd. *13 Mistresses of Murder* (New York: Ungar, 1986), pp. 1–5

CLARKE, ARTHUR C. (1917–   )

There are those to whom science fiction is nothing but a dreary catalogue of papier-maché monsters crunching down on matchstick reconstructions of the Golden Gate Bridge and the Empire State Building. There are others to whom it is but a slightly gaudier version of a western, with galloping spaceships and evil Martian uranium rustlers. There are also those to whom science fiction offers a look into the murk of the future. To these last, Arthur C. Clarke belongs.

He has a thorough grounding in science, and, in addition, has a nimble and most receptive mind. Nothing reasonable frightens him simply because it seems fantastic, and—equally important—nothing foolish attracts him simply because it seems fantastic.

As concrete proof of his ability as a seer, it is generally accepted that Clarke, in 1948, was the first to suggest the use of satellites for long-distance communications. He did not build or launch Telstar, but he saw it in the sky years before anyone else did.

Isaac Asimov. *The New York Times Book Review.* April 14, 1963, pp. 22, 24

An important part of Mr. Clarke's success as a fiction writer (I exclude his achievements as a popularizer of science and of science-fiction prophecies, which is an entirely different kind of skill) can be attributed to the use—the unashamed use—he made of semierotic, semiirresponsible daydreams, which he told as soberly as though they were as worth taking seriously as hard truths. Instead of clinging to them in privacy, shame, or penuriousness, he voiced them for all of us, as though he were reporting an important part of the real world. And of course he was; hence, how could we have failed to be moved?

William Atheling, Jr. *More Issues at Hand* (n.p., 1970), p. 48

It is interesting that one of the best-known science fiction writers, long a prophet of space travel and its implications, should espouse a fundamentally negative conception of nature, insofar as nature can be identified with matter. But such seems to be the case with Arthur C. Clarke, author of *2001: A Space Odyssey, Childhood's End,* and a spate of other fascinating inquiries into the world of science and the future. In *Childhood's End,* alien space creatures establish a benevolent dictatorship on earth, just as man is about to penetrate outer space. Poverty, war, ignorance, and disease are eliminated; there is even an attempt to erase the resulting boredom by the development of universal education and participation in the arts. Only one basic restriction is placed on man: He is barred from research in the field of parapsychology.

The golden age is disrupted when a young child begins having dreams during which his mind leaves his body and travels to distant planets. Other children begin to have similar experiences. The wandering child minds develop the capacity to manipulate matter. Then, as more children are affected, the minds begin to merge beyond the bodies. After a period of playing with their/its newfound power, the common mind leaves the earth, destroying it in the process. It ascends into the heavens to merge with an "overmind" which has infinite capacities to travel and manipulate matter. Man has ceased to exist. The creatures who arrived to rule the earth turn out to be the midwives of the "overmind," sent to earth to save man from self-destruction before the "birth" of the new form, and to keep him from aborting the birth of the children's common mind by stemming his advances in parapsychology. Salvation is attained in Clarke's novel by an elaborate process by which man is delivered from the tyranny of matter.

In the novel *2001: A Space Odyssey*—which Clarke published after his collaboration with Stanley Kubrick on the screenplay of the film—Clarke again introduces a freefloating mind. It is the power which intervenes at various points of human history and which lies behind the release of the astronaut at the book's end. In *2001,* the released mind seems to retain units of individual consciousness, but otherwise there is no change in Clarke's attitude toward matter.

Clarke's objectification of evil in matter can lead to a disregard of the natural environment, the consequent increase of sickness, and the encouragement of escapism and a distortion of truth in our perception of reality.

Another problem with *Childhood's End* and *2001,* if taken as possible sources of metaphysical speculation, is that individual freedom and self-consciousness are components which are devalued, and man is made subject to forces which he can neither comprehend nor control. Mind is all; it functions in a predetermined manner; it is finally a mere atom in the vague mass of "overmind."

Lois and Stephen Rose. *The Shattered Ring:*
Science Fiction and the Quest for Meaning (n.p.:
John Knox Press, 1970), pp. 48–53

Mr. Clarke's fantasy in *2001* shows us that science fictionists cannot escape a compulsion toward metaphysics even while they have to express it in a style conducive to their own habit of thinking in terms of gadgets. . . .

Clarke, an inveterate and hardheaded despiser of philosophers, seems to stammer in amazement as he finds himself caught up—one suspects greatly to his surprise—in the ancient dreams some philosophers have harbored about "Spirit . . . and even beyond." "If there was anything beyond *that,* its name could only be God."

There is something gratifying in seeing a fanatic of technology like Clarke become converted to the mysticism of Father Teilhard de Chardin. His conversion would be more satisfying, however, if this advance toward the spiritual were understood as something more and other than an increased skill with computers and information machines. And we notice too that obsessive habit of technological utopians, to which E. M. Forster has called our attention in "The Machine Stops," to debase the poor archaic vessel of the body until here, in this most advanced technological phase, it is simply shed like an inefficient and worthless husk.

William Barrett. *Time of Need: Forms of Imagination in the Twentieth Century* (New York: Harper & Row, 1972), pp. 357–58

Although it lacks some of the metaphysical fireworks and haunting visionary poetry of *Childhood's End* or *The City and the Stars,* this thoughtful scientific romance, *Rendezvous with Rama,* is happily representative of the man who is both our most distinguished writer of speculative fiction and one of the important literary figures of our time. Clarke handles his generic stocks-in-trade—the strange creatures and hallucinatory landscapes—with splendid imagination, but *Rendezvous with Rama,* like all of his work, is essentially an expression of wonder in the presence of Mystery, for this excellent scientist and entertainer has remained above all a moralist, preoccupied with the transformations of man, the infinite possibilities of time, the reverence for life, and the transcendental destiny of the human spirit. One customarily praises a science fiction by remarking that it is original or ingenious, but Clarke's books inspire a search for more ambitious adjectives. Try "lofty" or "noble"—or even "saintly."

Virginia Quarterly Review. Winter 1974, pp. vii, x

Mr. Clarke has specialized in the exploration of space, and so enjoys an edge when he comes to write fiction concerned with it. A story set in the future is not thereby a prophecy, and he is too good a novelist to make the confusion; but an intimate knowledge of the possible and the plausible greatly assists in that naturalizing of the marvelous which is the characteristic achievement of the best science fiction.

With the heavy stuff out of the way, let it be said at once that Mr. Clarke's *The Fountains of Paradise* is no easier to put down than any of his others. It takes us to the twenty-second century and the equatorial island of Taprobane.

The book becomes an action story instead of a metaphysical romance, but the action is tense enough. As I read I kept pushing myself further and further back in my chair, squealing with vertigo. This is not Arthur Clarke's best novel, though the blurb says he says it is; the most that can be said is that it's delightfully written, always interesting and at times almost unbearably exciting.

Two grumbles: the miles I have quoted are my own conversions; the author has gone metric. Must he? (Does he think it's more *scientific*?) The year of the story is 2142, and the changeover will almost certainly be complete by then, but my calendar only says 1979. And really, honestly, have we got to call it Sri Lanka? I dare says its inhabitants do call it that, but it's Ceylon in English, which is what I'm using. Next thing you know it'll be Deutschland, Ellas, Suomi, and the bloody old CCCP.

Kingsley Amis. *New Statesman.* January 26, 1979,

pp. 119–20

In *2010: Odyssey Two* Arthur C. Clarke has accomplished what few modern science fiction authors seem to be able to do. He has created a story that contains elements of both fantasy and classical science fiction on the grand cosmic scale, while maintaining a vivid sense of reality—staying true to the human realities of space travel, incorporating new facts gleaned from the 1979 Voyager Space probes, and making believable scientific projections based on those facts. . . .

Beginning where *2001* left off, *2010* follows three major story lines: Bowman's fate, the investigation of the Jupiter monolith by the spaceship Leonov, and the rehabilitation of Hal. . . .

Clarke's science fiction, as the art of making projections based on established fact, successfully creates such things as an amazing core for Jupiter and intriguing life forms beneath the icy crust of Jupiter's moon, Europa.

Only rarely does Clarke indulge in the kind of preachiness that keeps science fiction firmly locked within its genre. "What shocking linguists we Americans are!" says the central character, and he doesn't leave it at that. The story's opening nationalistic generalizations and conflicts are studiously antichauvinistic and unimaginative, hence disappointing.

As the story progresses, Clarke manages to work in some good characterizations: a sternly expert female Soviet Commander; a boisterous American engineer; the repressed, competent Bowman; and a self-effacing Indian computer scientist, who is frighteningly defensive about Hal. The computer's erratic personality adds several facets of suspense and interest, since its rehabilitation is held in question to the very end.

Even though Bowman and Hal are somewhat neglected and eventually shunted aside for the larger theme, Clarke's story drives on to an exciting finish in which the mix of fantasy and fact leaves the reader well satisfied with a book masterfully written.

Cary Neeper. *The Christian Science Monitor.*

December 3, 1982, p. B3

Profiles of the Future is an intriguing attempt to outline some possible parameters of future technology, although the author recognizes the futility of detailed prediction. As he describes the book's purpose: "It does not try to describe *the* future, but to define the boundaries within which possible futures must lie.'' Clarke is uniquely suited to glimpse what's coming in that he combines a solid scientific background with the elasticity of imagination found in a seasoned science fiction writer.

The work leads off with two fascinating chapters concerning some ''Hazards of Prophecy,'' detailing pertinent examples of past celebrated scientists making such myopic assertions as the impossibility of heavier-than-air flight, space flight, and even domestic use of the ordinary light bulb. This results in a statement of the well-known Clarke's First Law: ''When a distinguished but elderly scientist states that something is possible he is almost certainly right. When he states that something is impossible, he is very probably wrong.''

Other topics discussed in lucid and entertaining fashion are the nature of time, the brain-body interface, and even the chances for teleportation. I, myself, try to maintain a balance, falling into neither pitfall of hopeless technophobia or unquestioning technophilia. On the one hand, Clarke's scientific optimism is contagious, offering hope in the face of constant doomsaying. Conversely, I think he can go a bit far, for instance in espousing the inevitability of authentic Artificial Intelligence, largely glossing over deeper questions about what intelligence really is.

Interestingly, the book reflects many of the same strengths and weaknesses embodied in Clarke's science fiction. In reminding us of the wonders inherent in both the Cosmos and ourselves, it succeeds admirably, though at times the author does verge on violating his own First Law.

Paul Granahan. *Best Sellers*. May 1984, pp. 75–76

COLLINS, WILKIE (1824–1889)

In *The Woman in White* the spirit of modern realism has woven a tissue of scenes more wildly improbable than the fancy of an average idealist would have ventured to inflict on readers beyond their teens. Mr. W. Collins has for some years been favorably known to the general reader as a painstaking manufacturer of stories, short or long, whose chief merit lies in the skillful elaboration of a startling mystery traceable to some natural cause, but baffling all attempts to solve it until the author himself has given us the right clue. Some praise is also due to him for the care with which these literary puzzles are set off by a correct if not very natural style, a pleasing purity of moral tone, and a certain knack of hitting the more superficial traits of character. When we have said all we can for him, we have said nothing that would entitle him to a higher place among English novelists, than the compiler of an average school history would enjoy among English historians.

Take the plot away from *The Woman in White*, and there is nothing left to examine. There is not one lifelike character: not one natural dialogue in the whole book. Both hero and heroine are wooden, commonplace, uninteresting in any way apart from the story itself.

What character his personages have, the author prides himself on bringing out in a way which other novelists will do well not to imitate. If they neither say nor do aught characteristic on their own account, yet in connection with the story most of them have a good deal to write about themselves or about each other. This, indeed, forms the main peculiarity of the book. As Collins claims in his preface: "The story of the book is told throughout by the characters of the book," each of them in turn taking up the wondrous tale at the point where his or her shadow falls most invitingly across the scene. What movement the story has could have been imparted by much simpler means; and we would rather have seen the characters developed in the usual way, than by a process about as credible and straightforward as that employed by the spirits who are supposed to move our drawing-room tables.

But the attempt to combine newness of form and substance with reality of treatment has led to failure of a still more glaring kind. Throughout the book circumstances grotesque or improbable meet you at every turn. You are bidden to look at scenes of real modern life, described by the very persons who figured therein, and you find yourself, instead, wandering in a world as mythical as that portrayed on the boards of a penny theater or in the pages of a nursery tale.

Dublin University Magazine. February 1861,
pp. 200–204

I have gone through . . . [*No Name*] at a sitting, and I find it *wonderfully fine*. It goes on with an ever-rising power and force in it that fills me with admiration. It is as far before and beyond *The Woman in White* as *that* was beyond the wretched common level of fiction writing. There are some touches in the Captain which no one but a born (and cultivated) writer could get near—could draw within hail of. And the originality of Mrs. Wragge, without compromise of her probability, involves a really great achievement. But they are all admirable; Mr. Noel Vanstone and the housekeeper, both in their way as meritorious as the rest; Magdalen wrought out with truth, energy, sentiment, and passion, of the very first water.

I cannot tell you with what a strange dash of pride as well as pleasure I read the great results of your hard work. Because, as you know, I was certain from the *Basil* days that you were the Writer who would come ahead of all the Field—being the only one who combined invention and power, both humorous and pathetic, with that invincible determination to work, and that profound conviction that nothing of worth is to be done without work, of which triflers and feigners have no conception.

Charles Dickens. Letter to Wilkie Collins,
September 20, 1862. In Laurence Hutton, ed.,
Letters of Charles Dickens to Wilkie Collins (New
York: Harper & Row, 1892), pp. 112–15

The Woman in White, with its diaries and letters and its general ponderosity, was a kind of nineteenth-century version of *Clarissa Harlowe.* Mind, we say a nineteenth-century version. To Mr. Collins belongs the credit of having introduced into fiction those most mysterious of mysteries, the mysteries which are at our own doors. This innovation gave a new impetus to the literature of horrors. A good ghost story, to be half as terrible as a good murder story, must be connected at a hundred points with the common objects of life. . . . Less delicately terrible, perhaps, than the vagaries of departed spirits, but to the full as *interesting,* as the modern novel reader understands the word, are the numberless possible forms of human malignity. Crime, indeed, has always been a theme for dramatic poets; but with the old poets its dramatic interest lay in the fact that it compromised the criminal's moral repose. Whence else is the interest of *Orestes* and *Macbeth?* With Mr. Collins . . . the interest of crime is in the fact that it compromises the criminal's personal safety. The play is a tragedy, not in virtue of an avenging deity, but in virtue of a preventive system of law; not through the presence of a company of fairies, but through that of an admirable organization of police detectives. Of course, the nearer the criminal and the detective are brought home to the reader, the more lively his "sensation." They are brought home to the reader by a happy choice of probable circumstances; and it is through his skill in the choice of these circumstances—his thoroughgoing realism—that Mr. Collins has become famous.

Mr. Collins's productions deserve a more respectable name than sensation novel. They are massive and elaborate constructions—monuments of mosaic work, for the proper mastery of which it would seem, at first, that an index and notebook were required. They are not so much works of art as works of science.

Henry James. The Nation. November 9, 1865,
pp. 593–94

Of Wilkie Collins it is impossible for a true critic not to speak with admiration, because he has excelled all his contemporaries in a certain most difficult branch of his art; but as it is a branch which I have not myself at all cultivated, it is not unnatural that his work should be very much lost upon me individually. When I sit down to write a novel I do not at all know, and I do not very much care, how it is to end. Wilkie Collins seems so to construct his that he not only, before writing, plans everything on, down to the minutest detail, from the beginning to the end; but then plots it all back again, to see that there is no piece of necessary dovetailing which does not dovetail with absolute accuracy. The construction is most minute and most wonderful. But I can never lose the taste of the construction. The author seems always to be warning me to remember that something happened at exactly half-past two o'clock on Tuesday morning; or that a woman disappeared from the road just fifteen yards beyond the fourth mile stone. One is constrained by mysteries and hemmed in by difficulties, knowing, however, that the mysteries will be made clear, and the difficulties overcome at the end of the third volume. Such work gives me no pleasure. I am, however, quite prepared to acknowledge that the want of pleasure comes from fault of my intellect.

Anthony Trollope. *An Autobiography of Anthony Trollope* (New York: Harper & Brothers, 1883), n.p.

Exit the novelist; enter the characters; that is Collins's idea. One never sees him, never thinks of him, from first page to last. What he wishes you to know he makes his characters, his incidents tell for him; the purpose of the book, always advancing, gradually reveals itself, and grows slowly into shape we hardly know how, as incident follows incident. And in all the books this purpose is sustained, consistent, and worthy. Occasionally in the preface to the story he tells us himself what this intention has been, tells it plainly, simply, manfully, and leaves the reader to say whether or not it has been achieved. That Wilkie Collins was a great (one of the greatest) novelists we *know;* we, who have studied his works, have marked their range and power, their sincerity of purpose, their perfection of expression; but we know more than this, we know that in an age of self-advertisement, jealousy, and pretense, he was a type—not without faults, but still a type—of a genuine, kindhearted, helpful-to-others *man.* He had blood, as well as brains, generosity, as well as intelligence, artistic pride and purpose in his work, as well as popular success.

Harry Quilter. *Universal Review.* 1889, pp. 207, 224

All the works of Wilkie Collins which we remember with pleasure are works of art as true as his godfather's pictures, and in their own line as complete. His excellent sense, his perfect self-command, his modest devotion to his art, are qualities not more praiseworthy than they are obvious. And if it were but for their rarity they should command no less attention than respect. His most illustrious friend and contemporary did not always show himself at once so loyal and so rational in observance of intellectual or aesthetic propriety. Collins never ventured to fling down among his readers so shapeless or misshapen a piece of work, though doubtless he could not furnish them with a piece of work so excellent in parts and sections, as *Little Dorrit.* It is apparently the general opinion—an opinion which seems to me incontestable—that no third book of their author's can be ranked as equal with *The Woman in White* and *The Moonstone:* two works of not more indisputable than incomparable ability. *No Name* is an only less excellent example of as curious and original a talent. *The New Magdalen* is merely feeble, false, and silly in its sentimental cleverness; but in *The Fallen Leaves* there is something too ludicrously loathsome for comment or endurance. The extreme clumsiness and infelicity of Wilkie Collins as a dramatic teacher or preacher may be tested by comparison with the exquisite skill and tact displayed by M. Alexandre Dumas in his studies of the same or of similar subjects. To the revoltingly ridiculous book just mentioned I am loath to refer again: all readers who feel any gratitude or goodwill towards its author must desire to efface its miserable memory from the record of his works.

Algernon Charles Swinburne. *Fortnightly Review.*
1889, pp. 591, 593, 596

The special power of Mr. Wilkie Collins, as afterwards developed, was for the construction of plots, and the use of all the most elaborate machinery of the story. His was the art which keeps the reader breathless, not through a scene or act of adventure, but during the long and elaborate following out of intrigue and incident, those tangles of the web of fate, or intricate combinations of circumstance, conducting certainly to an often unsuspected end—which never lose their effect so long as they are skillfully and powerfully done, as was the case in the earlier works of this novelist. He did not possess the still more interesting and far higher gift of creation. There is no character, no living being in his works, with the exception, perhaps, of Count Fosco, of whom the reader will probably at this distance remember even the name; but, notwithstanding this, his power of holding his audience spellbound, and of rousing the same kind of curiosity and eager interest with which we watch day by day the gradual unfolding of the links of evidence in a great trial, was unsurpassed, we might say unequaled, in his day. The sensation produced by the *Woman in White,* the first and consequently most striking of the series of stories in which he has displayed this power, and which came out in a serial form in *Household Words,* thus doubling the excitement of those who had to wait from week to week for a fresh installment of the story—was prodigious. It was the subject of conversation and speculation everywhere, and the reader followed every turn, and commented upon every incident, as if some personal interest of his own hung upon the identification of the gentle, witless creature who was the shadow heroine, and the unhappy lady who was the real object of all those highly wrought and intricate snares.

Margaret O. W. Oliphant. *The Victorian Age of English Literature* (n.p., 1892), p. 482

An extremely uneven writer, Collins is less appreciated today than his merits and influence deserve. He will not bear comparison with Le Fanu in his treatment of the weird, though he was earnestly ambitious to succeed in this line. His style was too dry and inelastic, his mind too legal. Consider the famous dream in *Armadale,* divided into seventeen separate sections, each elaborately and successively fulfilled in laborious detail! In the curious semi-supernatural rhythm of *The Woman in White* he came nearer to genuine achievement, but, on the whole, his eeriness is wiredrawn and unconvincing. But he greatly excels Le Fanu in humor, in the cunning of his rogues, in character drawing, and especially in the architecture of his plots. Taking everything into consideration, *The Moonstone* is probably the very finest detective story ever written. By comparison with its wide scope, its dovetailed completeness and the marvelous variety and soundness of its characterization, modern mystery fiction looks thin and mechanical. Nothing human is perfect, but *The Moonstone* comes about as near perfection as anything of its kind can be.

In *The Moonstone* Collins used the convention of telling the story in a series of narratives from the pens of the various actors concerned. Modern realism—often too closely wedded to externals—is prejudiced against this device. It is true that, for example, Betteredge's narrative is not at all the kind of thing that a butler would be likely to write; nevertheless, it has an ideal truth—it is the kind of thing that Betteredge might think and feel, even if he could not write it. And, granted this convention of the various narratives, how admirably the characters are drawn! The pathetic figure of Rosanna Spearman, with her deformity and her warped devotion, is beautifully handled, with a freedom from sentimentality which is very remarkable. In Rachel Verinder, Collins has achieved one of the novelist's hardest tasks; he has depicted a girl who is virtuous, a gentlewoman, and really interesting, and that without the slightest exaggeration or deviation from naturalness and probability. From his preface to the book it is clear that he took especial pains with this character, and his success was so great as almost to defeat itself. Rachel is so little spectacular that we fail to realize what a singularly fine and truthful piece of work she is.

The detective part of the story is well worth attention. The figure of Sergeant Cuff is drawn with a restraint and sobriety which make him seem a little colorless beside Holmes, . . . but he is a very living figure. . . . The scenes in which his shrewdness and knowledge of human nature are contrasted with the blundering stupidity of Superintendent Seagrave read like an essay in the manner of Poe.

While each one of Collins's astonishing contrivances and coincidences might, taken separately, find its parallel in real life, it remains true that in cramming a whole series of such improbabilities into the course of a single story he does frequently end by staggering all belief. But even so, he was a master craftsman, whom many modern mystery mongers might imitate to their profit. He never wastes an incident; he never leaves a loose end; no incident, however trivial on the one hand or sensational on the other, is ever introduced for the mere sake of amusement or sensation.

In *The Moonstone,* which of all his books comes nearest to being a detective story in the modern sense, Collins uses with great effect the formula of the most unlikely person and the unexpected means in conjunction. Opium is the means in this case—a drug with whose effects we are tolerably familiar today, but which in Collins's time was still something of an unknown quantity, de Quincey notwithstanding. In the opium of *The Moon-*

stone . . . we have the distinguished forebears of a long succession of medical and scientific mysteries which stretches down to the present day.

Dorothy L. Sayers. Introduction to *Omnibus of Crime* (New York: Harcourt, Brace, 1929), pp. 25–26

Collins's best novel—or, at any rate, the only one of Collins's novels which every one knows—is *The Woman in White*. Now *Bleak House* is the novel in which Dickens most closely approaches Collins (and after *Bleak House, Little Dorrit* and parts of *Martin Chuzzlewit*); and *The Woman in White* is the novel in which Collins most closely approaches Dickens. Dickens excelled in character; in the creation of characters of greater intensity than human beings. Collins was not usually strong in the creation of character; but he was a master of plot and situation, of those elements of drama which are most essential to melodrama. *Bleak House* is Dickens's finest piece of construction; and *The Woman in White* contains Collins's most real characterization. Every one knows Count Fosco and Marion Halcombe intimately; only the most perfect Collins reader can remember even half a dozen of his other characters by name. . . .

The one of Collins's books which is the most perfect piece of construction, and the best balanced between plot and character, is *The Moonstone;* the one which reaches the greatest melodramatic intensity is *Armadale.*

The Moonstone is the first and greatest of English detective novels. . . . Sergeant Cuff, far more than Holmes, is the ancestor of the healthy generation of amiable, efficient, professional but fallible inspectors of fiction among whom we live today. And *The Moonstone,* a book twice the length of the "thrillers" that our contemporary masters write, maintains its interest and suspense at every moment. It does this by devices of a Dickensian type; for Collins, in addition to his particular merits, was a Dickens without genius. The book is a comedy of humors.

T. S. Eliot. *Selected Essays* (New York: Harcourt, Brace, 1932), pp. 374–77

In Wilkie Collins the unraveling of the skein of crime is the work, not of the hand of the law, but of some person with a compelling interest in the elucidation. Sometimes there is no crime, but only a mystery. The same skill is lavished on both; and Wilkie Collins has never been excelled as a contriver of complicated plots. His first outstanding success, *The Dead Secret* (1857), was followed by the unsurpassed "thriller," *The Woman in White* (1860). Other successes are *No Name* (1862), *Armadale* (1866), *The Moonstone* (1868), and *The Law and the Lady* (1875). Wilkie Collins has the power of generating an atmosphere of foreboding, and of imparting to natural scenes a desolation which suggests depression and horror of spirit. The beginnings of his books are sometimes so tremendous that the conclusion fails to maintain the level. This is true, for instance, of *Armadale*. The main defect of the Wilkie Collins method is an abuse of machinery—not indeed of the machinery of detection, but of the machinery of narration. We get diaries, papers, memoirs, confessions, and so forth, which, designed to give verisimilitude, end in giving tedium.

George Sampson. *The Concise Cambridge History of English Literature* (Cambridge: Cambridge University Press, 1941), p. 796

Wilkie Collins is supposed to have succumbed not only to bad health and the addiction to laudanum but to the urge toward social criticism. An obvious danger in using fiction for social criticism is the subordination of the elements of plot to the social purpose. Another, seen in the perspective of several generations, is that the social disorder of one age may seem trivial in the next; the twentieth century does not forgive Mercy Merrick so much as overlook her. For his social fiction, Collins has suffered on both counts. It is not accurate, however, to propose that toward the end he suddenly became a social critic, as another man might deteriorate in another way. As early as *Antonina,* Numerian comes forth to illustrate the social evils of religious fanaticism; and there is no more intense exposure of the horrors of the crass middle-class life in an industrial civilization than *Basil.* The absurdity of moral distinctions based upon wealth dominates *The Dead Secret,* and the inadequacy of the laws of inheritance and marriage is a principal theme in *The Woman in White, No Name,* and *Armadale.* The point is not that Collins succumbed in his last years to the urge to write social criticism but that he became less restrained in doing it.

Collins could hardly write anything else. His world is the world of social relations, of nineteenth-century man, deep in his industrialization and his attempts to rule himself, deprived of much of the authoritarian solace of the past. It is a world of the individual bounded by men living together but in an alien universe. Ultimately, the social relationship, interpersonal and intersubjective, becomes all, the source of value and of fulfillment. And the writer may turn his attention to what underlies that relationship. Collins made the commitment in his works to the world he knew, and in this lay his success and his failure.

William H. Marshall. *Wilkie Collins* (New York: Twayne, 1970), p. 134

In Collins's novels the whole legal system is fraudulent in its relation to sexual matters. Daughters and sons are disinherited in his melodramatic plots because he sees a massive deprivation of secure, satisfying identity in the entire culture's sexual practices. In a more bitter sense, daughters and sons are deprived of their inheritance because the patriarchal culture has little to bequeath in terms of sexual roles but shame, violence, oppression, and starved, denatured personalities.

Yet Collins stops short of explicitly confronting the patriarchal view of marriage embodied in the law that defined a wife as the property of her husband, a being without any legal identity. In this stance, Collins reveals the ambivalence he shares with Dickens, Trollope, and Thackeray. On the one hand, he creates characters, situations, and symbolic structures that implicitly indict a society that oppresses women. On the other hand, through his ambivalent depictions of those characters and situations, he stops short of acknowledging the basic premises of Victorian society. Just as in so many Dickens and Trollope novels, the actual themes and symbolic structures created within the novel are more radical than the author seems willing to admit. Thus many Collins novels, like many Dickens and Trollope novels, end by insisting on redemption through marriage, though the novels themselves have undermined that solution.

> Richard Barickman, Susan MacDonald, and Myra
> Stark. *Corrupt Relations* (New York: Columbia
> University Press, 1982), pp. 148–49

The originality of Wilkie Collins's *The Moonstone* lies in its sustaining of suspense throughout the novel—and a lengthy novel at that—on the single question of who has taken the diamond. . . .

In the superb creation of Sergeant Cuff, Collins extends the development of the fictional detective begun by Dickens in the portrait of Inspector Bucket in *Bleak House*. Like his prototype, Cuff is a splendid representative of the London Detective Police whom Dickens so much admired. Through his work with Dickens on the staff of *Household Words* in the early 1850s, Collins had met the Scotland Yard officers and shared Dickens's interest in the new force. Like Bucket, Sergeant Cuff has earned a reputation for competence. When Franklin Blake hears that Cuff is being sent from London, he is delighted, telling Gabriel that "if half the stories I have heard are true, when it comes to unravelling a mystery there isn't the equal in England of Sergeant Cuff!" Cuff's first inquiries into the disappearance of the diamond give him the chance to show his powers in contrast with the pompous local officer, Superintendent Seegrave, who heads a long line of inept plodders serving as foils to great detectives in literature. When Seegrave refers to the smear of paint on Rachel's door as a "trifle," he is promptly rebuked by Cuff:

> I made a private inquiry last week, Mr. Superintendent. . . . At one end of the inquiry there was a murder, and at the other end there was a spot of ink on a tablecloth that nobody could account for. In all my experience along the dirtiest ways of this dirty little world I have never met with such a thing as a trifle yet. Before we go a step farther in this business we must see the petticoat that made the smear, and we must know for certain when that paint was wet.

Cuff combines scientific methods with psychology. He examines smeared paint with a magnifying glass to exclude its having been made by human hands; he recognizes and analyzes the importance of the time element in the drying of the paint; at the same times, he sees the damage done by Seegrave's alienation of the servants and sets about charming them into cooperation, infecting even the reluctant Gabriel with "detective fever" as he studies the laundry book or traces footsteps in the sand. . . .

Unlike his successors in detective fiction, Cuff is not infallible. Although his methods are impeccable, his first solution to the mystery proves to be quite wrong. His retirement to the country to grow roses prefigures Sherlock Holmes and his bees or Hercule Poirot and his vegetable marrows, but unlike those sleuths, Cuff is not the central figure in the story. He disappears for a long segment of the novel, reappearing in the end to trace the missing diamond. . . .

The Moonstone is an altogether delightful work. Most of the events of the story take place in a sunlit world of everyday reality. Even the wonderfully haunting scenes at the Shivering Sand are part of the realistic life of the country house and the fishermen's village. Yet hovering over this picture of mid-Victorian English life is the exotic story of the Indian diamond and its violent history. The novel closes with the memorable picture of the shrine in a wild and remote region of India, observed by the traveler Mr. Murthwaite:

> There, raised high on a throne, seated on his typical antelope, with his four arms stretching toward the four corners of the earth, there soared above us, dark and awful in the mystic light of heaven, the god of the Moon. And there, in the forehead of the deity, gleamed the yellow Diamond, whose splendor had last shone on me in England, from the bosom of a woman's dress.

Audrey Peterson. Victorian Masters of Mystery.
(New York, Ungar, 1984), pp. 57–66

CRICHTON, MICHAEL (1942–   )

The Andromeda Strain is the *reductio ad absurdum* of that much discussed subliterary genre, the nonfiction novel. While I do not like this book very much, I must confess to feeling that Michael Crichton deserves a great deal of credit—if for nothing more than his willingness on the first try to test the outer limits of the logic of his genre. Eschewing the dramatically easier subjects of such writers as Irving Wallace, Fletcher Knebel, or Robert Serling—the Nobel Prize committee, a military cabal, or the possible workings of the Presidential airplane—he has attempted no less than a fictional construction of the world's first biological crisis.

As he is careful to point out to us, scientific crises are increasingly familiar to us. Moreover, it is logical to suppose that the next such crisis will occur in the most rapidly expanding scientific discipline, biology. Finally, he is clever enough to realize that we laymen know even less about that subject than we do about physics or rocketry and that we will, therefore, snap up (as we did *The Double Helix*) anything that looks like a convenient, readable trot on it.

So he has imagined a space shot that returns from outer space contaminated by a deadly bacterium against which man has no natural immunity and which could, if not neutralized or destroyed, wipe out the race. And he gives us an indecipherable blend of true, half-true, and imaginary theories about the nature of the invading organism and the strategies for dealing with it that is fascinating, believable, and seemingly informative—though the problem of what, precisely, to believe does nag at one. Finally, he has found an interesting form for his work, casting it as a journalistic-historical work written a few years after the Andromeda crisis has passed. There are acknowledgments of fictional informants, a made-up bibliography, computer print-outs, and exact typographic reproductions of what purport to be government documents.

Indeed, he has spared no effort in his attempt to make us believe *The Andromeda Strain* could happen here. Except one—the creation of people. Granted the ability of the nonfiction novelist to characterize is not his great strength. Were it, he would not, perhaps, become a hyphenated novelist. But the lack of interest in this matter is, in Mr. Crichton's case, amazing. Perhaps so much creative energy went into imagining his basic situation that none was left for people. Perhaps he is trying to tell us that high-level scientific technicians, obsessed with their work, are, in fact, inhumanly traitless. Still, one would have liked some human quirks to get hold of, if only to help keep the names straight. By the end of the book I would have settled for a few of Irving Wallace's walking clichés, even a few physical descriptions. Just for fun. Or as an acknowledgment of literary tradition and the expectations we still bring to a work that must still be called, for want of the better term that is surely coming, a novel.

Richard Schickel. Harper's. August 1969, p. 97

The Andromeda Strain is a science fiction novel masquerading as a suspense thriller. Its excellent disguise has fooled a good many already. First of all, it fooled Alfred Knopf, presumably—for whoever heard of his Borzoi imprint going on a piece of science fiction? And it must have fooled the Literary Guild, too, for had they known what it is they would surely not have sent it out. And by this time, finally, it must have fooled a lot of readers, as well. They must have supposed it just a very up-to-date thriller, since the novel is set in the present, since its space hardware (only incidental to the story in the first place) is of no more than contemporary sophistication, and since the "aliens" who invade the earth are mere microbes.

But nevertheless *The Andromeda Strain* is science fiction. What else are you going to call a novel that begins out on the desert like one of those scary old science fiction movies from the fifties—*It Came from Outer Space* or *Them,* for instance—with the discovery of a town that has been mysteriously wiped out? The cause is soon made clear: a NASA probe vehicle has returned to earth nearby, been broken open, and an unknown strain of microbes picked up from outer space has infected the small community. The mystery is solved; the panic is on. A team of doctors, biologists, and specialists of every sort is hastily assembled from all parts of the country, and the remainder of the story is an account of their efforts to isolate, identify, and deal with this new strain they dub Andromeda.

Nothing very new in this, of course. The basic plot is one that has been done and redone innumerable times in science fiction. What is impressive here, however, are the many exact scientific details the author has included and the narrative skill with which it is written. The pace is fast and absorbing; the writing is spare and its quality generally high; and the characters, if not memorable, are at any rate efficiently sketched in and have been given little personal touches of their own.

Does this make it *good* science fiction, as opposed to the stuff you see on your drugstore racks? No, it's not quite as simple as that. For whatever else it may be, science fiction is the last solid redoubt of the imagination. And the writers who command that fort may not always be the most skilled writers of fiction by the usual standards but they are the ones with the most fertile imaginations—the Blishes, the Pohls, and the Heinleins. And while *The Andromeda Strain* may rate as superior in science and as a marked improvement in fiction, it lacks something of the catalytic glow of imagination that under the best circumstances seems to spark when those two disparate elements are conjoined.

Alexander Cook. *Commonweal.* August 8, 1969,
pp. 493–94

The packaging of this collaborative effort *Dealing* by the phenomenal young author of *The Andromeda Strain,* Michael Crichton, and his kid brother Douglas, screams of countless hilarities to come: far more than a mere wrapping, the dust jacket is a heady experience of bubbling mirth. On the back, where a photograph of the author usually grimaces or smiles sardonically, or looks wistfully into the distance, there is a family-album photo of two small boys. The caption reads "Michael Douglas" in quotes; and the credit line, with boyish simplicity: "Mom." Now get this title: *Dealing, or The Berkeley-to-Boston Forty-Brick Lost-Bag Blues.* Oh, wow!

And that's not all, not by a country mile. The usual legal disclaimer is modified to read that any resemblance to real persons is "either coincidental or the result of stoned paranoia" and all of it is dedicated "To the Lawmakers of Our Great Land: Play This Book Out LOUD!" And then, after four epigraphs (Thoreau, Art Linkletter, Billie Holliday, and Fats Waller), you arrive, battered, breathless but quiveringly expectant, at the beginning of the novel itself.

Now you may not find any of this ingratiating, but stay a while; for this book wants to tell us something—and it does, though not always what it intends. "Dealing," as any child knows, is trafficking in dope; and here, as the very type-font proclaims, the dealer is Peter Harkness, not only the protagonist-narrator but the hero of his own tale. What's more, square society, with its booze and armamentarium of pills, is represented by the most vicious of cops, a sadistic, corrupt narc named Murph, himself a dealer in soft goods lifted from his victims. Masks in place, the forces of Light and Darkness are thus aligned.

But even masks need a few features, so the authors provide them, beginning immediately with the entire hip lexicon, strung across the opening pages like day-glo baubles, the principle being that those who authentically speak in tongues must be beautiful, especially if they burn their margin of profit by turning on. Naturally the hero happens to pass Sproul Plaza during a demonstration and a police riot. And then there must be a girl, and her name, if at all possible should be Sukie. In fact her name is Sukie. Damn if she hasn't just come from the Sproul Plaza scene. They meet cute. They turn on, again and again and again; and then they are ready. But it is not meant to be: at *the* critical moment, the fuzz break in and bust them.

Yet, this turned-on Government major from Harvard is all guts. Under interrogation by the narcs—by the dreaded Murph himself—he more than holds his own, more than stands up, he gives better than he gets. Even when he's kicked in the groin, twice, he doesn't yield an inch.

Not that Peter is political, unless postpolitical is political. He has some fun early on putting down a Black Power spokesman and a self-designated "Marxist-Leninist." Nor is he into any sector of the peace movement. Dealing is his scene—and scandalizing the bourgeoisie. Back in Cambridge, he goes to a garden party. A garden party, for God's sake! Everyone is dressed as for a garden party—but Peter comes decked out in his credentials, a "pair of greasy blue jeans, a rumpled, plasticly-freaky shirt, a tired old blazer, and sneakers." Once there, he amuses himself by spilling numerous bottles of "hooch" all over the lawn, and when the "fun of hassling the old dudes" wears off, he engages in the rich comedy of conning some incredibly square chick into actually believing he's the rock star "Lucifer Harkness."

The boy is as nasty a little prig as you're likely to meet anywhere between Boston and Berkeley, bereft of the smallest redeeming feature or shred of social utility; and yet the authors don't have the slightest doubt that we'll love him as they do, no questions asked. The implied plea (Legalize Pot) is spurious, a clumsy attempt at blackmailing us into assent. We know all about the narcs and the insane laws they execute. And since the book is nothing more than a shoddy plastic construction, whom is it for? One must conclude with dismay that there is abroad in this land a vast audience of "young people" of all ages, all of them tuned into the same drummer, all of them decked out in the same plasticly-freaky shirt bought in the same trendy shop who will take any sleazy commodity providing the right signs are flashed, so they know where they're supposed to be at.

Saul Maloff. *The New Republic*. February 6, 1971, pp. 25–26

Michael Crichton's goal (and his achievement) seems to have been technical virtuosity. His best work has a stylistic ease and pace that make writers with greater literary reputations seem like work horses.

He is a complex writer, and not the simplistic "computer" one critic tried to reduce him to. Like many highly intelligent and sophisticated writers who have written to make money, but also to make life more interesting, he seems to have reached a stagnation point in aesthetic and philosophical goals, tending toward both fantasy and the trivialized concrete.

His plots—the hallmark of the mystery-thriller—are weak. His early thrillers written as John Lange, and a weak collaboration with his brother on drug traffic among youth, contain only a modicum of ingenuity, but the John Lange adventures can be above-average entertainment. But, some of his best touches—the snake containers concealing a compartment for double dealing in underground traffic, an exciting chase through the Alhambra in Granada, or the bureaucratic entrapments that inspire a skilled crook into near heroic endeavor to loot an Egyptian tomb—are largely wasted on conventional plot and characters.

His villains are only a shade more villainous than many of his heroes, but his women, sophisticated with an out-of-the-ordinary intelligence that makes them attractive, are interesting. His best-selling science-documentary thrillers, *The Andromeda Strain* and *The Terminal Man,* achieved wide attention, but are not his most successful literary accomplishments. An underappreciated strength is his excellent ability to pace the shorter novel; the best example is *Binary.*

His one first-rate mystery is *A Case of Need,* written as Jeffrey Hudson. The appeal is in the focus of hero-pathologist's mind tracking down the evidence of death, making the story engrossing and believable. The plot is somewhat helter-skelter, but the angle of approach and the coordination of style and characterization draw it together. The pace is swift, almost unique in such a complex mystery.

The Great Train Robbery is an effort in the Victorian mystery, a hybrid form that took many skillful writers years to evolve into good entertainment. The form has a particular built-in contradiction to Crichton's forte of fast-paced action, as it substitutes history for plot, the chronicle for invention. Crichton was unable to transfer the pace of *Binary* into film, but, in his one good film effort, he improved upon the pace of the printed version of *The Great Train Robbery* by cutting data and focusing on action in the film.

The promise of Crichton is a unique background from which the values of science (a proper springboard for adventure and romance) might be resolved in the appropriate form of the mystery. The disappointment has nothing to do with his penchant (and success) in marketing, but with his confusion and/or rejection of other than technical values. To integrate the dichotomy of man's mind-body duality and channel creativity into a rational, moral course, is a "case of need" of not only Michael Crichton, but an entire culture.

Newton Baird. In John M. Reilly, ed., *Twentieth-Century Crime and Mystery Writers: Second Edition* (New York: St. Martin's Press, 1985), p. 220

CROSS, AMANDA [CAROLYN G. HEILBRUN] (1926–   )

Read in the order of their publication, Amanda Cross's Kate Fansler books reveal an increasing interest in feminist questions concomitant with a diminishing commitment to the murder mystery as traditionally defined. With *The Question of Max* (1976), Cross begins to ask what effects male-dominated society has on women, offering a series of tentative answers symbolized by the male criminals and the female victims of the novels. *Max* says that some men will destroy women to maintain their privileges, while also showing the ways in which exclusively male institutions warp men. *Death in a Tenured Position* (1981) looks at three possible female responses to exclusion—imitation of men, entire avoidance of men and of patriarchal institutions, and bonding with other women while continuing to participate in patriarchal institutions in hopes of changing those institutions from within—with the mystery's solution effectively demonstrating the danger of the first of those responses: Janet Mandelbaum dies because she finally despairs of acceptance as an honorary man. The victim in *Sweet Death, Kind Death* (1984) is a brilliant, independent woman whose theories about the aging process challenge received wisdom about women's lives and threaten the infinitely more conservative work of the man who kills her (aided by his wife, a male-identified woman). The solution to the mystery in *No Word from Winifred* (1986) underscores male fear of women bonding together: Winifred "disappeared" because her lover threatened to kill his wife and children unless Winifred removed herself from his world. The man's motive for such desperate measures is his discovery that Winifred and his wife have become close friends. These last four novels probe women's writing, female friendship, and female development, with these themes most deeply explored in *Winifred,* which is also the least conventional of Cross's Fansler novels, despite its many references to Kate as Holmes and to her niece Leighton as Watson.

In the first of Cross's novels, *In the Last Analysis* (1964), the mystery presented is an end in itself, with the solution of the puzzle presumed to be the dominant interest of the reader, as it is of the detective and, apparently, of the author. Kate Fansler is the only fully developed character in this novel, with even Kate's lover Reed Amhearst and her friend Emanuel Bauer, the falsely accused psychiatrist for whom she undertakes the investigation, remaining flat characters who serve limited functions and who excite little interest beyond their relationships to Kate and to the puzzle.

In *In the Last Analysis,* the fact that the (second) victim is female matters as little as the fact that Kate is female; what counts in this novel is not gender but work, especially intellectual work, and honor, as traditionally defined for men. By the second Kate Fansler novel, *The James Joyce Murder* (1967), Cross has begun to ask, "Who kills what kind of woman and why?" but the answers in *The James Joyce Murder* and in *The Theban Mysteries* (1971) are tinged with antifeminism, as the female victims are perceived as monsters who somehow deserved killing. Beginning with *The Question of Max,* though, all of the Cross novels offer more complicated and compelling answers to these questions, with the answers forming part of a carefully constructed critique of society from a feminist position.

The murder in *Poetic Justice* (1970) takes place at an English Department party and is one part of a larger plot focusing on the very idea of the university, as faculty members fight over the fate of an adult education division; further, this plot is interwoven with consideration of campus radicalism and student opposition to the Vietnam War.

The best characters in *Poetic Justice* are dedicated to their work but able to achieve balance in their lives, unlike the most radical students, who are portrayed as seeking only to destroy, and the most reactionary professors, who seek only stasis.

Cross's four novels following *Poetic Justice* consider academe anew, but in two—*The Theban Mysteries* and *The Question of Max*—the academy considered is not a university but a private secondary school, one a girls' and the other a boys' preparatory school. The girls' school, the Theban School, is portrayed as nurturing, responsive to its students' needs, and dedicated to the ideal that learning should be a mutual experience. In contrast, the boys' school described in *The Question of Max* reflects the values of the Watergate conspirators and of the so-called "me decade" of the 1970s, with the headmaster of St. Anthony's covering up several boys' cheating. When read together, *Death in a Tenured Position,* set at Harvard, and *Sweet Death, Kind Death,* set at a women's college in western Massachusetts, operate as revisions of *The Question of Max* and *The Theban Mysteries,* respectively, with *Sweet Death, Kind Death* also acting as a corrective to the implication of *Death in a Tenured Position* that it is prestigious, originally all-male colleges that most oppress women. The women's college in *Sweet Death, Kind Death* as an institution embodies Janet Mandelbaum's attitudes, hostile to feminism and to feminists, run by a president who is doing her best to be an honorary man.

There is no woman in *The Question of Max* who fully accepts the patriarchal order, but such a woman features prominently in *Death in a Tenured Position,* whose solution illustrates the dangers of accepting that order's definition of women. . . . Janet Mandelbaum, the woman who is happy to be chosen as Harvard's token, believes in the face of overwhelming evidence to the contrary that her sex is irrelevant, that women's studies is ''nonsense'' and that if women were ''good enough'' (like her) they would be employed at prestigious universities. Her ex-husband says that . . . Harvard hired her *because* of her sex, that she can never really be ''one of the boys,'' that gender matters. . . . Janet takes cyanide, but it is clear that she has been metaphorically poisoned long before her actual death and that the male world in which she had achieved by imitating men murdered her. There is no need for a man like Max to kill a woman like Janet, since she cooperates in the obliteration of (female) self, proving the truth of Kate's earlier observation that ''there is no place for women'' at Harvard.

Maureen T. Reddy. *Sisters in Crime: Feminism and the Crime Novel* (New York: Continuum, 1988), pp. 49–68

Kate Fansler, Professor of Literature at a New York City university, is well-to-do, well dressed, and well educated. Kate has been raised in an atmosphere of privilege and has a clear sense of her self-worth. She teaches for the love of it and enjoys the company of most of her colleagues. Her life is comfortable and well ordered and as the series opens, she is more than a little content with her unmarried status.

In the first Amanda Cross novel featuring Miss Fansler, *In the Last Analysis,* Kate becomes involved with murder when a former student of hers is found stabbed on the analytic couch of the top-notch psychiatrist Kate has recommended. Dr. Emanuel Bauer, a close friend and former lover of Kate's, is charged with the murder of his patient and Kate is determined to clear him. In this book we also meet Reed Amhearst, another of Kate's close friends who just happens to be an assistant district attorney. Kate may be a bit vague about exactly what Reed's duties are but she does not hesitate to ask for his assistance in getting her the official information she needs to pursue her inquiries. Only slightly shaken by Reed's news that the police have received an anonymous letter accusing her of the murder, Kate presses on with even more determination.

Throughout the series the ultimate clue for this professor is often a literary one. In the first book, armed with little more than a feeling she has about an individual who has been affected by a particular passage by D. H. Lawrence, Kate formulates an improbable and seemingly unprovable scenario. She asks Reed to help her get the evidence to prove her literary-based intuition. His agreement is reluctant and qualified.

"Will you help if I promise?"

"I won't even continue this conversation until you promise. I want your word. All right. Now, let me call hospitals. They will tell me none of their clerks works on Sunday. No one works on Sundays, except you and your friends. I will then threaten and cajole. But we may have to wait even so. I don't know to what degree the New York Police Department is willing to flex its muscles. Now stop evolving schemes. I'll call if and when I get any news. And remember your promise."

Kate had to wait until the afternoon when Reed called again.

Reed does obtain the one piece of physical evidence needed to clinch the case. The mystery is solved and both Kate and Dr. Bauer are exonerated.

There are eight Fansler novels. In each, we learn a little more about Kate, her family, her colleagues, and, of course, her relationship with Reed Amhearst—which eventually leads to their marriage. She appears in a variety of settings, from the hallowed halls of Harvard to an isolated cabin in Berkshire Wood. We discover that her wit and erudition are as well suited to rural simplicity as they are to urban elegance. While Professor Fansler takes scholarship seriously and has earned the respect of both students and colleagues, she takes herself a bit more lightly and can even laugh at her tendency to use seven syllables where two would do.

> Victoria Nichols and Susan Thompson. *Silk Stalkings: When Women Write of Murder* (Berkeley: Black Lizard Books, 1988), pp. 11–12

Amanda Cross, a skilled detective story writer, has given us a lighter side of "Joyceana" in her *The James Joyce Murder*. She has kept pace with the Joyce "industry" and has given us a series of quite plausible events leading to a murder and its curious aftermath.

Each chapter is ingeniously titled after a story from *Dubliners*. Amanda Cross manages this with a minimum of awkwardness. She must stretch a bit to call a Berkshire town "Araby" and to arrange for a full-scale discussion of "Ivy Day in the Committee Room" to justify the titles of two chapters. Yet she is so at home with Joyce lore and scholarship that everything proceeds with great fluency and ease.

I suspect that Amanda Cross is intimately in touch with the latest developments in fiction, especially with the post-Joycean antics of the *nouveau roman*. *The James Joyce Murder* strikes me as being very close at times to certain procedures of Alain Robbe-Grillet, Nathalie Sarraute, and Michel Butor. There is something gently mock-detective about it, in the best tradition of these French contemporaries and also of the Truman Capote of *In Cold Blood*, the William Styron of *Set This House on Fire*, and the Colin Wilson of *Ritual in the Dark*. Even though Amanda Cross's murderer is apprehended in the end, there are many false starts and stops, there are detectives who are more expert at literary criticism than solving crimes, and other mock ingredients.

Amanda Cross has a fine ear for academic conversation. She does occasionally overdo it. There is too much "hash-joint-cum-bar," "buddy-cum-tutor," and "cleaning woman-cum-cook"; even academics do not talk this way. But generally the dialogue is convincing.

Melvin J. Friedman. *The Modern Language Journal*. October 1967, p. 373

There are a few structural limitations or "faults" which amateurize the Cross books a little.

To begin with her dialogue, which is more important in Cross than for another style of writer: Cross adopts the technical convention that each important *speaker*—as opposed to "character"—shares the same conversational style; by implication, the same background.

This dialogue convention is adopted unconsciously by very bad writers because of course bad writers are tone deaf, employ limited vocabularies, etc.: these are all weaknesses not applying to Amanda Cross. On the other hand, one reason bad writers, including bad mystery writers, are bad, is that they are morally stupid and therefore assume that everybody else "really" agrees with them except those who "pretend" to disagree. To this last vice, I think Cross becomes a little more susceptible.

Her dialogue convention—which is also used by Henry James, "witty" playwrights, and nearly all narrative poets—receives its most interesting modern use in the William Haggard spy thrillers. This conversational device is artistically more successful with Haggard than with Cross, because any reader of a book is grateful and noncritical when the minor characters are able and willing to communicate in shorthand.

By contrast, Cross's characters (and those of her main influence, Sayers) labor to convince us that they are educated, while at the same time not quite concealing the fact that they don't really trust us, the readers, to catch too elliptic allusions or references.

Complaint No. 2 about Cross is more seriously derogatory of her novels as purist mysteries than my technical point about dialogue. This is the complaint that, beneath a veneer of educated allusion, the Cross mysteries are fairly simpleminded, considered as mysteries. The special technical characteristic of the purist detective story is, after all, the play of appearance and of illusion in social relationships.

However "sophisticated" her admirers and reviewers find Cross, her books are *naif* in the sense that the seemingly "bad" (disapproved) characters stay "bad" and the seemingly "good" (approved) people stay "good"—just like with Mickey Spillane or Nancy Drew. Cross is so simplistic with this important matter of mystery characterization that the first-time reader of one of her books must often be double-bluffed, the way Christie did it deliberately in her *Mysterious Affair at Styles*. Perhaps Cross's most incredible gaffe, by purist-mystery rules, occurs in her debut: *In the Last Analysis*.

Herein a nightmare identifies one particular character as a serious suspect, and by God he turns out the murderer!

Another technical difficulty concerns Cross not individually but representatively, in terms of the closed-society, upper-crust, comfortable-people style of book she and Sayers-Innes-Christie all write.

One cannot pretend Cross is an isolated offender, though *Poetic Justice* could, both in mainstream and in mystery terms, have been her best book because she had the fascinating idea of attempting herein to turn her distinguished colleague and apparent friend, Lionel Trilling, into a mystery villain.

Not only, as readers of *Justice* know, does Cross "cheat" by making the homicide in *Justice* accidental, the result of a stupid practical joke: not only does she back away from turning "Trilling" into a killer but, more seriously (and unlike C. P. Snow) she also fails to invent for her fictional "Trilling" a criminal act or moral offense that will articulate whatever serious criticism she is making of him. (The question is not whether the real-life Trilling, contrary to his public image, played practical jokes.) The point is that, under the sophisticated Cross veneer, we once again find some taint of amateurism in bread-and-butter matters of plot and theme.

Cross is generally treated by the reviewers as a "satiric" comic writer. However, she never satirizes the characteristic most commonly observed by educated writers who study our intellectual community: its tendency to indulge in cant, or to think, speak, and write in a truistic terminology borrowed from each other. Indeed, most imaginative writers with talent who do books about the American intellectual find themselves *obliged* to write parodies. Already in the 1930s, Sig Perelman was a more accurate observer than Dos Passos or the early O'Hara because of his parodic talents. And later students of our clerisy—from Mary McCarthy to Tom Wolfe—have made careers out of quoting and citing intellectual cant.

"Amanda Cross"—created Michelangelically by Professor Heilbrun and given leave to produce Kate Fansler and Kate's whole "secondary" world—enjoys herself by putting her view of the U.S. into print, writing off the top of her head to some extent, faking at times on matters of theme and structure, and never seriously attempting the more disturbing world of illusion and betrayal that we find in the structurally skilled mystery novel.

J. M. Purcell. The Armchair Detective. Winter
1980, pp. 37–40

Although Carolyn G. Heilbrun's pseudonym, Amanda Cross, is reminiscent (surely intentionally) of Agatha Christie, her true literary ancestor is Dorothy Sayers, who, like herself, was a noted scholar and feminist. Heilbrun has discerned in Sayers a delight in the comedy of manners, erudition, and formal English that she finds missing in contemporary mysteries and wishes to revive. She has also been pleased by the intellectual challenge of Sayers's puzzles, though, like Sayers herself, she has come to find the emphasis in classic detective fiction on an elaborate, multiclued puzzle both confining and destructive to other literary values. . . .

What is distinctive—and at least as fascinating—in the Amanda Cross canon is her irony, her ability to construct a mystery around the ideas of a single literary or intellectual figure, her application of her research on androgyny and a feminist history, the increasing complexity and appeal of her detective, Kate Fansler, and her responsiveness to the crises of her time, such as the student rebellions of the Sixties and the Vietnam War.

Her first novel, *In the Last Analysis,* is the most conventional, remaining firmly within the Sayers tradition at its most puzzle bound, as in *The Five Red Herrings.* As in the majority of classical detective novels, the only fully developed character is the detective, though some minor characters are lively and interesting. Wit abounds, as always in the series, and there are some perceptive observations on Freudian psychoanalysis and departmental politics at bureaucratically run universities. However, the major source of interest is unquestionably the puzzle. This puzzle is probably the most intriguing and best developed in the series, but it is an end in itself; the solution to it makes only the conventional point that order—personal, social, moral—can be restored through reason. The novel, though engrossing and entertaining, is therefore minor; it succeeds in its aims, but its aims are limited.

In her first appearance, Kate Fansler seems like a combination of Lord Peter Wimsey and Harriet Vane. Like Lord Peter, Kate is a rich amateur detective who undertakes cases out of friendship for the falsely accused and curiosity. . . . Like Harriet Vane, she is a professional intellectual (Harriet was a writer; Kate is an English professor) with an unconventional attitude toward sex and an uncommon integrity. She has too great a love for independence and for her work to desire marriage.

At the same time, Kate is also an individual with a personal history. *In the Last Analaysis* presents some important facts about her that are not repeated in subsequent mysteries: (1) She was a member of a "reform political club" during "the short period of political activity in Kate's life" and it was there she met Assistant District Attorney Reed Amhearst for whom politics had been a "more continuous affair"; (2) she "rescued" Reed from some unspecified trouble he had gotten into through "a series of impulses and bad judgments"; and (3) she met Emanuel Bauer, the psychiatrist falsely accused of murder, "at that identical point in their lives when each was committed to a career, but had not yet admitted the commitment" and the two of them became lovers and afterwards remained friends. The relationship between Kate and Emanuel illustrates a point which Heilbrun, writing under her own name in *Toward a Recognition of Androgyny,* made about George Bernard Shaw: "The friendship of a man and woman is one of the most unexplored of all human experiences, only Shaw, for example, recognizing that when a man and woman have ceased to be lovers, a friendship, a love, awaits them that is as ardent as an account of it is rare.''

Steven R. Carter. In Earl F. Bargainnier, ed., 10
Women of Mystery (Bowling Green, Ohio: Popular
Press, 1981), pp. 270–71

Many academicians have written mystery stories under pseudonyms, often (they say) because they fear that their more serious work would be compromised or undervalued if it were widely known that they also indulge in a bit of pleasure from time to time. This is rather like suggesting that the author of a standard text in biology would lose credentials were it known that he kept a mistress on the side. Carolyn Heilbrun, for example, did not reveal to her colleagues in the Department of English at Columbia University that she was also Amanda Cross until she was voted tenure. This compromise must still rankle, since her most recent book, *Death in a Tenured Position,* is her best, angriest, most pointed. Carolyn Heilbrun is a distinguished scholar. She has written an authoritative and utterly compelling book on the theme of androgyny in literature. She has pursued the Bloomsbury group. She has written one of the best essays ever written on Dorothy Sayers, whom she takes seriously. She is, I think, a highly skilled novelist of manners in an academic setting, and she has chosen the device of the mystery because she enjoys it, because she admires Sayers, and because she saw earlier than many that behind the alleged snobbery of Miss Sayers is a deeply committed feminism.

Robin W. Winks. Modus Operandi: An Excursion
into Detective Fiction (Boston: David R. Godine,
1982), pp. 33–34

The Players Come Again is an extremely skillfully told story, featuring the twisted fortunes of a celebrated modernist writer, Emmanuel Foxx; his wife, Gabrielle Foxx (who may or may not have been responsible for more of his works than hitherto acknowledged); and a gallery of other women, all more or less deserving the epithet ''strong,'' including his granddaughter, Nellie Foxx. There is also that feature of many of the best mysteries including *Wuthering Heights*—the memoir that gives the tale within the tale. *The Players Come Again* involves not only complicated legitimate and illegitimate family relationships (I have to say that I was a little slower than Kate Fansler in picking them all up and began to wonder why we did not have a family tree—although I later realized that would be impossible, for reasons connected to the plot), and literary themes, but above all, relationships between women.

All of these are familiar topics to readers of the Kate Fansler mysteries. I salute the latest work as being among the best [Amanda Cross] has written, if not the best. The actual crime element in *The Players Come Again* is perhaps a little weak, even hurried over somewhat at the end, but the wonderful pleasure of reading Amanda Cross resides not so much in her plots as in the creation of Kate Fansler and, more than that, in the brilliant manner in which Ms. Cross has allowed Fansler to age—gracefully, of course—in the last twenty-five years. This is a bold decision, and not one every crime writer has made. It has been calculated that Hercule Poirot would have been well over one hundred, had he aged normally in the fifty-five years between his first appearance and his last.

In allowing Fansler her own logical development from 1964, Ms. Cross has managed to chronicle the history of women during this key period in the most accessible way as well as to provide volumes of literate, witty entertainment. This is no mean feat. In fact, were I to be writing the history of women and women's education in the United States since the 1960s, I can think of no more important, illustrative texts than the Kate Fansler mysteries, and certainly none more diverting.

Antonia Fraser. *New York Times Book Review.*
October 14, 1990, p. 2

DAVIS, DOROTHY SALISBURY (1916–   )

The work of Dorothy Salisbury Davis indicates her keen perception as a student of human nature. A distinguishing feature of her writings—ironic, perhaps, in one so opposed to physical violence—is the preoccupation with crime and criminal psychology. Following the early success of *The Clay Hand* and *The Judas Cat,* this interest became apparent in such works as *A Gentle Murderer,* with its sympathetic portrayal of a killer who must be found in order to avert further tragedy. Davis's explorations of the criminal mind are far from morbid. Rather she seeks for the minor flaws of character, the unforeseen shifts of circumstance, that lead certain human beings to break the confines of the law, and the often disastrous consequences of their actions. The theme is central to one of her most celebrated books, *Death of an Old Sinner,* where a retired general finds himself drawn into blackmail and eventually pays with his life. So intrigued was the author by the character she had created that the lovable rogue is revisited in a "prequel," *Old Sinners Never Die.* Much of the interest of the Davis novel stems from the battle of wits between hunter and hunted, with close parallels often being drawn between the detective and his prey. *The Pale Betrayer* is a good example, its "criminal" a college lecturer who finds himself involved in an act of espionage which gets out of hand and results in the death of a friend. In the ensuing course of the detection, where Mather at last atones by the sacrifice of his own life, he and the detective Marks come to a close understanding of each other's innermost nature. Similar themes pervade the excellent *Enemy and Brother* and *Where the Dark Streets Go. God Speed the Night,* written with Jerome Ross, is set in occupied France. A Jewish refugee is helped by a nun who disguises herself as his wife after the latter dies in the local convent. The two are pursued in a duel of wits by the dissolute, hen-pecked Vichy police chief, whose power as a hunter of criminals is his only claim to self-respect. As always, the subtle workings of the human mind are set down in the clean unadorned style which is Davis's hallmark.

An excellent writer of short stories, Davis's skill and psychological penetration serve her well in the shorter forms of fiction. Some of her later works might be described as "straightforward" detective stories, with the difference that her probing intelligence gives them a depth denied to most. Marks, the detective, returns in *The Little Brothers,* a fast-paced thriller involving a teenage gang, murder, and drug trafficking. *Shock Wave* investigates a similar crime against a backcloth of racial unrest in the Deep South. Most recently, she has produced two fine novels starring the female sleuth

Julie Hayes. *A Death in the Life* has her tracking down a murderer in the red light district, while art theft is the theme of *Scarlet Night*. Julie Hayes is a lively and credible—if unorthodox—detective, and a tribute to the subtle skills of her creator.

Geoffrey Sadler. In James Vinson, ed., *Twentieth Century Romance and Gothic Writers* (Detroit: Gale Research, 1982), pp. 195–96

In her mysteries Dorothy Salisbury Davis has attempted to express her hatred of violence and her sympathy for the underdog. Often, her protagonists are undergoing crises of religious faith. This is especially true of *A Gentle Murderer* (1951), which most critics cite as containing characterization and insight seldom found in the mystery, and of *The Pale Betrayer* (1965), *Where the Dark Streets Go* (1969), and *The Little Brothers* (1973), all with New York City settings. She also received high praise for *Enemy and Brother* (1967) and *God Speed the Night* (1968), set in Europe.

Mrs. Davis's second book, *The Clay Hand* (1950), is set in the coal mine area of Kentucky and deals sympathetically with poverty in Appalachia. Drawing upon her own experiences, she has written two mysteries set in Illinois college towns, *A Town of Masks* (1952) and *Shock Wave* (1972). The latter tells of politics and race riots at a university where a world-famous scientist has been killed.

Dorothy Salisbury Davis's considerable reputation is based as much on her short stories as on her novels. She won second prizes in *Ellery Queen's Mystery Magazine* contests for "Spring Fever" (1952), "Backward, Turn Backward" (1954), and "By the Scruff of the Soul" (1963). She won a third prize for "Born Killer" (1953), a penetrating psychological study of a Wisconsin farmboy. A 1964 short story, "The Purple Is Everything," received a Mystery Writers of America Edgar nomination, as have five of her books.

Chris Steinbrunner and Otto Penzler. *Encyclopedia of Mystery and Detection* (New York: McGraw-Hill, 1976), p. 117

One of the finest of American suspense authors, Dorothy Salisbury Davis's work is distinguished both for creativity and for skill. The main body of the work centers on serious studies of character against environment. Only recently has she taken on the diversion of the New York street scene played for comedy not tension, and this is as rewarding as her serious novels. Mrs. Davis has received many Edgar scrolls both for novel and for short story.

H. R. F. Keating. *Whodunit?: A Guide to Crime, Suspense, and Spy Fiction* (New York: Van Nostrand Reinhold, 1982), p. 147

"If she's very lucky, a writer will sometimes receive a gift. I've had a couple of gifts in my lifetime. *A Gentle Murderer* was one. A gift from God, if you will. It came so easily, that book. It went so beautifully and so straight and so *right* from the beginning. I knew the first sentence was to be 'Bless me, Father, for I have sinned,' and that's how it went, all the way through. It was my third book, published back in 1951, and it's since been republished four times."

That's Dorothy Salisbury Davis speaking, a writer's writer, admired by her peers and by the critics and perhaps not as well known among the general reading public as she should be. . . .

Crises of faith, sexual conflicts, and identity problems are what Davis writes about. Her love/hate relationship with the Roman Catholic Church, and the fact that she was an adopted child, account for the exploration throughout her works of articles of faith, of commitment, and of the search for one's roots, which give her readers more than the one-dimensional look of many standard mystery books. . . .

Davis's first novel, *The Judas Cat,* was set in a small midwestern town and concerns a young newspaper publisher's inquiry into the death of a reclusive old man. The author's next book, *The Clay Hand,* also reaches into the past as a sheriff looks into the death of an investigative reporter who intrudes upon a West Virginia mining town. Her third book—Davis's personal favorite—was *A Gentle Murderer.*

Throughout the fifties, she produced almost a mystery novel a year, alternating in background between her native Midwest and her new home, New York. She next devoted herself to two novels outside the mystery field. *Men of No Property* is about the coming of the Irish to New York in the midnineteenth century, while *The Evening of the Good Samaritan* is a novel of generations in a large midwestern city. . . .

Davis once wrote, "A woman, to get in on a murder, has to be either dead or deadly, the victim or the murderer." Since she wrote that, and indeed since the advent of the woman's movement, there has been a strong flow of women detectives to join the mainstream of mystery fiction. Davis's contribution is Julie Hayes, housewife, reader, and advisor, who becomes involved in crime investigation in *A Death in the Life,* written in 1976.

Hayes, in her late twenties, involved in a somewhat restive marriage to a *New York Times* correspondent who frequently travels without her, is about to be fired as a legman for a *Daily News* gossip columnist. Part of Julie's problem is that she has no consistent job for her own, so when she is dropped she sets up as a fortune teller in Times Square. In this first book, Julie has a running dialogue with her analyst. Davis has even more fun with Julie in *Scarlet Night,* a caper. The third Hayes book, *Lullaby of Murder,* was published in the spring of 1984.

Davis considers herself a "passive activist" as far as the woman's movement goes. "I've been sympathetic. I suppose when they started, I felt, 'Gee, I'm doing all right in a man's world; what do I need this for?'

But then I came along. I knew Betty Friedan, who was living near me in Rockland County when she wrote *The Feminine Mystique*. I think that the movement has gone hither and yon and sometimes has been quite ridiculous. I, for one, don't want to be a 'chairperson.' I don't even want to be a chairwoman. On the other hand, they have made some valid points.''

She says she is now consciously raising the role of women in her own fiction.

Living close to New York, the Davises enjoy visiting in each others' worlds—mystery writing and show business. Her husband, the actor Harry Davis, is no great mystery reader, but he enjoys mystery writers, while Dorothy has been known to use a show-business background in her writing, notably with Julie Hayes.

Elaine Budd. *13 Mistresses of Murder* (New York:
Ungar, 1986), pp. 21–25

Davis's interpretation of evil appears to be more or less theological rather than literary. The evil that inhabits the psyches of her characters is a very real thing—not simply an outer label attached to an actor in a drama. It is up to the detective to isolate that evil; not for nothing are her investigators frequently men of the cloth.

The interest in a Davis novel generally involves reaching back into the past to untangle the threads of conflict that have skewed the characters in one direction or another and then in reaching out in the present to unmask and thwart the evildoer or evildoers.

Unlike her contemporary, Elmore Leonard, whose characters are various shades of gray, from very evil to mildly evil, and whose eventual actions and reactions are existentially resolved without benefit of judge or jury, Davis clearly characterizes her people as deserving or undeserving of punishment by their actions.

And unlike Robert B. Parker, whose characters act in concert with a very elaborate set of politically and sociologically correct values, Davis rates her characters on a simple scale of ''good'' or ''bad'' with the reader in her confidence.

Neither existential (like Leonard's) nor politically correct (like Parker's), Davis's literary themes reach back into theology and classic mythology for their psychological evaluations. Her books are rich in in-depth characterization and paced with an eye toward suspenseful investigation. Their stress on psychological analysis makes them quite possibly more ''whydunits'' than ''whodunits''—with the emphasis on the *reason* for evildoing rather than the identification of the evildoer. In the end, it is the evil that men (and women) do that is important—so important that it should *not* be allowed to live after them.

One of her most popular series characters is Julie Hayes, a housewife and surrogate detective, who first appears in 1976 in *A Death in the Life*. At the time a legman for a Broadway columnist whose marriage is in danger of breaking up, Hayes becomes immersed in trying to solve a murder in a seamy New York district where her qualities of intelligence and courage eventually bring her through to a successful solution of the crime.

In *Scarlet Night* (1980) Hayes returns to immerse herself in the midst of an international scam involving priceless artifacts in the world of art. Later, in 1984, she appears in *Lullaby of Murder,* involving the murder of her boss, the Broadway columnist, and centering on the world of the dramatic arts.

In this latter, Davis is aided perceptibly by her own background: she is married to Harry Davis, an actor, and spends a great deal of her time in the company of dramatists, producers, and actors.

Bruce Cassiday. The Literature of Crime and
Detection (New York: Ungar, 1988), p. 156

DEIGHTON, LEN (1929–   )

In *The Ipcress File* Len Deighton has combined picaresque satire, parody, and suspense, and produced a hybrid more humorous than thrilling. Inevitably, his comedic attack on modern espionage agencies and his burlesque of the fictional techniques of Ambler, Fleming, and Greene reduce the intensity and intrigue of his narrative. But even in itself his tale of espionage lacks distinction, and, despite some revelatory material on "brainwashing," its familiarity breeds boredom. Fortunately, the story seems less important than the comedy.

Deighton's plot, while using the customary obfuscation of the genre, is relatively simple. If the conventional narrative details are in part Deighton's burlesque of espionage fiction, they seem too often to be working both sides of the street. Moreover, his disclosure of the "inside man" is clearly intended as a part of the suspense, and yet it is as stereotyped as the material being parodied.

Where Deighton allows his humor to dominate, he is bitingly and savagely funny. He recognizes that the spy—whose survival depends on his guile, cunning, and adaptability—is today's picaro. Like some modern Le Sage, Deighton uses the picaresque to satirize the hypocrisies, deceits, and trickery in the community of secret agents. He exposes the lust for authority and money that subverts men's loyalties. Combined with his parody of the literary clichés of the genre, the satiric power raises the work above the mediocrity of its narrative.

Robert Donald Spectar. New York Herald Tribune
Book Week. November 17, 1963, p. 32

I am no unconditional admirer of Len Deighton, whose British Intelligence narrator-hero is a kind of determinedly proletarian James Bond. But it must be conceded that *The Billion Dollar Brain* has its points. With all his usual dexterity the author suggests a world in which, if we are not careful, machines may be ruling men. Triggered by the murder of a Finnish political commentator, action shuttles between London and Helsinki, over to Leningrad and Riga, across the ocean to New York and San Antonio, Texas, then back to Europe for the payoff. The antiheroine here is Signe Laine, a Finnish blonde with some curious traits; the bad guys are represented by Harvey Newbegin, neurotic American agent, and General Midwinter, that wicked conservative.

The day is long past when Americans in English novels (John S. Blenkiron of the Richard Hannay saga, for instance) talked a jargon no American in history has ever talked. The late Ian Fleming could draw admirable American scenes and characters. Alistair MacLean can do it. So can John Gardner. . . . Mr. Deighton's unnamed narrator manages tolerably well except when—his overmastering passion—he tries to be too in. Of him one American character is made to say, "He doesn't know a squeeze play from a loud foul." Do they hit many loud fouls in *your* league? The narrator understands baseball as little as he understands conservatives; in fact, with regard to so many things American, he doesn't know his you-name-it from third base.

John Dickson Carr. *Harper's.* July 1966, pp. 84,

86, 88

Suspense abounds in *Horse under Water.* It is not of the rat-tat-tat, double-barreled-action variety, but rather a subtly disturbing quieter kind of tension. The impatient reader wants Len Deighton to get on with it and resolve an expounded situation while, paradoxically, this same reader insists that Deighton not omit a single detail en route. In his earlier, highly popular, *Funeral in Berlin,* and *The Ipcress File,* Deighton employed the same formula. In fact, in classic suspense-story style, it is not until very near the end of *Horse under Water* that the by-now-befuddled reader has any inkling what the whole thing is all about nor is it until virtually the final page that the mystery is unraveled.

We seem to be living in a decade that is fortuitous for the spy story aficionado. Deighton's operations compare to those depicted by le Carré and Ian Fleming. His writing is without the extra gimmicks of James Bond. True, there are girls and there are cars, and food, and weapons, and international settings. None of these, however, intrude upon the main action. Character development is, happily, an integral part of the Deighton technique. At all times, the discerning reader is directly involved in a game of matching wits with Len Deighton and his nameless hero even to a clever puzzle linking Chapter headings with Table of Contents.

Jane Oppenheim. *Best Sellers.* January 1, 1968,

pp. 388–89

Deighton's sure handling of technicalities is reminiscent of Kipling, who could absorb unfamiliar detail and then write about it so convincingly that, for instance, men who had spent a lifetime at sea were convinced that he, too, must have been a sailor. Deighton's picture of men going through well-learned movements while their senses were being assaulted by great fear on the one hand and stimulated by the primitive exhilaration of killing and destroying on the other, reminded me of Stephen Crane who, though without experience of battle himself, wrote more truthfully about it than many who had actually fought.

In the thirteen stories which make up *Declarations of War* the research, as meticulous as ever, no longer obtrudes (as it did, one critic charged, in *Bomber*) and we are at least as interested in the characters as in their machines and their technique. Some of the characters—an ex-colonel, now a car enthusiast, a battered First World War ace, a young GI in Vietnam, a regular Army sergeant in India—have been touched with the rare magic which makes them live on in the memory long after their story is forgotten. Two or three of the stories are only a little short of masterpieces.

The exciting thing about Len Deighton is that he develops with each new book. He could have gone on repeating the formula of *The Ipcress File* with undoubted success, but instead he tried for more subtlety, for more convincing, more substantial characters. I do not think it is too farfetched to suggest that one day Len Deighton will write a novel which will warrant the most careful critical attention and will rank him among the best.

Peter Elstob. *Books and Bookmen.* December
1971, p. 60

In *The Ipcress File* (1963) and his subsequent books, Len Deighton . . . gave a new twist to the [spy story]. His anonymous central character (called Harry Palmer in the films) is a working-class boy from Burnley, opposed to all authority, who dislikes or distrusts anybody outside his own class. He is set down in a world of terrifying complexity, in which nobody is ever what he seems. The Deighton stories are elliptically—sometimes too elliptically—told, but their sudden shifts of tone and scene are extremely effective, and the technological expertise is impressive because it is not just there for show. Deighton's fascination with what in another writer would be gimmicks comes through . . . and there is something almost lyrical about his re-creation of the dangerous and transitory lives of agents, as well as something sharp and knowing. From his most brilliant performance, *The Billion Dollar Brain* (1966), one carries away admiration for a plot as intricate as the lock of a good safe and for the characterization of the clownish double agent Harvey Newbigin, but even more for the evocation of General Midwinter's dotty neo-Fascist organization in Texas and the wonderfully vivid picture of the shooting of Harvey in the snow outside the Russian train. Writing of this quality, combined or contrasted with the constant crackle of the dialogue, makes Deighton a kind of poet of the spy novel.

Julian Symons. *Mortal Consequences: A History—*
From the Detective Story to the Crime Novel (New
York: Harper & Row, 1972), pp. 245–46

By 1969 Len Deighton had written his four best spy thrillers, beginning in 1963 with *Ipcress File,* and going on quickly to *Horse under Water* and *Funeral in Berlin.* By 1969 the Deighton touch was clear, both the plots and the style almost instantly recognizable. In fine, Deighton had carved out his own niche by then.

What was this special niche? Roughly Deighton had decided to apply to the reader, and therefore to his style, the principle so honored in spy fiction (if not necessarily in real life), that of "need to know." His plots seem more complex than they are, as most mundane lives no doubt do, because very little is stated explicitly, sequences appear to begin in midpassage, and only through observation of the action does one come to understand either the motives of the villains, or the thought processes of the heroes. Deighton had patented a style in which every third paragraph appeared to have been left out.

It worked stunningly well, not only as pure thriller, but as a not too subtle way of sharing [his protagonist's] confusion with the reader. In a sense, Deighton's interest was increasingly in the question of what an agent might be led to believe was true rather than in any fictional truth to be revealed to the reader. Appearances increasingly became everything. . . . Appearances are deceiving, but what is stated—and that is often very little—is true.

So now Len Deighton has thumbed his nose at us and written his best book since *Funeral in Berlin,* all in the same gesture, which is surely a kind of grace. For he has written a book *[Yesterday's Spy]* which reviewers may well hail as Deighton returning to the style and mannerisms of his earlier successes. Having tried to grow and experiment, without critical success, Deighton has written a book that is self-parody so cunningly constructed as to please at almost any level.

Yesterday's Spy is, on the surface, about one Steve Champion, a hero of World War II who was a top operative for the British in occupied France.

But is is Deighton who is truly Yesterday's Spy, and he knows it. It is in this that he succeeds—taking us back to an earlier time in order to "return to form." This is a story written to the attitudes, the manners, the very style of the 1960s in which he won his audience. It will win that audience back, and will deserve to. And by doing so, by taking us back to the time when Muhammad Ali was Cassius Clay, Deighton has both written his best-seller and grown in the way in which he wanted and yet could not otherwise have done. *Yesterday's Spy* is all of us.

Robin W. Winks. *The New Republic*. December
13, 1975, p. 32

XPD belongs firmly in the "secret history of the war" genre. As with others of its kind, its main contention is the folkloristic one that the real truth of history has been covered up, that secret fortunes have been made, and that it only needs the removal of one card to bring the whole thing tumbling down. Since *The Ipcress File,* Deighton has shown himself to be the most protean of British best-sellers.

For all its diversity, there are certain core elements in Deighton's fiction. His novels all betray the other ranks' hatred of the commanding-officer class. It is the front-line men, agents, pilots, detectives, who are admirable. Another core element is Deighton's urge to demythologize. This is at its most aggressive in his recent work of history, *Fighter,* which presumes to dismantle the Churchillian myths about the heroism of the few. There's clearly a lot of writing energy and creative disgruntlement left in Deighton. I hope it produces better things than *XPD.*

John Sutherland. *London Review of Books*. April 1,
1981, pp. 21–22

Somebody once told me that to write a book for the movies you must do it in episodes—act 1, scenes 1, 2, 3, 4, and so on. If you write spy novels intended for the movies (and I can only conclude that such was the intention of the author of *XPD*), you must have regular violent episodes, the violence preferably mayhem, but an occasional accident will do if it is screechy enough.

I wish Len Deighton had let the movie people do his plot and had only then decocted a novel from the script, because what he has brought forth is most painfully unreadable, the violent episodes like telephone poles meandering over the landscape, stringing along a plot line that keeps sagging to the ground. When you reach a murder, an assassination or other butchery, your attention is temporarily hyped, but the business in between is so drained of literary or emotional interest that you are left feeling as benumbed as you would after looking at a hundred pictures of murdered corpses to identify a person with whom you are concerned—though you are unlikely to be concerned with anyone by the time you have flogged your way through Mr. Deighton's tedious scrapbook.

The author is unwilling to leave to the imagination of his readers the importance of the [Hitler] Minutes, and his intuition may well be justified since with the encumbrance of an imagination how could a reader plow through such passages as abound in *XPD?*

" 'Oh, my God,' said the M.I.5 man [on hearing about the Minutes from M.I.6]. 'Every last bloody friend Britain has in the world would be enraged overnight if this sort of stuff was ever made public.' " That's in case the reader is unwilling to imagine the gravity of the Hitler Minutes. It is, unhappily, characteristic of Mr. Deighton's verbal imprecision that he should at once urge that such Minutes are unique, and refer to them as "this sort of stuff," i.e., like just another embezzlement.

But Mr. Deighton has not hit his stride. Further on in the conversation the head of M.I.6 says to the head of M.I.5, "Do you realize what this would do to our delicately balanced economy? Foreign investors would flee from sterling and the stock market would crash . . . the social consequences of that would be terrible to contemplate." The reader at such a point would welcome the collapse of sterling in place of any prolongation of such conversation between the wooden Indians who by agonies of affirmative action have been elevated to chiefs of British Intelligence.

Perhaps there are readers who expect that admirals of the ocean fleet speak to each other in such fashion, but, in Mr. Deighton's book, so also speak the mates. . . . One has the sensation of being in a movie theater reading subtitles written by a translator unfamiliar with the idiom. The author's anxiety to stress the importance of the Minutes does not let up: "But we are playing for big stakes, my friend. Who knows what money can accrue from a careful and skillful utilization of this fine asset? But make no mistake about the price of failure. How long do you think it will be before they make . . . an attempt upon your life too?" It eludes understanding how such tone deafness can make its way into print, even if what was intended was merely a few Xeroxed copies of a screen script for Hollywood.

Such tusheries beget a similar treatment of violence. Example: "Billy Stein had no way of knowing who they were, because their killers had hindered identification by cutting off and taking away the hands and heads of both men." Good for a quick jolt, until the reader wonders why the killers' anxiety to hinder identification didn't prompt them to remove the victims' bodies from their home.

Historical invention is justified in spy novels. But (I think) the invention should not be pressed so hard as to suggest that the author is begging the reader to believe that It Was Actually So. In the concluding chapter—which gives us the only ingenious surprise in this endless volume—Mr. Deighton overdocuments his thesis, so to speak, as if whispering to the reader: "Just between you and me, such an encounter between Churchill and Hitler *did* once take place."

If so, it was the lesser of the two villainies that confront the reader on closing the covers of *XPD*.

William F. Buckley, Jr. *The New York Times Book Review*. May 3, 1981, pp. 12, 31

Len Deighton published *Berlin Game* in 1983, followed it up with *Mexico Set* and now comes forward with *London Match*. The analogy with tennis is sketchy, since a good many games have to be played to win a set and several sets to win a match. But we are, I suppose, meant to conclude that by the end of the present volume there has been a decisive climax to a long and complex action, and that one player or side has gained a victory. The characters, however, turn out to have little sense of this. "It's not game, set, and match to anyone," the protagonist says on the final page. "It never is."

Is this perhaps a neat way of hinting that there may be more to come about Bernard Samson of London Central, his wife Fiona—whose sheer inconceivability establishes once and for all the robust character of Mr. Deighton's imagination—and a prodigal array of men and women nearly all of whom have some connection with espionage? If this be so, the writer is well entitled to his reluctance to have done with them and their environments in London, Mexico City, West and East Berlin. The characters, although liable to bore a little during their frequently over-extended verbal fencings, are tenaciously true to themselves even if not quite to human nature. Ben Jonson himself would have approved of them. The places, whether urban or rural, can be described only as triumphs alike of painstaking observation and striking descriptive power.

Sometimes, indeed, Mr. Deighton's linguistic resourcefulness is at odds with *vraisemblance,* but this happens less frequently than in the earlier books. In *Mexico Set,* for example, we come on somebody with "a hard unyielding face, smooth like a carefully carved *netsuke* handled by generations of collectors, and darkening as elephant tusk darkens when locked away and deprived of light." It seems not probable that this elegant fancy should come to Samson when it does.

With what he thinks of as an English upper crust Mr. Deighton is linguistically less assured. Thus a woman called Daphne has, we are told, the loud voice and upperclass accent that go with weekends in large unheated country houses, where everyone talks about horses and reads Dick Francis paperbacks. This is fair enough, down even to Dick Francis. But then Daphne suddenly says, "I'm sorry we can't go into the lounge." In England (as Mr. Deighton, who is London born, ought to know) only quite shockingly vulgar and plebeian people call a drawing-room or living-room a lounge. Lounges are located in hotels or at airports. Daphne has let Mr. Deighton down.

London Match is full of this class stuff, which is conceived of largely in terms of expensive dressing and eating and drinking, with plenty of authentic brand names thrown in. This general expensiveness, although irritating and often seemingly no more than inconsequent padding, is by no means without its function in the total picture. It all comes to us from Bernard Samson on a note of ready compliance masking alienation, and we thus feel him to be what a secret agent should essentially be: a loner in disguise.

But what is this book—what are these books—*about?* The answer, if it has to be given in a word, is treachery. Is such-and-such a man or woman a double agent, or susceptible of being "turned"? If apparently successfully "turned," is the success illusory and the agent's true allegiance still where it began? In *Berlin Game,* indeed, there is somebody in East Berlin who has been transmitting to England specific information in the field of economics and finance. But in general the rival secret services are concerned only with their rivalry. And at London Central, there is another and wholly interiorized network of suspicions and treacheries. Everybody—to express the thing loosely—is after everybody else's job. Almost everybody, moreover, is after—or suspected of being after—everybody else's husband or wife. The spectacle is not without a certain power to entertain. But, like Restoration comedy, it is a purely speculative scene of things.

J. I. M. Stewart. *Washington Post Book World.*
December 15, 1985, pp. 1, 14

DELANY, SAMUEL R. (1942–   )

Delany is, of course, deeply concerned with myth; no doubt, any science fiction writer must be so concerned, since the writing of science fiction is, at its best, a myth-making process. However, Delany does not concern himself with any particular myth so much as he concerns himself with the rationale behind all myths; that is, he explores the reason why men need and create myths. Delany is essentially concerned, not with ideas, but men; he allows his characters to create mythos out of other characters, and then proceed to show the human truth that is masked by the mythic façade.

Delany chooses to explore the rationale of human myth making. His heroes are very often poets, musicians, singers—figures who may be termed "prophets" or "seers." In *The Einstein Intersection,* for example, he postulates a universe in which the figures of imagination and myth are real; and the artist-hero, Lo Lobey, assumes responsibility for confronting and dominating a variety of mythical creatures, including dragons, minotaurs, and, ultimately, "Kid Death."

In his novel *Nova,* Delany again includes an artist among his major characters; in this case, Mouse, a Greek-Turkish Gypsy jack-of-all-trades who, finding vocal expression difficult because of a congenital defect of the larynx, expresses himself through sound and color by means of a technologically sophisticated instrument called a "sensory syrinx." Although Mouse is not precisely the "hero" of *Nova,* it is he who ultimately becomes the most important figure, as I shall try to demonstrate.

The nominal hero of the novel, Lorq Von Ray, can indeed be typified as a "Frontier hero," a gigantic figure who reaches into the unknown depths of space to bring back wealth and power in the form of Illyrion, a powerful element formed in the explosion of a star (that is, a nova).

Because of the damage done to his nervous system, Von Ray, while successful, is unable to tell of his success. It is, therefore, the role of Mouse, who had been among Von Ray's crew on this voyage, to tell the tale for him; to portray, in sound and color on the "sensory syrinx," the myth of

Von Ray's quest. We can see in this novel that, while heroes exist and fill certain roles, the hero is nothing without the singer, or myth maker, to carry the tale to the people, and interpret it for them. Ultimately, the singer or myth maker is the true hero of his own myth.

It can be deduced from such examples as the works of Delany that, while science fiction is, indeed, literature of ideas and essentially concerned with myth, we cannot isolate any single myth or cluster of myths that science fiction is concerned with. Moreover, it must be seen that, in those novels which are concerned with the myth-making process, individuated characters are not . . . inconsequential. It is true that, in the "myth" which the singer-hero finally produces, individuated character may be lost, and replaced by a personification of some idea; but, if we are to study the myth-making process, as Delany does, we must see very clearly the individual and action upon which the myth is based, if only to better understand the new creatures who exist only in the myth.

Ronald M. Jacobs. The CEA Critic. March 1974,
pp. 37–39

The book in question is Delany's collection of critical essays and reviews called The Jewel-Hinged Jaw; Notes of the Language of Science Fiction. Grammatical, stylistic, and factual howlers abound. But when one actually experiences the clotted precocity of his prose, with its uneasy condescension and agglutinative gumminess, then the multitude of typos and other errors does seem more forgiveable, because translatorese is always hard to get a grip on; the Rube Goldberg unworkableness of much of the writing in this book, especially in the earlier and middle essays collected, does in fact make the task of winkling out paraphrasable content almost impossible. Ultimately I failed. I could not even patch together an adequate sense of what I had failed to understand; after all, as Delany does say in a clear moment, style and content are intersecting models of one another. I'm paraphrasing him. At the heart of this failure of mine—beyond the word-deaf gaucheries of the style, beyond the intrusive self-congratulatory garish foregrounding of the auctorial voice with all its morose cheeriness and duckpond aggro— lay a sense that when I did think I understood the terms and assumptions shaping a paragraph, by the dint of a lot of deconstruction work, what I was left with was a kind of shambles strewn with disqualified data and beheaded arguments, a spastic Guernica.

Bits of the arguments about the nature of science fiction as opposed to "mundane" literature, though tendentious and embarrassing in their attempts to restrict the imaginative scope theoretically realizable within a "mundane" text, are at least arousing. And the late long essay on Ursula K. Le Guin's The Dispossessed (1974) is a brilliant demolition job. Delany is at his best when he's forced to stick close to a given text.

John Clute. The Magazine of Fantasy and Science
Fiction. January 1979, pp. 45–49

Some writers in the science fiction genre have been accused of not having all the lights on in their marquees. Samuel R. Delany, on the other hand, is charged with having so many lights on in his that what is spelled out there is sometimes lost in the brilliance and glare.

Delany, who surfaced in the sixties, is the award-winning author of brilliant shorts ("Aye, and Gomorrah," "Driftglass") and novels *(The Einstein Intersection, Babel-17)* and of the long self-indulgent critical failure, *Dhalgren. . . .*

Delany is a wordsmith, a craftsman who creates images that are by turns shocking and full of wonder. His best works make their own pictures. He certainly doesn't need this kind of package, or this kind of hype from his publisher.

The stories range from award winner to throwaway (though the worst that can be said of his stories, like "We in Some Strange Power's Employ, Move on a Rigorous Line," included here, is that they don't *work*). A couple of pieces of major Delany, an okay story, some trivialities, and lots of Quaker Puffed Air between the words.

Howard Waldrop. Washington Post Book World.
August 30, 1981, p. 6

"Science fiction has been a kind of marginal writing," according to Samuel R. Delany, "a highly conventionalized writing in many ways; so you have a writing situation where you have many hard and fast conventions. Of course, looked at from another direction, you can do absolutely *anything* in it. But when you can do *absolutely* anything, what you tend to do is to fall back on the conventions."

Delany went from being a middle-class black youth in Harlem to become one of the top ten best selling science fiction writers by the age of forty. Science fiction offered him not only a means to recognition as a writer, and a means to earning a living, but it also offered him a fascinating combination of freedom and restraints.

But freedom for what? What conventions does science fiction have that Delany would want to use? If science fiction offers freedom, what is it that Delany wants to say? At what point does society press upon Delany so much that he desires this freedom?

So much of the non–science fiction literature of our society is based on exclusively heterosexual assumptions. On the other hand, most science fiction is not really sexual at all. The characters and plots of science fiction are not usually concerned with sex. If sex is mentioned, it is usually heterosexual.

From about the age of nine or ten, Delany knew he was more interested in sexual relations with men than with women. He was married to Marilyn Hacker in 1961 and divorced in 1980, and fathered a child, Iva Alyxander in 1974; but his primary sexuality has been that of a gay man, growing up gay in a predominantly heterosexual culture.

Society treats gays nearly as poorly as blacks; few science fiction writers are gay, and few public figures in any field are willing to identify themselves as gay to their public.

But all through his work, one can see where male homosexuality serves as the model for the situation the story describes. One thinks immediately of his award winning story in Harlan Ellison's *Dangerous Visions* anthology, "Aye, and Gomorrah. . . ." Even though it features a woman buying the sexual services of someone who was once, biologically, male, the situation, jokes, and exchanges that occur in the story are far closer to those that occur between young men selling themselves sexually to older males, as occurs in all the large cities of the world. They are not the exchanges of the more common heterosexual prostitution.

Even in the early novels that make up Delany's *Fall of the Towers* trilogy, there are references to homosexuality among the sexually segregated prisoners who mine the valuable "tetron" ore.

Sexuality and sexual roles are a strong part of all of Delany's works. He has dealt with both heterosexuality and homosexuality well, and has been one of the pioneers in science fiction who was able to write about sexuality and sexual roles. He still writes for a mixed audience of gay and straight. His own sexuality has clearly shaped the way he thinks and writes about sex, sexuality, and sexual roles.

Seth McEvoy. Samuel R. Delany (New York:
Ungar, 1984), pp. 11–13

Perhaps the most exciting event in science fiction this month is the publication of Samuel R. Delany's new novel *Stars in My Pocket Like Grains of Sand*. It is the first half of what the author calls a "diptych," but it stands well on its own, both as a story of complex human relationships and as a tour de force of novelistic structure.

Delany has not written a science fiction novel for almost ten years. He first rose to prominence with such novels as *Babel-17* and *Nova,* works that superimposed, upon the old cliché-prone space opera plots, dazzling new linguistic techniques. His gargantuan *Dhalgren*, over a thousand pages of recursive, dense writing, was a kind of Rubicon for him, and was the most vehemently debated science fiction novel of the midseventies. Traditionalists condemned the novel's apparent lack of plot and what they perceived as murky self-indulgence. His next novel, *Triton,* was an uneasy compromise between the new Delany and the old; there followed a series of works of literary criticism, heavily influenced by semiotics and infiltrated with jargon, sometimes undigested. Then came a fantasy series set in the universe of Neveryon, which took the trappings of sword-and-sorcery and lampooned them with such lofty humor that few saw the jokes.

But the novel in hand marks a return to science fiction . . . to the galaxy-busting universes with which Delany first made his name. The tightly controlled plotting is back. What's new is that he has distilled his decade of experimentation and critical soul-searching and finally made it all work. This is an astonishing new Delany, more richly textured, smoother, more colorful than ever before—and without the lumps of pretension that have disfigured other work of the past few years. This is one of Delany's finest novels, and as such must be considered one of the finest in science fiction.

Stars in My Pocket Like Grains of Sand is constructed as a series of set-pieces, and set-pieces within set-pieces. In the prologue we meet Rat Korga, a man reduced to zombie-like servitude by means of "radical anxiety termination," a sort of super-lobotomy that rids one forever of psychological problems—and much else besides.

The long central portion of the book chronicles roughly a day in the life of Marq Dyeth, an urbane citizen of the galaxy who inhabits an astonishingly complex universe. He is an industrial diplomat, and as such must deal constantly with planets with wildly differing societies and mores. There is a galactic information war going on, one of whose weapons is the destruction by massive cultural pollution of pristine planets. In Marq's overculture of humans and aliens, all sentient beings are known as "she" and all sex objects as "he"; and by this tiny shift in language Delany renders insecure all the reader's notions about how a culture should behave. To this world comes Rat Korga. He and Marq fall in love—and their relationship literally sunders the fabric of galactic civilization.

That Delany actually brings off so hyperbolic a plot is astonishing. But more than that: there are enough novel images and weird concepts for a dozen books here, and they come at you relentlessly. Despite its length, this is not a flabby book. It is terse and muscular and explosive, and its author more in control than ever before. It is Delany's first true masterpiece.

Somtow Sucharitkul. *Washington Post Book World*. January 27, 1985, p. 11

In *The Einstein Intersection* (1967), Samuel R. Delany made his own eloquent statement of the science fiction genre. The hero Lobey is a twenty-three-year-old freak. The villain is Kid Death, an obvious representation of Billy the Kid; but also Kid Death is a specific monster out of mythology, and in one episode even becomes the Bull of Minos. Lobey in turn takes on various characteristics. In the Bull of Minos sequence, he becomes Theseus, and strangles the Bull in a cave, later meeting Kid Death on a color television screen, recognizing him for what he is. Eventually another figure enters the story—this one called Green-eye. Green-eye is a Christ figure, the only one Kid Death cannot control. Lobey finally manifests his own power—as great in its way as Kid Death's and Green-eye's: Lobey can play music. It is the creation of music—read, art—that makes Lobey/Delany triumph in the end. Even Green-eye/Christ must use the artist to guide and instruct. Implicit in the entire reading process, and indeed in the wanderings of the hero Lobey, is the difficulty of distinguishing reality from illusion. The difference between the real and the illusive during the 1960s was a most important daily consideration. The inability to differentiate between the two—because of the drug culture, the Vietnam War experience, and ethnic struggles, the assassinations, the unreality of the world—led to the destruction and self-destruction of many people during that time. Delany's work reflects that and elaborates on it—in a "new" kind of science fiction vein.

Dieter Wuckel and Bruce Cassiday. *The Illustrated*
History of Science Fiction (New York: Ungar,
1989), p. 201

DOYLE, ARTHUR CONAN (1859–1930)

A detective story is usually lively reading, but we cannot pretend to think that *The Sign of Four* is up to the level of the writer's best work. It is a curious medley, and full of horrors; and surely those who play at hide and seek with the fatal treasure are a curious company. The wooden-legged convict and his fiendish misshapen little mate, the ghastly twins, the genial prizefighters, the detectives wise and foolish, and the gentle girl whose lover tells the tale, twist in and out together in a mazy dance, culminating in that mad and terrible rush down the river which ends the mystery and the treasure. Dr. Doyle's admirers will read the little volume through eagerly enough, but they will hardly care to take it up again.

The Athenaeum. December 6, 1890, p. 773

For those to whom the good, honest, breathless detective story is dear, Dr. Doyle's book, *The Adventures of Sherlock Holmes* will prove a veritable godsend. Of its kind it is excellent; there is little literary pretension about it, and there is hardly any waste of time about subtle character drawing; but incident succeeds incident with the most businesslike rapidity, and the unexpected always occurs with appropriate regularity. Of the dozen stories of which the book is made up there is not one which does not contain a thorough-paced mystery, apparently insoluble; but the solution is always satisfactorily wormed out by that marvelous amateur detective, Sherlock Holmes.

The adventures are all vastly improbable; but no matter; that has never detracted from an orthodox detective story. For genuine horror Dr. Doyle has a lively turn; in "The Speckled Band" and "The Engineer's Thumb" (mark the subtle suggestions of terror in the titles) the reader is worked up to such a pitch of nervous excitement that he is ready for almost anything; the first of these is worthy of Wilkie Collins. The chief defect of the book is the attempt to infuse vitality into Sherlock Holmes. It would have been better to leave him more of a detective machine; as it is, one gets rather wearied of his swaggering assurance, of his nights of silent thought, and of his habit of mystifying inoffensive strangers by describing to them all their little weaknesses. Still, much may be forgiven him for his wonderful cute-ness and for his hardly veiled contempt of our official detective police—a trait which is said to tell with the British public. The English is not always irreproachable: "If you will keep the two corner seats I *shall* get the tickets," for example, is bad.

The Athenaeum. November 5, 1892, p. 626

In looking over the work of Dr. Doyle during the past three or four years, one realizes with the keenest sort of regret the unfortunate mistake he made in putting an end to Sherlock Holmes. There are many tales which we lay down with disappointment simply because we feel how much better they would have been woven about the strange gifts, the personality, the omnipotence and omniscience of Sherlock Holmes. A notable story of this kind was "The Story of the Lost Special," which appeared in the columns of an English magazine about two years ago, but which, to the best of the recollection of the present writer, has not yet been brought out in book form. It was simply the story of a train—locomotive, tender, and two passenger-coaches—which, running in broad daylight through one of the most thickly populated districts of England, disappears without leaving the slightest clue of importance as to its fate. One could not readily conceive more startling and daring a plot, yet when the mystery is ultimately cleared away the whole thing seems possible enough, and had the explanation been brought about, as it should and might easily have been, by Sherlock Holmes and the science of deduction, the story would have taken rank with the very best that have come from Dr. Doyle's ingenious pen.

Arthur Bartlett Maurice. *The Bookman.* May 1900,
pp. 223–25

Sir A. Conan Doyle would appear to be deserting letters for affairs, so that it is difficult at present to judge of his true quality as a writer of fiction. Evidently he began with a more romantic feeling and a finer sense of the adventurous than he went on with. His fire seems to have decreased; he gives the impression of becoming more deliberate and less imaginative, and of attaining philosophy inconsistent with true artistry. It looks as if in his maturer years this ready writer were precipitating in the average British way. He always had an element of deliberation, such as one dissociates at once from inspiration and the "daemonic" force of art. Yet what an admirable piece of work was *The White Company,* which suffered no whit because it was descended from Charles Reade's *The Cloister and the Hearth* and Walter Scott's *Quentin Durward! Micah Clarke,* too, stands high among historical novels. . . . *Rodney Stone* is not a tale, but a cinematograph of the Regency period. It is vivid, wonderfully well studied, and understanding to a fault; but it falls short of fiction. The same hole may be picked in *The Stark Monro Letters,* which, for all that, contain some of the best material that the author has put together. It strikes one as odd and unfortunate that, with the author's power of visualizing a scene, he should have been, on the whole, so little successful in visualizing a character. He has invented some, no doubt, and several of these are in *Micah Clarke*. He has also hit upon an excellent type in Brigadier Gerard. But he shows no gallery of portraits; they lack life, but are set generally in a moving landscape. It is some kink in the imagination. The work that has made this author popular is the series of tales, admirable in their way, associated with Sherlock Holmes, a character, as is now generally known, imitated from Poe. Sherlock Holmes has so seized the popular ear that he almost alone of the abundance of men and women provided by living authors supplies a familiar reference used everywhere, an ineffaceable part of the English language. Such impression of a figure on the public is an achievement of the rarest (it is only equaled, as far as we recall at the moment, by the case of Jekyll and Hyde), but in this case it is an achievement which has little to do with letters.

The Athenaeum. January 9, 1904, p. 40

Evidently, I am growing old. Sherlock Holmes is dead, and to young readers it may be that he is not even a dear memory. But I was at an impressionable age when he burst upon the world; and so he became a part of my life, and will never, I suppose, be utterly dislodged. I cannot pass through Baker Street, even now, without thinking of him. Long ago I had decided exactly which were the two windows of the sitting room where Watson spent his wondering hours; and, only the other day, I had a rather heated dispute with a coaeval who had also long since "placed" that sitting-room— "placed" it, if you please, on the side of the street opposite to that where it really was (need I say that I mean the right-hand side as one goes towards Regent's Park?). My sentiment for Sherlock Holmes was never one of reverence unalloyed. Indeed, one of the secrets of his hold on me was that he so often amused me. I would have bartered a dozen of his subtlest deductions for that great moment when he said (presumably on the eve of his creator's departure for a lecturing tour in America) "It is always a joy to me to meet an American, for I am one of those who believe that the folly of a monarch and the blundering of a minister in far gone years will not prevent our children from being some day citizens of the same worldwide country under a flag which shall be a quartering of the Union Jack with the Stars and Stripes." I learned that speech by heart, years ago; and, to this day, I generally try it on any American to whom I am introduced—sometimes with most surprising results. Sir Arthur (then mere Mr.) Conan Doyle's own attitude toward life, and his own extraordinary versions of the familiar things around us—what would Sherlock have been without these assets?

Max Beerbohm. *The Saturday Review.* May 6,
1905, pp. 373–76

Sir Arthur Conan Doyle certainly weakened his excellent series of stories about Sherlock Holmes by being occasionally serious; especially he weakened it by introducing a sort of sneer at Edgar Allan Poe's Dupin, with whom he sustained no comparison. Sherlock Holmes's bright notions were like bright Cockney flowers grown in very shallow soil in a suburban garden; Dupin's were flowers growing on a vast, dark tree of thought. Hence Dupin, when he quits the subject of crime, talks in the tongue of permanent culture of the relations of imagination to analysis or of the relations of the supernatural to law. But the greatest error of the Sherlock Holmes conception remains to be remarked: I mean the error which represented the detective as indifferent to philosophy and poetry, and which seemed to imply that philosophy and poetry would not be good for a detective. Here he is at once eclipsed by the bolder and more brilliant brain of Poe, who carefully states that Dupin not only admired and trusted poetry, but was himself a poet. Sherlock Holmes would have been a better detective if he had been a philosopher, if he had been a poet, nay, if he had been a lover. It is remarkable to notice (I assume that you are as intimate with Dr. Watson's narratives as you should be)—it is remarkable to notice that the very same story in which the biographer describes Holmes's inaccessibility to love and such emotions, and how necessary it was to the clear balance of his logic, is the very same story in which Holmes is beaten by a woman because he does not know whether a certain man is her fiancé or her lawyer. If he had been in love he might have known well enough.

The only real danger is that Conan Doyle, by spreading the notion that practical logic must be unpoetical, may have encouraged the notion, too common already, that imagination must be absent-minded. It is a false and dangerous doctrine that the poet must be absent-minded. The purely imaginative man could never be absent-minded. He would perceive the significance of things near to him as clearly as he perceived the significance of things far off.

The real moral of the popularity of the adventures of Sherlock Holmes lies in the existence of a great artistic neglect. There are a large number of perfectly legitimate forms of art which are almost entirely neglected by good artists—the detective story, the farce, the book of boyish adventure, the melodrama, the music-hall song. The real curse of these things is not that they are too much regarded, but that they are not regarded enough; that they are despised even by those who write them. Conan Doyle triumphed and triumphed deservedly, because he took his art seriously, because he lavished a hundred little touches of real knowledge and genuine picturesqueness on the police novelette. He substituted for the customary keen eyes and turned-up collar of the conventional detective a number of traits, external and pictorial, indeed, but honestly appropriate to the logical genius, traits such as an immeasurable love of music and an egotism which was abstract and, therefore, almost unselfish. Above all, he surrounded his detective with a genuine atmosphere of the poetry of London. He called up before the imagination a new and visionary city in which every cellar and alley hid as many weapons as the rocks and heather bushes of Roderick Dhu. By this artistic seriousness he raised one at least of the popular forms of art to the level which it ought to occupy.

He wrote the best work in a popular form, and he found that because it was the best it was also the most popular. Men needed stories, and had been content to take bad ones; and they were right, for a story in itself is a marvelous and excellent thing, and a bad story is better than no story, just as half a loaf is better than no bread. But when a detective story was written by a man who refused to despise his art, who carried all their dreams to fulfillment, they preferred him to the bungling and irresponsible authors who had catered for them before.

> G. K. Chesterton. *A Handful of Authors: Essays on*
> *Books & Writers* ([t.c.]: Sheed and Ward, 1953),
> pp. 171–74

It is a great convenience to the critic to be able to compare what he is writing about with something else. But I cannot think of anything to which to compare Sherlock Holmes. He does not seem to be descended from either Sergeant Cuff or Monsieur Dupin. His relationship to Lecoq is quite superficial. He has had, on the other hand, a numerous progeny. So has Professor Moriarty. Only Mycroft Holmes, that colossal genius, has, so far as I know, no descendants. In Arsene Lupin, even in Raffles, we distinguish the features of the Robin Hood type. But Holmes was always reticent about his family: in fact he has no family to be reticent about. Another, and perhaps the greatest of the Sherlock Holmes mysteries is this: that when we talk of him we invariably fall into the fancy of his existence. Collins, after all, is more real to his readers than Cuff; Poe is more real than Dupin; but Sir A. Conan Doyle, the eminent spiritualist of whom we read in Sunday papers, the author of a number of exciting stories which we read years ago and have forgotten, what has he to do with Holmes? The only analogies are such as make the case more puzzling. We can think of Sam Weller without thinking of Dickens, or of Falstaff or Hamlet without thinking of Shakespeare: yet we do not compare Conan Doyle with Dickens or Shakespeare. Even Holmes's reality is a reality of its own kind. Never is he impeccable. He employs the most incredible disguises.

It is of course the dramatic ability, rather than the pure detective ability, that does it. But it is a dramatic ability applied with great cunning and concentration; it is not spilt about. The content of the story may be poor; but the form is nearly always perfect. We are so well worked up by the dramatic preparation that we accept the conclusion—even when, as in "The Red-Headed League," it is perfectly obvious from the beginning. Also, it must be remarked that the author (for we must mention Sir Arthur now and then) shows wisdom or instinct in keeping the sentimental interest down. Several times he trips. But on the whole Sir Arthur kept the sentiment in its place; and it is superfluous sentiment that dates a detective story. . . .

[Every writer of detective fiction] owes something to Holmes. And every critic of The Novel who has a theory about the reality of characters in fiction, would do well to consider Holmes. There is no rich humanity, no deep and cunning psychology and knowledge of the human heart about him; he is obviously a formula. He has not the reality of any great character of Dickens or Thackeray or George Eliot or Meredith or Hardy; or Jane Austen or the Brontës or Virginia Woolf or James Joyce: yet, as I suggested, he is just as real to us as Falstaff or the Wellers. He is not even a very good detective. But I am not sure that Sir Arthur Conan Doyle is not one of the great dramatic writers of his age.

T. S. Eliot. The Criterion. April 1929, pp. 553–56

Conan Doyle took up the Poe detective story formula and galvanized it into life and popularity. He cut out the elaborate psychological introductions, or restated them in crisp dialogue. He brought into prominence what Poe had only lightly touched upon—the deduction of staggering conclusions from trifling indications in the Dumas-Cooper-Gaboriau manner. He was sparkling, surprising, and short. It was the triumph of the epigram.

A comparison of the Sherlock Holmes tales with the Dupin tales shows clearly how much Doyle owed to Poe, and, at the same time, how greatly he modified Poe's style and formula. Read, for instance, the opening pages of *The Murders in the Rue Morgue,* which introduce Dupin, and compare them with the first chapter of *A Study in Scarlet.*

See how the sturdy independence of Watson adds salt and savor to the eccentricities of Holmes, and how flavorless beside it is the hero worshiping self-abnegation of Dupin's friend. See, too, how the concrete details of daily life in Baker Street lift the story out of the fantastic and give it a solid reality. The Baker Street menáge has just that touch of humorous commonplace which appeals to British readers.

Compare, also, the conversational styles of Holmes and Dupin, and the reasons for Holmes's popularity become clearer than ever. Holmes has enriched English literature with more than one memorable aphorism and turn of speech.

So, with Sherlock Holmes, the ball—the original nucleus deposited by Edgar Allan Poe nearly forty years earlier—was at last set rolling. As it went, it swelled into a vast mass—it set off others—it became a spate—a torrent—an avalanche of mystery fiction.

Dorothy L. Sayers. Introduction. The Omnibus of
Crime (London: Payson and Clarke Ltd., 1929),
pp. 9–47

The whole Sherlock Holmes saga is a triumphant illustration of art's supremacy over life. Perhaps no fiction character ever created has become so charmingly real to his readers. It is not that we take our blessed Sherlock too seriously. . . . But Holmes is pure anesthesia. We read the stories again and again; perhaps most of all for the little introductory interiors which give a glimpse of 221B Baker Street.

The character of Holmes, Doyle has told us, was at any rate partly suggested by his student memories of Dr. Joseph Bell of the Edinburgh Infirmary, whose diagnostic intuitions used to startle his patients and pupils. But there was abundant evidence that the invention of the scientific detective conformed to a fundamental logic in Doyle's own temper. One example was his ingenuity in transmitting news of the war in cipher to British prisoners in Germany. This he did by sending books in which he had put needle pricks under various printed letters so as to spell out the desired messages; but beginning with the third chapter, believing that the German censor would examine the earlier chapters more carefully. Of his humor there is a pleasant income tax story. In his first year of independent medical practice his earnings were. £154, and when the income tax paper arrived he filled it up to show that he was not liable. The authorities returned the form with the words *Most Unsatisfactory* scrawled across it. He returned it again with the subscription *I entirely agree*. As many readers must have guessed, *Round the Red Lamp* and *The Stark Munro Letters* were very literally drawn from his own experiences in medicine.

Those of us who in earliest boyhood gave our hearts to Conan Doyle, and have had from him so many hours of good refreshment, find our affection unshakable. What other man led a fuller and heartier and more masculine life? Doctor, whaler, athlete, writer, speculator, dramatist, historian, war correspondent, spiritualist, he was always also the infracaninophile— the helper of the underdog. Generous personality, his virtues had always something of the fresh vigor of the amateur, keen, open-minded, flexible, imaginative. If, as Doyle utterly believed, the spirits of the dead persist and can communicate, there is none that could have more wholesome news to impart to us than that brave and energetic lover of life.

A blessing, then, on those ophthalmic citizens who did not go to that office at 2 Devonshire Place, near Harley Street, where in 1891 Dr. A. Conan Doyle set up consulting rooms as an eye specialist. It was there, waiting for the patients who never came, that he began to see the possibilities in Sherlock Holmes. No wonder that Dr. Watson too sometimes rather neglected his practice.

Christopher Morley. *Internal Revenue* (New York:
Harper & Row, 1933), pp. 70–80

Too many ecstatic superlatives have been written about Sherlock Holmes; yet it is no exaggeration to say that after more than half a century he remains the best known and best loved detective in literature. But for him there might have been no detective story in the modern sense.

Stanley J. Kunitz and Howard Haycraft. *Twentieth
Century Authors* (New York; H. W. Wilson,
1942), pp. 396–97

My contention is that Sherlock Holmes *is* literature on a humble but not ignoble level, whereas the mystery writers most in vogue now are not. The old stories are literature, not because of the conjuring tricks and the puzzles, not because of the lively melodrama, which they have in common with many other detective stories, but by virtue of imagination and style. These are fairy tales, as Conan Doyle intimated in his preface to his last collection, and they are among the most amusing of fairy tales, and not among the least distinguished.

The Sherlock Holmes stories, almost as much as the Alice books or as Edward Lear's nonsense, were the casual products of a life the main purpose of which was something else, but creations that in some sense got detached from their author and flew away and had a life of their own. Conan Doyle, it seems, worked conscientiously to document his historical romances, which he considered his serious work, but he regarded Holmes and Watson as the paper dolls of rather ridiculous and undignified potboilers, and he paid so little attention to what he wrote about them that the stories are full of inconsistencies, which Doyle never bothered to correct. . . .

The stories have also both form and style of a kind very much superior to what one finds in our padded novels, though sometimes, it seems to me, the requirements of length for short stories in the *Strand Magazine* compelled Doyle somewhat to skimp his endings. . . . The writing, of course, is full of clichés, but these clichés are dealt out with a ring which gives them a kind of value, while the author makes speed and saves space so effectively that we are rarely in danger of getting bogged down in anything boring. And the clichés of situation and character are somehow made to function, too, for the success of the general effect.

Edmund Wilson. *Classics and Commercials* (New York: Farrar, Straus and Giroux, 1950), pp. 267–268, 270–71

It isn't easy for an author to remain a pleasant human being: both success and failure are usually of a crippling kind. There are so many opportunities for histrionics, hysterics, waywardness, self-importance; within such very wide limits a writer can do what he likes and go where he likes, and a human being has seldom stood up so well to such a test of freedom as Doyle did. The eccentric figure of his partner, Dr. Budd, may stride like a giant through the early pages of his biography, but in memory he dwindles into the far distance, and in the foreground we see the large, sturdy, working shoulders, a face so commonplace that it has the effect of a time-worn sculpture representing some abstract quality like Kindness or Patience, but never, one would mistakenly have said, Imagination or Poetry.

Graham Greene. *The Lost Childhood* (New York: Viking, 1951), p. 88

Like all true disciples, I have always recurrently dipped into the Sacred Writings (called by the vulgar the Sherlock Holmes stories) for refreshment;

but not long ago I reread them from beginning to end, and I was struck by a singular fact that reminded me of the dog in the night. The singular fact about the dog in the night, as we all know, was that it didn't bark; and the singular fact about Holmes in the night is that he is never seen going to bed. The writer of the tales, the Watson person, describes over and over again, in detail, all the other minutiæ of that famous household—suppers, breakfasts, arrangement of furniture, rainy evenings at home—but not once are we shown either Holmes or Watson going to bed. I wondered, why not? Why such unnatural and obdurate restraint, nay, concealment, regarding one of the pleasantest episodes of the daily routine? . . . Right at the very start, on page 9 of *A Study in Scarlet,* I found this:

> It was rare for him to be up after ten at night, and he had invariably breakfasted and gone out before I rose in the morning.

I was indescribably shocked. How had so patent a clue escaped so many millions of readers through the years? That was, that could only be, a woman speaking of a man. In the second paragraph I saw:

> The reader may set me down as a hopeless busybody, when I confess how much this man stimulated my curiosity, and how often I endeavored to break through the reticence which he showed on all that concerned himself.

You bet she did. She would. Poor Holmes! She doesn't even bother to employ one of the stock euphemisms, such as, "I wanted to understand him better," or, "I wanted to share things with him." She proclaims it with brutal directness, "I endeavored to break through the reticence." Indubitably she was a female, but wife or mistress? I went on. Two pages later I found:

> . . . his powers upon the violin . . . at my request he has played me some of Mendelssohn's *Lieder* . . .

Imagine a man asking another man to play him some of Mendelssohn's *Lieder* on a violin!
And on the next page:

> I rose somewhat earlier than usual, and found that Sherlock Holmes had not yet finished his breakfast. . . . My place had not been laid nor my coffee prepared. With . . . petulance . . . I rang the bell and gave a curt intimation that I was ready. Then I picked up a magazine from the table and attempted to while away the time with it, while my companion munched silently at his toast.

A man does not munch silently at his toast when breakfasting with his mistress; or, if he does, it won't be long until he gets a new one. Then who was this person whose nom de plume was "Doctor Watson"? Where did she come from? What was she like? What was her name before she snared Holmes?

Let us see what we can do about the name, by methods that Holmes himself might have used. . . . There are sixty of the tales all told. The first step is to set them down in chronological order, and number them from 1 to 60. Now, which shall we take first? Evidently the reason why Watson was at such pains to conceal her name in this clutter of titles was to *mystify* us, so the number to start with should be the most *mystical* number, namely seven. And to make it doubly sure, we shall make it seven times seven, which is 49. Very well. The forty-ninth tale is "The Adventure of the Illustrious Client." We of course discard the first four words, "The Adventure of the," which are repeated in most of the titles. Result: "ILLUSTRIOUS CLIENT."

The next most significant thing about Watson is her (his) constant effort to convince us that those things happened exactly as she (he) tells them; that they are on the *square*. Good. The first square of an integer is the integer 4. We take the title of the 4th tale and get "RED-HEADED LEAGUE."

We proceed to elimination. Of all the factors that contribute to an ordinary man's success, which one did Holmes invariably exclude, or eliminate? Luck. In crap-shooting, what are the lucky numbers? Seven and eleven. But we have already used 7, which eliminates it, so there is nothing left but 11. The 11th tale is about the "ENGINEER'S THUMB."

Next, what was Holmes's age at the time he moved to Baker Street? Twenty-seven. The 27th tale is the adventure of the "NORWOOD BUILDER." And what was Watson's age? Twenty-six. The 26th tale is the adventure of the "EMPTY HOUSE." But there is no need to belabor the obvious. Just as it is a simple matter to decipher the code of the Dancing Men when Holmes has once put you on the right track, so can you, for yourself, make the additional required selections now that I have explained the method. And you will inevitably get what I got:

> *Illustrious Client*
> *Red-Headed League*
> *Engineer's Thumb*
> *Norwood Builder*
> *Empty House*
>
> *Wisteria Lodge*
> *Abbey Grange*
> *Twisted Lip*
> *Study in Scarlet*
> *Orange Pips*
> *Noble Bachelor*

And, acrostically simple, the initial letters read down, the carefully hidden secret is ours. Her name was Irene Watson.

But not so fast. Is there any way of checking that? Of discovering her name by any other method, say a priori? We can try and see. A woman wrote the stories about Sherlock Holmes, that has been demonstrated; and that woman was his wife. Does there appear, anywhere in the stories, a woman whom Holmes fell for? Whom he really cottoned to? Indeed there does. ''A Scandal in Bohemia'' opens like this:

> To Sherlock Holmes she is always *the* woman. . . . In his eyes she eclipses and predominates the whole of her sex.

And what was the name of *the* woman? Irene!

But, you say, not Irene Watson, but Irene Adler. Certainly. Watson's whole purpose, from beginning to end, was to confuse and bewilder us regarding her identity. So note that name well. Adler. What is an adler, or, as it is commonly spelled, addler? An addler is one who, or that which, addles. Befuddles. Confuses. I admit I admire that stroke; it is worthy of Holmes himself. In the very act of deceiving and confusing us, she has the audacity to employ a name that brazenly announces her purpose! . . .

All this is very sketchy. I admit it. I am now collecting material for a fuller treatment of the subject, a complete demonstration of the evidence and the inevitable conclusion. It will fill two volumes, the second of which will consist of certain speculations regarding various concrete results of that long-continued and—I fear, alas—none-too-happy union. For instance, what of the parentage of Lord Peter Wimsey, who was born, I believe, around the turn of the century—about the time of the publication of ''The Adventure of the Second Stain''? That will bear looking into.

Rex Stout. Abridged from ''Watson Was a Woman''
in Howard Haycraft, *The Art of the Mystery Story*
(New York: Biblio & Tannen, 1976), pp. 311–18

When we attempt to place a final evaluation on the work of Sir Arthur Conan Doyle we must pause. Obviously in Holmes and Watson he has created two of the most popular and famous characters in literature, characters that are truly immortal in the same sense that Hamlet, Don Quixote, Tom Jones, and Tiny Tim are immortal. But after we make that statement we must also acknowledge that Conan Doyle's work belongs to a tradition that has largely gone out of style in literary study today. Doyle and other writers of his era who sought primarily to entertain—authors such as H. Rider Haggard, Edgar Rice Burroughs, H. G. Wells, and Robert Louis Stevenson— have been displaced by the tradition of cerebral ''serious'' literature that began with writers such as George Eliot, George Meredith, and, most important, Henry James.

Doyle is not ''studied'' today because there is no subtext there to study. One does not usually finish a Holmes story and ask what it ''means,'' for the story that is presented overtly is the meaning; there is essentially no covert theme to be teased out of the characters and the action. *Moby-Dick* is a novel about a whale that is really not simply a whale; *The Hound of the Baskervilles,* which is in many ways Doyle's most "literary" novel, is about a dog that in the end is really just a dog after all. And although we can see in *The Hound of the Baskervilles* a touch of naturalism, a hint of symbolism, the suggestion of a philosophical message, most critics today would relegate the novel to the category of "subliterature," because it merely entertains and does not broaden our understanding of the human condition.

But the lack of a philosophical subtext in the fiction of Conan Doyle does not mean that Doyle has no philosophy to give us. His message is somewhat easier to see in the collected body of his work than it is in any one selected story or novel. He is opposed to pettiness, greed, lying, meanness of temper, and low character. He values courage, chivalry, truth, valor, honor, and loyalty. Most of all we see in him, as we see in his fictional characters, what it means to have principles and to remain loyal to these principles—no matter what. What raises Holmes, Watson, Gerard, Challenger, Sir Nigel Loring, and Doyle himself above the masses is our assurance that these men will remain true to their convictions; they will not be compromised.

Don Richard Cox. *Arthur Conan Doyle* (New
York: Ungar, 1985), pp. 233–34

Doyle had read Edgar Allan Poe's tales and the novels of Collins and Gaboriau before creating his own detective whom he allows to mock the Chevalier Dupin and Monsieur Lecoq, maintaining that not one of them can match his powers of detection. "Numerous small fry" he calls them, none of whom could handle a really big affair. Holmes was largely modeled on Dr. Joseph Bell, Doyle's Professor of Surgery at Edinburgh University, who constantly surprised his students by a snap diagnosis or an unexpected conclusion based on logical "deduction."

Where earlier in the nineteenth century legal men had taken to crime writing it now became the turn of medical men. In a more effective way than Poe, Doyle provided his readers with a memorable hero and popularized the crime story. He understood the rapid progress being made in the natural sciences in the nineteenth century and featured the scientific approach in his story telling. In his view, close observation to factual details was the only sound basis for arriving at sensible conclusions. This modern attitude appealed to a public longing for a change from the somewhat wearied fin-de-siècle atmosphere that permeated the writing of the time. The "master" himself—Holmes— believed that when all other possibilities were exhausted the most *unlikely* possibility might be the explanation. At times Doyle pushed his detective close to the brink of irrational thought, only to bring him back to reason by the process of careful deduction. The reader was flattered that he too was required to use his intelligence. In that way he stood between Holmes and Watson and was given a definite part to play in the detection. As the plot progressed, he could search for the solution on his own. Naturally he was not as clever or knowledgeable as Holmes and the denouement always took him by surprise. Tension, maintained to the end, allowed the reader to remain happy in the knowledge that he was at least as intelligent as the good Dr. Watson, if not more so. In this fashion Doyle turned a mere monologue into a lively dialogue.

In contrast to his literary ancestors, in particular Poe's Dupin, Holmes did not limit his detective work to the armchair variety. It was full of action as he roamed through London, going into pubs, disguising himself at times like Vidocq, and spending whole nights following up clues. He might perhaps get lost in lonely places, yet he usually managed to arrive at the scene of the crime before the police.

Doyle, who had always considered himself a historical novelist rather than a detective-story writer, tired of the exploits of Holmes and killed him off in a duel to the death with master criminal Professor Moriarty at Reichenbach Falls in 1893. Nevertheless, readers demanded his return. Doyle had to give in.

In 1902 Holmes appeared again in a sensational case—*The Hound of the Baskervilles*—related by Watson in the role of executor. Doyle had heard the old legend of a ghost hound from a friend, and decided to turn it into a detective story. In the novel the tension is maintained by interrogation, quick questions and answers, and a series of exciting adventures. Even with all the success Sherlock Holmes had brought him, Doyle never forgot the primary rule of writing—"Tell a good story." . . .

The success of the Holmes stories is reflected in the many translations and imitations that were made, some pretty poor and none really fitting into the category of literature. At the coronation of Edward VII, Conan Doyle was knighted. The honor was bestowed on him for a nonfiction book he wrote on the Boer War. Many maintained that it was Sherlock Holmes who really earned it for him. It was perhaps a lucky coincidence that *The Hound of the Baskervilles* appeared at that time, fascinating the public then as it does to this very day. Among the many congratulations Doyle received for this honor was one for Sherlock Holmes!

Waltraud Woeller. The Literature of Crime and
Detection (New York: Ungar, 1988), pp. 90–101

Although Sherlock Holmes will always be the most memorable fictional creation of Conan Doyle, Doyle's stories of adventure bordering upon science fiction, as typified by the Professor Challenger series, have also had a strong following and made an undeniable impact upon fiction and the twentieth-century's popularizer of fiction-film. The first story in the series—*The Lost World* (1912)—is also the most important, for it has practically created its own cinematic genre. For the hero of this novel, Professor Challenger himself, Doyle turned to his medical training at Edinburgh, and, as he did when he selected Professor Joseph Bell as the model for Holmes, created a fictional character from a real-life character he had never forgotten. This time, however, the professor Doyle selected was not the shrewdly deductive, intellectual figure he had been attracted to in the person of Bell. Professor Challenger was based on Professor William Rutherford, an outspoken, eccentric physician with a bushy beard and somewhat explosive temperament. One could scarcely imagine a figure more the opposite of the quiet aesthetic Holmes. Even though quite different from the more quiet detective, Challenger became a popular fictional figure, and *The Lost World*, which some have compared to the tales of Jules Verne (most notably *A Journey to the Center of the Earth*) and others to *Robinson Crusoe*, inspired a silent movie made during Doyle's lifetime, and countless other movie variations on the theme, including the famous *King Kong*.

There is not, of course, a giant gorilla in *The Lost World*, but the intrepid adventurers, the strange isolated plateau peopled by savages unfamiliar with the outside world, and most of all, the dinosaurs and unknown reptiles that inhabit this "lost world"—these elements of Doyle's novel, like Holmes, have taken on a life of their own.

The epigraph to the novel—

> I have wrought my simple plan
> If I give one hour of joy
> To the boy who's half a man,
> Or the man who's half a boy

—reflects this adventure tale's intended audience, an audience of males seeking escape—escape from mothers and wives, schools and jobs, problems and responsibilities. And as a fantasy-adventure this novel succeeded in capturing and holding thousands of these readers under its spell. Just as important, for Conan Doyle at least, was the fact that he had created in Challenger another hero who, like Holmes, captured his readers' imagination, a hero whose exploits could be followed up in future volumes. Unfortunately, Doyle was unable to equal *The Lost World* in his future Challenger stories, probably because there were not enough lost worlds left for Challenger and his friends to explore.

Don Richard Cox. Arthur Conan Doyle (New
York: Ungar, 1985), pp. 184–89

DU MAURIER, DAPHNE (1907–   )

Miss du Maurier comes of such a gifted family that the excellence of her first novel does not take one quite by surprise. Still it is rare to encounter in the work of so young a writer so much that is of value. *The Loving Spirit* is by no means perfect—the story is sometimes forced and there are crudities that would not have appeared in the work of greater experience—but it is full of a promise from which I foretell for Miss du Maurier a high position among the novelists of this generation, if, as is to be hoped, her work develops logically from so auspicious a beginning. Her prose is clear, cool and flowing, and her dialogue, astonishingly enough, deteriorates as she approaches the present day.

She has a real feeling for the green hills and rugged cliffs of Cornwall, and real understanding for the Cornish villagers, dominated by the sea and the endless rhythms of the tides.

Helen Gosse. French Review. April 1931, p. 576

Jamaica Inn makes one realize how high the standard of entertainment has become in the modern novel. I do not believe R.L.S. [Robert Louis Stevenson] would have been ashamed to have written *Jamaica Inn*, with its smugglers, wreckers, wild moors, storms, its sinister inn, misplaced confidences, pretty and gallant heroine, and romantic love story. There is here all the melodrama that one can desire—and let nobody say "It is an old fashion." The old fashion was good.

Sean O'Faolain. The Spectator. January 24, 1936,
p. 144

So Cinderella married the prince, and then her story began. Cinderella was hardly more than a schoolgirl, and the overworked companion of a snobbish woman of wealth; the prince was Maximilian de Winter, whom she had heard of as the owner of Manderley in Cornwall, one of the most magnificent show places in England, who had come to the Riviera to forget the tragic death of his wife Rebecca. There was some mystery about Rebecca's death; but the book is skillfully contrived so that it does not depend only on knowledge of it for its thrill; it can afford to give no hint of it till two-thirds of the way through. But the revelation, when it comes, leads to one of the most prolonged, deadly, and breathless fencing matches that one can find in fiction, a battle of wits that would by itself make the fortune of a melodrama on the stage.

For this is a melodrama, unashamed, glorying in its own quality, such as we have hardly had since that other dependant, Jane Eyre, found that her house too had a first wife. It has the weaknesses of melodrama; in particular, the heroine is at times quite unbelievably stupid, as when she takes the advice of the housekeeper whom she knows to hate her. But if the second Mrs. de Winter had consulted with any one before trusting the housekeeper, we should miss one of the best scenes in the book. There is also, as is almost inseparable from a melodrama, a forced heightening of the emotional values; the tragedy announced in the opening chapter is out of proportion to the final outcome of the long battle of wits that ends the book. But it is as absorbing a tale as the season is likely to bring.

Basil Davenport. *Saturday Review.* September 24, 1938, p. 5

In the thirties, Miss du Maurier was a kind of poor woman's Charlotte Brontë. Her *Rebecca,* whatever one's opinions of its ultimate merits, was a tour de force. In its own way and century, it has achieved a position in English Literature comparable to "Monk" Lewis's *The Bleeding Nun* or Mrs. Radcliffe's *Mysteries of Udolpho.* Today Miss du Maurier the novelist is Miss Blurb's favorite Old Girl whose published appearances are heralded with the brouhaha of a privileged ex-hockey captain come down to give the home team a few hints about attack. This, one imagines her telling newcomers to St. Gollancz's, is how it should be done. Frankly, I cannot help feeling that Miss du Maurier's books have been successfully filmed so often that by now she may be said not so much to write a novel as shoot it. The present scenario [in *My Cousin Rachel*] is a honey for any Hollywood or Wardour Street tycoon. Slick, effective, utterly mechanical, the book is a triumphant and uncanny example of the way in which a piece of writing can be emasculated by unconsciously "having it arranged" for another medium. Close-ups, fade-ins, sequences by candlelight or long shots from the terrace—it has all been taken care of in the script and there is little call for anything in the way of imagination on the part of the director. . . .

Producers, admiring the general effect, will forgive such occasional anachronisms, as "forget it," "slapped my bottom with a hair-brush," and "Why not tell these gossips I'm a recluse and spend all my spare time scribbling Latin verses? That might shake them." Boyish sulks, mares in slather, and a lot of old lace at the throat and wrist, eked out with constant cups of poisoned tisane, complete the formula. A rare and irresistible bit of kitsch, whose clichés will soon be jostling and clashing in merry carillions up and down the premier cinema circuits of the English-speaking world.

John Raymond. *New Statesman.* August 11, 1951, p. 163

Daphne du Maurier's entertaining collection of stories, *Not after Midnight,* illustrates the fact that she is the nearest thing we have to a female Somerset Maugham. One might qualify this by saying that she possesses only in modified form those three characteristics which he considered to be his distinguishing features as a writer. His lucidity is sometimes her brightness; his simplicity is occasionally her banality; and his euphony is usually her homeliness.

Piers Brendon. *Books and Bookmen.* September 1971, p. 53

Francis Bacon seems an odd choice for Daphne du Maurier [in *The Winding Stair: Francis Bacon, His Rise and Fall*, 1977], with her fine wayward imagination and her gothic suggestiveness. Few Elizabethans had less of the mantic about them than Bacon; few steered a less infernal course. . . . Bacon was humdrum both in his grandeur and his decadence. He went meekly, if glumly, to his disgrace, arraigned as a Poulson and not as a Trotsky.

When we reach the time of the Shakespearian First Folio, the Baconian heresy naturally provides "food for speculation." The biographer disappears briefly behind an intrusive passive voice which suggests the possibility of collaboration between Bacon and Shakespeare. Not a shred of evidence is brought to support this half-hearted contention, and indeed it scarcely could be. The true Baconians, with their ciphers, anagrams, and hermetic signals behind Shakespeare's back, would find such lukewarm advocacy disappointing. The answer is that Dame Daphne would like to add *Macbeth* and *Twelfth Night* to Bacon's claims as The Most Brilliant Intellect: on the other hand, she is forced to emphasize as always, the poverty of physical evidence. Daphne du Maurier has many literary gifts, but I am not sure that this book has fully enlisted them. Her archaizing vein ("But stay, what was this?") is perhaps more suited to Cornish romance, and her cozy relationship with her hero "Francis" consorts oddly with his fiercely private nature and conscious dignity. Against this must be set a brisk narrative pace, an avoidance of pedantry, and some shrewdness in judging people. As an all-round character study, I am still inclined to prefer Catherine Drinker Bowen's *The Temper of a Man* of a decade ago. But there is always room for another book on anyone as complex and diversely gifted as Bacon. The man who took all knowledge as his province should not be left to specialists and scholars; he deserves a revival, and if Daphne du Maurier has not taken us to the inmost recesses she has made a good studio portrait of the outer man.

Pat Rogers. *The Spectator*. July 31, 1976, p. 20

The literary establishment clearly wants nothing to do with Daphne du Maurier. There are no critical essays or books about her. Her only critics to date have been the many book reviewers who, for the most part, heralded each novel as a gift of genius, though most agree that she never surpassed the level of excellence she achieved in *Rebecca*. The fact that millions of people read her novels certainly works against her approval by literary critics, who are not inclined to prize what the popular audience does. By the standards of contemporary literary criticism, most of du Maurier's works do not hold up well. Her prose, while straightforward and clear, is not especially interesting. There is little imagery, symbolism, or ambiguity in her writing. Her characters are often undeveloped, and her plots become all-important. Her style is conventional, her sentences unmemorable, and her story lines contrived. Compared with authors like Graham Greene or John Steinbeck she seems shallow and commercial.

Why, then, have her novels been so successful? Why is it that she has so many closet readers, sophisticated people who enjoy her works but who are reluctant to proclaim their enjoyment? Despite her failure as a thinker and as a stylist, du Maurier is a master storyteller who knows how to manipulate female fantasies. She creates a world that is simple, romantic, usually unambiguous, adventuresome, mysterious, dangerous, erotic, picturesque, and satisfying. It is a world that contrasts sharply with the mundane realities of ordinary existence, and it is a world that does not require the reader to suffer the pains of introspection and analysis. It is, in short, a world that brings considerable pleasure to millions of readers, especially women.

Three of her novels, however, transcend the narcotic effect of the body of her work: *The Progress of Julius, Rebecca,* and *The Parasites.* In these three works, du Maurier exhibits a powerful psychological realism reflecting her intense feelings about her father and, to a lesser degree, about her mother. The vision that underlies these novels is that of an author overwhelmed by her obsession with her father's sexual and authoritarian presence. This vision lends the stories a special vitality. Furthermore, the style of these novels stands out from that of the others in its relative simplicity, in its heightened attention to small detail, and in its depiction of unspectacular characters and events. A novel like *Frenchman's Creek,* for example, depends upon extravagant action, a broad land and seascape, and fairy-tale characters, while *The Parasites* works within the small compass of a living room within a twenty-four-hour period and focuses upon a neurotic but believable family. The love between Dona and her French pirate has no substance: it is a fairy tale, a projected fantasy. The incestuous feelings between Niall and Maria, on the other hand, vibrate with genuine emotion and are rooted in the particulars of their unusual past. Similarly, the narrator's involvement with both Maxim de Winter and Mrs. Danvers sweeps the reader into the midst of the triangle. Even the melodramatic murder of Gabriel Lévy in *The Progress of Julius,* through its oedipal significance, has a powerful psychological impact on the reader. The feelings in these works are believable and dynamic, as if conjured up from the depths of the human psyche. In these three novels, du Maurier manages to create a compelling vision of human character that transcends melodrama, creaky plots, and contrived endings.

Rebecca, "The Birds," and "Don't Look Now" also stand out among her works as landmarks in the development of the modern gothic tale. Du Maurier has breathed new life into the old forms of the gothic novel to come up with a classic tale of the Other Woman. Millions of women have identified with the plain, nameless narrator of *Rebecca,* a woman who defines her personality by overcoming the mother figure of Rebecca to win the lasting love of her father-lover. "The Birds" and "Don't Look Now" establish the twentieth-century sense of dislocation. The accepted order of things suddenly and for no apparent reason is upset. The great chain of being breaks, and people find themselves battling for their lives against creatures they always assumed inferior to themselves: birds and children. The continuity of time itself is in question in "Don't Look Now" as the future bleeds into the present.

Perhaps du Maurier wrote too much, catered too cynically to the popular taste of her audience, but she created the "classic" gothic novel of the twentieth century, setting the stage for hundreds of imitators grinding out formulaic tales in the Harlequin Romance series and others. Du Maurier has done her fair share of grinding out stories as well, but she has the talent to rise to the surface of literary respectability that many of her followers lack. The unseen Rebecca, Mrs. Danvers, and Manderley itself have become etched indelibly upon the imaginations of millions of people who have read *Rebecca* or have seen the motion picture. If Daphne du Maurier had written only *Rebecca,* she would still be one of the great shapers of popular culture and the modern imagination. Few writers have created more magical and mysterious places than Jamaica Inn and Manderley, buildings invested with a rich and brooding character that gives them a memorable life of their own. Although du Maurier does not subscribe to a conventional religious belief, she transformed the places she inhabited or visited—such as Ferryside, Jamaica Inn, and Menabilly—into gothic paradises, sacred structures of her imagination. Perhaps the passage in the Bible that best summarizes both her obsession with her father and her religious sense of place is that of St. John: "In my Father's house there are many mansions. . . . I go to prepare a place for you."

Richard Kelly. *Daphne du Maurier* (Boston:
Twayne, 1987), pp. 142–44

DÜRRENMATT, FRIEDRICH (1921–   )

Friedrich Dürrenmatt has written three detective novels. None of them has that aura of philosophical profundity which surrounds his other works: plays like *Der Besuch der alten Dame* [The visit], for instance, or prose works like his "noch mögliche Geschichte," *Die Panne* [Traps]. But the detective novels do have a reason for being.

In many of his works Dürrenmatt is concerned directly or indirectly with an almost obsessive idea: justice. In each of the detective novels it is the main idea and in each one it is treated differently. To be more precise, we might say that these novels are variations on a theme.

Dürrenmatt's optimistic philosophical conclusion in *Der Richter und sein Henker* [The judge and his hangman], *Der Verdacht* [The quarry], and *Das Versprechen* [The pledge] is this: If man wants justice, he must pursue it, but more often than not, the certain attainment of it is something he must leave to Heaven. What literary form is better suited to that "message" than the detective novel? It *is* the literary form in which the seeker of justice pursues the perpetrator of injustice. Dürrenmatt's only problem is to exalt the form, to make us realize that justice does not lie solely in the hands of the ingenious Scotland Yard man or the private eye.

The dramatic technique of which Dürrenmatt is a master pervades *The Judge and His Hangman.* The prose style has a clarity and simplicity which one does not expect in a philosophically inclined work (though Dürrenmatt's prose style is another problem in itself because it is of such a variable nature and because it has hidden intricacies). While the author now and then veers from his purpose (at one point becoming a character in his own novel) to engage in good-natured satire, generally speaking he is economical and he makes every sentence count. Every detail of the book, except for these occasional excursions, is a part of the theme that if man strives eternally, Heaven will be on his side; it is a theme which would be juvenile in the hands of a lesser man.

Dürrenmatt exalts the detective genre to express his basic concept of the absolute certainty of justice, of man's relationship to the power which governs it, and of the validity of the human pursuit for a better world. He considers it a part of his philosophical business to reach a mass audience through his novels without diluting that one main idea which permeates much of his writing: justice.

William Gillis. *The German Quarterly.* January
1962, pp. 71–74

Dürrenmatt has produced a series of comic plays and detective stories where the crime is major (murder), the criminal minor (all of us), the solution either absurd or, what is worse, rational. Chance or accident, he implies, is one of the chief initiating factors in human affairs—this with the authority of Aristotle and other comic metaphysicians who attempt a logical exposition of what they have just defined as illogical.

Tragedy, Dürrenmatt has said, is impossible in the atomic age, and the writer must use comedy to reveal the tragic condition of man. This apparently paradoxical esthetic is no more mystifying than Sartre's *No Exit,* which in fact exemplifies it. Does this make Dürrenmatt an Existentialist? No. He is a kind of moral logician writing plays and novels. The novels, of which *Once a Greek . . .* is the latest, are not so well known as the play *The Visit,* in which revenge for an ancient wrong is a sardonic sonata played savagely. . . .

In *Traps* Dürrenmatt turned an intellectual game, in which justice is examined, into a grisly conclusion; and in *The Pledge* he began to see the limitations of moral argument presented as mystery. To be sure, the mystery thriller with its format of clue and implication seems close to moral argument with its logical parade of data, development, and conclusion. It may be rejoined that sexual promiscuity, in part the theme of *Once a Greek. . . ,* is close in biological programming to sacred matrimony; but it cannot on that count alone receive holy sanction. That is because bizarre details, however realistically they may be urged upon us, do not determine the form of an act, but only its outward trappings. The detective thriller, like the promiscuous adventure, trades on what is exotic, unexpected—in a word, accidental. . . .

Dürrenmatt tried nobly in *The Pledge* to rescue the thriller as moral agent; he failed, and produced another engaging murder story with heady overtones. He then switched to satiric farce for *Once a Greek*. . . , thus suggesting that his comic-play technique is equally applicable to the novel.

Once a Greek . . . is a novel from which every serious consideration has been removed except the point, which is, as in the past, the assertion that chance plays sardonic tricks on us. The best will in the world, though informed by morality, justice, economy, and industry, all geared to what is predictable, cannot triumph over what is not. The importance of this message, in an age of totalitarian dedication, cannot be overestimated. . . .

Satiric farce offers the widest latitude: it can be poetic, as with Molière; scathing, as in the case of Sheridan; highly polished and glittering, as with Wilde. Dürrenmatt steers a safe, effective middle course. The result is a play disguised as a novel, amusing and easy to read.

Arthur Darack. *Saturday Review*. July 17, 1965,

p. 36

Dürrenmatt writes in German, and has obviously been much influenced by expressionism. His work is relentlessly moralistic, and every social point is driven home with the insistent irony of an Emil Jannings film. The most important of his short novels is *Der Richter und Sein Henker* (1952), translated as *The Judge and His Hangman* (1954), a book masterly in its control of the crime-story medium for the author's symbolic and moral purposes. . . .

Dürrenmatt's other crime stories do not fuse the investigatory and symbolic elements quite so successfully, but they are all remarkable for their originality. *Der Verdacht* (1953), translated as *The Quarry* (1962), finds Barlach in hospital, slowly recovering from what had been thought a fatal illness. The doctor treating him thinks he identifies in an old picture from *Life* a German concentration-camp doctor who took pleasure in operating on inmates without anesthetics. Has this man committed suicide, or is he in fact still alive and the head of a clinic which takes in only wealthy patients? There follows a struggle of wits and wills between Barlach and this man, which is also a struggle between freedom and nihilism. . . .

Das Versprechen, translated as *The Pledge* (1958), is about the transformation of Inspector Matthäi from an emotionless machine into a man with a passion for justice, intent to discover the murderer of three young girls. In pursuit of the man, Matthäi becomes for years a petrol station attendant, and with the utmost ruthlessness uses another young girl as bait for the killer. The bait is not accepted; the girl becomes a sluttish prostitute; the defeated Matthäi sinks into a sodden wreck. At the end of the story, it is revealed that he was "a genius, more so than any of your fictional detectives,'' and that all of his deductions were correct. Again, what might have been a mere clatter of ironies is kept finely under control.

> Julian Symons. *Mortal Consequences: A History— From the Detective Story to the Crime Novel* (New York: Harper & Row, 1972), pp. 195–96

On the face of it Dürrenmatt's first essay into the detective story, *Der Richter und sein Henker,* contains sufficient traditional elements to explain its abiding popularity. Written as it was in installments it enjoys all the sculptured, architectonic advantages of the *Roman Feuilleton.*

On first reading Dürrenmatt's *Der Richter und sein Henker* one is struck by the strangeness, the disconcerting oddity of the overall impression which this novel leaves. Where, one asks, is that feeling of delight, that essentially cathartic, reassuring feeling that things have turned out right? In its place one experiences a disconcerting *je ne sais quoi,* a nagging, worrying feeling that the equation has worked itself out unsatisfactorily. Initially one is inclined to dismiss this reaction, perhaps attributing it to Dürrenmatt's failure to cope with what was, for him at the time, a new form. But this too is unsatisfactory. The reader is left with no alternative but to reread—and read more closely, paying particular attention to Dürrenmatt's departures from the "classic" tradition.

The figure of Kommissär Bärlach dominates this novel from the earliest stages until the close; small wonder, then, that it is here that we find the causes for the reader's unusual reaction to this novel as a whole.

The unreflecting acceptance so characteristic of the usual response to escape literature has no place here. The reader is forced to reexamine, to criticize.

The apparently benign Kommissär is presented in a way which initially makes critical examination rather difficult, for he is clearly the most sympathetic character in the novel.

One feels that his inhumanity, total absence of moral scruple and willingness to involve himself in crime as a matter of whim, without any apparent gain to be drawn from it, marks Gastmann as a very particular kind of criminal. Written only seven years after the end of the war in Europe, the novel echoes ominously the gratuitous criminality and the inhuman treatment of the individual during the Nazi period. This particular thematic strand is central to the sequel, *Der Verdacht,* written one year later, 1952, which likewise has Bärlach as its hero.

> G. F. Benham. *Revue des Langues Vivantes.* No. 2, 1976, pp. 147–54

Mystery stories are usually noted for their adventurous but plausible events; in *Der Richter* as well as in *Das Versprechen,* the plot is very gripping without being unbelievable. In *Der Verdacht,* however, the reader, even by stretching his imagination to the extreme, will not be able to believe that a criminal surgeon like Dr. Emmenberger "who kills out of love," could run his hellish sanatorium in the center of a big city undisturbed by the relatives of the murdered rich people and unsuspected by the authorities.

The portrayal of Dr. Emmenberger (a mixture of Raskolnikov and Dr. Faustus), and the many unbelievably gruesome crimes he commits and philosophically justifies, make him the personification of evil rather than a real and convincing character. Also the way the other figures talk, act, and react, shifts this story towards the allegorical, the grotesque, and even the absurd. The reader is not only encouraged, but strongly urged to look for deeper meanings and profounder significance.

All of these elements combine to make *Der Verdacht* less of a mystery story and more of a literary novel. By increasing the intellectual substance and the poetic merit of this book, Dürrenmatt has created a highly sophisticated work of literature instead of a pure adventure story as he had originally intended. *Der Verdacht* is undoubtedly Dürrenmatt's only "mystery" novel which invites serious literary examination and tolerates different philosophical interpretations. But at the same time, and because of this, it is his most labored and tedious story.

Saad Elkhadem. *The International Fiction Review.*
July 1977, pp. 178–82

Friedrich Dürrenmatt's *The Execution of Justice* is not a murder mystery per se, but rather a master of the genre's sardonic study of the ethics and morality of justice. There is essentially no mystery in the novel; the reader knows from the start who kills whom. In fact, it is the convicted murderer, a well-off, multimillionaire politician, serving a term in prison, who hires the "detective"—a third-rate lawyer—to investigate the crime and come up with a plausible alternate theory to prove that someone else, now at large, committed the murder, and *not* the murderer. And, what's more, he does! The actual murderer is then acquitted, and lives happily and wealthily ever after. Even when the narrator decides to take justice into his own hands and do away with him, he is thwarted in a wicked turn of events. This allegory on ethics and morality resonates with the currently provocative and interesting Woody Allen movie, *Crimes and Misdemeanors*. Although the two vehicles are entirely different, their moral, if you will, is similar: the bad prosper; the good suffer. On his last page, Dürrenmatt writes: "Did [Spat, the lawyer-detective] then have to find a murderer who did not exist, just as man, once he had eaten of the fruit of the tree of good and evil, had to find the God, who did not exist, or the devil? Is that not the fiction of God by which he justifies his wayward creations? Who is the guilty party? The one who commissions the job, or the one who takes it on? The one who forbids, or the one who disregards the prohibition? The one who passes the laws, or the one who breaks them?"

Bruce Cassiday. *Border Patrol.* Summer 1990,
p. 3

FRANCIS, DICK (1920–   )

Francis improves with every book as both a writer of brisk, lucid prose and as a concocter of ingenious and intricately worked-out plots. He has acquired something of Ian Fleming's easy expertise in handling technical information, though his travels in Norway and South Africa led him in recent books into unnecessarily detailed diversions. In *Knock Down* the information was at his finger tips and the sales ring scenes are hair-raisingly convincing. Where he has followed Fleming less satisfactorily is in the increase in goriness and the stretching of improbability. He opts for a dozen crimes where one would do; as with Simon Raven, a writer of similar skills in the building-up of suspense, his imagination takes hold at crucial moments and finally runs off with him. He has now got a good enough horse under him to ride a waiting race. Meanwhile, a course of Simenon and a pair of blinkers would not come amiss.

Philip Pelham. *London Magazine*. February–March
1975, pp. 142–43

It is undeniable that Francis works to a formula—the hard-done-by chap blindly at grips with an unknown evil, the threads of which he gradually unravels. Frequently—perhaps too frequently—he is subjected to physical torture described in some detail. His heroes are hard men used to injury and pain and they learn to dish it out as once they had to learn to take it. Racing has made them stoics.

But, formula or no formula, Francis gets beneath the skin of his characters in a way few thriller writers manage. He does this best about his racing personnel but with each book his range has widened. The crooked trainer, Humber, in possibly his best book, *For Kicks,* is a living and lasting portrait, while the scenes in his dreadful stable have a Dickensian ring.

Fear stalks through these books; not the fear of the weakling but that of the strong, or, perhaps, once strong, man, doubting his strength under stress. He explored this first in his second book, *Nerve,* and in this book, *Whip Hand,* it is further developed, to an excruciating degree.

Finally, Francis can make a race come alive off his pages in thrilling fashion. One can hear the smash of birch, the creak of leather and the rattle of whips. The sweat, the strain, the tears, tragedies, and occasional triumphs of the racing game are all there, as well as its seductive beauty. In this—as in much else—no other racing novelist can touch him. He has made racing into a microcosm of the contemporary world, with its flawed values and ruthless manipulation. But he can convey tenderness and fidelity too.

John Welcome. *London Magazine.* March 1980, pp. 95–96

It was the late Edmund Crispin who recommended Dick Francis to me. "If you can stand the horse parts," he said, "the mystery parts are quite good." I found this an understatement in reverse. The horse parts, as everyone knows by now, are brilliant vignettes of a tiny portion of English life: the world of steeplechase racing. Novel by novel we meet the jockeys, the trainers, the owners (usually being taken for a ride in another sense), the bookmakers, the bloodstock agents, the sporting journalists. We learn what it is like to be a stableboy at a skinflint North Country trainer's, to ride in freezing February fog (the first sentence of the first novel is "The mingled smell of hot horse and cold river mist filled my nostrils"), to be Clerk of a run-down course that wrongdoers are determined to close. But the mystery parts, if inevitably less realistic, arise naturally from the greed, corruption, and violence that lie behind the champagne, big cars, and titled Stewards; they concern horse-pulling and betting frauds, and lead to wads of used notes in anonymous envelopes, whispered warnings by telephone, and sudden hideous confrontations with big men in stocking masks.

The elements of steeplechase racing and mystery are welded into adult reading by the Francis hero. Francis has no recurrent central character, no Bond or Marlowe; his heroes are jockeys, trainers, an owner who manufactures children's toys, a journalist, a Civil Service screener. But they tell the story in the first person, and they tend to sound alike. Their narratives are laconically gripping, and graphic in a way that eschews Chandler's baroque images and Fleming's color-supplement brand names. They combine unfailing toughness with infinite compassion.

There is a lot of pain in Francis novels, which puts some people off. But there can be liberating happiness also: the loner heroes often find warm-hearted unselfish women (Francis's women are usually as nice as his men, with the exception of a few fiendish bitches), and the love scenes, usually long deferred, are unpretentiously honest.

It would perhaps be pushing it a little to say that each Francis novel is a different story enclosing the same story, but it seems like this at times, as if the whole sequence were an allegory of the suffering individual inside endless inimical environments.

One hesitates to criticize a Francis novel, but *Reflex* displays in a less extreme form a defect of its predecessor *Whip Hand,* in which three themes proved in the end to have nothing to do with each other. I have a feeling that Francis is tending to put too many themes into his books at present to compensate for the lack of real dominance of any one, and is failing to relate them satisfactorily: this, coupled with a certain blandness in the writing, suggests there may be a limit to the number of imaginative thrillers to be derived from the steeplechase scene. One can't exactly complain about this: Francis has written a dozen superb novels in less than twenty years, but there have been occasions since 1972 when the vein has shown signs of being worked out. This is one of them.

Philip Larkin. *The Times Literary Supplement.*
October 10, 1980, p. 1127

It seems to me that the most astonishing thing about Dick Francis's work is his ability to juggle three elements—mystery, horses, and exotic information—in each of his novels and keep them suspended magically in the air. It is not easy to juggle a horse. It is even more difficult to ring in so many variations on horses while simultaneously keeping those other two elements airborne. In *Banker,* Mr. Francis's new novel, horses and exotic information are more heavily weighted than mystery, and perhaps die-hard fans may carp at the imbalance. But the author has written a brief introduction to allay their fears. . . .

In *Twice Shy* Mr. Francis tried something daring for a thriller and succeeded admirably. In each of the novel's two sections separate heroes faced the same frightening villain fourteen years apart. In *Banker* he has taken a similar risk. His new book *must* span three years because foals—like humans—aren't conceived and born overnight, and the "harmless-seeming seeds" Mr. Francis mentions in his introduction need time to germinate. That he manages to capture our attention and hold us spellbound over the course of those three years is further proof of his juggling skill. And when the unraveling finally does come, it comes with all the breathless pace we have come to expect of this superb writer.

I for one am very happy that Mr. Francis no longer rides horses.

Evan Hunter. *The New York Times Book Review.*
March 27, 1983, pp. 15, 20

Dick Francis is not only one of the most popular crime writers of our times, he is also one of the finest, having for several years been that most happy of men—the author who can truthfully say that his best book is the one most recently published. Although horses and the world of racing are invariably involved at some stage in his narratives, he tends nowadays to choose different central themes, often highlighting some unusual profession or arcane specialization. Dick Francis has an unobtrusively stylish gift for conveying interesting background information at the same time as telling a good story, and he writes with humble, honest respect about believable, rounded characters who have not lost sight of the possibility of integrity, love, faith, courage, and compassion. He also handles the difficult first-person narrative technique with grace and skill.

James Melville. *British Book News.* October 1984,
p. 617

It is difficult to place Dick Francis in the context of crime fiction or to identify him with one particular school or style. As a writer of racing thrillers he could be compared with Nat Gould or Edgar Wallace, but his literary standard and his explorations of positive themes and character motivation put him on a higher plane. Francis himself dislikes the label "racing thrillers." "I consider my books to be adventure stories rather than thrillers," he says, and cites Desmond Bagley, Gavin Lyall, and Alistair Maclean among the authors with whom he would be happy to have his style associated. Although not an adventure novelist, Ed McBain is another contemporary author whom Francis admires. All these writers, it should be noted, use the crisp and economical technique favored by Francis; they do not waste words if to do so would be to retard the action or impair the readability.

It is with Ian Fleming that Francis has been frequently compared, sometimes by prominent scholars of literature and to Francis's advantage. C. P. Snow has remarked upon Francis's "considerable inventiveness, both in plot and in technical devices, so that on the superficial levels his books would compare favorably with the James Bond stories." Philip Larkin has referred to Francis's best features in greater detail, itemizing "the absolute sureness of his settings, the freshness of his characters, the terrifying climaxes of violence, the literate jauntiness of style, the unfailing intelligent compassion," and concluding that "all these make him one of the few writers who can be mentioned in the same breath as Fleming." Snow nevertheless believed Francis to be superior in terms of his readability, tautness, and lack of pretentiousness, and saw greater similarities with the early work of the sadly neglected Nigel Balchin. This might be an idiosyncratic view, but it is undoubtedly more fruitful to look for parallels with such writers as Fleming and Balchin than to group Francis with the writers of "racing thrillers" or "sports mysteries." Psychological drama and the conflict between good and evil are salient points of comparison, as is the theme of the lonely protagonist who is motivated to behave in a particular fashion by certain influences, pressures, and obsessions. Taking the latter point, Jessica Mann has mentioned Francis in passing when considering the work of Geoffrey Household.

Francis's versatility has come through, in spite of the frustrations that could so easily have been caused by readers who seemed always to expect a strong horse-racing element. He has proved himself to be an excellent novelist rather than a fictionalizer of the specialized world he knows best, and could effortlessly produce a first-class thriller or adventure story with no racing connection whatsoever if he chose to do so, but it is unlikely that there will ever be such a Francis novel. "I doubt," he says, "if my regular readers would want it or accept it."

Even when viewed simply as a popular novelist, Francis is frequently regarded as being head and shoulders above most of his contemporaries. John Mortimer is prepared to accept Francis at his face value and declare him to be excellent: "Mr. Francis's work might be said to be perfect holiday reading. . . . He has the magical power of making you forget the sunburn and the mosquito bites, the gyppy tummy and the sickly smell of Ambre Solaire mixed with frying calamaris.''

It is a constant source of complaint by crime writers that their work receives scant attention from the critics. Why, they ask, can distinction not be recognized in those novelists who happen to be specially accomplished in one genre? Why, they have asked from time immemorial, must they turn to mainstream fiction in order to be deemed respectable? Raymond Chandler found the problem irksome as long ago as 1949: ''The sort of semi-literate educated people one meets nowadays . . . are always saying to me, more or less, 'You write so well I should think you would do a serious novel.' You would probably insult them by remarking that the artistic gap between a really good mystery and the best serious novel of the last ten years is hardly measurable compared with the gap between the serious novel and any representative piece of Attic literature from the Fourth Century B.C.'' The question of the critical recognition of crime writers remains to this day, although Dick Francis is among the few who have received more serious attention than would have been forthcoming a few years ago. He is a good example of a popular novelist who displays no self-indulgence, writing for his readers rather than for himself, which should surely be no reason for failing to acknowledge that he writes extremely well.

Melvyn Barnes. Dick Francis (New York: Ungar, 1986), pp. ix–xvi

Dick Francis utilizes many of the elements of the classic murder mystery, but he does not really write a detective story. He utilizes many of the elements of the private-eye novel, too, but his amateur sleuths are usually not investigators per se. What Dick Francis does is feature one more face of the ''thriller''—call it the crime thriller if you will. Neither a puzzler nor a P.I.er, a Francis book nevertheless exploits tension to create suspense, working on the emotions of the reader for its emotional effects. . . .

Francis never had a formal education; his wife, the former Mary Brenchley, was university educated and became more or less his firmly guiding hand in matters literary. When it became time to begin the background research for a new project, she would always step in and do the nitty-gritty cut and paste for him.

By the very nature of the crime thriller, however, the surface values of diction and description have little to do with the ability of the story itself to grip the reader. What Francis brought to this type of psychological crime novel was something that was his exclusive province: he knew exactly how to *pace* his writing, when to let the action subside and even lag and when to pour on the pressure and push the reader into turning the pages.

Most critics appreciate Francis's clear and lucid writing style; it is hard not to when the prose that results is so crisp and even. But clarity sometimes sacrifices depth and psychological probing. Francis has been criticized for not getting into his characters all the way.

He finds himself also the target for critics who claim he indulges in too much sadism. True, he does subject his heroes to all kinds of horrendous physical torments. Francis's answer is a simple one: as a rider, he points out, he suffered dozens of falls, all painful, all requiring weeks and months to heal. He has lived with pain and he knows the human body can stand pain. Therefore, why not let his heroes suffer it too?

Whatever is to be said about his diction and his tendency to sadism, he understands not only the psychology of his characters, but the psychology of his readers as well. The fact that all his books are still in print at the time of this writing is proof of his ability to reach out and grip his readers. And it is his knowledge of psychology that, with each new title, makes them come back for more.

Reading a Dick Francis book is probably just about as exciting as watching Dick Francis, in his younger days, race a horse around a track. What more could one ask?

Bruce Cassiday. The Literature of Crime and
Detection (New York: Ungar, 1988), pp. 167–68

What better praise can be given a popular writer than that millions of people enjoy his work? This, perhaps: that he does not cheapen sensation, pander, or diminish the power of his art. All of this is true of Dick Francis. His writings are a high-wire act. They hold an impressive balance over enormous canyons. They are violent but not titillating. They are moral but not oppressive. They are formulaic but not repetitive. They are didactic but not dull. The prose is plain but not pretentiously so. The themes center on manhood but are not chauvinistic. The protagonists are heroic but not superhuman. Realism is his objective, yet he does not take away the fantasies. Francis proves annually that to be moderate is not necessarily to be mediocre and to be entertaining is not necessarily to be tawdry. There rages still an ongoing debate on whether certain films, television, and writings are harmful to those who consume them. I cannot be certain that this is not so. Of this, however, I am certain: no one is a worse person for having read Dick Francis, and I sincerely suspect we are all made a bit more determined to do better against adversity.

J. Madison Davis. Dick Francis (Boston: Twayne,
1989), pp. 138–39

In 1962, so the story goes, Dick Francis needed a new carpet for his sitting room. He decided to write a book to get the money. Drawing upon his past as a successful jockey, he wrote a thriller set in the world of horse racing. That was *Dead Cert*. He now has homes in both the U.S. and Great Britain, and I bet they all have fine carpets. In Francis's latest novel, *Longshot,* the hero, John Kendall, is a struggling writer. He is down to his last few pence when the pipes freeze in his rooms and he is forced to seek temporary accommodations. About this time, he meets Tremayne Vickers, a successful horse trainer who feels the need to have his biography written. Although Kendall knows little of horses and less of Vickers, he succumbs to the lure of room and board. Kendall arrives at Vickers's estate amid a swirl of controversy about a trial concerning the death of a young lady at a party given there. Tensions mount as the skeleton of another girl, who has been missing for some time, is found in a nearby wood. As the list of suspects narrows to the Vickers group, we find the usual Dick Francis nail-biting, page-turning climax.

With one exception, Dick Francis does not use a continuing series character in his novels. John Kendall is, however, a typical Francis hero—competent, likable, and decent. He is thrust, reluctantly, into an alien environment where he must use all of his skills to survive. Luckily for this hero, a past job was to research and write a series of survival manuals. Unfortunately, the information in these manuals not only helps Kendall survive, it also provides the killer with a source of deadly ideas.

Dick Francis is my favorite writer of thrillers (at least this week he is). His novels can always be counted on for pulse-quickening suspense. His talent is such that you may actually find yourself breathing a little faster, pulling at your hair, and groaning a bit with the characters before you reach the end of the book. There are few books that I know I will enjoy just from the author's name. The Dick Francis novels are on this list. A definite must-read.

Rick Mattos. *The Armchair Detective*. Spring
1991, p. 228

GARDNER, ERLE STANLEY [also known as A. A. FAIR] (1889–1969)

The present American mystery owes its birth and development mainly to the efforts of three men—Dashiell Hammett, Erle Stanley Gardner, and Raymond Chandler.

None started out intending to write mysteries, yet each, in his own way, came to the genre, took what was a British formula and turned it into an American original. When they were finished, their influence extended from the pulps through novels, radio, TV, and the movies. These three were not the only fathers of what has come to be known as the hard-boiled school of mystery writing, but they did the most to make it prosper, develop and advance, as well as being linked as few others in that field were.

Without them, we might still be reading the genteel parlor formula developed in turn-of-the-century England, in which much was said and little was done, and the atmosphere of the Victorian drawing room pervaded throughout. . . .

This form was all the rage in post–WW I America when Dashiell Hammett, ex-Pinkerton detective and future creator of such memorable heros and villains as Sam Spade, Nick and Nora Charles, Caspar Gutman, Joel Cairo, and the Continental Op, took crime from the parlor into the street, where it belonged.

This did not mean the traditional mystery form had been destroyed or the quality diluted. On the contrary, Hammett refined and elevated the crime adventure, gave it an American character, turned the lowly private eye into someone noble and made him a man of the common people, rather than some lofty lord or count, using first the nameless, faceless Continental Op and later the intrepid Sam Spade.

Crime became real and violence a powerful force. Characters and scenes moved; machine guns sparkled with fire; grenades were lobbed from fast moving cars passing through the dark streets of night. The seamier side of reality; tough cops, cons, and others, were brought out of the closet and onto center stage.

Hammett put San Francisco on the map as a detective city much as Sir Arthur Conan Doyle turned the fog-enshrouded London of Sherlock Holmes into a place of adventure, mystery, and murder. Since Hammett, numerous detectives have moved across those steep San Francisco hills, but none as memorable as Sam Spade.

Incidently, the 1941 filming of *The Maltese Falcon,* the third screen version, propelled Humphrey Bogart into superstardom and typecast the film version of how a private eye should look and act. Both the book and movie are now classics.

Not all of Hammett's tales occurred in San Francisco, though his characters, wherever they went, soon set themselves apart from and above all other creations.

When *Black Mask,* the most important and popular of the pulp magazines, decided on a new editorial policy, they made Hammett the foundation of all their future efforts.

In his private life Hammett and Lillian Hellman, the famed playwright, were lovers. It was around the two of them that Nick and Nora Charles of "The Thin Man" [films] were fashioned.

During the formative twenties period a writer rose to the fore. Eventually he would outshine Hammett and dominate the pulps as later on he would dominate the paperbacks. His name was Erle Stanley Gardner.

Gardner's work reflected both the Hammett touch and his own views. He also gave us one more American crime fighter, the lawyer. His Perry Mason proved so popular that Gardner became the best-selling author of his age.

Mason was modeled after Gardner, the lawyer, just as Sam Spade was modeled after the private detective Hammett had once been. Gardner also had his Nick and Nora Charles team in the form of Perry Mason and Della Street.

His writing was faster than Hammett's, but the stories were less mature. Still, they had color and often unusual characters, among them Sidney Zoom and his police dog, Speed Dash, The Patent Leather Kid, and Lester Leith, gentleman thief.

Gardner proved one could have swift action and tension without being a private eye or having a bloody fire fight, as Hammett often did. He wrote mostly about California, helping set the trend of the West Coast crime story, which still persists.

Gardner paralleled Hammett in other ways. Both were born outside California and adopted it as home. Both had been in rough places: Hammett in two world wars and up against hard characters during his Pinkerton days; Gardner had lived in mining camps, been to the Klondike and had fought in amateur boxing matches. Like Hammett, he too had a common-law wife, but unlike Hammett he did try marriage.

Gardner proved his admiration for Hammett when the latter was threatening to quit *Black Mask,* because of low pay. Gardner felt that without Hammett *Black Mask* would fold, losing him an important selling outlet. To circumvent this, he offered to take a cut in pay so Hammett could get his raise.

In 1934, Gardner made his first foray into Hollywood with the filming of several Perry Masons. Hammett's *Maltese Falcon* had already been filmed three years earlier. Gardner was not to emulate Hammett's success and had to wait for radio, TV, and paperbacks to make him a household name.

In those years while Hammett was making the Hollywood screen scene, entering the army and going to jail for Communist activities, Gardner was expanding and improving his output and quantity. One of the men he would meet and who would effect him even more than Hammett was an ex-oil company executive named Raymond Chandler.

Chandler arrived on the mystery scene a good dozen years after his contemporaries. He had lived for a while in England and was fascinated by the differences in American and English speech patterns. Like the others, he also became an important *Black Mask* contributor.

More than any writer, Chandler would inherit the Hammett crown and set the direction of the private eye mystery school.

If Hammett can be considered violent, Chandler was less so. If Hammett's writing can be described as a mosaic of elegant black etchings, Chandler's must be likened to wide, sunny, brilliantly hued brushstrokes across the vast canvas of California. He also adopted this state as his own and did his part in helping make it the private eye and crime lawyer capital of the world.

Chandler was the originator of the semiseedy, hard-drinking hero and helper of the underdog, which is now the stereotyped classic private eye mold. It was Chandler who could paint word pictures of people, places, and homes, with such vividness that the reader almost felt as if he or she were waiting with bated breath in some darkened bedroom as the murderer slowly emerged from some shadowed corner.

For perhaps the second time in his life Gardner was influenced to write mysteries that can best be described as Chandleresque: one fine example being the classic 1941 Perry Mason novel, *The Case of the Empty Tin.*

Both writers were good friends, often exchanging letters, ideas, opinions, even borrowing and rewriting each other's stories, then publishing them.

In *The Case of the Dangerous Dowager,* Perry Mason travels to a foggy coastal town, takes a ferry out over the three-mile limit to a gambling ship, and there confronts the owner. The same scene, more vividly written, appeared in a Chandler pulp story later cannibalized to form a major portion of *Farewell, My Lovely.*

Chandler also followed Hammett, going in for strange and unusual people: Moose Malloy, Eddie Prue, Arthur Gwynn Geiger, Dr. Verringer, Amthor and his Indian medium.

Chandler went farther. He copied Hammett, hoping perhaps to do him one better. Arthur Gwynn Geiger, the blackmailer in *The Big Sleep,* and his young homosexual lover, mirror Caspar Gutman and his gunsel in *The Maltese Falcon,* right down to Marlowe's fight with Geiger's lover. This theme was repeated in *The Long Goodbye* fifteen years later. There, Marlowe met the phony Dr. Verringer and Erle, his lethal, moronic ward, who enjoyed dressing up and pretending to be Valentino.

The Geiger death scene and the rescue of the naked, drugged daughter of General Sternwood in *The Big Sleep* parallels the altar death scene and the Continental Op's rescue of the naked, drugged Gabrielle Leggett in *The Dain Curse.* Both books have as a main theme the search for an errant younger daughter.

The fake mystic, fleecing the rich, of *The Dain Curse,* finds his equal in Amthor of *Farewell, My Lovely,* in which story Marlowe is drugged, imprisoned, beaten up, and escapes. The same thing, more brutally done, happens to Ned Beaumont, hero of *The Glass Key.*

Chandler would follow Hammett in becoming a Hollywood writer, and he would also establish the reality-fantasy image of glittering, hard-drinking, viperish, danger-filled Hollywood. It was never like that, but this is the view the public bought as real.

Looking back today, at that period from the twenties to the sixties we see three men who did extremely well as writers. Their books sold in the millions of copies. People emulated them. All of Hammett's books and most of Chandler's and Gardner's became movies, radio, or TV shows, some several times over.

This does not mean they always lived mirror image lives. There were some sharp differences. Of the three, only Hammett turned to Communism. Only Chandler remained faithfully married to one woman, . . . even ignoring his work to take care of her. After her death he turned to drink and almost committed suicide. Hammett would later succumb to depression, emphysema, and lung cancer. Only Gardner was not to suffer a tragic ending.

When looked at in total, their lives, works, and connections, both personal and literary, plus their influence over the mystery genre, makes a fascinating history.

Paul Hofrichter. *Bookman's Weekly.* May 3, 1982,
pp. 3460–64

The largest numerical field in the American as in the British detective story during these years [1941–1968] has been, inevitably, the routine or straightaway police novel (whether the hero be professional or amateur) of the purely entertainment school. King of the "time-killers" among American writers today, at least if sales are a criterion, is Erle Stanley Gardner with his frenetic Perry Mason and Douglas Selby stories. There is at least a little of Hammett in the Gardner method, but there is more of the author's own background of years spent in writing for the "pulps." With no pretensions to literary style, but with a solid understanding of "action" fiction, the Gardner yarns are a sure two-hour cure for anybody's boredom.

Howard Haycraft. *Murder for Pleasure: The Life
and Times of the Detective Story* (New York: Biblo
and Tannen, 1968), pp. 217–18

Although Erle Stanley Gardner, a lawyer, began writing about the same time that Hammett and Chandler did, and also appeared in *Black Mask,* he eventually abandoned the persona of the detective and substituted a protagonist more suitable to his talents—the lawyer. After several years of writing short stories for the pulp magazines, he admittedly made a comprehensive analysis of hundreds of currently popular detective novels, synthesized his findings into a formula, and began writing a series of "detective" novels featuring a lawyer-hero as private-eye surrogate.

Using himself as a model, he sketched in the character of his protagonist Perry Mason, basing the efficient Della Street on his own secretary. In effect, his crime novels *began* where those of Hammett and Chandler *ended:* in the courtroom.

Mason never pretends to be a detective, nor does he do any routine detective work; he leaves those chores to Paul Drake. Nevertheless he tries to help his clients by the skilled use of legal procedure, often twisting the law for his own purposes. Mason theorizes that it is stupid to tell the simple truth when that truth is hard to believe and cannot usually be verified anyway. To clear an innocent person and see justice done, Mason believes a lawyer can frequently "bend the law."

And bend the law Perry Mason continually does. The real fun in reading a Gardner detective novel is in watching Mason rearrange clues and spread misinformation, and in following the convoluted machinations of Gardner's story line. Gardner knows how to spin out a yarn and keep the reader turning one page after another, even though the "plot" behind the façade of "mystery" may strike the reader as somewhat thin in the end.

In contrast to the "mean streets" characters that people a Hammett or Chandler novel, Mason's clients and citizens are solid middle-class types. Business executives, housewives, ordinary laborers, professional men and women—these are the usual dramatis personae of a typical Mason story, people easily recognizable to the reader.

> Waltraud Woeller and Bruce Cassiday. *The*
> *Literature of Crime and Detection* (New York:
> Ungar, 1988), pp. 137–38

On December 12, 1935, the editor of *Country Gentleman* offered Gardner ten thousand dollars to produce for the magazine an acceptable hero for a new novel-length serial. Three days later Gardner sent off a tentative outline, and on January 13 he submitted the final installment of *The Thread of Murder*. The narrative was then published in book form under the title *The D.A. Calls It Murder* (1937), and thus Gardner began his second major series. The ninth and final volume, *The D.A. Breaks an Egg,* appeared in 1949.

In quality as in quantity, the D.A. series is the least of Gardner's three principal novel series. The D.A. concept is even more tightly constricted by formulas than that of Perry Mason. A few stereotyped relationships form the predictable core of every Mason novel: Mason-female client, Mason-district attorney, Mason-Della Street. These necessary tensions are infinitely repeatable because they are inherent in the institutional premises: a lawyer must have a client and a secretary; he must confront a district attorney. The conventions which prescribe the essential relationships in the D.A. series are both too many and too accidental.

As the inaugural volume opens, young Doug Selby has just been elected to the office of district attorney on a reform platform. His position remains precarious throughout the nine novels: the old establishment which ran the small county seat of Madison prior to Selby's election appears ever-ready to exploit Selby's slightest miscue as an excuse for turning him out. The establishment newspaper, *The Blade,* constantly editorializes against Selby, and usually publishes its own hasty conclusions in a vain attempt to upstage him. An unreformed chief of police regularly assists in the effort to undermine Selby's authority. Unlike Mason, Selby cannot be readily threatened with disbarment. Gardner therefore contrives this implausibly persistent political/publicity threat to Selby's professional security.

On Selby's side—elected on the same ticket—is County Sheriff Rex Brandon. Brandon is actually an improvement over Paul Drake. He is a more complete individual, an older man, more experienced and less volatile than Selby. Something of a father figure, Brandon and his wife embody the practical wisdom and homey virtues of small-town America. Selby's Della Street is Sylvia Martin, star reporter for *The Clarion,* the reform newspaper.

Each of the D.A. novels follows a definite pattern. Someone commits a murder. *The Blade* blames Selby for acting too slowly to apprehend the perpetrator (or, in the several cases where Selby's office initially misidentifies the corpse, for acting too precipitously). *The Blade* outlines its own theory of the crime (imitating the district attorney's counterplot in the Mason series). Selby, Brandon, and Sylvia rush around the countryside interviewing witnesses until they uncover the real culprit. *The Clarion* celebrates Selby's triumph.

As the series continued, Gardner inserted two other recurring conventions. One involves the introduction of Selby's old flame, Inez Stapleton, a dark beauty who has decided to earn his respect by becoming a lawyer herself. Inez offers Selby one predictable legal adversary; Alphonse Baker Carr offers another, more important one. "Old A.B.C." is what Perry Mason would recognize as a most competent jury-bribing pettifogger. Carr is in some ways Gardner's revenge on Mason; he is a Mason with an unlocked id. Mason exercises his exciting lack of scruples on behalf of innocent clients; Carr merely extends his unscrupulousness to include his choice of clients. Though he always comes up just short in his struggle with Selby, Carr's witty self-possession makes an attractive contribution to the series.

Ultimately the action of the D.A. novels is too forced; the motivations too contrived. The symmetries are not subtle: *Blade/Clarion,* police chief/sheriff, Inez/Sylvia, Carr/Selby. There is simply no reason for *The Blade* to keep insisting upon its naive counterplots; and the abundance of misidentified corpses suggests that Gardner was hard-pressed to invent temporary advantages for Selby's opponents. The characters in short are too obviously puppets, and the action is too clearly programmed by external considerations. After completing a volume or two, the reader returns to the series not to wonder at Selby's ingenuity, but at Gardner's. He ceases to identify at all with the actors in the fable.

Nonetheless Gardner's ingenuity is sufficiently wonderful to be enjoyed as such. And the small-town environment he evokes has its pleasant aspects. His portraits of the comfortable Brandon kitchen or, in *The D.A. Calls a Turn* (1943), of solidarity of the large Freelman family, suggest a nostalgia for domestic values largely missing from his other two more cosmopolitan series.

J. Kenneth Van Dover. *Murder in the Millions*
(New York: Ungar, 1984), pp. 76–78

The "Donald Lam—Bertha Cool Mysteries" comply with the normal requirements of the detective story genre—crisis-confusion-resolution—and they were by no means unpopular. The success of the series justified twenty-nine titles, the last of which, *All Grass Isn't Green,* was published posthumously. And, because their superficial form was a bit more liberated, they are generally better written than the Mason cases.

Gardner began the series in 1939 in part as a challenge to his publisher. He submitted the original manuscript through his agent under a pseudonym. Only after it was accepted for publication did Gardner acknowledge authorship, and he continued to maintain the imposture publicly for a number of years. Eventually he allowed the book covers to read "Erle Stanley Gardner writing under the name of A. A. Fair."

In the first Lam-Cool mystery, *The Bigger They Come* (1939), Donald Lam, a twenty-eight year old, one hundred twenty-eight pound disbarred lawyer, applies for a position at the B. Cool Detective Agency, a one-woman outfit dealing primarily with routine divorce cases. Bertha Cool, "somewhere in her sixties" and weighing two hundred twenty pounds (later reduced to a still substantial one sixty-five), is a hard-boiled, tough-mouthed, penny-pinching private eye. After hiring Donald, she instructs him to buy himself an 85¢ shirt, a 25–35¢ necktie, and a 20¢ breakfast. ("Now listen, Donald, don't you go blowing that money. Twenty-five cents is absolutely tops on breakfast.") Avarice is her humor; caution is her practice: Bertha frequently complains about the dramatic complications Donald involves the firm in. At least once a novel she exclaims, "Fry me for an oyster!"

Gardner clearly intended the Lam-Cool mysteries as a sport upon the contemporary fashion in detective stories. In Bertha he proposed a hard-boiled female; in Donald he proposed a detective viewed by everyone, including himself, as "a little runt." Whenever he encounters physical aggression, Donald puts up a good, but invariably losing fight. As he informs Bertha at their initial interview, he has learned to compensate with his wit. Lam often mentions that his disbarment resulted from his discovery of a perfectly legal way to commit murder and to escape conviction.

Lam always provides the driving intelligence of the series. Bertha may be the senior partner, but Donald is the traditional masculine risk-taker who stuns everyone with his ingenious solutions to the questions of the crime. Gardner's sport is not really that subversive.

Donald Lam conducts his investigations more through action than ratiocination. He is a highly mobile detective who prefers to confront individuals rather than examine evidence. And he races toward his conclusions—the police are always threatening to lift his license or even to arrest him for the crime. An endangered and attractive working girl is usually implicated in some aspect of the murder, and the characters all come from the middle classes.

Like nearly all fictional detectives, Bertha and Donald do not age visibly during their thirty-two-year career. They have pasts. Bertha's weight is a response to the discovery of the unfaithfulness of her ex-husband. At the beginning of *Spill the Jackpot* (1941) her doctor registers her in a sanitarium, where she loses some sixty pounds. In the same year, through a neat bit of extortion, Donald becomes a full partner in the firm (*Double or Quits*). Donald then appropriates Elsie Brand, the hard-worked secretary, as his personal Della Street. Donald, having debuted as a penniless embodiment of the depression job-seeker, responds to World War II by enlisting in the Navy (*Owls Don't Blink* [1942]). During the next two adventures (*Bats Fly at Dusk* [1942] and *Cats Prowl at Night* [1943]), he remains largely offstage. He returns in *Give 'Em the Ax* (1944), having been invalided out of the service after contracting "bugs—tropical bugs."

All the adventures except the two which occur during Lam's hitch in the navy are narrated by Donald. His voice is not a subtle interpretive instrument. Lam's asides are not strongly colored by his character, but the presence of the "I" at least serves as a reminder that reality depends upon perspective.

J. Kenneth Van Dover. *Murder in the Millions*
(New York: Ungar, 1984), pp. 78–82

Notably absent from the Queen's Quorum listing of the important volumes of mystery short stories is the name of the most popular mystery writer of our time, Erle Stanley Gardner. Ellery Queen has now edited the first volume of short stories and novelets by Gardner, and this may change that situation. In addition, as a welcome bonus, in *The Case of the Murderer's Bride and Other Stories* he has provided the reader with an informative and unusual introduction regarding Mr. Gardner. . . .

It is surprising that so many of us have forgotten how proficient Gardner was in the shorter mystery. For at least a decade before the publication of his first hardcover book in 1933 he was one of the most popular and prolific writers for pulp magazines. Only one of the seven stories in this volume represents that period. It is a still readable 1931 adventure of one of Gardner's series characters, Lester Leith, the confidence man.

The other stories reprinted in this book come from the period when Gardner was writing short fiction for the "slick" magazines. It should be noted that frequently the background of these stories is more interesting and more authentic than that found in the hardcover Gardner. For example, "Death Rides a Boxcar" (1944) takes place in the busy Los Angeles freight yards. "Only by Running" (1952; originally known as "Flight into Disaster") is set in some very rugged Wyoming country and reflects the author's knowledge of the outdoors life. Finally, there is a short story set in Canton, China. This is my personal favorite among all of Gardner's works. It is called "To Strike a Match" (1938; originally known as "The House of Three Candles"), and I suspect that many readers would have difficulty identifying this story as one by Gardner if the author's name were omitted.

Since 1967 there has been a renaissance in critical and historical writing about the mystery story. . . . Perhaps this volume of Gardner's shorter works is a harbinger of a rebirth in this area of the mystery. After all, Poe started it all with a short story.

Marvin Lachman. The Armchair Detective.
Summer 1970, p. 203

In twenty-nine A. A. Fair novels from 1939 to 1970, the Mutt-and-Jeff team of Bertha Cool and Donald Lam develops from employer and employee to a legal, contractual detecting partnership. . . . Bertha Cool is the instigator of this partnership, having hired Lam for her own agency; however, the narrative structure joins with characterization and plot to undermine Cool's role as an effective detective.

In all but two of the novels, Donald Lam narrates; he also solves all the cases himself. His ability to maneuver is established in the first novel, *The Bigger They Come,* as he proves it is possible to get away with murder. In all the subsequent cases, he evades the criminals, the police, and the well-meaning but misdirected Bertha to increase his successes. In the two novels where Donald is absent, serving in the Navy in World War II, Fair does not continue the established pattern of detective-storyteller by now using Bertha Cool to narrate; instead he turns to a third-person narrator, indicating clearly how devalued the female point of view is in this series. The plots further this conclusion; in both instances (*Bats Fly at Dusk* and *Cats Prowl at Night*), Bertha bungles the cases by trying to think like Donald because she has come to mistrust her own instincts and value his. Naturally, she has to be rescued; once, she is saved by Donald who has figured out the problem from censored letters and solved the case in a thirty-six-hour emergency leave. Even when Fair does not make Lam his principal detective and narrator, he persists in using the male partner as the exclusive crime solver. Cool becomes merely a humorous adjunct or a troublesome sidekick.

Their contrasting abilities are paralleled in Fair's persistent references to their appearance and attributes. Almost every novel opens with Cool's physical description and emphatic references to her size: "Bertha Cool is middle-aged, weighs a hundred and sixty-five pounds, has a broad beam, a bulldog look, little glittering green eyes, and is just as hard and tough and difficult to handle as a roll of barbed wire.'' Little changes, in either Fair's style or Cool's size, in fifteen years. Both Bertha Cool and Donald Lam reassure clients worried about Lam's slight build by insisting that ''brains count in this organization.'' Donald does not need brawn: ''I figure things out. I always have. If a man starts pushing me around, I find a way to make him stop, and before I'm through he's sorry he ever started pushing. I don't mind hitting below the belt if I have to. I guess I even get a kick out of it. That's because of the way I'm made. A runt is apt to be mean.'' Since Bertha's description contrasts her size with Donald Lam's, she must be the brawn to match his brains. This implication minimizes her role since brains are ordinarily valued over mere brute force no matter how strong. However, the novels go further in undercutting Cool, since, with one or two exceptions when she sits on female suspects to prevent their escape, she doesn't use brawn successfully either.

Like narration and characterization, Fair's plots demonstrate the clear-cut superiority of the male partner. Donald's instincts, skills, and judgment are so complete that he has no need for a colleague; the female—''bulldog'' Bertha—is a plot device used to intensify the impact of his success. Although ''B. Cool—Investigations'' had successfully concentrated on small cases before Donald Lam's employment, Bertha is portrayed as incapable of even accepting a client much less solving a case after Lam's arrival. She admits this when he returns from wartime duty: '' 'When you went away,' Bertha said, 'you'd got us into the big-time stuff. Damned if I know how you did it. You could take even the most insignificant little case, and before you got done it developed into big business and big money. Then after you left, I could take what seemed to be the biggest case and it would peter out into little business and little money. I did all right for a while. Two or three cases went just as though you'd been here. And then the bottom dropped out and it's been a whole procession of little stuff like this.' '' With Donald's efforts, this ''little stuff'' also turns into a major case with a sizable fee. Although greed and financial management are supposed to be her specialties, Donald invariably has to unravel cases Cool has taken on too quickly and thoughtlessly just for the fee. On other occasions accepting a case despite her criticism and carping, Donald brings the agency a huge fee or bonus. Invariably, Big Bertha makes erroneous decisions and has to accede to lamblike Donald.

The apparent humor of Fair's novels disguises a misogynistic subtext. . . . These works disparage women through the persistent mockery of Bertha Cool whom the genre would designate the cohero. Caricatured as the leading male characters are not, she shares none of their redeeming talents. Unlike many examples in this study, Fair's submerged text shows that as both a married woman and a detective, Cool is a failure: both her husband and her partner outsmart her. Her only revenge is eating; the results—her weight, diets, appearance, meals—only elicit further mockery from Fair and his narrator, Lam. Nothing she is or does can be right; she is always ludicrous.

Kathleen Gregory Klein. *The Woman Detective: Gender and Genre* (Urbana and Chicago: University of Illinois Press, 1988), pp. 191–93

GILBERT, MICHAEL (1912–)

Accuracy in legal matters distinguishes the detective novels of Michael Gilbert, a London solicitor, whose stories range over a wide variety of subjects and settings. His first, *Close Quarters* (1947), deals with a "sealed room" problem in the precincts of a cathedral. Organized crime in London, routine police work and judicial procedure are the subjects of *They Never Looked Inside* (1947) and *The Doors Open* (1949). *Smallbone Deceased* (1950), set in the office of a London lawyer, is less striking, but *Death in Captivity* (1952) shows originality in its presentation of a murder mystery in an Italian prisoner-of-war camp. His next novel, *Fear to Tread* (1953) is outstanding and gives an alarming, authentic-seeming picture of the gangster violence behind large-scale pilfering on the railways. Mr. Gilbert has not yet surpassed this achievement, and of his later works perhaps the most entertaining is *The Claimant* (1957), an ingenious reconstruction of the Tichborne Case.

A. E. Murch. *The Development of the Detective Novel* (New York: Philosophical Library, 1958), pp. 238–39

The first novel of Michael (Francis) Gilbert was *Close Quarters* (1947), an orthodox detective story of what might have been pre-1939 vintage. It even included a map of the Cathedral Close as ornamentation for an ecclesiastical murder case. Gilbert quickly moved away from this classical pattern, and in *Smallbone Deceased* (1950) made splendid use of his own professional legal knowledge to construct a puzzle that also offered a nicely comic view of life in the office of Horniman, Birley, and Craine, solicitors. Since that time, Gilbert has wavered between a wish to be fairly realistic in depicting people and a feeling that one shouldn't be too serious in a crime story.

He is not tied to a series character—his first investigator, Chief Inspector Hazlerigg, was replaced by the insomniac Bohun, who disappeared in favor of Sergeant Petrella and others. And he is not afraid to experiment with settings—one of his best books, *Death in Captivity* (1952) is set in a prisoner-of-war camp, and in *The Crack in the Teacup* (1966) he concentrates very successfully upon some apparently petty crookedness in the affairs of a local Council. He has written skillful and enjoyable thrillers and short stories. Yet there remains an impression that he is not quite content to be appreciated just as an entertainer, but that some restraint (legal caution, perhaps) checks him from writing in a way that fully expresses his personality. *The Crack in the Teacup* was his best book for a long time, and it is possible that future stories may offer some development of the implicit social comedy in that book.

Julian Symons. *Mortal Consequences* (New York:
Harper & Row, 1972), pp. 200–201

There are not many mystery writers whose entire oeuvres I could recommend reading without literary interruption—the similarities, not so readily noticed when the fare is varied, usually become uncomfortably apparent when it is not.

Let me approach my subject from another direction. In covering some 800 books for the *New York Times Book Review,* I found two kinds of book which were hard to review for their very different reasons. The one represents the mass of average mysteries, for how does one say the same thing in different ways about hundreds of books? The other is represented by that exceptional work, about whose plot it is unfair to give many details in a review, for to the author rightly belongs the privilege of scheduling and staging these revelations.

Which brings me to Michael Gilbert, an author of uncommon ability whose every work is an individual achievement, and to *The Body of a Girl.*

With this book Mr. Gilbert comes more within the usual confines of the genre than some of his recent novels. We journey to Stoneferry, upriver on the Thames. A placid sort of manor this, and its soon-to-retire Superintendent of Police would just as well keep it that way. Enter Detective Chief Inspector Mercer, promoted to take charge of the plainclothes branch. Mercer is an odd chap, with a mind that seems gone off into at least three irrelevancies at any time. He quickly alienates the Super, makes himself unpopular inquiring about the doings of one of the town's solidest citizens—with whom he is seen in frequent alcoholic camaraderie, and generally constructs an ominous cloud over his own head. A strange way indeed for a honest copper to be carrying on, and his handling of the matter of the titular cadaver also excites no groundswell of confidence. More I will not say—in tardy obedience to my own stricture—except that after the rather flat year in mysteries in 1971 *The Body of a Girl* is an eminently satisfying example of what the form is capable in the hands of the truly creative.

Allen J. Hubin. *The Armchair Detective.* Summer
1972, p. 163

Michael Gilbert has drawn all of his London procedural short stories about Patrick Petrella together as *Petrella at Q.* Despite some attractive features about the last, none of them work. Some critics maintain that the short story is the best form for the mystery to take; I maintain that it is the worst.

Petrella may be a pleasant person to have around, but he becomes insufferable when he solves a dozen cases in a two-hour read, always right and always at the same pace. The short story is to the mystery what soccer is to football: simply so perfect in the shape of its specific moments, and so predictable as to what must be done to eliminate all elements of suspense, all misdirecting, all second guessing. Has anyone ever heard of a Monday morning quarterback in soccer?

Robin W. Winks. *The New Republic.* November
26, 1977, p. 37

In *Close Quarters* and in most of his subsequent tales of detection, Michael Gilbert employs the classic seven-step plot first used by Poe in the Dupin stories, which has become the conventional formula for organization of formal-problem detective stories. The structure is fairly obvious in *Sky High* where, after some preliminary episodes to establish background and atmosphere, the Problem—step 1—is introduced in the death of Lieutenant Macmorris, killed by an explosion in his home. Then comes the Initial Solution by the police (traditionally, in this type of story a mistaken one), to the effect that Macmorris was a burglar who kept in his home some explosives, which had been set off by accident. The third step is the Complication, in which the first solution proves to be mistaken: in this case the development of evidence that the accidental-explosion theory is untenable. Next is the Period of Confusion, wherein one of the three amateur detectives, acting on his own, follows up a clue with which he alone is familiar, another is almost killed in a thinly disguised accident, and the police continue with their own routine investigations. Step five is the Dawning Light, in which things begin to fall into place, the discovery of a vital piece of evidence and the apprehension of the murderer's accomplice, followed shortly by the Solution, the identification of the murderer, and the Explanation, this final revelation being an account of a highly ingenious means of setting off an explosion. Gilbert is fairly conservative in his use of the formal-problem plot structure. Although it is a tight formula it lends itself to almost unlimited variety in sequence (the Complication, the Period of Confusion, and the Dawning Light can be repeated several times, for example, and Solution and Explanation can be reversed), but Gilbert's detective tales customarily hold closely to the classic order.

There is one type of structure that has come to be a Gilbert specialty. This is the mystery that opens with a deceptively mild atmosphere, lures the reader into an attitude of serene security, and then jolts him rudely with the incursion into the story of violent death. A particularly happy instance may be found in the early chapters of *Smallbone Deceased,* where the locale is the quiet chambers of a firm of solicitors, and the action is chiefly lawyer talk, centering around such conveniences as the Horniman Self-Checking Completion System, designed to keep infallible account of the whereabouts of documents. Incredibly, a scream resounds through these peaceful surroundings, announcing the discovery of the mortal remains of Marcus Smallbone in a most unexpected place. That scream, by the way, must be the best heralded in mystery fiction: first, a conversation between two of the partners ends with one of them asking, "Is that someone screaming?"; five pages later a discussion of golfing is terminated with "What on earth was that?" "It sounded like a scream, didn't it?" Early in the next chapter we are told the cause, and the shock of recognition is much sharper as a result of the contrast. The corpse of Marcus Smallbone is a considerably more shocking affair in the chambers of Horniman, Birley, and Craine than if it had been found in an opium den or fished out of the Thames. The same device is employed (with modifications) in the opening chapters of *The Etruscan Net,* where the civilized security of the English colony in Florence is disrupted by murder, and in *The Night of the Twelfth,* where the locale is a boys' school. Of course the intrusion of violence into the peaceful community has always been basic to the myth of the detective story, but Gilbert has become a master of the art of heightening the effect by means of contrast. . . .

Any discussion of Gilbert's craftsmanship must include some comment upon his ability to manage the English language, in which respect he is an obvious master. On occasion his sentences snap with the unexpectedness of a well-told joke, as when he observes in *The Doors Open,* "Living together, as Anne of Cleeves was once heard to remark, can be a trial to both parties." His figures of speech are customarily not only richly suggestive but also neatly precise, as when Laura Hart in *After the Fine Weather* senses that the wine "had a resinous tang which touched the back of her throat as a man's hand will touch, for a fraction of a second, the hand of a woman he desires." It rarely rises to the level of pure magic, but when it does, it is singularly effective, as in one of the stories in *Game without Rules,* in which Mr. Calder and Rasselas are sleeping in the open on a down. Rasselas growls softly:

> Mr. Calder raised his head. During the time he had been asleep the wind had risen a little, and was blowing up dark clouds and sending them scudding across the face of the moon; the shadows on the bare down were horsemen, warriors with horned helmets, riding horses with flying manes and tails. Rasselas was following them with his eyes, head cocked. It was as if, behind the piping of the wind, he could hear, pitched too high for human ears, the shrill note of a trumpet.
> "They're ghosts," said Mr. Calder calmly. "They won't hurt us." He lay down, and was soon asleep again.

Whatever his other abilities, Michael Gilbert is not a character-portraitist. Nor does he need to be; the kind of story he writes well demands the effects of careful plotting and the tone of melodrama, but no great depth or breadth in the development of people. Many of Gilbert's most memorable people are caricatures. Some are as obvious as the obtuse Patrick Yeatman-Carter in *The Doors Open,* who considers everything enjoyable "a good show," and whose response to the possibility of a beating by gangsters is to suggest that he is quite capable of taking care of the situation: "I mean, I've done a bit of amateur boxing." Another undisguised caricature is Wilfred Wetherall, the crusading schoolmaster of *Fear to Tread.* Gilbert is too skillful a writer to make Wetherall a buffoon, but he touches him with a distrait quality that manifests itself when, during conversation, he catches an example of a grammatical function in his own speech, stops and makes a note for use in his grammar class. The most fully developed character in a Gilbert novel is Oliver Nugent of *The Dust and the Heat,* who might have been the subject of a Gatsby-like portrait if the writer's purpose were directed toward the figure of a personality in society, but who becomes rather a vehicle for the development of suspense; actually, we never get a direct look at Nugent, but must see him through the eyes of the other people in the story, with the result that his image is never complete. . . .

With such an array of technical skills at his command, it is no wonder that Michael Gilbert does not object to classification among the Entertainers. Ultimately, he is not likely to be ranked with the portrayers of complex characters or the developers of great ideas. His excellence lies rather in his control of the art of suspense, in his ability to make the English language crackle, and in his command of those narrative techniques that produce the well-made story.

George N. Dove. In Earl F. Bargainnier, ed.,
Twelve Englishmen of Mystery (Bowling Green,
Ohio: Popular Press, 1984), pp. 185–94

GRAFTON, SUE (1940–   )

Kinsey Millhone likes small, cramped spaces, is not particularly domestic, and would be content to live out of her car. The '68 beige VW is well prepared for it. Files, law books, boxes, and a case of motor oil adorn the inside. On appropriate occasions, the back seat has surrendered pantyhose and black spike heels. Her efficient apartment in Santa Teresa is a converted one-car garage, about fifteen square feet, properly apportioned into bedroom, kitchen, living room, and laundry facility. Even her office is small, occupying a corner of the California Fidelity Insurance Company.

Kinsey is thirty-two and twice divorced. When she was twenty, she attended the police academy and on graduation joined the Santa Teresa Police Department. She found that there were too many restrictions to the job, and continually having to prove that she was tough was frustrating for the independent and self-reliant person she had become. After an internship as an investigator for the California Fidelity Insurance Company, she began a business of her own, bringing to it the tools of the trade as well as the procedure of police work.

> In any event, I was going to have to check it out item by item. I felt as if I were on an assembly line, inspecting reality with a jeweler's loupe. There's no place in a P.I.'s life for impatience, faintheartedness, or sloppiness. I understand the same qualifications apply for housewives.
>
> Most of my investigations proceed just like this. Endless notes, endless sources checked and rechecked, pursuing leads that sometimes go no place. Usually, I start in the same place, plodding along methodically, never knowing at first what might be significant. It's all detail; facts accumulated painstakingly.

In Sue Grafton's *"A" Is for Alibi,* the first book in the series, Millhone is hired by Nikki Fife, recently released from prison and out on parole. Nikki maintains that she is innocent of the murder of her philandering husband, Laurence, and wants Kinsey to locate the real killer. Though the case is eight years old and success is less than predictable, it is still intriguing and Kinsey takes the job. Quite a few people wanted the shrewd and despicable, but irresistible, Laurence dead, and Kinsey thoroughly retraces the steps which lead to his demise.

In *"B" Is for Burglar,* two weeks after she winds up the smoldering Fife case, Kinsey is hired by the expensive and slightly crazy Beverly Danziger to find her sister, Elaine. Kinsey travels from Santa Teresa to Boca Raton, Florida, to search for the missing heiress and is assisted by two wonderfully feisty little old ladies, Tillie Ahlberg and Julia Ochsner. These amateur sleuths provide helpful long-distance clues for finding Elaine and the identity of the mysterious, hissing woman.

"C" Is for Corpse, opens with Kinsey working out at the gym, and recuperating from the ravages of her second case. She meets Bobby Callahan, a badly injured and frightened young man, who thinks that someone is trying to kill him and asks Kinsey to help him. Though bits and pieces of Bobby's memory have been wiped out from a deadly car crash, he feels that he still carries information vital to his enemy. The young man proves to be correct and the investigation shifts to one of murder.

Delightfully warm and colorful characters recur in Kinsey's life. Henry Pitts, her sexy eighty-one-year-old landlord, is a former baker. He still creates delicacies for neighbors and friends, occasionally caters small affairs, but currently earns a living devising impossibly complex crossword puzzles. Rosie, who is somewhere in her sixties, runs the neighborhood bar just a half block from Kinsey's apartment. It is a familiar stop for Kinsey, for dinner or for meeting clients or suspects. Rosie runs the bar, does the imaginative cooking flavored with a Hungarian touch, and deals with Life. Her rust-colored hair and distinctive eyebrows add a certain unnecessary flair to her appearance.

Grafton plans on giving readers the entire alphabet's worth of Kinsey Millhone mysteries. We applaud the idea because we have enjoyed watching Kinsey develop from an aggressive investigator who is simply competent and tough to an individual more at ease with her charge. While she doesn't give much away about who she really is, she is straightforward in her dealings with people and is respected and even liked by those she meets in the course of an investigation. The plots are for the most part believable, though Grafton exceeds several limits as the third book draws to its conclusion. At the rate the series has progressed to date, we predict that this character will continue to provide readers with pleasant surprises.

Victoria Nichols and Susan Thompson. *Silk
Stalkings: When Women Write of Murder*
(Berkeley: Black Lizard Books, 1988), pp. 217–18

"The basic characteristics of any good investigator," observes Kinsey Millhone, in *"A" Is for Alibi* by Sue Grafton, "are a plodding nature and infinite patience. Society has inadvertently been grooming women to this end for years." Kinsey, a decidedly unplodding cop-turned-private eye in Santa Teresa, California, is hired by Nikki Fife, who eight years earlier had been wrongly convicted of poisoning her husband, Laurence. With a trail as cold as the corpse, Kinsey must track down the real killer. . . .

This is Kinsey Millhone's debut in what her author hopes will be a series, and Grafton has sketched only the bare essentials of her detective's life—she is thirty-two, divorced, eschews the trendy, favors the slob school of fashion, runs. Still, she has created a woman we feel we know, a tough cookie with a soft center, a gregarious loner. Equally important, Grafton populates her cosmos with what one hopes will be a regular supporting cast: Henry Pitts, Kinsey's eighty-one-year-old landlord, who bakes bread, devises fiendish puzzles and has "an amazing set of legs"; Con Dolan, a cuddly grizzly-bear cop; and Arlette, an obese motel manager who lobbies for the rights of her fellow fatties—"her eyes squeezed almost to invisibility by the heavy cheeks. I wondered when she'd last seen her own neck."

Katrine Ames. *Newsweek*. June 7, 1982, p. 72

Sue Grafton's Kinsey Millhone encounters as many problems in personal relationships with men as she does in professional ones, but she does not usually suspend her doubts in order to become involved with men, seeing sexual relationships as risky. In the first book of the Millhone series, *"A" is for Alibi,* the dangers of the job and those of heterosexual relationships merge, as Kinsey has an affair with the man she ultimately realizes is the killer for whom she is searching. When first attracted to him, Kinsey compares the feeling to a suicidal impulse: "It's the same sensation I have sometimes on the twenty-first floor when I open a window—a terrible attraction to the notion of tumbling out. I go a long time between men and maybe it was time again." This man has already killed one woman and kills two more before attempting to murder Kinsey, so her early analogy is quite accurate: involvement with Scorsoni *is* suicidal. In some ways, *"A" Is for Alibi* is very close to traditional hard-boiled stories, with a sex-role switch: the detective puts aside suspicions, becomes sexually involved with a person who turns out to be the killer, discovers the truth, and punishes the dangerous lover. Considered from this angle, *Alibi* fuses *The Maltese Falcon* with Mickey Spillane-style violence as Kinsey finally kills the man who duped her. However, the alteration in sex roles is not the only revision Grafton makes, as the novel's central theme is women's position in marriage, with Scorsoni's cool murdering of three people to cover his embezzling set against a woman's poisoning of the ex-husband who cruelly punished her for years. The crime of passion committed by the woman pales in comparison to the man's cold determination to destroy anyone who gets in his way. Kinsey's killing of this man is in self-defense and is further mitigated by the thematic context in which it occurs. Nevertheless, *Alibi* does come uncomfortably close to a mere reversal of hard-boiled conventions, with all the men in the novel potentially dangerous but all the women granted subjectivity and individuality, with their crimes and failings excused by their subordination to men.

The treatment of male-female relationships is more complex in the next three novels in the Millhone series, with none of these making the simplistic gender divisions of *Alibi*. Kinsey's experience with Scorsoni in that first novel, though, provides an important context for her unwillingness to take risks with men in the next three books; in *"B" is for Burglar* Kinsey finds herself deeply attracted to a man but does not act on that attraction until *"D" is for Deadbeat* (1987), when she finally overcomes her "bone deep caution," deciding that she is usually too "careful not to make mistakes. Sometimes I wonder what the difference is between being cautious and being dead." Even the involvements with men Kinsey does allow herself are more physical than emotional; she says in *"C" is for Corpse* "I like my life just as it is," and any deep emotional entanglement would inevitably change that life in some way. She sees her sexual relationships as following a cyclical rhythm:

> About every six or eight months, I run into a man who astounds me sexually, but between escapades, I'm celibate, which I don't think is any big deal. After two unsuccessful marriages, I find myself keeping my guard up, along with my underpants.

She has important relationships with her landlord, Henry Pitts, who lives in the main house on the property where her one-room apartment, a converted garage, is located, and with Rosie, the proprietor of a rather seedy neighborhood bar. Both of these characters are more than twice Kinsey's age and may at first seem to fit neatly into the roles of substitute father and mother, but that would be a gross oversimplification of their function. Each does fulfill a few of the traditional requirements of parents, with Henry worrying about Kinsey's safety and Rosie providing food, but their roles in Kinsey's life do not fit into any established patterns. Neither exerts—or attempts to exert—the kind of power over Kinsey generally wielded by parents over children and neither stays within sex-role boundaries (Henry also bakes bread, for instance, while Rosie offers advice on a case).

Most importantly, Kinsey's relationship with each is an egalitarian one, with both Henry and Rosie respecting her independence and professional competence. In *"E" is for Evidence* Grafton dramatizes the significance of chosen families and their superiority to the nuclear variety by enmeshing Kinsey in a case that turns on ugly family secrets. With Rosie and Henry both out of town for the Christmas holidays, Kinsey at first feels alone and lonely, cut off from the special warmth and affection she imagines siblings share. The more Kinsey learns about the Wood family, though, the more she values her freedom to choose her relatives, so to speak, and the more she appreciates the life she has fashioned for herself.

Maureen T. Reddy. Sisters in Crime: Feminism
and the Crime Novel (New York: Continuum,
1988), pp. 108–10

Born during the Korean War, Kinsey Millhone is naturally a product of both the new feminist movement and the traditional view of women's lives. She is often caught between the two. Author Sue Grafton also invests Kinsey with most of the typical detective's trappings, accommodating her gender and potential self-awareness in only minor ways. Neither too young nor too innocent of the world to be a plausible detective, Millhone is a thirty-two-year-old, twice-divorced woman without children, plants, or housepets; she is a loner whose friendships do not seem to pass beyond a carefully modulated phase. She comes closest to establishing ties with just two women and two men—her eighty-one-year-old landlord, the black female owner of her favorite bar, an arthritic retiree who jokes about becoming her partner, and a recently divorced cop who is willing to help her. Her attitude about intimate relationships is equally self-protective: "Whatever the surface appearances, most human beings come equipped with convoluted emotional machinery. With intimacy, the wreckage starts to show, damage rendered in the course of passions colliding like freight trains on the same track. I'd had enough of that over the years." Ironically, her professional life contradicts the isolation of her personal one. Naive, frustrated, and idealistic, she left the police force because "back then, policewomen were viewed with a mixture of curiosity and scorn. I didn't want to spend my days defending myself against 'good-natured' insults, or having to prove how tough I was again and again." She did not go immediately into independent private detective work but held several noninvestigative jobs before apprenticing two years with a small detective firm. With five years of being in business for herself, she is well established even to the point of having a connection with California Fidelity Insurance Company, which trades her a two-room office in exchange for investigative work. Although three of her clients are vastly different women, she tends to overgeneralize: "I like older women as a rule. I like almost all women, as a matter of fact. I find them open and confiding by nature, amusingly candid when it comes to talk of men." And despite this avowal, she can be snide about other women she meets in her investigations; despite some feminist inclinations, she is not uniformly sympathetic to women.

Kinsey's style of operation is a twofold blend of traditional women's and men's work. She notes that most of her job consists of tedious, monotonous, boring checking and cross-checking—plodding and patient routine. Wryly she acknowledges in both books that society has inadvertently been preparing women for these roles for years, turning on its head the stereotype of the macho detective, knight-errant, man in a man's world of mean streets. In defining her performance, Kinsey continually tests herself; more than just being a detective, she is fitting herself into an external model she has seen. Methodically, she runs daily "for the same reasons I learned to drive a car with a stick shift and drink my coffee black, imagining that a day might come when some amazing emergency would require such a test." When she is wrong, she criticizes herself and then more fairly reconsiders, recognizing that she had made only the same mistakes as everyone else. Even so, she admits that feeling good about her professional behavior is as important as the money she earns for solving a case.

The novels' conflicts are more the result of Millhone's errors than either the criminals' cleverness or the pace of the investigation; this device makes it difficult for Grafton to recover her protagonist's stature. In all three of the cases described, Kinsey significantly misjudges the situations with client, criminals, or friend. Most important, she trusts and sleeps with a murderer who is trying to keep her from the truth. Her attraction to Charlie Scorsoni is immediate and powerful. Their relationship is marked by her self-consciousness at being so vulnerable to his sexual charm and, eventually, a nagging recognition that mixing business and lovemaking is both unprofessional and dangerous. A sharp irony arises: early in their affair, he makes her feel comfortable and safe; at the end of the case, she is forced to kill him when he hunts her down with a butcher knife. Before she calls a temporary break from seeing him, he forces an argument about how she is using him, pumping him for information. At first, she is angry—"I've never been good at taking shit, especially from men"—and labels his offer of compromise as giving away half of what is rightfully hers. But later she apologizes, wonders if she has misjudged him, and hops back into bed from which she emerges feeling smug about their sexual compatibility. Until almost the end of the case, she is ambivalent about her decision not to continue seeing him, worrying that she is using her job and her claims of integrity to avoid commitment. Grafton uses this concern, expressed only for an intimate heterosexual relationship, to reassure readers of this strong woman's traditional femininity rather than to develop her character or personality.

Grafton has created a thoughtful, self-aware if sometimes self-deluded woman who is also a detective; her work gives Millhone both reasons and opportunity to consider her own life: "I tried to imagine myself dead, someone sorting carelessly through my belongings. What was there really of my life? Canceled checks. Reports all typewritten and filed. Everything of value reduced to terse prose. I didn't keep much myself, didn't hoard or save. Two divorce decrees. That was about the sum of it for me. I collected more information about other people's lives than I did about my own, as though, perhaps, in poring over the facts about other people, I could discover something about myself. My own mystery, unplumbed, undetected, was sorted into files that were neatly labeled but really didn't say much." With this attitude, she has stripped down her life; when in doubt she falls back on routine. Even on a case, she wants to cut through the surrounding game-playing, hoping for straight answers without conniving and manipulating. Although she saves herself from Scorsoni and later from the Grices and Dr. Fraker, Kinsey questions her own professional judgment. Killing Charlie Scorsoni leads her to reconsider how she can be a good person if she has killed; attacking and shooting Leonard and Marty Grice causes her to wonder "how many times I'll dance with death." Guilty at not being able to forestall Tony Gahan's suicide, she muses, "Perhaps in this case, all of the accounts are now paid in full . . . except mine." She worries that she has made peace with corruption—or been a detective too long.

Her relationship with authority is contradictory. Millhone recognizes that her sense of self in the power structure is based on being sent to the principal's office when a schoolgirl. As a result she alternates between trying to inform the police about her case, promising Jonah Robb not to "be stupid," being nervous when a cop offers to pass along privileged information, and refusing to report a break-in at her apartment because she feels harassed by the cops. This ambivalence traps her between being independent and unconsciously expecting to be protected by the system. Even when she seems to take reasonable precautions for her own safety independent of police protection, it is just barely enough. So, she must bail herself out of trouble. Later, her victorious feelings of escape and self-preservation vie with others of guilt and regret.

What eventually emerges about Millhone's relationship with the patriarchal system is conventional, even traditional. Her personal ties with police officers may be both hostile and congenial but they signal her acceptance of the system despite her personal inability to fit into it. When she kills Scorsoni, she reports the shooting to both the police and the Bureau of Collection and Investigative Services; when she captures Leonard and Marty Grice and Dr. Fraker, she turns them over to the police. Even though Millhone is cautious about assuming that the courts will punish them, she takes her use of the legal system for granted. Her professional behavior is at odds with her awareness, but she still does not see herself challenging the process. The closest she comes to challenging the prevailing attitude is to acknowledge how simplistic (at least in the John Daggett case) her conventional view of morality is. Her latent feminism is individual rather than communal; she sees both problems and solutions in personal rather than systemic change.

Kathleen Gregory Klein. The Woman Detective:
Gender and Genre (Urbana and Chicago:
University of Illinois Press, 1988), pp. 203–5

At the Vagabond Motel, two chunky, middle-aged honeymooners are enjoying their wedding night. The woman next door is not. To block the noise, Kinsey Millhone ties a sock-stuffed bra around her head. "I lay there, a cone over each ear like an alien, wondering at the peculiarities of human sex practices. I would have much to report when I returned to my planet."

Wit is the most versatile weapon in Sue Grafton's well-stocked arsenal, and she uses it with disarming precision in her seventh Kinsey Millhone venture, *"G" Is for Gumshoe.* When you're laughing, you may momentarily forget about the particularly lethal hit man (he doesn't need the money, he just loves his work) who's pursuing Millhone.

A well-dressed neurasthenic hires detective Millhone for a simple task: to bring home her elderly mother, a scruffy sunbird living on an abandoned military base in the Mojave. But trouble begins as soon as Kinsey checks into the nearby Vagabond, whose thin-walled rooms smell faintly of "eau de bug." With a sociopath on her trail, she must pack not only a gun but a bodyguard (with whom she shares a palpable sexual tension). While tracking down her client's mother, she unearths grisly family secrets of a tormented woman. Millhone, whose background has made her believe that all families are dysfunctional, has unwittingly taken on another case of domestic violence. Grafton excels in this milieu. Never morally oblique, here she is slyly didactic about (among other things) attitudes toward the mentally ill. Good news: she's already started *"H" Is for. . . .*

Katrine Ames. Newsweek. May 14, 1990, p. 66

New to the best-seller lists is Sue Grafton, whose seventh mystery featuring female Southern California private investigator Kinsey Millhone, *"G" Is for Gumshoe,* is proving to be her "breakout" book.

Several elements make *Gumshoe* one of the best entries yet in this consistently appealing series. The out-of-nowhere appearances by the assassin—a spooky guy who brings his little boy along on jobs—provide genuine jolts, bursts of adrenaline that interrupt Kinsey's usual wisecracking mode and induce a giddy vertigo. The mystery proper has some of the intriguing qualities of a Ross Macdonald puzzle, dank with long-buried secrets and lingering guilts.

Major, minor, and recurring characters of all ages are quirky and vivid, like the ensemble company of the greatest TV show you'll never see. (Creating interesting and believable older women and men is something the author is especially good at.) And Millhone's distinctive running monologue, full of pithy descriptions and sardonic observations, pulls all this together in a most engaging manner.

Whatever the formula, its entertaining results make Ms. Grafton's alphabetical *Gumshoe* seem an especially deserving best seller. May it have at least nineteen equally successful sequels.

Tom Nolan. *The Wall Street Journal*. June 8, 1990, p. A8

Sue Grafton's Kinsey Millhone keeps turning up in a series that began with *"A" Is for Alibi* and goes through the alphabet for its titles. The latest Millhone mystery is *"H" Is for Homicide*. It continues to show the author in strong storytelling form in her Southern California locale.

If her first-person private investigator sometimes sets a scene like Dashiell Hammett or Raymond Chandler or Ross Macdonald, well, why not emulate the best? She treads in the footsteps of masters when she writes semi-tough or overwrites lyrically: "A moon the size of a dinner plate was propped up on the balcony outside my window, and the light falling across my face was almost bright enough to read by." And again, building suspense when she's alone on the job at three in the morning, staking out a suspected murderer: "The moon was full and rode high in the night sky. The Los Angeles city lights projected an ashen reflection across the heavens, blotting out the stars."

But there is a fundamental difference between Ms. Grafton's protagonist and the classic male private detective. For one thing, there's added tension and a greater sense of danger when her vulnerable heroine is walking down some dark alley, stalking and being stalked. Even more important, Ms. Grafton brings a woman's perspective to her people and their romances. One of her characters is described this way: "Her face was Kabuki white, her mouth a pout of bright red. Her hair had been newly bleached to the color of typing paper, standing up in spikes as if somebody'd folded it in quarters and cut it with a pair of scissors. The effect was of an albino rooster."

"H" Is for Homicide finds Kinsey Millhone working on a case involving the death of a claims adjuster for a California insurance company. The story takes her into the Los Angeles barrio in pursuit of a violent criminal, into jails and hospitals, and into a grungy bar named the Meat Locker. The plotting gets a little overwrought, but count on Millhone not only to corner

the murderer but also to make a statement against the foibles of the insurance game. The lady can write.

Herbert Mitgang. *The New York Times*. May 8,
1991, n.p.

See also under SARA PARETSKY: Carolyn G. Heilbrun, *Ms.*, March/April 1991.

GREENE, GRAHAM (1904–1991)

Graham Greene divides his fiction into "novels" and "entertainments." Superficially there is no great difference between the two categories. There is no Ruth Draper switch from comic to pathetic. "Novels" and "entertainments" are both written in the same grim style, both deal mainly with charmless characters, both have a structure of sound, exciting plot. You cannot tell from the skeleton whether the man was baptized or not. And that is the difference; the "novels" have been baptized, held deep under in the waters of life.

Mr. Greene's style of writing is not a specifically literary style at all. The words are functional, devoid of sensuous attraction, of ancestry, and of independent life. Literary stylists regard language as intrinsically precious and its proper use as a worthy and pleasant task. A polyglot could read Mr. Greene, lay him aside, retain a sharp memory of all he said and yet, I think, entirely forget what tongue he was using. The words are simply mathematical signs for his thought. Moreover, no relation is established between writer and reader. The reader has not had a conversation with a third party such as he enjoys with Sterne or Thackeray. Nor is there within the structure of the story an observer through whom the events are recorded and the emotions transmitted. It is as though, out of an infinite length of film, sequences had been cut which, assembled, comprise an experience which is the reader's alone, without any correspondence to the experience of the protagonists. The writer has become director and producer. Indeed, the affinity to the film is everywhere apparent. It is the camera's eye which moves from the hotel balcony to the street below, picks out the policeman, follows him to his office, moves about the room from the handcuffs on the wall to the broken rosary in the drawer, recording significant detail. It is the modern way of telling a story.

Mr. Greene is a storyteller of genius. Born in another age, he would still be spinning yarns. His particular habits are accidental. The plot of *The Heart of the Matter* might well have been used by M. Simenon or Mr. Somerset Maugham.

He makes of his material a precise and plausible drama. His technical mastery has never been better manifested than in his statement of the scene— the sweat and infection, the ill-built town which is beautiful for a few minutes at sundown, the brothel where all men are equal, the vultures, the priest who, when he laughed "swung his great empty-sounding bell to and fro, Ho ho, ho, like a leper proclaiming his misery," the snobbery of the second-class public schools, the law which all can evade, the ever-present haunting underworld of gossip, spying, bribery, violence, and betrayal. It is so well done that one forgets the doer. The characters are real people whose moral and spiritual predicament is our own because they are part of our personal experience.

Evelyn Waugh. Commonweal. July 16, 1948, pp.
322–23

The Confidential Agent is secular in its outlook in the same sense as *A Gun for Sale;* and it exhibits the same characteristics—the chase, the revenge, the motif of flight and pursuit. Greene's hero is a middle-aged scholar sent by his government to negotiate a contract with the British mine owners for badly needed coal. He is balked by counteragents and in the end defeated by them. But though he does not secure the coal his country needs, he has the satisfaction of knowing that the enemy will not have it either. . . .

D., the hero, is an elderly scholar who had at one time discovered an important manuscript of *The Song of Roland*. The war, which seems to parallel the war in Spain, had cut short his literary activities and forced him to devote himself to his political party. He is alone, and the death of his wife at the hands of Fascists has paralyzed his feelings. He has nothing to hold on to, not even belief in God. And he cannot be certain of the integrity of the cause for which he fights. . . .

Although he thinks he is past all feeling, D. is touched by the mute appeal of the child, Else, and by the unhappiness of the girl, Rose Cullen, the daughter of Lord Benditch, D.'s contact for the coal. D.'s pity leads him, eventually, to a "happy" ending; he goes off at the novel's end with Rose.

D. is aware of the evil in the world, but he is passive in the face of it until Else is murdered by the manageress of the hotel in which he lives. (D. had entrusted his identity papers to the child, and she is killed because she remains faithful to the trust.) Once D.'s humanity is aroused by the brutality and senselessness of the murder, he is no longer the pursued but the pursuer. . . .

D. can indulge in the chase to satisfy his sense of outraged humanity; and as long as he adheres to the world's dictum regarding right and wrong, he can allow himself the luxury of revenge, an eye for an eye, a tooth for a tooth. There is no God, so vengeance is D.'s. . . .

The Confidential Agent does not demonstrate the conciseness and economy of *A Gun for Sale*. And its ending seems somewhat arranged, even considering the melodramatic contrivances of the plot. Greene allows D. to escape the web of evidence that has connected him with the murder of Else, the death of K., the political intrigue in which the government is involved—and all this is done to bring about the "happy" ending which is one of the distinguishing features of the thriller.

A. A. DeVitis. *Graham Greene* (New York: Twayne, 1964), pp. 59–61

Arthur Rowe was a murderer. "Mercy killer," the papers had said. "Mad," the court had decided, and sentenced him to an asylum, from which he was soon released. Rowe was not so certain of the nature of his act. He knew only that he was a murderer, and by that fact not quite part of mankind. Not until he accidentally won a cake at a bazaar for the Mothers of the Free Nations—a cake that should have gone to a man who could undermine the safety of those nations.

What happens from there on in *The Ministry of Fear* could very easily have been just another story of spies and intrigues. The plot is clever and the settings realistic enough to raise it above the Oppenheim level. It might, say, have been on a par with Eric Ambler. But Graham Greene is even more than such a brilliant romancer as Ambler. He is something so close to a great novelist that it is hard to see the difference; perhaps there is none.

The fine storytelling, the craftsmanlike construction are never relaxed; but beneath them Mr. Greene is concerned with problems of ethics and character wider in their implications than any plot, the ageless problems of man's relationship to his God and to his fellow man. It is possible that Greene probes deeper into humanity here than even Steinbeck has with his angry sentiment or Saroyan with his indiscriminate love. But because his plot is that of a thriller, and a damned good thriller, it is unlikely that the moral philosophers of the Book-of-the-Month Club will be particularly concerned.

Labeling Greene as just spy stuff is a little like labeling Dostoyevsky as just blood and thunder. But don't shy off for that reason; if it's just spy stuff that you want, you won't find any better than this. And you may find in it, to boot, an unexpected nourishment.

Anthony Boucher. *San Francisco Chronicle.* May 23, 1943, n.p.

Graham Greene's subconscious seems to have been at work when he jotted down on the back of an envelope an idea for a novel, about a man raised from the dead. The narrator attends the funeral of a friend and is astonished to see him walking down a London street a week later. When Alexander Korda commissioned him to write a movie story about the four-power occupation of Vienna, Greene used the idea to create a basic thriller situation. *The Third Man* was published in 1950, a year after the movie itself appeared.

As Greene points out in his introduction, the story was not written to be read. The finished film is the vital product, Carol Reed's direction a vital part of it. Writer and director collaborated on revisions to the story, all of them improvements except for an over-extended chase scene through the sewers at the climax. This director's cadenza was Reed's mistake, minor in comparison with the insights he brought, the edgy atmosphere and cutting, actors perfectly cast and handled, the ironic use of a zither accompaniment, the imaginative reversal of Greene's ending. But the material itself, though slight, remains unmistakably Greene's.

Gavin Lambert. *The Dangerous Edge* (New York: Grossman, 1976), pp. 158–59

What is the meaning of the word "entertainment" as Greene uses it? What relationship have these entertainments to the mystery story genre? Does this thriller form carry any serious intent? If any distinction between the two types of work "entertainments" and "novels" is valid, I suspect it will have more to do with a shift in the entertainments from theological to political emphasis than with the evaporation of seriousness.

In what is conventionally called the "novels" such as *The Power and the Glory* and *A Burnt-out Case*, Greene gives us a religious vision with political overtones; whereas his entertainments, *A Gun for Sale* or *Ministry of Fear*, give us a political world with religious implications. The distinction between the two types is less than absolute. Do "novels" never entertain? . . .

The thriller form is the shape of the modern predicament, not only in its portrayal of flight and pursuit, but in its treatment of the search for identity among the real and the fantastic. . . .

Fiction is surely meant to be agreeable even in a negative sense, so the word "entertainment" does not separate the thriller from the novel form. . . .

Greene's disposition to depict the atmosphere of dream and mystery, the romance of the primitive terror, also links his entertainments to the gothic mystery of the late nineteenth century. The heroes of the latter wander the city to solve the riddle of the ghostly terror of their dreams. They are both the pursuer and the pursued. Unlike the detectives of a later generation who coldly rationalize the puzzle with mental gymnastics, the heroes of gothic fiction seek themselves in their tale of terror. This insistence upon scientific detachment—an undeniably attractive escape mechanism which makes the typical detective story something like a crossword puzzle or a game of chess—is not escape for Greene because it represents the culture washed clean. He returns to the old metaphoric terror, for the supernatural allegory he finds in concrete things. In his hands the detective's detailed game of chess turns into a morality play with the pieces taking on significance as they move. The entertainment is not in the puzzle but in the players.

Greene's novels are not patterned after the Newgate Calendar as were earlier detective stories: his characters are not to be found in police files nor does the solution depend on the scientific method of Scotland Yard. His heroes are jaded and disillusioned. They flee from the middle-class delight in crime detection that keeps one's possessions safe. The desire for a power-structured authority to intervene is the dream they struggle against: the man with the surgical gloves—the evil in prim, formulaic convention—presses against the door.

Greene's hunted heroes, like those of romantic mystery fiction as a whole, struggle between two kinds of evil—the primitive evil, Henry James's "fairy-tale side of life" or Jacques Maritain's "creative unconscious"—and the jaded evil of a representative superego that gradually paralyzes us as we grow into civilization.

The role of fantasy in Greene's thrillers does not exclude the social context. It is true that Greene drops a puzzling array of religious articles throughout the pages: Jansenist crucifixes, plaster manger scenes, votive candles. This seeming religious atmosphere, along with the interiorization of sin, has lead some critics to view Greene's Catholicism as more central than any other consideration. The thriller form with its visionary quality still cannot avoid the social, political commentary upon the source of man's crimes. None of Greene's entertainments ignore the political upheaval of Europe through the thirties and forties.

Greene's thrillers still catch the aesthetic of our age. In a time when the best-sellers are "nonfiction novels" about brutal, senseless murders, and the last days of a mad Germany, Greene's observation that "thrillers are like life" makes it increasingly difficult to distinguish between melodrama and what we thought was reality.

Carolyn D. Scott. In Harry J. Cargas, ed., Graham Greene (n.p.: B. Herder, n.d.), pp. 1–27

Graham Greene's "entertainments," as he now calls books like *The Confidential Agent* and *The Ministry of Fear,* to distinguish them from his later "serious" novels, reflected perfectly the pervasive anxiety of the Hitler-Mussolini age. In these thrillers the average man, the muddled and anxious man who usually appears in Greene's fiction as if he had stepped in a grimy mackintosh out of a London tube station, personified everyone's feeling of dread before the inhuman monsters of Nazism-Fascism. At the same time, the Greene hero personified that acute and enigmatic sense of guilt, usually arising from some surprising passion in his personal life, which so often made one irrationally feel that Hitler-Mussolini expressed the dark side of *everyone's* nature.

The sense of guilt is the essential theme of all Greene's fiction. It explains the chase after the hero in his "entertainments," and as the aftermath of adultery it results in the inner struggle on the brink of damnation that is the stuff of supposedly more "serious" books like *The Heart of the Matter* and *The End of the Affair.* The protagonists in both the entertainments and the novels are essentially decent and haunted human beings who are led into sins of violence and despair by the unexpectedness of some human attachment. They are fools, martyrs, and clowns of love, and through their love we see parallel lines—love for a human person, love of the divine law—that cannot meet in time.

Alfred Kazin. *Contemporaries* (Boston: Atlantic-Little Brown, 1962), pp. 158–61

Our Man in Havana is, among other things, a delightful satire with a serious edge, one of the funniest books to appear in many a day, and a complete change of pace for Greene the artist. . . .

Set in the near future, which appears uncomfortably like the immediate present, *Our Man in Havana* is like the other entertainments: an economical, tightly constructed, exciting satire on the exploits of the British Secret Service abroad. But, unlike the other entertainments, it is amusing, witty; in short, entertaining. Chief agent for Phastcleaner vacuum cleaners, Jim Wormold is one of the commercially unsuccessful, a group of people whom Greene dearly loves. Middle-aged, walking with a limp, early deserted by a beautiful wife but blessed with a beautiful daughter whom he has promised to bring up a Roman Catholic although he himself has no formal religion, Wormold finds his position in Havana difficult but not impossible.

His chief difficulty is economic, for his daughter Milly has expensive tastes. . . . Wormold solves his financial difficulties by becoming a spy for the British Secret Service; he then invents spies, borrows names from the Country Club registry, and by borrowing for his "spies" and for himself against an expense account manages to secure Milly's future. Eventually Wormold's creations spring unaccountably to life, and he is forced to a reckoning. By fabricating facts and passing them off as secret data, Wormold brings about the deaths of a young aviator and his best friend, Dr. Hasselbacher. His sense of guilt leads him to avenge their deaths; and, luckily for him, he succeeds, without being technically responsible for the death of the counterspy Carter. Deported from Havana and back in London, his exploits now known by his employers, Wormold wonders what is to be done with him, for legally he is not guilty of espionage—all his information had been invented and his one actual attempt at espionage had proved a failure. To his embarrassment, the Secret Service presents him with a medal and makes him an instructor in the espionage school, an ironic reward for his bungling. . . .

Ultimately Greene is important for the scope and originality of the novels that have provoked critics and readers alike into philosophical and religious arguments. But, as has already been pointed out, Greene is primarily a creative writer who happens to be a Catholic, not a Catholic writer. . . . The entertainments are first rate in their genre, books that any writer of thrillers or light fiction would be proud to have written. And they demonstrate, above all, the versatility of the writer—his many parts, to use the Elizabethan expression. No wonder then that Greene is thought by many to be one of the greatest writers of our language and, perhaps, our finest living novelist.

A. A. DeVitis. Graham Greene (New York:
Twayne, 1964), pp. 68–71

Graham Greene's heroes are never quite right for the parts fate forces them to rehearse. They are not competent to deal with large questions, and like Macbeth complaining to Ross, "Why do you dress me in borrow'd robes?" they find themselves in circumstances of smothering complexity. But Macbeth is not the best analogy. Chaplin in his baggy pants is better, and Greene's Sad Sack characters have latterly come to resemble that little baffled man, too small for tragedy, too earnest for farce, but the right size for comedy; after all, a sad tale's best for comedy. The cinematic nature of Greene's novels, which have the pace and structure of films, only heightens this impression, and in *The Honorary Consul* the characters acquire Chaplinesque dimensions from the towering hugeness of South America. . . .

Something that has always interested me about Greene's stories and novels is a note of undisguised mistrust and often outright loathing he has for Americans. It is an English trait, for the English sense of fairness which allows them to speak impartially about every subject under the sun, always breaks down when America is mentioned. Greene's attitude is tinged as well with Third World objections. His novels are full of American knaves and fools, and though he has never set a novel in the United States (a riddle that would make a good starting point for an essay), our country always hovers as a ridiculous threat at the edge of his fiction.

Paul Theroux. Washington Post Book World.
September 30, 1973, pp. 1–3, 10

Graham Greene divides his work into serious literature and "entertainments" and I, for one, have always preferred his entertainments to his serious literature, largely because the former are free from the Catholic shop talk of the latter. The "entertainments" also reflect Graham Greene's passionate interest in old crime and spy stories, those humble but vastly pleasurable and unpretentious types of straightforward story telling which could often serve as models for more ambitious but also more boring forms of literature. It was a splendid idea of Graham Greene's to follow the recent triumph of *Sherlock Holmes* with a revival of E. W. Hornung's counterpart to the great detective, that equally great gentleman amateur cracksman and test cricketer, A. J. Raffles. If Holmes had returned from the Reichenbach Falls, why should not Raffles rise from the dead of Spion Kop?

William Gillette's *Sherlock Holmes* was melodrama seriously meant; Graham Greene's *Raffles* is nostalgic pastiche, but none the worse for that. For lovingly tongue-in-cheek parody is a far more conscious, deliberate genre than naïve melodrama, it operates on more and subtler levels of irony and reflectiveness. And certainly Graham Greene is a better writer and a more accomplished artist than William Gillette could ever have been.

By lovingly reconstructing the late Victorian milieu, moreover, Graham Greene is enabled to say a great deal, indirectly, about his own time by contrast as well as tragic irony. In the figure of the aging Prince of Wales on the eve of becoming Edward VII he finds a brilliant spokesman for much that needs to be said about the virtues of *his* society and, by implication, the barbarisms of ours. And at the same time he enables us, enlightened, liberated denizens of a ''permissive'' age to laugh about the barbarisms of that period, its naïve patriotism, imperialism, love and sport and stuffiness.

Greene's Raffles is a far more sophisticated character than E. W. Hornung's; he is a philosopher, albeit a hedonistic one, as well as an elegant thief. And Graham Greene has put him into the world of Oscar Wilde and Lord Alfred Douglas, so that he becomes part of a fin de siècle aesthetic circle.

Martin Esslin. Plays and Players (Richmond, Va.:
John Knox Press, 1976), p. 30

The achievement of Graham Greene is difficult to assess. He is a complete man of letters, having written twenty-four novels and entertainments, several volumes of short stories, five plays, a two-volume autobiography, three travel books, numerous literary and political essays, hundreds of film and book reviews, a biography of Lord Rochester, four children's books, and ten screenplays. He also has edited *British Dramatists* (1942), *The Best of Saki* (1950), *The Spy's Bedside Book* (1957), *The Bodley Head Ford Madox Ford* (1962), *Victorian Detective Fiction* (1966), and *An Impossible Woman, the Memories of Dottoressa Moor of Capri* (1975).

Despite the variety of literary forms that Greene has explored, his greatness clearly lies in his fiction. Unlike other writers of the 1920s and 1930s, he has practically ignored the experimental novel. Rather, he has followed the loose tradition of such diverse writers as Charles Dickens, Wilkie Collins, Robert Louis Stevenson, Rider Haggard, Joseph Conrad, Henry James, Ford Madox Ford, François Mauriac, and Marjorie Bowen. Greene's main achievements in the novel are two: (1) he is a master storyteller, one of the chief reasons for his popular success; (2) he has created a unique vision of the world, having turned his obsessions into works of art. Greene both lives and writes on ''the dangerous edge of things,'' and in the world of his novels he has recreated the bittersweet conflict between the fascination of innocence and the hell-haunted drama of human existence.

Greene's exciting, fast-paced narratives have an illusive transparency about them, as if one can see and hear the characters and visualize their surroundings without the distractions of the author's presence or stylistic mannerisms. This authorial invisibility may derive from Greene's experience in writing film scripts and from the many years he spent in reviewing motion pictures. It is interesting to note in this connection how few of his novels or entertainments are written from the first person point of view, a perspective clearly unsuited to a motion picture script.

Although many of his novels are based on topical events—whether in London, Mexico, Vietnam, or Haiti—Greene's personal involvement in those events as a reporter and student of human nature allows him the perspective of an insider. And so, in his novels it is almost as if he would not ask his characters to do or think something that he himself had not done or thought. Life to Greene is a series of risks and moral choices; the dangers are betrayal, corruption, and failure. The central quest of his obsessed heroes is for the peace and innocence of their lost childhood, an adventure that is characterized by great tension and suffering, and one that ends often only in death.

Greene has the distinction allotted to few authors of being a popular writer who has the respect of the literary establishment. Some critics, however, believe that a writer with popular appeal cannot be a serious artist. In Greene's early novels he deals with this very issue through the characters of Quin Savory, the cockney novelist, who hopes to "bring back cheerfulness and 'ealth to modern fiction"; Maurice Bendrix, who imagines his literary ranking to be "a little above (Somerset) Maugham because Maugham is popular"; and Rollo Martins. Speaking to a group of literary snobs, Martins acknowledges that an important influence on his writing is Zane Grey, to which someone replies, "He was just a popular entertainer." Furious with this patronizing remark, Martins snaps back, "Why the hell not? . . . What was Shakespeare?"

Thus Greene defends the popular novelist while at the same time worrying about his reputation among serious critics. His classification of his fiction into *novels* and *entertainments* reflects this worry and seems to say, defensively, that some of his stories he simply tossed off for popular consumption, but that the others are serious novels worthy of serious critical judgment. It is as if he solves the conflict between popularity and artistic integrity by assuming the guise of two writers: the author of thrillers for the masses, in the tradition of Rider Haggard and Robert Louis Stevenson, and the author of important novels that examine the complexities of human psychology for a more sophisticated audience, in the tradition of Joseph Conrad and Henry James. In fact, before he came up with the term *entertainment,* Greene had toyed with the idea of publishing his early work under an assumed name as a means of protecting his future reputation.

Richard Kelly. *Graham Greene* (New York:
Ungar, 1984), pp. 179–83

The Tenth Man is a vintage Greene thriller (what he usually dubbed an "entertainment"), mordantly eerie and quite enjoyable. Greene himself, in a perplexed and slightly indignant introduction, finds the novel "very readable—indeed I prefer it in many ways to *The Third Man.*" He was in fact working on *The Third Man* in 1948—and already, he admits, all memory of anything called *The Tenth Man* had slipped away.

This is weird. Greene's reputation as a novelist, both serious and sleuthing, was well established by 1944. The acclaimed *Brighton Rock* (1938) had been followed by *The Confidential Agent, The Power and the Glory,* and most recently *The Ministry of Fear,* which was published in 1943 while Greene was still working for the Foreign Office. The following year he quit that position and, to make ends meet (for acclaim was hardly bankable in those days—*Brighton Rock* sold eight thousand copies and *The Power and the Glory* had a wartime print of only thirty-five hundred), sold himself to MGM.

How he must have hated those two years, to have suffered such amnesia; the unrevised canon continues with *Nineteen Stories* (1947), *The Heart of the Matter* (1948), and then *The Third Man* (1950). Or perhaps he didn't consider *The Tenth Man* really his. Certainly MGM didn't—either then or nearly forty years later when it dug the manuscript out of its vault and startled hawking it to publishers.

A friend of mine, full of literary suspicion, thinks it will all turn out to be a ruse, a clever sales gimmick to hype a brand new Graham Greene novel that might otherwise receive only ho-hum notice. MGM is going along with it, he hisses, to hype the inevitable movie. I don't believe it—though if *The New Yorker* can be sold to a chain, I suppose anything is possible.

The Tenth Man is eerie and detached, and also relentless in suspense. There are neat, concise observations along the way, about class distinction and the dislocation of time: "When a war ends one forgets how much older oneself and the world have become; it needs something like a piece of furniture or a woman's hat to waken the sense of time." All of Greene's themes are here—the atmosphere of oppression, the corruption of authority, the pessimism not quite balanced by the presence of grace, manifesting itself in moral paradox—but one eats them on the fly, as it were. This is a brief, fast story, and so resolutely unpretentious that when the most common food-for-thought is offered—"People are quite aware of the sorrow there always is in lust, but they are not so aware of the lust there is in sorrow"—it goes down like caviar.

The book's ending is unhappy, but there's a pleasing twist or two. It's not the deepest stuff, but as entertainment it has a cutting edge. In short, *The Tenth Man* is a professional job, and I don't care when it was written, though it's always fun to speculate, as Greene, I think, knows.

Eliot Fremont-Smith. *The Village Voice.* March 26, 1985, p. 39

Perhaps the most useful way to understand the distinctive qualities of Greene's fiction is to view it in terms of the writers who served as models for its development. Its sense of place, its stress on exotic places or on the strangeness of the familiar world of Greene's England, draw on the writings of

Joseph Conrad. Its sense of plot, its emphasis on action, draw on writers from Greene's youthful reading—Robert Louis Stevenson, Stanley Weyman, John Buchan, G. E. Henty, and most importantly H. Rider Haggard—and, to a lesser extent, the American cinema. Its sense of character development, of the structure of narrative, arises from the influence of Henry James and Charles Dickens, from whom Greene learned the art of dramatizing inner conflicts, the conflicts of the heart.

Crucial to Greene's fiction is a sense of story, of adventure. In fact, this has had as much to do with enduring popularity as has any quality in his work, and in that regard puts him somewhat at odds with the modernist tradition, where plot tends to be subordinate to character formation, where states of mind and epistemological development, or the internal drama, take precedence over the external narrative. Greene acknowledges often his indebtedness to the adventure novel, particularly to the romance tradition of Sir Walter Scott as it was inherited by Robert Louis Stevenson and H. Rider Haggard. From Greene one can always count on a compelling story. Oddly enough, it was probably his interest in the novel of intrigue—or, as he labeled it, the entertainment—that encouraged him to be a consummate storyteller.

Greene's approach to plot utilizes Dickensian as well as Haggardian elements and hinges on an Aristotelian idea of *kinesis,* or action, in which the plot begins in the middle of a problem and moves toward resolution. What distinguishes the entertainment from the novel is that in the entertainment there is solution with resolution; in the novel there is only resolution, a sense that the action is at an end, though the problem remains unsolved.

By far the most recurrent pattern in the action is that of pursuit, of someone on the run. So Pinkie and Rose do their best to escape Colleoni and his gang in *Brighton Rock,* the whisky priest tries to elude the civil authorities in *The Power and the Glory,* Charlie Fortnum hopes to escape the terrorists in *The Honorary Consul,* Maurice Castle is desperate to escape MI6 and find sanctuary in Moscow in *The Human Factor.* In the entertainment the pattern is toward success and escape (and hence a certain feeling of unreality) and in the novel toward failure and a resultant loss of freedom but a heightened sense of tragedy—though Greene's heroes inevitably fall short of tragic stature, with the exception perhaps of the whisky priest.

All-important to Greene are his characters. To better understand his approach to character development one needs to consider Greene's deep interest in psychoanalysis, in the unconscious, in dreams as revelations of inner lives. One cannot point to some crucial moment in Greene's development to find this strong interest in characters; it is there in the earliest work, in his first novel, *The Man Within,* in which the protagonist Andrews is torn apart by having to betray his friends. If in every Greene novel there is a macrocosmic world of the Englishman caught in native and hence alien culture, there is also a microcosmic world in which the character, usually male, is at war with himself—"There's another man within me that's angry with me,'' as the epigraph reads that Greene chose from Sir Thomas Browne for his first novel. All Greene's protagonists suffer from this war with self— Pinkie in *Brighton Rock,* the whisky priest in *The Power and the Glory,* Major Scobie in *The Heart of the Matter,* Querry in *A Burnt-out Case,* Castle in *The Human Factor.* There is no escape from it.

Greene would be the first to admit his debt to Henry James for providing him with models for the psychological novel; secondly, his debt is to Ford Madox Ford. He has written on James and Ford, has edited Ford, and mentions having read *The Good Soldier* several times over and learned much about narrative technique from it. The result in the novels is a sophisticated attention to point of view and a highly skilled use of it, if in fact at times an obsession with it. Within Greene's work one can find any number of variations in technique, from the rapidly shifting third-person point of view of *Brighton Rock* to the focused use of first person in *The Third Man,* where that use of point of view is transferred to the film screen as well, and then is perfected in *The End of the Affair* and *The Quiet American.*

Some final remarks about Greene's style. He has admitted to being dominated in the early novels by the luxuriance of Conrad's prose, but after those excesses he soon settled into a style well honed, lapidary, almost journalistic at times, a style learned not only from great writers but also from years of copy-editing the work of others, as he did during the time he spent as subeditor on the *Times,* and from his years doing interminable reports for MI6, or writing accounts of unrest and war in faraway places like Kenya, Malaya, Indochina, and other trouble spots in the Third World. A fine introduction to the salient qualities of Greene's style is given by Samuel Hynes. Hynes points specifically to Greene's precision, sense of pace, ability to heighten by understatement without losing anything to a lack of clarity. While not a minimalist, nevertheless by the height of his career Greene had developed a style that focused on the reportorial, on seeing not through the omniscient narrator but through the minds of his characters, by exploring their skill at perceiving the events they play out and their ability to apprehend and comprehend their environments, whether they be male or female, adult or child.

R. H. Miller. *Understanding Graham Greene*
(Columbia, South Carolina: University of South
Carolina Press, 1990), pp. 6–14

HAMMETT, DASHIELL (1894–1961)

It is doubtful if even Ernest Hemingway has ever written more effective dialogue than may be found within the pages of this extraordinary tale of gunmen, gin, and gangsters, *Red Harvest*. The author displays a style of amazing clarity and compactness, devoid of literary frills and furbelows, and his characters, who race through the story with the rapidity and destructiveness of machine guns, speak the crisp, hard-boiled language of the underworld. Moreover, they speak it truly, without a single false or jarring note, for Mr. Hammett, himself an old-time Pinkerton detective, knows his crime and criminals through many years of personal contact. Those who begin to weary of the similarity of modern detective novels, with their clumsily involved plots and their artificial situations and conversations, will find their interest revived by this realistic, straightforward story, for it is concerned solely with fast and furious action and it introduces a detective who achieves his purposes without recourse to higher mathematics, necromancy, or fanciful reasoning. It reads like the latest news from Chicago.

Herbert Asbury. *Bookman*. March 1929, p. 92

Until the coming of Mr. Dashiell Hammett in *Red Harvest* and now in *The Maltese Falcon*, the memorable detectives were gentlemen. The everdelightful M. Lecoq and his copy, Mr. Sherlock Holmes, are fair gods against the gnomes. Their only worthy successor, Father Brown, is a priest. Now comes Mr. Hammett's tough guy in *Red Harvest* and his Sam Spade in *The Maltese Falcon*, and you find the Pinkerton operative as a scoundrel without pity or remorse, taking his whiffs of drink and his casual amours between catching crooks, treating the police with a cynical contempt, always getting his crook by foul and fearless means, above the law like a satyr—and Mr. Hammett describing his deeds in a glistening and fascinating prose as "American" as Ring Lardner's, and every bit as original in musical rhythm and bawdy humor.

There is nothing like these books in the whole range of detective fiction. The plots don't matter so much. The art does; and there is an absolute distinction of real art. It is the genuine presence of the myth. The *events* of *The Maltese Falcon* may have happened that way in "real" life. No one save Mr. Hammett could have woven them to such a silver-steely mesh.

Donald Douglas. *The New Republic*. April 9, 1930, p. 226

More and greater mysteries reside in the mental and emotional makeup of Mr. Hammett's characters, who provide fascinating problems in all directions. What one reader wants to know, just out of idle curiosity, is this: Are there people like that? And is life like that? And if so, can anything be done? Meanwhile you get a story in *The Glass Key* positively without rubber stamps, a brilliant study in the ugly and abysmal which should be read by authors of all kinds and distributed as tracts to the mystery mongers.

Will Cuppy. *New York Herald Tribune Book*
Review. April 26, 1932, p. 13

Now that Dashiell Hammett is beginning to be taken seriously by the high-brows, my first enthusiasm for him is beginning to cool a little. Not that *The Thin Man* is not a first-rate murder story and one that only Dashiell Hammett could have written. But, perhaps because he has turned the trick so easily before that he is now getting a little tired of it, perhaps because we are beginning to notice that he sometimes repeats his effects, *The Thin Man* seems a less excitingly fresh performance than, say, *The Maltese Falcon*. It is still head-and-shoulders above any other murder story published since his last one.

One reason why Hammett's books have been so outstanding, aside from the naturalism of his style, the careless humanity of his characters, is that his murders are gangster-political affairs; they come naturally out of his tough backgrounds, instead of being the kind of academic and farfetched bridge problems in a vacuum of the ordinary detective story writer.

T. S. Matthews. *The New Republic*. January 24,
1934, p. 316

Of all the detective novelists of the period 1918–1939 only one, the American Dashiell Hammett, happened to be both a first-rate writer and to have had a long experience of crime, in his capacity as a Pinkerton Agency manager. Yet even after his *Thin Man* became a screen success, his *Red Harvest, The Glass Key, The Maltese Falcon, The Dain Curse,* and *The Thin Man* itself were practically unread in England.

Robert Graves and Alan Hodge. *The Long Week*
End (London: Macmillan, 1941), p. 290

Because of their startling originality, the Hammett novels virtually defy exegesis even today—though their external pattern is by now all too familiar by process of overmuch imitation. As straightaway detective stories they can hold their own with the best. They are also character studies of close-to-top rank in their own right, and are penetrating if often shocking novels of manners as well. They established new standards for realism in the genre. Yet they are as sharply stylized and deliberately artificial as Restoration Comedy, and have been called an inverted form of romanticism. They were commercial in inception; but they miss being Literature, if at all, by the narrowest of margins.

The *Bookman's* comment in 1932 that "it is doubtful if even Ernest Hemingway has written more effective dialogue" may seem a trifle over-enthusiastic today, but only a little. And Hammett's talents in this direction are, if anything, exceeded by his ability to delineate character by sharp, frugal, telling strokes admirably suited to the form.

> Howard Haycraft. *Murder for Pleasure*
> (Philadelphia: Appleton-Century, 1941), p. 171

Perhaps no other writer of detective fiction in the present generation has so changed and influenced the form as Dashiell Hammett. For all their external speed and violence, Hammett's novels are among the best examples extant of the blending of detection and the psychological study of character.

> Stanley J. Kunitz and Howard Haycraft. *Twentieth Century Authors* (New York: H. W. Wilson, 1942), pp. 607–8

Hammett gave murder back to the kind of people that commit it for reasons, not just to provide a corpse; and with the means at hand, not handwrought dueling pistols, curare, and tropical fish. He put these people down on paper as they were, and he made them talk and think in the language they customarily used for these purposes.

He had a literary style, but his audience didn't know it, because it was in a language not supposed to be capable of such refinements. They thought they were getting a good meaty melodrama written in the kind of lingo they imagined they spoke themselves. It was, in a sense, but it was much more. All language begins with speech, and the speech of common men at that, but when it develops to the point of becoming a literary medium it only looks like speech. Hammett's style at its worst was as formalized as a page of *Marius the Epicurean;* at its best it could say almost anything. I believe this style, which does not belong to Hammett or to anybody, but is the American language (and not even exclusively that any more), can say things he did not know how to say, or feel the need of saying. In his hands it had no overtones, left no echo, evoked no image beyond a distant hill.

Hammett is said to have lacked heart; yet the story he himself thought the most of is the record of a man's devotion to a friend. He was spare, frugal, hard-boiled, but he did over and over again what only the best writers can ever do at all. He wrote scenes that seemed never to have been written before.

> Raymond Chandler. *The Atlantic Monthly*.
> December 1944, p. 58

Understand, there is a great difference between *type* and *style*. After the success of *The Maltese Falcon,* many writers began to imitate Hammett's *style,* which was distinct and original with him. I think of all the early pulp writers who contributed to the new format of the detective story, the word "genius" was more nearly applicable to Hammett than to any of the rest. Unfortunately, however, because Hammett's manner was so widely imitated, it became the habit for the reviewers to refer to "the Hammett School" as embracing the *type* of story as well as the *style*. This has caused some confusion. Carroll John Daly did as much, or more, than any other author to develop the *type*.

Erle Stanley Gardner. In Howard Haycraft, ed.,
The Art of the Mystery Story (New York: Simon &
Schuster, 1946), pp. 204–5

I went back and read *The Maltese Falcon,* called by Alexander Woollcott "the best detective story America has yet produced" and since, at the time of its publication, it had immediately caused Dashiell Hammett to become—in Jimmy Durante's phrase, referring to himself—"duh toast of duh intellectuals." But it was difficult for me to understand what they had thought—in 1930—they were toasting. Mr. Hammett did have the advantage of real experience as a Pinkerton detective, and he infused the old formula of Sherlock Holmes with a certain cold underworld brutality which gave readers a new shudder in the days when it was fashionable to be interested in gangsters; but, beyond this, he lacked the ability to bring the story to imaginative life. As a writer, he is surely almost as far below the rank of Rex Stout as Rex Stout is below that of James Cain. *The Maltese Falcon* today seems not much above those newspaper picture-strips in which you follow from day to day the ups and downs of a strong-jawed hero and a hard-boiled but beautiful adventuress.

Edmund Wilson. "Why Do People Read Detective
Stories?" *Classics and Commercials: A Literary
Chronicle of the Forties* (New York: Farrar, Straus
and Giroux, 1950), pp. 235–36

Hammett is the acknowledged founder of the hard-boiled school which specializes in word savagery—savagery in style, sophistication, sex, slugging, and sleuthing. Just how does Hammett achieve, against a background of sheer melodrama, the brittle lacquer of realism which we now associate with the hard-boiled species? The secret lies in his method: Hammett tells modern fairy tales in *terms* of realism. He combines extreme romanticism of plot with extreme realism of characterization. His *stories* are the stuff of dreams; his *characters* are the flesh-and-blood of reality. The stories are flamboyant extravaganzas, but the characters in those stories are authentic human beings who talk, think, and act like real people. Their speech is tough, earthy, two-syllabled; their desires, moods, frustrations are laid bare with probing frankness.

Ellery Queen. *Queen's Quorum* (Boston: Little,
Brown, 1951), p. 101

Dashiell Hammett was the great innovator who invented the hard-boiled detective novel and used it to express and master the undercurrent of inchoate violence that runs through so much of American life.

In certain ways Hammett's heroes are reminiscent of unreconstructed Darwinian man; *McTeague* and *The Sea Wolf* stand directly behind them. But no matter how rough and appetent they may be, true representatives of a rough and appetent society, they are never allowed to run unbridled. Hammett's irony controls them. In fact he criticized them far more astringently and basically than similar men were criticized by Hemingway. In his later and less romantic moments Hammett was a close and disillusioned critic of the two-fisted hard-drinking woman-chasing American male that he derived partly from tradition and partly from observation, including self-observation.

Even in one of his very early stories, first published by Mencken in *Smart Set,* Hammett presents a character who might have been a parody of the Hemingway hero, except that he was pre-Hemingway. This huge brute is much attached to his beard. To make a short story shorter, the loss of his beard reveals that he used it to hide a receding chin and make him a public laughingstock. This isn't much more than an anecdote, but it suggests Hammett's attitude towards the half-evolved frontier male of our not too distant past. Shorn and urbanized, he became in Hammett's best novels a near-tragic figure, a lonely and suspicious alien who pits a hopeless but obstinate animal courage against the metropolitan jungle, a not very moral man who clings with a skeptic's desperation to a code of behavior empirically arrived at in a twilight world between chivalry and gangsterism.

Like the relationship of Charles Dickens and Wilkie Collins, the Hemingway-Hammett influence ran two ways. Hammett achieved some things that Hemingway never attempted. He placed his characters in situations as complex as those of life, in great cities like San Francisco and New York and Baltimore, and let them work out their dubious salvations under social and economic and political pressures. The subject of his novels, you might say, was the frontier male thrust suddenly, as the frontier disappeared, into the modern megalopolis; as Hemingway's was a similar man meeting war and women, and listening to the silence of his own soul.

Hammett's prose is not quite a prose that can say anything, as Chandler overenthusiastically claimed it could. But it is a clean useful prose, with remarkable range and force. It has pace and point, strong tactile values, the rhythms and colors of speech, all in the colloquial tradition that stretches from Mark Twain through Stephen Crane to Lardner and Mencken, the Dr. Johnson of our vernacular. Still it is a deadpan and rather external prose, artificial-seeming compared with Huck Finn's earthy rhetoric, flat in comparison with Fitzgerald's more subtly colloquial instrument. Hammett's ear for the current and the colloquial was a little too sardonically literal, and this is already tending to date his writing, though not seriously.

Analysis of any kind is alien to this prose. Moulding the surface of things, it lends itself to the vivid narration of rapid, startling action. Perhaps it tends to set too great a premium on action, as if the mind behind it were hurrying away from its own questions and deliberately restricting itself to the manipulation of appearances. It is in part the expression of that universally-met-with American type who avoids sensibility and introspection because they make you vulnerable in the world. At its worst such prose can be an unnecessary writing-down to the lowest common denominator of the democracy. But at its best it has great litotic power, as in some of Hemingway's earlier stories, or in the haunting chapter where Sam Spade makes devious love to Brigid by telling her the story of Flitcraft:

"A man named Flitcraft had left his real-estate office, in Tacoma, to go to luncheon one day and had never returned. He did not keep an engagement to play golf after four that afternoon, though he had taken the initiative in making the engagement less than half an hour before he went out to luncheon. His wife and children never saw him again. His wife and he were supposed to be on the best of terms. He had two children, boys, one five and the other three. He owned his house in a Tacoma suburb, a new Packard, and the rest of the appurtenances of successful American living."

Sam Spade is Flitcraft's spiritual twin, the lonely male who is not at ease in Zion or in Zenith. He is inarticulate about himself, like Babbitt is aware only of a deep malaise that spurs him on to action and acquisition. *The Maltese Falcon* is a fable of modern man in quest of love and money, despairing of everything else. Its murders are more or less incidental, though they help to give it its quality of a crisis novel. Its characters act out of the extreme emotions of fear and guilt and concupiscence, anger and revenge; and with such fidelity to these passions that their natures almost seem coterminous with them.

Driven by each and all of them, Sam Spade strips away one by one the appearances which stand between him and the truth, and between him and the complete satisfaction of his desires. His story ends in drastic peripeteia with the all but complete frustration of his desires. His lover is guilty of murder; the code without which his life is meaningless forces him to turn her over to the police. The black bird is hollow. The reality behind appearances is a treacherous vacuum. Spade turns for sardonic consolation to the wife of his murdered partner (whose name was Archer). It is his final reluctant act of animal pragmatism.

Probably Hammett intended the ultimate worthlessness of the Maltese falcon to be more than a bad joke on his protagonist. I see it as the symbol of a lost tradition, representing the great cultures of the past which have become inaccessible to Spade and the men of his time. It represents explicitly the religious and ethical developments of the Mediterranean basin, Christianity and knight-errantry. Perhaps it stands for the Holy Ghost itself, or rather for its absence.

In any case the bird's lack of value implies Hammett's final comment on the inadequacy and superficiality of Sam Spade's life and ours. If only his bitterly inarticulate struggle for self-realization were itself more fully realized, the stakes for which he plays not so arbitrarily lost from the beginning (a basic limitation of the detective story is that its action is preordained, in a sense, by what has already happened), Sam Spade could have been a great indigenous tragic figure. Maybe he is. I think *The Maltese Falcon,* with its astonishing imaginative energy persisting undiminished after a third of a century, is tragedy of a new kind, deadpan tragedy.

Ross Macdonald. *Mystery Writers' Annual.* 1964,

pp. 8, 24

I had known Dash when he was writing short stories, but I had never been around for a long piece of work. Life changed: the drinking stopped, the parties were over. The locking-in time had come and nothing was allowed to disturb it until the book was finished. I had never seen anybody work that way: the care for every word, the pride in the neatness of the typed page itself, the refusal for ten days or two weeks to go out even for a walk for fear something would be lost.

Lillian Hellman. *New York Review of Books.*

November 25, 1965, p. 20

The detective, before Hammett transformed him in the 1920s, had been the guardian of good against evil, a knightly character, pure and without reproach, the urban equivalent of the cowboy. Hammett's world blurred the distinction between good and evil, and his heroes were not without blemishes of their own. Their virtues were distinctly personal—courage, dignity, and patience; and to them the hero clung for their own sake, not because the client for whom he fought had any worth. Honor to Sam Spade was conformity to a code of rules which he himself invented, a means of demonstrating his own worth against the world.

The character he created corresponded to the felt needs of Hammett's personality. The detective in almost all his stories was "I"; and it was no coincidence that he gave the first name he himself discarded (Samuel) to his best-known hero. He took his writing seriously no matter how trivial the subject because through it he projected his experience.

Oscar Handlin. *The Atlantic Monthly.* July 1966,

p. 137

The characteristics of Hammett's "daemonic" tough guy, with significant variations in the last two novels, can be schematized as follows: he is free of sentiment, of the fear of death, of the temptations of money and sex. He is what Albert Camus calls "a man without memory," free of the burden of the past. He is capable of any action, without regard to conventional morality, and thus is apparently as amoral—or immoral—as his antagonists. His refusal to submit to the trammels which limit ordinary mortals results in a godlike immunity and independence, beyond the power of his enemies. He himself has under his control the pure power that is needed to reach goals, to answer questions and solve mysteries, to reconstruct the (possible) motivations of the guilty and innocent alike. Hammett's novels present a "critique" of the tough guy's freedom as well: the price he pays for his power is to be cut off behind his own self-imposed masks, in an isolation that no criminal, in a community of crime, has to face.

> Robert I. Edenbaum. In David Madden, ed.,
> *Tough Guy Writers of the Thirties* (Southern
> Illinois: Southern Illinois University Press, 1968),
> p. 81

What [Hammett's] stories have, even the earliest and least of them, is a flavor wholly individual. This flavor comes partly from the bareness of a style in which everything superficial in the way of description has been surgically removed, partly from his knowledge of actual criminal investigation, and partly from the wistful cynicism with which he wrote. . . .

With all his innovations of form and language, Hammett kept the puzzle element from the orthodox detective story. . . . The problems are composed just as skillfully as those in an orthodox detective story, but in the best of Hammett they are the beginning and not the end of the book's interest. *The Maltese Falcon* and *The Glass Key* offer a gallery of characters and scenes unexcelled in the crime story, all of them seen with a Dickensian sense of the truth in caricature.

> Julian Symons. *Mortal Consequences: A History—
> From the Detective Story to the Crime Novel* (New
> York: Harper & Row, 1972), pp. 137–39

The works Hammett didn't write must give way to the ones he did. To move from surmising about what never happened in favor of discussing the real and the achieved is to clear a path to the art of fast-paced adventure and intrigue. Hammett has the craft of good narration well in hand. He writes fresh, muscular prose; he controls his materials; he knows how to seize and then hold the reader. Much of Hammett's best work sustains this vibrancy by means of color, concreteness, and a sharp eye for both social detail and historical change. Sometimes, he wins the day by avoiding vibrancy. The precision of flat, bald factual statements recounted in toneless sequence conveys menace.

Most often, Hammett stirs our imaginations by using forms and norms traditionally associated with crime fiction. He knew the aesthetic limits of his medium and kept within them.

What other writers grope for, Hammett knows instinctively. He doesn't narrate. Instead, he makes things happen to people. Then he makes us wonder where the excitement came from and what it meant. There is little in his plots to stretch on the rack of literary theory. Hammett puts forth a personal vision that expresses itself in movement and conflict. There is little moral struggle, the characters having already lost their battles with conscience.

Before they come to us, they have decided to rob, deceive a husband, wife, or business associate, steal—even kill for—the falcon. Hammett heightens but won't brood or analyze, showing the effects rather than the development of psychological drama. Vivid in both conception and execution, these effects translate well to radio and screen.

Hammett avoids giving insights into his characters' thoughts and feelings in order to compel greater reader participation. The Op reacts neither morally nor emotionally to the twin discovery of a corpse alongside him and the apparent murder weapon, an ice pick, in his hand when he wakes from a drugged sleep in *Red Harvest*. His composure creates a high degree of intensity, yoking form to content while forcing the reader to question motives. But it also blocks expansiveness. If Hammett's people change or grow, they keep it to themselves. Rarely do we see a character converted or reborn. Experience teaches little in Hammett, even the experience of terror. . . .

Hammett's firsthand knowledge of crime stopping gave American detective fiction both a freshness and a command it never enjoyed before. The narrative drive resulting in part from his brisk, colorful documentation has also earned him acceptance as the founder of modern American detective fiction—the tough, realistic mystery centering on a lonely, cynical private eye.

Peter Wolfe. *Beams Falling: The Art of Dashiell
Hammett* (Bowling Green, Ohio: Popular Press,
1980), pp. 9, 18–20

There are a number of features or incidents in Dashiell Hammett's novels which seem to break sharply with previous conventions of the detective story. I do not refer to the important changes of direction brought about by the "hard-boiled" school and instanced by such matters as the professional detective, organized crime, dark urban streets and a spare, colloquial, "tough" style. Rather, I wish to concentrate on features which are unexpected even *in* the context of "tough-guy" writing and which occur unexpectedly in order deliberately and provocatively to remind the reader, in the midst of an easily identifiable style, of other styles and methods of inquiry into human behavior and, ultimately, of another and very different worldview which must be placed against the worldview of the rest of the novel. By adopting this technique, Hammett succeeds in drawing attention not only to the limitations of his particular kind of popular fiction but also to ways in which these very limitations can be used. The aspects of Hammett's novels to which I began by referring are not separated stylistically from the rest of the novel. But they nonetheless suggest to the reader that the first-person narrator might have to be viewed in a context other than that in which he normally presents himself for the reader's judgment (and, frequently, approval).

Hammett's detectives do indeed rely on their own strength and invention to maintain their security, yet their strength resides not in a stable personality but in the ability to change like a chameleon to meet the needs of a fluctuating world, to hold to the security of the present moment, and their invention is always powerfully destructive in human terms. They operate not from the base of a recognizable interior self but from a deliberately created void. They cannot be seriously damaged because there is nothing there to damage. Hammett has often been likened to Hemingway, but Hemingway's heroes, in a non-teleological universe, adopt a concrete style as a mimetic representation of physical action allied to narrow but recognizable rules (bull fighting, big-game hunting) or physical action whose consecutive, non-idealized function is a healing coalescence with natural rhythms ("Big Two-Hearted River"). The Continental Op and Sam Spade adopt self-generative language allied to the creation of their own rules and the rhythms of their work are anything but natural. Even when Hemingway's heroes retreat from the illusions of the past and the impotence of the present to the narrowest possible area of light ("A Clean, Well-Lighted Place") they harm noone. Hammett's heroes persistently do harm without ever leaving themselves the chance to feel guilty.

John S. Whitley. *Journal of American Studies.*
December 1980, pp. 443, 454

The preeminence of Dashiell Hammett's position in the world of twentieth-century detective fiction and his influence on the genre are a matter of more or less common consent: propositions that have attained the status of received truths. But when one considers the incredibly brief span of Hammett's career as a productive author, his stature as a writer becomes cause for astonishment. The five novels on which his reputation are based—*Red Harvest, The Dain Curse, The Maltese Falcon, The Glass Key,* and *The Thin Man*—were all published between 1929 and 1934, a period of barely five years.

The fact that Hammett published virtually nothing of any significance in the remaining two-and-a-half decades of his life has only deepened the fascination of latter-day Americans with this enigmatic figure.

More than fifty years after they first appeared in print, Hammett's novels and stories, later collected into book form, still captivate readers with the authority of their craft, the credible characters and wonderfully drawn action scenes, the canny air of authenticity with which they capture the mood and texture of the twenties underworld and the work of real detectives, and Hammett's own special blend of a sometimes chilling cynicism and a deeply rooted sense of honor. But, to be entirely honest, time has also taken a certain toll.

One hears from friends sent off to read Hammett that, while they enjoyed this or that novel or book of stories, they came away with a vague sense of disappointment, having expected something more startling, more sharply original from such a legendary writer. While they were, they admit, swept away in spite of themselves by certain scenes and sequences, they found themselves, at other times, with the uncomfortable feeling that they had heard this dialogue—or met this detective—somewhere before.

Such is the fate of being the first of the line. So numerous have Hammett's progeny been—indeed the whole subgenre of cops and robbers stories that still flourishes in our popular media was ushered in by Hammett's break with the tradition of detective fiction he inherited—that much of the stunning freshness which earlier readers encountered in his work has inevitably been lost. Hammett invented the modern urban detective story: its poses, its dialogue, its *rhythms,* its ethos, its heroes and villains. There was nothing like them before Hammett, and much of what has come after has been mere variations—however talented, however clever—on the forms he created.

It is, moreover, difficult to appreciate fully the impact Hammett's stories had on a generation whose anxious, colorful, naive and brutal, frantic and shell-shocked world he caught so perfectly. The special poignance of the new sense of vulnerability and peculiarly modern disillusionment with civilization many felt in the wake of World War I is difficult to imagine at half a century's remove—the way it must have felt to be embarking on the era of Prohibition not knowing, as we do now, that it would fail, indeed would usher in the reign of organized crime in America; the strange, unprecedented horror Americans, who had grown up with barbershop quartets and cotton candy, must have felt reading in their daily papers about machine-gun slayings in city streets and massacres of rival gangs in closed garages. Hard, too, to imagine the giddy exhilaration—the sense of excitement and danger—that must have accompanied the coming of the automobile, the emancipation of young women from Victorian mores, the naughty but oddly compelling theories of a Viennese psychiatrist named Sigmund Freud. (Hammett's frankness with respect to such things helped give his work an edge that is lost now.)

It has been said that Hammett's greatest innovation was that he wrote detective stories which were worth reading even if the last page was missing. True enough. Hammett's stories command our attention not with the startling revelations on the final page but with the many smaller revelations of a far more interesting sort strewn like so many crumbs of bread along the way—as though finding his way back to the person he was that morning is as important to Hammett's hero as finding his way to the heart of the crime.

For it was in the work of Dashiell Hammett that the fictional detective reached self-consciousness. Before Hammett, the emphasis—for all the eccentricities of character indulged for the amusement of the reader—was on the solving of the crime. With Hammett, the detective himself—his aches and pains, his motives, values, feelings, and needs, his fears of growing old—has become the real subject. The people with whom he deals fascinate him as much as the evil deed he is investigating. As does his own behavior. Hammett invested his fictions not only with a gift for memorable writing but also with an extraordinary feel for the human condition and a series of questions that lie at the heart of the twentieth-century experience: Is it still possible to be a good person in what is manifestly an evil world? Wherein, given the collapse of the traditional shared-value system, does that goodness consist? (In other words, how can we continue to tell the difference between the good folks and the bad folks?) How do we know what we know? And is it possible to live a life without trusting in something or someone?

In their characteristic blend of cynicism and idealism Hammett's fictional heroes mirror what seems to have been their creator's lifelong struggle with his own contradictory behavior. The perennial themes of guilt and punishment found in all detective stories are complicated, in Hammett's, by all the ambiguities and maddening uncertainties that haunt the real world. What makes Hammett's heroes interesting is not, finally, their endearing tough talk or the steel nerves with which they face their nemeses, nor even their touching moments of odd vulnerability (a lifelong theme of Hammett's), but the fact that they experience doubt, guilt, the judgment of time, a yearning to believe in someone or something, revulsion toward their own actions, the need for forgiveness, and—especially in the case of Sam Spade and the Continental Op—a real agony over what is happening to their humanity.

Hammett's deeper concerns, in other words, are essentially spiritual in nature—a fact that has not sufficiently been noted, though everybody talks about his sense of honor, and of the importance of commitment to a code. The present book follows this concern with spiritual issues, and what can only be described as the moral perspective, through Hammett's entire career—from his early days as a fallen-away Catholic of some ferocity, to his later years as a communist manqué and patriot rejected by his own country.

Hounded and harrassed by the Internal Revenue Service and various government committees through the last sickly years of his life, unable to write, and having turned away finally even from the solace of alcohol, Hammett clung to the same deeply rooted convictions—and demonstrated the same qualities of character—that had informed his craft and sullen art. As a writer he had asked important questions, and ventured some bold answers . . . and showed us things about our society and our very language—the way we talk and think about our lives—that have become a permanent part of what we know.

But perhaps the most remarkable thing of all about Dashiell Hammett is that he managed to accomplish all of these things in the course of turning out some of the best detective stories anybody ever wrote.

Dennis Dooley. Dashiell Hammett (New York:
Ungar, 1984), pp. vi–xv

See also under ERLE STANLEY GARDNER: Paul Hofrichter, *Bookman's Weekly,* May 3, 1982, p. xx.

HEINLEIN, ROBERT A(NSON) (1907–1988)

Robert A. Heinlein's own statement of his intent in writing *Stranger in a Strange Land* may well be noted; but it is not necessarily the reader's best guide in his perusal of it. "My purpose in this book," the author says, "was to examine every major axiom of the western culture, to question each axiom, throw doubt on it—and, if possible, to make the antithesis of each axiom appear a possible and perhaps desirable thing—rather than unthinkable."

An ambitious and comprehensive undertaking, surely. "Western culture," even though restricted to its major axioms—and who is to determine which they are?—is a complex of multiple concepts and behavior patterns. To stand each one of them upside down, with the avowed objective of discovering whether they may thereby appear more acceptable, is to subject each axiom to the warped mirror of ruthless reflection. Such a quixotic venture might well seem foredoomed to disaster.

But the author calls to his aid the helpful technique of science fiction, to lend a trace of plausibility to the preposterous. An experienced and expert practitioner in that occult craft, he launches his social critique by virtue of the rocket propulsion of this device.

Stranger in a Strange Land is an excellent yarn, creating its own atmosphere of fantasy and fascination as it proceeds. It is Alice in Wonderland for grownups of the space age. Disturbing vestiges of human actions and reactions in the characters who play their topsy-turvy roles in this extravaganza project a mirage of veracity that lures us on and on.

In the quaint vernacular of our everyday world, a man from Mars becomes the protagonist of the fable. It is he who justifies the title, as well as the author's avowed intention in writing the book in the first place. It is he who reveals our mores and our morals to ourselves. He forces us to see ourselves as others see us—some god has given us, through him, the gift to do so.

Even so, the earthbound reader may well be excused if he disregards this elaborate examination of our culture, except in passing, and finds his chief enjoyment, instead, in the wide-ranging fantasy of the story for its own sake.

R. A. Jelliffe. *Chicago Tribune.* August 6, 1961,
p. 5

The publication of *Stranger in a Strange Land* marked a drastic shift in Heinlein's writing, at least in social criticism and controversial subject matter. Theodore Sturgeon remarks in the *New York Times Magazine* that up till 1961 Heinlein's works "contain rather less objectionable material than the Reverend Bowdler would have been able to find had he been equipped with an electron microscope." He concludes though that *Stranger* "is not for kiddies." Whether or not *Stranger* should be read by youngsters is a personal judgment, but many parents would feel uneasy themselves concerning Heinlein's irreverent, satiric swipes at almost every sacred value held by Western society in general and America in particular. *Stranger* takes a caustic look at everything from "true confession" magazines to democracy, but in particular Heinlein is concerned with exposing and undermining stifling sexual mores and repressive religion. In this exposé Heinlein portrays the beginning of the twenty-first century as much the same as the last of the twentieth, but what he feels to be negative tendencies are accelerated.

Along with using science fiction's distinctive approaches for social criticism, *Stranger* also contains another element essential to good science fiction: high entertainment value. An evaluation of whether or not a particular work is entertaining is a highly subjective process, but *Stranger* contains the elements needed for a novel to be enjoyable. Most importantly, *Stranger* has an easily followed plot consisting of the story of Mike's arrival on earth as an innocent, the experiences that form his character and actions, and the events that culminate in his death. The specific incidents vary in tone and substance from crude slapstick to exciting melodrama to moving pathos. The characters are either people the reader would like to spend some time with or individuals the reader can have some enjoyable moments hating. Heinlein drew his characters full-size and with easily recognizable faults and virtues.

Ronald Lee Cansler. Journal of Popular Culture.
Spring 1972, pp. 944–54.

Robert A. Heinlein has that attribute which the mathematician Hermann Weyl calls "the inexhaustibility of real things": whatever you say about him, I find, turns out to be only partly true. If you point to his innate conservatism, as evidenced in the old-time finance of "The Man Who Sold the Moon," you may feel smug for as much as a minute, until you remember the rampantly radical monetary system of *Beyond This Horizon*.

With due caution, then, let me say that in art, at least, Heinlein seems to be as conservative as they come. He believes in a plain tale well told. Although he fancies his own Yukon-style verses, or used to, he has no patience with poetry-in-a-garret. The people he writes about are healthy, uninhibited, and positive, a totally different breed from the neurasthenic heroes of many of his colleagues. In a field whose most brilliant and well-established writers seem to flip sooner or later, Heinlein is preeminently sane.

Heinlein's greatest asset, I think, is the same perennial hero—essentially he's Heinlein himself, and Heinlein likes himself. This is a thing so rare in writers-by-necessity, who are insecure, self-critical men, that every now and then a writer-by-accident who has it, as Mark Twain did, cheerfully walks away with all the prizes in sight.

Heinlein's style, which I admire, is a flexible and efficient instrument, but so simple and conversational that it makes you think of Heinlein's work as a simple, standardized product, and of Heinlein himself as a simple, standardized man.

In reality, there are several Heinleins. One of them is a nineteenth century rationalist and skeptic, who believes in nothing he can't see, touch, and preferably measure with calipers. Another is a mystic, who strongly believes in the existence of something beyond the world of the senses, and keeps an open mind even toward the ragtag and bobtail of mystical ideas, flying saucers, and Bridey Murphy.

> Damon Knight. *In Search of Wonder: Critical
> Essays on Science Fiction* (Chicago: Advent,
> 1967), pp. 76–89

One reason for Robert A. Heinlein's success has been the high grade of machinery which goes, today as always, into his storytelling. Heinlein seems to have known from the beginning, as if instinctively, technical lessons about fiction which other writers must learn the hard way (or often enough, never learn). He does not always operate the machinery to the best advantage, but he always seems to be aware of it.

In the novel form, Heinlein has shown a special interest in the most difficult of all points of view: the first person story, told by the principal actor. Among the adult novels he has handled in this way are *The Puppet Masters, Double Star,* and *The Door into Summer.*

The only first-person narrator Heinlein has created who is a living, completely independent human being, is The Great Lorenzo of *Double Star.* Lorenzo is complete all the way back to his childhood—the influence of his father upon what he thinks is one of the strongest motives in the story—and his growth under pressure is consistent with his character and no-one else's.

In *The Door into Summer* Heinlein has apparently come to take this hero so for granted that he does not even try to set him forth clearly for the reader—a defect which is fatal to the novel. Presented with the task of showing us not one, but two future societies, Heinlein bungles both because he has failed to visualize precisely *who* is seeing what there is to be seen. Unless my memory has failed me, *The Door into Summer* is Heinlein's only major essay in time travel, and as such it should have been a major novel. Every other important subject of science fiction which Heinlein has examined at length has come out remade, vitalized, and made the author's own property. It didn't happen here, for the first time in Heinlein's long and distinguished career—and not because Heinlein didn't have something to say, but because he failed to embody it in a real protagonist. Evidently, Heinlein as his own hero is about played out.

> William Atheling, Jr. *More Issues at Hand.* (n.p.:
> Advent, 1970), pp. 51–58

Heinlein assumes that technology will continue to develop and thereby change society. The cosmos is infinite. With increased scientific knowledge man may roam the universe and even the fourth dimension. Unlike many science fiction writers who express an uncritical faith in technology or, like C. S. Lewis, who express a distrust of materialism and science, Heinlein's view shows more balance. He recognizes that technology may threaten the existence of independence and individual integrity, but he expresses a belief in the individual's ability to cope with strange conditions and to act in an independent, nondeterministic fashion. The portrayal of modern man's ability to shape his own destiny accounts in large part for Heinlein's continued popularity since this view is expressed concretely through fast-moving action and appealing situations.

Diane Parkin Speer. *Extrapolation.* December 1970, p. 33

Robert Heinlein is a storyteller of such talent that his novels outsell all others and his name remains fixed at the top of every list of favorites. He is a universe maker who believes in the future of mankind and in the endless frontier of the galactic civilization that is to be. In this day of despair and crises, that faith is more of a true beacon than all the frightened philosophies of the panicked dystopians.

Look through the bulk of his novels and you will find that faith always shining through. Whatever the nature of the novel, whatever his message may be, this is the one constant that Heinlein will not surrender. Humanity, whatever its faults, is the best darned thing going and will never be pinned to the mat.

Donald A. Wolheim. *The Universe Makers* (New York: Harper & Row, 1971), pp. 99–101

The one author who has raised science fiction from the gutter status of pulp space opera (still practiced by Hollywood) to the altitude of original and breathtaking concepts is Robert A. Heinlein. And there is no doubt that his latest novel, *Time Enough for Love,* an enormous work covering the next twenty-four centuries, played on nine planets, with several hundred vivid characters, will evoke the same reaction that his thirty-odd previous books have: a curious combination of admiration, awe, shock, hatred, and fascination.

For Heinlein is a delightful paradox, and the contrasts of his character show in his splendid, challenging, and sometimes infuriating writing. One thing is certain: Heinlein will never bore you, in life or on the page.

Alfred Bester. *Publishers Weekly.* July 2, 1973, pp. 44–45

In 1959, Robert Heinlein's *Starship Troopers* won the Hugo award as the year's best science fiction novel. Critics and reviewers have been apologizing for that fact ever since. Even admirers of Heinlein as a logician and storyteller condemn *Starship Troopers* as a "militaristic polemic" glorifying a violent, protofascist ethic, creating a polarized society in which heroic war veterans rule over "draft-dodgers, effeminate snobs, pacifists, and other animals of low standing."

Evaluating the charges of fascism and militarism is complicated by the fact that Heinlein's society is not presented in detail. Nevertheless, consideration of the social structure outlined in *Starship Troopers* in the context of recent scholarship on fascism and militarism suggests that, in fact, neither ideology is embodied in this work, and that critics of Heinlein's views and visions must find new pejorative terms with which to condemn the novel.

The charge of fascism can be most easily dismissed, since the world of *Starship Troopers* has literally none of the characteristics commonly associated with fascist societies. Such concepts as a revolt against bolshevism, a reaction to liberalism and positivism, and a desire to restore an organic community, can be neither supported nor extrapolated from the novel's context. More significantly, Heinlein offers no other common bench marks of fascism. There is no indication of a ruling party, a secret police, a charismatic leader, or an official ideology.

At least as significant in demonstrating that Heinlein's society is not fascistic is the absence of racism and xenophobia.

The society depicted in the novel is neither militarist nor fascist in the scholarly sense of these concepts. Critics might do well to familiarize themselves carefully with the past from which they believe a given work draws its social and political inspiration. Such knowledge can make possible conclusions and extrapolations in areas where an author intent on telling a story may present no more than the hint of an explanation. It might also indicate that science fiction writers are not entirely prone to rely on custom and analogy in developing their future societies.

Dennis E. Showalter. *Extrapolation*. May 1975,
pp. 113–24

In an attempt to account for the extraordinary popularity and influence of the novels of Robert Heinlein, it would be all too easy to assert that the masses are asses and let it go at that. Those of us academics who read Heinlein are likely to admit it with an apology, acknowledging that we realize his literary merit is probably small and our weakness in enjoying his work a minor character defect. We feel we should not relish his opinionated expressions. We note that frankly didactic literature has always had a relatively small but devoted readership, especially among those whose prejudices and biases coincide with the author's.

But Heinlein's appeal somehow seems to be broader than these general apologies account for. The fact is, though many of us disagree with Heinlein, or what we assume are Heinlein's "true" opinions, we're usually caught by the questions he raises. Contrary to the most widely accepted critical theories, the Heinlein addict reads his work, not *in spite of* the sermons Heinlein crafts, but actually *for* the pleasure of the challenge of considering the moral and political questions Heinlein raises. I also believe the secret of his successful sermons lies in his provocative use of irony and in his *not* providing clear answers to these vital questions; rather, at his best he raises issues for the serious adult mind to consider and trusts the reader to draw his or her own conclusions.

Science fiction in general and Heinlein's work in particular have often been considered as different—a thing apart—from the "mainstream" of literature. But I believe Heinlein's craft can be analyzed best by first placing it in context.

The most fascinating questions Heinlein raises are in the field of political power—our outward responsibilities to one another—and in the realm of personal freedom, particularly sexual freedom. In the former area, Heinlein's mastery of irony creates some of the most intriguing, albeit secular, sermons of modern literature. In the latter, he often lacks the perspective and balance required to intrigue someone not already in agreement. One feels he or she is being told rather than shown, and the viewpoint seems manipulated to fulfill the author's wish-dreams.

A master of paradox, he shows that machinery is "human" both in the sense of being created by people and in the notion of capacity to produce good or bad results in terms of our continued existence. What is good in the short term may prove ultimately bad, and vice versa.

Being human, Heinlein shows, is a process of becoming; only changes are permanent. His protagonists are usually becoming better or more aware, but whatever state of awareness in which he leaves his protagonist at the end of a novel, the reader is assured he has not stopped developing. "Truth" exists only in pragmatic moments when decisions must be reached on whatever evidence is at hand.

Elizabeth Anne Hull. Extrapolation. Spring 1979,
pp. 38–42

There are two ways to review Robert A. Heinlein's work since *Stranger in a Strange Land,* excepting *The Moon Is a Harsh Mistress.* With that exception, there is a pre-1961 Heinlein and then there is this "new" fellow.

The old Heinlein was a crisp, slick wordsmith of uncommon intelligence and subtlety. His gift for characterization was sharp within its narrow limits, and those limits were fortuitously placed to include the archetypical science fiction here. All his people talked alike. You could tell the stupid and villainous from the worthy and heroic only by their choices of subject matter. But his dialogue worked; its purpose was to propel the story, and it served quite well.

The Number of the Beast reflects the quintessence of the "new" Heinlein. Where the pre-1961 writer clung to the old pulp tenets—Tell your story quickly, clearly, basing the resolution on physical action emerging from inner growth, and for God's sake never give the reader a chance to realize there's a writer involved—the new one repudiates them, deliberately. The new Heinlein hero is perfect to begin with. The world is best served by acknowledging his perfection and acting in accordance as quickly as possible. The plot thread is a rambling one, strung with incidents whose one common purpose is to give the world, and the reader, time and evidence required to work out details of the hero's perfection. The nature of the incidents is not organic to the story. They do not grow out of the hero's exploration of his problem. They can't—he has no problems, only transient difficulties, and this is obvious from the first paragraphs.

Therefore, the incidents can take place anywhere, anytime, and must be attractive in themselves. They are not successively unlocked rooms in an unknown structure, through which the hero must pass to find the ideal egress. They are way stations on a circular tour of the hero's nature, and they must be furnished to engage the reader's interest as a reader, rather than as an involved rider in the searching hero's head.

That results in a kind of game, with Heinlein visibly his own hero. At times he invents new-ish settings which are actually recalls of typical Heinlein settings. At other times he directly borrows settings—E. E. Smith's Lensman universe, the Land of Oz, and the universe of Lazarus Long. In every case, the reference is to the relationship between conscious author and reader, not between hero and the reader's subconscious role-playing as a hero-surrogate. There can be no doubt on either side that at all times there is a book involved. The magic of forgetting that the reader is actually sitting in a quiet room surrounded by creature comforts—that special magic which is what reading does for most of us—cannot occur. *The Number of the Beast* is a book for critics; for the reader as critic, not as participant, it can be impressive. It has cut itself off, by first intention, from any attempt to be compelling.

Algis Budrys. The Magazine of Fantasy and
Science Fiction. October 1980, pp. 55–56

Robert Heinlein's following was ardent and instant with the appearance of his first short story in *Astounding Science Fiction* magazine more than forty years ago, and it has multiplied with each of his publications. His series of "juveniles" had a great deal to do with raising that category from childish to what is now called "young adult." His influence on science fiction has been immense; his knowledge of the hard sciences and his gift for logical extrapolation inspired many beginning writers—and a good many already established hands—to knit fact and conjecture with a little more care and a great deal more literary quality than previously. The net effect over the years has been to erode the snobbery placed on science fiction. Vladimir Nabokov, Doris Lessing, Kurt Vonnegut, Jorge Luis Borges, and other luminaries have found it a worthy metier with full awareness that it is, after all, not all zap guns and special effects. And throughout this swift and steady evolution can, almost always, be seen the Heinlein influence.

Heinlein's most recent books have been largely didactic, interior, sometimes pedantic, though each has its good measure of action. Some of his idolators mourned the lack of the Heinlein of the decisive hero, the blinding pace, the magnificent sweep of very possible near-future developments; above all, that element of capital-S Story.

Well, *Friday* has it all. Friday herself is a delight. She is as strong and resourceful and decisive as any Heinlein hero; in addition she is loving (oh, yes) and tender and very, very female. She also has an evolved ethos—the ability to discard past hatreds and dislikes and so to meet people, day by day, in terms of what they now are, and not to judge them by what they have been.

Heinlein's gift for invention—we owe him the remote manipulator that scientists call "waldoes" after a Heinlein story, and another gave us the waterbed—moves pretty far out from time to time. In this book he describes a completely Balkanized North America, complete with his typical meticulous analysis of its currencies, customs and political forms, its border guards and variegated moralities. This, like so many of Heinlein's works (particularly the earlier ones), is as joyous to read as it is provocative.

Theodore Sturgeon. *Los Angeles Times Book Review*. June 20, 1982, p. 4

We are approaching the thirtieth birthday of *Stranger in a Strange Land*. Valentine Michael Smith is the stranger. Raised by Martians on Mars, he is brought to Earth where he must adapt not only to our social prejudices, but to our strong gravitational field and rich atmosphere. Some sixty thousand words that were cut from Heinlein's manuscript for reasons of economy back in 1961 are at last taking their rightful place in the body of world literature. There is a preface by the author's widow, Virginia Heinlein, which speaks not at all of the neglect of her husband's work by the establishment. It tells the history of the uncut manuscript, which, if it weren't for her, might have remained in total darkness forever in a vault in the library of the University of California at Santa Cruz.

Is the story much improved by the restored passages? I leave it to someone else to compare the two versions line by line. The thought-provoking premise is unchanged and could scarcely be enriched. Nor did the consequences of that premise as extrapolated by Heinlein seem to me garbled or anemic or whatever in the abridged edition I read years ago. So I say of the restorations, "Icing on a cake which for people who like that kind of cake was already quite satisfactory."

Am I arguing that *Stranger in a Strange Land* is anywhere near as good as *Madame Bovary*? Good heavens no! No novel has come within a kilometer of the greatness of Flaubert's masterpiece. Not even *Anna Karenina*. Not even *The Bonfire of the Vanities*.

Kurt Vonnegut. *New York Times Book Review*. December 9, 1990, p. 13

HERBERT, FRANK (1920–1986)

Professional science fiction writers have rarely been encouraged to be good stylists. This is partly because science fiction publishing and marketing methods make little distinction between the kind of star schlock in which intergalactic cops battle hypothyroid blobs, and a well-wrought literary work in which far-reaching concepts and social problems are dramatized with intelligence, wit, and verbal skill.

More important, critics and reviewers who confer literary status rarely know much about science or technology. Even journeymen practitioners of science fiction are likely to know more about literature than most novelists and critics know about science. And in the twentieth century, ignorance of the fundamentals—and social implications—of physics, chemistry, biology, and mathematics constitutes an embarrassing form of illiteracy.

Despite much misunderstanding over the past half-dozen years, science fiction has undergone an explosive growth. In perspective, the interest in science fiction can be seen as part of the natural anxiety about the future of the planet.

Unlike many best-selling popular novelists who squint at headlines for topical book ideas, science fiction writers often prove to be commercially farsighted. One of the most spectacularly successful science fiction novels of recent years, Frank Herbert's *Dune*, is a good example of how public concerns and infatuations catch up with the science fiction imagination. It has been extremely popular with youth, which is greatly involved with the power of mysticism and the impieties of earthly industrial civilization.

Paul Atreides, the hero of *Dune,* is well equipped with psychic abilities and Christlike symbolism. A superior thought-hypnotist, swordsman (of the old school), and ecologist, he is descended from an ancient line of space migrants whose antitechnology religion is summed up in the commandment, "Thou shalt not disfigure the soul." Set on the nearly waterless planet of Arrakis thousands of years in the future, *Dune* is a swashbuckling account of how human civilization, as it is now known, is reborn in a desert.

Like most science fiction, *Dune* is conceptually rich. It has 541 pages crammed with the canned fruits of Herbert's researches into ecology, desert cultures, and history. There are even extensive appendices outlining the soil growth and planting schedules that Atreides projected for his centuries-long ecological project to make Arrakis bloom.

R. Z. Sheppard. *Time.* March 29, 1971, pp. 86–87

If you can't be great, be big! Frank Herbert's *Dune* (1965) is certainly big, and many people have found it great.

Dune is enjoying something like the same success as Robert Heinlein's *Stranger in a Strange Land,* and probably for the same reason, because its readers can indulge in a fantasy life of power and savor a strange religion.

But there is more than that to *Dune* and its successor, *Dune Messiah* (1969). Although Campbellian science fiction is still present, so, too, is an attention to sensuous detail which is the antithesis of Campbell; the bleak, dry world of Arrakis is as intensely realized as any in science fiction. The obvious shortage of water, for instance, is presented not just diagrammatically, but as living fact which permeates all facets of existence.

Dune and *Dune Messiah* are dense and complex books, repaying careful reading. While they contain many ideas, the main informing idea is an ecological one; which makes them—together with all the other things they are!—very trendy books.

Herbert has long been known as an impressive writer. His great *Under Pressure*—reprinted as *Dragon in the Sea,* and *21st Century Sub*—also has strong religious elements, and is well worth seeking out for its study of obsessed men engaged in undersea warfare some time in the future.

Brian Aldiss. *Billion Year Spree: The True History*
of Science Fiction (New York: Doubleday, 1973),
pp. 274–76

Few would deny that *Dune* is a "great read," as Tolkien's *Lord of the Rings* is a "great read." It gives us strongly defined heroes and villains, engages us in an action which is simple in essence but full of events, twists, complications. *Dune* and its sequel, *Dune Messiah*, first appeared as serial fiction, and they exhibit the frequent climaxes and moments of great suspense which the serial format requires. *Dune* is a romance of adventure, and it is not my intention here to suggest that this romance hides great speculative profundities. What makes it exceptional is the systematic way in which the narrational events are imbedded in a particular ecological setting, and the thoughtfulness and delicacy that have gone into the major characterizations. By choosing as his main location a planet that is naturally a desert, Herbert has alloted the ecosystem a major role in structuring his narrative. And he has developed this role with a wonderful rigor and attention to detail.

This is one great strength of *Dune*. Another is in Herbert's attention to the mechanisms by which religious and political "greatness" are achieved. The imaginary sands of *Dune* owe a good deal to the real sands of Arabia, and somewhere behind this novel stands T. E. Lawrence's *Seven Pillars of Wisdom,* in which Lawrence speculated on the curious propensity of the semitic geography for producing prophets and mystics. Paul Atreides, who becomes the religious leader Muad'Dib, finds himself cast for the role of prophet in a holy war. Herbert is saved from operating at the adventure story level—saved by a greater ability to transfer something of actual political maneuvering into narrative form, and to an even greater extent saved by his ability to characterize Paul as a young man who *knows* that he has been cast for a role, that he is enacting a myth with which he is not entirely in sympathy. Like the comic-mythic heroes of John Barth's *Chimera,* Paul Atreides has a powerful sense of the artificiality in his own situation. But where

Barth's bumbling heroes struggle to enact their mythic roles fittingly, forcing us to laugh at their comic ineptitude, Paul simply takes a sardonic attitude toward "greatness" and tries to ride the mythic whirlwind and tame it for the sake of the people on his adopted planet.

Herbert wisely avoids loading the story with a greater conceptual weight then the romance of adventure can comfortably handle, nor does he often try to philosophize beyond his own intellectual range. He works within the traditional formula, achieving his effects through care and consistency, and through considerable tact in the use of extraordinary mental and physical events. Paul's prophetic powers, for instance, reveal not one future to him, but many possible futures, projections of present history which he may try to actualize or avoid. The other extraordinary mental feats performed by various characters are logical, almost reasonable extensions of the practices of yoga or the possibilities of biofeedback. Tact, consistency, and restraint, are what make this adventure story an exceptionally mature and interesting one. And nowhere do these qualities emerge more clearly than in Herbert's presentation of the ecology of *Dune* and the various human responses to that ecology. Here he is most structural, most aware of system and necessity, and this awareness is the backbone of the book.

> Robert Scholes. *Structural Fabulation, An Essay*
> *on Fiction of the Future* (South Bend: University
> of Notre Dame Press, 1975), pp. 67–70

That we are in for a portentous rendering of great issues in philosophy is signaled at the outset of Frank Herbert's *Santaroga Barrier* by the name of the hero, Dr. Gilbert Dasein. *Dasein* in German means "being there" and is the key concept of existential thinking in the philosophy of Karl Jaspers, whose own name figures in the drug with which the townsmen of Santaroga infuse their beer, cheese, and other foods.

Karl Jaspers is associated with a number of critics of modern society who together have built what is probably the most influential social theory of our day: the theory of mass society. They are concerned less with the general conditions of freedom in society than with the freedom of those persons who possess the intelligence to cultivate a sense of the individual self over and above the dim self-awareness of mass man. The criticism of mass society brought to bear by Karl Jaspers is above all an aristocratic critique. Therein lies the source of his appeal: the defense of creative individuality.

The decline of cultural standards in order to meet the consensus needs of the classless multitudes of average people has brought about a crisis of individual consciousness. In the absence of a cultured elite born or educated to command, true leadership is replaced by organization men who strive for position and power with an opportunistic cunning that stands in the way of responsibility for one's actions, with the result that true selfhood is denied to others as well; for where power depends on the mobilization of popular appetites in politics and business, leadership cannot tolerate individuality, reason, or self-expression in the target population. It is a world of mass mediocrity, from top to bottom. Given this cultural decline, is the realization of the self still a possibility?

To that question the inhabitants of Santaroga, a small town in California, answer *yes*. They have erected a barrier against mass society behind which the personal values of their counterculture may flourish. But their unanimity of purpose is mediated by a drug, Jaspers, whose pernicious effects result in the heightening of empathy and the awareness of others at the expense of self-awareness. But ironically, in their reliance on the drug Jaspers to restore a traditional sense of community which the individual may imbue with his selfhood, they too are reduced to a mindless mass of functional parts.

In the course of finding an answer to the question of why Santarogans won't trade with outsiders, Dr. Dasein himself, an outside investigator, becomes a Santarogan.

In tracing the hero's philosophical progress, Frank Herbert is faithful to the essential pessimism of Karl Jaspers's message: that people in general lack the capacity to resist deception; that both the manipulators and the manipulated in mass society lack the will to see reality as it is actually constituted. And the reality is human mendacity; people are not, in fact, honest or kind. The discovery that life among dishonest men is not worth living is the discovery made by the Santarogans, and Dr. Dasein joins with them in creating a community of like minds. The stress in the philosophy of Karl Jaspers is the dependence of the self upon social and linguistic interaction. The Santarogans are living examples of Jaspers's belief that we humans are what we are only through a community of mutually conscious understandings, that truth is communicability.

The fallacy that makes Santaroga a black utopia is that it is a community of vital sympathies merely, minus the freedom to reject the communications of one's fellows in favor of the promptings from an inner source. This enforced awareness of others, mediated by the drug Jaspers, makes for a caricature of everything Karl Jaspers the philosopher ever stood for. It is all group awareness and no individual freedom. In fact, the Santarogans are not aware individually that their collective will communicates hostility to outsiders. They murdered a number of outside investigators but actually believe these deaths resulted from unfortunate accidents.

The first thing that Dasein notes about Santaroga, when it is his turn to investigate it, is its conservatism; it resists change.

Far from pioneering an exportable counterculture against mass society, as it believes it is doing, the rest of the world is moving away from it.

In the end, Dasein understands the Santarogans so well that he becomes one of them. But not before he is addicted to Jaspers for life when he ingests a massive dose of the drug abstracted from a wheel of Jaspers cheese. Up until this time he had escaped unharmed from all attempts to murder him.

The collective will to kill him finally almost succeeds in the person of Jenny, but like the others she lacks any individual knowledge of this; Dasein understands and forgives her. After his conversion, he himself murders Dr. Selador, a psychiatrist colleague, in the same unconscious manner.

The unconscious communication of hatred for outsiders is Santaroga's version of raw, ungoverned power; the Santarogans take Jaspers as their "Consciousness Fuel," but it fuels a sense of communal awareness at the total expense of individual awareness. With his engagement to Jenny, Dasein leaves behind all such attempts to intellectualize his experience:

> He settled his mind firmly then onto thoughts of the home Jenny had described, pictured himself carrying her across the threshold—his wife. There'd be presents: Jaspers from "the gang," furniture. Santaroga took care of its own.
> *It'll be a beautiful life, he thought. Beautiful . . . beautiful . . . beautiful. . . .*

These concluding words are meant to be ironic; the Santarogan utopia turns out to be a totalitarian utopia, in which men are domesticated for community life at the sacrifice of their souls. Like all utopian goals, those of Santaroga are beyond human reach—they intended nothing less than to overcome the sum of human alienation caused by the rise of modern civilization. But the result was a replication of the worst feature of mass society—"all people everywhere alike." In addition, there were a number of individuals who did not respond well to the drug; it turned them into nullities, moronic rejects who were chained to the production lines of Santaroga's cheese industry. For the others, all that remains in place of a spiritually informed existence is a collectivity of primal selves.

In conclusion, I believe that Frank Herbert's presentation of Santaroga as a black utopia is the means by which he criticizes the theory of mass society itself and its romantic hostility to the modern world. Everyone is against atomism and for organic living, but if we substitute "totalitarian" for "organic" and "individualistic" for "atomistic," the argument is turned around. The picture of mass society as debauched by concessions to popular taste is overdrawn. And if it be granted that mass society is superficial in personal relations, utilitarian, competitive, acquisitive, and mobile, the good side must also be shown—the right to privacy, the free choice of occupation and friends, social status on the basis of merit not pedigree, a plurality of norms and standards rather than monopolistic control by a single dominant group.

For mass society, Dr. Counterculture prescribes Jaspers beer and cheese. Once again, the cure is worse than the disease.

Leon E. Stover. *Extrapolation.* May 1976,
pp. 160–67

Frank Herbert's long-awaited finale of his *Dune* trilogy, *Children of Dune,* cannot be dismissed casually as just another space opera. To be sure, there is plenty of traditional science fiction action for the true believer, but, as with the earlier novels, *Dune* and *Dune Messiah,* there's much to satisfy ecologists, anthropologists, and speculative theologians, as well.

Arrakis, the desert planet, sole source in the universe of a genuine life-prolonging drug, is the real hero. *Children of Dune* opens as the changes begun decades before are taking place. The vast spectrum of characters, many of whom illustrate some Jungian mythic archetype, are either unaware of, or unconcerned with, these changes. The consequences make up the plot of *Children of Dune.*

In the hands of skilled writers like Herbert, science fiction becomes a tool or a device to say something meaningful about our contemporary world. In this sense, science fiction verges on allegory, but without the burden usually associated with that word. We need to understand what we are doing to our own environment, Herbert seems to be saying, that, because of some of the things we've done, e.g., disruption of the ozone layer, the earth may already be beyond redemption, with disastrous consequences for human life. But Herbert is too good a writer to draw such obvious conclusions in his novel. Rather, he stimulates the reader to think about these problems, while he goes on telling a rattling good story.

Moreover, some of the questions it asks are ones not normally associated with science fiction: Given a genuine avatar, what will be the psychological (and ecological) effects on him and his planet if, because of the violent nature of the planet, he must choose as his method of redemption, not the traditional means of mercy and love, but violence? What are the effects of a ritualistic religion on a planet undergoing a change from static to dynamic?

Dune was deservedly a popular success, and it has become something of a cult object among its readers. *Children of Dune* will be no disappointment to them, and its quality may finally convince those who haven't yet accepted the fact that science fiction can be good.

Willis E. McNelly. America. June 26, 1976,
p. 570

What makes *The Heaven Makers* unique among mind-invasion science fiction stories is its historical orientation. It attributes the madness and misery of past and present to mind-warping incubi—vampires feeding on man's creative energy or string holders of the Punch-and-Judy show called history, whose scenario human beings imagine they have written.

The Heaven Makers stirs recollections of Samuel Johnson's satiric criticism, "A Review of Soame Jenyns' *A Free Inquiry into the Nature and Origin of Evil.*" "He [Jenyns] imagines," Johnson writes, "that as we have not only animals for food, but choose some for our diversion, the same privilege may be allowed to some beings above us, *who may deceive, torment, or destroy us for the ends only of their own pleasure or utility.*"

Johnson proceeds to demolish Jenyns's speculations, pricking him with exquisite ridicule, and concludes, "The only end of writing is to enable the readers better to enjoy life, or better to endure it: and how will either of those be put more in our power by him who tells us, that we are puppets, of which some creature not much wiser than ourselves manages the wires." Yet that is the thesis of Herbert's story.

The Chem, immortal, invisible, goblin creatures, imprisoned in eternity, find relief from oppressive timelessness by molding "voices and faces and entire races" for their amusement. Having little else to relieve their boredom but voyeurism, the Chem have made earth (and other worlds too) one vast theatrical stage. From his storyship beneath the ocean, director-scenarist Fraffin had sent shooting crews "filming" the pageants of history to entertain the Chem on universal "pantovive" (a kind of television). "I touch a nerve," says Fraffin, explaining his art to a Chem visitor. "Greed here, a desire there, a whim in the other place—and fear. Yes, fear. When the creature's fully prepared, I arouse its fears. The whole mechanism performs for me then. They make themselves ill! They love! They hate! They cheat! They kill! They die! And the most amusing part, the most *humorous* element, is that they think they do it of and by themselves."

It is curious that the mind-invasion stories of Herbert should lean toward an interpretation of history. Does this approach signal the beginning of a trend? Shakespeare's metaphor, "All the world's a stage, And all the men and women merely players," has been held literally, as theology and superstition reveal. If man continues to move inexorably toward yawning, calculable hells, will fiction—will man—look to demonism for answers?

There is an ironic moment in *The Heaven Makers*, which touches its philosophic core. Fraffin, looking through his scanners for some activity among "his creatures," focuses upon a pitchman's flea show, the fleas dancing and leaping, wrestling, and racing. The Chem wonders, "Do those fleas know they're someone else's property?" The mind-invasion story asks, Whose property is man?

Harold L. Berger. *Science Fiction and the New Dark Age*. (Bowling Green, Ohio: Popular Press, 1976), pp. 111–16

What makes Frank Herbert's work unique (beyond even the depth of his thought) is his willingness to consider alternative futures that appear distasteful to present-day readers. In a work such as *Hellstrom's Hive*, this willingness serves chiefly as a spur to thought. A statement made in *Destination: Void* reveals a deeper meaning in Herbert's attitude:

> There's a serious question whether humans actually can break out of their self-regulated pattern. It takes audacious methods indeed to explore beyond that pattern.

As suggested in the discussion of *Children of Dune,* Herbert seems to subscribe to a kind of evolutionary ethic, which uses survival as a touchstone for evaluating species behavior. This ethic is also the subject of one of his most effective short stories, ''Seed Stock'' (1970).

A colony has been landed on an alien planet. It is dying. There is no return. The colonists are trying to reproduce Earth; they cannot understand why their efforts do not work. There is a strange force that warps embryos and seedlings so they do not flourish. The experts choose the most normal-born of the plants and animals to nurture, with no success. They cannot see (because it is unthinkable) that it is the seemingly most stunted and sickly of the plants and animals that are adapting. Kroudar, the laborer, listens with his body; he *feels* the different rhythm of life on his new planet. He does not try to maintain the old ways. He nurtures the new.

In this one fable is all of Herbert's wisdom. When people want the future to be like the present, they must reject what is different. And in what is different is the seed of change. It may look warped and stunted now, but it will be normal when we are gone.

Herbert's insistence throughout the story that one cannot *know* this principle, but must *feel* it, suggests a warning about the analysis of his books: By exposing Herbert's intentions, one may circumvent them. ''If you say, 'I understand' . . . you have made a value judgment,'' reads a Laclac riddle quoted in *Whipping Star.* And on Pandora, a planet like Arrakis or Earth itself, which demands human adaptation, Avata says, ''If you understand, then you cannot learn. By saying you understand, you construct barriers.'' Understanding can convince one that a problem has been solved and nothing remains to be done. Feeling, a perception that remains in touch with its source, cannot be so deceived. This is the final reason why Herbert tries to speak to the unconscious of his readers, not just with hidden verbal or conceptual allusions, but with rhythms and perceptual demands that evoke the feelings he is trying to depict. ''Seed Stock'' slouches toward that undefinable evolutionary difference that Kroudar feels in his blood. Like the design of the *Dune* trilogy, the style is its own argument, from which the reader cannot come away unchanged.

Such an effect argues that imagination, in the older, more limited sense of the ability to summon up the fantastic or the impossible, is the aging mother of science fiction. In a few precious works, such as Herbert's best, it is replaced by a new scion, an imagination that draws its strength, like fabled Antaeus, from its ability to touch the ground of experience. Science fiction readers are stereotypically escapist, but their need is real. They want more life than they can get their hands on. Science fiction supplies adventure, romance, a feeling of being on conceptual frontiers, shifts of awareness that are real: a spectrum of answers to that one basic need. Herbert's spectrum is merely broader than most. The *Dune* trilogy is more than just an analogue that mirrors our society in ways that illuminate it; for some it is a reality in itself, which creates a novelty of experiences not yet common, which helps to create the very futures it depicts.

Timothy O'Reilly. *Frank Herbert* (New York: Ungar, 1981), pp. 187–92

The late grand master of the short-short story, Frederic Brown, wrote one in which the most powerful, most complex computer ever devised was asked its first question: "Is there a God?" Its response: "There is now."

There we have, in a nugget, theme, content, and basic statement not only for *The Lazarus Effect,* but for its weighty predecessor *The Jesus Incident.* That one established the settlement of the watery planet Pandora by humans, their conflicts with the indigenous life forms, including a sentient kelp, and their abandonment by their supercomputerized ship (hereafter known as Ship). Having achieved self-awareness, Ship left them with the injunction "Find ways to worShip me." The current volume deals with the appalling results of the humans' almost total obliteration of the kelp.

So: many astonishments. And the greatest is that in so convoluted a structure there are so many simplistic characters. In Creative Writing 101, paragraph (a), Verisimilitude, Dictate One is: Nobody is all good; nobody is all bad; no one is ever all anything. In this narrative the heroine is Good; the hero is Brave; the old Judge is Wise, and oh, how Evil is the villain. Further, one knows at the instant of introduction which couple will ultimately Make It, which of course they do when everything Comes Out All Right At The End.

This is perplexing. I don't know the work of poet Bill Ransom, coauthor of *The Lazarus Effect* (though I suspect that many deft phrases, like a man's mind "coming apart at the dreams" are his) but Frank Herbert (whose output includes the *Dune* series) certainly has earned his high credentials. His forte, clearly, is metaphor; and in that case, one might have a gentler response to this intrusion of absolutes. To apply advanced tectonics to the terrain through which pilgrims progress, is pedantic foolishness.

Or it just might be the high glee (for Frank Herbert is, at base, a gleeful man!) of expanding to two volumes and most of a thousand pages, the ultimate pun on the three words deus ex machina.

Theodore Sturgeon. *Los Angeles Times Book Review.* August 28, 1983, p. 4

Since its inception as a celebration of technology, science fiction has become bored with hardware and turns to something else instead: an allusive penny mysticism not the result of poetic scholarship but of a shoddy ransacking of paperback reflections on the occult, the ancient gods, and sacred scripture—anything, that is, to efface the fact that the future—or a mythical past—is unknowable and unknown, since as Joyce has said somewhere, we still must wipe our glosses with what we know. As scenario for the future, the genre has become moribund and self-conscious, so immired in its own conventions we have to look elsewhere for such things: to Huxley still, to Burgess always. Even C. S. Lewis helps; and always, it seems beyond this clubby group of writers who feel compelled, like the writers of pulp horror and gothics, to hold conventions, give awards, and publish apologiae for what looks like xenophobia in the ranks, and probably is.

In *The Lazarus Effect* coauthors Herbert and Ransom deck the hackneyed conventions with nothing new, nothing marvelous at all; and the novel's surprise is that nothing surprising happens at all. Plot and characterization become interchangeable with others of the genre. In place of Arthur C. Clarke's Hal, we have Ship—a computerized, mechanical intelligence who demands (punning inexcusably) WorShip from its human creators. In place of H. G. Wells's animal experiments on the island of Dr. Moreau, we have properly updated clones and mutants—Mutes, for short, in accordance with most science fiction writers' passion for the abbreviated, the colloquial, and the mundane.

Read it and rail against Nietzsche and all the supercilious, facile distinctions between Apollo and Dionysus ever made. Read it and wish that Jung had never written the words collective unconscious, or that Teilhard de Chardin had never mused about an Omega point, and know that the self-consciously created archetype—whether sentient kelp or Apollonian mermen—is always second-rate, and more than a little boring. Even to criticize such pulp strikes one as a vulgar practice, far too easy and far too slick a service: not tilting at windmills, but at paper kites.

Gregory Mercurio. *Best Sellers*. September 1983,
p. 203

HESSE, HERMANN (1877–1962)

The language of nature-mysticism was Hermann Hesse's answer to his religious problem up to the beginnings of World War I. One must avoid calling it pantheism, for pantheism means addressing nature or the cosmos or the universe as God. Hesse shuns every personal image or definition of God, but he still believes in the existence of a deity. Nature is its appearance, but not its essence. The proper term for such a view, in which God comes first and the universe second, is theopanism.

Psychoanalytic concepts helped Hesse considerably. They also serve as a key to a better understanding of his later works. But he did not become an amateur psychologist who used psychoanalysis namely for artistic purposes. It made him more aware of the role of the subconscious in artistic creation. Life and thought now appeared as a battle between conscious and subconscious tendencies, and a total picture of man emerged which no longer was simple or one-sidedly rational.

Stylistically, *Demian* signaled Hesse's definite break with his early Regionalism and Impressionism. To be sure, his new style still preserved some realistic elements. Kromer, Demian, Pistorius, and even Demian's mother are entirely possible in real life and behave like human beings. But for Sinclair they represent archetypal experiences in his struggle for integration. They hold one meaning as persons of real life and another as archetypes of Sinclair's psychological world. The proper name for such a contrapuntal style would be Surrealism, if by Surrealism is meant the employing of real objects to express nonobjective experiences. In Hesse's case one can see the affinity of this style to Romanticism.

Hesse's view of man can best be described as a poetic image of the total personality adumbrated by anthropological psychology. Here the individual stands in the spheres of nature and society just as much as he is indissolubly linked with history and with the forces of transcendency. Since we still largely connote scientific thinking with a strictly compartmental, rationalistic approach, Hesse's poetic vision for many contemporaries may provide an even better idea of modern psychological orientation than a strictly scientific description of it.

Ernst Rose. *Faith from the Abyss: Hermann Hesse's Way from Romanticism to Modernity* (New York: New York University Press, 1965), pp. 156–57

Hesse's works are filled with symbols of unity and totality. Most of them, of course, can be fully comprehended only within the context of the work itself, but by way of anticipation let us mention briefly a few of the more outstanding symbols. In *Demian* Hesse employs the god Abraxas, who represents in Gnostic mysticism the unification of God and Satan; and in the same novel he makes use of the egg, traditionally a symbol of totality. The Magic Theater in *The Steppenwolf,* as a projection of Harry Haller's inner nature into the outside world, is an externalization of the multifarious poles of his existence that, as he discovers, are by no means mutually exclusive. Here also, as in *Demian,* totality and delimitation are symbolized by the hermaphroditic nature of the women loved by the heroes. The Glass Bead Game, in the novel of that title, is an abstraction of all values of human culture that are invoked simultaneously in the game itself. Finally music, for Hesse, represents in almost every instance the symbolic manifestation of totality because in the counterpoint and harmony of music the most disparate elements can be brought together in a harmonious whole. It is not an exaggeration to say that every important symbol in Hesse's works is basically a representation of totality.

Like every major artist of his generation, Hesse faced the central problem of the early twentieth century: the breakdown of traditional reality in every area of life. The solution he found is explicitly a "magical" or mystical one that manifests itself in magical symbols and motifs in his works.

To this extent Hesse represents one of the strong currents in modern literature, for the resolution of conflict on a superrational level is a central theme of the reaction against positivism.

Hesse's novels from *Demian* on represent the search for a realm of timeless values that he ultimately defines most perfectly in the ideal vision of Castalia in the introduction to *The Glass Bead Game*. In this sense, his works after the years of crisis are a journey to Castalia, the aesthetic realm in which all values are reunited in an all-embracing totality and in which the threat of death is canceled out. To this extent Hesse's work is representative of his generation—the writers who, like him, sought the answers to life in an absolute world of art.

Theodore Ziolkowski. *The Novels of Hermann Hesse* (Princeton, New Jersey: Princeton University Press, 1965), pp. 341–60

Hermann Hesse has moved away from the position of pure contemplation that seemed to constitute his ideal in the twenties and early thirties. In the terms of the novel he is striving for a synthesis of the *vita activa* and the *vita contemplativa*. In *The Glass Bead Game* the ideal is symbolized by music, which requires a constant compromise between practice and theory, the abstract and the concrete, the spiritual and the sensual. Hesse's last novel is in no way a depiction of the charms of disengagement, but rather a plea for human commitment and for an art nourished by life, for a life enriched by art.

Hesse's growth as a writer parallels the development of literature in the twentieth century from aestheticism to engagement. But he was always an amused observer, never a member of movements of a frantic participant in the contest to keep abreast of the times. He was drawn to themes that are perhaps more urgent today than in ages with accepted patterns of belief, but still universal: the quest for identity, the search for personal values, the impulse to moral commitment. Just as he was reluctant to concern himself with issues that are merely timely, he also refused to engage in pure innovation and stylistic experimentation. Even in the least conventional of his novels he simply reshapes existing forms. It is his achievement to have shown to what extent modernity is traditional, in its thought and in its form; his works bridge the gap, so to speak, between romanticism and existentialism. His range was narrow and his expression essentially lyrical, for he rarely went beyond himself. At most, after 1917, he transposed his themes from the minor key of the private to the major key of the symbolic. For this reason Hesse does not rank, as a novelist, with Proust, Joyce, or Thomas Mann; and in his poetry he never approached Rilke, Eliot, or Valéry. But in the realm of poetic fiction—a province marked out by his favorite romantic authors and explored by Rilke, Hermann Broch, Virginia Woolf, André Gide, and others—his best works are unsurpassed. Sometimes, in this difficult terrain, he stumbled through a landscape cluttered with thickets of allegory. But with *The Steppenwolf, The Journey to the East,* and *The Glass Bead Game* he added lasting names to the map of our poetic imagination.

Theodore Ziolkowski. *Hermann Hesse* (New York: Columbia University Press, 1966), pp. 44–46

Hermann Hesse is perhaps one of the most paradoxical and enigmatic of modern writers. An image of the self defined by fierce individuality is matched by an author who is many things to many men. A persistent thematic current running through all of Hesse's books, the search for stability above the chaotic pressures of contemporary life, is accompanied by characters who, for the most part, are notoriously unstable in confronting their demons of uncertainty.

Hesse is an original inventor of unique fictional devices, yet his work is shot through with borrowings from his contemporaries and predecessors until the reader wonders whether he can find an original bone in his literary body. He has been praised as one of the masters of the modern German novel, yet he has also been criticized for his lack of comprehension of the novel's form, for the flatness of his characters, for the poverty of his imagination. Academic critics have praised him for his intelligent use of ideas and art forms, and of various literary traditions, while antiintellectual readers have valued him precisely because he eschewed intellectual complications and because, with Gide, he has supposedly jettisoned all books. Hesse has been seen as belonging within the broad stream of European fiction by some and as decisively outside it by others. He has exemplified the changes in society since the beginning of this century and at the same time has remained resolutely aloof.

Ralph Freedman. *Contemporary Literature.* Vol. 3, No. 3., 1969, pp. 421–26

Hermann Hesse exhibits an uncanny comprehension of man's interior states and portrays them with awesome power and unusual artistic insight; he charts youth's constant search for self-identity and meaningful self-expression with uncommon poignancy; he strips the animal man down to the raw naked skeleton of existence and sets him on a dramatically moving journey to seek flesh by solving the riddle of his life, the only one he has. Having read Hesse you may dismiss him, but forget him? Never.

What is he really saying? Practically everything not a few young people are saying about religion, the world, institutions, the need "to do one's thing" amidst conflicting loyalties and confusing options. In Hesse, as indeed today, there is an awareness of the impersonalism of existence, the impoverishment of a materialistic culture, the struggle to construct spiritual moorings, the failure of structures to cope with human problems and the concomitant failure of those in positions of power and prestige to provide human solutions. There's a happy absence of clichés and enervating bromides in Hesse. His works are candid, straightforward documents delineating man's perpetual combat to know himself and at the same time attempting to define his relationship to others, especially to the Other.

Richard J. Ford. *Catholic World*. October 1970,
pp. 15–19

Hesse called his books "autobiographies of the soul," and, indeed, the striking aspect of his work is its continuity of theme, through novels, poems, and essays. It is a search which Stephen Koch has considered "adolescent," while Thomas Mann saw them as "prophetic of the future," calling the novels "great works of longing."

The expectation which constantly frustrates Hesse in his early novels is that of finding order through knowledge, of making an intellectual pattern out of chaotic interaction of the self and outer reality. The vision of the "realm of pure intellect" haunted Hesse until it found full expression in the construction of Castalia in *Magister Ludi*.

Following Nietzsche, Hesse expects a new order based on a change in the very substance of man. Yet neither had a program for that change. The task of Hesse's new man is not to create the new order but to recreate himself so as to be ready for it when it comes. This readiness means a complete self-knowledge, he must accept the potential validity of all ideas, the potential actualization of all deeds. For if a truly new man is to emerge, he must choose himself out of a full range of his potential, his choice must be made in full psychological and physical freedom, unhampered by past notions of "good" and "evil," of acceptable and unacceptable. Precisely because the new order is unknown, precisely because there is no program, there can be no predetermined choices. The evolving man must be able to "think of crime, to dream of it, to be acquainted with its very possibility," and yet to find his own basis for moral behavior.

All his subsequent work is an attempt to illuminate, work out, and understand, the consequences of that existentialism. What is fascinating about Hesse is that his personal turmoil so closely mirrors the philosophical groupings of his age, and we must be grateful that he gives us so much of himself in his work, for it is that blending of thought and experience which ultimately instructs us best.

Krystyna Devert. *TriQuarterly*. Winter/Spring
1972, pp. 302–17

Hesse is deeply loved by those among the American young who are questing.

His simplest, clearest, most innocent tale of seeking and finding is *Siddhartha*.

Hesse is no black humorist. Black humorists' holy wanderers find nothing but junk and lies and idiocy wherever they go. Not so with the wanderers of Hesse; they always find something satisfying—holiness, wisdom, hope.

An easy explanation of American youth's love for Hesse is this: He is clear and direct and well translated, and he offers hope and romance, which the young play hell finding anywhere else these days. . . .

But there are darker, deeper explanations to be found—and the clue that they exist is that the most important Hesse book to the American young, by their own account, is the wholly Germanic, hopelessly dated jumble called *Steppenwolf*.

Steppenwolf was the most profound book about homesickness ever written.

The politics espoused by the hero of *Steppenwolf* coincide with those of the American young, all right: He is against war. He hates armament manufacturers and superpatriots. No nations or political figures or historical events are investigated or praised or blamed. There are no daring schemes, no calls to action, nothing to make a radical's heart beat faster.

Hesse shocks and thrills the American young by taking them on a lunatic's tour of a splendid nightmare—down endless corridors, through halls of breaking mirrors, to costume balls, to empty theaters showing grotesque plays and films, to a wall with a thousand doors in it, and on and on.

Curiously, Hesse, a man who spoke for my father's generation, is now heard loud and clear by my daughters and sons.

And I say again: What my daughters and sons are responding to in *Steppenwolf* is the homesickness of the author. I do not mock homesickness as a silly affliction that is soon outgrown. I never outgrew it and neither did my father and neither did Hesse.

Kurt Vonnegut, Jr. *Wampeters Foma & Granfalloons* (New York: Delacorte Press, 1974), pp. 107–115

HIGHSMITH, PATRICIA (1921–   )

Patricia Highsmith is an acquired taste, which means a taste that some never acquire. . . .

Most of Patricia Highsmith's books have their origin in some sensational idea. In her first novel, *Strangers on a Train* (1949), a young man who meets another on a train proposes that each of them shall murder a person whom the other wishes to see dead. Since neither killer will have any connection with his victim, there is no reason why these should not be "perfect murders." In *The Blunderer* (1954), a clumsy amateur killer sets out to copy a crime committed by a more professional one and finds himself being pursued by the murderer. . . . In *The Two Faces of January* (1964), when the emotionally footloose Rydal Keener sees the petty crook Chester MacFarland kill a man, his immediate reaction is to attach himself to Chester and his wife rather than to report the affair to the police. In the opening scene of *Those Who Walk Away* (1967), Ray Garrett is shot at and wounded by Coleman, but again his reaction is to link himself more closely to the would-be murderer rather than to attempt to escape from him. . . .

But it is not the ideas behind [Highsmith's] books so much as the intensity and skill with which they are presented that make her such a rewarding novelist. . . . Her settings—Venice, Crete, Tunis—are chosen with care. In strange surroundings her characters become uncertain of their personalities and begin to question the reasons for their own conduct. . . . What takes her books beyond the run of intelligent crime stories is the intensity of feeling brought to the central figures. Violence is necessary to her, because the threat or actuality of it produces her best writing. . . . The deadly games of pursuit played in her best novels are as subtle and interesting as anything being done in the novel today.

> Julian Symons. *Mortal Consequences: A History—*
> *From the Detective Story to the Crime Novel* (New
> York: Harper & Row, 1972), pp. 182–84

In the chilling, clinical presentation of a wholly twisted world Miss Highsmith has managed an achievement—the creation of an ambience—perhaps superior to that of the early Eric Ambler novels.

But there is something else about her work, which came over even more strongly in conversation than it does on the printed page. Miss Highsmith is an excellent hater, and however patiently she unravels the criminal motivations of her characters, and with however such sympathy she delineates them, there is a powerful rage for justice always to be sensed just beneath the surface. "I hate," she said, "the Mafia above all" and, in *Ripley's Game* there is a clear distinction drawn between different kinds of baddies, different kinds of evil. Her instinct seems to be that the normal world—the world of good policemen, good detectives, good heroes—being unable to assert itself against the underworld, the underworld itself must find some way of keeping order. And behind the perception lies another awareness that dominates her books—the awareness of nemesis. As in a tragedy events seem to acquire a momentum of their own, so that as the villains weave their webs, the reader can sense an approaching, impersonal doom. The extraordinary power and intensity with which this sense of doom and nemesis is sustained throughout a book is the most distinguishing mark of the Highsmith creation, probably the most consistently excellent body of work of its kind produced since the war.

> *The Spectator.* March 23, 1974, p. 366

Critics have been unsure of where to place Patricia Highsmith's work, and it's easy to see why. To call her a "crime writer" sounds limiting, even patronizing, since, like Chabrol, Highsmith is less interested in the mechanics of crimes than in the psychology behind them. On the other hand you can hardly overlook the fact that most of her fictions end up with blood on their hands: she may command a high-art following, but there are those who read her to see how ingeniously and brutally she'll dispose of her characters. Very few of the twelve stories in *Slowly, Slowly in the Wind* slot neatly into a crime-suspense category, but there's no slackening of invention when it comes to the crunch. Vines sprouting out of a pond drag their victims underwater; a farmer's corpse is hung up as a scarecrow; Madame Thibault's Waxworks Museum acquires three additional exhibits.

The most chilling stories here are those in which the threat of violence or death, and the taking of measures to stave off that threat, have become a part of daily routine. There's a good deal of class and racial tension in these stories (middle-class whites protecting themselves against down-and-outs and blacks), but the ultimate horror show is one that a family inflicts on itself: a child dies after swallowing broken glass and sleeping tablets left on the floor by a neglectful mother and drunk father. This story, "Those Awful Dawns," reads at times like an exaggerated case-study for trainee social workers, but Highsmith's grasp of current social problems is generally greater than she's given credit for and she's at her most macabre when most mundane.

Blake Morrison. *New Statesman.* March 30, 1979,
pp. 454–55

Patricia Highsmith's novels are peerlessly disturbing—not great cathartic nightmares but banal bad dreams that keep us restless and thrashing for the rest of the night, with the sense that some awful possibility has been articulated only to be left unresolved. In dreams like these, you eat a sandwich, you go to the movies, you come home and a boa constrictor has swallowed your cat, and it all feels pretty much the same. . . . In her nineteenth novel, *Found in the Street,* nothing happens until very, very late in the story, and then, after the murder that is the book's first real event, nothing happens again—as if this brutally arbitrary act were just a blip on the monitor. . . .

As escapist literature, Highsmith's novels leave a lot to be desired. That no-exit feeling her books induce isn't ideal for, say, calming the nerves on a long plane trip. Twirling the rack of paperbacks in the departure terminal, you might pick up—at random, unsuspecting—something as nasty as *A Dog's Ransom,* in which a young and very naïve policeman is slowly stripped of everything he cares about by the combination of a smart psycho, a sadistic fellow-cop, and the grinding indifference of New York. Or as painful as *This Sweet Sickness,* the story of a man who refuses to accept that his first love has married someone else: he hounds her with phone calls and passionate letters; furnishes a house where, under an assumed name, he indulges in a pathetic fantasy of their lives together; cruelly rejects a girl who adores him; and, almost against his will, is responsible for three deaths. Or as nihilistic as *The Tremor of Forgery,* in which an American writer in Tunisia tries, and fails, to keep a grip on his identity, his principles, any connection to "civilized" society: he leaves unsure whether or not he's killed a man, and reasonably sure that he doesn't care. Or as cold-blooded as any of the four books about Tom Ripley, a charming American sociopath who assumes a number of false identities—including that of a friend whom he has, with a small twinge of regret, killed—in his pursuit of art, culture, wealth, the finer things. When you're in the grip of stories like these, your sense of the world's reliability is broken down: once the turbulence starts, you feel that nothing will be solid enough to hold you up.

Most of Highsmith's books depend on some sort of guilty recognition, a startled, reluctant acknowledgment of qualities we hadn't known we had or desired until we saw them reflected in someone else. In her famous first novel, *Strangers on a Train,* two very different men, the psychopath Bruno and the respectable professional Guy, meet by chance and end up weirdly implicated in each other's lives: they kill for each other. (In Hitchcock's film adaptation Guy doesn't commit his murder; in the book he does.) Her second thriller, *The Blunderer,* is about another ordinary guy, who wants to murder his wife but doesn't, and is obsessively attracted to a real wife killer; the murderer, who's still being questioned by the police, isn't happy about the unasked-for scrutiny. These odd affinities, these pairs of characters linked by dimly understood compulsions, are a constant motif in Highsmith. People attach themselves to others out of morbid fascination, childlike hero worship, or plain erotic attraction—or, often, all three—and Highsmith tracks her characters as they track each other, as if they were following a logic so mysterious and convoluted that it can only lead them back to themselves. In her fiction, surveillance and introspection are the same thing. . . .

Her best novel, *The Tremor of Forgery,* is all torpor and irresolution. An American novelist who has been sent to Tunisia to write a screenplay stays on much longer than he needs to, without quite knowing why: he's cut off from his New York friends, he's spooked by the Arab culture, he's bored and frustrated. The book is about as eventful as a trek through the desert, yet Highsmith keeps the reader lurching forward by constructing her narrative as a series of mirages—promises of defined, recognizable action, of suspense-novel thrills—that dissipate as we approach them. In this shimmery void, the only real movement is internal. *Found in the Street,* though set in a New York that's as overstimulating as Tunisia is narcoleptic, has a similar haunted stillness. The story progresses fitfully, wandering from one chance encounter to another with no apparent purpose, shifting the perspective from Linderman's to Sutherland's and back, attenuating the action (such as it is) over nearly a year. Yet there's something else here, hard to identify, pulling us along relentlessly, as thrillers do—an undertow, a surge of third-rail current. . . .

Elsie Tyler is this book's mirage, the object of everyone's desire. It's not just her beauty that gets everyone going but also her essential neutrality: she's so young, so agreeably unformed as a personality, that she can seem all things to all people. In a way, this easygoing dream girl (who becomes, in the course of the book, a successful fashion model) is Highsmith's ironic version of the thriller's classic object of obsession: she's this novel's Maltese Falcon, its Moonstone. . . .

Even when nothing appears to be happening in *Found in the Street,* we can feel the desperation of the characters' desire to acquire something valuable from the deadening, chaotic environment, to hoard a jewel plucked from the debris. The fact that Elsie is, in some sense, a tease, flickering in and out of view, gives this apparently placid novel an undercurrent of menace: we know, too well, how easily frustration turns to violence. . . . Sometimes we see events from the harsh, overdetermined perspective of Ralph Linderman, who follows Elsie openly and interprets his brief glimpses of her in lurid, tabloid terms. He misinterprets everything, and his protectiveness seems dirty, voyeuristic, potentially dangerous. The rest of the time, we're seeing things from the point of view of Jack Sutherland, who's altogether more sophisticated and detached. A commercial artist who finds Elsie a fascinating model for sketching, Sutherland is so rigorously nonjudgmental, so determined *not* to conjure a story out of the bits and pieces of Elsie's life, that he seems, finally, at least as peculiar as Linderman. Jack is an amiable monster of neutrality, and the funny thing is that he, too, misses the point. When the story of Elsie's life becomes clear, it's not as pulp-novelish as Linderman's version, but it's considerably more dramatic than Sutherland's blandly "objective" one, the yuppie nouveau roman he's been carrying around in his head.

At the end of *Found in the Street,* both men mistake blond girls on the street for Elsie: she's become a kind of permanent mirage, an everyday apparition. . . . Patricia Highsmith is no mean tease herself. She keeps us off guard, never quite sure what she's up to or why, the hard surface of her prose encouraging us to find our own reflections in it. . . . And then—final humiliation—we discover that we've accepted, and felt weirdly stimulated by, this stripping of our identity, these awful desert hallucinations. In this sense, Highsmith's books are the queasiest fun imaginable—stroke books for neurotics. But when her novels turn on themselves, as the good ones, like *Found in the Street,* do, they become something more: fiction too abandoned to care what it's called, literature or trash, that celebrates restlessness and volatility. She keeps moving, darting in and out of our field of vision, making afterimages that will tremble—but stay—in our minds.

Terrence Rafferty. *The New Yorker,* January 4, 1988, pp. 74–76

HILLERMAN, TONY (1925–   )

Until someone I trust praised Tony Hillerman's fiction, I had not read any of his mystery novels featuring a Navajo policeman. The detective as gimmick—be he blind, wheelchair-bound, or homosexual—usually portends a one-note performance with everything hinged to the differentness of the gimmick being exploited. Such superficial invention usually means the reader is in for a long night.

Not so with *The Dark Wind,* a convincing argument for examining each case on its own merits, for not filling in the quick pigeonhole. Hillerman's book works on the levels a good mystery should. It is a compact story that engages, an implicit commentary on the Indian society it portrays, a mini-study of arcane subjects that bear directly on the plot.

Jim Chee becomes involved in solving several murders tied to a cocaine shipment hidden in the Southwestern high desert country he patrols. Though his jurisdiction does not extend beyond Indian borders, Chee commits himself to finding out who killed on his turf and why.

As in better police procedurals, we learn, concretely, how professionals work. Chee's forte is tracking—thorough hands-and-knees stuff that requires an intimate knowledge of the terrain and those who live on it. He knows just how high the sun must be for the slanting light necessary in reading the faintest of tracks. Nor is Chee's talent a cultural hand-me-down only. He has learned modern methods to discern differences of tire treads quicker than you can say Mark C. Bloome.

Chee's investigation takes us into Navajo and Hopi communities where poverty is indexed by hard facts. The nearest movie is one hundred miles away; there is little electricity; the Indian telephone book encompassing a territory larger than New England can be carried by Chee in his hip pocket.

When he is troubled, this modern-day detective falls back on his cultural heritage.

Language as well as philosophy melds with narrative, as in the scene when Chee asks a woman about her son:

> "You are hunting for him," she said. Navajo is a language which loads its meanings into its verbs. She used the word which means "to stalk," as a hunted animal, and not the form which means "to search for," as for someone lost. The tone was as accusing as the word. Chee changed the verb. "I search for him," Chee said.

Throughout, the language is equally precise and plain as befits its subject and stoic protagonist. Chic phrases and flashy metaphors are for faraway places like Santa Fe or Las Vegas, places Jim Chee does not know.

Like his Navajo policeman, Tony Hillerman never loses his sense of place.

Ralph B. Sipper. *Los Angeles Times Book Review.*
July 25, 1982, p. 6

Tony Hillerman transcends the mystery genre without betraying the elements that have special appeal for its followers. First, he tells a good story.

A Thief of Time opens with stunning impact as a solitary figure—a woman anthropologist—backpacks along a remote cliff ruin in search of Anasazi Indian clay pots.

> The moon had risen just above the cliff behind here. . . . Sometimes when the goat trail bent and put the walker's profile against the moon, the shadow became Kokopelli himself. The backpack formed the spirit's grotesque hump, the walking stick Kokopelli's crooked flute. . . .
>
> If an Anasazi had risen from his thousand-year grave in the trash heap under the cliff ruins here, he would have seen the Humpbacked Flute Player, the rowdy god of *fertility* and lost people. But the shadow was only the shape of Dr. Eleanor Friedman-Bernal blocking out the light of the October moon.

It is the disappearance of Dr. Friedman-Bernal that involves Lieutenant Joe Leaphorn of the Navajo Tribal Police, who appeared in 1970 in Hillerman's first novel, *The Blessing Way*. Also featured is Sgt. Jim Chee, Hillerman's other series character. It is an uneasy, wary collaboration. The younger, more mystical Chee is training to be a Navajo singer. He respects but does not really like Leaphorn. Leaphorn does not practice the old rituals and has a legendary reputation among the Navajo tribal policemen.

Leaphorn is on terminal leave. "Just tired," he tells his superior officer when he hands in his letter of resignation after the death of his wife, Emma. Nothing seems to interest him, and he decides to try to find the missing woman rather than sit in an empty apartment.

Meanwhile, Chee is chasing the Backhoe Bandit, who has stolen heavy digging equipment from a police parking lot. He finds the stolen backhoe, and two corpses, at an illegal digging site. The diggers are pothunters, "thieves of time," seeking to take advantage of soaring auction prices.

The threads of the separate investigations by the two Navajo policemen are pulled together in the finale, which is literally a cliffhanger.

The question is: Why hasn't Hollywood filmed a Hillerman novel?

Hillerman's characters are etched in the mind—Houk, the powerful rancher-politician who manages a quick note ("Tell Leaphorn she's still alive") before he is murdered; the effete New York collector who relishes the bloody history behind the artifacts he collects; the Indian who has become a born-again evangelist, financing his tent revivals with sales of clay pots; the arrogant anthropologist with an Ivy League background who collects jawbones with a genetic flaw of a surplus molar in the left mandible.

A Thief of Time is one of the best Hillermans.

Jean M. White. *Washington Post Book World.*
June 19, 1988, p. 8

The course of Tony Hillerman's growth as a writer is steady. He moves, in a career spanning almost two decades, from journalistic reportage to fictional but thoughtful considerations of the complex interaction of time, space, place, and circumstance. What his future works will reveal of the lives of Joe Leaphorn and Jim Chee can only be conjectured; however, the works already extant establish his place in Western American letters. His West is not that of the formula story, with its feathered Indians, dusty streets, and choreographed gun battles, nor is it the urbanized West of present-day cinema and television. It is, instead, a West in which—alongside the steel-and-glass cities and the chaos of the modern world—tradition, landscape, history, and myth, quietly endure, helping those who accept their teachings to become persons at one with region and society. It is a veritistic West that Hamlin Garland would applaud.

Hillerman brings to this West the professional reporter's ingrained respect for fact. His journalistic training and his reporter's eye let him create clear, precise accounts with the telling details quietly emphasized. He does this consciously, knowing that fact is the stuff of fiction as surely as of journalism: as he says, "the details must be exactly accurate—from the way a hogan is built, to the way a sweat bath is taken, to the way it looks, and sounds, and smells at an Enemy Way Ceremonial at 2:00 A.M. on a wintry morning." His accuracy adds authenticity to his work, but it also carries another benefit: his works are acclaimed by Navajo readers as enthusiastically as they are by Anglos.

He brings as well the storyteller's regard for a good narrative. As comfortable with a tongue-in-cheek tall tale as he is with a carefully constructed mystery, he never loses sight of the professional writer's obligation to be entertaining. "My readers are buying a mystery," he says, "not a tome of anthropology. Therefore, my first priority must be to keep the story moving. . . . The name of the game is telling stories." Tell stories he does, in volume after volume of prose combining the clarity of the good journalist with the careful construction and economical characterization of the accomplished mystery-writer. Whatever else his books may do, they never fail to entertain.

Above all, though, he brings to his writing the veritist's consciousness of the compelling power of place. He tells of the Southwest's diverse cultures, demonstrating how their qualities determine life itself; his mysteries, in fact, build upon the unique Navajo vision, so that "the solution to the crime requires that the policeman be Navajo." He tells of the region's diverse environment, quietly establishing the myriad ways in which climate and terrain pervade and shape human life. And he tells of the pertinence of the region's past to its present: "It's important to show how aspects of ancient Indian ways are still very much alive and are highly germane even to our ways." He does, in short, all that Hamlin Garland asks of the veritist, opening the life of a region to embrace the concerns of all mankind.

The historian Frederick Jackson Turner called the map of the United States a palimpsest, from which can be read the history of successive generations of American life. Nowhere is that metaphor more pertinent than in the Southwest, as Hillerman's books attest. Weaving myths of the past and problems of the present into police procedural novels, he dramatizes the intricate intermingling of cultures that shapes the region's life. He goes beyond Turner, however, to remind his readers that the mingling process transcends regional boundaries to affect the nation at large. The problems that Joe Leaphorn and Jim Chee face are in many ways peculiar to the Southwest, yet in other ways they are those of any citizen of the twentieth century, for every region and every culture has its demands and its unescapable rules. Leaphorn and Chee, as Navajos, give readers a sense of the demands of Southwestern life. In a larger sense, though, that they are Navajo is incidental; they are human as well as Navajo, and as they, like every other person, grapple with the realities of their people, their place, and their time, their responses help all readers to decipher the palimpsest of human life in all its complexity and all its majesty.

Fred Erisman. *Tony Hillerman* (Boise, Idaho:
Boise State University, 1989), pp. 46–48

HIMES, CHESTER (1909–1984)

Should the books of Chester Himes . . . be classed as police novels? It is certainly hard to know what else to call them, and his black detectives, Coffin Ed Johnson and Grave Digger Jones, make an exhilarating black comic comment on the activities of all other policemen. From *Cotton Comes to Harlem* (1964) onward, Himes has recorded the activities of these fierce thugs in a world more sluggish still, in rattlingly vigorous prose, and with equal feeling for violence and for comedy. Coffin Ed has been quick on the trigger ever since a glass of acid was thrown into his face by a hoodlum, and when we first meet Grave Digger he has been off duty for six months after being shot up, although, "other than for the bullet scars hidden beneath his clothes and the fingersize scar obliterating the hairline at the base of his skull where the first bullet had burned off the hair, he looked much the same." The humans among whom the detectives move are credulous, lecherous, treacherous, greedy, and savage.

Julian Symons. *Mortal Consequences: A History—
From the Detective Story to the Crime Novel* (New
York: Harper & Row, 1972), pp. 207–08

Chester Himes, in his two psychological novels, *Lonely Crusade* and *If He Hollers Let Him Go,* bears the imprint of Richard Wright's psychological probing. But Himes lacks Wright's intensity.

He also shows the influence of James Cain who wrote *Past All Dishonor* and *The Postman Always Rings Twice.* Like Cain in *Butterfly,* Himes describes industrial conditions. There is a similarity as to style and the psychological presentation of characters.

Lonely Crusade develops a thesis similar to that of *If He Hollers Let Him Go*. Himes exhibits, nevertheless, a more advanced conception of his medium. He uses the steel-cage technique, that is to say, the Negro is in a steel cage on the economic level with whites in control of the wealth. Himes is consistent, and his themes deal with materialism and communism.

Himes's forte is the psychological novel, and his projected narrative and characterizations are convincingly done.

The protest novels by Negro authors, such as *Lonely Crusade* by Himes, say that the Negro is proud of his American heritage for the most part. He continues to point out in effect that by choice and birth he will remain a part of the American scene. He seeks an improvement of his condition nevertheless. Rejection of a contrary system and faith in the efficacy of the American experiment form the basis of his protest.

Lonely Crusade is a novel in which Himes paints a distasteful picture of the Communist Party activities in America according to Lee Gordon's experiences. His book is tantamount to a Negro writer's complete estrangement from such a conflicting ideology.

Carl Milton Hughes. *The Negro Novelist* (New York: Citadel Press, 1953), pp. 68–76, 255–60

Although Chester Himes has published over a dozen books—a number of these have been popular thrillers—it is still the first, *If He Hollers Let Him Go* (1945), that warrants attention. It is set in a southern California shipyard in wartime (war projects, because of the need for workers, were one of the first large-scale instances in America of unsegregated hiring); the hero is race-mad almost to the point of hysteria, packed with dry high explosive, waiting for the match.

Himes's subsequent novels play cruder variations on the race-war theme. In *Lonely Crusade* (1947) he mixed in heavy doses of a communism that made the novel more attractive to European than American tastes. *The Third Generation* (1954) is the sordid, late-naturalist chronicle of the utter decay of an entire Negro family, under the pressure of a light-colored, cannibalistic mother who despises her black husband and his race. The book's harrowing frenzy suggests that Himes may have been settling some long-rankling childhood scores. In *Pinktoes* (1965), Himes turned to the newly profitable genre of Olympia Grove Press comic pornography, asserting his status as a highly commercial writer. The book is an interracial sex fantasy that reviewers will call "wildly funny." It is the kind of thing, in Dr. Johnson's phrase, that anyone could go on writing indefinitely, "if he would but abandon his mind to it."

David Littlejohn. *Black on White: A Critical Survey of Writing by American Negroes* (New York: Viking, 1966), pp. 142–43

Himes in his detective fiction sees Harlem as the intensification, the logical absurdity, the comic horror of the black experience in America. And not naturally, Himes draws on his own violent American years as being symptomatic of that experience.

What Himes seems to draw mainly from his American background—middle class, working class, lumpen lower class, and criminal years—is that the one central fact of the black man's life in America is violence. Himes, despite the slapstick and sometimes surreal quality of his work, speaks from the ''inside.''

Himes's two black police detective heroes, Grave Digger and Coffin Ed, tread their way through arabesques of venality, sin and corruption, official and otherwise, before they can get to the bottom of things. In the course of their investigations, they appear to take violence, cupidity, betrayals, and brutality as norms of human behavior and they rarely delude themselves about the true nature of their jobs. There exists, one feels, a peculiar sense of distance in Himes's early potboilers, as if the author stands aside from his material and points to it with a long stick for the edification of his readers. Possibly it is this long-range perspective, literary as well as literal, that allows Himes the freedom to laugh at the violence of his vision. For it is humor—resigned, bitter, earthy, slapstick, macabre—that protects author, readers, and detectives from the gloom of omnipresent evil.

From one point of view Himes's humor derives from the pop, campy, pulp magazine character of his stories. What Himes does in effect is carry the dime detective format to its logical absurdity—the genre then becoming its own moral, metaphysical, and social comment. For Himes, the significance of pulp fiction lies in the unconscious assumptions it makes about existence (violent), power (malevolent), and sex (eroticless), the full implications of which are announced in Himes's thrillers. That these assumptions conform more or less to Himes's view of the black experience suggests that his authorship of these thrillers is something more than expedient. The message is of course basically comic in the way *Measure for Measure* is comic; that is, Himes focuses on the venality of society and men's failings, baseness, and depravity, rather than their virtues. But comic in this sense does not necessarily mean funny, and it is the burlesquable aspects of the pulp thriller that give these books their particular bite.

Similarly Himes draws on the feverish violent action of pulp thrillers to announce grim jokes in the kind of grotesque slapstick one associates with Keystone Cops and animated cartoons.

Some of Himes's humor is verbal, burlesquing old-fashioned American shibboleths that pulp writers occasionally throw in as a sop to readers who may feel they have been wallowing too long in gore and sex. Quite as often though Himes's humor reflects the hard cynical wit of the urban poor who know how to cheat and lie to the white world to survive physically, and cheat and lie to themselves to survive psychologically.

On occasion Himes's humor turns in on itself as if the suffocating squalor of Harlem has indeed pressed its inhabitants into molds of dehumanized darkies. From the darkened squares of tenement windows ''crescent-shaped whites of eyes and quarter moons of yellow teeth bloomed like Halloween pumpkins.'' Himes even manages to draw some acid humor from his descriptions of the Harlem poor being fleeced by unscrupulous charlatans. (Some of the hustles he describes—especially those of ''men of God''—are, in their own fashion, highly imaginative.) But generally Himes's portrayal of Harlemites lies somewhere between open-mouthed gullibility and tough-minded sophistication. They usually possess bawdy, earthy, down-home qualities mixed with a kind of urban hipness.

One cannot be certain that Himes will be able to continue to pursue the humor of violent death. For Himes, civilization has become so eroded that in *Blind Man with a Pistol,* his detectives are unable to identify, let alone bring to heel, the true criminals. Perhaps then this is Himes's last laugh. Who, after all, has ever heard of a detective novel where the detective could not find the killer? But if somewhere in Himes's consciousness there arises a phoenix of hope regarding the prospects of a just order, we may well yet be allowed to follow the continuing adventures of Coffin Ed Johnson and Grave Digger Jones in the Harlem lower depths.

Edward Margolies. *Studies in Black Literature.*
Summer 1970, pp. 1–11

The five novels Chester Himes wrote between 1958 and 1961 [*For Love of Imabelle, The Crazy Kill, The Real Cool Killers, All Shot Up,* and *The Big Gold Dream*] are classic detective stories. Each poses a problem, or a series of problems, usually expressed in hideous physical violence, which extends its corruption into personal and communal life, and threatens the always precarious balance by which individuals survive in Harlem. Each network of dangerous mysteries is explained by a single discovery of guilt, which restores that balance and redefines the worth of those characters with whom we sympathize. The discovery, of course, is made by Grave Digger and Coffin Ed, the heroic figures who embody all the attributes of the traditional literary detective. Opposed by violence and unreason, they struggle courageously to uncover truth; trapped in a hopelessly venal institution, they remain incorruptibly honest; burdened with a body of law ludicrously inappropriate to the conditions of Harlem life, they are lonely dispensers of justice. They implement most of their solutions outside the law; many of their methods defy it. The responsibilities and dangers involved in the search for decency rest upon them personally rather than upon the institutional apparatus which supposedly protects them.

But Grave Digger and Coffin Ed are more than familiar literary heroes; their cultural antecedents ultimately give them the moral authority they exercise. Simply enough, they are the ''bad niggers'' of Black Folklore. Like all ''bad niggers'' they may seem at first glance improbable (or undesirable) models for humanity. But the ''bad nigger'' is an emotionally projected rather than a socially functional figure; he is valuable as a symbol of defiance, strength, and masculinity, to a community that has been forced to learn, or at at least to sham, weakness and compliance. As "bad niggers" Coffin Ed and Grave Digger are part of the continuing evolution of a black hero, and are thus studies in cultural lore rather than examples of individual character. In the Harlem series they lay all of their traditional qualifications on the line in a desperate fight against the crimes that endanger the integrity, even the collective sanity, of the black community.

Raymond Nelson. Virginia Quarterly Review.
Spring 1972, pp. 265–67

Chester Himes, himself, as explorer of black experience represents a considerably alienated sensibility. In addition, he is extremely individual, a writer of many parts although frequently all parts do not come together in a single piece. Yet his examination of black experience in America has created a place of its own. There is little doubt that his detective stories, notably *Cotton Comes to Harlem* which was made into a film, provided some inspiration for the current spate of hard-boiled black movies.

In his confrontation with the black experience, it is tempting to see his hard-boiled approach (touched often with sentiment underneath) as his strongest strain. He seems to incorporate both the James M. Cain type fiction with the rebellious hero, made famous by Richard Wright in the novel *Native Son* (1940). In *If He Hollers Let Him Go* (1945), his first novel, Himes pitted a tough but frustrated hero of black middle-class status against relentless racism of a war-time shipyard. In *Lonely Crusade* (1947), he involves the same general type of hero in a struggle with Communist ideology, interracial sex, and racial discrimination. In *Cast the First Stone* (1952), he took advantage of a knowledge of prison gained from serving seven and a half years of a twenty-five year sentence for armed robbery; however, the book is about white characters. In *Third Generation* (1954), he gave an often tender and searching exploration of his own pathos-filled family background, and in *The Primitive* (1955) he explores again the high-tensioned and frustrated black hero of middle-class status, in relationship to general suffering, violence, sex. Afterward come a long spate of detective stories in the hard-boiled vein.

The contents of *Black on Black* thus represent the shorter pieces which Himes was also doing. His stand-out pieces often reveal a gutted black life, although he ranges into lugubrious humor, the whimsical, the satirical, and the character study. There is no illusion about a black life wired in as moral beneficiary of the larger society.

Himes reports that the French critics who read *Baby Sister* called it a Greek tragedy. The scenario has no gods, no suggestion of the viability of transcendent values. What it has is *inevitability* and *fate*.

To make his point, Himes has stripped the resources from the black experience—perhaps a bit further than warranted.

Perhaps in an acted version, the scenario would reveal moments of poetry. Read, it confines itself to naturalistic shocks which further violate the humanity of the black experience. Although one can see the advantage of keeping Baby Sister relatively inarticulate regarding her yearnings, it would seem that the author could give her more mental suggestiveness than the statement in which she wishes people would stop looking at her as if she had no clothes on.

All in all, the stories show considerable range and skill on Himes's part, but do not give the definitive evidence of the range of emotion, feeling, and search which the novels afford. The novels remain indispensable for a full understanding of Himes's talent.

George E. Kent. *Chicago Review,* v. 25, n. 3,
1973, pp. 76–78

Chester Himes's sudden turn to the detective story in the mid-1950s at first dismayed (and to a certain extent still does dismay) many of his readers who had become accustomed to the kind of confessional indictments he had written from *If He Hollers Let Him Go* down to *The Primitive.* The detective novels, beginning with *For Love of Imabelle* in 1957, seemed to be potboilers, attempts by a jaded, down-and-out expatriate who had never made much money from his "legitimate" novels to capitalize on a sensationalized and not always so accurately remembered depiction of a Harlem entirely in the grip of criminals.

But as Himes continued to write his Coffin Ed Johnson and Grave Digger Jones series, it became apparent that Himes had not only developed a new form of the detective story, but that he had found a means of expressing his vision of a racially obsessed and decadent America that none of his earlier books quite afforded. Recognition of Himes's achievement was slow to develop, but by the time *Blind Man with a Pistol* came out in 1969, hesitations concerning Himes's artistic integrity had been exchanged for critical enthusiasm. The effectiveness of Himes's protest and his art in his detective novels derives from the interplay of character and setting; that is, his powerful conception of his two black detectives and their role as Virgilian guides to an inner city that is at once Harlem, hell, and the nightmare center of white America.

Himes's detectives are black; they must operate in the Harlem of the 1950s and 1960s; and they never are allowed to deal with such classically simple crimes as a gangland bank robbery. Their personalities, the situations they find themselves in, and the philosophical implications of their actions are far more complicated than those of the Continental Op or those of any other hard-boiled heroes. Chandler's Philip Marlowe, however, has some affinity with Coffin Ed and Grave Digger, not only because the Los Angeles in which he works is developed symbolically somewhat like Himes's Harlem, but because he is an urban hero who is appalled by the corruption of the modern city and, in defiance of all reason, in a choice that is absurd, decides to take on search after search for the truth that solves the crime even though the solution often neither explains nor settles anything. Like Marlowe, Coffin Ed and Grave Digger move through a milieu that contains an incredible gradation of speech and class but is nonetheless a jungle, a wilderness of neon where the epitome of honor sometimes seems represented only by the conscience of a stool pigeon.

"As far back as Lieutenant Anderson could remember," Himes writes in *Cotton Comes to Harlem,* "both of them, his two ace detectives with their identical big hard-shooting, head-whipping pistols, had always looked like two hog farmers on a weekend in the Big Town." Their nicknames indicate the respect they receive in Harlem, whose residents know that Grave Digger and Coffin Ed each has an invisible line over which no one had better step. They drive the streets in a nondescript battered Plymouth with a hopped-up engine. They work mainly through sheer presence and chance along with a carefully maintained network of stool pigeons—junkies, blind men who can see when the moment is right, drunks who sober up fast—who appear whenever they see the black Plymouth pull to a stop in their neighborhoods. And they must deal with a part of the city in which the daily police reports include such events as a man killing his wife with an ax because she burned a pork chop, a man playing a fatal game of Russian roulette in a bar with a .32-caliber revolver, and a man picked up with a shotgun and a hound dog for hunting cats on Seventh Avenue.

Both detectives are coldly efficient, so coldly efficient that the police commissioner has to call them on the carpet repeatedly for excessive violence, or, to use the term, police brutality. Most of this violence is directed at other blacks and this, as many reviewers have noted, seems paradoxical given the social consciences of the two detectives who never become hardened enough to cease shaking their heads over the wholesale victimization of their race. But Coffin Ed and Grave Digger see no other way to control crime than through brute force—unless social change takes place, and that is not likely. . . .

Ross Macdonald in "The Writer as Detective Hero" writes that "A close paternal or fraternal relationship between writer and detective is a marked peculiarity of the form. Throughout its history, from Poe to Chandler and beyond, the detective hero has represented his creator and carried his values into action in society." If this is true, Grave Digger and Coffin Ed with their combination of toughness, honesty, and willingness to enforce justice through controlled violence are central to an understanding of Himes's ideas and Himes himself. And the development of the two detectives as they move from the relatively understandable setting of *The Crazy Kill* to the images of chaos that dominate *Blind Man with a Pistol* is a powerful statement in itself concerning a crucial decade in American history. . . .

Himes's Harlem is symbolic. It is not just that riots of the sort he describes did not happen in the actual Harlem of the 1960s. And it is not just that his Harlem geography is occasionally inexact. Harlem is presented not only as representative of all the inner cities of the United States, but

also as an inner city of the mind of white America. Harlem is black, isolated, and repressed, but it is there and it must be dealt with.

Himes gives the detective story added social purpose; and through the
creation of Grave Digger and Coffin Ed and the depiction of the inner city
in which they operate, Himes rawly projects what it is like and what it
means to be black in America. In this sense he himself becomes a balancer
of evil accounts and for white readers, at least, reading each of the Grave
Digger and Coffin Ed books is like being presented with a search warrant.
Search yourself, man.

James Lundquist. *Chester Himes* (New York:
Ungar, 1976), pp. 106–32

I know that Chester, whose friendship I value highly, is puzzled and annoyed by the comparative indifference of the American public to his books.
At World and at Putnam's we paid him modest advances. We recovered our
investment, not from hardback sales, but from the paperback reprints. But
the reprints, in turn, did not fare well. It is very hard to find any of Himes's
paperbacks in the bookshops of America, although most of them are in print.
Luckily, this is not true in Europe, especially France. The French readers
love him. Gallimard, the foremost publishing house in France, publishes
Himes's books with profit. Chester Himes is a VIP in Paris as anyone can
see who visits the French bookshops. This is also true in Barcelona.

Himes has talent to burn: he has wit, a fine comic sense, an understanding of scenic values; he's an inventive plotter; his characters are alive and
easy to become involved with: his stories have action, animal heat, tension.
He also usually has something vital to say. Added up, he should be popular
in America. But he isn't.

As an author his reward must come soon—I mean his American reward. Meanwhile, his *critical* reception continues good; the critics and the
aficionados love and understand him and his worth. When his autobiography
is completed and published (possibly in 1976) some dramatic changes may
occur for him—for the better.

William Targ. *Indecent Pleasures* (New York:
Macmillan, 1975), pp. 291–92

Himes's short fiction, almost without exception, can scarcely be classified
as such: his "stories" are powerful and disturbing and hate-filled polemical
essays or tracts involving fictional techniques. The ultimate is "Prediction,"
a devastating allegory written after he had "become firmly convinced" that
"the only chance Black Americans had of obtaining justice and equality in
the United States was by violence."

If there is less gore in other Himes stories, there is no less hatred and
indignation; his villains are not only the White Establishment of Police and
Sheriff who kick and beat to death the decorated black soldier returning
home for Christmas of "Christmas Gift" or fill full of bullets the narrator

of "One More Way to Die," but White Society itself epitomized by the "respectable" white man of "All He Needs Is Feet," who deliberately bumps into the black man who has stepped off the sidewalk to let him and his companions pass, and in one way or other in one story after another precipitates the chain of events leading to the destruction or humiliation of their victims.

Too over-simplified to be successful as fiction, the work of Chester Himes, like that of his superior Richard Wright, is a shocking mirror of our times; it makes us reflect, in the words of one of the author's few compassionate whites: "What have we done to him?"

William Peden. *Studies in Short Fiction*
(Newberry, South Carolina: Newberry College,
Summer 1975), pp. 234–35

Because of his political situation as a self-aware radical black writer Chester Himes substantially changed the hard-boiled detective genre that he inherited from Dashiell Hammett and Raymond Chandler. By looking at the ways in which he altered the genre, we can see some of the contradictions between the Chandlerian thriller and American racial reality.

The Chandlerian novel took on its distinctive shape in part because of its political vision of the nature of evil. It contrasts to the classical British detective story, as typified by Agatha Christie, in which evil springs from the diseased minds of disturbed individuals and is perpetuated primarily by deceit (which can be punctured by logic) rather than by raw power (which requires social transformation for its uprooting). The detective's task is thus fairly easy, with a resolution of the text's initial disorder readily achieved by a single intelligent, even unarmed individual. "Solving" the crime becomes more difficult, and even to the extent that the sources of particular evils can be determined, they are often so well entrenched in the political structure that nothing short of revolution can dislodge them. It's no accident that Poirot is characterized by his arrogance, Marlowe by his gloomy sense of despair—for Poirot succeeds in a way that Marlowe cannot.

Since the asymmetry of black and white in our culture rules out Chandlerian heroism for black protagonists, the author Chester Himes is left in an artistically difficult position. His vision of evil is closer to Chandler's than it is to Christie's, so his story line tends to be Chandleresque. The ingenuity of the crime itself (central to Christie's complications) is replaced by fast-paced plots and counterplots, crosses and doublecrosses, often involving people of considerable social and political standing. But since he recognizes that the Chandlerian resolution is a luxury that black cops in our society cannot afford, he has to look elsewhere for a satisfactory means of closure. At first, he seems to have fallen back on the kind of comic Christie-esque resolutions that Chandler and Hammett had more or less abandoned. Granted, while Christie will occasionally set a criminal free in order to give her plot an extra jolt, it happens more often in Himes, largely because of his more complex sense of the world—either because his heroes decide that it wasn't really a "crime" at all (in *The Real Cool Killers,* for instance, Grave Digger decides that it is appropriate for the black victim of a white sexual pervert to kill her tormentor), or because it's a necessary part of a deal (in *Cotton Comes to Harlem,* it's the only way to get the money back), or because someone is too well-placed politically (*All Shot Up*).

Nonetheless, most of Himes's detective plots resolve themselves in surprisingly genial ways. At the end of *A Rage in Harlem,* the impossibly naive Jackson, who has gotten himself entangled with a brutal gang that manages to knock off several people far more experienced than he is, gets back both his job and his girlfriend; *The Real Cool Killers* ends even more sentimentally, with the impending marriage between the equally square Sonny and Sissie, who is pregnant with the child of the dead gang-leader Sheik; in *Cotton Comes to Harlem,* Uncle Bud the junk man ends up with $87,000 with which to buy himself a harem in Africa. And while *All Shot Up* lacks the element of coupling, it too is upbeat: the stolen money is stolen back by Coffin Ed and Grave Digger and sent as an anonymous contribution to the Boys' Club. Indeed, the last words of that novel are those of the anonymous telegram they sent to political boss and swindler Casper Holmes: *"Crime doesn't pay."*

You cannot, however, just slap a Christie ending on a Chandlerian novel. The very incongruity of these finales seems a self-conscious questioning of the implications of the genre itself. In a sense, then, these novels make a political point about the asymmetries of white and black experiences through their internal contradictions, which show that the same literary forms are not appropriate to both. And from this perspective, perhaps, some of the violence in the novels—especially the violence of Coffin Ed and Grave Digger themselves—can be seen to undercut the genre, as well. Certainly, that violence is explicitly made problematic in the texts. Beneath the rapid-moving surface of the adventures, there's always something questionable: not only do people both black and white complain about their tactics, but for all their insistence that only the guilty have anything to fear, they often find themselves trouncing the innocent in their pursuit of justice. At the beginning of *The Real Cool Killers,* a teenage hood throws perfume at Coffin Ed, who, remembering the acid thrown at him in *A Rage in Harlem,* overreacts; in the aftermath, not only is the prankster killed, but an innocent bystander is shot as well.

But even if the violence were never explicitly questioned in the text, we could still see that it is generated by the novels' contradictions—not only the social contradictions in the situations of Coffin Ed and Grave Digger, but also the formal contradictions in the genre that emerge when it is asked to attend to black life. For the only way to arrive at a Christie-esque ending in a Chandlerian world is precisely through violence—that is, when it is power rather than deception that protects evil, you can only hope to get to the bottom of things by violent means. In a figurative sense, then, the violence is not only characteristic *of* the novels, but is also directed *against* them: the very incongruity of the genre and its subject matter produces a violent disruption. Perhaps that's why, in the last novel in the series, *Blind Man with a Pistol*, all attempt at a resolution is dropped, and the novel rips itself apart into chaos. A long goodbye to the detective story itself? Perhaps; but if so, it's a tacit recognition that when ideology and art collide, something has to give way. And since the genre stood in the way of Himes's own vision of what it meant to be black, who can say that his farewell was a wrong choice?

Peter J. Rabinowitz. In Barbara A. Rader and
Howard G. Zettler, eds., *The Sleuth and the
Scholar* (Westport, Connecticut: Greenwood Press,
1988), pp. 19–24

HOCH, EDWARD D. (1930–   )

One of the most prolific short-form writers in the mystery genre—Edward D. Hoch—turns out scores of stories every year, by one count in fact producing one of every twenty mystery short stories published annually in the United States!

Now the author of over 650 stories, Hoch writes under a half dozen pseudonyms, and has created at least two dozen series characters. He concentrates exclusively on clever plots. And he has come up with some dandies.

A carriage enters a covered bridge—and disappears. How? A young bicyclist rides down a lane to vanish from sight, leaving the bicycle behind on the ground. A man steals the water out of a swimming pool in front of the owner's eyes. How? And why?

Hoch's most popular hero, and the one about whom he has written the most stories, is Nick Velvet, a reformed thief, in the vein of Raffles, who continues to perform outside the law for "good causes." The shtick Hoch exploits in this series is the absolute *valuelessness* of the objects stolen. Water. Why? And so on.

Simon Ark is another series hero in Hoch's extensive cast of protagonists. Ark is a mystic, who is supposedly 2,000 years old, and generally utilizes his preternatural powers in carrying out investigations into puzzling enigmas.

In the subgenre of the espionage story, Hoch celebrates the exploits of Jeffery Rand, an ex-undercover agent, formerly a member of the "concealed communications" (cryptography) office of British Intelligence.

Captain Leopold is a Hoch-created policeman, a specialist in violent crimes, who solves various types of mysteries that come his way. Ben Snow is Hoch's "frontiersman" Westerner who solves crimes that take place at the turn of the century in sagebrush America. Dr. Sam Hawthorne does not go back quite so far as Snow; he is a simple New England country doctor who operates in the 1920s and 1930s, solving locked-room puzzles, and other classic mysteries that his creator dreams up for him.

Hoch won an Edgar award for his Captain Leopold short story, "The Oblong Room," and has been nominated several times.

Waltraud Woeller and Bruce Cassiday. The Literature of Crime and Detection (New York: Ungar, 1988), p. 186

If ever there was a member of an endangered species it's Ed Hoch, the sole surviving professional writer of short mysteries. Since his debut in 1955, in addition to five novels, he has published more than 650 such tales, including numerous non-series stories and a total of 22 separate series. Among his recurring characters are an occult detective who claims to be two thousand years old, a private eye, a Western drifter who may be a reincarnation of Billy the Kid, a priest, a British cryptographer-sleuth, a science-fictional Computer Investigation Bureau, a con man, two Interpol agents reminiscent of the stars of TV's *The Avengers,* a Lollipop Cop, and a New England physician-detective of the 1920's. His longest-running and perhaps best series are those dealing with Nick Velvet, the thief who steals only valueless objects and often has to detect while thieving, and Captain Leopold, the tough but sensitive violent-crime specialist on the force of a large north-eastern city.

In the stories of Hoch's pre-1960 apprenticeship the ideas are occasionally quite original (e.g., the murder of one of a sect of Penitents while the cult members are hanging on crucifixes in a dark cellar), but the execution tends to be crude and naive and the Roman Catholic viewpoint somewhat obtrusive. As his work matured it came to reflect the influence of several of his own favorite writers, including Graham Greene, Jorge Luis Borges, and especially John Dickson Carr and Ellery Queen. Such Hoch stories as "The Long Way Down," in which a man leaps from a skyscraper window but doesn't hit the ground until hours later, and "The Vanishing of Velma," in which a woman disappears without trace from a moving ferris wheel, are among the finest works in the tradition of Carr's impossible-crime tales.

Some of Hoch's most vividly written stories appeared in the *Alfred Hitchcock* and *Saint* mystery magazines during the 1960's, among them his Edgar-winning "The Oblong Room," in which Captain Leopold investigates a college campus murder with bizarre religious overtones. But from 1965 to the present his most consistent market has been *Ellery Queen's Mystery Magazine* which, with very few exceptions, has featured at least one Hoch story per issue since the early 1970's. Although his EQMM output is usually written in the plainest nuts-and-bolts style, the story concepts are generally stimulating, and his best efforts for the magazine are lovely mini-aturizations of the classical fair-play detective novels for which Queen him-self is famous.

Francis M. Nevins, Jr. In John M. Reilly, ed.,
Twentieth-Century Crime and Mystery Writers:
Second Edition (New York: St. Martin's Press,
1985), p. 460

Edward D. Hoch once wrote, "I've written more stories than I can count." He has certainly written more than most devoted fans of the mystery short story can count—nearly seven hundred short stories.

Not only is Ed Hoch the most prolific mystery short story writer ever, he has other noteworthy distinctions. He holds a record which will probably never be equalled, the mystery-writing equivalent of Lou Gehrig's 2,130 consecutive games played and Joe Di Maggio's 56-game hitting streak. As the listing of his magazine fiction shows, *every* issue since May 1973 of *Ellery Queen's Mystery Magazine,* the most prestigious short story magazine in the genre, has contained a Hoch story.

Hoch reached his current position the hard way: he earned it. He mas-tered his trade by publishing stories in such now-forgotten pulp and digest-sized magazines as *Crack Detective and Mystery Stories, Fast Action Detec-tive and Mystery Stories, Keyhole Detective Stories, Killers Mystery Story Magazine, Off Beat Detective Stories, Terror Detective Story Magazine, Tightrope Detective Magazine,* and *Two-Fisted Detective Stories.* Even *they* didn't publish him until 1955, after he had endured eight years of rejection slips. (John Creasey, the most prolific mystery novelist, had *only* seven years of rejections, but he had 743 of these, far more than Hoch.)

Like many prolific mystery writers, Hoch has used pseudonyms, begin-ning with "Stephen Dentinger," a combination of his confirmation and middle names. Another early pen name, not used since 1957, was "Irwin Booth," the names of two famous real-life murderers: Robert Irwin and John Wilkes Booth. Hoch has also been "Pat McMahon" (his wife's maiden name), "R. L. Stevens" (a shortening of Robert Louis Stevenson), and "Anthony Cir-cus." For five years he wrote an *EQMM* column as "R. E. Porter," report-ing on current happenings in the mystery field. (In addition to these col-umns, he has written about one hundred other short works of non-fiction.) As "Mr. X" he wrote a six-part serial in *EQMM,* one which was later reprinted under his own name. He was even "Ellery Queen" for a paper-back original novel. Recently, such has been the increasing recognition of his own name, that he has rarely resorted to pseudonyms.

Hoch has created a small army (twenty-four) of series detectives, and they have appeared in more than half his stories. He would be the last to claim that it is possible (or even desirable) to present an in-depth character study within the confines, usually about six thousand words, of a short story.

Yet Hoch's folks are distinctive and so are the milieus in which they operate. Many of his stories explore themes of considerable depth.

Marvin Lachman. Introduction to June M. Moffatt
and Francis M. Nevins, Jr., eds., *Edward D. Hoch
Bibliography 1955–1991* (Van Nuys, California:
Southern California Institute for Fan Interests,
1991), pp. v–viii

HUXLEY, ALDOUS (1894–1963)

Brave New World may well prove to be Aldous Huxley's most lasting book.
Purely satirical and brilliantly prophetic, it is the last destructive work by an
essentially destructive writer. By the time *Eyeless in Gaza* was published in
1935 Mr. Huxley had become a disciple of Gerald Heard. From now on, an
increasing concern with mysticism was to take control of Mr. Huxley's life
and work, and the final pages of *Eyeless in Gaza,* which contain Anthony's
spiritual meditation, point the way to all his future writing, including his
last book about mescaline. Why does this development, so boldly constructive and apparently so consistent, not entirely satisfy? A certain element in
his treatment of what he thinks disgusting, weakens, in his novels, the force
of his striving towards what he thinks pure. In spite of the case made out
for withdrawal, Mr. Huxley, it seems, relishes life, and not at all in the way
of which Mark Rampion would approve. Several episodes in *Eyeless in Gaza*
are comic, but not straightforwardly so; one laughs less with the author than
at him for having invented them, and one suspects that he (a witty but
humorless writer) only thinks them funny to the extent that, in various ways,
they are potentially shocking. He seems, in fact, to be perpetually trying to
shock himself by emphasizing the inadequacies of physical life, by pointing
out that lovers look ridiculous when copulating, that the food we enjoy eating is revolting when raw and makes us belch and so on, but the shock
results in titillation rather than rejection and disgust. As the writer of pornography pays, in his fashion, a compliment to sex, so Mr. Huxley obliquely
honors the sensual life; but this is done in a series of highly cerebral diver-
tissements advocating discipline, control, and meditation as the means towards
spiritual peace and transcendent illumination. Yes, he is an excellent host;
there is something here for everybody. The quality is high, the menu varied,
but it is not, in the last analysis, a sustaining diet.

Francis Wyndham. In Robert E. Kuehn, ed.,
Aldous Huxley: A Collection of Critical Essays
(New Jersey: Prentice-Hall, 1974), pp. 23–25

Huxley has always shown a good deal of skill in giving us the illusion that
he is quite detached or neutral. It is, however, almost entirely the illusion

of one form of detachment, that which the intelligent writer may achieve—
or seem to achieve—by the practice of intellectual discipline. Unfortunately
for himself as a novelist he has practically nothing of that power—which
Joyce, for instance, possessed in abundance, and which is essential to the
truly effective novelist—whereby a writer associates himself sympathetically
(or, if one prefers, empathically) with his characters in all their feelings,
while skillfully concealing the fact from us. His intellect works too hard for
that. His human sympathy is limited.

These, then, are novels of ideas which are rationalizations of certain
sentiments, instincts, dispositions of soul in a number of characters selected
to convey the author's life view and to point his moral. But the general
conclusion, or moral, or practical lesson, or general principle of the author's
thought or life view does not in the end emerge with anything like the clarity
one expects from a man of such apparently superlative intelligence. All one
can do is to induce it confusedly and unsatisfactorily from the underlying
spirit of invective, which one feels to be just as instinctive and emotional as
in any congenital novelist. One is finally driven to conclude that all Huxley's intellectual paraphernalia conceals an intelligence at war with itself,
or struggling vainly for a clear position from which to attack. And while in
this essay I am interested directly only in the early novels, it would be
unrealistic not to bear in mind also the constant gropings and changes
of position in his later work.

The result has been that he has from the beginning attempted satire and
achieved only what I have called invective. The absence of a firm standpoint
made this inevitable, since of its nature satire implies a clear standpoint, or
acceptable norm, from which to castigate. . . . The impression a rereading
of these novels gives one today is of an arid and desiccated waste, bordering
at many points on jungles of odorous despair, always blessedly watered by
a constant dew of bitter wit and otherwise illuminated not by intelligence
but by brilliant intellectual pyrotechnics.

Sean O'Faolain. The Vanishing Hero (New York,
Grosset and Dunlap, 1956), pp. 5, 8–9, 22

The novel *Island* becomes, in effect, a series of talks on industrialism, the
family, flagellation, militarism, sexual technique, education, death, biology,
the rarer drugs, affluence, true and false mysticism. The familiar coruscation
of all Huxley's writing in this manner is here at its best. There is an interesting change from *Brave New World:* instead of the simple contrast of
scientific modernity and naïve primitivism, there is a last desperate grasp
towards integration. At a purely conceptual level, there is a consistency
based on a genuine humanity.

At the actual level of the novel, it is less easy to assent. The breathtaking synthesis of biology, Sanskrit and political theory has to live with a flock
of mynah birds trained to fly round the island singing (as spiritual reminders)
"Attention" and "Here and now, boys." Tense intellectual argument is cut

by extraordinary pseudopoems and suddenly disastrous slang; the happy Palanese, more than once, are offered to us for our admiration as "full-blown human beings." The theme is integration, and the identification of all the forces against it, but the experience (as so often in Mr. Huxley) is disintegration. The novel is new, but the critical problem (and, I would say, the decision) is what it has always been, since Mr. Huxley started writing.

Raymond Williams. *The Manchester Guardian*
Weekly. April 5, 1962, p. 10

Like Bacon's jesting Pilate, from whom he borrowed a title, he asked and did not stay for an answer. He moved on. Nothing short of universal knowledge was his aim. No traveler through cultures, no connoisseur of human habits, no asker had lapped up so much. As a writer, he became a mellifluous but active, ever-extending, ever-dramatizing encyclopedia and he had the gaiety and melancholy of mind to put it out in novels, essays, plays, and works of speculation and criticism. Endlessly educable, he was, in the family tradition, a hybrid—the artist-educator; an extraordinary filler-in of the huge gaps in one's mind. To the very young in the twenties, this was inestimable. One might clap a label on him ten years later but, in the meantime, the next decade had found him new. So it went on, until pretty well the present day. His range and his manner were irresistible to youth. The spell continued: to the latest appetites he offered the devils of Loudon; to the curious the merits of mescaline; to the pragmatic a therapy for blindness; to the terrified the possibility that man's survival was related to the non-human "otherness" he shared with Nature. One got from him a stereoscopic view of the world. One can call his method popularization; but really the attraction lay not only in the new facts, but in the opportunity for more speculation.

His mind had, of course, the tricks of the man who knew too much and too well how to express it. He was one of the last of the Victorian liberals. He was totally pacifist. Logically he refused to be implicated. His manner had a lot of old Bloomsbury in it. "Significant. But significant of what?" "Possibly. But possibly not." All the same these phrases were designed to drop us simple readers into a void where, defenseless, we were exposed to shock. Shock was one of the luxuries of the twenties. But, for Huxley, perhaps the most accomplished educator of his generation, to shock was to ensure the course of intellectual freedom.

V. S. Pritchett. *New Statesman.* December 6,
1963, p. 834

"As a man sows, so shall he reap." It is a favorite quotation of Mr. Propter's, in *After Many a Summer Dies the Swan,* and it is the moral of Huxley's later fiction. It is the theme of many great works of fiction, but what we are conscious of in Huxley is not the degradation, which is the consequence of wrong choice, but only of the jigging of puppets. The drama the puppets play out is horrifying enough, but we are unaffected because it is not played out in terms of flesh and blood. If it were, it would be unbearable. As it is, in the novels that follow *Point Counter Point,* one can scarcely help feeling that Huxley himself is indulging in sensation for sensation's sake.

From the beginning—one sees it in the early poems—Huxley has been agonizingly aware of the terrible contrast, the irreconcilable conflict within himself, between the idealization of art and the physiological, animal realities of human existence, the fact that, to hark back to an early poem, lovers among other things sweat. The conflict has continued throughout his work, apparently insoluble, reaching its climax perhaps—though *Ape and Essence,* published eight years later, falls little short of it—in *After Many a Summer,* where the consequences of the quest for an elixir of life are depicted in the spectacle of a man and woman who, at two hundred years old, have retrogressed into apes, savaging each other in a stinking cage. Here Huxley comes very near to literary coprophilia.

Since *Ape and Essence,* Huxley has written only three novels. The mystical reality he now accepts is intractable to dramatization in fiction. Perhaps his best work was always to be found in his essays and in the superb biography, *Grey Eminence,* which contains, among much else, the finest of his incursions into fantasy since *Crome Yellow.*

Walter Allen. *The Modern Novel* (New York:
Dutton, 1964), pp. 43–44

The spectacle of a society withering in a desert of make-believe and joyless gaiety, served novelists and dramatists in the 1920s and 1930s with material they turned to gruesome use. The most prominent of this group was Aldous Huxley. As a writer of fiction he had the useful gift of being, at least in his earlier works, irresistibly readable. He was well equipped as a humorist and wit, mainly sardonic and often savage enough to lead to his being regarded as a modern Swift. The inclination to consider him also as a follower of D. H. Lawrence had little foundation, for Huxley wrote, not as Lawrence did with the fervor of the blood, but in the deadly chill of a cerebral contempt which distilled vitriol. The contemporary Dance of Death had for him its moments of ludicrous humor, recorded in such books as *Crome Yellow, Mortal Coils,* and the more acerb *Antic Hay* in which the human being becomes something of a Gothic grotesque. As the political atmosphere grew more and more saturated with intolerance and hatred, Aldous Huxley's novels became more darkly charged with antagonism towards these tendencies. *Point Counter Point* is corrosive with detestations, so generously distributed as to leave few unscathed. *Brave New World* pictured horribly a possible future in which laboratory-produced creatures would be mechanistically conditioned to serve the will of their masters in a world where everyone performs the motions of life without, in any acceptable sense, living. The measure in which this "brave new world" was already existing for the radio and newspaper and otherwise "capitalistically conditioned" masses, gave Aldous Huxley's vision a more immediately sobering significance than any mere story of an inverted Utopia could have had. But as he became more immersed in the fearful contemplation of a threatening cosmic catastrophe, Huxley sacrificed his creative talent and therefore much of his readability, as was apparent in *Eyeless in Gaza,* though some of his original verve was recovered in *After Many a Summer.*

From that point Aldous Huxley as a novelist was a spent force and his *Time Must Have a Stop* and *Ape and Essence* stirred a more limited interest. His disgust with the world seemed to be less the repulsion of a superior intellect by the follies and enormities of common humanity than the outcome of protracted adolescence, an aspect of arrested development frequently found among twentieth-century intellectuals whose abnormal mental growth had been at the expense of emotional comprehension and human understanding. Some part of Huxley's later fiction was more vomitous than satirical.

> A. C. Ward. *Twentieth-Century English Literature*
> *1901–1960* (n.p.: Methuen-University Paperbacks,
> 1964), pp. 64–66

Brave New World is actually a satire not so much of the future as of the present: of the future as it is implicit in the present. Huxley resorts to future remoteness for the same reasons that other Utopian satirists had earlier resorted to geographical or past remoteness (e.g. More, Swift, or Anatole France): in order to gain the necessary distance and detachment to more effectively satirize the present. Huxley's satirical point in this novel is that if the present continues to "progress" as it is "progressing" now, then the inevitable result must be a brave new world.

That the United States is the present model for Huxley's vision of the future emerges even more clearly from an essay entitled, "The Outlook for American Culture, Some Reflections in a Machine Age," published in 1927. Huxley begins this essay with the observation that "speculating on the American future, we are speculating on the future of civilized man." According to Huxley, one of the most ominous portents of the American Way of Life is that it embraces a large class of the people who "do not want to be cultured, are not interested in the higher life. For these people existence on the lower, animal levels is perfectly satisfactory. Given food, drink, the company of their fellows, sexual enjoyment, and plenty of noisy distractions from without, they are happy."

Brave New World is the fictional extension of Huxley's earlier views on the nature of American "culture"; it is a portrait of the Joy City spread over the whole globe. And as Huxley was to remark with considerable alarm some three decades later in his *Brave New World Revisited,* it is a portrait which is beginning to seem more and more as if it were drawn from the life. In the only too near future, in Huxley's view, it may prove difficult not to revisit the brave new world.

The idea of the individual as opposed to the mass is of paramount importance to a proper understanding of the novel. For it is precisely this idea that the brave new world cannot tolerate. To be extraordinary or to be individual is to be criminal; thinking or feeling deeply are punishable offences.

In spite of all the efforts of technology and psychology directed at reducing man to an automaton, some semblance of humanity and individuality still survives—even if only accidentally. In this sense *Brave New World* can be seen as a not altogether pessimistic novel: the hope for a continuation of *humanity* is not altogether extinguished.

The problem, however, in the brave new world is that the conditioning is so complete and the pursuit of external happiness so compulsive that it is enormously difficult for the individual to increase his awareness of himself as an individual.

In the series of portraits of this twentieth-century society which Huxley satirically sketched in his earlier novels, the fatal flaw was always the isolation of the individual. He was alone, trapped in his own conception of reality. This is not the case, however, with the society of the brave new world, or, to a lesser degree, with that of the Indian *Penitentes*. In both of those societies the individual is solidly integrated, is an almost indistinguishable part of the whole. Too solidly, too indistinguishably—that is what is wrong with them. The individual is no longer isolated, but he is no longer isolated because he is no longer an individual. This is the paradox which is at the very heart of this novel: to be an individual is to be isolated, is to be unhappy; to be integrated is to be "happy," but happy in an inhuman fashion.

Peter E. Firchow. Modern Fiction Studies. Winter
1966–67, pp. 451–60

Huxley's death in November 1963 was ignored by the great world because it had another death to think about—the assassination of President Kennedy in Dallas, Texas, U.S.A. This event, like the assassination of Gandhi which starts off one of Huxley's last novels, the bitter and terrible *Ape and Essence,* could be taken as a self-evident proof of the existence of evil—a Huxleyan starting point which it was too late for Huxley to use. Huxley's awareness of good and evil found its first starting point in the awareness of human division which found expression in an early novel, *Point Counter Point*. His work before that had been gay, witty, erudite, vaguely pessimistic *(Crome Yellow)*, concerned with the lack of belief and lack of direction in the cultured classes of the nineteen twenties *(Antic Hay)*, half-convinced that there was a way out of the human mess *(Those Barren Leaves)* which was closer to Indian yoga than to European Christianity. The statement of *Point Counter Point*, however, was that in man too many irreconcilables are yoked together for happiness in this world—flesh and spirit, passion and reason, instinct and intellect. The musical implications of the title applied to the fictional technique he used—many plots proceeding at the same time, very nearly independent of each other, on the analogy of the melodic strands of a complex piece of counterpoint—a Bach fugue, say. . . .

For forty years his readers forgave Aldous Huxley for turning the novel form into an intellectual hybrid—the teaching more and more overlaying the proper art of the fiction writer. Having lost him, we now find nothing to forgive. No novels more stimulating, exciting, or genuinely enlightening came out of the post-Wellsian time. Huxley more than anybody helped to equip the contemporary novel with a brain.

Anthony Burgess. *The Novel Now: A Guide to Contemporary Fiction* (New York: W. W. Norton, 1967), pp. 39–43

Island (1962), Huxley's last novel, presents as many facets of his comprehensive vision for man and community as he was able to commit to print before his death in 1963. The book is Huxley's solemn and, in many ways, unique remedy for psychic atrophy and the specter of the bomb in the world of the 1960s.

Huxley's fairly complex vision stems from his conviction that any operative ideal would have to be based on a syncretic approach to the problem of existence.

Huxley distinguishes carefully the two main traditions of Hindu philosophy: the ancient Hinayana tradition, which taught total renunciation of the world and the quest for perpetual Nirvana; and the more recent Mahayanist tradition, which sought awakening through a responsible if delicate recognition of the world. In its tolerance and flexibility, Mahayana offers enlightenment not only to the monk in isolation but to the layman in society as well. That branch of Eastern thought which Huxley pursued left him intellectual elbow room to satisfy both his mystical and reformative urges.

One of Huxley's strongest ideals promoted in *Island* is the desire that Western and Oriental worlds accept and learn from each other. The merger between East and West in *Island* is not defined exhaustively. Like most sweeping ideals, it eludes complete description. But the direction of the union is toward a Tagorist synthesis of Western progress with Eastern spirituality. Huxley's comprehensive mysticism is not just a Western retreading of Taoist ideology, but also a positive counterpoint to the problems of separation, alienation, and incommunication which he delineates in his other novels. Huxley always sought an ideal which would permit him to experience and express existence as an entity rather than a fragment, and the educative ideals of *Island* aim toward a similar objective for Everyman.

Huxley conveys to his readers some of his more difficult ideology in *Island* through an interesting use of symbol. In truth, the nature of Huxley's subject frequently requires a symbolic description because many of his mystical precepts elude literal explanation.

The very title of the book, *Island,* suggests a pattern of symbolism latent in Huxley's thought for many years. For Huxley in the 1920s existence seemed bewilderingly pluralistic; the world appeared to be inhabited by a group of irreconcilably heterogeneous individuals. Huxley seems never to have altered his belief in the multiplicity and confusion of unmystical experiential reality. Through his conversion to mysticism, Huxley arrived at the conviction that while relativity and isolation were part of the human condition, they were not necessarily the sum total of human fate. In Huxley's last novel, the implications of the title suggest larger meanings for the symbol of people as islands.

The lesson that *Island* propagates through the connotations of Huxley's symbol is that, although people are admittedly alone on the surface of routine life, like islands, they are nevertheless united, like islands, beneath the uneasy, oceanic flux. Through their contact with a common base, their submarine connection with a more permanent, subsurface reality, they are joined in a unitive psychic land which, for Huxley, is the mystical "Divine Ground." The cynic, whose vision is limited to "outsight," to the surface, sees only separation and isolation in a pluralistic universe. The mystic, who is capable of genuine insight, perceives a unity beneath the heaving, relativistic chaos, a unity which is far more real than the separation of surface reality. The symbolism behind Huxley's title is, in this way, functional to the Palanesians' emphasis on awareness and to Huxley's own mystical reading of life.

Huxley's serious quest for a "reality revealer" pill and his personal experiments toward a perfect vision producer are among the more controversial items in his efforts to formulate a suitable mystical system of life for the masses. The goal of the perfect stimulant is total awareness of events and objects in the present, leading to the "awakeness" of the contemplative mind in meditation.

In *Island*, Huxley's faith in the potentiality of man receives its clearest and most noble expression. Since *Eyeless in Gaza* Huxley was convinced that any improvement of existence in the modern world would have to begin with the individual. He believed that every individual has within him a latent fund of insight and compassion. He felt that a small but alert number of men, perhaps his own version of Milton's "few but fit," were capable of enlightenment without external aid. In a favorable environment, Huxley seems to have thought, this core of leaders would be able to assist large numbers of people in realizing their latent goodness and mystical potential. In *Island*, Huxley illustrates what could be done in a community if it were built on the premise of "goodness politics" rather than power politics.

Huxley sought to frame an ideal knowing that its acceptance, perhaps even its tolerance, in a materialistic world was impossible, yet believing that its relevance to men as individuals was supremely real. And it is difficult not to wonder if *Island* is Huxley's final legacy to posterity, if somehow he hoped that someday the quest toward such an ideal on a more universal scale would not be so far removed from reality.

Donald J. Watt. *Twentieth Century Literature.*
October 1968, pp. 149–60

As utopian fiction, *Brave New World* has a great aesthetic success; it fuses what one presently recognizes as the dangerous incompatibles of this form into a telling unity. And the novel is, just as interestingly, a notable record of uncertainties and hopes proper not only to Huxley but also to the era in which he writes; in consequence, it can be used as a key to analysis of the times by persons who regard as somewhat irrelevant to their purpose questions of aesthetic success. Furthermore, the novel must be seen as expressive of the developing opinions of Huxley himself.

Huxley's two other utopian fictions—*Ape and Essence* and *Island*—are works that are aesthetically unsatisfactory. *Ape and Essence* is inferior simply because of the superficiality with which the utopian task is performed; and *Island,* a more ambitious work, fails to please because the interplay of the "mirrors"—one for reality, one for the author's speculations about reality—does not really take place.

Huxley's mature estimate of the meaning of human personality and his detection of its limitations draw together many items that, lacking this clue, dangle. This estimate—worked out systematically in *The Perennial Philosophy* and elsewhere, but embodied less systematically in works of fiction and casual essays—may be expressed thus: man must somehow be saved or improved. But what ordinarily goes under the heading *man* is not, in its own right, very estimable.

For the Huxley of *After Many a Summer Dies the Swan* and *Time Must Have a Stop,* the persons who achieve superior existence are those who have gone beyond the trammels of personality, the fear of death, and the constriction of being this man or that man at a particular time and place.

Harold H. Watts. *Aldous Huxley* (New York:
Twayne, 1969), pp. 72–74, 146–49

The work of Aldous Huxley developed through four of the most interesting decades in the history of Western Man and he responded all the time to what was going on around him: the breaking of Europe, the knowledge explosion with its technological revolution, the population explosion with the appearance of Mass Man, the economic revolution with its tantalizing promise for poor men everywhere. During these decades violent oppositions came into being. It became possible for whole populations to be properly fed, clothed, and housed; it became possible for them all to be destroyed together in a few minutes. The airplane and mass communications developed until what seemed a spacious world became a confined space in which the multitudes jostled one another. For the first time, on the other hand, it became possible to relieve mankind of its secular pain and anxiety.

Huxley was always sensitive to these oppositions, the eternal balance between good and evil in nature and in human societies. He was prepared to take a full look at the worst; but he spent more time in exploring the new possibilities of advantage to man. He believed in the individual, and he saw the possibilities of greater awareness for the individual. He believed that the balance could only come right if a sufficient number of individuals acted with steady good purpose. It is the Existentialist reaction in a time of flux, the Stoic attitude modified for the times. The unbelievably wonderful possibilities for good were frightening because they could become equally powerful possibilities for evil. But they had to be faced.

To all this Aldous Huxley reacted sensitively and energetically. He could not escape from his heredity, on the one side the Huxleys, on the other the Arnolds, two of the great intellectual families of the nineteenth century, when the responsible use of knowledge seemed to be replacing religion in the control of human societies. When Huxley was a boy, men believed in the steady progress of human betterment. The belief was based on the stability of society and it foresaw our knowledge explosion but not the breaking up of European societies. With his family background and the educational advantages of Eton and Balliol, Huxley could feel he inherited this world of progress. But he was born in 1894, and would have gone to war if he had not been nearly blind. The rich creative years of early manhood were spent in a society which was trying to forget the horrors of war, and the social earthquakes it had brought. He began with books of verse and intellectual satirical novels. The verses showed promise but never said much; a characteristic of most verses in England ever since. The prose was witty and ran clearly and nimbly. He discovered immediately a gift of style, which is a gift frequently denied English novelists.

Laurence Brander. *Aldous Huxley: A Critical Study*
(Lewisburg, Pennsylvania, Bucknell University
Press, 1970), pp. 11–12

To one school of ontology the world as a whole is unintelligible, whatever order we may discern in its parts. It has been said that there is no evidence that "all the systems and structures which we discover are parts of a single system." From *Eyeless in Gaza* on, Huxley assumes the opposite. He takes it on faith that there is a Nature, an Order of things, which we must both assume and within our limits try to grasp. We can confirm this immanence in our day-to-day existence if we are willing to use all our available resources, and subject all but the basic assumption to a pragmatic, existential test.

Island is Huxley's equivalent to Yeats's *Vision*. Both writers began as divided men, and poets; both were alert to contraries for most of their lives; both were ultimately reconciled to them; both were able to make final assertions of joy. *A Vision*, however, is a more symbolic work, *Island* a far more literal one. Both symbolize a belief in ultimate order, but *Island* offers a human order here and now. Contraries are resolved on the plane of the divine, yet the divine resolution can be—it really is—immanent in our lives. Even the least appealing heterodoxies urge us to examine cultural pressures and to withstand the destructive ones, however strong. Mankind may not be able to withstand them, but *Island* claims that if it has the will, it can. It denies that one thinker or one method can provide complete or final answers. It prophetically suggests "new psychophysical sciences" and affirms that answers are available if men will use a responsible intelligence, and look. Huxley's ideas, his whole adventure should become not a subject for dismissal on logical grounds, but instead what Whitehead calls a "lure for feeling." They should incite us to use our critical faculties toward greater usefulness and a larger understanding.

In Huxley's last book, *Literature and Science* (1963) and last essay, "Shakespeare and Religion" (1965), there are signs that his pluralism might have found more unified form. He sees both scientists and writers as purifiers of language, one for public and the other for essentially private truth. The scientist can learn from the artist's intuition while the artist should recognize the increasing accuracy of scientists who study aspects of the destiny of man. But theoretically a total unity is involved, since scientific observation is now recognized as a dialogue with nature, no longer involving a subject-object division. Huxley never could have engaged in the analysis he mentions, or worked out the philosophy for an existential religion. Driven even more by personal need than by his inquiring mind, he was little interested in Whitehead's speculations about God, or even in those of Julian's friend, Teilhard de Chardin. He could never emulate the scholarship of a Northrop, a Toynbee, or a Tillich. He knew, however, at least as well as they, that the West must be alive to the ways and riches of the East, that man cannot live without both science and art, that knowledge must serve a lived acceptance, or faith.

Charles M. Holmes, *Aldous Huxley and the Way to Reality* (Bloomington, Indiana University Press, 1970), pp. 199–200

Brave New World is obviously a satire as well as a fantasy, and at first glance it may seem just as appropriate to evaluate the book on the basis of criteria derived from a definition of satire as on the basis of those derived from a concept of fantasy. Huxley's novel, like *Gulliver's Travels* and *Erewhon*, employs fantasy as a vehicle for satire.

The World State, as it exists in the unverifiable year 632 A.F., is a satiric projection of popular values and associated uses of science in the real world of 1932. Nevertheless, to treat *Brave New World* as primarily a satire would involve difficulties which it might be wiser to avoid than to confront. In the first place, satire is much easier to recognize than to define; unlike fantasy, it is not so much a technique as a manner. The underlying assumption of fantasy is that the reader can distinguish between what is verifiable and what is not.

Second, *Brave New World* is wholly a fantasy (that is, unverifiable time and devices are integral to the novel) but not wholly satiric. John's suicide serves as a final symbol of universal death, or of the ultimate horror of the road civilization may be traveling, but it is not a satiric symbol. Much in the real world simply cannot be satirized. A satire of the concentration camps at Auschwitz is inconceivable. Yet the horror of the camps can be reflected in fantasy. Most modern fantasies with a political theme combine satire with reflections of those aspects of reality which must be treated differently.

Rudolf B. Schmerl. In Thomas D. Clareson, ed.,
SF: The Other Side of Realism—Essays on Modern
Fantasy and Science Fiction (Bowling Green,
Ohio: Popular Press, 1971), pp. 105–15

In *Time Must Have a Stop,* Huxley gently satirizes a young intellectual named Paul De Vries in his quest for "bridge-ideas" that might link the "island universes of discourse"—span the "gulfs separating art, science, religion, and ethics." In some ways, Huxley is probably satirizing his own penchant for trying to find connections between the disparate fields of knowledge; for throughout his career as a prolific writer of both fiction and nonfiction, his theme and his approach was that of integration—the integrated life and the integration of knowledge from universes often regarded as incommensurable. Turning again to the idea of bridge building in the series of lectures delivered in 1959 at the University of California, Santa Barbara, he suggests that the role of *pontifex,* or bridge builder, is an appropriate one for the literary person concerned with "the human situation": "The function of the literary man in the present context, then, is precisely to build bridges between art and science, between objectively observed facts and immediate experience, between morals and scientific appraisals."

He also admits in these lectures that "there is a great problem facing the man of letters who tries to build bridges." What he has in mind is the difficulty the artist faces in making of the facts and theories of science the emotionally engaging material for art; but there is also the problem, as Huxley's fiction reveals, of rendering these materials dramatically within an art form. More concerned with ideas than fictional technique, more by inclination a moralist than a fictionist, Huxley wrote first to inform and only secondarily to entertain. And if, as Anthony Burgess says, his fiction sometimes "nags at human stupidity when it should be getting on with the story— well, we accept the didacticism as an outflowing of the author's concern with the state of the modern world." From the standpoint of drawing from the many universes of discourse to address the contemporary problems, no artist has proven to be a more adept *pontifex* than Aldous Huxley.

Guinevera A. Nance. *Aldous Huxley* (New York:
Continuum, 1988), pp. 136–37

INNES, MICHAEL [J. I. M. STEWART] (1906–   )

It fell to literary figure, J. I. M. Stewart, a don at Oxford, to spin out what must be the longest and most consistently entertaining line of erudite mystery novels to bridge the time span from the absolute peak of the Golden Age in 1935 through World War II and to the present day.

Innes's output—Innes is the "I." of J. I. M. Stewart—is almost incontrovertibly intellectual, with story lines that involve spectacularly convoluted plots and long, intriguing segments of conversation woven through their pages. From the very beginning, with the publication of *Death at the President's Lodging* in 1935, and the almost immediate reprise in *Hamlet, Revenge!* in 1936, the Innes canon has consisted mostly of urbane, intellectualized, "donnish" works. "President" in the first title, incidentally, refers to a university president and not the President of the United States, causing the book to be retitled in America—somewhat insipidly—*Seven Suspects*.

Featuring Inspector John Appleby, later Sir John Appleby, the main body of Innes's work involves plots that are somewhat unconventional, although they tend to sacrifice the ingenuity of the best of Ellery Queen or S. S. Van Dine to accommodate the irrepressible jocularity of the court jester that cohabits with the writer in the Innes body. *Hamlet, Revenge!*, for example, involves a complex murder plot with the solution wrapped up in layer upon layer of detailed scholarship regarding the proper and improper manner of producing Shakespeare's plays.

His work can generally be broken down into four basic types of mystery subgenres: the classic puzzle mystery, the "university" mystery, the art-world mystery, and the espionage-adventure mystery of flight and pursuit.

At his best, Innes is an exciting, amusing, and literary writer, providing page-turning episodes that propel the reader through alarmingly extensive morasses of conversation and explication, through sometimes contrived and hard-to-believe developments, but always eventually to satisfactory denouements.

In his "art world" mysteries, Innes is adept at producing sleight-of-hand forgeries—even forgeries *of* forgeries—to keep the ball rolling. His art information is valid and esoteric, and his knowledge of treasures and antiques extensive, providing a gold mine of trivia for the reader as the various characters romp through the plot turns.

In spite of Innes's university background and his first-hand knowledge of college life as a don himself, he rarely uses his settings or his characters to exploit social problems or to espouse political causes. Essentially con-

316

servative, he presents both leftists and rightists as potential fanatics, and rarely takes side with either, but rather distances himself from what he seems to feel are intrusions in the general format of the mystery.

Bruce Cassiday. *The Literature of Crime and Detection* (New York: Ungar, 1988), pp. 148–49

English mystery novelists, heedless of the example of Wordsworth's nuns, have a way of fretting at their narrow room. They forever seek to widen the limits of the form, and sometimes end by passing those limits entirely. But their publishers may ignore the fact, and a brilliant "straight" novel may thus be addressed solely to the somewhat baffled fan of whodunits.

The case in point is this latest Michael Innes. Mr. Innes himself once described his novels as "on the frontier between the detective story and the fantasy." Now, in *The Daffodil Affair,* that frontier has been definitely crossed.

The story starts out from New Scotland Yard, but on such a quest as Inspector French never knew. There are missing (a) a counting horse named Daffodil, (b) a Cockney girl with three distinct personalities, (c) a young and authentic witch from Yorkshire, and (d) a haunted house (once investigated by Dr. Johnson) stolen with piecemeal plausibility during a series of blitzes.

It is Inspector Appleby's Mycroftian aunt who puts her nephew onto the pattern of these thefts. Appleby, the delightfully civilized protagonist of the other Innes novels, and the splendidly somber Inspector Hudspith set out in pursuit, and wind up in the jungles of the Amazon as guests of the charming and horrible Mr. Wine. This gentleman has his own peculiar plans· for postwar reconstruction, in which Daffodil and the haunted house are equally essential.

The macabre intellectuality of the fantasy, the almost outrageous skill of the writing, the brilliance of the concept and treatment make this one of the finds of the season. The true mystery fan may frown more than a little; but the readers of Norman Douglas, Evelyn Waugh, John Collier, or the early Huxley will acclaim a new treasure.

Anthony Boucher. *San Francisco Chronicle.*
October 11, 1942, n.p.

Over the years, reviewers have often enough commented that the complications of Michael Innes's plots are apt to make one's head spin, but in *A Night of Errors* (1947) Innes produced a country-house murder mystery so complicated and so fantasticated that it may lay fair claim to being the most *migrainous* detective novel ever written.

This work was conceived in the spirit of a joke. Innes began work on it the night after he was inducted into the Detection Club of London. One of the rules of initiation was the taking of an oath not to transgress certain "rules of fair play," one of which was not to write a detective story turning on the plot device of identical twins. "Being donnish and intellectually arrogant, I thought poorly of this; indeed, the next day I started *Night of Errors,* a mystery novel turning on triplets," and taking off on *A Comedy of Errors.*

A satirical prologue offers a summary of the history of the Dromios, a Mediterranean family that naturalized itself in England in the sixteenth century and subsequently married into such distinguished families as the Moneytraps, the Overreaches, and the Whorehounds. The key thing about the family is an unfortunate tendency to produce triplets, a propensity particularly awkward with regard to inheritance laws.

The previous baronet, Sir Romeo Dromio, forty years earlier found himself faced with both a ruinous financial position and a brand new set of triplets. One night a terrible fire at Sherris Hall decimated the nursery wing, from which Sir Romeo was able to rescue but one infant. Shortly thereafter Sir Romeo died mad.

Now, forty years later, his widow, a vague and confused sort of woman, lives at Sherris with Oliver, the remaining son, and also with Lucy, an adopted daughter, a rather mysteriously discontented and sharp-tongued young woman. Also on the scene is a rude and scoundrelly Uncle Sebastian and Mrs. Gollifer, Mrs. Dromio's best friend, a widow who lives with her son Geoffrey. Completing the household are Swindle, the laconic aged family retainer, and Grubb, a stupid and belligerent gardener.

It takes about a hundred pages or so to complete the sense of the complications that exist among these people. The matter is built up effectively, and incrementally, through a series of small but revealing domestic scenes. Mrs. Dromio has always suspected that her other two sons are really alive, that Romeo Dromio would never really have contrived to murder his own children. Only now, forty years later, has Mrs. Dromio taken the opportunity of a trip of Oliver's to America to write him about the existence of his long-lost brothers. Oliver is expected back at Sherris Hall, and already there are rumors of "two Olivers" having been seen in the neighborhood.

Oliver, a notorious womanizer, has been abusing the affections of his adoptive sister Lucy, who has tragically fallen in love with him. Lucy is actually the daughter of Mrs. Gollifer, his mother's friend, by a previous liaison; he has been blackmailing Mrs. Gollifer to keep silent about the fact.

Geoffrey Gollifer, who is earnestly in love with Lucy himself, makes the crushing discovery that Lucy is his half sister, and that Oliver has been blackmailing Geoffrey's mother over the secret of her birth.

Late at night on the eve of Oliver's return a loud crash calls attention to the vacant library, and a terrible smell emanating from it. What is discovered is the body of Oliver Dromio, killed by a vicious blow to the head, lying sprawled on the hearth, his arms actually burning in the fireplace. The young doctor who examines the body along with Inspector John Appleby and Hyland, the local inspector, comments about the dead man, "And I doubt if he had the stuff of martyrs in him. Take a pinch at the buttocks here and you'll see he was a flabby sort of cove."

Almost immediately the initial situation is further complicated: the gardener Grubb is found on the grounds with the murder weapon (a great decanter), and after an absurd chase through a formal garden labyrinth, he is shot dead by a purportedly confused Uncle Sebastian. Geoffrey then comes forward to confess killing Oliver. Lucy testifies that the body is *not* Oliver's after all!

The affair takes yet another dramatic turn when Sherris Hall is set on fire and becomes a mighty conflagration. By the time the blaze is brought under control, the greater part of the house, including Oliver's body, has been destroyed. Dental evidence then confirms that the body recovered from the fire is *not* Oliver's.

Appleby's investigation establishes that the gasoline used to start the fire was not taken from what was in fact the most convenient storage space— a place known only to the members of the household. Thus it seems certain that the arson, and presumably the murder, was perpetrated by an outsider. What this adds up to is the rather confusing conclusion that Oliver did not commit the crime.

In a final melodramatic development, Oliver actually makes an appearance behind the burning house in the distance, laughing maniacally. He then leads police on a wild, pyromaniac chase, setting fires here and there across the countryside in a seemingly random pattern. In the final encounter, Oliver is seen poised above a fire he has set in a quarry, again laughing maniacally, and a moment later his body is seen hurtling through the smoke into the quarry. Soon thereafter Oliver's—and it really *is* Oliver's—burned and battered body is recovered.

Oliver, Hyland concludes, killed one of his brothers, but tried to make it look as if he himself was killed. Thus Oliver arranged it so the hands would be burned, eliminating any immediate evidence that the body was not his own, and then destroyed the house and evidence entirely to prevent any revision of that identification.

Appleby announces that is precisely what the murderer *intended* the police to believe! Geoffrey Gollifer *did* quarrel with Oliver on the terrace, and there struck him on the head and left. At that point Oliver's twin brother Jacques, who had come back from America with Oliver, found the body and contrived an ingenious plan: to let the body be identified *at first* as Oliver's (which it was), but with the idea that on closer examination it would be thought *not* to be Oliver's after all.

The reason Jacques could count on the body ultimately *seeming not* to be Oliver's was that in America Oliver had been hospitalized and bedridden, thus undergoing a subtle change of physique. His consequent flabby buttocks were counted on as a misleading telltale sign here. The burning of the hands prevented any easy identification through fingerprints.

The next step was to plant a substitute body in the house, so that the remains, after the fire, would indeed be verified as *not* being Oliver's. The body he provided was none other than that of Geoffrey Gollifer, whom he killed in the garden after Geoffrey had bolted. Then Jacques, posing as Oliver, staged his mad pyromaniac act, while actually driving about the countryside with Oliver's bashed and partially burned body, until finally he found a place where he could contrive the necessary situation—"fire down below"—a fire at the bottom of the quarry. There he played mad Oliver one last time and then, under cover of the smoke, pretended to leap into the flames, while actually hurling Oliver's body into the quarry.

Thus, in short, *his idea was to stage the murder of himself and follow it with the apparent suicide of Oliver,* after which he could make his appearance *as the third brother* and claim the Dromio estate for himself!

George L. Scheper. Michael Innes (New York:
Ungar, 1986), pp. 179–83

John Innes Mackintosh Stewart, born near Edinburgh in 1906, distinguished himself in the world of letters while still at Oxford, and after a period as lecturer at Leeds University accepted an appointment in Australia, as Professor of English at Adelaide University. As "Michael Innes" he has written many novels and short stories of his Scotland Yard detective, Inspector John Appleby (later Sir John), a scholarly sleuth with a "weakness for cultivated reverie" and a habit of overfrequent conversational references to the classics and the lesser-known poets. The first in the series, *Death at the President's Lodging* (1936), with its very complicated plot, is set in a provincial university, described with satirical humor and a wealth of detail. *Hamlet, Revenge!* (1937) brings a detective drama to complicate an amateur Shakespearean performance in an English country house. In his third novel, *Lament for a Maker* (1938), Michael Innes came to full stature in the genre, and produced one of the most memorable detective novels of recent years. The title itself is derived from a fifteenth century historical poem, William Dunbar's *Lament for the Makaris,* the setting is Scotland, gloriously portrayed, while the method of presentation and the plot itself are cleverly modernized from Wilkie Collins's *The Moonstone.* The literary quality of this novel has not been reached again in Michael Innes's later work, though his popular detective, erudite as ever, has continued to appear in a long series of slight tales, with his name in the title of each volume, and has regained something of his former stature in *The Long Farewell* (1958), which shows Sir John grappling with a complicated mystery that calls for his own special blend of scholarship and detective skill.

A. E. Murch. The Development of the Detective
Novel (New York: Philosophical Library, 1958),
pp. 239–40

There is something about murder and the Scots.

Scotland has given birth to far more than her share of the truly unforgettable cases, from the blowing up of the King of Scots in 1567 to the fantastic doubly criminal career of John Donald Merritt/Ronald John Chesney in our own times; she provided the facts and the background for the greatest of black-and-red studies in murder in *Macbeth;* she has given us the king of scholars of true crime in William Roughead; and she has mothered such superb storytellers of death as Robert Louis Stevenson, John Buchan, and Michael Innes.

Lift a bumper of her other great export and drain it in a toast to Scottish blood: may it never cease flowing!

Superlatives are always rash; but it might be safe to say that Michael Innes—who was born near Edinburgh in 1906 as John Innes Mackintosh Stewart—is the most versatile of modern writers of suspense and detection.

He can write a stolid formal detective story as painstakingly as Freeman Wills Crofts, or an impossible phantasmagoria as extravagantly as M. P. Shiel. He can keep a story down to less than 1500 words or expand it to well over 100,000, and appear comfortably at ease in either length. He can flaunt erudition as arrogantly as S. S. Van Dine (and far more genuinely); he can examine the shadings of character and motive as minutely as Henry James; and he can tell a stirring, sweeping, wind-in-the-sails adventure as rousingly as Stevenson or Buchan.

In a quarter of a century of prolific writing, Innes has never (God bless him!) found a formula. He is almost a different literary personality with each book. But a few things one can always be sure of in any Innes volume: the prose will be graceful, allusive, and witty. There will be plentiful evidence of a fertile inventive mind at work. And the story (of whatever type it may be) will be paramount, even surmounting the temptations of grace and erudition.

Innes was a young Oxford graduate lecturing at Leeds when he was offered a professorship at the University of Adelaide. The long sea voyage to Australia resulted in the academic first novel of murder-in-cap-and-gown which so many of us feel compelled to start off with. The book (*Seven Suspects,* 1936) was in many respects delightful, in others trying. It was with his second novel, *Hamlet, Revenge!,* that Innes really hit his stride; and with his third, *Lament for a Maker,* it became apparent that he belonged (as Howard Haycraft classed him in 1941) with Margery Allingham, Nicholas Blake, and Ngaio Marsh, in the very vanguard of the modern British school of detection.

Since then Innes has unceasingly experimented. In recent years, in addition to his varied suspense stories, he has used his "real" name of J. I. M. Stewart for subtly Jamesian noncriminous novels; and the Innes and Stewart facets seem to have collaborated on the interesting novella (by Stewart) *The Man Who Wrote Detective Stories* (1959).

Which of these many kinds of Innes novels are you about to read? I suppose one might classify *Hamlet, Revenge!* as a splendid example of the detective-story-plus. It is, and very gratifyingly, a formal detective story, with brilliant deduction by not-yet-Sir John Appleby. But it is also a vivid novel—about people, about the theater, about Shakespeare—and lively melodrama. And one trick must, I think, especially have pleased Innes-the-Oxford-scholar: since *Hamlet* is based upon the device of the play-within-a-play, what could be more fitting than to let *Hamlet* itself serve here as the play-within?

Anthony Boucher. Introduction to *Hamlet,
Revenge!,* by Michael Innes (New York: Collier
Books, 1962), p. UK.

[Michael Innes certainly gave his books a thick] coating of urbane literary conversation, rather in the manner of Peacock strained through or distorted by Aldous Huxley. The Innes books were immediately acclaimed as something new in detective fiction from the publication in 1935 of *Death at the President's Lodging*, a title with misleading implications for the United States, where it was rather tamely renamed *Seven Suspects*. The *Times Literary Supplement* said that he was a newcomer who at once took his place in the front rank and, with the publication of *Hamlet, Revenge!* (1936), called him "in a class by himself among writers of detective fiction."

There was actually nothing very new about Innes's approach. J. C. Masterman, in *An Oxford Tragedy* (1933), had produced very much the same kind of "don's delight" book, marked by the same sort of urbanity. But Innes is the finest of the farceurs, a writer who turns the detective story into an overcivilized joke, by a frivolity which makes it a literary conversation piece with some detection taking place on the side. There is no greater quotation spotter or capper in crime literature than Inspector (later Sir John) Appleby, and few Innes characters of this period will flinch at playing a parlor game which involves remembering quotations about bells in Shakespeare. Appleby, when confronted by the "fourteen bulky volumes of the Argentorati Athenaeus," murmurs: "The Deipnosophists . . . Schweighauser's edition . . . takes up a lot of room. . . . Dindorf's compacter . . . and there he is." Appleby shows off, not out of sheer pretentiousness like Wimsey or Vance, but from genuine high spirits. The Innes stories cannot compare as puzzles with the work of Van Dine or Queen. Their strength is in their flippant gaiety, and perhaps the best of them all is *Stop Press* (1939), in which he dispenses with the almost obligatory murder, and keeps the story balanced on little jets of unfailingly amusing talk.

Julian Symons. *Mortal Consequences: A History—
From the Detective Story to the Crime Novel* (New
York: Harper & Row, 1972), pp. 126–27

If you recall all the epithets that have been used to describe Michael Innes's books in the past and repeat them about *Appleby and Honeybath,* you will be pretty near the mark. A country house weekend, a body in a library, a most knowing butler, and a houseful of rather eccentric guests, would seem to be a recipe for a cliché-heavy whodunit in the classic mold. Michael Innes does not exactly break the mold but he stands the clichés on their head with a flick of his whisk and turns stodge into soufflé. As in *Sheiks and Adders* we can only marvel at what a long way a little style will make the old ingredients go. Literature and art combine in the solution as they do in the book's composition. It is a slim volume but not one to gallop through, for its many pleasures of phrase, cameo, and characterization, should be sampled slowly by the discerning palate.

Books and Bookmen. June 1983, p. 28

JAMES, P. D. (1920–   )

Miss P. D. James is the leading present-day practitioner of the feminine character novel that is also a detective story. By and large she is, indeed, the only member of her clan who has substantial claims to rank alongside Dorothy Sayers and Margery Allingham. She writes and plots, usually, with a gemlike clarity that compels both attention and admiration. Unfortunately in *An Unsuitable Job for a Woman* the gem is flawed. Private detection is indeed no job for the dear little thing who is employed to uncover the motives behind the apparent suicide of a likable dropout. The atmosphere of suspicion and brooding violence surrounding a Cambridge clique of trendy youths is excellently conveyed, the background and switching scenes are handled with the same impeccable skill as ever. One is about to hail a minor masterpiece of the genre when, suddenly, the whole carefully constructed edifice collapses into an unlikely solution and an unsatisfactory aftermath. It looks, for once, like too-hasty plotting and one has, too, the horrible suspicion that Miss James is about to commit the cardinal sin of falling in love with her great detective. Let her beware and take thought of Miss Sayers who did just that and neither she nor Wimsey were ever the same afterwards.

John Welcome. The Spectator. December 23,
1972, p. 1011

P. D. James's *Death of an Expert Witness* is quite possibly her best book: certainly the characters are the most credible, the writing is the most controlled (after a slight lapse in *The Black Tower*), and the sense of rhythm is the most subtle. There is an unexplained red herring early on, and the reader is told a little too clearly that the solution is buried in the past, in a scene in which a scientific officer examines a coerolith, the skeleton of a microorganism from ancient seas now found in the chalk of East Anglia. But all else is perfect.

Adam Dalgleish is a sensitive, keenly intelligent officer from Scotland Yard whose growth is palpable from book to book; he is also a poet, and Miss James convinces us that he is a good one without making the mistake of giving us any of his poetry. He can quote Crabbe, the most English of poets, "and not only get it right but make it relevant." In the end the murderer forfeits the right to feel pain and Dalgleish must feel it for the murderer.

James appeals to fans of Dorothy Sayers, Margery Allingham, and Agatha Christie, but she appeals to fans of Ross Macdonald as well. Her sense of taste, even when dealing with the distasteful, is acute; her professional knowledge is that of a hospital administrator; her manner of depicting character is feminine, precise, compassionate, and clear eyed.

Robin W. Winks. The New Republic. November
26, 1977, pp. 34–35

There are a number of good things to be said about P. D. James, but that she is a "new Agatha Christie" is not one of them. I'm not even sure if James is a "queen of crime," as a further bit of well-meaning puffery proclaims her. However, she *is* without doubt one of the genre's noblewomen, and if there's anyone her oeuvre does call to mind, it's a fine author whose own place at court is secure: the late Elizabeth Mackintosh, or Josephine Tey.

To my way of thinking, what keeps both James and Tey just beneath the throne, as it were, is their good taste. They both lack that slight edge of eccentricity that enabled Christie to dream up Poirot, Dorothy Sayers (whom James claims as an influence) to concoct Peter Wimsey, or Margery Allingham to delineate Albert Campion. Tey's Alan Grant and James's Adam Dalgleish are a pair of handsome, brave, true, and intelligent Scotland Yard detectives; one wouldn't kick them out of bed and yet even though Dalgleish is a published poet who's won critical acclaim, one can't help having a fond yearning for Poirot's less intellectually taxing vegetable marrows, or Lord Peter's languid babble about incunabula. Lovable idiosyncrasies command a space of their own and have a staying power unmatched by characters who make do without.

Michele Slung. Ms. August 1979, p. 31

P. D. James is a mystery writer who with *Innocent Blood* has abandoned mystery. She began as a writer of orthodox detective stories in the English tradition. Her first book, *Cover Her Face,* opened with a tea party, and offered fairly conventional characters in a rural setting. But this book and its immediate successors seem not to have satisfied her, and in *Shroud for a Nightingale* (1971) she used her professional knowledge as a hospital administrator to give a realistic portrait of the Nightingale Training College for Nurses. *The Black Tower* (1975) is set in a home for incurables, and the crime is investigated by a detective who has just been reprieved from what was in effect a death sentence, a diagnosis of leukemia.

The detective, Commander Adam Dalgleish, appears in her first seven books, but the portrait of him is deepened and strengthened in *The Black Tower* and in the following *Death of an Expert Witness* (1978). Yet although these later books are pushing to extend the bounds of the detective story, there is a puzzle to be solved and a murderer to be exposed in all of them. With *Innocent Blood* this apparatus has gone. There is the threat of violence, but no mystery. There is no Dalgleish. No doubt this is the serious novel that Phyllis James had it in mind to write when she began. . . .

Innocent Blood shows among other things the risks of too much ambition. The puzzle element in a crime story has been a crutch for many. Chandler, for example, found creating a puzzle a bore, but the necessary construction work proved a great help in making the stereotyped heroines of his early books acceptable. Throw away the crutch and you stand on your own two fictional legs, with the need to justify action by means of character, not of mystery. And judged by its characters, *Innocent Blood* is strikingly implausible.

First, Philippa. An ordinary girl of eighteen, on learning that her mother is a murderess, might feel that she did not want to renew the family connection. Philippa's determination never falters, however, and in an attempt to make her very unlikely actions plausible, the author turns her from a human being into a quotation machine, a sure winner in any literary quiz. It is true that we have been told she is a clever girl, but she seems rather to be crammed with facts, facts which she is dismally eager to communicate. . . .

This is indeed a highly literary novel, in which even a private detective employed by Scase quotes Thomas Mann. What would mother and daughter have talked about if Mary, as seems more probable, had been an ordinary woman damaged or brutalized by prison life, not interested in visiting the Brompton Oratory to see the Mazzuoli marbles?

It is because the loving relationship between Philippa and her mother is essential to the plot that it is—not very skillfully—forced on us. . . .

The improbability of the plot (with which the story's unexpected final turn is quite in keeping) is to some extent concealed by the intelligence and detailed realism of the writing. . . . Here, as in her detective stories, P. D. James's writing has a solid stylishness touched by flashes of wit and observation. . . .

P. D. James is also a writer remarkably concerned with the details of things and places. The flat Philippa rents to occupy with her mother gets several pages of description, the room rented by Scase in a hotel is given a page, and so is the visiting room in prison. Often the details are strongly visual, giving us in Scase's hotel room the stained fawn carpet, a spot of dampness in one corner, the rickety wardrobe, and the dressing table "in veneered walnut with a spotted mirror." Such elaborate descriptive detail has always been one of P. D. James's strengths. Through it she often succeeds in giving us the feeling of a house or a community, and of the people in it. . . .

The book also attempts to get the feeling of contemporary London, chiefly through a concern with ways of traveling in it by public transport, especially by Underground. This immense accumulation of factual detail certainly gives us something, although it's hard to be quite sure what. Although it helps to make the localities convincing, it does nothing for the people in them. The characters with whom the author is less involved . . . are much more plausible than Philippa, her mother, and the unlikely avenger Scase. Nor do the settings help the plot, which is made more jarringly melodramatic by the solidity of rooms and furniture. There is no doubt about P. D. James's talent, but on the evidence of *Innocent Blood* one must hope for the return of Adam Dalgleish in her next book.

Julian Symons. *The New York Review of Books.*
July 17, 1980, pp. 39–40

P. D. James is a novelist who happens to write in the mystery form. That distinction—endorsed by the writer herself—is not merely semantic; it is, in fact, what [she] is all about.

Her plots, while appropriate to novels that deal with crime, transcend the mere puzzle aspect of the traditional mystery. Her characters have a depth that is neither necessary to nor common in the genre, and her themes strike chords of recognition in a wide audience. Who has not grappled with loneliness, been affronted by the terrible certainty of death, harbored thoughts—however brief—of retribution? Who has not wondered about his true identity? Who has never been touched by crime?

These are matters that concern most thinking people. P. D. James deals with them in such a way as to please both the conventional mystery buff and an ever-increasing general readership as well. She entertains, yes, but she also gives us a lot to think about, even after she's told us "whodunit."

"Civilized," "literate," and "complex" are just a few of the adjectives that are frequently used to describe her writing. Her style is all of that; it is very English, very intelligent, and above all, very readable.

Central to the whole concept of the mystery is, of course, plot. Is it logical? Believable? Clear, or muddled? The success of the story depends to a great degree on the answers to these questions. Agatha Christie became the most popular mystery writer in history on the basis of her convoluted plots and surprise endings, although she was not a great writer in the usually accepted sense. That didn't matter. She excelled in the one area where excellence is demanded.

While P. D. James does not create the same kind of plots as Christie did, James too excels in this all-important category. All the other writing skills she possesses—and they are many—would not have saved her as a mystery writer if she didn't build tight plots.

The mystery format demands that there be a crime, several suspects, numerous clues scattered here and there, and a detective capable of finding, analyzing, and interpreting them. If, along the way, the reader finds himself following some false trails, so much the better.

In all cases, even where a story is marred by melodrama, the plot is intricately devised and presented in an orderly manner. Clues are often subtle and derived as much from personality as from physical evidence. There are always enough "red herrings" to complicate things and make for genuine puzzlement.

Her methods of murder are many, and they range from the mundane—strangling, for example—to such ingenious horrors as disinfectant in the intragastric feed. Poison is a rare choice. When she does use it, it is not an unknown variety but something more common, such as nicotine. She is careful to set such use in a hospital or clinic setting, where the murderer has both knowledge of and access to poisonous substances. Even in this she strives for verisimilitude.

Motivation is important to James, and she has often said that her fictional crimes are the natural result of the situations she creates. While she does give people a variety of reasons for murder, she relies somewhat too heavily on one device: the will. In *A Mind to Murder*, in *Unnatural Causes*, in *An Unsuitable Job for a Woman*, in *The Black Tower* and even *Death of an Expert Witness*, the question of inheritance is crucial to the plot.

Pace is important to a novel, and James manages to keep her story moving, despite a paucity of action. Psychological movement is more crucial than physical. There are no fast fists, no cracking guns; rather, there is a careful unfolding of personality, a meticulous placing of detail.

James's major characters are many-layered, and she can make her minor ones memorable with only a sentence or two. Equally impressive is her ability to create atmosphere and mood. Whether she is writing about a clinic in London or a nursing home in East Anglia, she paints a vivid and complete picture, filled with interesting detail and brilliantly alive with minutiae.

One thing that is always marked in a discussion of James's style is her "literacy." Critics hail her as being "in the great British tradition" of writers whose people, middle and upper class, discuss art and quote poetry, even as they concoct devilish ways to do each other in.

A favorite device is to give her characters some of her own literary tastes. Her own favorite author, for example, is Jane Austen, whose "peace, sanity and order" she finds restful. It is not surprising that Adam Dalgleish, who after all does share some of his creator's likes and dislikes, prefers Jane Austen too and keeps at least one of her books on his bedside table at all times. Dalgleish and James share also a respect for Thomas Hardy and for the poet George Crabbe. . . .

James's literary interests are not confined to the past. She can drop modern names as easily as older ones, as when she has Frederica Saxon say of Enid Bolam, "Who would suppose that Bolam would want to see Anouilh? I suppose she was sent a free ticket."

Nor does James slight earlier writers, those of the seventeenth century. Her very first title, *Cover Her Face*, comes from Webster's *Duchess of Malfi* (c. 1613), and she refers again to the Jacobean period in *Death of an Expert Witness*, as Maxim Howarth reflects on his love for his sister Domenica, a love of which his own wife was jealous and of which Dom's husband was painfully aware:

> He remembered Charles Schofield's gauze-cocooned head, the dying eyes still malicious behind two slits in the bandages, the swollen lips painfully moving.

"Congratulations, Giovanni. Remember me in your garden in Parma."

What had been so astounding was . . . that he had hated his brother-in-law enough to die with that taunt on his lips. Or had he taken it for granted that a physicist, poor philistine, wouldn't know his Jacobean dramatists?

The play thus obliquely referred to is John Ford's *'Tis Pity She's a Whore* (c. 1627), a tragedy about the fatal attraction of Giovanni for his sister Annabella. The play takes place, of course, in Parma. None of this is explained, however, by James, who assumes that the reader will be as well-read and as thoroughly educated as she is herself.

For nearly everyone James's writing is a pleasure to read: colorful, clear, precise, ample without being padded, often dryly humorous, insightful, compassionate, kind. That she understands her characters, there is never any doubt. It is obvious, too, that she has a psychologist's comprehension of human nature, with an ability to put herself in the other person's mind, to feel his emotions and predict his actions. Such is her power of description that the reader will often sympathize with a "bad" character because he has been made aware of the complex motivations that lie behind every action. She does not sketch in black and white; indeed, her character studies might be titled, "Variations on a Shade of Gray." There's good—and bad—in everyone.

Perhaps most indicative of James's own mood is the generally upbeat way in which she ends her stories. Hers are not the kind of mysteries that build up to an O. Henry twist on the final page and leave the reader breathless. On the contrary, the action moves to a climax, the mystery is solved, and then the story winds down gently, with all loose ends tied. There is an almost nineteenth-century nicety about the way she puts everything in place at the end. And in almost all cases the bad are punished, and the good, if not rewarded, at least left to continue their lives in peace.

James's strong feelings about criminal behavior require her to punish wrongdoers, by an "act of God" if not by the law. This satisfies her need for retribution, although it may seem too "fictional" for a story that purports to depict real life. In a like manner she has, in most of her books, added information about marriages, job changes, and various positive moves for many of her main characters.

As recently as *The Black Tower,* her sixth book, there is a very positive ending, with a strong hint of a future relationship between Dalgleish and Cordelia. Only *Death of an Expert Witness* fails to reflect James's generally optimistic outlook on life. Since the publication of that book James has stepped beyond the narrow confines of the mystery form to write *Innocent Blood,* a novel that deals with crime but is not in itself a mystery.

She is now squarely in the mainstream of popular fiction. Her great commercial success in that area, however, will not put an end to her mystery career. She admits to being "extremely fond" of the mystery form. She finds working within the genre's strict rules very challenging and will, she has stated, "certainly be doing it again."

Norma Siebenheller. *P. D. James* (New York: Ungar, 1981), pp. ix, 129–40

That element of good writing variously called the author's philisophical stance, worldview, or general attitude, is best discerned in parts of the novel that do not pertain directly to plot, setting, or characterization. It appears in expository embellishments to the main story or in apparently incidental observations of characters or author. Such material in P. D. James's novels may be divided thematically into three areas: aesthetic, intellectual, and ecclesiastical. An examination of themes from these perspectives indicates an emerging pattern: characters most sophisticated about art and scholarly pursuits often are deficient in moral perceptions, and vice versa. With the striking exception of the chapel murder scene in *Death of an Expert Witness,* however, the church is consistently a symbol for order and altruism.

To support this thesis it need only be pointed out that among James's murderers are a scholar, an artist and an art connoisseur. But James's references to art do not stop there. When Adam is called to the murder case at the Steen Clinic, for instance, he recalls that that is the place with an original Modigliani. In the course of Cordelia Gray's investigation, she notices that what she has thought is a print is an original Renoir. The single painting in Maxim Howarth's sitting room is "a Sidney Nolan oil of Ned Kelly." These details are almost always used in conjunction with an unsavory group or individual. In James's world evidence of aesthetic acuity is an implicit indictment of, if not sheer villainy, at least an unsympathetic attitude toward other members of one's society.

People associated with intellectual pursuits represent a more eclectic attitude on the part of James: some are reprehensible, but some, on the contrary, are to be admired. Edwin Lorrimer in *Death of an Expert Witness* and Sir Ronald Callender of *An Unsuitable Job for a Woman* seem as accomplished as they are unpleasant. On the other hand, Henry Carwardine of *The Black Tower* and Dalgliesh himself are both sympathetic and erudite characters. Often Dalgliesh demonstrates his ability at philosophical colloquy. Usually, however, this kind of activity is in reference to one of the more sinister characters in the novels.

Religion is treated quite differently from philosophy and art. Two clergymen, Father Baddeley in *The Black Tower* and Canon Hubert Boxdale in the short story, "Great Aunt Allie's Flypapers," are thoroughly good men. Religious ceremonies and church buildings themselves are frequently mentioned and usually emphasize moral responsibility. Some characters, to be sure, suffer from an excess of religious fervor, as is the case of Enid Bolam in *A Mind to Murder* and Nurse Pearce in *Shroud for a Nightingale.* Significantly, each of these characters tries to impose her religious practice upon her colleagues and each is a murder victim. Most of the references to ecclesiastical habits or theology, however, indicate that James sees religion as a positive force in society.

Finally, P. D. James is distinguished not only because of her deftness in creating plot, setting and character, but also because of her demonstration of moral sensitivity and humanistic concerns. These attitudes permeate the novels, manifesting themselves in her awareness of societal reform and her acceptance of physically and psychologically maimed human beings as being worthy subjects. In "The Art of Fiction" Henry James deals with the moral sense of the novel and makes as a final point "the very obvious truth that the deepest quality of a work of art will always be the quality of the mind of the producer." It only belabors the obvious to aver the high quality of P. D. James's art.

Nancy P. Joyner. In Earl F. Bargainnier, ed., *10 Women of Mystery* (Bowling Green, Ohio: Popular Press, 1981) pp. 121–22

KAFKA, FRANZ (1883–1924)

The Kierkegaardian system of belief was responsible for much of the form and content of Franz Kafka's novels. And it does seem as though the Danish philosopher's conception of a religious way of life transcending human codes and sanctions was peculiarly profitable in stimulating Kafka's approach to his material. For whether or not we care to admit from a doctrinal point of view the possibility of a teleological suspension of the ethical, there can be no doubt that something of this kind is assumed whenever one asserts the universality of a work of art.

In Kafka's view there is a way of life for any individual that is the right one, and which is divinely sanctioned. So much is perhaps admitted by most of our moral novelists; but to Kafka this fact itself constitutes a problem of tremendous difficulty, because he believes the dichotomy between the divine and the human, the religious and the ethical, to be absolute. Thus, though it is imperative for us to attempt to follow the true way, it is impossible for us to succeed in doing so. This is the fundamental dilemma that Kafka believes to lie at the basis of all human effort.

One has only to run one's mind over the more significant literature of Kafka's generation, from *St. Mawr* and *The Waste Land* to *Ulysses* and *Manhattan Transfer* to realize how prominent a part this view of modern European civilization has played in determining the artist's attitude to his material. Preoccupation with this problem—the problem presented by the corruption, not of the individual as such, but of the interhuman relationships that give him significance as a member of civilized society—recurs throughout Kafka's work, and is realized most effectively in his short story "The Hunger-Artist." Its more positive aspects are persistent throughout *The Castle,* where the hero's whole efforts are directed immediately towards an attempt to establish himself in a home and a job, and to become a member of the village community—to come to terms, in fact, with society.

Kafka's particularization of the teleological problem doesn't stop at the social level, however. Just as the attempt to follow the religious way of life is seen as a social problem, so the social problem is in its turn seen as one that appears in terms of individual human relationships. The complexity of relationship that exists between the individual and the undiscoverable way of life emerges as the complexity of the relationships between the hero and the other characters in Kafka's novels. In this his method isn't essentially different from that of most other novelists; the difference lies in that, in his treatment of interhuman relationships, Kafka's concern is always for their more general implications, their significance for the social, and ultimately for the religious, problem, and the framework and properties of the novels are constructed with this consideration in mind.

The effect of the prose in *The Castle* is to produce the sense of physical effort appropriate to the situation. The short phrases and the jerky movement of the sentence suggest the feeling of frustrated effort that K. experienced, striving to get nearer the Castle, but repeatedly being prevented.

It is necessary to insist on this fusion of the mental and the physical in Kafka's work for two reasons. In the first place, it is the basis of his allegorical method. The whole of his hero's experience—whether spiritual, mental, emotional, or physical—is regarded as absolutely continuous, and the distinctions that for the sake of exposition I have drawn between the religious, the social, and the individual levels simply do not exist in the actual writing. The objectification of emotional experience into physical that I have noted emerges in the large as the concrete visualization of the individual's sense of the wider issues of existence in terms of the institutions and officials that characterize his novels and stories. Secondly, it is this preoccupation with the concrete and the physical that forces itself first on the reader's attention, and the remoter implications of the hopeless struggle are realized only over a wide area; the stress, that is, is on the struggle and not on the hopelessness, and the preoccupation with this struggle in the most immediate sense engages the reader's emotional energies, directs and disciplines them, and offers him a positive interest amid what would in abstraction be described as a philosophy of pessimism.

R. O. C. Winkler. *Scrutiny.* December 1938, n.p.

With much admiration for Kafka, I find it impossible to take him seriously as a major writer and have never ceased to be amazed at the number of people who can. Some of his short stories are absolutely first-rate, comparable to Gogol's and Poe's. Like them, they are realistic nightmares that embody in concrete imagery the manias of neurotic states. And Kafka's novels have exploited a vein of the comedy and pathos of futile effort which is likely to make "Kafka-esque" a permanent word. But the two of these novels, *The Trial* and *The Castle,* which have become for the cultists of Kafka something like sacred writings, are after all rather ragged performances—never finished and never really worked out.

Must we really, as his admirers pretend, accept the plights of Kafka's abject heroes as parables of the human condition? We can hardly feel toward Kafka's father, whose aspect Kafka's God always wears, the same childish awe that Kafka did—especially when the truth is that Kafka himself cannot help satirizing this Father-God as well as his own pusillanimity in remaining in bondage to him. A good deal has been made of the influence on Kafka of the Danish theologian Kierkegaard; but we learn from Max Brod that Kafka was at least equally influenced by Flaubert, and his work is full of a Flaubertian irony which the critics have tended to disregard.

I do not deny that the enslaver, the master, is often given, in Kafka's stories, a serious theological meaning; but this side is never developed in anything like equal proportion to the ironical self-mocking side. Is the man condemned to death in *The Trial,* and finally convinced of his guilt for some crime which is never named, really either adapted or intended to illustrate Original Sin?—or is Kafka not rather satirizing the absurdities of his own bad conscience? In *The Castle,* there is also self-irony, but, besides this, a genuine wistfulness in K.'s longing to settle down and find a modest place in life for himself. But neither—unless one takes them as parodies of the Calvinist doctrine of Grace—seems to me to possess much interest as the expression of a religious point of view. The Christian of *Pilgrim's Progress* had obstacles to overcome and required moral fortitude to meet them; but all the struggling, such as it is, that is done by Kafka's K. is against an omnipotent and omniscient authority whose power and lights he can never share but to whose will he is doomed to succumb. . . . These stories too often forfeit their effectiveness as satires through Kafka's rather meaching compliance, his little-boy-like respect and fear in the presence of the things he would satirize: the boring diligence of commercial activity, the stuffiness of middle-class family life, the arid reasonings and tyrannous rigidities of Orthodox Judaism (which have a good deal in common with those of our old-fashioned Puritan Protestantism).

What he has left us is the half-expressed gasp of a self-doubting soul trampled under. I do not see how one can possibly take him for either a great artist or a moral guide.

Edmund Wilson. *Classics and Commercials: A*
Literary Chronicle of the Forties (New York:
Farrar, Straus & Giroux, 1950), pp. 383–92

Kafka's novels evoke a world as self-coherent and characteristic as that of Dickens, of Dostoyevsky, of Proust, of Poe, of Hawthorne. Like Hawthorne's and Poe's, Kafka's is a limited, a lyric, world. Kafka is a metaphysical poet in symbolist narrative.

Kafka's is a world known in nightmares—a rational, unnatural world in which unnatural situations are rationally worked out—in which everyone is able, like Lewis Carroll's creatures, to argue long, ingeniously, and convincingly. It is a nightmare world in which the "I," all innocent and eager to submit, all desirous to propitiate, is pushed about, pursued, regimented by potencies veiled of visage—in which one is forever being orally examined by dignitaries who forever flunk one. The self and the world are juxtaposed in opposition. If one is not being pursued by the world or carried off by the world, one is running after it. There is the image of the old father trying to catch the ear of the Castle dignitaries—trying in vain, for the officials go at a gallop, their carriages "race like mad." It is the world of a Mack Sennett comedy—one of chase and pursuit, of intense movement, horizontal and vertical: of running and climbing. It is a world of uncertainty and insecurity, of fear and trembling.

It is a world of hierarchy, created by Kafka in the parodic imitation of the Austrian bureaucracies under which he lived, within which, as underofficial, he worked. In its chief traits it could be a feudal estate or it could be an American department store or a chain of restaurants or a metropolitan public library. Hierarchy provides, negatively, for deferment of responsibility or infinite regress. One's complaint always reaches the wrong office; one is passed on from office to office, in general moving up the scale of delegated authority, only to find that the proper official to handle the complaint is out of town, or the necessary documents are lost, or by delay one's claim is outlawed. Wonderful is the efficiency of an order so complexly graduated that every expert is inexpert at satisfying the simple need for justice.

Kafka's novels can be taken as burlesques of bureaucracy. Satiric, of course, they are. Yet they lack satiric norm, a contrasting model of elegance and humanity. The hero is too uncertain of himself to sit in judgment on duly constituted authorities and too intent upon learning their ways to have leisure for criticizing them. As for bureaucracy, it is even at its worst a corruption of order; and order is a state so blessed, so indispensable, that even its parodies deserve respect.

Doubtless there is an ultimate authority, but we never reach it except through its intermediaries: there is no direct vision.

Kafka's world is one of mystery.

His method offers a superficial analogy with that of Hawthorne. But Hawthorne offers alternatives—usually supernaturalism and some form of naturalism.

It is not Kafka's method thus to contrast a supernatural with a natural reading. It is, for him, in and through the natural that the supernatural operates and—with whatever intermittence and illusion—is revealed.

Kafka's world is neither the world of the average sensual man nor yet fantasy. It is the world seen slightly askew, as one looks through his legs or stands on his head, or sees it in a distorting mirror. Nor does his adjustment take, like Swift's in *Gulliver,* the method of segregation. With Swift, the fantastic is safely corralled and tucked away in the initial assumption; with Kafka, realism and fantasy move in more close and sensitive relation. In *The Trial* and *The Castle* the whole sequence is so improbable as to suggest some kind of pervasive allegory, but at no point (or almost no point) does one encounter downright impossibility.

Kafka's "mystery" is, then, the apparent sign of how elusive is the truth. What happens is tolerably easy to ascertain, but what it means is precarious as well as important.

Such scrupulosity of interpretation recalls a characteristic feature of hierarchy everywhere prominent in Kafka's novels—the connection between promotion, pleasing, and propitiation. Kafka's worlds are patriarchies or theocracies. One's success or failure depends on one's skill in divining the wishes of the great man; and among underlings there develops a necessary skill in calculating his mood by his complexion, step, tone of voice.

Like Kierkegaard, whose *Fear and Trembling* starts from and repeatedly returns to the story of Abraham and Isaac, so Kafka, delighting in speculation, yet offers his story as a mythic fable the meaning of which is anterior to and unexhausted by any included commentary.

Myth is not allegory; and Kafka is not an allegorist. An allegory is a series of concepts provided with a narrative, or a narrative accompanied by a conceptual parallel. Strictly, it is a philosophical sequence which systematically works itself out in images.

A narrow, moving writer, Kafka is both an artist and a symbol. The appeal of this symbol has been extraordinarily wide to Europeans and Americans in the past decade. One secular hope after another has failed. Kafka can be the symbol for what is left. He is illiberal, unrelenting, unsentimental; as Spender has said, he combines the power of the visionary with the self-criticism of the skeptic, so that he communicates the sense of their being something to believe without the claim of being able to define what it is. It is difficult today to believe in the reality of a world of comfort, good sense, and progress; we doubt that we shall ever see such a world again; we think it wise to prepare ourselves spiritually for worlds more exacting and metaphysical; and of such worlds Kafka is initiate.

Austin Warren. *Rage for Order* (Ann Arbor,
Michigan: University of Michigan Press,
1948), n.p.

Franz Kafka's work is probably not absurd. . . . His work is universal (a really absurd work is not universal) to the extent to which it represents the emotionally moving face of man fleeing humanity, deriving from his contradictions reasons for believing, reasons for hoping from his fecund despairs, and calling life his terrifying apprenticeship in death. It is universal because its inspiration is religious. As in all religions, man is freed of the weight of his own life. But if I know that, if I can even admire it, I also know that I am not seeking what is universal, but what is true. The two may well not coincide.

In the fullest sense of the word, it can be said that everything in that work is essential. In any case, it propounds the absurd problem altogether. If one wants to compare these conclusions with our initial remarks, the content with the form, the secret meaning of *The Castle* with the natural art in which it is molded, K.'s passionate, proud quest with the everyday setting against which it takes place, then one will realize what may be its greatness. For if nostalgia is the mark of the human, perhaps no one has given such flesh and volume to these phantoms of regret. But at the same time will be sensed what exceptional nobility the absurd work calls for, which is perhaps not found here. If the nature of art is to bind the general to the particular, ephemeral eternity of a drop of water to the play of its lights, it is even truer to judge the greatness of the absurd writer by the distance he is able to introduce between these two worlds. His secret consists in being able to find the exact point where they meet in their greatest disproportion.

Albert Camus. *The Myth of Sisyphus and Other Essays* (New York: Alfred A. Knopf, 1955), pp. 136–38

The fundamental quality that makes Kafka different—in his time almost uniquely different—from the received tradition of the nineteenth and early twentieth centuries is his abrogation, or more graphically, his collapsing of the aesthetic distance that was presumed to separate the writer from his reader. He does not merely vary it, now letting the reader come close to the work, now contriving to widen the distance again—he abolishes it entirely, from beginning to end. The reader is given Gregor Samsa turned into an insect as, even before, the story begins. Gregor does not become for a while less an insect, for a while more an insect, nor is his insectness revealed at the end—or anywhere else—to have been a dream or an illusion. Gregor dies an insect, with the dessicated body of an insect. Except in narrative retrospect, the reader has never seen him as anything else.

The continuing reaction of the reader to this seemingly unmediated closeness is to be shocked out of his or her capacity to reflect. One is obliged to confront the fictional catastrophe without the solace of contemplation that was earlier provided for by aesthetic distancing. Reflection, moreover, and analysis and interpretation are no longer external to the fiction. Those processes were formerly performed by the reader more or less at his leisure, but, with Kafka, they are part and parcel of the fiction itself. The reader's problem with authorial analysis and interpretation as performed by Kafka is that the processes and the results never seem fixed and definitive. They are repeated, modified, subjected to dialectics, to irony, to humor. So that the careful reader, probably to his discomfort, has learned to be wary of subscribing very wholeheartedly to such internal glosses, anticipating always a revision which, like its predecessors, may in any case affront his sense of logic—or simply prove all but impenetrable.

Kafka's preference for orientation to the individual may bring the reader to examine with especial stringency the apparent implication in, for example, "In the Penal Colony," that the *era* of the old commandant was superior to that of the new commandant. As far as that goes, were the good old days really better? Only in the most ironic sense, if one applies the autobiographical criterion, which is often more appropriate than the social or the Nietzschean. Similarly in "The New Advocate" one ought to examine closely the critical consensus that Dr. Bucephalus is a somewhat unwisely indulged survivor of a more vigorous, regrettably past, era. Or, in "A Country Doctor," that olden times were somehow better, when the church exerted a greater influence and a medical doctor was not called upon to do a priest's work. One's reference points are, in fact, individuals. The implications or the inferences transcend the individual. Those above probably are cautious enough if one keeps Kafka's preferred focus in mind. It would on the other hand seriously misrepresent Kafka to allegorize Josef K. or K. into an Everyman. They are not; they are fictional personae of Kafka himself— as indeed are most of his heroes.

Richard H. Lawson. *Franz Kafka* (New York:
Ungar, 1987), pp. 151–54

KING, STEPHEN (1947–   )

Stephen King's *Salem's Lot* (Jerusalem's lot) is a novel of such chilling beginnings that we look forward to losing sleep over it. It is the kind of goose bump fiction that makes grown men afraid of the dark.

It is to Stephen King's credit as a stylist that he has charmed us into such familiar territory. Sparing the endless atmospheric creaks and cobwebs and cupolas of this New England landscape, he thrusts us into the private terror of his characters. A wise choice. An equally familiar assortment of types achieves a personal dimension and life's blood that grounds us. King gives this stock company a contemporary resonance and wit. Instead of stalking among their dusty antiques, he lets us peek into their souls.

It is here that the writer proves a master of this genre. He juggles character vignettes into a structural crossfire that is hypnotic. A thousand detailed portraits become the broad canvas of *Salem's Lot*.

Unfortunately, we mystery fans are an odd lot, opting for a good story over a well-written one any night of the week. And it is here, ultimately, that *Salem's Lot* disappoints. No one minds a good retelling of an old legend when there is a new finale. But the final confrontation is labored, obvious, and familiar. King has added nothing new to this legend.

Walter Bobbie. *Best Sellers*. January 1976, p. 304

The Shining has flaws, some minor and some serious.

But when all's said, the novel *works!* It makes one tremble in anticipation of the day when King gets it all together and writes a "perfect" book. King's style is his most obvious fault. It's all *good* writing, it's all pertinent, but it goes on and on. Setting a realistic scene and creating believably complex characters are laudable traits, but King seriously overdoes it.

King builds his mood slowly, at first establishing the idyllic setting of the peaceful old Overlook. Minor ominous incidents occur at intervals between lengthy flashbacks to Jack's and Wendy's youth, showing the childhoods that molded their personalities. Gradually the story stabilizes in the present as the hallucinations become more vicious, and the Torrances are increasingly hard-pressed to rationalize them as imaginary.

King continues to add detail, building upon minor incidents, filling in a mosaic of horror which has unsuspected depths.

There's another annoyance that's obvious; King does not portray Danny as a five-year-old child. He's too mature; he seems nine or ten at least. Even granting that a telepathic boy might be emotionally older than his peers, it's important for plot reasons that Danny be no more than five. Whenever King switched to a lengthy scene with the boy, the story suddenly became less convincing. There are also some subplots that don't really fit the story; they're too obviously just to give the reader some extra chills.

Most of the flaws are in the nature of loose ends that the reader is bothered at finding unresolved. Some may be setups that King decided to drop, such as an old canvas firehose that has a "disturbingly coiled" aspect, we are told several times, but which never does do anything. Some may be due to deliberate vagueness; King doesn't seem to want us to be sure at what point the hotel's manifestations pass from the illusory plane to the actual one. A list of other loose ends would be tedious to those who haven't read the book yet, so I'll just say that the totality leaves the reader with a distinct wish that King had spent less time on the Torrances' past and on their emotional complexes, and more on finishing the story in a complete manner.

But it's still the goddamnedest best horror novel I've read in over two decades.

Frederick Patten. *Delap's Fantasy and Science
Fiction Review.* April 1977, p. 6

The stories of *Night Shift* all begin in our normal world, where everything is safe and warm. But in almost every instance, something slips, and we find ourselves in the nightmare world of the not-quite-real.

Such stories require a willing suspension of disbelief, of course, but they also require an author who is an expert manipulator, one who can make horror seem not only plausible but almost logical. King is an expert, and many of these stories will not be easily forgotten. Perhaps "The Mangler" is the best example of King's skill at what he does. The idea of a steam ironer possessed by a demon seems laughable, but no one who reads "The Mangler" is going to laugh for very long.

Bill Crider. *Best Sellers.* April 1978, pp. 6–7

The haunted hotel of *The Shining* is a stock sort of device, left over from the days when people were still writing straight ghost stories. The struggling family offers the pathos that no doubt is in part responsible for the book's popularity—real characters, beautifully handled for the most part, though some of the development toward the end is a bit too hasty. Even the child with the "gift" is a common theme of Stephen King's. But herein they are combined, redeveloped, slowly woven into a dark, unfamiliar tapestry—something dreadful and inevitable and ultimately terrifying.

King's creation of atmosphere is masterful—the first irrational hint I had that anything unusual might happen terrified me as fully as the later, more logically constructed episodes. In fact, where the novel falls short is in the fact that the conclusion is not nearly as frightening as the mood that has been predicting it. King takes the stance that he should give the reader a hint of the ultimate horror early in the game, and then—when they're sure to be afraid that it's actually going to happen—give them exactly what they've been nervously waiting for. It's a technique that works rather well, though in this case the intimations of doom are more frightening than the doom itself.

Marc Laidlaw. Nyctalops. Vol. 2, No. 7, 1978,
p. 34

In 1980, America dies for its sins (pollution of both landscape and spirit) in a shifting antigen plague leaked from some cavern of government-sponsored biological warfare. But the purge leaves certain issues of good and evil unresolved. In *The Stand*, Stephen King divides the survivors up like tiddledywinks into two camps, one devoted to good, the other to the devil. Will it be Walden III or the Fourth Reich? In the panorama of mass disaster—and with such moral freight to consider—King loses his characterizations in a clutter of place-names and products.

The devil (otherwise known as Randall Flagg, an agent provocateur out of the Rolling Stones's "Sympathy for the Devil") successfully raises hairs on the arms. The prose flows well, describing multiple plague deaths, swollen corpses, and the rantings of idiot savants. But *The Stand* is not a horror story like King's *Carrie* or *The Shining*, and that's why it ultimately bores. Horror lies in that area where known becomes unknown, where ordinary turns menacing.

Too much of King's new book deals with a little leaguer's vision of American democracy somehow smiling through apocalypse; good and evil are set up like so many kindergarten blocks. Bad is Las Vegas where those survivors who sell their souls gather; good is Boulder, Colorado, and the American constitution. Similar equations act like dry rot on the plot.

Anne Collins. Maclean's Magazine. December 18,
1978, p. 51

Firestarter is another smasheroo from a writer whose books haunt best-seller lists as well as impressionable imaginations. This is your advanced post-Watergate cynical American thriller with some eerie parapsychological twists, and it's been done so distinctively well that we'd better talk about genius rather than genre. Complex characterizations, credible dialogue and a no-nonsense prose style are among the uncommon virtues King brings to popular fiction, and his novels will be read long after this year's Prix Limburger winner has gone the way of all big cheeses for a season. As scary as *Carrie*.

Paul Stuewe. Quill and Quire. October 1980,
pp. 40–41

Some may object that King's writing is too enthusiastic, or, at least, too energetic. A true son of the 1960s, King in all his books makes the music coming out of the era one of his touchstones for decency and sensitivity. Even his love of parentheses, to indicate thought or menace or to heighten a mood, could be considered writing stereophonically. Sometimes a King novel or story is a veritable light show of italics, ellipses, and parentheses; one imagines him drumming it out on an electric typewriter with rock music blaring behind and the occasional blown fuse.

King also has a well-known predilection for brand-name products: Hush-Puppies, Adolph's Meat Tenderizer, Pledge, Woolco, Sara Lee, Cheez Doodles, Cremora, Hefty Bags, Shakey's Pizza, etc. Certainly these items were missing from Castle Dracula, as were such favorite King expressions as "pissant," "doodly-squat," and "shitcan." King also does very well with making modern appliances and machinery, like lawnmowers and trucks, ominous, even predatory: perhaps he will one day give us a killer Cuisinart.

Stephen King, in short, is not the kind of occult writer who would have gone out and joined a satanic society; brushed by the counterculture, he's still much more likely to be a pillar of the local Kiwanis. But his Sears catalog horror can be appealing, as it taps everyone from Edgar Allan Poe to Chuck Berry. Moreover, King's fiction fulfills, in its own way, Henry James's dictum that "a good ghost-story be connected at a hundred points with the common objects of life." James might have fastidiously recoiled from King's lumbering prose but he would have understood what he was about.

Michele Slung. The New Republic. February 21,
1981, pp. 38–39

H. P. Lovecraft once called Nathaniel Hawthorne's *The House of the Seven Gables* "New England's greatest contribution to weird literature." *Pace* Hawthorne scholars, there's a new contender, out of Maine, for the title. At least booksellers today would be unanimous in citing Stephen King, author of *Carrie, The Shining, Salem's Lot, The Stand, The Dead Zone,* and now *Firestarter,* best sellers all, as the northeast's preeminent scribe of the spooky.

King has not been taken very seriously, if at all, by the critical establishment. Unfortunately for him, it's all too easy to take cheap shots at his material by lifting bits of it out of context; what is ghastly when the mood has been set can be risible when the lights are up, so to speak.

But King's real stigma—the reason he is not perceived as being in competition with *real* writers—is that he has chosen to write about ghoulies and ghosties, about things that go bump in the night. Rats and vampires, necromancers and mind readers, deadly plagues and telekinetic children: it may sound silly but, as King is well aware, there's a long, as the saying goes, and honorable tradition.

It's a familiar list, these distinguished folk who've been intrigued with what Lovecraft termed "the overtones of strangeness in ordinary things": Dickens, Henry James, Kipling, Walter de la Mare, de Maupassant. And there are many best known for their work in the horror genre alone: J. Sheridan Le Fanu, Bram Stoker, Arthur Machen, Algernon Blackwood, M. R. James. References to these greats are dotted throughout the King oeuvre. It is apparent that he has read widely and appreciatively in science fiction, fantasy, and supernatural literature.

King began by borrowing freely. In his collection of short stories, *Night Shift*, two tales in particular call to mind earlier classics: "Jerusalem's Lot" (which sets the scene for the novel *Salem's Lot*) resembles Lovecraft's "The Case of Charles Dexter Ward" and "Gray Matter" seems to owe a bit too much to Arthur Machen's "The Novel of the White Powder." But overall, King has been moving in the direction of admirable originality; it is no mean trick to make the here-and-now creepy, without recourse to gothic ruins or the Carpathian Mountains.

Firestarter is dedicated to Shirley Jackson and takes its epigraph from Ray Bradbury, another writer whom King often calls to mind, specifically when he elegizes small-town America. *Firestarter* is, as Henry James would say, "an excursion into chaos," much as was *Carrie*, another novel in which a young female mind could upend the fixed laws of nature.

This time, however, the child is a grade-schooler, not a sexually strait-jacketed adolescent: Charlene Roberta McGee, a precocious seven-year-old when the story begins, is on the lam with her father, Andy, running from minions of "the Shop."

Flashbacks reveal that Andy and Vicky, the woman who became his wife, had volunteered as guinea pigs in a drug-testing experiment back when they were seniors in college. Their encounter with "di-lysergic triune acid"— administered by a faculty member, yet secretly controlled by the Shop—is an episode of unsettling gruesomeness that doesn't really end when the effects ostensibly have worn off. Not only do Andy and Vicky find themselves afflicted with low-grade psychic powers, but their genes are somehow affected as well. They realize the extent of the problem when the infant Charlene shows herself to be capable, if annoyed, of sizzling up the hairs on her teddy bear.

The bulk of *Firestarter*'s scenario is King's characteristic long-windedness; the rest is pursuit-and-flight and the anticipation of those moments when Charlie shows herself to be "capable of manufacturing hell, or a reasonable facsimile." Yet the whole is greater than the sum of the parts, and once again King has given the supernatural epic a good name, for those not afraid to meet it on its own terms. Though an inelegant writer King impresses, finally, by virtue of his enthusiasm and self-confidence, his faith in his own imaginative powers. I defend Stephen King as a science fiction writer now because I have a good excuse: *The Dead Zone*.

Technology doesn't enter into this tale. The occult does, however, for Johnny's talent *is* occult. It is of the light, though, not the dark; and he uses it to fight for the good. And here is the key to King's choice of themes. He writes of good versus evil, putting a usually shaded white up against the blackest black. He uses the occult, I suspect, solely because it lends itself to tales of horror, and perhaps because it makes good and evil seem more akin. Yet he treats it as rationally as he can, given its nature. It is a source of power, but one with limits that restrict his heroes. And, at least in *The Dead Zone,* it is not quite the sort of occult beloved of the masses. On that silliness King heaps scorn. Johnny's mother goes all out for flying saucers, interstellar and subpolar True Christians, and all the other goodies in the cosmic fruitcake. An occult-oriented tabloid seeks Johnny as a "house psychic" and gets the bum's rush. Fans are avoided like the ten plagues of Israel.

Does Steve King write science fiction? It's a fair question, for to most people he is a horror writer, a fantasist. But his premises that the occult (especially ESP) is real and evil can be personified are hardly foreign to our field. And he is as much a rationalist, free-will advocate, and moral reactionary ("absolutist," as opposed to "relativist"; he does not believe that society makes evil, even though he does use background to flesh out his evil characters) as that demigod of science fiction, Robert A. Heinlein.

King's works have their fantasy components, sometimes more strongly than others, but at least his latest are indeed science fiction. *The Stand* and *The Dead Zone* are both examples. And they are both ripping good stories. For all their length, I enjoyed both tremendously.

Tom Easton. Analog Science Fiction/Science Fact.
March 30, 1981, pp. 164–65

Stephen King's *Danse Macabre* is the horror writer's homage to his genre. Part autobiography, part analysis, the book connects King's own practice to the horror novels and films of the past thirty years. What links all of these, or King's selection from them, is a cathartic relief, close to laughter, as we face down our fears; this is true even at the extremes of H. P. Lovecraft, Carpenter's *Halloween,* Hooper's *Texas Chainsaw Massacre,* where laughter is, quite consciously, part of the horror. In the era of Treblinka, Manson's "Helter Skelter," the "White Night" at Jonestown, horror and science fiction movies build psychic bulwarks which compress and contain the whole process of alienation, always ending with the comforting news that "The present danger is over."

The unease King generates in *Danse Macabre* stems from a simple stylistic idiosyncrasy. He writes about "disestablishment and disintegration," "the set of reality," our "phobic pressure points" but instantly highlights the pomposity of much of this with slang expressions. There is little consistency of argument or tone. Lee Oswald becomes "a nurd with a fourteen dollar mail-order gun"; Albert Camus and pop star Billy Joel are flung together; both it seems, write (or sing) about Strangers.

King's embarrassment at the whole venture is instructive. As a working practitioner, and a phenomenally successful one, he is clearly ill at ease with the intellectual formulations which attach themselves to his chosen genre.

Horror, almost uniquely, links the graduate seminar with the best-seller lists; Erich Segal's *Love Story* fits no academic curriculum, *Carrie* does and has. King's belief that horror is central to our collective awareness, that it "dances" evilly through our lives, is best served when he avoids an acquired jargon. His gobbets of psychoanalysis and cultural sociology are spread only unevenly on his autobiographical base. It is never clear how well King understands his borrowed methodologies. His awareness of its artistic potential is constantly underlined by its irruption into everyday life: JFK's assassination; rock'n roll destruction; Vietnam; most poignantly, an October afternoon in 1957 when a matinee of *Earth vs. the Flying Saucers,* attended by the ten year old King is interrupted to announce the Cold War shock of Sputnik I.

The culture-shocked ten year old is still in there. So too in his books, the confusions of intent and register suggest much about our age and the writer's ambivalent role; what a dream to be paid for disgust and horror, and what an anxiety. Perhaps, as he constantly suggests, Stephen King is quintessentially the child of our times.

Brian Morton. The Times Educational Supplement.
August 21, 1981, p. 18

The movie is *Creepshow* directed by George A. Romero and the script is by Stephen King, whose novels *Carrie* and *The Shining* became stunning films by Brian De Palma and Stanley Kubrick, and whose second novel, *Salem's Lot,* was a CBS miniseries. That's the connection between King and Romero: a studio executive saw Romero's 1977 vampire movie, *Martin,* at a Utah film festival and asked him to direct *Salem's Lot,* a project from which Romero eventually removed himself. . . .

It took King two months to write *Creepshow,* a conscious and affectionate imitation of William M. Gaines's horror comics of the fifties, screamers like *Weird Science* and *Tales from the Crypt,* of which King was an avid reader as a child. Like them, *Creepshow* consists of five short stories interleaved with advertisements for *Grit* newspapers, Joy Buzzers, X-ray glasses, and novelties to "Amuse and Amaze Your Friends."

Wrapped around these five stories is a sixth, situated on Maple Street, in Centerville, U.S.A. A boy named Billy is in his room at night reading a comic book called *Creepshow*. When Billy's cruel father discovers his son's secret vice, he slaps the boy, snatches the comic book, and stuffs it into a garbage can in the street. Lightning flickers as the camera seeks out the book in the can. The cover is blown over, and we see Crayola-colored artwork: a family in a sitting room beneath the title, "Father's Day." Then the lettering vanishes, the splash page becomes a freeze frame, the actors move, and *Creepshow* the comic becomes *Creepshow* the eight million dollar film.

The situations in the stories are classic: an autocratic father returns from the grave after seven years to chasten his errant daughter; a shirttail farmer unearths a meteor that seeds his land and his face with weeds; a janitor and a student are both slaughtered by a ravenous monster inside a cobwebbed crate. . . .

Creepshow isn't like one of those hackabout horror films currently making the rounds. Romero's scenes are mitigated by what Rubinstein calls "violence so stylized that the audience can't forget they're watching a movie."

Ron Hansen. Esquire. January 1982,
pp. 72–73, 76

Creating stories about werewolves, vampires, and things without names are only part of Stephen King's gothic paraphernalia, the more blatant part. Frequently, less substantial creatures of a phantom world—often but not always, things *with* names—weave vaporously in and about his early stories, adhering to the imagination like gothic gossamers. They are the fleshless hands of the dead that reach out toward the reader, what "Apt Pupil" calls hands with "hungry fingers," cold but insubstantial— all the more ominously inhuman because, as "Breathing Method" observes of the terrors of the mind, one can shoot them or stab them but cannot kill them. Various devices may be used to achieve such haunted illusions. Among the most interesting is the introduction of a series of half-suggestions to evoke the image of a famous person, preferably someone young who died suddenly. Almost imperceptible, these semisuggestions are "pressure points" that work on the imagination through what King likes to call "trace memory"—though, unfortunately, not on every reader. In these tenuous matters apparently not all gothic readers are equally susceptible.

An intriguing example occurs in the February section of poetic, calendarlike *Cycle of the Werewolf.* The dark spirit of the famous matinee idol of silent films, the Latin lover Rudolph Valentino (who died suddenly and unexpectedly in 1926 at the age of thirty-two) is evoked by the subliminal technique of using the name Randolph, that sounds much like Rudolph, and the word "Valentines" in adjacent lines—"This year Stella *Randolph,* who runs the Tarker's Mills Set 'n Sew has received twenty *Valentines"*—immediately reinforcing the ghost-suggestion of a "dark lover" with the haunting names of other attractive male movie idols (Paul Newman, Robert Redford, and John Travolta), and by naming the girl who is having erotic Valentine night dreams about these distant lovers, the Hollywoodish "Stella" (Latin for "star"). This tissuey tomfoolery turns ominous enough when, some dozen or so lines later, a "dark [male] shape" blocks out the dreamy moonlight of Stella's window and seems to enter her bedroom through a "film" or "screen" of snow. But Stella soon realizes that the "clearly masculine shape," so "wickedly handsome," has disappeared and indeed was "never there." What takes the place of the Valentine movie illusion is a "beast" (the story's werewolf) with "shaggy fur in a silvery streak," its breath "hot but somehow not unpleasant." Despite the gross illustration that accompanies the incident, the "wolf-rape" is never graphically described in King's poetic prose, but veiled instead in quasi-romantic images that might have derived from John Keats's classic poem, "The Eve of St. Agnes." When the savage sex-wolf leaps into Stella's bedroom, for example, he is hardly more than a "cold vapor" as he softly shakes himself "spraying a sugarpuff of snow in the darkness," as if he were nothing more dangerous than an imaginary reindeer. Gentle romantic breezes from the open window cause one of the silent Valentine cards, all fictitiously sent from inaccessible male movie idols, to "fall and seasaw lazily to the floor in big silent arcs. . . ."

It is impossible to catalog all the astute literary devices that King can dream up to deal with his gothic world divided by the "filmiest of perceptual curtains"—that is, mixtures of comedy and tragedy, autobiography and uncontrolled fantasy, or psychology and demon lore. However, of King's many talents two things may be stated with confidence. Certainly one must acknowledge that his range of literary skills in psychology, character, comedy, gothic symbology, and natural-sounding dialogue is easily one of the most stunning in twentieth-century American fiction. But having acknowledged this, one is compelled to point out that much of his work is entrapped in the absurd confinements, crude vulgarities, and simple-minded exaggerations of late twentieth-century gothic fiction. In a satirical poem called "A Fable for Critics," nineteenth-century Harvard professor James Russell Lowell wittily summarized similar difficulties in the work of Edgar Allan Poe—an evaluation that readily applies to many gothic writers, but most especially to Stephen King: "There comes Poe, with his raven, like Barnaby Rudge, / Three fifths of him genius, and two fifths sheer fudge." In this neat but all-too-brief evaluation, Lowell recognizes that Poe has written some things "quite the best of their kind," but goes on to complain that sometimes the "heart is all squeezed out by the mind." While one cannot complain that mind-squeezing is exactly what fudges King's work, one feels compelled to concur with a perceptive observation by reviewer Annie Gottlieb in that King sometimes "loses credibility" (especially in his longer works) and that a "recurrent flaw" is the "loss of control of, and perhaps interest in, his material after the midpoint" in all too many of his narratives. Such penetrating works as *Salem's Lot,* "Apt Pupil," "The Body," "Night Surf," "Last Rung on the Ladder," and "Reaper's Image" prove that Stephen King has the genius to overcome the too-constrictive limitations and exaggerations of the gothic imagination.

Joseph Reino. *Stephen King: The First Decade,*
"Carrie" to "Pet Sematary" (Boston: Twayne,
1988), pp. 135–39

LE CARRÉ, JOHN [DAVID JOHN MOORE CORNWELL] (1931–   )

John le Carré began his writing career while he was still working at the British Embassy in Bonn, West Germany. His first two novels, *Call for the Dead* and *A Murder of Quality,* were more or less straightforward detective stories, but they did serve to introduce his famous character, George Smiley, who acted more like a detective than a secret agent. His third novel, *The Spy Who Came in from the Cold,* became a best-seller and made him famous as one of the main practitioners of spy fiction, a position he still holds today. *The Spy* brought a new vitality and literary style to the spy novel, winning le Carré the Crime Writers Association Gold Dagger Award in 1963, the Somerset Maugham Award in 1964, and an Edgar from the Mystery Writers of America in 1965.

The popularity of this novel can be partly attributed to the fact that it was so very different, in style and content, from the escapades of James Bond. But its success was also due to the new realism le Carré brought to the spy novel. In *The Spy* and his subsequent stories the Cold War is presented in a gray, menacing light; espionage is depicted as a sordid occupation, and the people involved are of questionable morals.

The Spy is centered around the character of Alec Leamas, a fifty-year-old British intelligence agent, who wishes to retire from active duties. But he is persuaded to take one last assignment before leaving. He pretends to defect to the East and gives false information to the East Germans in order to implicate one of their high-ranking intelligence officials. Leamas soon realizes that the information he has supplied has framed one official while protecting the identity of the real British spy.

Many critics have seen the work of John le Carré as an obvious reaction to the cult of James Bond, but the author himself denies this. It was not so much that he despised Bond, but that Fleming's stories left a "black hole," or a vacuum, that his novels were able to fill.

Le Carré belongs to the second tradition of spy fiction—the realistic approach, first adopted by Erskine Childers, and continuing with the novels of Maugham, Ambler, and Greene. Although le Carré's style and treatment are similar to his predecessors, his material, as critic Julian Symons says, is "firmly rooted in the revelations about Soviet agents that shook Britain in the fifties," a factor which is most obvious in the novels le Carré wrote in the mid-1970s.

Another similarity that le Carré shared with some of his literary predecessors, and which brings further authenticity to his novels, is that now he admits to have worked for the British Secret Service. Far from hindering his writing, this experience has further enhanced his reputation as one of the best authors of this kind of literature.

Like *The Spy, The Looking-Glass War* also explores the intrigues of Intelligence Services. It begins with the death of a courier sent to Finland to collect films taken by a commercial pilot who had, ostensibly, flown off course while over East Germany. Orders are given for planting an agent in this territory where, it is suspected, a new type of rocket site is being set up. Le Carré is at his best describing the plans for this operation, the recruitment of the agent, his training and briefing and the cynical, inhuman professionalism of the executive planners. Here is espionage in a team which lacks all esprit de corps, but which can cold-bloodedly plan the disavowal of an agent once it becomes clear that his slow transmission on single frequencies on an obsolete radio make his capture inevitable.

A Small Town in Germany is set in the British Embassy in Bonn. In this story a British diplomat, Leo Harting, disappears with very sensitive documents which may damage Britain's chances of joining the Common Market. Alan Turner is ordered to investigate his disappearance and discovers that Harting was amassing evidence that could damage and destroy the political structure of West Germany.

In *Tinker, Tailor, Soldier, Spy,* le Carré begins a loosely connected trilogy, in which George Smiley is pitted against the Russian master spy Karla. This story concerns finding the mole, deciding which of four men is the double agent at the center of British Intelligence. In order to do this Smiley goes back through the records of intelligence operations to try to detect a pattern of failures that could be attributed to the machinations of a particular agent.

Smiley's battle against the Russian Karla continues in *The Honourable Schoolboy,* which is set in Hong Kong, where British Intelligence is investigating a prosperous businessman who seems to be working for the Soviets. The central character is Jerry Westerby (although his actions are directed by Smiley), who wants to identify one of Karla's moles, who is working inside Communist China, and capture him for the West.

The trilogy ends with *Smiley's People*—the last confrontation between Smiley and Karla. Smiley decides to force his enemy out into the open so that his only choice is to defect to the West. This operation is conducted unofficially because the British Secret Service, due to political pressure, cannot be involved in an offensive intelligence operation. It becomes instead a personal mission for Smiley and his friends and espionage contacts that he has accumulated over the years.

The three novels which make up the Karla trilogy are very much dominated by le Carré's fascination with the history of British Intelligence in the 1950s, and in particular, the treachery of Kim Philby, which is reflected in his fiction. In each novel Smiley sets out to discover information that will entrap the Soviet masterspy, Karla. But somehow this quest appears irrelevant compared to the information that Smiley discovers on the way; in particular, the uncovering of the mole in the British Secret Service. Every action and thought before and after this discovery, called "the Fall" in the novels, seems to permeate the fictional world presented to us.

Le Carré's fascination with the real-life spies within the British Secret Service reaches beyond his fiction—many of his views and opinions can be found in his introduction to *The Philby Conspiracy* (1968) by Bruce Page, David Leitch and Philip Knightley.

In *The Little Drummer Girl* le Carré turns to the Middle East as the setting for his novel. There is a great deal more action in the story than is usual in a le Carré novel, and there is also a female protagonist, who is recruited by the Israelis to infiltrate a Palestinian terrorist group and set up its leader for assassination. One critic has written that "Without condoning terrorism, the book makes the reasons for it understandable—perhaps the first popular novel to do so."

Le Carré's recent novel, *The Perfect Spy,* describes the life of a British Intelligence officer and how he became a double-agent. This book contains a great deal of biographical material from the author's life, in particular his relationship with his father. As a result, it is highly introspective, and does not contain much activity. What action there is is described in a sequence of flashbacks in the life of Magnus Pym.

Le Carré's latest book, *The Russia House,* concerns a derelict English publisher who becomes the unlikely recipient of some of the hottest defense secrets to come out of the Soviet Union for years.

Donald McCormick and Katy Fletcher. Spy
Fiction: A Connoisseur's Guide (New York: Facts
on File, 1990), pp. 64–66

David John Moore Cornwell, who used the name of John le Carré for his first book, *Call for the Dead* (1961), was a member of the British Foreign Service at the time of its publication. This spy novel was followed by a straightforward and very good detective story, *A Murder of Quality* (1962). Neither book had more than moderate success, but *The Spy Who Came in from the Cold* (1963) found a response almost equal to that roused by the James Bond books, although of a different kind. The Bond stories were enjoyed as pipe dreams, le Carré's for their approach to reality.

It is right, I think, to see two traditions in the spy story as in the crime novel. The first is conservative, supporting authority, making the assertion that agents are fighting to protect something valuable. The second is radical, critical of authority, claiming that agents perpetuate, and even create, false barriers between "us" and "them." Fleming belongs to the first tradition, le Carré to the second. The actual texture of le Carré's writing owes something to Maugham and Green, but his material is most firmly rooted in the revelations about Soviet agents that shook Britain in the fifties. The messages of the unjustly neglected *Call for the Dead,* of the *Spy,* and of le

Carré's later books are that authority is not benevolent but often destroys those who serve it, that espionage and counterespionage work is often fumblingly uncertain in its aims and effects, that "our" men may be personally vicious and "their" men decent human beings—and, most of all, that an agent is generally a weak and not a strong character, powerless once he has been caught in the spy net.

The special qualities of le Carré's books are their sense of place, their sense of doom, their irony. The irony is most powerful in the *Spy,* because there it is most closely associated with the fates of individuals. As layer after layer of deceit is lifted in the story, and the way in which "London" has cynically used its own agent is revealed, the effect is to show the two apparently opposed organizations on one side and helpless human beings like Leamas and Elizabeth on the other. Le Carré shows a strong sense, both here and in *The Looking Glass War* (1965), that spying is a sort of game in which, without wearing comic noses or any kind of disguise, people pretend to be what they are not. The whole apparatus of the trial in the *Spy* is a game, and so of course are the ridiculous, out-of-date operations in the later novel. And the purpose of such party games is betrayal; this is what is required of human beings by the players "sitting round a fire in one of their smart bloody clubs." If none of le Carré's other admirably written novels comes up to the *Spy,* it is because here the story is most bitterly and clearly told, the lesson of human degradation involved in spying most faithfully read.

> Julian Symons. *Mortal Consequences: A History—*
> *From the Detective Story to the Crime Novel* (New
> York: Harper & Row, 1972), pp. 243–44

For le Carré, who sees nothing glamorous in espionage, the spy is not autonomous. The spy is a thing, created in dull security meetings and controlled by a board of drab directors. The double and triple agent becomes the truly absurd hero because, as a puppet, his only choice is to be a comedian, to act out his empty loyalties in order to show contempt for each of them. Le Carré is the best of the espionage lot, probably the best writer in the form after Graham Greene. His conclusions are close to what other serious fiction has been telling us about the world we have to live in, that it is physically shabby and seedy and spiritually sterile, without love, faith, or hope.

> Robert Gillespie. *Salmagundi.* Summer 1970,
> pp. 57–58

During a cold war, when battles are fought by spies instead of soldiers, spy novels, particularly those written in response to the exigencies of everyday political life, seem to flourish. In a world politically split, with neat *Schrecklichkeit,* into Us and Them, the spy novel boomed with hectic inventiveness. However farfetched and implausible, it nonetheless touched a raw nerve.

But as history moved beyond confrontation between the two superpowers to a more diffuse, amorphous, constantly shifting arena of multiple antagonisms and unpredictable alliances, the spy novel itself changed from a hyperbolic reflection of a comprehended world to a rather poignantly anachronistic echo of a world that is gone. As a result, the novels of John le Carré, who is unarguably the most brilliantly imaginative practitioner of the genre today, are "historical" novels even when they are ostensibly set in the present. And because of their historical perspective, they can register a skepticism and moral ambivalence, even outrage, about many aspects of espionage that would have been unthinkable to Ian Fleming and Helen MacInnes, the straight-and-true descendants of St. George. In contrast to the razzle-dazzle adventure tales of those authors, neither of whom harbored the faintest doubts about good and evil or which is which, le Carré's books appear to be enriched with the insight and subtlety of a complex literary sensibility—or, at the least, a muckraking insider's view of Intelligence work as a very dirty game, a brutal contest that leaves no one on either side clean or unbloodied.

As Kingsley Amis has acidly pointed out, this seeming philosophic detachment renders le Carré acceptable and "true" and "realistic" to highbrows who would ordinarily disclaim any interest in a writer of mere thrillers. Yet le Carré's genuine strength is precisely and strictly that of a first-rate spy novelist. To distort his admittedly unconventional view of British Intelligence, seeing in it a symbolic representation of Larger Issues; to draw high-toned moral profundity from the exhausted seediness of Alec Leamas, the spy who came in from the cold, is to misrepresent and distort le Carré's extraordinary achievements as an original and mesmerizing writer working within the strict boundaries of a difficult genre.

It is myopic and unjust to link le Carré with high art: The criteria for judging literary fiction are simply irrelevant to his superb entertainments and can only muddle a reader's pleasure. One takes up le Carré's books not for his style, though he writes with exceptional grace and wit; not for his delineation of personality, though many of his characters are drawn with a lively eye for their singular eccentricities and foibles; and certainly not for his pseudoprofound comments on the moral implications and underlying rot of Intelligence work, which he offers with extreme reticence and veiled, slyly mocking solemnity. Rather, le Carré is a master craftsman of ingeniously plotted suspense, weaving astoundingly intricate fantasies of discovery, stealth, surprise, duplicity, and final exposure. And the good news is that after *The Naïve and Sentimental Lover,* a recent limp venture into "straight" fiction, with *Tinker, Tailor, Soldier, Spy* he is back at the very top of his form.

Pearl K. Bell. The New Leader. June 24, 1974,
pp. 15–16

Le Carré's contribution to the fiction of espionage has its roots in the truth of how a spy system works. If in Ian Fleming's James Bond novels we meet fantasy and embrace it with a willing suspension of disbelief, in books like *The Honourable Schoolboy* we approach a truth, or at least a plausibility that must be accepted even if we would prefer to reject it. The people who run Intelligence totally lack glamor, their service is short of money, they are up against the crassness of politicians. Their men in the field are frightened, make blunders, and grow sick of a trade in which the opposed sides too often seem to interpenetrate and wear the same face. . . .

Since le Carré wants to present espionage as actuality, he must also cling to real places, where real espionage situations are available. Only Hong Kong seems to be left, and that is where the greater part of the action of this novel takes place.

Le Carré is so concerned with planting his story in a wide field of credibility that he spends far more time in mowing the field than in spudding in his shoots. This is a very long book for its subject, and there is scene after scene—usually back in London where the Circus operates—in which the old fictional principle of Occam's Razor (less is more) is relentlessly eschewed. On the other hand, le Carré has learned something about dialogue that is not apparent in the earlier books. His Hong Kong Chinese sound like the real thing, as do his Americans—the Cousins, as the Brits call them—and the horrible Bolshies and Yellow Perils of the Circus (so the specialists are facetiously called) speak like many varieties of Brit. . . .

Does this book have anything to do with literature? In the sense that literature is recognizable through its capacity to evoke more than it says, is based on artful selection, throws up symbols, suggests a theology or metaphysic of which the story itself is a kind of allegory, the answer has to be no.

Le Carré remains ingenious, veridical, documentary rather than imaginative. There is nothing wrong with that, but it is probably better for a novelist's soul? *Soul?* Souls are for the running dogs! Baptist miss missims.

Anthony Burgess. *The New York Times Book Review.* September 25, 1977, pp. 9, 25

The Master of Stasis has returned, driving his dense herd of auxiliary words to the glue factory. John le Carré is back again with the same novel as before.

Le Carré has to be an Olympic-class sprinter but not a distance runner. In those stretches of *Smiley's People* which are the nub and reason for his story, he is brilliant. He is a gifted short-form writer who has decided that the longer form could be more rewarding. *Smiley's People* seems to me to have been meant to begin at what is now chapter 11. Before that we have the same embarrassing fill as in the first ninety-odd pages of *The Honourable Schoolboy*—the short-form writer, worried that his novel won't be long enough for the marketplace.

Le Carré's stories are not what they seem to be about. They are about a world inhabited entirely by registered masochists. Le Carré, never a barrel of laughs, gives us George Smiley, a barrel of pain. His antagonists suffer just as much as his associates suffer, all of them gladly. That is undoubtedly what makes le Carré's novels so popular with his readers, to whom the pleasure of universal pain is as a hobby.

It is possible that le Carré's novels are memorable because they are so repetitious. No writer of popular fiction today rings the changes on what seems to be every sentence in his set pieces in the way le Carré does.

But when le Carré is not concerned with repetitions and obfuscations and his desperate requirement to overwrite, he is one helluva writer. It may be that readers bow their heads and take the punishment of le Carré's brutal fillers just to get past the set pieces and into the haunted places where his novels leave their sweaty footprints across the memory and where he has so few peers writing in his genre today.

Smiley's People is a direct sequel to *Tinker, Tailor, Soldier, Spy,* a novel which had all the faults of this one and which also was filled with haunting, helpless, useless pain—which said, in essence, "I am you and you are me, and what have we done to each other." It was the *ultimate* spy story.

Smiley's People is the subtle, wearily sophisticated story of revenge, pure revenge, eternal revenge, the sweetest and most terrible of macho motions. Le Carré takes an eternity of backing and filling and faking and padding to get to it, but when he does *Smiley's People* fulfills itself as a stark and moving novel.

Richard Condon. New York Magazine. December
24, 1979, p. 66

Mr. le Carré's *The Little Drummer Girl* is certainly the most mature, inventive and powerful book about terrorists-come-to-life this reader has experienced. It transcends the genre by reason of the will and the interests of the author. The story line interests him but does not dominate him. He is interested in writing interestingly about things interesting and not interesting. Terrorism and counterterrorism, intelligence work and espionage are, then, merely the vehicle for a book about love, anomie, cruelty, determination, and love of country. *The Little Drummer Girl* is about spies as *Madame Bovary* is about adultery or *Crime and Punishment* about crime. Mr. le Carré easily establishes that he is not beholden to the form he elects to use. This book will permanently raise him out of the espionage league, narrowly viewed.

Drummer Girl has here and there passages that demand diligent reading. And sometimes Mr. le Carré is drawn, annoyingly, to nondeclarative narrative. Disdain for narrative rigidity is probably closer. There is something of John Fowles in his style, in the liberties he gives himself to wander about as he likes, to dwell at any length that grips him or amuses him, serenely confident as he is that we will be, respectively, gripped and amused— and if not, we should go read other people's books. But he succeeds, almost always, because he is naturally expressive, dominant, and in turn dominating in his use of language. And so the liberties he takes tend to be accepted as a part of his tapestry—even if, looked at discretely, they can be, as I say, annoying and even logically dissonant.

Is there a message in *Drummer Girl?* Yes. A quite earnest one. It is that the intensity with which the Israelis defend what they have got can only be understood if one understands the intensity with which the Palestinians resent what it is that they have lost. The Israelis triumph in the novel, even as they do in life. But Mr. le Carré is careful to even up the moral odds. I have in the past been discomfited by trendy ventures in ideological egalitarianism, such that the reader ends by finding the Communist spy and the Western spy equally weak, equally heroic; and perhaps the ambiguist in Mr. le Carré would overcome him in any exercise in which the alternative was moral polarization. But having acknowledged that this may be in John le Carré a temperamental weakness, reflecting the clutch of ambiguity rather than any ultimate fear of moral fine-tuning, one must go on to acknowledge that he permits the Palestinian point to be made with rare and convincing eloquence.

He is a very powerful writer. His entertainment is of a high order. He gives pleasure in his use of language. And his moral focus is interesting and provocative.

William F. Buckley, Jr. *The New York Times Book
Review*. March 13, 1983, pp. 1, 23

Writing about Le Carré is chancy. Ever since 1962, when *The Spy Who Came In from the Cold* was published, he has been the standard by which other writers of the so-called international thriller are measured. A couple of years ago I got the garland "Le Carré of the Year." The next season it was passed to the succeeding pretender. Le Carré stayed the constant. With his new novel, *The Little Drummer Girl,* he remains ahead of us, dwelling at, exploring, the very end of espionage as the analogy he helped create. . . .

In each new book, le Carré becomes more involved and entangled in espionage as the professional technique it really is. This is the context and lesson of his work as it has developed: ever more detailed means, ever more obscure ends. . . .

This may be the best and most complete novel about espionage technique, about its psychoanalytical application, ever written. It's also the most balanced novel about Jews and Arabs, outrage for outrage and tear for tear, I've read. Still, for all that, there is no touch of le Carré's great characters—no Leamas, no Smiley—in *The Little Drummer Girl.* While there is much to be learned about how to tear apart the psyche of a second-rate actress and remake her into a spy, there remains a vacuum for a central human. Charlie is essentially an innocent bystander, a fellow traveler, and the willing slave of love; she is shrewdly observed but so suggestible as to give us no constant person we can live in. Leamas, *Spy*'s centerpiece, has here developed into Gadi Becker, an Israeli intelligence officer, still middle-aged and scarred but smoother, handsomer, a deliberate seducer. He acts the part of a young Arab with painstaking exactness and utter denial of his own character and emotions, and he becomes more a blur the further we go into this long book. There are interesting secondary characters, but in the center no one alive. Espionage itself, with its self-deluding detail and obsession with manipulation, is the main character of *The Little Drummer Girl*.

It may be said that when espionage no longer delivers new characters, only finer gears, it has ceased to be a creative metaphor. Yet this is a bleak and daring novel for all its hollowness, because of its hollowness, and because it delivers a message with no comfort. *The Little Drummer Girl* is in part a primer on what it means to be a spy. Klaus Fuchs, the "Atomic Spy," once said he could work with, admire, and be a close friend to the people he was betraying because he operated with a "controlled schizophrenia." That schizophrenia is what le Carré and Gadi teach; it is what all spies eventually must learn.

Martin Cruz Smith. *Esquire*. April 1983,
pp. 106–7

George Smiley, a central figure in five of le Carré's ten novels and a significant presence in two of the others, has become to his creator what Sherlock Holmes is to Conan Doyle, Hercule Poirot to Agatha Christie, Lord Peter Wimsey to Dorothy Sayers, and Philip Marlowe to Raymond Chandler. Today, nearly a quarter of a century after Smiley made his entry in *Call for the Dead*, we have become so accustomed to him and to le Carré's idiom that it is easy to overlook how original that début was.

When le Carré published his first book, such distinguished "Golden Age" exponents of the classical detective novel as Agatha Christie and Margery Allingham were still writing, and even though that particular mode was long past its peak, its potential was not completely exhausted. In *Call for the Dead* le Carré makes use of the underlying formula of the classical detective story, but by building on it a realistic novel about espionage in the context of contemporary European politics rather than an intriguing murder case of the traditional type, he revitalizes and transfigures it in such a way that he produces a substantially different kind of fiction.

Le Carré does not describe the adventures of the spy as hero, but the process by which the spy is identified and tracked down as though a criminal. The point of view is not that of the spy but of the spy catcher. . . .

It is almost inevitable that reviewers and journalists should have speculated about the relationship between Smiley and le Carré himself. How much of le Carré has gone into his series character? There are obvious resemblances: in terms of class, both have indeterminate origins; both were educated at public school and Oxford; both are German specialists; both have belonged to British Intelligence. But the question is like asking how much of T. S. Eliot went into J. Alfred Prufrock.

It is in his political stance that Smiley most closely represents le Carré's own position. While admitting to Miriam Gross that he always votes "Socialist—with misgivings," he made it clear that he believes, "reluctantly, that we must combat Communism. Very decisively"; and turning to Smiley he said:

> His engagement against Communism is really an intellectual one. I think he stands where I stand: he feels that to pit yourself against any "ism" is to strike a posture which is itself ideological, and therefore offensive in terms of practical decency. In practice almost any political ideology invites you to set aside your humanitarian instincts.

A number of le Carré's political statements endorse Smiley's commitment to defend the values he upholds by means of his secret work. In his 1976 interview with Melvyn Bragg, le Carré justified the need for intelligence operatives because they are the people who "actually combine thought with deeds" and are therefore "the infantry of our ideology." In 1978 he told Michael Barber that "whether it's age or maturity" he found himself "committed more and more to the looser forms of Western democracy at any price. And I've become more and more disenchanted about the possibility of understanding with the Soviet Union as it's constructed at the moment." Over four years later he defended the activities of intelligence organizations to the *Newsweek* reporters: "It's bad enough to have an inefficient secret service, but to have none at all would be disastrous. . . . The dishonesty of politicians puts a premium on intelligence gathering." The moral problem of how far you can go to preserve a society without destroying the very values you are trying to defend pervades le Carré's fiction.

Peter Lewis. *John le Carré* (New York: Ungar, 1985), pp. 14–24

LE GUIN, URSULA K. (1929–   )

Ursula K. Le Guin grew up in a stimulating environment; her father was an anthropologist and her mother, a writer. She studied at Radcliffe College and Columbia University. During a Fulbright year in France (1953) she married a historian. Le Guin lives with him in Portland, Oregon; they have three children. She is a member of Phi Beta Kappa and Science Fiction Writers of America.

Le Guin's first science fiction novels were *Rocannon's World* (1966), *Planet of Exile* (1966), and *City of Illusions* (1967). They show an interest in anthropology and even in ESP, rather than in technology, which places them in the "New Wave" of science fiction. At the same time, their magical, romantic tone suggests a hint of "Sword and Sorcery."

These novels were followed by Le Guin's most unified work, the Earthsea trilogy, in which basic human problems are discussed in fairy-tale terms, complete with wizards and dragons. In *A Wizard of Earthsea* (1968), which won the *Boston Globe* Horn Book Award for excellence, she stresses the importance of coming to grips with the evil in one's own personality. In *The Tombs of Atuan* (1971), she shows a girl coming to trust a man whom she had seen as an intruder in her feminine world. And in *The Farthest Shore* (1972), which won the National Book Award for Children's Literature, she presents the fact that life is meaningless if one refuses to face the reality of death. But the relation of form to content is not that of the sugar helping the medicine go down: they are the same thing.

Le Guin describes herself at times as a Taoist. This means that she feels that wholeness is reached through a dynamic balance of opposites. This philosophy is expressed most directly in *The Left Hand of Darkness* (1969), which won the Hugo and Nebula awards. In this novel the imaginary planet Gethen is peopled by "androgynes," who have a biologically regulated, almost guilt-free sex life and do not, as yet, wage war. Her aim is to show what it means to be simply human, working one's way through conflicts that are not based on sex roles. It is interesting to see that we are still left with love and faith, disappointment and betrayal, face saving, incest, religion, politics, and the weather.

Many of Le Guin's novels and short stories have won Hugo and Nebula awards. "The Word for World Is Forest" (1972), combines insight into dream states with a scathing satire on American involvement in Vietnam. *The Dispossessed* (1974) shows a physicist from an anarchist moon colony who is obliged to go to the capitalist mother planet in order to be able to continue his research. Finally he returns to his own society in the hopes of leading it back to its original free principles. *The New Atlantis* (1975), in contrast, depicts a repressive, bureaucratic US, which is destroyed by a visionary cataclysm out of Edgar Cayce. Le Guin calls the stories in *The Wind's Twelve Quarters* (1975) "psychomyths."

Some of her most recent publications have been much closer to mainstream literature. *Orsinian Tales* (1976), a collection of stories about an imaginary East European country, is quite realistic. *Very Far Away from Anywhere Else* (1976), a novella for young adults, describes without any fantasy the pressures brought to bear on sensitive young Americans to force them into conformity.

On the whole, Le Guin has shown a preference for science fiction and fantasy over the techniques of the mainstream novel. She has great faith in the creative imagination and wants it to be free; science fiction and fantasy give her the scope for this. Probably it is because she allows so much free play to the imagination that she is able to be concerned with moral issues without appearing moralistic and to discuss politics without being forced into other people's molds. Liberty, in short, is her watchword.

Barbara J. Bucknall. *American Women Writers,*
vol. 1 (New York: Ungar, 1980), pp. 546–47

The Lathe of Heaven is really a very neat performance, accomplishing what science fiction is supposed to do. The time is 2002, the hero a passive man who discovers that his dreams are out of control. George's dreams change reality. Whatever George dreams comes true as he dreams it; moreover, his dreams cover their tracks, changing the past and what people remember as well. Naturally people are reluctant to believe George's story—but George is terrified. His "effective" dreams, as he calls them, began in a small way—a relative killed, a picture changed—but in time he dreams of the alteration of the world and history. The earth's population is decimated; its wars intensified and then halted; an alien planet attacks and all because George dreamed it. An ambitious psychiatrist discovers that under hypnosis George will dream what he is told and so the psychiatrist can play God, advancing both his own career and history as he wishes—except that, as we know from Freud, dreams like to play tricks.

Ursula Le Guin is extremely inventive. She shifts her continuum of the world and its past every few pages, playing expertly on alternative suggestions as to what we may expect from violence, war and overpopulation. She has a nice sense of irony, too: for all his tremendous power, George remains virtually a prisoner; for all the horror of his dreams, the world actually seems to improve. Science fiction is rarely able to offer a sustained view of an interesting alternative to the world we know, and Mrs. Le Guin does not attempt to do so; instead, she provides the brief glimpses, the partial speculations that I have suggested are essential to a story of this kind. Even her moral—that we cannot stand outside the world and direct it but must be content to be part of the whole—is gracefully developed. It is, after all, what the ecologists are still trying to tell us.

Peter S. Prescott. *Newsweek.* November 29, 1971,
p. 106

Though some would argue that Ursula Le Guin's political novel, *The Dispossessed* (1974), is her best work, and others might favor her ecological romance, *The Word for World Is Forest* (1972, 1976), or her young people's fantasy, *A Wizard of Earthsea* (1968), today's critical consensus is still that her best single work is *The Left Hand of Darkness* (1969).

In *The Left Hand of Darkness* Le Guin moves far from our world in time and space, to give us a planet where life has evolved on different lines from our own. This world, which happens to be in a period of high glaciation, has evolved political institutions in two adjoining countries that resemble feudalism on the one hand, and bureaucracy on the other. But the most important difference between this world and our own is that its human inhabitants are different from us in their physical sexuality. All beings on the planet Gethen have both male and female sexual organs. In a periodic cycle like estrus in animals, Gethenians become sexually aroused—but only one set of sexual organs is activated at this time. These people are potentially hermaphroditic. Most of the time they are neuter, but then they may briefly become a man or a woman, and in that time beget a child or conceive one. Thus the same person may experience both fatherhood and motherhood at different times. The major effect of Le Guin's imagining such a fictional world is to force us to examine how sexual stereotyping dominates actual human concepts of personality and influences all human relationships.

Ursula Le Guin has been attacked by radical feminists for not going far enough, for using male protagonists, as she does even in *The Left Hand of Darkness,* and for putting other issues, both political and environmental, ahead of feminism. In fact, it is probably wrong to think of her as a feminist. But I know of no single book likely to raise consciences about sexism more thoroughly and convincingly than this one. And that this is done gently, in a book which manages also to be a fine tale of adventure and a tender story of love and friendship, makes the achievement all the more remarkable. There are few writers in the United States who offer fiction as pleasurable and thoughtful as Ursula Le Guin's. It is time for her to be recognized beyond the special province of fantasy and science fiction or feminism as simply one of our best writers.

Robert Scholes. *The New Republic.* October 30,
1976, pp. 39–40

"An die Musik" and *Orsinian Tales* are acts of imagination that transform the calamity of history that is Central Europe into a celebration of the individual's ability to survive bad times. Le Guin has consistently occupied herself with her own inner life. She has always written fantasy, searching not in the outside world, but in her own creative unconscious, for the subjects of her fiction. The course of her development from the early sixties into the middle seventies has been a series of attempts to develop for herself the means of expressing her own suffering (which, of course, can be ethical and political as well as psychological) and its conquest more precisely and clearly. She would probably agree with Rilke's repeated assertion that we are "only just where we persist in praising." But she also feels the need to blame. The strength of her convictions and her ethical principles demands that. When her fiction blames, however, as *The Word for World is Forest* does, it is less just.

Ultimately, the real subject of *"An die Musik"* and the rest of Le Guin's fiction that explores ethical problems is not a group of ethical questions. These are means, not ends. Her purpose is to ask them, not to answer them. The real subject of *"An die Musik"* is celebration; the tale is a celebration of Gaye's devotion to his art, and beyond that, a celebration of art itself.

That is the meaning of its title. Like many other Le Guin characters, Gaye is an "enemy of the feasible." Le Guin places so many obstacles between him and his music not merely to wrestle with questions about the duty of the artist and the function of art, but to dramatize more vividly Gaye's capacity to endure and survive, and to pursue an ideal without compromising either himself or his goal.

James W. Bittner. *Science-Fiction Studies.*
November, 1978, p. 235

It is not uncommon, as a literary technique, to employ a critical individual who narrates as the action unfolds. Ursula Le Guin takes this device one step further, making of her protagonists participants-observers; in short, she transforms them into anthropologists. Her heroes all seem to have characteristics that separate them from the worlds in which they find themselves: they are either off-worlders whose job may be explicitly that of an ethnographer, such as Rocannon (*Rocannon's World*) or Genly Ai (*The Left Hand of Darkness*), or they are the skeptics and freethinkers in their native society, as in the cases of Selver and Lyubov (*The Word for World Is Forest*) and Shevek (*The Dispossessed*). Because they are outsiders with the outsider's critical viewpoint, they are cast in the mold of anthropologists, with the perspective and unique dilemmas of the discipline. Repeatedly in her fiction we confront individuals who are of society and yet not quite a part of it. The outsider, the alien, the marginal man, adopts a vantage point with rather serious existential and philosophical implications. For Le Guin this marginality becomes a metaphor whose potency is fulfilled in a critical assessment of society.

Le Guin squarely confronts the isolation and loneliness of her protagonists. Themes such as xenophobia, a suspicion and mistrust of all that is different, are developed in all her work, but reach a clear culmination in 1972 in *WWF*. Here there is an explicit presentation of the heroes (Lyubov and Selver) as anthropologists in their roles as outsiders and translators. Consistently her portrayal is pessimistic. Such individuals suffer heartily. Abandoned, misread, and psychologically disoriented, they often sacrifice themselves or are sacrificed for their understanding. Yet often they represent the only hope.

Le Guin has, essentially, two modes for presenting her protagonists as outsiders: either they are true aliens (for example, Rocannon, Lyubov, Genly Ai, and Falk-Ramarren [*City of Illusions*]) or they are natives of a society, yet their perception of social life nevertheless sets them apart (for example, Shevek, Selver, Estraven [*LHD*], Jakob Agat [*Planet of Exile*], and George Orr [*The Lathe of Heaven*]). In either case, their problems, and more importantly their solutions, are of a similar nature. Their apartness precludes their complete membership in, or commitment to, any particular society. Yet their critical viewpoint gives them an insight into the nature of social relations that eludes their fellows.

In the final analysis, however, Le Guin's anthropologists-outsiders have the edge over their fellows. For all their solitariness, their convictions are strengthened by their ordeals. They are no longer mystified by differences. They can grant humanity to others because they cease to glorify or stigmatize that which is not immediately comprehensible. The irony is that in their realization that opposition does not necessarily imply impenetrable boundaries, they erect barriers between themselves and their society. Because they recognize that the task of understanding is not impossible, they contribute to their own isolation. Their perception of balance is an appreciation of differences. And it is here that the paradox ultimately resides; for if there is an aloneness in the chaos of social life, there is even greater solitariness once order is achieved.

> Karen Sinclair. In Joe De Bolt, ed., *Ursula K. Le Guin: Voyager to Inner Lands and to Outer Space* (n.p.: Kennikat, 1979), pp. 50–52, 64–65

The Dispossessed has both implicit and explicit connections with anarchism and utopian tradition. Its very title recalls the English title of Dostoyevsky's controversial satire (*The Possessed*) on Nechayev and his nihilist gangster-ism, a movement related to anarchism through its influence on Bakunin. In its more obvious sense, though, "dispossessed" refers to the freedom from property that is central to anarchism and which is actualized in Odonian society. Indeed, elsewhere Le Guin has indicated her partiality for anarchism as a political ideal, stating that the thematic motivation of *The Dispossessed* was to accomplish for the first time the embodiment of that ideal in a novel. Similarly, the novel's subtitle (*An Ambiguous Utopia*) indicates that it is to be read as a contribution to the utopian tradition, while its structure, which alternates chapters narrating Shevek's experiences on Urras with episodes from his life on Anarres, conveys the dialectic of old world and new world that is central to utopian satire and vision.

> John P. Brennan and Michael C. Downs. In Joseph D. Olander and Martin Harry Greenberg, eds., *Ursula K. Le Guin* (New York: Taplinger, 1979), p. 117

In the nine novels and numerous short works which Ursula K. Le Guin has written between 1962 and 1976, the exploration of imaginary worlds has provided a framework for an exploration of the varieties of physical life, social organizations, and personal development open to human beings. At the same time, this richness and variety suggest the ethical concept underlying her work: a celebration of life itself, through a joyful acceptance of its patterns. This concept is expressed not only in the works themselves, but in her vision of the artistic process which brought them forth. In general, her characters are engaged in a quest, both a physical journey to an unknown goal which proves to be their home, and an inward search for knowledge of the one true act they must perform. The development of the plot, then, takes on a deeper significance than is usual in science fiction, with its emphasis on action for the sake of entertainment. The Le Guin character often initiates actions which have personal and social consequences. More important than the pattern of plot, however, is each character's movement to an understanding of this pattern: to an acceptance both of the integrity of each individual life, and of the place of each individual within the overall pattern of life.

Le Guin's weakness is a paradoxical tendency to impose moral and ethical patterns on her work, so that form and content work against her philosophy. This didacticism is most evident in *The Word for World Is Forest* (1972), *The Ones Who Walk Away from Omelas* (1972), and passages of *The Dispossessed.* The author's statement of values precludes their discovery, in contrast to the process, most notable in the Earthsea books, whereby the reader shares naturally in the characters' growing awareness of the right direction of their lives. Such a tendency is inevitable, however, given Le Guin's serious concern with human experience and conduct. It is this concern, usually embodied convincingly in individuals' actions and perceptions, which has made her one of the most notable writers to choose science fiction as a framework for discovery.

Ursula Le Guin's work, then, is mature art: rich and varied in content, skillful in presentation, joyous in its celebration of life, and, above all, thoughtful in approach, rooted in and developing a significant personal philosophy. The maturity is literal as well as literary.

Susan Wood. In Thomas D. Clareson, ed., *Voices for the Future: Essays on Major Science Fiction Writers* (Bowling Green, Ohio: Popular Press, 1979), pp. 154–56

Surely one sign of the serious artist is the willingness to subordinate the part to the whole. Somehow, through her faithfulness to the controlling conception of the work, the artist hopes to create a whole that transcends the sum of its parts. I think Le Guin has done this in *The Left Hand of Darkness,* but that is not all of her accomplishment. The artist's desire for coherence can lead to dogmatism; in this case, unity can easily become sterility. Freud observed that life resists order, that perfect order is synonymous with death. This observation is germane to *Left Hand,* not only because the dualism it implies is thematically relevant to Le Guin's holistic vision but because the book offers us both the satisfaction of artistic unity and the richness of a complex diversity. For almost every statement she gives us, Le Guin supplies a counterstatement. No truth is allowed to stand as the entire truth; every insight is presented as partial, subject to revision and another perspective.

Such subtle but pervasive insistence that every truth is a partial truth is, of course, wholly consistent with Le Guin's controlling vision for this book, since if she allowed any truth to stand as *the* truth, the sense that wholeness emerges from a tension between dualities would be lost. The delicate balance of conflicting possibilities that Le Guin posits means, for one thing, that the book is rarely in danger of becoming dogma. It also means that, for a complete expression of Le Guin's holistic vision, nothing less than the entire structure of the book will suffice. The final whole that emerges is the book itself. And this kind of unity, which encompasses within itself all manner of diversity, makes *The Left Hand of Darkness* itself an example of the creative fecundity that is possible when differences are not suppressed but used to create a new whole. For all these reasons, *The Left Hand of Darkness* is one of Le Guin's finest books, and an enduring literary achievement.

N. B. Hayles. In Joseph D. Olander and Martin Harry Greenberg, eds., *Ursula K. Le Guin* (New York; Taplinger, 1979), pp. 113–15

The importance of Ursula Le Guin's contribution to science fiction lies in her ability to use a distinctly Western art form to communicate the essence that is Tao. In many of her novels, Tao is the universal base upon which societies and individual characters act. The fact that Tao exists not in rational systems but in life and the imaginative construct of life that we call art makes the critic's task of revealing the methods and materials of Le Guin's imaginative integration a very difficult one. The Taoist mythos permeates the three novels—*City of Illusions, The Left Hand of Darkness,* and *The Dispossessed*—which I think best communicate it.

Le Guin is a deliberate, conscientious writer who not only creates fully developed cultures in each of her novels, but who has woven them together into an entire cosmogony, giving, in the course of all her novels and stories, a history of the spread of civilization from Hain-Davenant to the Ekumen of eighty worlds, of which Terra is a part. She weaves social and political commentary into her cultural presentation, as in the conflicts between Karhide and Orgoreyn in *The Left Hand of Darkness,* or Anarres and Urras in *The Dispossessed,* always set within the larger scale of humanity as an integral part of the balance of the cosmos. Finally, her style mirrors the balance of her themes. Her writing moves gently but inexorably. To use another analogy from Lao Tzu, it is like a deep pool of water, seemingly inactive, but actually teeming with life. She, too, like the Sage, influences by actionless activity. The value of her work lies in the combination of all these elements, and others, into a complete overview of what it means to be human, no matter on what world, in what cultural subdivision, humans find themselves.

Dena C. Bain. *Extrapolation.* Fall 1980, pp. 209, 221

Le Guin is a seeker who uses her imagination. If she returns again and again to fantasy and science fiction, it is not only because these genres are traditionally ones that make use of journeys and marvels. It is also because they offer great scope to the creative mind. Le Guin is convinced, as she explains in her essay, "Why Are Americans Afraid of Dragons?", that we must use imagination, as long as it is disciplined by art, for our minds to be fully alive and well.

She says this in defense of fantasy. But what is true of fantasy is, for her, also true of science fiction. She recognizes that they are different forms and, after her early novels, she has tried not to mix them. But, all the same, she feels that there is a similarity between them.

Le Guin is a romantic, and as a romantic she values love, nature, adventure, marvels, dreams, the imagination, and the unconscious. Like the romantics, she is aware of the dark side of things and is attracted by it, even when she prefers the light. She values the individual and his or her struggle for personal liberation. And she expresses that struggle in a language that, while straightforward, makes use of poetic metaphor. But like the Brontës, she manages to be romantic and realistic at the same time. Her early apprenticeship to the description of people's daily lives, even if those lives were led in a country that cannot be found on any map, taught her skill in handling specific detail. She uses that skill to good effect in her fantasy and science fiction.

However, it is hardly surprising that she did not find a publisher for her first novels. Romantics are not welcome nowadays in mainstream literature. It is in fantasy and science fiction that such an unfashionable attitude can find a home, since these genres offer a great deal of liberty to the writer. Certain conventions have to be observed, but within these conventions there is scope for the widest variety of outlook, approach, and style. Because of her love of personal freedom, Ursula K. Le Guin has chosen the genre that affords the greatest freedom to her mind, for which we can well be grateful.

Barbara J. Bucknall. *Ursula K. Le Guin* (New
York: Ungar, 1981), pp. 153–54

LEIBER, FRITZ (1910–1992)

You will recall from anthologies such brilliant Leiber stories as "Coming Attraction" and "A Bad Day for Sales" bitterly depicting a near-future American society in which present trends of sadism, exploitation, and hypocrisy have reached their nadir of decadence. *The Green Millennium* is a full-scale novel of that society, evoked with Heinleinesque skill at detailed indirect exposition—and of how men rose from that nadir because a technologically unemployed young man happened to adopt a green cat and to glimpse a female satyr. It's a story as imaginative, unexpected, even surrealist as that odd but accurate synopsis indicates; and it's also a thundering action melodrama, as it becomes apparent that the fate of the world hinges incredibly upon the green cat and every force in society, from the under-world to the Federal Bureau of Loyalty, concentrates on its capture. You may read this as an extraordinarily good suspense-thriller, or as the Writing on the Wall of a funhouse, reflecting in distorting mirrors the message that we are weighed in the balance; in either fashion, read it you must.

H. H. Holmes. *New York Herald Tribune.*
November 15, 1953, p. 14

"Adept's Gambit," built around the characters of The Gray Mouser (per-sonifying Harry Fischer) and the seven-foot sword-wielding giant Fafhrd (the romantic incarnation of Fritz Leiber, Jr.), is beyond question not only the first but the best of the entire series Leiber was to write about these characters. From the moment that the spell is cast upon Fafhrd that tempo-rarily changes every woman into a pig the instant he kisses her; on to the Gray Mouser's consultation with the seven-eyed Ningauble, gossiper with the Gods, about what to do about it; through the supernatural sword battle with Anara; to the finale, in which the adept turned to a mouse contempla-tively evaluates its chances of killing a bear cub, the story is a delight to read.

Leiber's sense of pace, rich background detail, taut battle scenes, fine characterization, fascinating supernatural elements, together with his ex-traordinary talent for weaving tasteful humor throughout the entire fabric of his story—a talent unsurpassed by any living fantasy writer today—make this a classic fantasy.

Before the appearance of *Gather, Darkness!* Leiber was regarded as an important writer. That one story placed him among the "big names." Only slightly less successful than *Gather, Darkness!* was *Destiny Times Three* to which "Business of Killing," a short story of the contemplated exploitation of simultaneous worlds, was a prelude. Fundamentally, the novel is a fan-tastic allegory, splendidly readable, with fast-moving action, and thoroughly polished.

Leiber's ideas on sex were presented in such impeccable good taste that there was little reaction to them. The opposite was true of "Coming Attrac-tion," which in every sense epitomized his second big successful period as a science fiction writer. "Coming Attraction" introduces a British visitor to post-atomic-war life in New York City, where it is stylish for women to wear masks (since many of their faces were seared by atomic blasts) and where a warped culture has arisen which Leiber artistically unveils with magnificent indirection and almost psychiatric insight to produce one of the masterpieces of short science fiction.

Leiber's award-winning novel *The Big Time* is a tale of a war fought by changing the past and the future, and it is told in the vernacular of a party girl who is a hostess of The Place, a timeless night club suspended outside the cosmos. The philosophical upshot is the comprehension by man-kind of a higher state of consciousness, and its evolution from time-binding (the unification of events through memory) to possibility binding (making all of what might be part of what is).

The Wanderer is about a lacquered planet which abruptly appears in space alongside the moon, causing earthquakes and tidal disasters on Earth. The story builds with increasing fascination into a highly advanced epic, conceptually in the vanguard of modern science fiction and to that degree gratifying to the seasoned reader sated with predigested pabulum marketable to the masses by virtue of a self-imposed limit on imagination. *The Wanderer* is flawed but far from a failure.

Throughout his writing career the "branches of time" theme has fascinated him. In three of his biggest novels, *Destiny Times Three, The Big Time,* and *The Wanderer,* as well as in many shorter works, he has speculated on what might happen if the reel of life could be rewound and played out again.

Sam Moskowitz. *Seekers of Tomorrow: Masters of Modern Science Fiction* (New York: World, 1966), pp. 283–302

Conjure Wife, by Fritz Leiber, is easily the most frightening and (necessarily) the most thoroughly convincing of all modern horror stories. Its premise is that witchcraft still flourishes, or at any rate survives, an open secret among women, a closed book to men. Under the rational overlay of twentieth-century civilization this sickly growth, uncultivated, unsuspected, still manages to propagate itself:

> I don't do much. Like when my boyfriend was in the army, I did things to keep him from getting shot or hurt, and I've spelled him so that he'll keep away from other women. And I kin annernt with erl for sickness. Honest, I don't do much, ma'am. And it don't always work. And lots of things I can't get that way.
> Some I learned from Ma when I was a kid. And some from Mrs. Neidel— she got spells against bullets from her grandmother who had a family in some European war way back. But most women won't tell you anything. And some spells I kind of figger out myself, and try different ways until they work.

Tansy Saylor, the wife of a promising young sociology professor at an ultraconservative small American college, is, like most women, a witch. She is also an intelligent, modern young woman, and when her husband happens to discover the evidence of her witchcraft (not his own easy advancement, which he ascribes to luck, but certain small packets of dried leaves, earth, metal filings, etc.) he's able to convince her that her faith in magic is compounded of superstition and neurosis. She burns her charms; Norman Saylor's "luck" immediately turns sour. But this is not all—the Balance has been upset.

This witches' warfare . . . was much like trench warfare or a battle between fortified lines—a state of siege. Just as reinforced concrete or armor plating nullified the shells, so countercharms and protective procedures rendered relatively futile the most violent onslaughts. But once the armor and concrete were gone, and the witch who had forsworn witchcraft was out in a kind of no man's land—

For the realistic mind, there could be only one answer. Namely, that the enemy had discovered a weapon more potent than battleships or aircraft, and was planning to ask for a peace that would turn out to be a trap. The only thing would be to strike instantly and hard, before the secret weapon could be brought into play.

Leiber develops this theme with the utmost dexterity, piling up alternate layers of the mundane and outré, until at the story's real climax, the shocker at the end of chapter 14, I am not ashamed to say that I jumped an inch out of my seat. From that point onward the story is anticlimax, but anticlimax so skillfully managed that I am not really certain I touched the slip cover again until after the last page. Leiber has never written anything better—which, perhaps, is all that needed to be said.

Damon Knight. *In Search of Wonder* (Chicago:
Advent, 1967), pp. 40–42

All I ever try to write is a good story with a good measure of strangeness in it. The supreme goddess of the universe is Mystery, and being well entertained is the highest joy.

I write my stories against backgrounds of science, history, and fantasy worlds of swords and sorcery. I write about the intensely strange everyday human mind and the weird and occult—about which I am a skeptic yet which interest me vastly. I always try to be meticulously accurate in handling these backgrounds, to be sure of my facts no matter what fantastic stories I build from them. . . .

I seem to have had four chief bursts of creativity, triggered off by the Second World War, the nuclear bomb, the sputniks, and the war in Vietnam. I'm glad I've been able to react to those dreadful stimuli with laughter as well as fears.

So, as I say, there you have them, the best of my science-fantasy stories. But I hope to write better ones. I'll never stop writing. It's one occupation in which being crazy, even senile, *might* help.

Fritz Leiber. *The Best of Fritz Leiber* (New York:
Doubleday, 1974), pp. 293–301

For more than thirty years. Fritz Leiber has been giving his readers glimpses of Heaven and Hell in his own special time machine/spaceship theater. One might describe it, if the metaphor is not too conventional, as the theater of his imagination. Such a metaphor is more accurate than usual in the case of Leiber, since he often designs his stories according to theatrical conceptions.

The influence of theater upon his work is more than just a simple costuming of his fantasy and science fiction stories in the paraphernalia of the stage, more than just the fact that his characters often perform plays or put on little shows or gather together for poetry and song recitals in the course of their adventures. The ideas, structures, and machinery of the drama, as practiced from the time of the ancient Greeks right up to the present, are such basic elements in his fiction that it is difficult to find a Leiber story or novel that does not, in some way, suggest his ties to the theater.

Leiber's work has been distinguished for his ability to create mood, especially the dark mood of the occult and supernatural, and to tell stories complex in plot and theme at a fast pace. He is perhaps better than any other fantasy-science fiction author at creating good dialogue (although in some science fiction circles, that observation might be classified as faint praise). He has the knack of writing emotionally charged dialogue that is believable and effective, without resorting to the kinds of melodramatic formulae so common to the genre. And he portrays character vividly, whether the character is human or alien. In a literature often accused of male chauvinist leanings, he has consistently etched effective characterizations of women and, in advance of the current women's liberation concerns, shown understanding of, and sympathy for, the role of women in a male-dominated society. In fact, many of Leiber's themes, derived perhaps from his continuing interest in liberal beliefs and causes, are underlain with politically radical ideas, especially when viewed in light of the generally reactionary themes of many of his contemporaries in the field. In addition to his work in fantasy and science fiction, he has made his mark in the related sword-and-sorcery subgenre with his memorable tales of Fafhrd and the Gray Mouser.

The most striking similarity to theater is Leiber's use of dialogue. The men and women who are his players often talk as if on a stage. Conflicts between characters are structured according to dialogue exchanges which are "built" in intensity, according to theatrical custom. Most important of all, it is well-written dialogue.

Robert Thurston. Introduction to The Big Time, by
Fritz Leiber (n.p.: Gregg Press, 1976), pp. v–xi

A Specter Is Haunting Texas resembles Fritz Leiber's very first science fiction novel—*Gather, Darkness!*—in being an intermittently satirical melodrama about revolution. The target of both satire and revolution in *Gather, Darkness!* was organized religion. The target in *A Specter Is Haunting Texas* is Texas—which is to say the American impulse toward gigantism.

The differences that twenty-five years have made are that the satire in *Specter*—while it lasts—is painted in broader strokes than the satire in *Gather, Darkness!* and that the revolution in the newer book is a temporary failure rather than a success. Otherwise, the books are much of a piece.

At its best, *Specter* is not particularly original. It covers ground covered better in the fifties by H. Beam Piper and John J. McGuire. Its greatest strength, in fact, is in conceits and occasional lines. And two-thirds of the way through it falls apart, its satire forgotten in favor of the melodramatic requirement of movement at any cost.

A Specter Is Haunting Texas, like *Gather, Darkness!* before it, is without the same claims to stature, similarly spoiled.

Alexei Panshin and Cory Panshin. *SF in Dimension: A Book of Explorations* (Chicago: Advent, 1976), pp. 11–18

In *The Golden Bough* Sir James Frazer deduced that in essence primitive magic was not like primitive religion, as most observers had assumed, but was instead *similar to science,* in its belief that the universe was subject to "immutable laws, the operation of which can be foreseen and calculated precisely." *The Golden Bough* makes this claim overtly. And it is a relatively short step from saying that magic is *very like* science to saying that it is actually *a form of* science. It is this further step which many science fiction authors have, with varying levels of seriousness, been happy to take.

The real potentials of the "Frazerian" story were exposed as well as anywhere by Fritz Leiber's unduly neglected novel, *Conjure Wife.*

Conjure Wife draws power from its cool and rational tone, its everyday setting, while its central images—the cement dragon, the Prince Rupert drop, the shattering mirror—all carry a physical as well as a magical explanation. The book's penultimate paragraph, indeed, offers a rational explanation (that all the women involved are psychotic) as an alternative to the fantastic one (that they are all witches), while the last words of all are Professor Saylor saying evasively "I don't really know." All this makes *Conjure Wife* fit one rather strict definition of fantasy, that it takes place just as long as one is uncertain about how to explain events. However, it also points out one way in which *Conjure Wife* does *not* fit the normal development of "Frazerian" science fiction, for all its pioneering motifs and explanations.

This is, that most "worlds where magic works" are alternate worlds, parallel worlds, future worlds, far-past worlds. *Conjure Wife* is one of very few to be set in a recognizable present. It gains from this, of course, in realism; but loses inevitably a quality of romance. It has witches, and spells, and even the glimpsed presence of He Who Walks Behind; but there are no centaurs, or werewolves, or mermaids, or basilisks, or any of the other ancient images of fantasy. The only dragon in *Conjure Wife* is a cement one. Yet there is clearly an urge in many writers and readers to resurrect these images and use them again, partly no doubt as a result of "escapism," but at least as much out of a kind of intellectual thrift: ideas compulsively attractive to mankind for so long, it is felt, are too good to throw away. Nevertheless this urge, powerful though it is, is met by an equally powerful current of skepticism. Twentieth-century readers, especially those with some scientific training or inclination, cannot even *pretend* to believe in anything that makes no sense, i.e., anything that has no rationalistic theory to cover it. Frazer and *The Golden Bough* provided a rationale for magic, as exploited by Leiber in *Conjure Wife*.

Tom Shippey. Foundations, nos. 11 and 12.
March 1977, pp. 119–34

Our Lady of Darkness is an absolutely superb book, Leiber's first novel of the supernatural since the incredible *Conjure Wife*.

While the novel is easy to read and follow, almost every page is filled with little subplots and commentaries that shift and slide with ambiguous purpose. The reader who is familiar with Leiber's own background may be convinced the book is only a thinly disguised autobiography embellished with interludes of supernatural horror. And those with a solid grounding in supernatural literature and the histories of its practitioners (especially H. P. Lovecraft) will understand how Leiber is creating a fantastically successful tour de force of the entire genre. The whole performance is a sophisticated sleight-of-hand creation that may seem perilous to "mainstream" readers but is not so esoteric that it cannot be enjoyed simply as a witty, amusing and, finally, terrifying tale of occult forces at work in the modern world.

What is especially remarkable about the book is Leiber's cast of characters, the most engaging ensemble to appear in many years.

None of the characters are introduced merely for the color they add, although all are extremely colorful and manage to even get away with some quite complicated dialogue ("bookish," as it is often called); but rather each has a definite and telling part to play as the web of horror draws tighter and tighter around the threatened Franz. Their characterizations are developed so that when they must do something vital to the plot, their actions are totally believable and in character.

Finally, there is Leiber's writing itself. Already acknowledged as one of the finest stylists in the field, versatile, sophisticated and armed with a perceptive wit that continually astounds and surprises with its offtrail directions, Leiber has here produced some of the best writing in his long and distinguished career.

The novel is quite obviously an homage to the Lovecraft oeuvre—the slow, steady build to a moment of supreme terror—but deliciously cut with worldly wise humor and sprightly sexual innuendo that make it palatable for today's less shockable readers. Along with the important and pervasive elements of pathos and kindness, this gives the book a distinctive taste of its own that should delight readers of every persuasion. Moreover, there are recurring images (the "spider" in the elevator, for example) that personify with exactitude Leiber's unique cross of modern and primeval fears.

Richard Delap. Delap's Fantasy & Science Fiction
Review. April 1977, pp. 4–5

Many of the pieces in *The Worlds of Fritz Leiber* are either overwritten or unimaginatively resolved, if not both together. To Leiber's credit is the fact that none of these stories pretends to be anything more than an entertainment—even though he manages to touch on such weighty subjects as political witch hunting, cold-war politics, the Bomb, father-and-son relationships, bungling bureaucracy, growing old, cats, and (obsessively but chastely, as if afraid to confront a healthy lust in anything but the most decorous or tangential terms) nubile and prenubile young women. Fine. The problem is that too many of these entertainments are so trivial as to be irritating or so facile in their resolutions as to border on clichés. Many would benefit from cutting.

"Catch That Zeppelin!" is fascinating and believable historical speculation, and Leiber's erudition shows to good advantage.

Structurally and stylistically, however, the story is a failure. Leiber resorts to the expedient of making one of his characters a "social historian" who lectures his father, the narrator, about all his most recent findings. And, at the story's end, when the narrator is finally cornered by an enigmatic Jew who has been following him, two puzzling but disgracefully convenient shifts of the temporal continuum return him safely to the present. That, friends— unless your name is Euripides, and maybe even then—is known as a copout.

But the collection's greatest disappointments, because they initially promise so much, are two fairly recent stories, "Waif" and "Night Passage." Each declines so rapidly into cliché that one is amazed to find them under Leiber's byline. And the latter is the worse offender. Set in a Las Vegas casino, "Night Passage" seems at first to promise the phantasmagoric fireworks of the author's award-winning "Gonna Roll the Bones." Instead, it explains away its briefly intriguing "mystery lady" and its sinister casino operators with their diamond-pupiled eyes as aliens engaged in a deadly game right under our unsuspecting noses.

As a partial antidote to the foregoing crankiness, I'd like to end this overview of *The Worlds of Fritz Leiber* on a note of unqualified praise. In the apparently little-known "Endfray of the Ofay," Leiber altogether successfully combines plot, character, speculation, and style, serving up an entertainment that so wackily glosses contemporary world affairs that one's laughter has a nervous edge. Here Leiber's wit, humor, and stylistic gymnastics are perfectly in tune with his subject matter; and the Endfray of the title, while being distinctly himself, reminds me of Harlan Ellison's nonconformist protagonist in " 'Repent, Harlequin!' Said the Ticktockman." This is the one story in *The Worlds of Fritz Leiber* that I believe I could read again with unfeigned eagerness.

Michael Bishop. Delap's Fantasy & Science
Fiction Review. April 1977, pp. 29–31

Here is a mistake from Fritz Leiber, though it warms the heart. *Our Lady of Darkness* is a mistake of displacement. Whatever one reads of Leiber, in whatever genre he presents to us his skill and touch, the implied author (the author visible in the text, all we have a right to know) who speaks to one seems to exhale a kind of shy sacrificial gravitas, however garish or commercial the story he's telling happens to be. It somehow seems *brave* for an adult person like Fritz Leiber to expose himself without condescension or disguise to a readership comprised of people like us—young, claquish, aggressive, intrusive, we tend to demand complicity of our authors, and to punish those who turn a blank face, or (like Silverberg) a mask of anguish. Perhaps anguish comes too close to the foul rag and bone shop to be amenable to claims of complicity. And perhaps Leiber was after all right, in *Our Lady of Darkness,* to avoid telling the tale of anguish and mourning that lies palpably at the heart of its inspiration, and instead to displace that story into a routine tale of externalized haunting, even though injected with elements of a science fiction rationale, a good deal of social realism scarifyingly illuminating about life in California now (and in our future soon enough), and some interesting speculative musing about what the modern world-city may be beginning to do to us.

The implied author of *Our Lady of Darkness* sounds singularly ill-at-ease in his efforts to present to us the story he does as though it were the real story. Thin ice does seem to bring out the jocosity in the best of us. And matters are not made any better when one realizes that the protagonist of the novel, whose name is Franz Westen, patently stands in as a kind of pun, whether or not a lying one, for the author himself. As the novel opens, he has apparently been comfortably reinstated in human society for some months after a three year period of drunkenness that followed the gruesome death of his wife by brain cancer. Franz Westen is all right now, you bet, as he seems to tell us, and as the implied author of the book insists in words that grin. But what reader is going to believe that? It sounds like a classic opening to a novel whose subject lies in the examination of forms of intolerable suffering. After ten pages, the reader is bracing himself for a descent into the Hell indoors, and each time the text protests that Hell is somewhere in the past the reader recognizes a conventional ploy.

Leiber makes some attempt to relate the external haunting that comprises the ostensible subject of the book (and most of its bulk) to an interior story of insecurely managed grief; the connection of wife to Scholar's Mistress to Noseless Whatsit, though made little of, comprises the real line of power and esemplasy in the novel. But what Leiber has done with this line of potency, however, is to reverse its thrust; the dead wife serves to illustrate and add resonance to the tale of a haunting, not the reverse, and it is precisely here that the displacement can be identified as having taken place. Reverse the thrust at this point, and the emotional force, the edgy somberness, the sense of walking on eggshells that permeates the novel begins to come clear, and the discursive yakking about the fatuous de Castries and crew comes to read as a sequence of desperate maneuverings away from the real trauma, the real horror. But one can only reverse the thrust abstractly, like this, after a selective synopsis: the novel itself resists this reversal strenuously and, to our loss, successfully.

So one reads Fritz Leiber—exuding the decency and gravitas he does exude in his texts—as telling a kind of fib, grimacing a little, dragging in Lovecraft Sauce and C. A. Smith and Lord help us Ambrose Bierce to protest too much along beside him, and one wonders what it was, what caused this forgivable treason. Perhaps it was only a marketing decision. Crap about paramental dingbats fits genre expectations; the dark night of the soul, on the other hand, is death on the stalls. And Fritz Leiber has to live. In some ways he's produced a pretty effective tale. But the face of the implied author stares at one from within the text, and I'm afraid I read that face as confessing all, and I thanked it.

John Clute. *Foundation #14*. September 1978, pp.
64–66

The Change War stories reflect Leiber's fascination with the instability of much of modern American life. In Leiber's best fictions he is able to endow this instability, this American capacity for change, with a profound supernaturalism that can turn the most freakish accidents of urban chance into nightmares of paranoic intensity.

The Change War is an exercise in thought that can be carried in many directions, and most other writers would have taken it elsewhere. By choosing as he has, Leiber scorns some easy crowd-pleasing effects in order to test the boundaries of science fiction and gothic horror as they apply to modern life. In this he is foregoing the traditions of both fields and attempting something new, exciting, and quite valuable. Leiber writes in the tradition of the English, French, and German gothic writers of the early nineteenth century who reacted to their revolutionary age by acknowledging the vastness of human ignorance. But Leiber also stands with the early optimistic science fiction writers, with Jules Verne and H. G. Wells, because of his faith in man's innate ability to adapt and equip himself for the future whatever it may hold. In this conjunction of praise and dispraise he follows only one gothic writer of real power, Mary Shelley. He simultaneously challenges the dark fearful past and the uncertain but possibly bright future.

It is no coincidence that Leiber chooses the early twentieth century, instead of any other historical or future era, as the Greenwich Standard Time of the Change War. The twentieth century is like no other for complexity and confusion on a worldwide scale—or within the individual mind. The Change War is a rationalizing metaphor for the inexplicable in modern life, a fantastic model for an even more fantastical universe in which nothing is just exactly as it appears. We are all part of the Change War in our secret fear that our private worlds will come tumbling down around us.

This personal horror is the source of many of Leiber's best fictions. It is at its most intense and provocative when he deals with modern, particularly urban life. This is the fabric of a modern peculiarly urban gothic mode— a transformation of a traditional horror form to the twentieth century cityscape—a transformation that takes its most complete and satisfying shape in the Change War saga.

The Change War stories proved to be particularly apt vehicles for the reworking of old forms. Their basic premise is the theory of change, a theory which Leiber has equipped with a science fictional apparatus as fascinating and telling as Isaac Asimov's Laws of Robotics. The basic theme of these stories is the consequences of change, particularly on the individual. Leiber seems to be telling us that we cannot live in an increasingly complex and manifold world without feeling some ill effects. His Change War stories emphasize the complected nature of modern life by mixing science fiction with gothically conceived descriptive elements (his spiders and snakes, wolves and ghosts) thereby attempting to reconcile technology with the supernatural mind with matter in the modern world.

Robert Thurston in his introduction to *The Big Time* makes a good case for theater as a device and metaphor in Leiber's fictions. With Leiber's theatrical and film background it comes as no surprise that he is adept at setting a stage and bringing players to life. Leiber's stories are in a very real sense psychological dramas, the action taking place in the character's minds. The settings, the science fictional and gothic props, serve the same staging purpose as, say, Yorick's skull—a point of departure for the real meat of the story, an individual's self-discovery.

Leiber's is a fiction of paradoxes if not opposites. Good and evil, ignorance and knowledge, inside and outside, praise and dispraise, past and future: all play their part in Leiber's world. Science fiction and gothic horror, too, are opposites which Leiber has successfully wedded in the Change War saga in order to better probe the scienti-supernaturalism of modern life. Fritz Leiber is one of the first to make this connection between the dark recesses of man's psyche and the swiftly eddying future.

John Silbersack. Introduction to *The Change War*
by Fritz Leiber (n.p.: Gregg Press, 1978),
pp. vii–xvi

Reflecting upon the body of work created by Fritz Leiber during his career, one finds certain themes and concerns that recur. Leiber has said:

> I would say that all of my writing has increased my interest in the problem of the relationship between fantasy and reality. . . . I tend less and less to think of separate worlds of reality and fantasy, but see them as interweaving, constantly, at all points.

From the early stories onward, Leiber's characters have been rather ordinary people who found themselves in unusual or harrowing circumstances. In many of their adventures, Fafhrd and the Gray Mouser have confronted illusions and spells placed in their paths by demons and sorcerers. The first of their published exploits, "Adept's Gambit," features a singularly unpleasant curse that causes any woman they kiss to be transformed into a sow. In a story written decades later, "Under the Thumbs of the Gods," the pair are thwarted in every attempt to seduce women they encounter, but the reason this time is that the women are seeking revenge for all the times Fafhrd and the Gray Mouser have been sexually exploitive. The reality of the women's movement seems to have made an impression on Leiber, and he later said that he supports women's rights and wanted to bring this topic into a sword-and-sorcery tale involving his two heroes.

Reality and fantasy interweave in many of Leiber's stories and novels. The autobiographical elements in *Our Lady of Darkness* included the fact that his own apartment building and rooftop astronomy were its starting points. In this first major work after his wife's death, Leiber wrote of a novelist who was just coming out of a long period of mourning and whose battle against alcoholism reached a crisis point. Just as Franz Westen reached out to people to end his isolation, so did Fritz Leiber reach out by writing an important novel.

Franz Westen grappled with a paramental entity that assumes the place once occupied by his late wife, Daisy. He questioned his own perception of reality throughout the novel, wondering if his eyes were playing tricks when he looked at the creature through his binoculars, and pondering whether he was being paranoid. At the end of the book, Franz and the reader are not really sure where fantasy begins and reality ends.

Individuality is another of Leiber's concerns. Fafhrd and the Gray Mouser strike out for freedom and adventure and hire themselves out to whatever patron has the money to send them on a mercenary assignment. While women seem to conspire to take the heroes' freedom away, the men strive to break out again. Scully maintains freedom of thought and action regardless of his shortcomings in *A Specter Is Haunting Texas,* and he leads a revolution to gain liberty for others. In *Gather, Darkness!* and *The Green Millennium,* repressive governments are in control, while rebellious Leiber heroes fight to overthrow them. The Wild Ones in *The Wanderer* are rebels, too.

The theme of pacifism is found in stories such as "Richmond, Late September, 1849" and the collection *Night of the Wolf.* Satire is used effectively in *The Green Millennium, The Silver Eggheads,* and *A Specter Is Haunting Texas.* Each also includes a rebellious Leiber hero and makes a statement in favor of the individual in society. The writers who try to do their own work when replaced by machines in *The Silver Eggheads,* and Phil Gish, who opposes the Department of Morality and the Bureau of Loyalty in *The Green Millennium,* are people whose lives have been controlled by others and who decide to fight back.

Women and their relationships with men are important in most Leiber works. The Fafhrd and Gray Mouser stories feature a particularly possessive and vindictive mother, whose Snow Women cohorts would rather have their men die than set free. Most of the other women in Leiber fiction appear in a more favorable light, and their relationships with men are vital to the outcome of the stories. Together, men and women mount a good battle against the forces they confront, but apart, they founder.

Tigerishka and Paul in *The Wanderer* do not get along at first, but their mating ends up influencing Tigerishka to heal the Earth's wounds and spare its people from greater losses. Before her relationship with Paul, she was totally uncaring about humans and disdainful of them. At one point, too, the Wanderer appears as a yin/yang symbol—representing the male and female principles of the universe in Chinese cosmology—while at another moment, observers on Earth call it an angry animal face. These images signify the joining of alien and man as Tigerishka and Don make love, the joining and cooperation of male and female which begins the healing process.

Tom Staicar. *Fritz Leiber* (New York: Ungar, 1983, pp. 116–20

LEM, STANISLAW (1921–   )

The uncontested master of science fiction writing in Eastern Europe is Stanislaw Lem, born in Poland in 1921. After completing school, he studied medicine until 1941, but then switched to motor mechanics and electrical engineering. After the war he reverted to medicine, completed his studies, and practiced as a doctor. . . .

One of Lem's most dearly held beliefs is that science fiction must first and foremost come up to a high literary standard—precisely because the vast number of books he has assessed give so often a negative impression in terms of their artistic quality. With such views, it is not surprising that Stanislaw Lem, who had long been an honorary member of the Science Fiction Writers Association in America, was expelled from this body because he had publicly criticized the fact that "this genre in the USA has gone to the dogs through sheer commercial pressure; because he [Lem] demanded that his colleagues should actively resist and not obey Mammon."

In addition, Lem would like to see science fiction literature "take seriously its connection with science, and acknowledge itself, according to the number of tasks allotted to science in today's world, its special responsibility."

Science fiction is for Lem equally poetic fantasy and a preview of an as yet only guessed-at future. "Even if we can present no exact detailed picture of future ages, it is still possible, building on the developmental trends of science and technology, to sketch such a picture in its essentials."

Thus Lem regards science fiction as a method of expressing "in the form of similes" the moral problems of our age.

The realization of these basic principles is at the core of all his publications. To date even the breadth of ground his interests cover—including engineering, medicine, biology, electronics, astronomy, cybernetics—is not easily comprehensible. But Lem remains, essentially, a "moralist, who wishes to hold a mirror to his age, a doubter who poses questions where everything seems clear already; he is a world improver, even though this may not be admitted."

Dieter Wuckel. *The Illustrated History of Science Fiction* (New York: Ungar, 1989), pp. 160–65

Stanislaw Lem is a Polish writer of science fiction in both traditional and original modes. His books sell in the millions, and he is regarded as a giant not only of science fiction but also of Eastern European literature—as well he should be. Lem is both a polymath and a virtuoso storyteller and stylist. Put them together and they add up to genius.

Lem's marriage of imagination and science creates various intricate worlds. Some are just around an indeterminate corner from our everyday one; some are just beyond the horizons of our own space age; some are far distant, parabolic extrapolations of the folklore of the past into a legendary future of statistical dragons and microminiature kingdoms, of psychedelic utopias that mask universal suffering, of autobionic mortals who persecute monotheistic robots—as though the tutelary spirit of Lem's fantasy were a mingling of Jonathan Swift and Norbert Weiner.

He has been steadily producing fiction that follows the arcs and depths of his learning, and a bewildering labyrinth of moods and attitudes. Like his protagonists, loners virtually to a man, his fiction seems at a distance from the daily cares and passions, and conveys the sense of a mind hovering above the boundaries of the human condition: now mordant, now droll, now arcane, now folksy, now skeptical, now haunted, and always paradoxical. Yet his imagination is so powerful and pure that no matter what world he creates, it is immediately convincing because of its concreteness and plentitude, the intimacy and authority with which it is occupied.

If there is any dominant emotional coloring to Lem's vision it is the dark surreal comedy that has flourished in this century in Eastern Europe, the principal charnel house and social laboratory of the modern age. (Indeed, Eastern European history seems like a scenario for science fiction in which a peaceable pastoral planet with centers of high culture is repeatedly invaded by lethal, authoritarian robots.) What gives Lem's writing its regional signature is its easy way with the grotesque—as in the corpse with a rose behind his ear, the stone-faced bureaucratic chief with a winklike tic, the community that is inanely proud of the cement factory that is destroying their environment and lungs, and so on throughout the postwar literature and films of Poland, Hungary, and Czechoslovakia.

Theodore Solotaroff. *The New York Times Book Review*. August 29, 1976, pp. 18–19

Mortal Engines shows Lem mainly in a jovial mood, as a light-hearted would-be La Fontaine of the cybernetic age. There are several stories which insist on the shiftiness, vengefulness, and general nastiness of human beings, who thus take on the mean, imperialist role which used to be assigned to Martians and Venusians and the like in fifties science fiction. This is a worthy enough revision, but it has become a standard gesture in recent science fiction, and good science fiction, in any case, has always known it was *us* and not *them* who caused trouble, indeed has always known that *they* could not be anything other than versions of ourselves, mirrors of our favorite fears and wishes.

Lem's special field, the theme which brings out his most vivid writing, is the puzzled relation between men and robots. And even here *vivid* is perhaps not the word. It is impossible to judge the texture of prose in translation, and Polish is no doubt fiercely difficult to render in English, but even apart from the tiresome and insistent whimsy, there does seem to be a jerkiness in Lem's writing, an unsteadiness of focus or of inspiration, which is probably more a quality of mind than an accident of style, or the casualty of travel between languages. Fine touches are constantly dissipated by a manner which simply marks time and misses chances.

Nevertheless, Lem has interesting things to say about men and robots. In "The Hunt," a man out to catch a robot gone berserk begins to feel a kinship with it, because he can guess its movements, and because for a moment he pretends to be its ally rather than its pursuer. He destroys the robot and accomplishes his mission, but is haunted by the sense that he has done away with a creature who was more his fellow than most of his fellow men—than the people who shot at him by mistake, for example, and against whom the robot actually defended him.

What is attractive in Lem is his view of humanity not as a matter of organic life or biological development, but as a matter of freedom—even if it is a freedom we may not in fact be able to exercise. We are brethren whenever there are even flickers of freedom, and the political implications of this view, in the work of a writer who lives in Poland, are clear. Lem seems to feel that reality is a system of betrayals, and in an interesting displacement of his concern from politics to metaphysics, it is the universe, not the world, which comes under attack: "this state of things that merits only derision and regret, called the Universe."

Michael Wood. The New York Review of Books.
May 12, 1977, pp. 36–37

Throughout his accounts of his adventures, the disparities between what the central character of *The Star Diaries* Ijon Tichy is, what he says he is, what he says the universe is, and what we know it to be, provide scintillating humor and entertainment, while at the same time subtly hinting at how time- and space-bound we all are in our imaginations.

The other half of Lem's oeuvre is quite unlike these works. It appeals to lovers of science fiction and, because of its superior quality, has won a large following. The most admired, *Solaris* (1961), explores in an artful way the difficulties—and ultimately the impossibility—of man's establishing communication with a "sentient ocean," a one-celled organism that is found to cover the entire surface of a distant planet, about the size of the earth, to a depth of several miles. This is quite an impressive and original novel, one which may serve as the epitome of the science fiction genre for some time.

The Star Diaries belongs to that half of Lem's work devoted to humor, satire, and parody, most of which is directed at the pettiness and vanity concealed within the motives behind human endeavors of all magnitudes. These works are all rich in hyperbole, fantasy, humor, and wordplay.

Tom J. Lewis. World Literature Today. Summer
1977, p. 465

I find Stanislaw Lem a master of utterly terminal pessimism, appalled by all that an insane humanity may yet survive to do.

We are pollution.

He wants us to feel no pity for Homo sapiens, and so excludes appealing women and children from his tales. The adult males he shows us are variously bald, arthritic, sharp-kneed, squinting, jowly, rotten-toothed, and so on, and surely ludicrous—save for his space crewmen, who are as expendable as pawns in a chess game. We do not get to know anybody well enough to like him. If he dies, he dies.

Nowhere in the works of Jonathan Swift, even, can I find a more loathsome description of a human being than this one, taken from Lem's "Prince Ferrix and the Princess Crystal," one of a dozen fables for the Cybernetic Age in his *The Cyberiad:* "Its every step was like the overflowing of marshy vats, its face was like a scummy well; from its rotten breath the mirrors all covered over with a blind mist. When it spoke, it was if a pink worm tried to squirm from its maw."

Lem gives me no reason in this or any other story I have read to feel regret when a human being is killed. The one in this particular fable is butchered and stuffed by the robots, and put into a museum.

I do not think Lem would have as many readers as he does . . . if he did not go to such lengths to say, in effect, what bitter nightclub comics often say: "Only kidding, folks." When he predicts that our reason will soon be destroyed by mind-altering chemicals in careless hands (*The Futurological Congress*), . . . or that, when we venture into space, we will become destroyers of all we cannot understand (*The Invincible*) or that our machines will soon be more intelligent and honorable than we are (the theme of tale after tale), he must be kidding, since, as Le Guin says, he is so "zany" all the time. I am moved to suspect now that most of our finest humorists, including Mark Twain, may have been not especially funny people who painstakingly learned their clowning only in order to seem insincere when speaking dismally of the future of mankind.

So we can expect to have many more tremendously amusing writers like Stanislaw Lem. Few will be his peers in poetic exposition, in word play, and imaginative and sophisticated sympathy with machines.

A technical matter to be dealt with here: It is absolutely impossible to write a good story that does not have at least one sane and respectable character in it, someone the reader can trust. Lem gets away with such stories again and again, seemingly but not really, for he himself is never invisible. He himself is that solid character without whose presence we would not read on. . . .

I will guess that he is at his funniest when he has looked so hard and long at hopelessness that he is at last exhausted, and is seized by convulsions of laughter that threaten to tear him to pieces. It was during such a fit that he wrote *The Futurological Congress,* I am sure. And anyone wanting to sample Lem, hoping to like him, should probably start with that book. The hotel sheltering the congress is reduced to gravel by rioters and police, and the surviving futurologists wind up with the hotel staff in a sewer.

Laffs aplenty. Why not?

Kurt Vonnegut. *The Nation.* May 13, 1978, p. 575

In postmodernist literature there is an obsession with the primacy of style and structure over "subject matter": The artist is willfully and ingeniously refined out of existence, as Joyce never was, so that the perfect art would be art in a vacuum—a *perfect* vacuum—not only self-referential but lacking a self to which to refer. Stanislaw Lem, a Polish writer of science fiction, states in the parody-review of a parody-introduction to his own book, *A Perfect Vacuum:* "Literature to date has told us of fictitious characters. We shall go further: we shall depict fictitious *books.* Here is a chance to regain creative liberty, and at the same time to wed two opposing spirits—that of the belletrist and the critic."

An ambitious project, fraught with intriguing perils: To create ghost books obliquely glimpsed in reviews (alas, they are really review essays and sometimes disquietingly lengthy) that are in turn written by ghost reviewers whose shadows fall upon the page, sometimes distracting us from the author's "true" thesis. Joyce did something similar in *Ulysses,* where each chapter is dominated by—is in fact filtered through—a "voice," and the reader is asked to deal with the voice as well as with the narrative that is *evidently* unfolding behind it; but Joyce's great work is so thoroughly grounded in the naturalistic world, in Dublin, that even the most befuddled reader, lost for paragraphs at a time, can nevertheless strike solid earth again and continue with the "story" as if it were there all along.

By contrast, Stanislaw Lem has put together a truly postmodernist (one might almost say post-Borgesian) book, a collection of reviews of sixteen nonexistent books. One of them is, naturally, a review of *A Perfect Vacuum,* in which the somewhat impatient reviewer calls the undertaking a "trick," because the book deals with ungranted wishes—Lem had wanted to write some of these books, in earnest, but dared not, or hadn't the skill, so he writes pseudoreviews that deal with them in miniature.

A most unusual book! But then again, is it really so unusual? Lem refers explicitly to Borges, as indeed he should, but had he not alluded to Borges (and to Calvino as well) we would nevertheless sense his presence, for his shadow falls darkly . . . across nearly every page of *A Perfect Vacuum*. But where Borges's ingenuity is saved from meretriciousness by the master's quick, deft, poetic style and the brevity of his fictions, Stanislaw Lem draws out each of his jokes laboriously, so that the reader, forced to read synopses of fatuous books, wonders (as readers of reviews assurdedly should not) whether it might be easier to read the books themselves. And then Lem's reviewers are not sufficiently cranky, or wrong-headed, or astute, to make us care about their opinions on these nonexistent books.

A second reading convinced me, as the reviewer of *A Perfect Vacuum* hints in *A Perfect Vacuum,* that the book really originated as a series of speculative pieces, perhaps even embryonic novels, that Lem did not feel like writing, for the pièce de résistance of the book (the phrase is Lem's reviewer's) *The New Cosmogony* is quite straightforward, and would have made a competent science fiction novel (though it bears a close kinship to Arthur C. Clarke's *2001*); and the Huxleyan satires, mordaciously amusing, cry out for development. These satires, particularly "Sexplosion," which deals with the Crash of 1998, when the public suddenly rejects the sex-saturated consumer society, and sex itself, and turns to gluttony, are the most successful pieces in *A Perfect Vacuum*. The lengthy parody of Joycean literary criticism will strike an American reader as outdated, and the speculative review-essays, in which "philosophical" propositions of the sort customarily debated in freshman philosophy classes are developed at staggering length, will seem self-indulgent.

But Lem *is* intermittently funny, and while *A Perfect Vacuum* isn't perfect, what is?

Joyce Carol Oates. The New York Times Book
Review. February 11, 1979, pp. 7, 40

Lem has been delighting European readers of science fiction for two decades, and has recently garnered laurels in the U.S. Though *A Perfect Vacuum* is not primarily science fiction, the blurb writer who maintains that Lem "here breaks away from the science fiction mold" is not strictly correct either.

Of the reviews of nonexistent books that make up this volume, most play with Lem's favorite speculative fiction themes: cosmology, cybernetics, probability, and the confusion of subjective and objective realities. Some of the most successful pieces come from this group, such as *Non Serviam,* a "book" detailing experiments conducted on *personoids,* rational entities created by scientists within the mathematical matrix of the computer, and allowed to develop their own culture and cosmology within that universe.

Lem's cosmic irony manifests itself in the theories and faiths these perso-noids formulate to explain their existence, and in the troubled noninterven-tion of the Creator in question, the author-scientist himself.

Lem also toys with purely literary ideas. The best of such pieces, *Gi-gamesh,* beautifully parodies James Joyce and his disciples, presenting an outline of the ultimate Joycean novel, one that goes beyond *Finnegans Wake* to include in its meticulous aesthetic puzzle, created in part by computer, every aspect of all human civilization. While few of the reviews are con-vincing as reviews, and a couple fail altogether—such as *Pericalypsis,* which merely sets forth a scheme for saving culture from itself by punishing any-one who creates or invents—the format allows Lem to discuss at length the concepts that inform his fiction, making the book particularly useful to those already familiar with his work. But even those unfamiliar with Lem should find his speculations drolly fascinating, and his parodies well aimed. The whole is a triumph of whimsical genius.

Stephen W. Potts. *Science Fiction & Fantasy Book Review.* June 1979, p. 60

Only recently discovered in England and America, Lem has for three de-cades written novels, plays, short stories, screenplays, pieces of literary crit-icism, sociological essays, and tomes on the science of cybernetics and the philosophy of chance—works of such significance that in Poland he is re-garded as a leading contemporary philosopher of science. At last count Lem had published some thirty titles in thirty-one languages for a total of eleven million books sold, making him one of the best-selling science fiction writ-ers in the world.

The Cosmic Carnival of Stanislaw Lem and *Memoirs of a Space Trav-eler* should draw many of the as yet uninitiated into the expanding circle of Lem admirers. Although described on its cover as an anthology of a dozen of Lem's "unforgettable stories," *The Cosmic Carnival* in fact contains only seven stories: four cybernetic fairy tales from *The Cyberiad* and *Mortal En-gines;* two voyages of Ijon Tichy, a kind of spaceage Gulliver, from *The Star Diaries;* and one of the *Tales of Pirx the Pilot.* The remaining five selections consist of four excerpts from various novels, *The Invincible, The Futurological Congress, Return from the Stars,* and *Solaris,* and one essay from Lem's collection of reviews of nonexistent books, *A Perfect Vacuum.* As such, *The Cosmic Carnival* is a diversified but fragmentary introduction to the work of a great artist. *Memoirs of a Space Traveler* is somewhat more consistent, containing all the material omitted from the 1976 English edition of *The Star Diaries:* two more of Ijon Tichy's voyages, his five reminis-cences, his encounter with Doctor Diagoras, and his open letter, "Let Us Save the Universe." Several of these pieces have appeared recently in *The New Yorker,* a rare distinction for a science fiction author in any language.

Perhaps the strongest tie between the two books is the sense, recorded by Michael Kandel in his informative notes to *The Cosmic Carnival,* that

Lem is at heart a didactic writer. Lem's authorial judgment hovers over every page, and it is fair to presume that he intends none of his fantasy or farce to be taken too lightly. But Lem is a master satirist in the manner of Swift, and he manages to score his points without treading too heavily on plot or characterization.

For his most obviously moralizing statements he has chosen a moralizing genre, the fairy tale, and updated it for the cybernetic age. The robots Trurl and Klapaucius, slapstick constructors of *The Cyberiad,* are summoned in their "Second Sally," a tale from *The Cosmic Carnival,* to the planet of cruel King Krool to construct a cybernetic beast for him to hunt. If they fail to create a worthy adversary, His Krooulty will reduce them to scrap metal like their predecessors. Trembling and rattling, they ask how many there have been before them. The king replies that he cannot recall how many constructors he has heaved down the scrap well—only that their screams of terror don't last as long as they used to, which means that the remains at the bottom are beginning to mount. In this archetypal fable it is not hard to predict where Lem's and our sympathies will lie. It would spoil the fun to describe how Trurl and Klapaucius try to escape from this predicament; suffice it to say that the ending is a happy one. . . .

In the "Seventh Voyage," a dozing Tichy, having failed to fix the broken hull, is rudely awakened by an insistent and familiar-looking stranger— the spitting image of himself, formed by his ship's passage through a high-gravity time loop. The Doppelgänger merely wants Tichy to help fix the ship, but the sleepy Tichy angrily chases him away. Soon there are dozens of identical timeloop Tichys, and as the ship drifts helplessly through space, all they can do is argue over which two should repair it. Lem's sobering message is all too clear. We have met the enemy, and he is us.

Peter Engel. The New Republic. February 7, 1983,
pp. 37–39

Diversity and ingenuity are the keys to plot and genre in Stanislaw Lem's work. The diversity appears in many areas. Some of Lem's books include sustained plots with conventional, Aristotelian structure, while others are radically anti-Aristotelian, as Lem denies the reader solutions to puzzles and merrily thumbs his nose at conventional notions of structure. Sometimes Lem is an old-fashioned spinner of intriguing tales, at other times a philosopher explaining his positions on meaty intellectual issues concerning man and science. Unlike a Faulkner, Lem is not a storyteller who concentrates on the same core of subject matter. Readers may question how the same man could have written all these different books and begin wondering if he may not have stumbled across a modern-day Proteus.

The reader encounters an elitist's schlemiel charged with revising history, a clone murdering its inventor, corpses that disappear, a Kafkaesque tale of a character lost in the Pentagon, a frightening foe in the form of Black Rain, playful tales about inventor/constructors who live in a Medieval rendition of the future, a famous scientist who grapples with evil, and a man tortured by a drug-induced nightmare. The diversity in plot explains in part why Lem's books appeal to so many different readers. More important, though, the diversity is a constituent element of Lem's genius—his powerful imagination.

Lem's imagination surfaces primarily in the ingenuity of his plots. The mind that conjures such unusual, sometimes bizarre, situations and events is rare. As Lem pursues inventive plots, he employs numerous techniques. The most salient are his surprise endings, his masterful twists in narrative perspective, and his skill with accurate, compelling detail.

Lem's talent with genre is also remarkable. He has experimented with thirty genres and subgenres. He is also master of numerous conventional forms such as the novel, the short story, detective fiction, science fiction, and satire. Far more striking, though, is his work in fashioning new genres and in combining traditional forms. His futuristic fables and his reviews of nonexistent books offer exciting, risky attempts to break through to new structures.

Overall Lem's characterization skill is not on a par with his ability in the areas discussed above, yet he has succeeded with his four character groups in creating noteworthy personages: Tichy, Pirx, Trurl/Klapaucius, and the consciousness types. Lem's cast of outstanding characters is small; nevertheless, the good ones have been lively and have appeared with sufficient frequency in the various books that character cults have begun to develop, with some readers looking for the Tichy books, others for those that involve Pirx.

His achievement with respect to scientific thought raises him to the pinnacle among intellectual artists. In this arena his contribution has involved popularizing contemporary scientific knowledge about physics, astronomy, biology, and probability. Most significantly, though, he makes a genuine contribution through his literary and nonfiction renditions of cybernetic issues.

In sum, Lem's artistic and intellectual contributions have been outstanding. Hence, Gerald Jonas may be correct in singling out Lem as the one science fiction writer capable of winning the Nobel Prize. The chief reason Jonas can risk such a statement is that Lem has the extra-artistic credentials as an intellectual to cause mainstream reviewers and literary historians to forgo their prejudice against science fiction.

Richard E. Ziegfeld. *Stanislaw Lem* (New York: Ungar, 1985), pp. 140–44

In *Microworlds: Writings on Science Fiction and Fantasy,* Stanislaw Lem argues that an age dominated by empiricism and technology needs a fiction conversant with the discoveries and speculations of science. As models he holds up H. G. Wells and Olaf Stapledon, who created new narrative forms to deal with such themes as the nature of intelligence and the fate of the universe. Precisely because he expects so much, he is appalled by the "pulp of materials, destitute of intellectual value and original structure" that he sees masquerading as science fiction today. His attitude is summed up in the title of one essay: "Science Fiction: A Hopeless Case—with Exceptions." The two principal exceptions he cites are the late American writer Philip K. Dick and the Russian brothers Arkadi and Boris Strugatsky. Mr. Lem feels that science fiction suffers most from a lack of honest, informed criticism, capable of discerning the rare good book amid an "ocean of trash." To this rescue operation he brings a wideranging erudition and a savage contempt for artistic compromise.

The New Yorker.
April 22, 1985, p. 143

LEONARD, ELMORE (1925–   )

Elmore Leonard's early books were Westerns, and several of them were made into movies, most notably *Hombre* and *Valdez Is Coming*. When he graduated from Westerns—if "graduated" is the word—several of his non-Westerns also made it to the big screen, including *The Big Bounce* and *Mr. Majestyk*—although, in the case of the former, I'm not quite sure what came first, the chicken or the egg.

I discovered Elmore Leonard in 1975, when I picked up a second printing of his novel *Fifty-Two Pickup,* and what a discovery he was for me. He writes hardboiled, streetwise books as if he were sitting right on the street with a typewriter. I've read many of his novels since then, including some of his Westerns, and I admit that I did not like all of them. When I think of Elmore Leonard, however, three particular novels come to mind, all of which I L-O-V-E-D.

The first is, as I said, the first I read, *Fifty-Two Pickup*. The story centers around Harry Mitchell, a self-made man with a wife, kids . . . and a young mistress. When Mitchell finds out that some films of him and the girl were taken, with her cooperation, it is from her two friends who attempt to blackmail him. Naturally, they expect him to back off and pay up, but that is not Harry Mitchell's style. No, even when the game escalates to murder, Mitchell doesn't fall apart, he "takes" apart. Beautifully written, wonderfully hardboiled, Harry Mitchell, businessman, is as tough as any of the hardboiled private eyes.

Unknown Man No. 89 deals with a professional rather than a tough amateur. Jack Ryan is known as the best process server in Detroit, but in this particular case he is hired simply to find a man, a missing stockholder who turns up dead, tagged in the morgue as "Unknown Man No. 89." The relationship that develops between Ryan and Lee, a young woman on the skids, is a major factor in the book being as enjoyable as it is. Again, the style is hard as you can boil, the pace lively, and the dialogue is straight from the street. Detroit comes alive in the typewriter of Elmore Leonard.

City Primeval, with the subtitle *High Noon in Detroit*, is just that. Raymond Cruz, a police lieutenant, is a modern-day Wyatt Earp, even down to the way he dresses and looks. Clement Mansell is a killer, as he's proved time and time again . . . at least to Lt. Cruz. Legally, however, Cruz hasn't been able to pin anything on Clement, partially due to his lovely female attorney, with whom Cruz ultimately becomes involved. This is a fencing match between Cruz and Clement, and Cruz finally decides to take matters into his own hands.

An authentic police procedural, *City Primeval* is a prime example of Elmore Leonard at his best. Fast, hard, real, the characters and the city leaping off the pages with extraordinary impact, these are elements of all of Elmore Leonard's books. He seems to switch, however, from lighthearted books such as *Swag* and *The Switch* to the cool, hard style of *The Hunted, Fifty-Two Pickup,* and *Unknown Man No. 89*. Whatever the mood, they are all well-written and enjoyable . . . but I like my Leonard hard.

Robert J. Randisi. *The Armchair Detective.*

Fall 1982, p. 416

Elmore Leonard strikes me as being the finest thriller writer alive primarily because he does his best to efface style, and has done this so successfully that few readers know about him at all. Since 1953, Leonard has written a remarkable series of novels, Westerns as well as thrillers, the latest of which is *Split Images*. There are no wisecrack-eloquent detectives or over-wrought similes in Leonard's writing. His characters are often lower-middle-class people who fall into crime because it's an easier way to make money than that tedious nine-to-five. Leonard's favorite plot is the revenge story—someone exploited by criminals commits a bigger, better crime that ruins his or her victimizers. . . .

Leonard resists mannerism instinctively; it's one reason he ditches his heroes from book to book, always inventing new crooks and detectives who weight the balance between good and bad in quirky disproportion. Early on in Leonard's best novels, there's always a disorienting, exhilarating period when you can't tell where your sympathy is supposed to fall; the first few chapters not only offer up the donnée of the thriller plot, but also spend a while picking, choosing, and discarding people—a cop who looks like a pip of a fellow in chapter one gets blown away in chapter three so that a seedy hood flitting around the back alleys of the story can step into the glare of Leonard's admiring prose. The best thing about *Split Images*, in fact, is that initially it looks as if we'll have to work up a fondness for rich, twitchy Robbie Daniels; what a relief it is when Bryan Hurd, as unassuming a gumshoe as you'll find this side of Jim Rockford, comes forward to mull over Daniels's nastiness.

This lovely trick of Leonard's—the ability to keep you in the dark about not only where the story is going, but also who its hero is—adds great force to the violence that rears up regularly; it permits the author to dispatch characters you may have been convinced were central to the drama. In all of this there's a kind of wicked amorality. Thriller writers can be the cruelest of artist-gods, lopping off heads in cynical, mean ways, as if envisioning the colorful scenes they'll make in the movie version. But Leonard is much more skillful, more scarily witty, than that. The violence in his books is quick, quiet, and brutal; it's the kind that can strike you as being true and realistic even though the actions are utterly beyond your experience. Can an artist receive a higher compliment than that?

Ken Tucker. *The Village Voice.* February 23,
1982, p. 41

Leonard's bandwagon had left the station by the time I heard its music, and I've had to do some running to catch up. But better late than never: Leonard is the real thing. He doesn't write "literature," and I'd be astonished if he claimed to; there's nothing in his fiction to suggest that he packs even an ounce of pretentiousness. But like John D. MacDonald, whom he resembles but does not appear to imitate, he raises the hard-boiled suspense novel beyond the limits of genre and into social commentary; he paints an acute, funny, and sometimes very bitter picture of a world that is all too real and recognizable, yet a world that rarely makes an appearance in the kind of fiction that is routinely given serious consideration.

It is a world in which people do business; they don't often do it honestly, but in one form or another business is what they do. This is the great untouched subject in contemporary American fiction: the focus round which American life revolves, yet which American writers resolutely ignore. As a character in *Stick* puts it: "Anyway, what's my goal, the American dream. What else? Put money in some gimmick everybody *has* to have, get rich and retire. No more worries, no more looking over your shoulder." Making a buck: it's a story rooted as deeply as any other in the American tradition, yet when it comes to telling it in fiction, only a handful of suspense writers and an occasional peddler of schlock are willing to take up the challenge. . . . Elmore Leonard has no tolerance for sham or pretense, in the prose he writes or the people he depicts. He's a funny writer—all the best suspense writers are—and an incisive, unsparing one. He does honest work, and reading it is great pleasure.

Jonathan Yardley. *Washington Post Book World.*
February 20, 1983, p. 3

Elmore Leonard's literary excellence is the result of artistic genius coupled with an approach to writing that can be expressed in three main tenets: (1) Get It Right; (2) Let It Happen; (3) Be Natural.

1. GET IT RIGHT: For Leonard this means doing research. Often the purpose of the research is simply to gather specific information: how do the local police investigate a killing? how does a drug dealer launder money? how does a casino surveillance system work? how do you make a bomb? Research of this type enhances the realism of the fiction by insuring authenticity down to the smallest detail and provides him a clear picture in his own mind of his main characters. He will often develop an entire history of a character before beginning to write. His characters then become as lifelike to him as real people. Even if much of this background information is never included in the novel, it nonetheless gives Leonard a vivid feel for his characters.

Leonard is a great listener. He possesses what one critic calls a "Panasonic ear" capable of recording the exact sounds he hears. Leonard doesn't use a tape recorder. When he listens, he isn't listening for specific dialogue but for rhythms of speech and cadences of sound. He has a particular liking for a certain sound. "It's the sound of savvy people, or people who *think* they're savvy and talk that way. To me, they're so much more interesting than educated people. . . . I guess I'm still a kid on the corner of Woodward Avenue listening to my friends, who were all blue-collar kids."

2. LET IT HAPPEN: Once Leonard begins writing his book, he switches to an entirely different approach. Instead of depending on research, he now relies on instinct. To borrow a phrase uttered by several of his characters, Leonard's philosophy of composition can be described as "letting it happen." As intimately as he knows his various characters, he never knows in advance what they'll do. Once he begins a book, he lets them "tell" him what will happen next.

Despite the unplanned method of their composition, Leonard's novels are far from shapeless. Though he begins without a definite plot in mind, Leonard takes great care in the organization of individual scenes, rearranging them to achieve the best pace and rhythm and the most effective balance between action and exposition. If there is too much exposition in one scene, he will break it up by intercutting it with another scene.

Leonard also takes care in shaping individual scenes. Many of his scenes end with a punch line, a zinger that puts a finishing touch on the preceding action or dialogue. He also takes care to get the right perspective for each scene, often rewriting from a different perspective to achieve better effect. As an experienced writer of screenplays, Leonard knows the importance of moving a story scene by scene. Few do it better than he does.

3. BE NATURAL: A corollary to his philosophy of "letting it happen" is "let it happen naturally." Leonard avoids situations that are artificial, contrived, or clichéd. His readers will not get what convention dictates but what develops naturally out of the characters and the situation. In his books personal confrontations between characters don't always result in fisticuffs or gun-

play, as they invariably do in the works of lesser writers who lazily depend on formula. Leonard likes to avoid the expected. He also likes the unexpected when it comes to violence in his books.

His crime novels paint a colorful portrait of an often overlooked segment of American life (perhaps more correctly, American lowlife). His subject isn't life among the rich and famous, or as it is lived behind the well-tended front lawns of suburbia. He's staked out as his territory the shadowy borderline between the cops and the crooks. His characters are usually simple people—jewel thieves and chauffeurs, blackmailers and process servers, con artists and morticians' assistants—who must work for a living. It's just that in his books, many of these individuals pursue occupations that take them outside the law. Out of such characters Leonard has created a series of novels noted for their drama, excitement, humor, thrills, and plain human interest.

David Geherin. *Elmore Leonard* (New York:
Ungar, 1989), pp. 126–35

Book by book (he publishes almost one a year), the tireless and ingenious genre novelist Elmore Leonard is painting an intimate, precise, funny, frightening, and irresistible mural of the American underworld. This mural is peopled with thieves, embezzlers, kidnappers, loan sharks, drug dealers, rapists, and killers, but there is no camp in it and no caricature. Leonard, laughing just loud enough to let us know that he has everything in perspective, slowly reveals his characters as the fools and clowns they are; inevitably, they go too far and are destroyed. This usually happens somewhere near the end of his books, and before it does we hear, see, and even smell these people. We learn where they came from and how they think and communicate—occasionally on a frequency we can barely understand. We learn how, for instance, a man graduates with a master's in business administration from the University of Michigan, teaches accounting, is fired for running a part-time abortion service (10 percent of the fee), embezzles from a chain of dress shops, and, slipping gradually sidewise, ends up seven years after his graduation as a blackmailer and killer. But Leonard never lectures or preaches or points a finger at his figures or at society; evil suborns evil in his books, then self-destructs. At the center of this turbulence are his wondrous heroes, who survive, no matter how badly scarred. The heroes include ex-cons, a California melon grower, a Miami cop, the owner of a Detroit machine-tool company, the wife of an ironworker, an ex-marine and Pompano Beach-motel owner, an ex-Secret Service agent turned Walker Evans-type photographer, and, in his newest book, *Get Shorty,* a reformed loan shark who works his way into the movie business.

Get Shorty is not red-tomato Leonard. Its plot within a plot—the loan shark, Chili Palmer, uses the story we are reading as his first script idea—moves at a surprisingly slow speed, and there is little of the tension that made *Killshot* and *Glitz* almost unbearable. The best thing to do when Leonard falters—he did recently in *Bandits* and *Freaky Deaky,* too—is to reread *Mr. Majestyk,* or *LaBrava,* or *The Hunted,* or even one of the lesser-known Leonards, such as the marvelous *Fifty-Two Pick-Up.* . . .

Get Shorty belongs to that vast vinegary canon known as the Hollywood novel. There is a crafty, movie-wise Roger Corman producer named Harry Zimm, whose reputation rests on pictures called *Slime Creatures* and *Grotesque, Part Two.* There is a sharp, tough, needling female big-studio producer and an equally sharp retired actress, who became famous for her screams in Harry's pictures. Best of all is the portrait Leonard gives us of a seven-million-dollar-a-picture star named Michael Weir. (Leonard's names are perfect. They make the characters they are attached to reverberate in just the right way.) Weir is a fine actor, a De Niro or a William Hurt, but he's spoiled, indecisive, and empty-headed. He is having dinner in a Hollywood restaurant with Harry and Chili Palmer:

> Then Michael had to look at the menu for a while, Harry willing to bet anything he wouldn't order from it. It was an unwritten rule in Hollywood, actors never ordered straight from the menu; they'd think of something they had to have that wasn't on it, or they'd tell exactly how they wanted the entrée prepared, the way their mother back in Queens used to fix it. The seven-million-dollar actor in the jacket a bum wouldn't wear told the headwaiter he felt like an omelet, hesitant about it, almost apologetic. Could he have a cheese omelet with shallots, but with the shallots only slightly browned? The headwaiter said yes, of course. Then could he have some kind of light tomato sauce over it with just a hint of garlic but, please, no oregano? Of course. And fresh peas in the tomato sauce? Harry wanted to tell him, Michael, you can have any fucking thing you want. You want boiled goat? They'll send out for it if they don't have one. Jesus, what you had to go through with actors. The ideal situation would be if you could make movies without them.

Leonard likes little inside jokes. When Chili Palmer first meets the smooth, deadly black dude Bo Catlett, he asks him if he is related to the great swing drummer Sid Catlett. Bo, looking dreamy, says, "Big Sid, huh? No, I'm from another tribe." Chances are that Bo, born around the time of Catlett's death, in 1951, would never have heard of him. Leonard wants us to know that *he* has, though.

Whitney Balliett. The New Yorker.
September 3, 1990, pp. 106–7

A typical Leonard novel, usually categorized a "crime suspense" variant, is noted for its intricate plot, its racy, "with-it" dialogue, and its lean, terse, and fast-moving writing style. Deadpan humor is an active ingredient of his technique, lending color to the prose and evoking the edgy argot of contemporary American speech and brilliantly painting the seedy settings of his backgrounds. Elmore Leonard's knack is in depicting in detail the tastes of no-class characters, conjuring up the feel of cheap glitzy swank in his settings, and packing his stories with secondary characters etched in indelible fashion by his highly individualized prose. A Leonard novel focuses on a main protagonist who is probably a man of murky morality, a bit frayed around the edges, just trying to make his way in a world that is as flawed as he. Morally, this hero, or antihero, has discovered that there is no true simplistic notion of good and evil, that indeed morality is really an ambiguous quality at best. His is a kind of existentialist attitude toward life that is shifting and constantly reinventing itself to surmount life's obstacles.

Although Leonard turned to the urban milieu with *Fifty-Two Pickup* (1974), a story of a man trying to survive blackmail, kidnapping, and murder; followed it with *Swag* (1976), about an auto thief involved in armed robbery; and *Unknown Man No. 89* (1977), about a seedy process server up against a dangerous con man; and then *The Switch* (1978), a kidnap caper that turns sour, it was *City Primeval* that made his name. *Split Images* (1982) followed, about a broken-down cop, a millionaire homicidal maniac, and his sadistic driver. *Cat Chaser* (1982) involves a motel owner, a group of corrupt con artists, and the wife of a rich Dominican exile. *Stick* (1983), starring a character originally in *Swag,* is the story of an ex-con trying desperately to readjust to life outside prison amongst a group of drug dealers and stock manipulators. *LaBrava* (1983) won the Edgar Allan Poe Award of the Mystery Writers of America. In it an ex-Secret Service agent tries to break up an extortion scam aimed at a former child actress. *Glitz* (1985) and *Bandits* (1987) both followed the general lines established in the four previous books.

In these 1980s works, Leonard found his voice after years in the literary wilderness. Although his thematic material and his technique of writing are only loosely concerned with the stern and uncompromising precepts of the conventional detective story format, he is a true follower of the Dashiell Hammett and Raymond Chandler school, the difference being that his protagonist has passed the stage of moral outrage at evil, has made his peace with the world, and has come to a loose constructionist position about other people's virtue. His main concern is staying alive—more observer than doer, but able to act, and act effectively, when it becomes necessary. This attitude strikes a chord in his readers and is the primary reason for Leonard's hard-earned but well-deserved literary success.

Bruce Cassiday. Encyclopedia of American
Literature (New York: Continuum, in preparation)

LESSING, DORIS (1919–   )

The hiatus between *Memoirs* (1974) and *Shikasta* (1979), first in Lessing's science fiction–fantasy series, is the lengthiest pause between major publications in her production since 1950. With the long-awaited appearance of volume one and subsequent rapid-fire publications of *The Marriages between Zones Three, Four, and Five* (1980), *The Sirian Experiments* (1981), *The Making of the Representative for Planet 8* (1982), and *The Sentimental Agents* (1983), Lessing's readers found themselves confronted with a very different kind of fiction indeed, and forced to make an at least partial reassessment of the author. Critics were quick to distinguish "the old" from "the new," now apolitical and nonrealistic Lessing. And more than one reader has expressed the sense of having lost a friend with Lessing's abandonment of earthlings. Far from settling into the comfortable niche of "modern classics," these works are still unrelenting in their insistence that a new, more dynamic, less restrictive view of life must be pursued.

The author now shifts her focus from the entanglements and reflections of single individuals to the universe and its aeon-long evolution, both real and imaginary. She concentrates on an empire called Canopus that benevolently colonizes and administers many planets. The one best suited to inhabitation is called Rohanda or Shikasta—it is earth. All colonized planets are visited by Canopean emissaries, such as Johor and Klorathy, who descend like the mythological gods from Mount Olympus to observe, advise, and meddle. In Lessing's universe, Canopus stands for "good," that is, respect for the laws governing nature and history, whereas the rival empire Puttiora (ruling planet Shammat) is equated with evil, and the Sirian empire wavers between the two.

Many readers' first question is, of course, why this virtuoso of down-to-earth realism should turn to the fantastic at all. Several explanations come to mind. Science fiction eludes compartmentalized definition—it shares common ground with detective stories, fairy tales, scientific and historical documents, as well as many other genres—and thus appears well-suited to an author who progressively disdains the conventional demarcation lines between literary genres, between truth and fiction, the sane and the mad, the objective and the subjective. Further, the novels of the early 1970s attest to the fact that the artistic concept of realism, even in the term's broadest sense, is largely exhausted for Lessing. Its boundaries are too confining, and it is too political to accommodate her increasingly apolitical viewpoint. Like many ex-Communists of her generation, she no longer believes in literature as a consciousness-raising tool. Utopian fiction, in contrast, has two advantages. While on one hand it provides escape from an altogether imperfect reality, it furnishes on the other hand a detached and often impartial perspective for scrutinizing the human condition. Since utopian scenarios—be they called Lilliput, Erewhon, or Zone Three—disclaim any connection to current events in real places, they are freed from the restraints of actual or self-imposed censorship. The writer who describes the distant universe or far-off future is free to say more—a fact well illustrated by the ideas in Orwell's *1984,* which could hardly have flowered under the title "1949" (when the book was published). Lessing, who once said she was "tormented by the inadequacy of the imagination," now too gives her fantasies full rein.

At the same time, she denies that her focus is substantially changed: "I see inner space and outer space as reflections of each other. I don't see them as in opposition." And undeniably, her essential theme of the relationship between the individual and the whole remains constant, even if the whole involved assumes cosmic proportions.

Lessing now examines this question from the viewpoint of an intergalactic traveler and obtains results very different from those of the earlier novels. In *Canopus,* the whole consists of empires and planets evolving through the course of millennia, and assumes uncontested validity as good and right. Collectives (such as earthly political configurations) remain unchanged in their self-defeating and futile status. Individuals, however, are the big losers. They are no longer allowed to question authority—often they don't even know who this authority is, but they know it is to be obeyed. The space novels' continued concern with individual cogs as they fit into the larger pattern reflects once more Lessing's preoccupation with the dogma of communism. And ironically, her current verdict on individuality—requiring it to submit to the master plan at all costs—alludes to the fallacy that has plagued so many Communist collectives. For while communism aspires in theory to guarantee each individual equal rights and privileges, in practice personal rights are often sacrificed to the collective interest. Therefore, while Lessing may have come a very long way from her initial involvement in communism, the magnetism of its ideas—and pitfalls—is as evident in her works as ever.

Mona Knapp. *Doris Lessing* (New York: Ungar,
1984), pp. 130–32

The second of the *Canopus in Argos* series of novels is finer-grained and stronger than *Shikasta* [the first]. *The Marriages Between Zones Three, Four, and Five* may be read for the pure pleasure of reading it, a tale unencumbered by metaphysical machinery. The Canopans and Sirians, the superhuman powers of good and evil of *Shikasta,* stay offstage this time. . . . The powers of good, the Providers, command Al·Ith, ruler of Zone Three, and Ben Ata, ruler of Zone Four, to marry. Both obey the order not happily but unquestioningly. Theirs not to reason why (why not?). Once they meet, however, the two human beings begin to behave very humanly indeed, and what might have been a fable enacted by wooden puppets twitching on the strings of allegory becomes a lively and loveable novel—a novel in the folktale mode, bordering on the mythic.

The theme is one of the major themes of both myth and novel: marriage. Lessing's treatment of it is complex and flexible, passionate and compassionate, with a rising vein of humor uncommon in her work, both welcome and appropriate. Marriage in all modes. Marriage sensual, moral, mental, political. Marriage of two people, an archetypally sensitive lady and an archetypally tough soldier. Marriage of female and male; of masculine and feminine; of intuitional and sensational; of duty and pleasure. Marriage of their two countries, which reflect all these opposites and more, including the oppositions wealth-poverty, peace-war. And then suddenly a marriage with Zone Five is ordered, a second marriage, a tertium quid, startling and inevitable.

It may be worth noting that this series of oppositions does not overlap very far with the old Chinese system of opposites, the Yin and Yang. Her dialectic of marriage takes place almost wholly in terms of Yang. Its process therefore is Hegelian, struggle and resolution, without the option of a maintained balance (the marriage cannot last). This is worth mentioning as illustrative of the extreme Westernness of Lessing's ethic and metaphysic. The *Canopus* books propose a cosmic viewpoint: but it turns out to be so purely European an explanation of human destiny that anyone even slightly familiar with other religious or philosophical systems must find it inadequate, if not presumptuous. Lessing's parochialism is disturbing.

The landscapes and societies of Zones Three, Four, and Five (and, most tantalizingly, Two) are sketched, not detailed. One cannot live in these lands, as one can in Middle Earth. These are the countries of parable, intellectual nations which one can only travel through in a closed car; but the scenery is vastly interesting, and one may wish one could at least stop and get out.

At first the protagonists also appear at a distance, a bit larger than life, all of a piece, heroic. Perhaps the Ben Hur lurking in the name "Ben Ata" is even deliberate (though I wish the Alice trying to lisp her way out of Al•Ith were not so audible). As the two enter upon their difficult marriage, however, and are driven through all the changes of fear, patience, lust, rage, liking, masochism, ecstasy, jealousy, rebellion, dependence, friendship, and the rest, they become smaller, more distant, more complicated. They get older. Their heroism is no longer easy; it has become painful; it has become real. By having the courage to use these great stock characters, the queen and the king, and to take them seriously as people, Lessing has presented a personal drama of general significance, skillfully and without falsification. Her portrait of a marriage is perfectly clear-sighted and admirably inconclusive. Moralist that she is, she makes no judgment here. Character is destiny: her characters make themselves a human destiny, far more impressive than any conceivable pseudo-divine five-year plan for the good of Zones Three to Five. They might even have risen to tragedy, had the author not opened heaven's trap-door to them to prevent that chance.

Though accurate, that last sentence is probably unfair. After all, *The Marriages* aspires to myth, not to tragedy. . . . Perhaps it is only mean-mindedness that makes me distrust Zone One, fearing that it will turn out to be not simply better, but perfectly good, and therefore longing to find something wrong with it. . . .

Indeed the Manichaean-Calvinistic hierarchy, the closed system implied by the structure and the more vatic bits of *Shikasta*, seems here to give way to an open course of relative values—a way, a human way. Or does Lessing not agree with the Chronicler who a way, tells her tale so well? I think she does. . . .

> I tell you that goodness—what we in our ordinary daylight selves call goodness: the ordinary, the decent—these are nothing without the hidden powers that pour forth continually from their shadow sides. . . .

However the tale is not a fearful one, but kindly, careful, cheerful; its teller, knowing the darkness, faces the light.

Ursula K. Le Guin. *The New Republic.* March 29, 1980, pp. 34–35

In her recent series of "space fictions," generically titled *Canopus in Argos: Archives,* Doris Lessing frequently appears to be twitting her admirers, challenging them, with the literary equivalent of a Mona Lisa smile, to put up or get out. She is quite aware of the consternation the series has created and has now taken to addressing readers directly in exasperated, somewhat gnomic prefaces and afterwords, while insuring that the effort involved in putting up becomes ever more arduous. She's enjoying herself. Disdain for the conventional novels she once wrote so masterfully shows up in these extramural remarks, and though it's not likely that science fiction or experimental-novel fans will clasp her to their bosoms, she hardly needs them.

The story so far: Three sets of space invaders have colonial or exploitative interests in our Earth, and have indeed been meddling with us since about the Pliocene Epoch. The Northern Hemisphere has been colonized by representatives from Canopus, a high-minded group of *pukka sahibs* concerned about the planet and about the various breeding and teaching programs they have devised for us.

The Sirians control the Southern Hemisphere in a much more bureaucratic and less responsible manner, tending to refer to the natives as "animals" and to be dispassionate—we would say callous—in their experiments with agriculture, genetics, and social structures. The colonial parallels are obvious. Canopus feels superior to Sirius (Sirians are not *pukka*), and Sirians are envious, resentful and respectful of Canopeans.

Meanwhile, acting against everybody's interests, a crew of "low-grade space pirates" (Lessing's phrase in one of those prefaces) is hard at work pillaging, raping, looting, and carrying on as space pirates will. These villains represent Shammat, and, as you can easily imagine, they've had quite an influence here on Rohanda—or Shikasta, as the Canopeans insist on calling us now that we've fallen from Grace.

Shikasta, the shortened title of the first book, gave us the history of our planet from about the paleolithic period up through World War III (you remember World War III: it turned up in *The Four-Gated City* and in several novels that followed). Much of this is familiar to us from the Bible and related Middle Eastern literature, while more comes from the instructive writings of Erich von Daniken, Charles Berlitz, Charles Forte, and other promoters of alien influence. Through the reports of Canopean agents, we learn of the Fall of Man and the rise of cruelty, bigotry, obscurantism, ignorance, and suffering. Some of this is Shammat's fault, but we've done fairly well on our own.

The third book, *The Sirian Experiments,* takes us through some of the same material but in a more personal way. The events are seen through the eyes of a Sirian agent, a sort of Martha Quest figure who is well meaning but often fed up and at fault, and who comes to share, slowly, some of the Canopeans' concern for us. This book explores colonial attitudes, a long-time Lessing concern, from the point of view of the colonists.

The Making of the Representative for Planet 8, the book more or less under review (less rather than more, for reasons I'll get to), is very short. Thank God in Her mercy for that, for it is so grim, so relentless, so actually painful to read, that 122 pages is more than enough. This time, the point of view is that of the colonized. Planet 8 is the supposedly temporary home to a group of human beings who are being readied by Canopus for removal to Rohanda as genetic seed material, just as soon as conditions are right. But conditions never do become right—instead Rohanda, as we know from the earlier books, goes from bad to worse. Planet 8 freezes, and Canopus permits the colonists to freeze with it, sending an agent, Johor (familiar to us from the first book), to encourage the settlers to hold out against death longer than most of them want to. But they do die, and their souls soar joyfully upward.

That's it. Just the cold, bare bones of a straightforward narrative of suffering, betrayal, and despair—and then that ending. Philosophically, it's a puzzler. For most of the book, I was dead certain that its author was offering an homage, forty years after the publication of *The Myth of Sisyphus,* to Albert Camus's uplifting brand of romantic existentialism, the call to clear thinking and right conduct in the face of an absurd universe with no Paradise or Rohanda in the offing. But then how to explain the hearts and flowers? One expects Steve Martin to break out in a chorus of "Pennies from Heaven" as he is reprieved from the gallows.

Even though I know the details of Lessing's universe, and that she appears to believe in an afterlife, a sort of reincarnation and a journey toward salvation, I find that ending hard to figure out. If the settlers had given up earlier, would they not have been saved? What happened to the ones that did give up? What if their motives were altruistic, as with Captain Oates on Robert Scott's expedition to the South Pole, who walked off into a blizzard so as not to delay his colleagues? Why was Johor hanging around anyway? Just checking out the results of the Canopean experiment on Planet 8—seeing if this stock takes well to being frozen? Beats me. Camus would have despised it. But he would have liked what comes next.

Mona Lessing is not about to explain herself to us, but she is willing to add a twenty-three-page afterword. This turns out to be an essay on the polar expeditions of Scott and Roald Amundsen. Aha, we say. But we are wrong. No, this isn't an afterword to Book Four, *The Making of the Representative for Planet 8,* at all; it is instead a misplaced *fore*word to Book Three, *The Sirian Experiments.* And the author reserves a special sneer for "casual or literal-minded readers" who insist on connecting the suffering and freezing to death of Scott's band with the suffering and freezing to death of Planet 8, rather than with the adventures of Ambien II of Sirius in Atlantis and Aztec America.

Trying not to be casual or literal-minded, I set to work trying to apply this essay (and it is a brilliant essay, out of context) to *The Sirian Experiments.* Some points seemed apt: she compares Amundsen's efficient, practical, colorless (surely Canopean?) approach, which won the Pole but lost the audience, with the lofty, exalted emotionalism that fired the very badly prepared Scott team and made lasting heroes of Captain Oates, the noble but whacko Edward Wilson, with his yen for King Emperor penguin eggs, and the rest of the band of gallant bumblers.

Yes, bumblers. For Lessing wants to remind us that history is constantly revised. World War I ended that era of nineteenth-century romantic endeavor, and to our modern eye, Scott can be considered a damn fool. One moment the Gang of Four are cultural leaders, the next they are disgraced. "The heresies of one year are the pieties of the next," says Doris Lessing.

Well, sure. And Ambien II does go through quite a few shifts of perception and atmosphere in *The Sirian Experiments* (which is not exactly under review here, sorry, but Lessing is causing the difficulty, not me). There is a connection, perhaps, in that both essay and book are really about the nineteenth century, the high point of uncomplicated colonial endeavor, national rivalry and patriotic heroism. The spirit of the times has changed.

But there she is, smiling again. It's pointless to go on with the exercise. Quite a number of people might contend that it's equally pointless to go on with this series, which seems to get odder and harder to read with each book. To that I can only say that, despite recent appearance, Doris Lessing really is a major author. She is one of the very few writers in the world who are writing about the world, who are willing to tackle the Big Subjects: history, politics, the working of the human mind, the way we treat one another. She has been through a lot, and she has taken us through a lot. And perhaps we should indulge her whim.

But next time I hope she writes about Shammat. Pirates are a lot more fun than people freezing to death.

Alice K. Turner. *The Nation.* March 6, 1982,
pp. 278–80

LEWIS, C. S. (1898–1963)

C. S. Lewis was a man with wide interests, a man who wrote with distinction in many fields—literary history, philology, criticism, Christian apologetics, science fiction, myth, poetry, and children's literature. His readers are thus drawn from many walks of life. Some know him only as a literary historian; others only as a Britisher who has delighted them while defending the orthodox faith. Only as a poet has he had a limited audience.

James W. Sire. *Prairie Schooner*. Winter 1966–
67, pp. 364–66

Lewis's society on Mars is peopled by creatures which suggest a good deal about the author's conception of man. The three groups—sorns, or the scientists and intellectuals; hrossa, or the poets, musicians, and fishermen; and pfifltriggi, the craftsmen, miners, and sculptors—suggest elements or parts within man; out of these parts come certain characteristics which are Good. Such a conception of man is a bit arbitrary; it ignores the possibility that man is an indivisible unity, not to mention the insight of psychoanalysis that man's strengths and weaknesses may be one and the same, that the strongest positive characteristics carry with them the strongest negative possibilities. While Lewis makes no moral distinction between the intellectual, the aesthetic, and the physically active, he makes precise distinctions concerning these faculties, with a premium on docility and resignation and an attitude of condescension toward aggression and rebellion.

In *Perelandra*, Lewis casts further light on his view of man. The hero, Ransom, is treated by the author (unconsciously perhaps) as a lovable but rather dumb child. He does the same with the good folk in *That Hideous Strength*—Ransom having attained a certain stature. The evil antagonist, Weston, is often compared to a nasty little boy. His "naughtiness" is epitomized by his cruel teasing and senseless torture of animals. It seems that Lewis regards men from the viewpoint of a nineteenth-century British nursery. Abstract allegory tends here to remove traces of depth or complexity; what is left tends to be devoid of constructive meaning.

There can be no doubt, however, that Lewis, for all his primness and tendency to abstraction, introduces a valuable dimension into the discussion by insisting that there is a *reason* for man's ill nature. But this sad state is hardly cured by the assumption that a perfect world is based upon hierarchical principles. It almost amounts to a medieval concept of "know your place"; or perhaps it's an English gentleman's view of good and bad.

The universe which C. S. Lewis gives us is, with minor adjustments, the formal world of Anglican orthodoxy. Fallen man is in thrall to the forces of evil which keep him from realizing himself. However, Lewis is weak at the point of redemption precisely because his understanding of evil and of man is lacking in dynamism and complexity. He fails to see that *redemption can never be the same thing as unfallen innocence.*

Lois and Stephen Rose. *The Shattered Ring:*
Science Fiction and the Quest for Meaning (n.p.:
John Knox Press, 1970), pp. 63–67

Quite how a novel such as *That Hideous Strength*, or the trilogy of which it forms a part, may be considered "theological," much less an apology for church orthodoxy, is difficult to understand. One may grant that C. S. Lewis's stress upon human frailty and his recasting of the Biblical Genesis in *Perelandra* derive from his deeply felt Christianity. Yet Lewis's concern in *Out of the Silent Planet* and *Perelandra* is neither religious nor theological, but moral. Lewis is interested in the human response to choices of good and evil. The novels are set in a theocentric cosmos because Lewis was a believer, just as Olaf Stapledon's novels are set in a godless universe because he was not. Yet the focus of Lewis is upon the moral challenge posed to Ransom, upon the moral deterioration of Weston, and upon the monumental temptation offered to the Green Lady. The conflict in *Perelandra* would be little less forceful if divinity or demon had never been specifically mentioned.

The third novel of Lewis's trilogy differs markedly from the first two. Lewis himself writes in the preface to *That Hideous Strength* that "it concludes the trilogy . . . but can be read on its own." The great difference between the first two novels and the last is in the shift of scene from the "moral laboratory" of the planets back to the world of everyday experience. Ransom tells Merlin, "The Hideous Strength holds all this Earth in its fist to squeeze as it wishes." *This* earth. One leaves Mars and Venus for a small, sleepy English university town. Thus the trilogy follows an archetypal pattern well established in literature. Just as Shakespeare's characters in *As You Like It, Midsummer Night's Dream,* or *The Tempest,* having become wiser through a visit to a fantasy world, must eventually return to the mundane world from which they have come, Ransom has journeyed to the unfallen worlds of Mars and Venus to achieve a kind of enlightenment, but it is to Earth that he must return, and it is on Earth that his greatest battle must be fought. *That Hideous Strength* puts the moral insights of the first two novels to the test. They must be applicable to a recognizable world. *That Hideous Strength* becomes at once the "proof of the pudding" for Lewis's insights into good and evil, and a coda that unites and expands all the themes developed before.

The shift of setting with the third novel is accompanied by a shift of mode from the romantic, with its allegorical strain, to the ironic, with its satiric one. While in the first two novels, Lewis sought to involve the reader, now he tries to disengage him. As does Jonathan Swift in *Gulliver's Travels,* Lewis inserts a series of grim jokes to prevent our becoming too sympathetically engaged, to keep us at a certain critical distance. For example, the diabolic institute is "N.I.C.E.," the truncated head of a criminal is literally the "head" of that institute, and some of the symbolic names have a comic ring: "Fairy Hardcastle" for a lesbian, or "Mr. Fisher-King" for Elwin Ransom. Lewis wishes his reader to treat the surface of the story with a certain detachment, so that he may perceive overtones which make the fictional plot a means of attacking real social perils.

Although Lewis has as acute a Christian consciousness as had Swift, he, like Swift, refrains from preaching. He renders his morality into the image, symbol, and dramatic situation of art. Satire has often been rendered by its masters as a conflict between two societies, one real and one fictional.

In sum, Lewis accedes to no moral relativism. The garden of St. Anne's, the garden paralleled to a woman's body, suggests a harmonious order of nature, an order in terms of which man must live if he is to be human. Lewis believes, in contradiction to Feverstone and Filostrato, that man does not "make himself," but that his reason is capable of apprehending a rational universe, and thus, that there is a natural moral order. Such a stance places him in opposition to all principles of infinite human progress, to all philosophies of the superman. Lewis would accept Blake's maxim that "in trying to be more than man, we become less."

In such views, Lewis is traditional rather than "modern." Yet more often than not great satirists have been conservative traditionalists, lashing out at excesses of "modern" thought. Lewis shares this role with both Jonathan Swift, who attacks the Enlightenment in *Gulliver's Travels,* and with Samuel Johnson, who attacks it in *Rasselas.*

Patrick J. Callahan. *SF: The Other Side of
Realism—Essays on Modern Fantasy and Science
Fiction* (Bowling Green, Ohio: Popular Press,
1971), pp. 147–56

The fantasy of C. S. Lewis, taken as a whole, begins in autobiography, moves into apologetics, and then returns—but with a difference—to autobiography. The fiction for which he is best known was published between 1938 and 1945, almost precisely in the middle of his career as a writer. These books—*Out of the Silent Planet, Perelandra,* and *That Hideous Strength* (the so-called space trilogy), along with *The Screwtape Letters* and *The Great Divorce*—function in part as implicit apologetic, as a defense of the Christian faith, which takes particular account of the skepticism or hostility of the nonbeliever.

In *The Pilgrim's Regress* C. S. Lewis (like Bunyan before him and like Saint Augustine before both of them) writes as an adult convert to Christianity, examining his past in order to understand for himself and make known to others how he has become what he now is. Just as John Bunyan in his earlier years had fed his imagination on popular tales of knights and giants and dragons, so Lewis's memory is filled with the fantasies of George Macdonald, William Morris, and H. G. Wells.

Lewis says of his way [to conversion]: "It is a road very rarely trodden"; Bunyan's was, in his day at least, a more typical conversion. The times make a difference too. C. S. Lewis is very conscious of writing for an audience which does not share the presuppositions that have become his as a convert. Thus he must bring to life allegorically not only the hindrances and helps in the way, but also the intimations or "inklings" that have drawn him toward belief. For both endeavors he enlists the aid of fantasy.

Because so many of the stumbling blocks are associated, for Lewis, with intellectual concepts or ideologies, and because he feels many of these to be merely unfortunate fads, much of his fantasy carries out a satirical function, occasionally degenerating into invective. At other times it serves to intimate the beauty and desirability of what is ideal or ultimate, often in passages of "heightened" prose which are singularly unsuccessful.

Out of the Silent Planet departs in several respects from Lewis's practice in the more strictly allegorical works. One notices first of all the "popular" form, that of the space voyage, which makes possible once again the twofold reference, through satire and myth, to this world and the other. It is to emphasize the otherworldly reference that Lewis eliminates the dream framework and turns to science fiction. Here we have myth handled as "fact" and the natural metaphors within the myths as cosmic "facts."

C. S. Lewis speaks often of his adherence to "plain, central Christianity" or "mere Christianity." Within this traditional structure of doctrine, however, he concerns himself chiefly not so much with questions concerning Redemption (Atonement, Salvation, Sanctification) as with the relationship of God as Creator to his creation. This is consistent, of course, with his often stated special interest in the *praeparatio evangelica* as distinct from *evangelium* itself. But when we ask what Lewis conceives to be the actual qualities of the relation between Creator and creature, we discover an imbalance. In every confrontation between man and the Eternal Word who mediates the love and power of God's being, between man and the supernatural instruments of God's will, or between man and the natural reflectors of God's self-disclosure, there is an excessive sense of "otherness." Lewis tends, in short, very greatly to emphasize transcendence over immanence, eternity over time, objectivity over subjectivity, and the supernatural over the natural. Even if, as some would maintain, this is a tendency inherent in traditional Christian theism itself, we would have to see in Lewis something of a "skewed" orthodoxy.

> Gunnar Urang. *Shadows of Heaven: Religion and*
> *Fantasy in the Writing of C. S. Lewis, Charles*
> *Williams, and J. R. R. Tolkien* (Toronto: United
> Church Press, 1971), pp. 5–50

Lewis's purpose in his "space" trilogy, *Out of the Silent Planet, Perelandra,* and *That Hideous Strength,* was to combine an old love with a newer, to combine the romance of the far off and faerie with the religion of his maturity, to unite what the imagination loved with what the intellect was convinced to be true. In short, his purpose was to romanticize religion.

Christianity—the very story of Christianity as well as many of its dogmas—is translated into mythology in order that Christianity may seem more wonderful (not more wonderful than it is, perhaps, but more wonderful than we ordinarily conceive it). Romance, beginning as a means to Christianity, is now used as a servant to Christianity. The whole trilogy is full of the old Chestertonian device of making something marvelous by describing it in terms that we never use for it, of making us see something as if for the first time. The drama of the Incarnation takes on a strange new light in being told by a naked green woman on a floating island on Venus, as the Fall assumes new grandeur by being almost repeated. Maleldil, so truly in motion that He is still (a psychophysical parallel of God's infinite act?); Maleldil the Young locked in battle with the Dark Eldil of Thulcandra, setting an impassable frontier against him across the face of the moon; Maleldil reviving Merlin after fifteen hundred years so that he may join the Pendragon and the planetary Oyeresu in the fight against the Bent One—what could be more wonderful, what could be less like not only what Newman called "the dreary, hopeless irreligion" of the time, but less like the very religion itself of the time? Lewis's religion seems hardly to belong to the same century, or the same world, as Eliot's *Thoughts after Lambeth,* or Jaspers's and Bultmann's discussion of myth and religion, or the work of Camus.

I do not suggest that Lewis's romantic Christianity is identical with Anglicanism as such, any more than the romantic religion of Macdonald or Chesterton was identical with their formal religions. I do suggest that Lewis has come to terms with dogma in a typically romantic way learned from Coleridge, that he has done this in order to go beyond dogma to experience, the romantic experience of longing which he can now see as of religious significance. Lewis's transcendental Christianity preserves the value of both dogma and experience by explaining both as attempts to reach the same end, by showing that *Sehnsucht* approximates the Practical Reason or the will. Romantic longing is for what never was on sea or land, for the beyond "partly in the west, partly in the past"; Lewis's transcendental Christianity provides an ultimate reality that is opaque, unapproachable, and unknowable except through the will. Christianity itself, in Lewis's transcendental terms, may be thought of as a myth or accommodation, so far as it is understood rather than perceived spiritually by moral means. Just so far as Christianity is formal and dogmatic, it is a limitation of the transcendent God, a form of perception like quantity or substance by which we mutilate and distort the I AM WHO AM. In order to know God we must love Him; there is no discursive way. Lewis's transcendental Christianity, like romantic longing, puts its good in "the High Countries," where the heart is.

R. J. Reilly. *Romantic Religion: A Study of
Barfield, Lewis, Williams, and Tolkien* (Athens,
Georgia: University of Georgia Press, 1971),
pp. 98–147

Lewis, in the Ransom trilogy, plays with the notion of something like the Platonic ideas taking flesh and walking (or stalking) the earth. How does one read such scenes? How does one read the end of *The Last Battle,* when Narnia becomes the new heaven and new earth? Certainly a willing suspension of disbelief is the last response Lewis asks from the reader. Like a gospel, a fiction by Lewis draws the reader in and forces him to accept the author's position, even in all its hyperbole, or reject it, and be damned with the Calormenes, Weston, and all the rest. Lewis certainly was not writing novels. He has little sympathy for most of his characters, who either come up to his standards or get thrown away; his plots are pedestrian. He excels at fantastically imagined archetypal situations, that draw the reader in with a sense of *déjà vu*. If he judges the reader harshly, the options for good he provides are so beautiful as to be painful.

Gerard Reedy. *Commonweal*. March 29, 1974,
pp. 93–94

As a scholar of English literature Lewis made a considerable contribution. He placed a stamp on the English school at Oxford which was to last for a quarter of a century although, even before his death, the study of the hated modern poets was making inroads into the walled garden of the Anglo-Saxons and the Medievals which he had labored so valiantly if narrowly to create. His major work of scholarship, *The Allegory of Love* is one of those rare academic works that survives its own time. Yet it is the writings which spring more directly from his Christian imagination, such as the incomparable seven of Narnia—the children's books which are certainly that but also very much more—and the great popular theological tracts, *The Problem of Pain, The Screwtape Letters, The Four Loves,* and *The Letters to Malcolm,* which will form the basis of his lasting fame.

They sprang as did his conversion to Christianity from his own deep inner life and they were given form not only by his literary sensitivity but by his deep commitment to theology.

Norman St. John-Stevas. *The Spectator*. July 20,
1974, p. 85

Lewis's delight in argument made him the foremost apologist for Christianity in the English-speaking world.

Two qualities, literary sensitivity and unrelenting logic, characterize Lewis's published works as they did his conversation and account, in large measure, for the enduring popularity, eleven years after his death, of his forty-odd books. *The Allegory of Love, The Discarded Image,* and *English Literature in the Sixteenth Century* will endure. Anyone studying medieval literature will inevitably come upon the first two, while the last must rank as the most engagingly written of all the tomes in the Oxford literary history series. It also contains, in a section on the English divines, the most concise and lucid analysis of the spirit of the Lutheran reform I have ever seen:

> In reality, . . . morality or duty . . . never yet made a man happy in himself or dear to others. It is shocking, but it is undeniable. We do not wish either to be or to live among, people who are clean or honest or kind as a matter of duty: we want to be, and to associate with, people who like being clean and honest and kind.

Much of Lewis is in those three sentences: his profound interest in religious questions; his peculiar ability to see, and capture in uncluttered prose, the bond that ties theological speculation to human experience; his insistence that Christianity is about a gift, not a set of rules. The themes echo throughout his apologetic and inspirational works, and can be found as well, in mythic form, in his space trilogy and the Narnia tales. When he applied them to concrete cases, he sometimes sounded an eerily prophetic note, as in his famous essay on the allurements of the "Inner Ring."

John B. Breslin. The New Republic. December 21, 1974, p. 17

Often discussed as if it were merely Christian fable, the interplanetary fiction of C. S. Lewis retains considerable interest for readers of science fiction; it is among the first to portray an ideal world invaded by humanity. Malacandra and Perelandra have a mythic quality that penetrates to a deep level of the mind; after we have read about them, it is difficult not to seek *eldila* in space or to think of Venus without its floating islands and heraldic colors. These books should last as myth, as romance, as science fiction, but they cannot be considered great novels. *That Hideous Strength* is even less successful as a novel, although it contains excellent ingredients.

When Lewis turned from adult fiction to the fairy tale, he remarked, with admirable self-awareness, that the form was helpful because it checked the "expository demon" in him. It is certainly true that the major weaknesses of the space trilogy can be attributed to that demon, particularly when characters begin to sound like Lewis delivering a lecture. While the mythic elements of the trilogy have enduring value, it is likely that Lewis's reputation as a fiction writer will increasingly rest on the Chronicles of Narnia, a series that is already considered a children's classic, and on the haunting novel *Till We Have Faces*. This final novel is more completely mythic than any of his previous writing and at the same time is a deeper study of character. Far more demanding than the other fiction, it also returns more to the reader. . . .

Of course any predictions about which works will last are dangerous. Lewis may well continue to be known as the author of the Chronicles of Narnia, as a science fiction writer, as a mythmaker, a literary scholar, and a Christian apologist. But complete alterations in literary tastes might leave all those accomplishments in oblivion and resurrect his reputation two hundred years hence, labeling him a great twentieth-century poet. Lewis would have enjoyed the irony of such a situation.

Margaret Patterson Hannay. C. S. Lewis (New York: Ungar, 1981), pp. 260–68

LOVECRAFT, H. P. (1890–1937)

The Lovecraft tales generally fall into two major classifications, and one combination; that is, the tales are either fantastic, somewhat after the Dunsany pattern; or they are weird and terrible tales of cosmic outsideness, after a pattern which, though a compound of Poe, Machen, Chambers, and Bierce, manifests the influence of Arthur Machen and Algernon Blackwood, and yet manages to remain individually Lovecraftian to such an extent that it has influenced many another writer in the genre. The combination, manifestly, is of these two developments, and has not been notably successful. The weird and terrible tales subdivide into "New England" tales and stories of the Cthulhu Mythos. The best of these early tales are stories of pure horror, such as the unforgettable "The Rats in the Walls," the Poesque "The Outsider," "The Picture in the House," etc. Of the Dunsanian pieces, "Dagon," "The Cats of Ulthar," and "The Strange High House in the Mist" are the best of the earlier stories, and "The Statement of Randolph Carter," "The Silver Key," and "Through the Gates of the Silver Key" the best of the later tales. The one surviving fantasy novel, *The Dream-Quest of Unknown Kadath,* has a kind of eerie charm, but seldom any genuine terror; it has a dreamlike quality, almost an Alice in Wonderland kind of fantasy, and is quite unlike the other short novel, *The Case of Charles Dexter Ward,* which is one of Lovecraft's most carefully wrought fictions.

The Dunsanian influence waned rather quickly, though Lovecraft occasionally returned to the manner, considerably modifying it each time; and he devoted more of his creative energies to the fashioning of memorable tales in the purest Gothic tradition. To this second period belong, apart from those titles already mentioned, such fine stories as "The Shunned House," "The Music of Erich Zann," "The Picture in the House," and "Pickman's Model." The last and most promising phase was that of the Cthulhu Mythos, which some commentators are prone to think came into being with the story, "The Call of Cthulhu," which is not factual, since the Mythos was evolved piecemeal, and very slowly, and the most that can be said for "The Call of Cthulhu" is that it began to give shape to the mythos and the pattern Lovecraft was beginning to evolve. As a matter of record, there is everything to show that Lovecraft had no intention whatsoever of evolving his Cthulhu Mythos until that pattern made itself manifest in his work; this explanation alone would account for certain trivial inconsistencies. . . .

As examples of something new and different in the Gothic tradition, the Cthulhu Mythos stories of H. P. Lovecraft place him at once in the forefront of writers of the macabre in American letters. Without any suggestion of imitation, he belongs in the tradition of Poe, and in the line of Poe and Ambrose Bierce, rather than in that of Hawthorne, Mary E. Wilkins-Freeman, and Edith Wharton.

Lovecraft's prose style in his major work is suggestive of his beloved eighteenth century. It is grave and stately; it is deliberate, rather than studied; and there is throughout his later prose work an air of leisurely compulsion, however paradoxical that may sound—a compulsion which affects the reader with a desire to carry on and stems from that careful leisureliness of manner so typical of Lovecraft at his best. This is the mature style, as against the earlier manner of Lovecraft; it is the style which Lovecraft himself questioned as "verbose." The need to set the stage meticulously is a necessary aspect of the supernatural story, and Lovecraft held to the tradition. In its prose style alone, however, Lovecraft's work is akin to the past; for his recurrent preoccupation with time and space, with the tantalizing enigmas of the neverending quest for scientific knowledge and the attempt to comprehend the universe and man's place in it belong to our own time.

There is no basis for comparison of Lovecraft's work to that of any other contemporary writer; . . . comparison has thus had to be made to the Gothic writers of the last century, and as a result there is too often a kind of careless suggestion that there are great similarities between the work of Lovecraft and that of Poe or Bierce. That is simply not so. Apart from the single tale, "The Outsider," which is similar, there are none of the similarities to Poe, so carelessly imagined; and of Bierce's work, only "An Inhabitant of Carcosa" and "The Death of Halpin Frayser" suggest any similarities. Nothing more. Lovecraft was an original in the Gothic tradition; he was a skilled writer of supernatural fiction, a master of the macabre who had no peer in the America of his time.

August Derleth. H. P. L.: A Memoir (Sauk City,
Wisconsin: Arkham House, 1945), pp. 67–68

There were three important elements in Lovecraft's style which he was able to use effectively.

The first is the device of *confirmation* rather than revelation. In other words, the story ending does not come as a surprise but as a final, long-anticipated "convincer." The reader knows, and is supposed to know, what is coming, but this only prepares and adds to his shivers when the narrator supplies the last and incontrovertible piece of evidence. . . .

So closely related to his use of confirmation as to be only another aspect of it, is Lovecraft's employment of the terminal climax—that is, the story in which the high point and the final sentence coincide. . . . Use of the terminal climax made it necessary for Lovecraft to develop a special type of story telling, in which the explanatory and return-to-equilibrium material is all deftly inserted before the finish and while the tension is still mounting. It also necessitated a very careful structure, with everything building from the first word to the last.

Lovecraft reinforced this structure with what may be called *orchestrated prose*—sentences that are repeated with a constant addition of more potent adjectives, adverbs, and phrases, just as in a symphony a melody introduced by a single woodwind is at last thundered by the whole orchestra. "The Statement of Randolph Carter" provides one of the simplest examples. In it, in order, the following phrases occur concerning the moon: "waning crescent moon . . . wan, waning crescent moon . . . pallid, peering crescent moon . . . accursed waning moon." Subtler and more complex examples can be found in the longer stories.

All these stylistic elements naturally worked to make Lovecraft's stories longer and longer, with a growing complexity in the sources of horror. In "The Dreams in the Witch-House" the sources of horror are multiple: ". . . Fever—wild dreams—somnambulism—illusions of sounds—a pull toward a point in the sky—and now a suspicion of insane sleepwalking. . . ." While in "At the Mountains of Madness" there is a transition whereby the feared entities become the fearing; the author shows us horrors and then pulls back the curtain a little farther, letting us glimpse the horrors of which even the horrors are afraid!

It must be kept in mind that no matter how greatly Lovecraft increased the length, scope, complexity, and power of his tales, he never once lost control or gave way to the impulse to write wildly and pile one blood-curdling incident on another without the proper preparation and attention to mood. Rather, he tended to write with greater restraint, to perfect the internal coherence and logic of his stories, and often to provide alternate everyday explanations for the supernatural terrors he invoked, letting the reader infer the horror rather than see it face to face.

> Fritz Leiber, Jr. In August Derleth, ed., *Something about Cats* (Sauk City, Wisconsin: Arkham House, 1949), pp. 290–303

The principal feature of Lovecraft's work is an elaborate concocted myth which provides the supernatural element for his most admired stories. This myth assumes a race of outlandish gods and grotesque prehistoric peoples who are always playing tricks with time and space and breaking through into the contemporary world, usually somewhere in Massachusetts. One of these astonishing peoples, which flourished in the Triassic Age, a hundred and fifty million years ago, consisted of beings ten feet tall and shaped like giant cones. . . . They propagated, like mushrooms, by spores, which they developed in large shallow tanks. Their life span was four or five thousand years. Now, when the horror to the shuddering revelation of which a long and prolix story has been building up turns out to be something like this, you may laugh or you may be disgusted, but you are not likely to be terrified—though I confess, as a tribute to such power as H. P. Lovecraft possesses, that he at least, at this point in his series, in regard to the omniscient conical snails, induced me to suspend disbelief. It was the race from another planet which finally took their place, and which Lovecraft evidently relied on as creations of irresistible frightfulness, that I found myself unable to swallow: semi-invisible polypous monsters that uttered a shrill whistling sound and blasted their enemies with terrific winds. Such creatures would look very well on the covers of the pulp magazines, but they do not make good adult reading. And the truth is that these stories were hack work contributed to such publications as *Weird Tales* and *Amazing Stories,* where, in my opinion, they ought to have been left.

The only real horror in most of these fictions is the horror of bad taste and bad art. Lovecraft was not a good writer. The fact that his verbose and undistinguished style has been compared to Poe's is only one of the many sad signs that almost nobody any more pays any real attention to writing. I have never yet found in Lovecraft a single sentence that Poe could have written, though there are some—not at all the same thing—that have evidently been influenced by Poe. . . . One of Lovecraft's worst faults is his incessant effort to work up the expectations of the reader by sprinkling his stories with such adjectives as "horrible," "terrible," "frightful," "awesome," "eerie," "weird," "forbidden," "unhallowed," "unholy," "blasphemous," "hellish," and "infernal." Surely one of the primary rules for writing an effective tale of horror is never to use any of these words— especially if you are going, at the end, to produce an invisible whistling octopus.

Lovecraft wrote also a certain amount of poetry that echoes Edwin Arlington Robinson—like his fiction, quite second-rate; but his long essay on the literature of supernatural horror is a really able piece of work. He shows his lack of sound literary taste in his enthusiasm for Machen and Dunsany, whom he more or less acknowledged as models, but he had read comprehensively in this special field—he was strong on the Gothic novelists—and writes about it with much intelligence.

Lovecraft's stories do show at times some traces of his more serious emotions and interests. He has a scientific imagination rather similar, though much inferior, to that of the early Wells. The story called "The Color out of Space" more or less predicts the effects of the atomic bomb, and "The Shadow out of Time" deals not altogether ineffectively with the perspectives of geological aeons and the idea of controlling the time sequence. The notion of escaping from time seems the motif most valid in his fiction, stimulated as it was by an impulse toward evasion which had pressed upon him all his life.

Edmund Wilson. *Classics and Commercials: A Literary Chronicle of the Forties* (New York: Farrar, Straus & Giroux, 1950), pp. 286–90

Lovecraft carried on a lifelong guerrilla warfare against civilization and materialism, albeit he was a somewhat hysterical and neurotic combatant.

What is so interesting about Lovecraft is the extraordinary consistency of his attempt to undermine materialism. His aim was "to make the flesh creep": more than that, to implant doubts and horrors in the minds of his readers. If he had been told that one of his readers had died of horror, or been driven to an insane asylum, there can be no doubt that he would have been delighted. In a tale called "The Unnameable," the writer claims that one of his horror stories, published in 1922, had caused a magazine to be withdrawn from the bookstalls because it frightened the "milksops." Whether this is true or not, there can be no doubt that Lovecraft wished it to be true.

He wanted to horrify the world. . . . To increase the illusion, he never set his stories in the remote past; in fact, he took care to date them close to the time they were written . . .

It must be admitted that Lovecraft is a very bad writer. When he is at his best, his style might be mistaken for Poe's. (A tale called "The Outsider," about a monstrous-looking man who does not realize that he is monstrous until he finally sees himself in a mirror, owes something to "William Wilson" and perhaps to Wilde's *Birthday of the Infanta;* it might easily pass for an unknown work by Poe.) But he makes few concessions to credibility, in spite of his desire to be convincing. His stories are full of horror-film conventions, the most irritating of which is the trustful stupidity of the hero, who ignores signs and portents until he is face to face with the actual horror.

But although Lovecraft is such a bad writer, he has something of the same kind of importance as Kafka. If his work fails as literature, it still holds an interest as a psychological case history. Here was a man who made no attempt whatever to come to terms with life. He hated modern civilization, particularly its confident belief in progress and science. Greater artists have had the same feeling, from Dostoyevsky to Kafka and Eliot. Only Kafka's approach was as naïve as Lovecraft's. He also relied simply on presenting a picture of the world's mystery and the uncertainty of the life of man.

All the same, Lovecraft is not an isolated crank. He is working in a recognizable romantic tradition. If he is not a major writer, he is psychologically one of the most interesting men of his generation.

Colin Wilson. *The Strength to Dream: Literature and the Imagination* (New York: Houghton Mifflin, 1962), pp. 1–10

A disparaging remark I once made about H. P. Lovecraft brought several long letters of rebuttal from his partisans. Mrs. R. J. Snyder of Canoga Park, California, Allan Howard of Newark, New Jersey, and James Wade of Chicago all pointed out that I had erred in calling Lovecraft's monsters inexplicit. Fritz Leiber made the same comment, adding, "It seems to me that Arthur Machen made more use than Lovecraft of the idea of 'unspeakable' horrors—and with Machen one gets the idea that these horrors were unspeakable because they involved abnormal sex, being generally associated with some pagan or witch cult. Of course Lovecraft did use the 'unnameable' device in a few stories like 'The Statement of Randolph Carter'—and 'The Unnameable'!—but I think the tediousness (for some readers) of his later stories comes from something else—chiefly his liking for writing stories as if they came from the pen of a rather fussy long-winded New England scholar . . . sort of Gibbonesque prose . . . something very apt to happen to the first-person narrative done by a thoughtful writer who has a hero rather like himself."

The Shuttered Room and Other Pieces, by H. P. Lovecraft & Divers Hands, gives me an opportunity to enlarge on this topic. Here are some phrases and sentences culled from "Dagon," a story which Lovecraft's followers consider one of his best:

"When you have read these hastily scrawled pages you may guess, though never fully realize, why it is that I must have forgetfulness or death"; "the carcasses of decaying fish, and of other less describable things"; "Urged on by an impulse which I cannot definitely define"; "A closer scrutiny filled me with sensations I cannot express"; "Of their faces and forms I dare not speak in detail; for the mere remembrance makes me grow faint."

In spite of these examples it *is* true that as a rule he did make a practice of bringing his monster or alien on stage once, near the end of each story, for one brief, static glimpse. In this respect, "The Shuttered Room" is typical. The story broadly hints, over and over (until the protagonist's continued obtuseness drives the reader to chew paper), that a froglike monster, capable of enormously increasing its size, is living in a boarded-up room in an old mill. At the end of the story, we meet this being:

> There, squatting in the midst of the tumbled bedding from that long-abandoned bed, sat a monstrous, leathery-skinned creature that was neither frog nor man, one gorged with food, with blood still slavering from its batrachian jaws and upon its webbed fingers—a monstrous entity that had strong, powerfully long arms, grown from its bestial body like those of a frog, and tapering off into a man's hands, save for the webbing between the fingers.

At this point, the monster springs, and the protagonist pots it with a kerosene lamp. End of monster.

Now, this is my real objection to Lovecraft and his imitators (aside from their arthritic styles): the monster does appear, sometimes, but only as a sort of peepshow. It is never brought onstage, as Leiber's and Sturgeon's monsters are, to act and react against the other characters. Thus the story remains in embryo, is never developed; one of the primary requirements of fiction is not fulfilled. A story has a beginning, a middle, and an end: Lovecraft's pieces are only endlessly retraced beginnings.

Damon Knight. *In Search of Wonder* (Chicago: Advent, 1967), pp. 223–24

Supernatural Horror in Literature is a magnificent achievement from many points of view. Structurally it is an accomplished tour de force, since it transmuted what might have been a catalogue with opinions into an organic unity. It reveals a mind of power and subtlety, a fine critical sense, and a feeling for development and cultural milieu that any historian might envy. Very few of Lovecraft's judgments have been overturned, even in mainstream criticism, and Lovecraft's acumen has been praised by critics as diverse as Vincent Starrett and Edmund Wilson.

One ability Lovecraft demonstrates to a supreme degree in *Supernatural Horror in Literature*. No other writer has ever been able to summarize a supernatural story in a more enticing manner, penetrating to the heart of the work and restating it accurately, yet with an appeal that may at times exceed that of the original work. In his letters Lovecraft comments on a related facet of his mind: his memory keeps reworking the books he has read, and he is forced to retrace his steps to avoid distorting ideas. Yet he was successful in avoiding such contamination. Many passages in his essay, too, refute the charge that Lovecraft always wrote in a leaden and pompous style. The reader who has covered the same literature can marvel that Lovecraft could always find something fresh to say about what might seem an exhausted subject.

E. F. Bleier. Introduction to *Supernatural Horror in Literature,* by Howard Phillips Lovecraft (New York: Dover Publications, 1973), pp. iv–v

The long-awaited Lovecraft biography is finally here. Frankly, I could have awaited it twenty or thirty more years without serious discomfort, but there is a large and perennially adolescent subculture in America that will no doubt be grateful to have the book now. As a biography it is, at best, of sparse interest, but as a kind of casebook on the history of a phenomenon—i.e., the popularity of a totally untalented and unreadable writer—it is not without its curiosity.

It is quite clear that, emotionally and intellectually, Lovecraft never progressed beyond adolescence, and it is thus not surprising that adolescents have kept his name alive. Weird-fantasy, the genre in which Lovecraft worked, has always been a weak strain in Western literature; Lovecraft's antecedents were the German and English Gothics of the early nineteenth century—some of the most unreadable books ever written. Poe took this strain up and brought a certain thin genius to it, but it clearly peaked with him.

What the pulp writers of the twenties and thirties did was to achieve a kind of marriage of Gothicism a la Poe with the boy's adventure story, a la Henty, Kirk Monroe, etc. This was an awful mixture then and it is still an awful mixture, but it appeals precisely to adolescent morbidity and the adolescent need for the private and the arcane. The private kingdoms of the weird-fantasiasts offer adolescents an escape from their sense of misfittedness; if they didn't, the genre would have died with Monk Lewis.

There were a number of pulp writers who at least managed to write plain prose—Frank Gruber, Ernest Haycox, and the prodigious Frederick Faust. Lovecraft, unfortunately, was the master of the turgid and the inflated. His chief gift seems to have been for the creation of vaguely Druidic, vaguely Celtic, nomenclature. What is one to make of a man, for example, whose sonnet sequence is called "Fungi from Yuggoth"? One of his most famous stories is called *The Dream-Quest of Unknown Kadath*. It contains dholes, ghouls, gugs, ghasts, and small furry creatures called zoogs. De

Camp admits that these names lend a juvenile flavor, but he appears to feel that they are offset by the story's atmosphere. Yet this famous Lovecraftian atmosphere—it is all he really ever had to offer, since, as his biographer admits, he was totally uninterested in the creation of character—seems to me to consist largely of more names. In that one story, for example, we find such names as Barzai, Hatheg-Kla, Pnakotic, Atal, Mount Ngranek, the isle of Oriab and something called Nyarlathotep. And if the reader thinks those names something, let me assure the reader that they are nothing compared to the names of Lovecraft's one-act Cthulhuvian operetta *Fen River.*

Finally, one might say that attempts to respectabilize the pulp writers of the twenties and thirties just don't work. The pulp writers were phenomenal producers but terrible writers; take away Raymond Chandler and the pulps were zilch, an almost totally subliterary medium. They survive as a collecting fad largely because of their cover art, and not because of the writing between their covers.

Larry McMurtry. Washington Post. February 17, 1975, p. D4

Lovecraft is one of the few authors of whom I can honestly say that I have enjoyed every word of his stories. His study, *Supernatural Horror in Literature,* makes one feel he could have been a remarkable interpreter of literature. And while his poetry seems to me mostly written "with his left hand," it includes that marvelous bacchanalian song (in "The Tomb") with the magnificent line,

> Better under the table than under the ground

which makes one think he might under some circumstances have been a fine poet. But it was a writer of weird fiction that he chose to be primarily, and that choice seems to me justified by what he wrote.

His gifts were unusual. He was a scientist at heart, and that gave him a love of clarity. But he was also a dreamer, and could command the record of his own dreams, so as to make his readers yield "to shadows and delusions here." But mere style and clarity and careful planning cannot make a writer outstanding. There must be a narrative power for the writer of stories to excel, and that narrative power was the greatest of Lovecraft's gifts. It could outbalance his one greatest weakness—as recognized by himself, a tendency to melodrama, to kill off a dozen victims where one would have served better. It could have outbalanced a dozen weaknesses he did not have.

From time to time he is compared to Poe. There is little basis and no necessity for comparison. He was a great appreciator, admirer, and even interpreter of Poe (his recognition of the central theme of the "House of Usher" as the possession of but one soul by brother, sister, and the house itself seems to have been as novel as it is obviously correct) and he shared to a large extent Poe's views of the purpose of literature and the attitude the artist should have toward the weird. The chief difference is hard to explain although it is easy to feel; Poe was more interested in method of thought, Lovecraft more in a record of ideas; yet Lovecraft tried to make his tales consistent with each other, while Poe could allow the devil to read human minds in one tale and not in another with insouciance. It is also notable that Poe, like most writers, was only occasionally interested in the weird, while Lovecraft confined himself to a single genre.

But Lovecraft is not to be thought of as an imitator of Poe. Lovecraft can stand on his own feet, and does this without reference to his influence or the influences upon him. Few writers have ever won their way with less ballyhoo. I think it too soon to say what place Lovecraft will have in American literature, I have no doubt that it is an honorable place that should be accorded this truest amateur of letters.

T. O. Mabbott. In S. T. Joshi, ed., *H. P. Lovecraft: Four Decades of Criticism* (Athens, Ohio: Ohio University Press, 1980), pp. 43–45

"The trouble with most of my stuff is that it falls between two stools," Lovecraft once lamented. "My tales are not bad enough for cheap editors, nor good enough for standard acceptance and recognition." Today, more than fifty years after his death and nearly one hundred years after his birth, he remains on the fringe of literary respectability in his own country. (He has received more attention abroad, especially in France, Italy, Germany, and Japan, owing in part to their lack of prejudice against imaginative fiction.) Distinguished American critics, when they have deigned to comment at all, have often been severe. In his notorious *New Yorker* notice of the forties, Edmund Wilson grumped that "the only horror here is the horror of bad taste and bad art," while more recently Jacques Barzun has snorted, "How the frequently portentous but unintelligible H. P. Lovecraft has acquired a reputation as a notable performer is explained only by the willingness of some to take the intention for the deed and by a touching faith that words put together with confidence must have a meaning. . . ."

Critics can mellow. According to L. Sprague de Camp, for example, Edmund Wilson in his last years took delight in the first volume of the *Selected Letters.* Colin Wilson, a few years after dealing harshly with Lovecraft in *The Strength to Dream,* wrote two Lovecraftian science-fiction novels, *The Mind Parasites* (1967) and *The Philosopher's Stone* (1969), which in their philosophical basis reveal an understanding of his work missing in the mass of Mythos fiction perpetrated by more worshipful imitators. The *Columbia Literary History of the United States* (1988) may contain no mention of him, but in the Columbia University Bookstore paperback copies of Lovecraft's tales are located on the literature shelf, flanked by such august neighbors as Jack London and Norman Mailer. A reviewer of the latter's Egyptian novel, *Ancient Evenings* (1983), reports, "Some years ago Gore

Vidal cheekily remarked that Mailer was starting to sound like H. P. Lovecraft. . . . In this book Mailer has larded Lovecraft's deep-purple, fungoid weirdness with slabs of James Michener Informative.'' While hardly complimentary, such mention is another small indication that this peculiar New England gentleman, for so long the object of only an obscure "cult," is well on his way toward seeping, like one of his insidious horrors some might say, into the literary consciousness of America.

Peter Cannon. *H. P. Lovecraft* (Boston: Twayne, 1989), pp. 123–26

McBAIN, ED [SALVATORE A. LOMBINO]
[also known as EVAN HUNTER and
RICHARD MARSTEN] (1926–   )

When the prolific English mystery writer John Creasey published *Gideon's Day* in 1955, the first in a successful series of police procedurals featuring Commander George Gideon of Scotland Yard, the book was greeted with raves from both critics and readers. Its auspicious debut prompted an Americanized rival series to appear, this one written by a New Yorker and featuring the homicide detectives of the so-called 87th Precinct, a made-up number in a made-up city (Isola—Italian for "Island"; thus, "Manhattan").

Ed McBain, the author, was actually the writer Evan Hunter, a second pseudonym for a man who had been writing mystery stories under the Hunter byline and others, including "Richard Marsten." The subgenre of the American version of the French *roman policier* into which McBain plunged with such enthusiasm and obvious talent with *Cop Hater* in 1956, one year after Gideon's first adventure appeared, was not entirely vacant at the time.

Early ground had been broken for the American police procedural just before and during World War II by Lawrence Treat—*D as in Dead* (1941), *H as in Hangman* (1942), *O as in Omen* (1943), *V as in Victim* (1945)— but it was Hillary Waugh who with *Last Seen Wearing* in 1952 set the postwar tone in America that McBain took up. The detailed procedure by which a small-town police chief and his detective sergeant in Connecticut solved the murder of an eighteen-year-old freshman coed at a nearby college is painstakingly chronicled, with the thoughts, conversations, and actions of the detectives the focus of the story. It is not speed and action that grips the reader, but the meticulous, frustrating, wearying details that must be dealt with to uncover the murderer.

To Waugh's quiet Connecticut countryside McBain added the drama and dynamism of the big city, created characters with memorable personality shticks, invented "homicide division-type" dialogue that amused the reader and moved the story forward at the same time, sprang plot twists that brought the reader up sharp, and finally, evoked an unforgettable atmosphere and smell of tension, frustration, hard work, cynicism, and compassion—components of the true New York scene. . . .

An interesting feature of a typical McBain work is the manner in which he deliberately inserts pages and pages of dull textbook material taken verbatim out of some medical or forensic reference book by simply putting the words in the mouths of his characters and adding in appropriate grunts and exclamations to make it seem exciting. The same is true of his ability to insert an unimportant action—walking across the street to buy an egg cream at a stand—in the middle of an important and frustrating case, and make it seem as important as the unraveling of the mystery itself.

It was McBain's success with the formula that eventually led to the later success of Joseph Wambaugh, a Los Angeles police officer who began writing fiction based on the day-to-day action in which a policeman must involve himself such as *The New Centurions* (1970) and *The Blue Knight* (1972).

The *roman policier* will always be certain of a public somewhere, a public interested in the work of the police and in technical and scientific innovations in the realm of criminology.

Waltraud Woeller and Bruce Cassiday. *The Literature of Crime and Detection* (New York: Ungar, 1988), pp. 182–83

The most consistently skillful writer of police novels is undoubtedly Ed McBain. Under his real name of Evan Hunter . . . he has written some highly successful novels, and he has used other pseudonyms, but the formula of the police novel suits his talent particularly well. He began with Steve Carella, a detective working for an unnamed big-city police force, and equipped him with a wife named Teddy, who is beautiful but both deaf and dumb. As the series developed, Carella's fellow detectives—like Cotton Hawes, who was named after Cotton Mather, and Meyer Meyer, whose father thought it would be an excellent joke to duplicate surname and first name—were introduced. Sometimes half a dozen detectives appear in a book, sometimes only one or two. The cases vary from the macabre to the comic, and the stories are told largely in crisp believable dialogue between detectives and suspects, or between the detectives themselves. Often the dialogue has a nice note of deadpan comedy.

Julian Symons. *Mortal Consequences: A History— From the Detective Story to the Crime Novel* (New York: Harper & Row, 1972), p. 205

In the [police] procedural story, you get what you see. The mystery is not hidden by the words, for the intent of the artist is to use an entire squad room as the hero, a composite portrait of men embedded in an organization, of organizational man at work, triumphing through care, effort, weary repetition: through procedure. For this reason dialogue plays an important part in [Ed] McBain's novels. Entire chapters consist of nothing but dialogue, much of it irrelevant (and clearly so at the time), the function of which is to strengthen the awareness of a procedure embedded within the system of a squad, a family by which the men come to know each other, and later, through the knowing, may work effectively together, and by the book, to a conclusion. Yet almost always chance plays a rôle, and if genius consists of the prepared mind, then the solution to the mystery in a McBain book arises from the observant policeman who grasps the meaning of an accident; for seldom does detection in the normal sense of the word take place in procedural fiction. This, too, is surely true, for if it is realism we seek, we must realize how often policework must wait, depending on the lucky break, the informer, the simultaneity of chance occurrences.

Robin W. Winks. *Modus Operandi: An Excursion into Detective Fiction* (Boston: David R. Godine, 1982), p. 113

McBain's Ladies, by Ed McBain, might just as well be titled *Kling's Ladies,* since four out of five of the female characters spotlighted are the hapless officer's girlfriends. (The fifth is Steve Carella's deaf wife, Teddy.)

Bert Kling, we see in these passages excerpted from a couple dozen "87th Precinct" procedurals, usually has a time of it landing a new girl; enjoys her company for a time; but ultimately ends up a loser. How he becomes a loser, we won't give away here, but suffice it to say, the romantic aspect is equal to the mystery/crime one in this collection.

The book culls its selections from the usually intermingled plotlines of the regular novels. This volume shows, as if we needed reassurance, that the threads hang together, distractions or no.

McBain is the first popular fiction writer since Western writer J. T. Edson (*J.T.'s Ladies,* 1980) to isolate segments featuring female characters from previously published adventures. In McBain's case, one minor point stands out: only one of the five women featured is a police officer—Kling's fourth ladyfriend, Eileen Burke, who frequently plays a decoy for muggers. The reader can only suggest: more women cops.

Bernard A. Drew. *The Armchair Detective.*
Summer 1990, p. 359

It's easy to tear through an Ed McBain 87th Precinct novel, completely caught up and reluctant to set the book down, without ever crediting the author for being a superb storyteller. But he is, and *Kiss,* his forty-fourth police procedural set in an imaginary city of very mean streets, is McBain in top form. Detective Steven Carella must investigate the attempted murder of beautiful Emma Bowles while his father's murderer is tried in the city's courts. Emma's wealthy, handsome stockbroker husband imports a bodyguard for her from Chicago, who stays on the job even after the man who twice tried to kill Emma is found shot *and* hung. Carella and partner Meyer Meyer know something's not right, and doggedly keep investigating. Stoically, Carella also sits in court wondering if his father's killer will be convicted. McBain fans will understand the use of words like *dogged* and *stoic*. New readers need to know there's no Dirty Harry action, no car chases, no explosions. Instead, there's solidly researched police procedure, regulations, and culture. There's great dialogue and unexpected plotting. Best of all, there's McBain's artful artlessness. In *Kiss,* there's scarcely an errant word to remind readers that he is a master.

Thomas Gaughan. *Booklist.* December 1, 1991,

p. 660

McCAFFREY, ANNE (1926–   )

In *Dragonsong* young Menolly, whose greatest love is music, rebels against the harsh life in a fishing Hold after her father forbids her even to sing. Leaving the safety of the Hold, Menolly is befriended by a group of fire lizards and eventually realizes her dream about becoming a musician. The author explores the ideas of alienation, rebellion, love of beauty, the role of women, and the role of the individual in society with some sensitivity in a generally well-structured plot with sound characterizations.

Joan Barbour. *School Library Journal.* April 1967,

p. 91

Details of the apprentices' lives—rigorous curriculum and teaching methods, food, clothing, and societal relationships—give verisimilitude to *Dragonsinger,* a superbly crafted fantasy in the heroic tradition. Yet these details, essential to the evocation of the setting, are so thoroughly integrated into the story that they complement and extend the action rather than serve merely as a framework. Poetic introductions to each chapter appropriately suggest ancient ballads and sagas, thus supporting the motif of song as the cement of a people, and the idea that crafters of song are historians and effectors of change. Unlike many sequels, this maintains the dramatic tensions of its predecessor.

Mary M. Burns. *The Horn Book Magazine.* June

1977, p. 320

Get off the Unicorn is a delightful collection of science fiction short stories. McCaffrey—a master story teller—makes the collection even more enticing by adding an introductory anecdote for each tale. While the book as a whole shines with warmth and humor and makes fine entertainment, several stories are exceptional. "Changeling," dealing with homosexual parenting, and "A Proper Santa Claus," describing a small boy's concept of the "right kind" of Santa, are moving human studies whose quality is far and above the usual fare.

Evie Wilson and Michael McCue. *Wilson Library*

Bulletin. October 1977, p. 177

Science fiction's "Dragon Lady" has written several novels, but none more popular and durable than the sagas of the Dragonriders of Pern: *Dragon-*

flight, Dragonquest, and the new *White Dragon.* No random magic here, no Tolkienesque created language—Pern is supposedly a long-lost Earth colony—but a meticulously logical civilization, finely crafted. Social structure, tensions, legends, and traditions, are all based on the fundamental ecological battle and on the empathetic kinship between a dragon and his rider.

The ideal of empathy is at the root of Pern. . . .

The people of Pern fight internal disunity and the cultural stagnation that threatens their society's very survival. Each Dragonriders novel marks a victory for a world that revitalizes ancient traditions to fit modern demands. The heroine, or hero, upholds the spirit of the law rather than its letter, taking a moral stand against a dogmatic society. . . .

These kinds of conflicts aren't easily disposed of, and McCaffrey's books often end with ellipses: People don't pair off neatly, dragons die, solutions are acknowledged as merely temporary. Of course, unresolved endings are useful when you're writing a continuing series, and McCaffrey willingly mocks her own habit. *Dinosaur Planet,* the first volume of a new, less subtle, trilogy, ends with her protagonists hanging, literally, from a cliff. . . .

Why dragons in the first place? "They had bad press. And I liked the thought of them being so big, and controlled by a bond of love." Ties of trust and telepathy are a constant theme of McCaffrey's.

Debra Rae Cohen. Crawdaddy. June 1978, p. 51

Rich detail, warm, memorable characters in an interesting, tradition-based society, dragonlike animals with psi powers, absorbing action, and a dash of sex and romance add up to Anne McCaffrey's highly successful "Dragonriders of Pern" series.

This series is so popular that it has almost transcended genre categorization. Anne McCaffrey succeeds so well because she presents a colorful, ideally traditional culture in which each person has his or her place, with corresponding duties and privileges; in which the moral choices are clear; and in which, "if you try hard enough, and work long enough, you can achieve anything you desire." *The White Dragon* is a major work that should be in all collections.

Gary K. Reynolds. Science Fiction & Fantasy
Book Review. July 1979, p. 70

In *Dragondrums,* Piemur reaches puberty and loses his glorious voice, so he is apprenticed to Olodkey, the Drummaster.

Dragondrums does not stand well alone, however, but should be read as part of the sequence. The six novels about Pern fit together perfectly. Although her writing style has become a bit pedestrian in *Dragondrums,* McCaffrey has sustained reader interest by the addition of the message drums, their uses and their language. The reader barely remembers that planet-wide means of communication were lacking in the earlier books. *Dragondrums* leads into the exploration of the Southern Continent that is so much a part of *The White Dragon,* and finally lets us know how Mirrim impressed her green dragon Path. The appearance of this new book will undoubtedly compel fans to reread the entire series, to their great enjoyment. Pern, like Darkover and Dune, is a living world; may the dragons return to us in many novels to come!

Susan L. Nickerson. *Science Fiction & Fantasy*
Book Review. July 1979, p. 71

The seventies saw many more women writers entering the field. Some, like Anne McCaffrey . . . worked through the decade, adding to their reputations and followings of the sixties. McCaffrey had won a Hugo for "Weyr Search" (1967) and a Nebula for "Dragonrider" (1968), accumulating a whole sequence of novels throughout the seventies, all set on Pern, where the threads fell threateningly from the sky and the dragonriders flew up to meet the menace.

Brian W. Aldiss. *Trillion Year Spree: The History*
of Science Fiction (New York: Atheneum, 1986),
p. 366

MACDONALD, JOHN D. (1916–1986)

John D. MacDonald, one of the most prolific and successful of action-adventure writers, died December 28, 1986. He was seventy.

Best known as the creator of Travis McGee, the eccentric antihero detective who became the sixties' answer to Raymond Chandler's Philip Marlowe, MacDonald's career spanned more than forty years, including at least seventy-seven books and five hundred short stories.

In all, his books have sold more than seventy million copies. Of these, twenty-one were novels about McGee, the salvage expert-amateur detective and adventurer who lived on a Florida houseboat, the *Busted Flush,* won in a poker game.

Beginning in 1964, with *The Deep Blue Goodbye,* McGee solved crimes and, indulging his creator's dislike for many of the trends and customs in contemporary life, delivered shrewd commentaries on modern life as the mysteries unraveled.

In McGee mysteries and other novels as well, MacDonald's voice was one of a social historian, particularly of the Southern coast. In a first person McGee-MacDonald voice, the detective lamented the "locust population" of large cities advancing south, and the sad transformation of Florida's paradise of birds and marshes turned "flashy and cheap, tacky, and noisy."

In *Barrier Island,* published in 1986, MacDonald sketched "the laidback life of golf, boating, long cool drinks, the peculiar callousness bred by hot climates and luxurious comfort, better than anybody since Graham

Greene,'' author Stephen Vizinczey said in a review. He won two major awards, the Edgar Grand Master award from the Mystery Writers of America in 1972, and the American Book Award's mystery competition in 1980.

John Dann MacDonald was born in Sharon, Pennsylvania, on July 24, 1916. He attended the Wharton School of Finance and the Syracuse School of Business, then received a master's degree from the Harvard School of Business in 1939.

He earned his first paychecks from pulp magazines, selling stories while serving in the U.S. Army during World War II. He spent thirty months in the China-India-Burma theater, mostly with the Office of Strategic Services, and rose to the rank of lieutenant colonel.

In the first four months after he was discharged he wrote 800,000 words, and virtually never stopped writing. At first, he lived in Utica, New York, selling to the pulps as well as to *Esquire* and *Cosmopolitan,* often using a number of pseudonyms.

In 1950, his first book, *The Brass Cupcake,* was published. By 1964, when his first McGee mystery appeared, he had already written forty-three novels.

''When McGee was created, I set about coldly to devise a character who would be likable, yet substantial enough for me to be involved with for a series,'' the publicly reticent MacDonald said in a rare interview, in 1973. ''In the first novel, he was too somber. . . . I threw it out. In the second version, he was too much of a smart-ass—too quick and funny, too much of a winner. But by my third try, a character emerged that I enjoyed: a physically tough man who was vulnerable, yet strong.''

He admitted that McGee, moralistic yet supremely knowledgeable about travel, food, drink, and women, was ''my Walter Mitty projection, in the sense that every banker likes to think secretly that he can pull off that big job.''

In a 1984 television interview, he called his hero a ''tattered knight on a spavined steed.''

In later years, the non-McGee novels tackled corporate swindles and greed, as in the 1977 *Condominium,* about corporations grabbing land in Florida, or *One More Sunday* (1984) about spiritually bankrupt evangelical church leaders who raise funds through television and computers.

A lover of boats—like McGee—MacDonald also enjoyed chess, poker and was once a semi-pro bridge player. A disciplined writer, he kept regular hours, working from 8:30 a.m. to 6 p.m., producing from nine hundred to nine thousand words a day.

Penelope McMillan. *Los Angeles Times.* December 29, 1986, n.p.

John D. MacDonald has the uncanny ability to create believable characters with whom we can identify as victims and equally convincing and frightening villains. Although Travis himself is as indestructible as most mythic heroes, we realize that his friends are less immortal. Often we meet them first after they have already been victimized, and are fully aware of how much they have suffered, and how cruel and destructive any further suffering would be. We are therefore almost as psychologically vulnerable as they are themselves to the idea of further pain, and we cringe when such violence recurs. In *Bright Orange for the Shroud* (1965), Vivian Watts is raped by the animalistic yet shrewd Boone Waxwell. She is ravaged not only sexually, but also psychically, a cruel abasement that leaves her no choice but suicide.

The McGee novels (and in fact almost everything written by MacDonald) are morality plays: Travis engaged in an endless struggle on behalf of defenseless victims, a force of Good against the multifarious Evil rampant in our harsh society. Though protean in their form the MacDonald villain is generally greedy, sexually twisted, and amoral; in short, a sociopath, total madness only a flicker away. MacDonald's moral vision is conservative and manichean: McGee strives to preserve traditional values which he honors as an act of social good.

Yet in some of the recent novels one senses a certain ennui creeping into Travis's soul. He seems to be more remote with his friends, his women, even his enemies. In *The Dreadful Lemon Sky,* he turns down Carrie Milligan's offer of herself for no apparent reason except indifference, he remains strangely distant with Cindy Birdsong, in spite of himself; he can't make up his mind whether the clearly amoral Freddy Van Harn is really such a bad guy; and finally when his cop colleague, gutsy Captain Harry Max Scorf, has his head blown off by Hascomb, McGee uses Hascomb's moment of stunned "incredulous horror" to win the shootout, but then passes over Captain Harry's death without even a word of tribute.

Perhaps Travis and John D. both need a vacation, a time for McGee to savor his putative retirement, and a chance for MacDonald to work on a different type of novel for a while, to freshen his extraordinary narrative gifts. One remembers McGee's lament early in *The Dreadful Lemon Sky,* that his favorite Plymouth gin is no longer bottled in England: "It isn't the same. It's still a pretty good gin, but it is not a superb, stingling dry, and lovely gin."

David A. Benjamin. The New Republic. July 26,
1975, pp. 28–31

Travis McGee has joined the small but select company of fictional characters who manage to transcend the boundaries of the books in which they appear. However, thanks to John D. MacDonald's care in creating a character with substance as well as stature, McGee has also become an effective spokesman for public and private themes. An endlessly fascinating man, his growth, development, and faithful adherence to principles of moral behavior in an increasingly amoral world are sources of continuing interest. Equally important, he serves as a prism through which MacDonald is able to reflect his own views and opinions on dozens of issues of contemporary relevance. Whether assailing the venality and corruption he sees around him, bemoaning the regrettable decline in the quality of much of our contemporary culture, or deploring the shameless assaults on the environment, McGee has become an impassioned commentator on the way we live today—a feature that elevates his exciting adventures to a level of seriousness beyond mere escapist entertainment.

MacDonald is a gifted storyteller, a talent he learned early in his career as a young writer trying to break into the pulp market, which placed a premium on fast-paced, action-filled narratives. Neither as byzantine as Ross Macdonald's nor as loose and desultory as Raymond Chandler's, MacDonald's plots are well-woven, artfully constructed arrangements of action sequences. They are neither needlessly complex nor do they exist simply to obscure the identity of the villain until the final chapter. A master at creating and sustaining mystery, suspense, tension, and drama, MacDonald understands all the tricks of readability; turning the pages in one of his novels is always a pleasure, never a duty. And although each of the McGee books adheres to the general outlines of a simple recurring pattern—McGee is roused from the *Busted Flush* to retrieve or restore some valuable item for a person in distress, usually a woman, and then retires to his boat again at the completion of his mission—MacDonald is skillful enough to avoid duplicating situations. Finally, his plots generate enough narrative energy to keep the reader moving at a brisk pace throughout the books, yet are flexible enough to allow for the inclusion of quiet, gentle scenes, as well as the many mini-sermons that have become such a characteristic feature of the McGee books.

As important as story is, however, it isn't everything to MacDonald; his novels always feature believable characters about whom, thanks to his skill in making them real as well as interesting, the reader comes to care deeply. His success in achieving such credibility in his characterizations can be traced to the same feature that makes his prose so effective—concretization of detail. Normally he introduces a character by focusing on a single vivid detail in order to give that figure a substantial presence on the page.

Although one encounters the full spectrum of humanity in his novels, it is possible to divide his characters into two main groups: manipulators, usually men, who are driven by the need to accumulate, compound, launder, or extort money; and victims, usually women, who are conned, abused, and mistreated by them.

But whether they be heroes or villains, saints or sinners, featured performers or background figures, MacDonald's characters are invariably believable and interesting. Thanks to his instinctive choice of the right gesture, mannerism, speech pattern, quirk, and tic, even the most insignificant character is allowed his brief and shining moment in the limelight before being retired to the obscurity of the background once more. In the richness of his characterizations and the perceptive delineation of their innermost selves, MacDonald creates a world of recognizable beings who are driven by the same emotions—fear, love, hate, greed, loneliness, compassion—that compel us all. More than any other feature, it is MacDonald's skill in creating credible and convincing characters that gives his work the look and feel of solid reality. . . .

MacDonald has been an acute chronicler of the American Dream as it has moved south and taken up residence in the Sun Belt. If his works can be said to have a central theme, it is money: there is perhaps no writer who knows better than he how money works and how it weaves its magic spell over people. His concern is not with the very rich or the very poor but with that segment of the populace driven by avarice to accumulate, often by shady means, all it can. It is such con men, swindlers, and hustlers who provide him with his plots, serve as his villains, and produce the victims for his keenly observed chronicles which, thanks to his concentration on the human factors of each situation, achieve a powerfully compelling emotional resonance.

Whether for the sake of convenience one categorizes his works as mysteries, adventures, or thrillers, it is clear that such labels are inadequate in conveying the full extent of his accomplishment. By creating a substantial body of thoughtful and provocative entertainment for an enormously diverse and widespread audience, MacDonald has justly earned for himself the right to be considered a serious American novelist worthy of the highest distinction.

David Geherin. *John D. MacDonald* (New York: Ungar, 1982), pp. vii–viii, 171–81

In *Slam the Big Door,* by John D. MacDonald, forty-year-old ex-combat correspondent Mike Rodenska, trying to get over the loss of his wife, is staying at the Florida home of his World War II Marine buddy, Troy Jamison. A few years back, when Troy, at the peak of his advertising career, had a nervous breakdown and lost his job to alcohol and his wife to his compulsive adultery, Mike took care of Troy and helped him put his life back together. Now Troy is returning the gift of life to Mike.

Troy has settled down with his new wife, Mary, a lovely, wealthy widow, and is operating a small construction business. The Jamisons have invested everything they own in the development of a large piece of land. All is well, the sun is warm and the drinks are cold, and Mike is beginning to relax.

But little anomalies start cropping up. Like any good reporter, Mike puts together bits of information and learns that the Jamisons' development is going to fail and that their marriage, despite Mary's attempts to hide the truth, is in bad shape. Troy has begun drinking again and, Mike suspects, is having an affair. To add to the complications, Mary's seductive, newly divorced daughter, Debbie Ann, is living with them and seems to be looking for trouble.

Mike realizes that, instead of having been invited by his friend to relax, the invitation is Troy's way of begging for help again. Mike's investigations show that the troubles at the development are not accidental and may have been caused by the desire of a group of wealthy, powerful men to grab the land for themselves. There is nothing for Mike to do but to get fully, dangerously involved with the development and, unavoidably, with the whole Jamison family.

Although the names are different, and Mike Rodenska is not as big, strong, and tough as the colorful salvage expert, this is really the first Travis McGee book. And, I think, the best of that series, than which there can be no higher compliment to a John D. book. It is not really a mystery (to me, a mystery implies a puzzle; Penzler needs only a crime) or even a crime story, unless you consider drunk driving or assault and battery sufficient for the labeling. There is practically no violence, and the sex is not only intrinsic, it is essential to the story, yet the book is gripping, exciting, and enthralling, and shows what can be done without car chases, shootouts, or gratuitous sex and violence. Provided it is done by a master. Which it is.

Slam the Big Door is one of the four John D. books not yet published in hardcover. I hope that the Mysterious Press will print the other three. Soon. I wish this could have been done while John was around to see it happen. *Slam the Big Door* was his favorite of all his books. He was so right. As usual.

Herbert Resnicow. The Armchair Detective. Spring
1988, p. 201

MACDONALD, ROSS [KENNETH MILLAR] [also known as JOHN ROSS MACDONALD] (1915–1983)

Dashiell Hammett and his many admirable pulp colleagues gave a vitally needed blood transfusion to the detective story with a more nearly realistic approach to crime and punishment, a faster tempo, and added narrative vigor, and a prose at once simpler and more colorful than that prevalent in the trade at the time. Yet, just as the overardent admirers of Charles Fort have turned the conjectures of that valiant antidogmatist into a dogma of their own, so the imitators of the hard-boiled school have turned a fresh approach into the tiredest of formulas.

The entrance upon this jaded scene two years ago of John Ross Macdonald was highly welcomed. *The Way Some People Die* is probably his best novel to date—and thereby automatically the top hard-boiled novel of the year. Macdonald has the makings of a novelist of serious caliber—in his vivid realization of locale; in his striking prose style, reminiscent of Chandler and yet suggesting the poetic evocation of Kenneth Fearing; in his moving three-dimensional characterization; and above all in his strangely just attitude toward human beings, which seems incredibly to fuse the biting contempt of a Swift with the embracing love of a Saroyan.

The plot of the latest Macdonald (starring, as usual, the private detective Lew Archer) is a complex study of the heroin racket and its impingement on an assortment of characters of all social and cultural levels; but for all its complexity, it's a tighter and better organized plot than that of either of his previous stories. Which makes this (to stick my neck out) the best novel in the tough tradition that I've read since *Farewell, My Lovely*, and possibly since *The Maltese Falcon*.

Anthony Boucher. *The New York Times Book Review*. August 5, 1951, p. 16

The hearse which gives occasion for Mr. Macdonald's title [*The Zebra-Striped Hearse*] does not figure prominently in his story, nor do the beach bums who drive it to Malibu or Zuma play more than an incidental part. But the indecorum of the vehicle is significant, and its owners are representative of the society in which the action moves—they are rootless and immature, without firm purpose, without character. Archer, Mr. Macdonald's private eye, responding sensitively to the world to which he is condemned, accepts it with resignation, and is thoroughly at home in the police stations and mortuaries, the seedy back streets and restaurants, the artists' colonies, bars, and motels through which he passes in his resourceful, persistent search for a half-dozen victims and their destroyer.

Mr. Macdonald, always a superb contriver of puzzles, again gives his reader a full measure of excitement and suspense, and of satisfaction with the resolution of his plot. The first problem presented is the identity of Burke Damis, a mysterious painter, talented, but hostile and uncommunicative, who carries off the infatuated Harriet Blackwell very much against the will of her father, a wealthy retired colonel. The discovery of Damis's true name and history proves to be not very difficult; but as the clues are followed up they lead into a perplexing tangle of relationships, ambitions, intrigues, and violent acts, all of which must be unraveled before the fate of Harriet can be known. Archer is tireless, determined, incapable of admitting defeat. Except for Damis, all the people with whom he deals are familiar—he has met them before, under different names, and he reads their natures quickly and accurately. They are not, to be sure, very profound.

Mr. Macdonald writes excellent dialogue, and his descriptions of people and places are masterly in their economy and precision. The fastidious reader is occasionally brought up short by gaudy splashes of figurative language; but since these passages never occur in the language which Archer reports, but only in the paragraphs in which he tells what he himself observes, they may be attributed to his taste rather than to lapses on the part of his creator, and help to define his persona as author.

Warner G. Rice. *Michigan Quarterly Review*. Summer 1963, p. 212

Without in the least abating my admiration for Dashiell Hammett and Raymond Chandler, I should like to venture the heretical suggestion that Ross

Macdonald is a better novelist than either of them. He owes an immeasurable debt to both in the matter of technique and style; but he has gone beyond their tutelage to develop the "hard-boiled," private-eye novel into a far more supple medium, in which he can study the common and the uncommon man (and woman) as well as the criminal, in which he can write (often brilliantly and even profoundly) not only about violence and retribution but simply about "people with enough feeling to be hurt, and enough complexity to do wrong"—to quote from his latest *The Far Side of the Dollar.*

A seventeen-year-old boy has run away from a curious sort of psychotherapeutic prep school, and private detective Lew Archer is called in to find him. It is a quest which illumines the war of the generations, odd corners of Hollywood, a twenty-year-old sin and even a part of Archer's own past. It involves above all a compassionate understanding of people, old and young, caught up in this moment of time.

> Anthony Boucher. *The New York Times Book Review.* January 24, 1965, p. 42

A few years ago Ross Macdonald wrote a series of stunning psychodramas that still remain generally neglected: *The Galton Case, The Wycherly Woman, The Zebra-Striped Hearse.* But subsequent books fell into repetition of these successes, and now the latest, *Black Money,* sets out to do something different. It begins—and few writers create the sense of starting out as well as Ross Macdonald—with what seems a standard tale about the way underworld money corrupts the respectably wealthy, and proceeds to show how Lew Archer, Ross Macdonald's private detective, wrongly assumes, as if because he watched too much television, that when you find the underworld king you solve the case. Archer has the rug neatly pulled out from under him—the solved case leaves everything unsolved—but then, author and hero, sadly, have nothing left except shreds of a wornout tangle and some not very clearly articulated anti-academic biases. Someone coming to Ross Macdonald first via *Black Money,* then, has every right to feel he is only another private eye novelist. But those who know this curiously modest and pretentious writer can still invoke his entire career and say he may be started on something new.

> Roger Sale. *The Hudson Review.* Spring 1966, pp. 127–28

Ross Macdonald writes detective novels, so he is seldom dealt with in serious literary quarters. This is everyone's loss. He is a skillful and intelligent novelist, albeit a minor one, who provides those essential insights into character and milieu which are the major functions of his craft. But, since his protagonist is a California private detective, Macdonald is usually spoken of as a follower of Dashiell Hammett and Raymond Chandler—to the disadvantage of all three. While he is not without some indebtedness to Chandler, the body of his work is very much his own; he has found his particular subject and his personal way of handling it.

His investigator, Lew Archer, is an ex-Los Angeles police detective who has weathered the aftermath of a disastrous marriage and, for undisclosed reasons, gone into private practice. He is a man of realistic compassion and understanding, called upon to look into the details of the private and nonvillainous lives of individuals living in more or less quiet desperation in the anomic world of Los Angeles and its environs.

Macdonald depicts the members of the Southern California middle classes, the real subjects of his novels, as rootless, usually without real connections where they have chosen to live. Archer's efforts to make sense of their shattered lives, in this microcosmic climate of physical comfort and moral collapse, can provide no relief other than knowledge, and knowledge uninformed by an organizing principle to make the miniscule tragedies and crimes either bearable or expiable.

Though the violence of the third-rate private detective thriller is conspicuously absent, Macdonald's universe is replete with malevolent activities and psychological violence—more convincingly frightening as the reader realizes the veracity of the account.

Black Money is, I think, his best book yet. The usual Macdonald themes are present, but they are treated with even greater lucidity and sharpness than before. His portrait of life in a state college and the desperate striving for accomplishment is consistently pointed and concise. The interconnections in American life between the Las Vegas casinos, the new underworld of quasi-respectability, and the middle classes are conveyed in human terms, with all parties damaged by the reticulated corruptions.

Macdonald combines the elegiac theme of *The Great Gatsby* with scrupulous observation of the minute details of modern life—all rendered in neatly balanced prose that make his characters both individuals and types. In these days of dreary fiction, Ross Macdonald is a boon.

Henry A. Woodfin. *The New Leader*. April 11, 1966, p. 26

Unlike the snarling private eye heroes of Hammett and Chandler, Mr. Macdonald's Lew Archer is a decent sort with whom any reader can sympathize. His toughness is never mere bad manners; he knows how to behave in good society, carries no chip on his shoulder, and does not insult everybody as a matter of principle.

John Dickson Carr. *Harper's*. July 1966, p. 85

It seems evident that Ross Macdonald is constantly maturing as a writer of detective stories. His previous novel, last year's *The Instant Enemy,* is probably his finest performance. *The Goodbye Look,* though lacking its predecessor's dazzling narrative drive and impact, is nevertheless a worthy successor and has been called ''a stunning addition to the Archer books'' by novelist William Goldman (author of *Harper*'s screenplay) in a front page review in the *New York Times Book Review* of June 1, 1969.

The Goodbye Look starts placidly when Lew Archer is hired by a lawyer to investigate what appears to be the simple and unimportant matter of a stolen Florentine gold box. However, as you would expect, many outward spirals of unexpected plot ramifications develop amidst a set of conflicting emotions and purposes whose basic motivations retreat a quarter of a century into the past.

All of these currents are related in a clean and relatively uncluttered plot progression that moves forward in stately cadences which become more spare and stark as the maelstrom of incident and character revelation whirl toward their inevitable conclusion.

Charles Shibuk. *The Armchair Detective*. Fall
1969, p. 274

Not since W. S. Gilbert brought to jolly culmination the Victorian obsession with children who somehow mislay—or are mislaid by—their parents, has a writer been as successful with entertainments revolving around what might loosely be termed the Oedipal theme as Ross Macdonald. His last two novels have enjoyed front-page coverage in the *New York Times Book Review,* he has recently been the subject of a *Newsweek* cover story, and, most important of all, he has broken through the barrier that normally segregates the detective novelist from the rest of literature. . . .

It is the failure to evoke a milieu, and the related failure to develop a wide range of memorable characters to populate it, that represents Macdonald's great defect as a novelist. His cast remains remarkably similar from book to book, with only the names, sketchy physical descriptions, and occupations varying while the psychological typology remains constant. What is more curious is his obsession with the upper-middle class and the rich. It is nearly always to their enclaves, many of them well outside Los Angeles, that Lew Archer is called to duty. . . .

At best, Macdonald is a writer of severely limited capabilities and a rather weak inheritor of the tradition of what Edmund Wilson once called "the boys in the back room." He is, moreover, an entertainer who has wiped the grin off his face and is thus able to confront the historical moment with that measure of decorum the middlebrow public deems suitable to its seriousness.

Richard Schickel. *Commentary*. September 1971,
pp. 96–99

Lew Archer from the start has been a distinguished creation; he was always an attractive figure and in the course of the last several books has matured and deepened in substance to our still greater pleasure. Possessed even when young of an endless backlog of stored information, most of it sad, on human nature, he tended once, unless I'm mistaken, to be a bit cynical. Now he is something much more, he is vulnerable. As a detective and as a man he takes the human situation with full seriousness. He cares. And good and evil both are real to him.

Archer knows himself to be a romantic, would call it a weakness—as he calls himself a "not unwilling catalyst" for trouble; he carries the knowledge around with him—that's how he got here. But he is in no way archaic. He is at heart a champion, but a self-questioning, often a self-deriding champion. He is of today, one of ours. *The Underground Man* is written so close to the nerve of today as to expose most of the apprehensions we live with.

In our day it is for such a novel as *The Underground Man* that the detective form exists. I think it also matters that it is the detective form, with all its difficult demands and its corresponding charms, that makes such a novel possible.

Eudora Welty. *The New York Times Book Review.*
February 14, 1971, p. 29

In *The Underground Man* Ross Macdonald keeps entirely within the formula but broadens it by providing a great California fire as the background of his book. This fire is an "ecological crime" linked more than fortuitously to the cigarillo dropped by Stanley Broadhurst, the murdered son. Stanley belongs to a "generation whose elders had been poisoned, like the pelicans, with a kind of moral DDT that damaged the lives of the young." By combining ecological and moral contamination Macdonald creates a double plot that spreads the crime over the California landscape. Superb in snapshot portraiture of California life, Macdonald gives us a sense of the wild life flushed out by the smoke, the way people lean on one another when they fear crime and fire.

Geoffrey Hartman. *The New York Review of Books.* May 18, 1972, pp. 31–32

Ross Macdonald's early books, written under his own name of Kenneth Millar, are uneven, but they show that vividness in the use of metaphor and simile which from the beginning pulled his work out of the ruck of reasonably well-written hard-boiled stories. *Blue City* (1947), the best of these early books, is about the son of a murdered man coming back to a Midwestern town to find his father's killer. The development owes something to Hammett, but the turns of phrase are striking. . . .

In the first half-dozen Lew Archer stories, written under the name of John Ross Macdonald, the setting is always California, sometimes its rich face and often its dirty backside; the plots are densely complicated; there is a great deal of gun play. The books are written with the exuberance and zest of a man intoxicated by his own skill with epithets. Chandler criticized Macdonald harshly, much too harshly, for saying that a car was "acned with rust" and for calling the words and drawings on lavatory walls "graffiti."

. . . If you turn to almost any page, you are likely to be jerked to attention rather than lulled into repose, and that must be a good thing. A random opening of pages in three different books, all of them early Archer, gave "He had a bulldog face whose only expression was a frozen ferocity intended to scare off trespassers." "I caught glimpses of glass-and-aluminum living machines gleaming like surgical equipment in the clinical moonlight." "Geoff had lived too long among actors. He was a citizen of the unreal city, a false front leaning on scantlings." There is occasionally a sense of strain about such writing, but more often it seems finely appropriate to the frenetic world that is being described. If all this talent and energy could be more closely harnessed, if there were a little less violence and a little more detachment, it seemed that Macdonald might be not merely the lineal successor to Hammett and Chandler but even their superior.

The development that one hoped for has not quite taken place. Macdonald's later books are in many ways better than the early ones. They are composed with less violence, more subtlety, more satisfactory plots. The quality of the observation gives pleasure; the view of California as a place of immense beauty made ugly by man is expressed with passion; there is a lot of sympathetic and discerning characterization, particularly of the young. All these later books are good, and it is only naming personal preferences to mention particularly *The Zebra-Striped Hearse* (1962) and *The Far Side of the Dollar* (1964). Yet an impression that Macdonald has repeated too often the quest for personal identity and the investigation of the past that marks these books, that he has been too easily content with the things he can do well, remains. Perhaps it is a pity that he has retained Archer in every story; perhaps his talent would have flowered more finely and more variously if he had sometimes looked for a setting and a theme outside California. But of course a writer must be judged by what he has actually done, and such conjecture is more or less idle. At his best, Macdonald is as good a writer as Chandler, and that should not be taken for light praise.

Julian Symons. *Mortal Consequences: A History—
From the Detective Story to the Crime Novel* (New
York: Harper & Row, 1972), pp. 189–90

Detective novels are by their very nature a kind of puzzle. One begins reading a detective mystery with the assumption that there is a puzzle to be figured out—the puzzle of the crime. Who did it? And why? Too often readers and critics confine their analyses to how well individual novels succeed as puzzles and completely disregard the larger structure of the writer's entire body of work. Ross Macdonald has a much larger purpose than the construction of individual games for intellectual distraction. He analyzes contemporary society and the shaky psychological substructure on which it rests. Frequently his plots reflect classical mythology twisted or distorted by modern circumstances to reveal a new mythology, one depicting California as the symbol of man's inability to cope with himself, his fellow man, and the world.

Any effort to place his literary achievement—whether within the restricted field of detective novelists or the broader spectrum of modern fiction—should first attempt to separate criticism of the genre from criticism of Macdonald as practitioner of that genre. One of the few literary critics of stature to take the genre seriously and to direct his attention to Macdonald specifically is Geoffrey Hartman. Professor Hartman makes some interesting observations, which can serve as a point of departure. He says:

> to solve a crime in detective stories means to give it an exact location: to pinpoint not merely the murderer and his motives but also the very place, the room, the ingenious or brutal circumstance. We want not only proof but, like Othello, ocular proof.
>
> . . . sophisticated art is closer to being an antimystery rather than a mystery. It limits, even while expressing, this passion for ocular proof.

Hartman sees the detective story as clearly preferring "the horror of the visible . . . to what is unknown or invisible," suggesting finally that the genre is incapable of dealing with the subtler shadings of psychology and circumstance. While he admits that there are, of course, differences among the styles of American mystery writers and says, for example, that "Macdonald's characters . . . are more credible than Chandler's, because they are more ordinary," Hartman presses on to another significant criticism. In his opinion, the genre avoids moral issues in favor of an "exploitative element" that plays upon a popular desire to believe "that one just man (the detective) will succeed" even though reality, for Hartman, suggests this is not the case. He draws particular attention to *The Goodbye Look* and finds fault with that part of the plot which has Nick Chalmers, at the age of eight, shooting his estranged father, Eldon Swain. He interprets Swain's performance and motivations as "only an act of sentiment and boozy affection" and concludes that "grim mistakes of this kind belong to folklore or high tragedy."

Such criticism implies several misreadings of Macdonald. To suggest that Eldon Swain's actions are purely the result of "sentiment and boozy affection" is to disregard all the evidence amassed in the plot concerning Swain's *possible* motivations (blackmail, kidnapping, child molesting) and the chronicle of Swain's spiraling moral decline (from banker, to embezzler, to purchaser of another man's daughter). And to speak of Archer in terms of exploiting the reader's gullible desire to believe in perfect heroes is to overlook Macdonald's careful and explicit avoidance of the Chandlerian hero ("neither tarnished nor afraid") in favor of a character as capable of selfishness and failure as any human. In Hartman's final summation, he remarks, perhaps more to the point, that:

the trouble with the detective novel is not that it is moral but that it is moralistic; not that it is popular but that it is stylized; not that it lacks realism but that it picks up the latest realism [Freudianism in Macdonald's case] and exploits it.

While his criticisms apply with more force to some detective novelists than others (perhaps more to Spillane than to Hammett, for instance), they make very little room for the unique achievements which are possible in the genre and which Macdonald frequently exemplifies.

It may be instructive at this point to reflect upon Hartman's further criticism of detective fiction that "when all is finished, nothing is rereadable." This assertion is rooted in his belief that detective stories lack the dramatic irony characteristic of great tragedy. The multiple layers of meaning which an author is able to suggest by his use of irony are often used as a measure of the author's stature.

The classic example of dramatic irony occurs in Sophocles' *Oedipus* where the king engages in a hunt for the evil-doer who has brought a plague upon Thebes and the object of the hunt proves to be the king himself. The point is that it is possible to argue the existence of a kind of dramatic irony in Macdonald's work, that this irony is only apparent upon rereading, and that the rereading makes the author's ability and his message shine in a new light.

To give just one example: when we have read *The Zebra-Striped Hearse* and know that Harriet is the real murderer, that Mark Blackwell's psyche was largely shaped by the tyranny of his own mother, that he has fathered a child by Dolly, and that he finally commits suicide in an attempt to absolve himself of his guilt in the whole affair, then we begin to look very differently on Mark and his bungling belligerence, and on such early statements as: "You don't know the pressures I live under. The combined forces of the females in my life—"

In this light, Macdonald's efforts might be seen as a kind of anti-mythology or mythology on its head—the negative mythology of individual avarice and desire. It is a world without communal value where man is systematically consuming himself and ravaging nature.

As the novels are absorbed into the reader's consciousness, they leave there a personal, residual mythology of characters and plots on the edge of man's technological advance westward that serve the very contemporary purpose of explaining "why the world is as it is and things happen the way they do," that help us become conscious of the evil within our collective unconscious—a mythology of the mass mind, of contemporary society.

Finally, the novels reflect not only a cultural mythology but also, as with all great fiction, the record of the author's own personal struggles to comprehend the world and his own place in it. As Macdonald has described the writing process:

> The character holding the pen has to wrestle and conspire with the one taking shape on paper, extracting a vision of the self from internal darkness—a self dying into fiction as it comes to birth.

The struggle of the self for identity, whose record Macdonald has left for us in the pages of his novels, offers a brilliant, vivid image of contemporary consciousness in conflict with itself and surely justifies William Goldman's calling these "the finest series of detective novels ever written by an American." Perhaps in time, when our views of contemporary fiction are less myopic, even some of the restricting qualifiers to greatness in that phrase will fade away.

> Jerry Speir. *Ross Macdonald* (New York: Ungar,
> 1978), p. vii, 154–60

Ross Macdonald, the true successor to Hammett and Chandler, worked in almost the same vein as his models. His detective, Lew Archer, is an ex-cop who has left the police force to get away from the constant menace of corruption.

His clients' cases typically begin as family affairs but the subsequent investigations lay bare intricate networks of avarice formed by lust for power, by jealousy, and by greed, all of which lead eventually to murder. Gangsters, even whole families, all belong to the same complex, degenerate world.

The crimes in Macdonald's novels are committed frequently in the wealthier parts of Southern California, in white-washed villas, surrounded by palm trees, with the rich wicked and the police corrupt. Again and again somebody is in need of protection and, difficult as it may be, Lew Archer simply has to survive to help uncover the morass of complicated motives lying beneath the integument of the laid-back and permissive society.

Almost in a Freudian sense, the identification of the ills in society is enough to start the client on the road to recovery. Archer can keep himself aloof from the relationships of the people he encounters in the same way a psychiatrist distances himself in a personal way; his duty is simply to unmask the evil and let it show in all its hideousness. Rehabilitation is up to the patient.

> Waltraud Woeller and Bruce Cassiday. *The*
> *Literature of Crime and Detection* (New York:
> Ungar, 1988), p. 141

MARSH, NGAIO (1895–1982)

Ngaio Marsh's characters seem mostly fantasy. The sheer business of trying to be psychologically plausible about a small group of people (usually with subterranean pasts) who are meant by the rules of the genre to have performed some almost gymnastically ingenious act, has often defeated the detective story writer. And from that basic implausibility poor character drawing may hurtle the characters (or "cast" as Marsh calls them) into ridiculous love affairs and little lives as pat as their actions. What has always distinguished Miss Marsh from the rest has been her gift for narrative clarity, for linking striking situations together. The little pasteboard men are shoved around the board with great dexterity.

David Hare. *The Spectator*. December 12, 1970,
pp. 772–73

Tied up in Tinsel is *not* a reprint, though it might be and surely will often be! As, mark you, *Death in Ecstasy* which appeared in 1936 has been. The incredible ease with which Miss Marsh conceals the skill and effort of her constructions under a surface of bright light humor is no more remarkable now than it was all those years ago. She has not *needed* to develop, to improve—she was always just right. Apart from a few details, this country house staffed entirely by convicted murderers might have figured in a thirties whodunit, though the then-legal processes might have made such characters less freely available. Alleyn and Fox don't seem a day older than when we first met them, and well-deserved promotion seems to elude them, too.

Leo Harris. *Books & Bookmen*. June 1972, p. 82

Dame Ngaio has now reached that classic state where she is almost above criticism.

Dame Ngaio has an extraordinary gift for the drawing of characters just this side of eccentricity (and sometimes those on just the other side, as in *Surfeit of Lampreys*), as well as an amazing sense of the visual: her atmospheres and scenic set pieces are always pure magic. Her detection is, of course, usually excellent, but her achievement in scenes and tones serves to remind us of how important it is for the detective story writer, expecially one in the traditional mold, to create a separate and slightly artificial world for his or her characters. It is in the precision and completeness of these fictional worlds that the detective writer most readily manages to suspend the disbelief of the reader, and if the writer's mind has a turn for the bizarre, as Dame Ngaio has, the world becomes one providing particular delight for the reader.

The Spectator. May 4, 1974, p. 550

Ngaio Marsh invariably constructs her plots following one specific formula. None of her novels begins with the crime but they start with several chapters which provide atmosphere and introduce the characters who will later become suspects and victim. Then comes the murder. Following the murder the police take over and perform tests and conduct extensive interviews with the suspects. Near the end of the interviews there is a recapitulation scene in which one of the subsidiary detectives sums up the known information and presents it as a list of suspects with notations on motive and opportunity. Then Marsh often, but not always, adds an adventure sequence, like the communist business in *A Man Lay Dead,* or a second murder, as in *Enter a Murderer* and *Artists in Crime.* This is followed by the confrontation scene or reenactment where the murderer is exposed, and the book closes with a very short—atypically short for a detective novelist—summary which ties up and explains events which have not been explained before. The formula, then, is: introduction, murder, interviews, recapitulation, action, reenactment, and summary. It always happens this way. What is so unusual about this pattern? Most detective novelists follow it. That is true, but Marsh varies from the norm in the atypically short summary and in the tenacity with which she sticks to the pattern. With Marsh the murder cannot occur on the first page and the summary cannot take more than a few pages. This is because she constructs her detective novels following the traditional structure of the drama which every beginning student of the drama knows . . . from Aristotle. . . . According to ancient dramatic criticism, every play has three structural parts: the prostasis, the epistasis, and the catastrophe. The prostasis introduces characters, sets the scene, provides background material, and incites the subsequent action of the drama. For Marsh the application is obvious: she sets the scene, gives background, introduces characters, and then brings in the murder which incites the rest of the action in the first stage of her plots. Epistasis: the epistasis according to classical theory is the actual action of the play during which there is an increase in tribulations for the hero, and the writer confronts the audience with surprises and crises. For Marsh, the middle of the book contains the characters' (the detective and his assistants) collection of a mass of testimony, which gives various surprises to the detectives and the readers; it complicates what seemed to be clear-cut issues, and it gives rise to various crises for suspects and detectives alike. When the midbook recapitulation comes there should be a ready and easy solution to the problem (and there is one since the detective, but not his friends or the readers, knows the answer) but it is not apparent. Finally comes the catastrophe, the last part, in which the problem is solved through action, the threads tied up, and the stage emptied. This is the place where Marsh's books are most obviously made on the pattern of the drama. If one wants to insult or attack a drama—or at least a traditional one—all that has to be done is to whisper the word "anti-climax." Try to find a critic who believes that act five of *Henry V* is structurally fitting and you will see the point. Drama is supposed to stop soon after the most important action has been performed. Marsh knows this and she also knows that the detective's summation can be and is a long, boring lump on the end of many detective novels, which makes them anti-climatic. Therefore, she never includes windy summary chapters in her books, but sticks to the reenactment because it is structurally more fitting—more dramatic.

Coming as she does at the end of the Golden Age, Marsh was better able to fit her fictions to the postwar world than her fellow writers. In part this was because she was not infected so strongly with the spirit of play and in part because she did not have to work at breaking down clichés of the thriller—this had already been done for her by others. . . . She had no past to live down and could start at the point at which the others finished. Consequently, her realistic view of police and crime, her sensitive detective hero, and her perceptive drawing of subsidiary characters fit in with the new mold. Her books were not as frank or disturbing as much postwar detective fiction in both America and Britain, but they were still realistic and used techniques which readers had become accustomed to through their years of reading the other detective writers. Marsh survived the break in cultural continuity brought about by the Second World War because she put both worlds into her books—the old, comfortable arcadia, and the new and disturbing country without a name.

LeRoy Lad Panek. *Watteau's Shepherds: The Detective Novel in Britain 1914–1940* (Bowling Green, Ohio: Popular Press, 1979) pp. 196–97

Much of the structure of Marsh's novels is naturally determined by the conventions of classic detective fiction. When she began to write, she modeled her novels on those prevalent in the 1930s. Therefore, her early works reflect the devices and techniques already used by Sayers, Christie, and others, and many of these continue into the later novels: maps, connected chapter titles, repeated characters, mention of previous cases, the midnovel recapitulation, the lists of various sorts (clues, questions, suspects), the detective's laying traps for the murderer, the action's stopping with the arrest of the murderer, the final summation by the detective, and on and on. The rule of fairness to the reader was made much of in the Golden Age, and Marsh has been scrupulous in laying out all of the necessary information. A recheck of any novel after the final summation demonstrates that. Her fairness may be clearly seen in her habit of presenting the murderer's thoughts shortly after the crime. Whether the murderer is frightened, remorseful, jubilant, or contemplating his next move, that he is the murderer can be deduced—with a correct reading.

The structural feature of Marsh's novels most often criticized is the amount of time Alleyn spends interrogating one witness or suspect after another. The early novels especially are characterized by a long parade of interviews, sometimes repetitious, with chapter titles giving the names of the persons questioned. It can be argued that, though weak from a narrative standpoint, such a series of interviews is a prime illustration of Alleyn's continual insistence that most police work is routine and even tedious. Also, they indicate Marsh's interest in character, since they emphasize the reactions of those involved, and the influence of her theatrical work, for each is a dramatic scene, practically all dialogue.

From these interviews, Alleyn not only pieces together the sequence of the crime, discerns motives, and eliminates some suspects, but also obtains verbal clues by his questioning, whether lies or truth. What is surprising, however, is that most of the cases hinge not on verbal clues, but on physical ones. . . . Half an onion, a notched stethoscope, trout scales, a dead cat, color blindness, a glove, an angled mirror, a lost diamond clip, a druidic costume, a fishing line, a new flashbulb for a camera, a damp sheet of music—these are just a few of the physical clues which lead Alleyn to solutions.

Before he reaches them, Marsh makes his job more difficult by throwing all sorts of red herrings in his path. She is fond of including another crime, which complicates the investigation of the murder. Most often that crime is drug dealing. It appears in seven novels. . . . Blackmail, theft, and illegal gambling are other "extra" crimes present, as well as communist plots. . . . Another type of red herring appears in the novels in which murder occurs within a large family; this is the Golden Age convention of the members being either at cross purposes or attempting to shield each other. It is enough to say that Marsh is never at a loss to find ways of impeding Alleyn's process of discovery, which only makes his ultimate success even more brilliant.

Earl F. Bargainnier. *10 Women of Mystery*
(Bowling Green, Ohio: Popular Press, 1981), pp. 99–101

In *Color Scheme,* the real trouble starts when Roderick Alleyn presents Carolyn Dacres with a Maori tiki. Her husband Meyer then facetiously bows to the ornament for good luck, and Alleyn whispers to Dr. Te Pokiha "I half regret my impulse." Te Pokiha's reply is significant: "So may my great grandparents have laughed over the first crucifix they saw." Of course, shortly after this scene Meyer is killed and Te Pokiha tells Alleyn "The tiki is revenged." Marsh implicitly vindicates the moral order when the sacrilege of *tapu* objects returns with an unexpected irony upon these reckless and obtuse Europeans.

Te Pokiha's account of the initial desecration of the tiki by a European is a damning piece of narrative, and one of his laments about European colonization is that Maoris "have become a sideshow in the tourist bureau—our dances—our art—everything." Can it be that, in spite of her honorable intentions, Marsh herself unwittingly used the Maori element for plot enhancement? The issue seems to focus around Alleyn's instinctive admiration for Te Pokiha, the Oxford-trained, pureblooded Maori aristocrat with "the most exquisite manners." Alleyn's attraction to him is undoubtedly founded on respect, but that respect is itself clearly based upon the Doctor's presence and bearing. We have previously heard Te Pokiha summed up by Wade; that although athletic and brainy ("Best type of Maori"), the Doctor is only "ninety percent civilized. See him when he goes crook!" True to form, Te Pokiha rises to provocation, his lips coarsen "into a sort of snarl," his teeth are bared like a dog's and the ever-suave Alleyn purrs, "By Jove, the odd twenty percent of pure savage.'' It was this passage of *Vintage Murder* that so enraged Bill Pearson when he wrote about writers (usually not New Zealanders) who showed in their stories ''that all Maoris, no matter how educated, are incomprehensible savages at heart.''

As if to set the record straight, Marsh tried to present a less ambivalent portrait of a Maori *rangitira* in the next New Zealand story, *Color Scheme.* In this novel Ngaio Marsh exhibits a deep reverence for Rua Te Kahu, a chief of the Te Rarawas. She is less successful at avoiding cliché with his great-granddaughter Huia, the memorable yet vaporous Maori help whose ''voice was as cool and deep as her native forests.'' But in the person of Rua, Marsh wishes to create a symbol for the Maori people over a long stretch of time. Rua's father was a *tohunga* who had signed the Treaty of Waitangi and therefore he is a well equipped figure to declaim on his ''children,'' like the half-caste (''a bad *pakeha*-Maori'') Eru Saul. He remarks that

> The reason may put on new garments but the heart and the blood are constant. From the shaft of the weapon there flows an influence darker and more potent than all the *pakeha* wisdom I have stored in my foolish old head.

This is not a piece of subtle racism (it is far less liable to misinterpretation than Alleyn's ''odd twenty percent of pure savage''), nor is Marsh using the Maori notion of *tapu* as a sensational bit of superstitious supernaturalism. The affair of Questing (his name being suitably ironic), in search of native relics to sell, serves as a deeply critical comment on the cupidity and lack of spiritual values of the European.

Bruce Harding. Landfall. December 1982, pp. 447–60

Even as a novelist whose work spanned nearly fifty years, Ngaio Marsh was unsure of her achievement, struggling with plots, waiting anxiously to hear from her agents, grateful beyond belief for praise. Nevertheless, of the four Queens of Crime who dominated the 1930s—Margery Allingham, Agatha Christie, Ngaio Marsh, and Dorothy L. Sayers—Ngaio Marsh reigns supreme for excellence of style and characterization. She expanded the genre in a fresh and creative way, adding psychological depth and a welcome strand of humor to the basic murder investigation.

Even today, when the classic Golden Age formula of detective fiction has diversified along many different paths, the novels of Ngaio Marsh continue to be republished for a new generation of crime fiction readers. Like a vintage car, or her own cherished Jaguar XK150, they have ceased to be old-fashioned and have the timeless qualities that always go with sound craftsmanship and good style.

Writing to friends just before she died, about her last novel, *Light Thickens,* and the profound uncertainties that she felt about the manuscript, she concluded characteristically, "I'm glad I tried." What better epitaph could anyone request? Except, perhaps, the words of the late Sir Anthony Quayle, actor, director and a friend for many years, who wrote about Ngaio, "She was a generous, intelligent, warm-hearted spirit and made the world a richer place."

Margaret Lewis. *Ngaio Marsh* (London: Chatto & Windus, 1991), p. x

MILLAR, MARGARET (1915–   )

Margaret Millar has always worked in the format of the detective story, producing novels that usually transcend the genre and approach the literary mainstream. She won the Mystery Writers of America's Edgar Allan Poe Award for best mystery novel for *Beast in View* (1955) and was named Grand Master of the Mystery by that organization in 1986.

Beginning her career in the 1940s with a number of books written in the traditional format of the detective story, she soon broke away from the established conventions to probe more deeply into the psychological motivations of murder. The theme of vengeance, carefully camouflaged in some cases even from the avenger, runs strongly through her works. Complex crosscurrents of love and hate force her characters into cerebral as well as physical acts of destruction. Her later stories, set mostly in California, show a simpatico and appreciation of the Chicano population in a primarily Anglo environment. She uses background and sociology skillfully to highlight the aberrations of her main characters.

In *Beast in View,* the work that established her as a major writer of psychological suspense novels, the motivation of the principal character is a tangle of conflicts that creates a psychotic individual capable of being both killer *and* victim. *Beyond This Point Are Monsters* (1970) involves an ethnic conflict between Anglo and Chicano that screens the true motive for murder, pointing up the danger of bigotry and prejudice in trying to uncover any truth. In *Ask for Me Tomorrow* (1976), a clever avenger performs her actions in front of the reader's eyes, but with all motivation carefully out of sight. In *Spider Webs* (1986), a courtroom drama, the avenger is present, seated quietly and waiting to act if the guilty party should be declared not guilty.

While the conventional detective novelist focuses primarily on a detector or pursuer, Millar, in her later books, focuses on the actions and reactions of a (usually) female protagonist whose psychological twists, conflicts, or aberrations set the story in motion. In the end, the author is concerned with what makes a killer kill, not with how a detective stalks a murderer. Frequently her detectives are surrogates—lawyers, interested parties, and so on. They play a secondary role in the final revelation of the psychological twists and turns of the protagonist's mind.

A Millar story line frequently violates the straight-line narration of mystery-genre convention, circling warily around before finally zeroing in on the source of evil, the killer, at the end—although clues have been liberally strewn throughout to satisfy the traditional detective fan. In fact, without her in-depth psychological study, without her expertly presented backgrounds, without her evocative characters and spritely dialogue, Millar's plots would stand on their own as models of the genre.

Bruce Cassiday. *Encyclopedia of American Literature* (New York: Continuum, in preparation)

In *Wall of Eyes,* Margaret Millar concerns herself with an oddly sorted household dominated by a blind and vindictive younger sister who holds her power by holding the family purse strings. To be sure, this presumed an unsympathetic limpness on the part of her victims—the father, drained by his wife; the housekeeper-sister; the simple, hulking brother; the young and sensitive pianist—but Mrs. Millar's skill mitigated this in part. The blind tyrant is murdered and the ultimate object of the tale is the object of any detective story: to uncover the murderer.

But the method of the narrative is to present the tale through the perceptions of its characters and obviously, if she is to keep her murderer a secret, Mrs. Millar must at the same time lose her richest opportunity for exploring the murderer's mind. She must so sharply select his thoughts that she presents him piecemeal until, after all, it appears that what we have had is not a psychological study but some exceedingly adept sleight-of-hand. We have been in the fairly improbable position of sharing a murderer's mind fully, except for what after all must be occupying most of it—the matter of murder itself.

Mrs. Millar's latest novel, *The Iron Gates,* uses the same technique. Once more she is dealing with an uneasily ingrown family. At first the narrative is directed chiefly through the consciousness of Lucille Morrow, second wife of a distinguished gynecologist whose first wife has been hacked to death some years earlier while returning from an evening at her successor's house. The author establishes very deftly the pride of the second Mrs. Morrow in her possession of her husband, marks easily her humorous tyranny over him and the enmity felt toward her by her two stepchildren. And then, suddenly, after a ragged stranger's visit to deliver a box, Lucille disappears. Later she is found, raving. The second part of the novel describes her short stay behind the iron gates—the protecting gates—of Penwood asylum. But the gates are not impregnable, and Lucille's overwhelming fear that she will be murdered (why she fears we do not know; we share her fear but not its source) drives her to suicide. The third part of the novel is the unraveling, the diagnosis of madness and of murder's motive. Once more Mrs. Millar's concern has been to observe the workings of the terrified mind.

But she has insisted, as well, upon hiding the causes of the terror so that she can surprise us at the last. And because of this, it would be a good deal more accurate to call her novel not a psychological novel but a tale of terror. For as a psychological study it is, by its own limitations, necessarily superficial.

James Sandoe. *Poetry Magazine*. June 1946, n.p.

Margaret Millar fits no more neatly into the generic category of detective fiction novelist than she does into that of gothic romancer. She is neither a Hammett nor a du Maurier, but the dialectic between established form and artistic purpose in her fiction reveals her to be, at the very least, a fundamental revisionist attempting to reimagine the premises of the mystery story. Millar's sort of revision should not be confused with purely technical variation. For example, when Agatha Christie violates the rule of detective fiction that proscribes the use of a narrator as the murderer, or wittily applies the axiom governing probability (eliminate the impossible, and whatever remains, however improbable, must be the truth) to reveal that since no single person is the murderer, everybody on the Orient Express sleeper must be, she is approaching the minor conventions of the detection puzzles as technical materials for bafflement. She transgresses the rules to place her signature upon the form, but the effect of surprise depends upon the rules remaining valid except in one case.

Contrasting with pure technical variation of this sort is Millar's reversal of detective function in *Ask for Me Tomorrow*. In that novel the attorney Tom Aragon is hired by Gilda Lockwood Decker to locate her first husband in Mexico. Key informants meet with accident, and worse, before Aragon can interview them; still, he pieces together evidence to formulate a satisfactory hypothesis about Lockwood's disappearance. The final pages of the novel, however, completely redefine Aragon's role. Lockwood, the victim of a stroke, is living with Gilda as a second husband under the name of Decker. He had truly gone to Mexico, been imprisoned and otherwise abused, then remarried Gilda. She had vowed to avenge her husband and accomplished the vendetta by employing Aragon to seek out the people who had been instrumental in Lockwood's Mexican period. She had then sent his male nurse to execute them. Unknowingly the detective has become a fingerman; the distressed client is the criminal; and the missing man has never been lost.

Such comprehensive reversal must be described in terms of variations upon features of the narrative that our experience with detective stories has led us to expect, but in their significance they go well beyond technical bafflement to suggest a fictional environment very different from the one where we first developed our now disappointed expectations.

Millar's revisions in generic patterns must also be distinguished from the practice of enriching a story by the addition of secondary themes. Her provision, for example, of a Chicano background for the detectives Steve

Pinata and Tom Aragon, and her relation of ethnic prejudice to events are not patently didactic as is, say, the information about Judaism offered by Harry Kemelman in the Rabbi Small stories. Nor is Millar's revision of the same sort as Dorothy L. Sayer's integration of the interestingly adult relationship of Harriet Vane and Lord Peter Wimsey into the detective story. Sayers gives detective stories a greater range and modifies their characteristically male outlook, but she leaves the essential patterns of the classic story intact, since they can well accommodate her innovations. In contrast to Sayers, Millar finds that her innovations are necessary in the first place, because her basic suppositions will not readily accommodate to the available patterns.

John M. Reilly. In Earl F. Bargainnier, ed., *10 Women of Mystery* (Bowling Green, Ohio: Popular Press, 1981), pp. 227–29

Margaret Millar's reputation is not as widespread as her husband's (he is Ross Macdonald), but among her followers it ranks as high, and appreciation is intense. Her specialty, beginning with *An Air That Kills* (1957), has been the interweaving of menace and anxiety with rather subdued or inessential mystery. Before that date, she had evidently tried classic-style detection (see *Wall of Eyes,* 1943) and given it up; but lately her stories—always intent on strong effects—have reinstated search and detection. *Beyond This Point Are Monsters,* the one under review, set in southern California, deals with the effort to establish the death of a man missing for eighteen months. The method—court testimony—makes for some repetition but does not lessen suspense. The dialogue is brisk, though not sharply characterized, and the surprise ending has a touch of ambiguity, but plot and physical clues are first-rate. In the same vein, see *Ask for Me Tomorrow* (1976).

Jacques Barzun and Wendell Hertig Taylor. *The Armchair Detective.* Summer 1981, pp. 228–29

"Among the crime writers who have come into prominence since the war she has few peers, and no superior, in the art of bamboozlement. She presents us with a plausible criminal situation, builds it up to a climax of excitement, and then in the last few pages shakes the kaleidoscope and shows us an entirely different pattern from the one we have been so busily interpreting." I wrote these words about Ross Macdonald's wife, Margaret Millar (1915–   ) a long while ago. They still seem true, although one would have to add the qualification "at her best." She is one of those novelists whose imagination is sparked off by the element of mystery, and the four "straight" novels she published in the forties and early fifties are much inferior to her best mystery stories. Even as a mystery writer her early books were comparatively commonplace. It is the half-dozen books beginning with *Beast in View* (1955) that show the full scope of her skill as a novelist whose chosen theme is almost always a mystery with roots deeply hidden in the past.

The skill is shown at its finest in *How Like an Angel* (1962) which begins when Joe Quinn, a former casino cop at Reno who has lost his money gambling, lands up at the home of the True Believers in California, out in bleak mountainous country, forty-five miles from the nearest large town. The True Believers is a religious cult whose members believe that they are preparing for the ascension of a Tower which has five levels, of the earth, trees, mountains, sky, and at the top "the Tower of Heaven where the Master lives." . . . The practical good sense of Sister Blessing, the silence of Brother Tongue of Prophets, the excitement when a new convert arrives to join the slowly disintegrating group, are conveyed with a powerful sense of pathos and absurdity, joined to respect for a way of life. The tension of the novel is partly created by the contrast between the simplicities of the group, and the complexity of the investigation which Quinn undertakes on behalf of Sister Blessing into the background of Patrick O'Gorman, who apparently died five years earlier in a car accident. The puzzle is there all right, and its solution on the last page lives up to those phrases used about Millar's work, but by that time many readers will have become so much concerned with the fate of the characters that the problem itself is a secondary thing.

The best of the other Millar books show her ability to create an atmosphere of uneasiness and terror which in other hands might have become merely Gothic, but in her case is used to show developments based on the conflict of character. *Beast in View*, with its perfectly fair bit of conjuring on which the whole story depends, *The Soft Talkers* (1957), *The Listening Walls* (1959), with its apparent double bluff and brilliant trick ending, and *A Stranger in My Grave* (1960), are all very good. Millar's recent books have been less firmly plotted, and only occasionally successful.

Julian Symons. *Bloody Murder: From the
Detective Story to the Crime Novel* (New York:
Viking, 1985), pp. 174–75

In dealing with the psychopathology of crime, Margaret Millar weaves her web and holds up her mirror to madness with infinite care. Her silences speak as eloquently as her words. She has been creating this magic for many years. Her nearest lineal descendant among the newer crime writers is Britain's Ruth Rendell.

It is interesting to note (perhaps coincidentally) the way in which Rendell's titles parallel titles of earlier Millar books: There is Millar's award-winning *Beast in View*, about a paranoid schizophrenic woman; and there is Rendell's *A Demon in My View*, which won Britain's Gold Dagger award, about a paranoid schizophrenic man. *The Devil Loves Me* was one of Millar's earliest books; Rendell's *Make Death Love Me* is of more recent vintage.

These (both Millar's and Rendell's books) are skillful studies in the broken pathways of the psyche, and bear about as much resemblance to those one-dimensional books (in which a seemingly sane person is suddenly designated on the next-to-last page as a nut case who committed the crime) as gold resembles dross.

Rendell's writings, however, are relentlessly evil. Millar's are leavened with a pocketful of wry. Her collection of crazies range from the truly demonic to the gently daft. One of her most daft—and most engaging—is the elder Mrs. Osborne in *Beyond This Point Are Monsters.*

Elaine Budd. *13 Mistresses of Murder* (New York:
Ungar, 1986), p. 90

In the subgenre of the psychological suspense mystery, women are absolute craftmasters. Margaret Millar, an underrated writer, is probably used to a certain amount of this because, as the wife and then the widow of Ross Macdonald, she has consistently been in the shadow of his career. (Personally, I find her a superior writer.)

Millar wrote her first novel, *The Invisible Worm,* in 1941; since then, she has written approximately thirty novels, most of them in the psychological-suspense genre. She is a subtle and, I think, genuinely original writer who creates suspenseful stories through her understanding of the pathology of crime. Her studies of the psychology of children are indeed extraordinary, and I direct you particularly to *Banshee.* Here she writes with exquisite sensitivity of a lonely child who invents playmates to console herself. The beauty of this portrait is its insistence on the child's honesty.

During an interview, I once asked her about her uncanny insights into the minds of her child characters. "Why is it that adults don't seem to take children seriously?" she asked me in return. I couldn't tell her, so she went on: "A kid will come home from school and tell his parents something important that happened; and the parents will say, 'Oh, the little bugger's lying again!' " This seemed to annoy her, because she said: "Adults always assume that the child is lying or having a fantasy. I, however, would always tend to believe the child and assume that the *adult* is having the fantasy."

I consider Millar one of the very few writers of suspense fiction who truly speaks for children's rights. Her young characters are always human beings, which is what makes her descriptions of childhood horrors so compelling. I think that Millar also understands that the essence of suspense involves the threat of evil to innocence—something which takes on extra frisson when the innocent is a child. There is also the drama, in suspense stories, when the victims are unable to communicate this threat of evil to those who might help them. With Millar's children, this becomes more poignant because they are doubly vulnerable, unable to communicate their fears to adults who either won't listen or won't believe them. That's genuine suspense—not those gory, pornographic, woman-loathing, slice-and-dice novels so often mislabeled "suspense" mysteries.

Marilyn Stasio. In Barbara A. Rader and Howard
G. Zettler, eds., *The Sleuth and the Scholar*
(Westport, Connecticut: Greenwood Press, 1988),
p. 74

MULLER, MARCIA (1944–   )

With a fairly average—for California—middle-class upbringing, Marcia Muller's Sharon McCone graduated from the University of California, Berkeley, with a degree in sociology. Unable to find a job in her field, she went back into security work—which she had done part-time while a student—and was trained as a detective. Now, she is the staff private eye for the All Souls Legal Cooperative in San Francisco. In typical, laid back, California style, the Coop provides people with low cost legal counseling and pays correspondingly low salaries to its partners. To make up for the low pay, several of the attorneys, including Sharon's good friend and boss, Hank Zahn, live in the old Victorian house which serves as the office as well. Sharon doesn't live there herself, and actually spends more time in the field than in her small office, but it serves as a center for her messages and the inevitable monthly bills.

Sharon takes her job seriously and applies a high standard of professionalism to the work she does. One of the reasons that she is good as an investigator is that she has an innate respect for the people she has to deal with as well as enough objectivity to sort out the good guys from the bad ones. In return, she demands respect for herself and her profession, but does not wear a chip on her shoulder in defense of a less than traditionally feminine choice of work. In the first book, *Edwin of the Iron Shoes*, Sharon meets Lieutenant Greg Marcus, a homicide detective with the San Francisco police. Their relationship is marked by constant bickering and many of the issues of disagreement between them center around Sharon's work as a P.I. The relationship ends at the end of *Ask the Cards a Question*.

Some of Sharon's investigations begin with murder. Others begin as something else but turn to murder as the case progresses. She relies on her skill in drawing people out for most of her information and is good at assessing the answers she receives. Occasionally she needs to run some risks in obtaining clues or evidence. In these situations, not all of her decisions are wise and Sharon finds herself in jeopardy. In *Double*, written jointly by Muller and Bill Pronzini, she has been shot, stranded on the desert at midday with no water, and is at the mercy of a murderer who has already killed twice. The Nameless Detective—Pronzini's own series character—a man with whom she is working on the case, arrives in the nick of time to save her.

This character has evolved through the seven books in which she appears. Any risks she takes seem to be a bit more calculated and she is using her intellect more than her gun to resolve sticky situations. Her relations with the police have improved and she is less antagonistic with officers of the law than she was in the early books. Perhaps Don Del Boccio, a disc jockey with whom she has become romantically involved, can be given some of the credit for these changes, as he gives her the respect she requires and a great deal of latitude to be who she is and to do what she does.

Most of Sharon's work takes place in and around the city of San Francisco. Author Marcia Muller is a San Francisco Bay Area resident herself and provides wonderful descriptions of places all up and down the Peninsula. In *Games to Keep the Dark Away,* Sharon travels south to the small fishing community of Salmon Bay in search of a missing woman. Even though Salmon Bay itself is a fictional location, San Jose, Salinas, King City, and Highway 101 are real, and well sketched, if briefly, by Muller.

Victoria Nichols and Susan Thompson. *Silk Stalkings: When Women Write of Murder* (Berkeley: Black Lizard Books, 1988), pp. 212–14

In the first of Marcia Muller's Sharon McCone novels, *Edwin of the Iron Shoes* (1977), the detective develops an uneasy relationship with a police lieutenant, Greg Marcus, who alternately encourages and patronizes Sharon. By the end of the novel the two are moving toward sexual involvement, but it seems clear to the attentive reader that theirs is a doomed romance, with Marcus's insistence on addressing Sharon by an endearment that she finds offensive—"papoose"—one clear indication of trouble ahead. This nickname suggests that Marcus sees Sharon as a child and as an object identifiable strictly by race. In the second of the McCone books, *Ask the Cards a Question* (1982), the reader finds Marcus wooing Sharon with chocolate—still unable to take her seriously—but agreeing in the end to accept Sharon's terms for their relationship, a relationship that meets its inevitable end in *The Cheshire Cat's Eyes* (1983).

Muller eventually creates a relatively conflict-free romantic relationship for her detective, as the three most recent Sharon McCone novels—*Games to Keep the Dark Away* (1984), *Leave a Message for Willie* (1984), and *There's Nothing to Be Afraid Of* (1985)—incorporate subplots following Sharon's involvement with a disc jockey who is a near paragon of feminist manhood: he really listens to women, respects Sharon's commitment to her job, never expects that theirs will be a traditional relationship, etc. In *Leave a Message for Willie,* Sharon worries that Don will be like other men in her past who have hated her job, and then that his moving to San Francisco, where she lives, will doom their relationship: "It seemed to me that relationships between men and women didn't last very long these days. And it also seemed that, the more you were together, the more you hastened that almost certain end.'' Over time, Don proves himself to be unlike other men Sharon has known, with his differences finally persuading her that their relationship might last. Nevertheless, even this character ultimately interferes with Sharon's work on a case, blundering into a very delicate and dangerous situation because, he tells her, ''I couldn't just sit there, knowing you might be in danger.'' Although Sharon claims to be furious with him—''I wanted to scream at him. I wanted to hurl the gun at his head''—she quickly forgives him, and they strike a deal, each agreeing to stick to his or her own turf. Muller is more interested in providing her detective with an ongoing sexual relationship than in seriously exploring the ramifications of gender-based conflict within personal relationships.

Maureen T. Reddy. *Sisters in Crime: Feminism
and the Crime Novel* (New York: Continuum,
1988), pp. 92–93, 105–6

Three levels of action—a modern-day museum director trying to learn more about an 1894 San Francisco detective's tracking down a mystery which took place in 1846—make *Beyond the Grave,* by Marcia Muller and Bill Pronzini, fascinating reading. Structurally, it is a fictional variation on Sidney D. Kirkpatrick's nonfiction *A Cast of Killers,* in which a modern-day biographer finally uncovers director King Vidor's account of how he solved a 1921 Hollywood murder.

Muller's Elena Oliverez, who has been featured in two earlier books, attends an auction, hoping to acquire an early Mexican wedding coffer and other items for the Museum of Mexican Arts. The coffer reveals a secret drawer which contains a ninety-year-old manuscript, a report from San Francisco private detective John Quincannon (who has appeared in an earlier Pronzini novel). Quincannon had been hired to track down a cache of statuary and artifacts missing since 1846, when Mexican defenders buried it during a skirmish of the Bear Flag Rebellion.

The story line alternates between time periods, with Muller writing in the first person, Pronzini in the third. Their styles blend well, and the writers do a fine job of creating mystery without (until well along) having a murder to solve. The amateur detective and the professional, separated by nine decades, develop ''an eerie connection.'' And it is Elena, even though distanced by time, who has the necessary background to see a clue which Quincannon cannot, and finally solve the much earlier puzzle.

There is richness here both in character and in setting. Elena is worried about her mother, in the hospital with an ulcer, and about her boyfriend, who has just broken with her. Quincannon also has personal worries, how to get closer to his detective partner Sabina Carpenter. One sees modern-day Santa Barbara, nineteenth-century San Francisco, and glimpses of the 1840s *ranchos grandes* era in the southern part of the state.

The two writers previously collaborated on *Double* (1984), which paired their other series characters, Nameless and Sharon McCone. In this book, they seem more comfortable with the dual format. It's a good read.

Bernard A. Drew. *The Armchair Detective.*
Summer 1987, p. 300

My personal favorite among the amateur female detectives is Marcia Muller's Elena Oliverez, of *The Tree of Death* (1983), *The Legend of the Slain Soldiers* (1985), and *Beyond the Grave* (1986), the last cowritten with Bill Pronzini. Muller, also the author of the Sharon McCone series, combines some unusual elements in these novels. Not only is the detective a woman, but she is also Chicana, one of only two female minority detectives I have come across in a great deal of mystery reading.

Muller sets the Oliverez novels almost entirely within the Mexican-American community of Santa Barbara, with Elena's cultural and ethnic heritage a central fact of her character and of the crimes she investigates. Elena resents those who see her ethnicity as "something to be ignored or even forgiven," because "in the last couple of years I'd come to identify more and more with my heritage and my own people. It hadn't always been that way—I'd had more than my share of Anglo friends and a penchant for Anglo boyfriends—but recently that was changing. Maybe it was working at the museum [of Mexican Arts]; maybe it was simply coming of age." Most refreshingly, the reader also gets a look at cross-cultural relationships from a perspective seldom encountered in popular culture, as Elena finds herself attracted to a police detective and considers whether she should allow herself to become involved with an Anglo.

More than one critic has remarked on the astonishing literariness of characters in detective fiction, but little attention has been paid to the role of the musical and visual arts, both of which feature prominently in mysteries. The solutions to the mysteries in both Oliverez novels require some knowledge of art on the part of the detective, and Muller incorporates a sort of minicourse on Mexican-American art and history into her novels. As *The Tree of Death* begins, Elena has recently been named curator of the Museum of Mexican Arts, which is about to open in new quarters. By the end of the book, Elena is the director of the museum, having solved the murder of the original director.

Muller does an admirable job of interweaving Elena's vocation and her avocation, while simultaneously planting clues to the mystery, sketching out Mexican-American culture and traditions, and deepening Elena's character, delicately balancing all the elements of the novel right to its closing pages. Muller gives Elena a background that enriches one's understanding of and regard for her, providing her with a free-spirited, proud mother who did domestic work to send her daughters to college (Elena has a sister who is a professor at the University of Minnesota) and who is now happily retired to a mostly Mexican-American trailer park, where the murder in *Soldiers* takes place. That Elena now lives in the house where her mother raised her is a revealing detail, typical of Muller's light but sure touch: metaphorically, Elena has chosen to follow her mother's path. The mutual regard of mother and daughter, despite their differences, plays an important role in the novels.

Muller's Oliverez series is feminist in the deepest sense of the term. Women are at the center of the world she creates, with relationships between women seen as basic to every woman's life and women portrayed in all their realistic variety. Muller seems very sensitive to differences among women—differences of age, race, class, ethnicity, personal circumstances—and the first two Oliverez novels celebrate those differences, that variety. The killers in both novels are women, and their victims are men, which may seem both unrealistic and unfeminist—women are far more likely to be victims than murderers—but the motives offered in each instance make psychological sense. Each killer is an idealist who acts on a mistaken conception of honor: Isabel, in *Tree,* kills the museum's director in a fury at his betrayal of the museum she loves through running a lucrative smuggling business in Central American artifacts, while the murderer in *Soldiers* kills first when she believes her lover to have betrayed both her and the labor movement and forty years later when she realizes that the first murder is about to be revealed by a historian.

The only really discordant note in the first two Oliverez books comes in their conventional endings, in which the killer is captured, order is restored, and Elena draws closer to the Anglo police lieutenant, Dave Kirk. Given Elena's status as a minority woman who is intensely aware of social injustice, it seems odd that she trusts the official system of justice so freely, aiding the police in their inquiries and evidently satisfied that a trial will conclude each case. Muller explains Elena's attitude in *Tree* by making her the police's prime suspect and having her embark on an investigation as a way of saving herself, and, less successfully, in *Soldiers* by making the (second) victim her mother's good friend and having her mother initiate the investigation, as she does not believe the police will find the culprit. Nevertheless, taking a nontraditional detective and a nontraditional criminal and then ending their stories in a completely conventional way strikes me as less satisfying than other possibilities.

Maureen T. Reddy. *Sisters in Crime: Feminism and the Crime Novel* (New York: Continuum, 1988), pp. 33–36

One of the most promising women detectives of [the early feminist] period, Marcia Muller's Sharon McCone has become conventional by her seventh appearance. McCone, just under thirty when introduced, is staff investigator for the All Souls Cooperative, a legal and residential commune in San Francisco working with middle-class clients. This alternative to the corporate model of litigation parallels Sharon's apparent disdain for rigid, official systems. Intensely interested, she is willing to risk her license by investigating two cases without having a client, continuing a third when the client ends the case, and talking a fourth prospective client into joining the cooperative to legitimate her already initiated investigation. With a background that includes department store security, night security while working on a sociology degree at Berkeley, and being fired from a large detective agency for not following orders, she is well satisfied with the casual independence allowed by All Souls.

McCone is a fairly traditional investigator, using some logic, some intuition, and plenty of legwork to solve the thirteen murders which seem to dog her personally and professionally. She considers her strongest point to be her ability to ask the right question without also answering it herself; responses come because she looks like a person in whom others can safely confide. Quick thinking in a tight spot, hard working enough to stay up all night or drive monotonously long distances several times, and determined to continue despite opposition, Sharon has come to terms with both the demands and the ethics of her profession. She can rationalize breaking-and-entering or entrapment in her own cause. Luckily, she has both friends and supporters who help her by supplying information, offering cautionary warnings, or hiding her from police scrutiny. She carries false identification, uses judo on thugs, or cuts a deal with the police to solve her cases. But, too often she takes unreasonable risks. Traps she has set lead to suicide or shooting, leaving her to wonder: "But there were more deaths, and the older I got and the more violence I saw, the more I wondered if I could go on like this indefinitely. And when I wondered that, I also wondered what I would do if I couldn't go on. What on earth *could* a former private eye with a useless sociology degree do for a living?" When Sharon considers her choices, the direction is unclear; she knows only that she loves her work, feels she's "a person who lives it every hour, every day." She sees the difference between herself and high school friends with striking clarity on a visit home; she recognizes both vicarious excitement and distance in their eyes. But her older brother also reinforces this divided reaction: he admires her drive and success but insists that she's played safe by never allowing herself to be in a position where she could lose too much.

McCone runs into the usual array of reactions to the combination of her gender and profession. She is surprised when Lieutenant Marcus doesn't pull the standard "what's-a-nice-girl-like-you" routine on her and only slightly amazed when a woman-hating inspector uses her supposed reputation as a troublemaker to make a pass. With her lovers, Sharon encounters vastly different responses: the cop is so persistently hostile to private investigators that her gender is negligible. Her second lover is taken aback by the gun in her glove compartment: "You're for real, aren't you? . . . It's one thing hearing you talk about an investigation, but seeing that. . . ." Her mother wants her to settle down, marry, have kids. Other professional women note, without comment, her choice of profession. The real hostility is voiced by an angry bail-bondsman/suspect/thief; he hopes to insult her—''little girls playing detective''—then threaten, then frighten her off the case. But, Sharon McCone also aligns herself with this last attitude; when she succeeds in standing up to a tough ghetto lawyer, her self-congratulations are for the ex-cheerleader and homecoming princess that she was, not the competent investigator she is. She is surprised to discover her own strength.

Kathleen Gregory Klein. *The Woman Detective:*
Gender and Genre (Urbana and Chicago:
University of Illinois Press, 1988), pp. 206–9

ORWELL, GEORGE [ERIC ARTHUR BLAIR] (1903–1950)

George Orwell's novel *1984*, written in 1948 and published in 1949, stands out mainly for the totally pessimistic future it paints, and for the adroit managing of the plot. Also to be considered is the fact that Orwell was incorporating and commenting on negative sociopolitical developments of the 1930s and after.

Orwell's book is only fully to be understood with reference to the inner development of the writer. Eric Arthur Blair (Orwell's real name) was born in 1903 in Motihari, Bengal, and educated at Eton. He served for five years from 1922 to 1928 in Burma in the Indian Imperial Police. He turned against the methods of the colonial service, and left his position. For some years he led a varied life in different professions. He eventually found his way into journalism.

At this period, Orwell became interested in and joined in the general democratic-socialist movement of the era, with its anarchist-trotskyite overtones, and fought in the International Brigade in the Spanish Civil War in the mid-1930s. When reports began coming in of the personality cult of Stalin, and violations of the Leninist norms in Soviet life grew in frequency, Orwell gave up his communist ideas. He later came to adopt the position of the British Labour Party. He joined the regular staffs of various London newspapers, and was on the staff of the BBC during World War II. In 1945, he published his first dystopian satirical novel, *Animal Farm,* in which he campaigned against dictatorial power structures by means of a parable. In 1949, Orwell published the book that ensured his worldwide fame and that became a supreme example of science fiction literature that dealt with society and politics. Orwell died in 1950. Six years later, a film version of *1984* produced by Michael Anderson introduced it to further millions.

Orwell sets his fiction in the near future, the date determined simply by swapping the numbers in the date of composition (48 and 84). He thus produced a utopia of the near future, distanced by a mere thirty-six years. This time has now passed, and it is easy to make carping indictments of the work by pointing to the many details and the main idea itself by arguing that what Orwell prophesied has not in fact come to pass. But it is important to remember that science fiction is not in the business of foretelling the future, nor is it obliged to paint a literal picture of what is to come; its premises are based in the present, and though the problems it probes may be estranged by being set in the future, its arena is the present.

Dieter Wuckel. *The Illustrated History of Science Fiction* (New York: Ungar, 1989), pp. 139–41

Mr. Orwell stands apart from the imaginative writers of the Left; he spoils for trouble, dislikes his own side more than the enemy, is closer to continental writers. On the continent he found that drama and the suffering which, with mingled Quixotism and misanthropy, he always sought. It is not only this that sets him apart from the rest of the English intelligentsia. What has made him different is that, like a kind of Kipling turned upside down, he has seen the Empire and knows that the violent English political drama is enacted there and not at home.

V. S. Pritchett. *New Statesman and Nation.*
February 16, 1946, p. 124

Orwell was incapable of self-love or self-pity. His ruthlessness towards himself was the key to his personality; it determined his attitude towards the enemy within, the disease which had raged in his chest since his adolescence.

His life was one consistent series of rebellions both against the condition of society in general and his own particular predicament; against humanity's drift towards 1984 and his own drift towards the final breakdown.

The greatness and tragedy of Orwell was his total rejection of compromise.

The urge of genius and the promptings of common sense can rarely be reconciled; Orwell's life was a victory of the former over the latter. For now that he is dead, the time has come to recognize that he was the only writer of genius among the littérateurs of social revolt between the two wars. Cyril Connolly's remark, referring to their common prep-school days: "I was a stage rebel. Orwell a true one," is valid for his whole generation.

He was the only one whom his grim integrity kept immune against the spurious mystique of the "Movement," who never became a fellow-traveler and never believed in Moses the Raven's Sugar-candy Mountain—either in heaven or on earth. Consequently, his seven books of that period, from *Down and Out* to *Coming up for Air* all remain fresh and bursting with life, and will remain so for decades to come, whereas most of the books produced by the "emotionally shallow Leftism" of that time, which Orwell so despised, are dead and dated today.

A similar comparison could be drawn for the period of the war. Among all the pamphlets, tracts, and exhortations which the war produced, hardly anything bears rereading today—except, perhaps, E. M. Forster's *What I Believe,* a few passages from Churchill's speeches, and, above all, Orwell's *The Lion and the Unicorn.* Its opening section, "England Your England," is one of the most moving and yet incisive portraits of the English character, and a minor classic in itself.

Animal Farm and *1984* are Orwell's last works. No parable was written since *Gulliver's Travels* equal in profundity and mordant satire to *Animal Farm,* no fantasy since Kafka's *In the Penal Settlement* equal in logical horror to *1984*. I believe that future historians of literature will regard Orwell as a kind of missing link between Kafka and Swift.

Arthur Koestler. *The Observer*. January 29, 1950,

n.p.

In allegorical form *Animal Farm* tells the story of the betrayal of the Russian Revolution. However, its main warning is not of how a dictatorship can dupe its electorate, but of how the rulers of a dictatorship can rewrite the history of the past: in short, make nonsense of the term history. Herein resides the significance of *Animal Farm,* for it is the point of departure for *1984*.

1984 is also allegorical. The animals have become human beings, but for all that they are living the life of animals. They are without conscience and memory, for in destroying the memory the conscience is obliterated. Winston Smith—a mixture of Flory, Bowling (from *Coming up for Air*), and Orwell himself—attempts to remember what it *felt* like to be independent. But it is as dangerous for the State for its citizens to feel as to think. Along with the other senses, the tactile one must be destroyed. Everything is planned to the last dot and Smith brought into subjection. The past is rewritten to conform with the present and the files of all newspapers are accordingly constantly being revised. Systematically, proof of earlier civilizations is wiped out. "The command of the old despotism was 'Thou shalt not.' The command of the totalitarians was 'Thou shalt.' Our command is *'Thou art.'* " Negative obedience is not enough; there must be surrender, and it must be total. One must give up opposition not through fear of torture, but of one's own free will. There must be no martyrs. One must die loving Big Brother.

This is a depressing note on which to end, but it is in the note on which George Orwell's work ends; it is what he saw as the completion of "a gloomy story," and he was far too honest a writer to allow false optimism to cloud his vision. From his standpoint, it was the logical conclusion. Moreover, it is a vision which calls to mind H. G. Wells's vision of *Things to Come,* although there are certain obvious differences between these two authors as Utopians. For it is only in *1984* that Orwell can stand comparison with Wells—and then not in outlook so much as in imaginative insight into what may happen in the future.

Neville Braybrooke. *The Fortnightly*. June 1951,

pp. 403–9

1984 is the work of an intense and concentrated, but also fear-ridden and restricted imagination. A hostile critic has dismissed it as a "political horror-comic." This is not a fair description: there are in Orwell's novel certain layers of thought and feeling which raise it well above that level. But it is a fact that the symbolism of *1984* is crude; that its chief symbol, Big Brother, resembles the bogeyman of a rather inartistic nursery tale; and that Orwell's story unfolds like the plot of a science fiction film of the cheaper variety, with mechanical horror piling up upon mechanical horror so much that, in the end, Orwell's subtler ideas, his pity for his characters, and his satire on the society of his own days (not of 1984) may fail to communicate themselves to the reader. *1984* does not seem to justify the description of Orwell as the modern Swift, a description for which *Animal Farm* provides some justification. Orwell lacks the richness and subtlety of thought and the philosophical detachment of the great satirist. His imagination is ferocious and at times penetrating, but it lacks width, suppleness, and originality.

The lack of originality is illustrated by the fact that Orwell borrowed the idea of *1984,* the plot, the chief characters, the symbols, and the whole climate of his story from a Russian writer who has remained almost unknown in the West. That writer is Evgenii Zamyatin, and the title of the book which served Orwell as the model is *We.*

It has been said that *1984* is the figment of the imagination of a dying man. There is some truth in this, but not the whole truth. It was indeed with the last feverish flicker of life in him that Orwell wrote this book. Hence the extraordinary, gloomy intensity of his vision and language, and the almost physical immediacy with which he suffered the tortures which his creative imagination was inflicting on his chief character. He identified his own withering physical existence with the decayed and shrunken body of Winston Smith, to whom he imparted and in whom he invested, as it were, his own dying pangs. He projected the last spasms of his own suffering into the last pages of his last book. But the main explanation of the inner logic of Orwell's disillusionment and pessimism lies not in the writer's death agonies, but in the experience and the thought of the living man and in his convulsive reaction from his defeated rationalism.

Of course, Orwell intended *1984* as a warning. But the warning defeats itself because of its underlying boundless despair. *1984* is in effect not so much a warning as a piercing shriek announcing the advent of the Black Millennium, the Millennium of damnation.

Isaac Deutscher. *Heretics and Renegades: And Other Essays* (London: Hamish Hamilton, 1955), pp. 35–52

Animal Farm is written on many levels. It is already a children's story in its own right. It is an attack on Stalinism—and it should be pointed out that it is an attack from the Left. Rightwing journalists tried to extract more comfort from it than was warranted. I have shown how Orwell believed that one of the difficulties Socialists had to contend with is the familiar belief that Soviet Russia is Socialist, and that therefore any criticism of Russia is a criticism of Socialism. *Animal Farm* is a Socialist's mockery at the expense of Soviet Russia. It contains very little real comfort for an English Conservative because it will make very few converts. Most Englishmen believed in *Animal Farm* before it was written, but they were delighted by the form in which their beliefs appeared. The book is also a lament for the fate of revolutions and the hopes contained in them. It is a moving comment on man's constant compromise with the truth. In a very short compass it contains most of Orwell's main ideas about men and politics.

John Atkins. *George Orwell* (New York: Frederick
Ungar, 1954), p. 222

Why is it that, even before the recent spate of publicity, I met ten people who knew *1984* for one who knew *Animal Farm?* Here we have two books by the same author which deal, at bottom, with the same subject. Both are very bitter, honest, and honorable recantations. They express the disillusionment of one who had been a revolutionary of the familiar, *entre guerre* pattern and had later come to see that all totalitarian rulers, however their shirts may be colored, are equally the enemies of Man.

Since the subject concerns us all and the disillusionment has been widely shared, it is not surprising that either book, or both, should find plenty of readers, and both are obviously the works of a very considerable writer. What puzzles me is the marked preference of the public for *1984*. For it seems to me (apart from its magnificent, and fortunately detachable, Appendix on "Newspeak") to be merely a flawed, interesting book; but the *Farm* is a work of genius which may well outlive the particular and (let us hope) temporary conditions that provoked it.

To begin with, it is very much the shorter of the two. . . . In this instance the shorter book seems to do all that the longer one does; and more. The longer book does not justify its greater length. There is dead wood in it. And I think we can all see where the dead wood comes.

In the nightmare State of *1984* the rulers devote a great deal of time—which means that the author and readers also have to devote a great deal of time—to a curious kind of antisexual propaganda. Indeed the amours of the hero and heroine seem to be at least as much a gesture of protest against that propaganda as a natural outcome of affection or appetite. . . .

But this is only the clearest instance of the defect which, throughout, makes *1984* inferior to the *Farm*. There is too much in it of the author's own psychology: too much indulgence of what he feels as a man, not pruned or mastered by what he intends to make as an artist. The *Farm* is work of a wholly different order. It becomes a myth and is allowed to speak for itself. . . .The satire becomes more effective. Wit and humor (absent from the longer work) are employed with devastating effect. The great sentence "All animals are equal but some are more equal than others" bites deeper than the whole of *1984*.

Thus the shorter book does all that the longer does. But it also does more. Paradoxically, when Orwell turns all his characters into animals he makes them more fully human. . . . The greed and cunning of the pigs is tragic (not merely odious) because we are made to care about all the honest, well-meaning, or even heroic beasts whom they exploit. The death of Boxer the horse moves us more than all the more elaborate cruelties of the other book. And not only moves, but convinces. Here, despite the animal disguise, we feel we are in a real world.

Finally, *Animal Farm* is formally almost perfect; light, strong, balanced. There is not a sentence that does not contribute to the whole. The myth says all the author wants it to say and (equally important) it doesn't say anything else. Here is an objet d'art as durably satisfying as a Horatian ode or a Chippendale chair.

C. S. Lewis. *Time and Tide.*
January 8, 1955, pp. 43–44

Whereas his previous books had never had more than small and struggling sales, *Animal Farm* at once caught the public fancy in almost every country of the world—particularly in the United States—was translated into every one of the leading languages, established him as one of the best-selling authors of the day, and incidentally gave him for the first time in life a tolerable income.

Fortune favored him in the timing of the publication which it imposed upon him. *Animal Farm,* a short book of less than a hundred pages, was written between November 1943 and February 1944. It was, said Orwell, "the only one of my books I really sweated over." What would have been its fate had it immediately found a publisher and appeared in the winter of 1944, when Russia was still fighting and Western statesmen were full of optimism about the possibility of just arrangements with her, it is hard to say. Influences and the climate of opinion might well have prevented it from gaining any but a small and eccentric market. Happily for Orwell, four publishers in succession rejected it on the ground that it would be against public policy at such a time to put on the market a book attacking our Russian ally. As a result it only appeared through Messrs. Secker and Warburg in the early summer of 1945, in the month of the German surrender, when fighting had come to an end, and its first circulation exactly coincided with the beginnings of popular disillusionment with Russian policy, as people in the West saw to their dismay the ugly methods by which the Russians were establishing themselves in the East. By chance it exactly struck the public mood and was the first book to strike it.

Christopher Hollis. *A Study of George Orwell*
(Chicago, Illinois: Henry Regnery Co., 1956), pp.
139–40

How remarkable a book *1984* is can be discovered only after a second reading. It offers true testimony, it speaks for our time. And because it derives from a perception of how our time may end, the book trembles with an eschatological fury that is certain to create among its readers, even those who sincerely believe they admire it, the most powerful kinds of resistance. It already has. Openly in England, more cautiously in America, there has arisen a desire among intellectuals to belittle Orwell's achievement, often in the guise of celebrating his humanity and his "goodness." They feel embarrassed before the apocalyptic desperation of the book, they begin to wonder whether it may not be just a little overdrawn and humorless, they even suspect it is tinged with the hysteria of the death-bed. Nor can it be denied that all of us would feel more comfortable if the book could be cast out. It is a remarkable book.

Irving Howe. *Politics and the Novel* (New York:
Meridian/World, 1957), pp. 236–37

Like a number of other writers who had thought themselves ill-used by pre-war society and had been unconsciously looking forward to Armageddon and social shipwreck, George Orwell consoled himself by constructing a fantasy of universal ruin. *1984* is not a rational attempt to imagine a probable future; it is an aggregate of "all the things you've got at the back of your mind, the things you're terrified of." Most of these, in *1984,* are of an infantile character, and they clearly derive from the experience described in "Such, Such Were the Joys." At Crossgates, women—the headmaster's wife and the "grim statuesque matron"—were particularly dangerous; they seemed to be spying on Orwell all the time, and whenever they caught him doing anything they handed him over to "the head" for physical punishment. This idea crops up early in *1984.*

The whole pattern of society shapes up along the lines of fear laid down in "Such, Such Were the Joys" until the final point of the dread summons to the headmaster's study for the inevitable beating. In *1984,* the study becomes Room 101 in the Ministry of Love, and the torturers correspond closely to the schoolmasters; in fact, they use some of the tricks Orwell complains of in his picture of Crossgates. Even the idea of Big Brother, which seems to be drawn from a rational examination of the propaganda technique of dictatorship, goes back to the same source. Big Brother, the feared dictator whom everyone pretends to love, is really Bingo, the headmaster's wife.

Whether he knew it or not, what he did in *1984* was to send everybody in England to an enormous Crossgates to be as miserable as he had been.

Anthony West. *Principles and Persuasions: The
Literary Essays of Anthony West* (New York:
Harcourt Brace Jovanovich, 1957), pp. 164–76

Among the writers of this century, Orwell stands out, like Hilaire Belloc, as a master of unadorned English prose. Even when one disagrees with what he is saying, one has to admire the vigor and lucidity with which he says it. Like the Austrian Karl Kraus, he knew that corruption of the language must corrupt society. . . . As a novelist, he is, I think, most successful when he is least "fictional," that is to say, when he narrates what he himself has personally felt and witnessed. Though I am very glad for his sake that he wrote *Animal Farm* and *1984,* since they freed him from financial anxieties, neither, in my opinion, quite comes off. When one compares his encounters with the poor in the early nineteen-thirties with those of his great predecessor, Henry Mayhew, in the eighteen-fifties, one is struck, and saddened by the decline in their powers of verbal expression. Compared with the Dickensian exuberance of Mayhew's interviewees, Orwell's seem almost inarticulate. I rather fear the cause may be universal elementary education, which has destroyed their instinctive native speech, but not trained them to do more than read the cheaper newspapers.

About other writers he shows keen insights and astonishing fair-mindedness. Though himself a man of strong political and moral convictions, he is always ready to recognize aesthetic merit in those of whose politics and morals he disapproves: he even manages to say a good word for Dali. Indeed, the only writers whom, it seems to me, he has gotten all wrong are the poets, including myself, who began to publish in the thirties, The Movement, as he calls us. We were, he says,

> didactic, political writers, aesthetically conscious, of course, but more interested in subject-matter than technique.

To this, I can only say, that all my life I have been more interested in poetic technique than anything else. What is true is that I am technically more conservative, more conscious of my debt to the nineteenth century (Yeats was too for that matter) than poets like Eliot and Pound. Then aside from a few plays, very little of the poetry I wrote in that decade was overtly political: basically I have always thought of myself as a comic poet. More seriously, he charges us with refusing to admit that we were bourgeois. The term *bourgeois*, like *proletariat*, has no meaning in English-speaking countries, but if he means that I was ashamed to be, like himself, professional upper middle class, I have never thought of myself as anything else. At times, to be sure, I wrote satires about my class, but one can only satirize what one knows at first hand.

As a commentator on the contemporary political and social scene, he reminds me of Cobbeu: he exhibits the same independence of party and the same vigor. Both of them, too, were not under the illusion that political action can solve all problems.

He did, I think, have one blind spot. His fanatic, essentially religious hatred of Christianity, prevented him from seriously studying the subject. Thus, while I am sure he was well read in Communist literature, I very much doubt if he had read much theology or ecclesiastical history. He seems to have imagined that Christianity, like Manicheism and Buddhism, is an "other-wordly" religion. In fact, from the accession of Constantine to the present day, the charge which all too often can justly be brought against the Churches, both Catholic and Protestant, is that they have been all too "worldly," all too willing to make shady deals with temporal powers that would protect their power and wealth. The English Catholic apologists of this century, Belloc, Chesterton, Beachcomber, etc., all had very definite views about politics, society, history. One may disagree with them—I do myself—but the one thing one cannot accuse them of is a lack of concern for the things of this world. I suspect that the cause of Orwell's obsessive hatred was probably his experiences at his prep school, St. Cyprian's, which seems, when I compare it with the one I attended, to have been exceptionally nasty. I also suspect that his upbringing in early childhood had more effect on his sensibility and character than he realized. If I were asked to name people whom I considered true Christians, the name *George Orwell* is one of the first that would come to my mind.

W. H. Auden. *The Spectator*. January 16, 1971,
pp. 86–87

Orwell's last book [*1984*] is in many ways a nightmare, but this particular nightmare could only have been dreamed by a writer of this century, circa 1947, post Russian revolution, post World War I, post Spanish civil war, post World War II. With all Shakespeare's knowledge of history and court intrigues, he could not have imagined this totalitarian world. Nor could Milton with all his knowledge of the classics, the Bible, and the cruelty of civil war.

When we realize that this novel could not have been written at any other time, we understand its relationship to us. The shadow of barbed wire, of the truncheon, of the boot, of unholy tortures in unholy settings, of thousands upon thousands executed for "deviational thinking," of sadism cloaked in political institutionalism, falls upon all of us. We are free not to like *1984*. We are free to reject it as extreme. We are not free to reject it from our political awareness. The question to ask about *1984* is not how precise its predictions are, but to what extent it approximates a direction, and how germane its vision of totalitarian power is to our century.

Roberta Kalechofsky. *George Orwell* (New York:
Ungar, 1973), pp. 133–34

1984 is Orwell's major work on language. The fact that this work is a novel, and not an essay or treatise, raises special difficulties of interpretation. A novel's content is refracted through its form. It is an elementary kind of misreading to regard every opinion in a novel as the author's, yet the majority of commentators on *1984* have done just that. The result has been to make him seem more definite and more simple-minded than he was. But the ideas in *1984* always have a source in the novel itself, which is clearly distinguished from the author's consciousness. The world of the novel is seen mostly through the eyes of Winston Smith, whose experience is totally contaminated by the manipulative techniques of Ingsoc. Into the narrative is inserted a treatise by Goldstein, arch-heretic against Big Brother, or probably another fiction from high up in Minitrue, the Ministry of Propaganda. Attached to the work is an Appendix on "Newspeak," the language program of Oceania. Whose voice speaks in the Appendix—Orwell's? Hardly. These are the opinions of an orthodox worker from the middle levels of Minitrue, someone like Syme but less critical. Orwell himself is everywhere but nowhere. The novel presents deliberately limited ideas, along with some of the means for understanding and criticizing these limitations, tracing them to sources in a particular social and political order. How far Orwell consciously worked through this critique we can never know, and this novelistic method of presenting ideas encourages such uncertainty. When does Orwell's understanding end, and his readers' own speculation begin? It is often impossible to say. In this situation the critic can only try to avoid two extremes. One is to claim Orwell's critical activity as his own, the other is in effect to rewrite Orwell's novel so that it confirms a new orthodoxy. Both perversions would find a happy home somewhere in Minitrue—another illustration of how relevant Orwell's satire is to the conditions of intellectual production in our society. But Orwell leaves us no single choice. By writing in this form, he has produced something that is tailor-made to be appropriated by contrary interests. Qualities that are admired in works of art, like irony, ambiguity, and multiple levels of meaning, are kinds of doublethink.

Bob Hodge and Roger Fowler. In Roger Fowler,
Bob Hodge, Gunther Kress, and Tony Trew, eds.,
Language and Control (London, Routledge &
Kegan Paul, 1979), p. 9

PARETSKY, SARA (1947–   )

Chicago is not a gentle place to live. Its mean streets are about the meanest in the entire country. The mob still holds a great deal of power in the city—a holdover from the twenties and the prohibition era—and racial tension is manifested by the young members of Puerto Rican, Chicano, and black street gangs. Unions are strong in the Windy City and their burly representatives can be found at the docks and rail yards.

Sara Paretsky's V. I. Warshawski is both tough and capable. She runs, has a black belt in Karate, and is a law school grad. She is self-supporting and autonomous.

> It makes an enormous difference. I'm the only person I take orders from, not a hierarchy of officers, aldermen, and commissioners.

In every novel in which she appears, this lone-wolf operator is challenged and meets danger head-on, in full combat stance. Warshawski's speciality is financial investigations, but all of her chronicled cases involve murder. Inevitably, she treads on some toes and, in a couple of her investigations, is actually asked to withdraw. As tenacious as she is tough, Warshawski can't let go until she has reached a conclusion which satisfies her. Along the way, V. I.'s actions also upset the lives of those only peripherally involved. Beatings, madness, and suicide are not unknown outcomes of her detecting.

While V. I. brings intelligence and competence to her job and maintains cool detachment throughout the series, this facade barely masks underlying feelings of anger and bitterness. Daughter of a Polish cop, V. I. still has connections with the Chicago police. Bobby Mallory, her late father's closest friend, frequently encounters her in the midst of a case and invariably tells her that she should be happily married and making babies instead of pursuing this dangerous career. Every time he throws down this gauntlet, V. I. reacts to the challenge with counter provocation.

With her family, as with the police force, V. I.'s antagonism runs high. In *Deadlock,* readers are introduced to some of the members of the Warshawski family at the funeral of her cousin Boom Boom, a former hockey star. In *Killing Orders,* the other side of the family is presented through her Aunt Rosa and Cousin Albert. Both sides make a point of wondering when she plans to settle down and raise a family. V. I.'s responses to these queries are predictable. These two books give readers information about her background and upbringing and pose some interesting explanations of this detective's abrasive nature.

Paretsky has done a good job with aspects of this series. Chicago comes alive under her pen. Riding with Warshawski, one can see the buildings, thoroughfares, and intersections clearly. The heat, the cold, the presence of the lake, and the people who inhabit this major metropolis are very true to life. The plots are tight and the stories capture readers from the first page and hold them to the last. Unfortunately, Warshawski, with her anger and her aggressive pugnacity, is one of the least attractive heroes we've recently encountered. She may have a sense of justice but it seems self-serving at best. She'd as soon shoot some of her suspects as question them, and will not hesitate to practice the tricks of street fighting on anyone foolish enough to surprise her.

These readers think that the world really does not need any more stereotypical, hard-boiled private eyes. The mean streets aren't going to get any nicer unless those who have elected themselves private guardians rise above the dregs of humanity. In these books, those qualities such as tenderness, empathy, and nurturing, are often set aside in favor of a *macha bravada* we find detrimental and counterproductive not only in the cause of feminism but humanism as well.

Victoria Nichols and Susan Thompson. *Silk
Stalkings: When Women Write of Murder*
(Berkeley: Black Lizard Books, 1988), pp. 215–16

When Christie Opara, a policewoman in the N.Y.P.D., was introduced to readers of detective fiction ten years ago, it appeared likely that Dorothy Uhnak's competent and believable heroine would soon be followed by several more of her sex and profession. The flood has not materialized, but Sara Paretsky's *Indemnity Only* marks the entry into the field of the woman private eye, modern style. Sara Paretsky is a Chicagoan who obviously knows the insurance business from the inside. Her heroine, "Vic" Warshawski, faces in her first murder case a complex but clearly presented tangle of corruption engineered by big business *and* deadly union tactics. Vic's part is not over-played; she goes in for the conventional trailing of suspects, gets vandalized and beaten up, and winds up successful. The shoot-out shows her competence. There are several well-drawn characters, a bit of love-interest, and some veiled but plain enough sex. A newcomer worth watching.

Jacques Barzun and Wendell Hertig Taylor. *The
Armchair Detective.*
Fall 1982, p. 371

Female detectives have been snooping around in crime fiction for decades, but rarely do they operate as independently as V. I. Warshawski, who ruins some of her best silk blouses breaking people's arms and kicking their kidneys on those frequent occasions when she's attacked by hoodlums. Indeed,

Sara Paretsky had a hard time selling her first manuscript, in part because publishers wanted to equip V. I. with a male partner. (The Chicago setting was a problem, too; New York publishers feared a Midwestern city would seem "alien" to readers.) But *Indemnity Only* appeared in 1982 with setting and heroine intact, winning excellent reviews and a host of fans. Paretsky promptly wrote two more: *Deadlock* and *Killing Orders;* and her latest, *Bitter Medicine* has just arrived in bookstores. . . .

Paretsky, forty, who holds a Ph.D. in history from the University of Chicago, writes mystery novels chiefly because she always loved to read them; but she did create V. I. Warshawski with an eye to countering the usual female stereotypes in detective fiction. "*The Maltese Falcon* is a classic in its way, for depicting a woman who is a reprise of Eve," she says. "Brigid O'Shaugnessy is incredibly beautiful and deceptively virginal; she tries to use her body to get this good boy to do bad things, but she's not able to do it because he's morally superior. It's a recurring theme—you have a sexual woman and she's evil." She also sees a trend toward more violence and sadism in mysteries. "It's not enough to have the woman killed, now she has to be raped and chained," she points out. "You never saw this years ago, at least not in books that get reviewed nationally." . . .

Paretsky's work does more than turn a genre upside down: her books are beautifully paced and plotted, and the dialogue is fresh and smart. As for V. I. Warshawski—gobbling a taco salad as she drives out to a Chicago suburb prepared to meet an ambush—she's the most engaging woman in detective fiction since Dorothy Sayers's Harriet Vane, who was certainly never pictured with chili dribbling down her shirt.

Laura Shapiro. *Newsweek.* July 13, 1987, p. 64

According to one critic, Dashiell Hammett's much-discussed bare style, especially his creation of a skeptical, tough voice for his detectives, represents the "voice of Male Experience," directly connected with male sexuality and with fantasies of male power. The pen seems to be a substitute penis for Hammett; women in Hammett's books are always depicted as the "other" "to a central male consciousness." In both Hammett's and Chandler's novels, women are usually amoral or predatory, with Chandler's heroes in particular exhibiting repugnance amounting to horror toward women's sexuality. In *The Big Sleep,* Philip Marlowe says, "I hate women," a statement he proves by slashing his bed after a woman has lain in it, hoping to seduce him; Mike Hammer, like Marlowe before him, takes pleasure in hitting women.

One way to begin answering these questions is to examine some of the authors' treatments of another phallic substitute and staple of hard-boiled detective fiction, the gun. V. I. Warshawski buys a gun for self-protection in *Indemnity Only,* reasoning that she is at a disadvantage in facing armed thugs while herself unarmed. She knows how to use a gun, having been taught by her father, and recognizes while remaining suspect of the power guns embody. The difference between V. I. and those enamored of guns is succinctly summed up in her taunting of a hired thug who has beaten her up and wants to shoot her: "You big he-men really impress the shit out of me. . . . Why do you think the boy carries a gun? He can't get it up, never could, so he has a big old penis he carries around in his hand."

Whereas the treatment of women as objects in male hard-boiled detective fiction results in a simple, clear pattern—women are all potentially destructive and predatory, with some women redeemed by their willingness to submit to patriarchal rule—women's private-eye novels encode no simple reversal of this pattern. Indeed, there is no pattern at all, or at least no single pattern, in these novels' depiction of either men or women. In Paretsky's *Killing Orders,* for instance, the total dedication of several patriarchal women to the system that deprives them of real power leads them to serve as accomplices to murder; most horrifyingly, one such woman is an accessory to her own daughter's death, representing in fiction the feminist analysis that women who ally themselves with the patriarchy destroy their own and their daughters'—actual and metaphoric—life chances. In the novel's most chilling scene, V. I. comes across this woman sitting in an attitude of attentive waiting and realizes she is listening for the sound of the shot she expects to end V. I.'s life.

Maureen T. Reddy. *Sisters in Crime: Feminism and the Crime Novel* (New York: Continuum, 1988), pp. 91–120

Known as Vic only to her friends, Victoria Iphigenia Warshawski uses her initials otherwise—V. I. Warshawski—because patronizing her is more difficult when men don't know her first name. Appearing in four novels to date, she is one of the best developed and most convincing female private eyes in contemporary fiction. Virtually every aspect of Sara Paretsky's novels relates to gender. The reader is always made aware of Vic as both a woman and a feminist, both in her positively attributed independent stance and in defensive responses appearing in dialogue, descriptions, and thoughts. As a first-person narrator, Vic reveals a great deal about her life; as a feminist she devotes considerable thought to women's roles and their treatment in explicit gender-role terms. She clearly recognizes oppression, paternalism, and patriarchalism in the behavior of others around her and reinforced by society at large.

Paretsky provides the background details which make these concerns plausible; Vic is no newcomer to either detection or political awareness. After her graduation from the University of Chicago Law School, Warshawski entered the public defender's office, a starry-eyed rookie whose experience in an underground abortion referral service, and in Louisiana freedom marches, had previously put her on the other side of the law. Although her father had been a cop, clearly her mother's drive was the more important influence in Vic's life; but, she believes, neither parent would have approved of her decision to become a detective. After their deaths, this attitude is echoed resoundingly by family friend Lieutenant Bobby Mallory who criticizes her decision, subverts her investigations, threatens her license, and urges her to marry so she can bear children. Divorced after just fourteen months from a man who could only admire independent women from a distance, she is wary of commitments. Her mother's advice is more to her liking: "Any girl can be pretty—but to take care of yourself you must have brains. And you must have a job, a profession. You must work." And work is what V. I. Warshawski does best.

V. I. has become a private investigator not only to be her own boss but also—"a la Doña Quixote perhaps"—to redress the imbalances between guilty and innocent she'd seen in the public defenders office. As a detective, she contrasts herself unfavorably with Lord Peter Wimsey, who would have charmed rather than bullied; favorably with Mike Hammer, who could barely think; and grudgingly with the host of hard-boileds: "Of course, a hard-boiled detective is never scared. So what I was feeling couldn't be fear. Perhaps nervous excitement at the treats in store for me." Law school colleagues remind her of maverick approaches and bullying in moot court; her closest friend, Dr. Lotty Herschel, calls her a pit dog and Jill-the-giant-killer. Vic's own description of her methods is more benign: "My theory of detection resembles Julia Child's approach to cooking: Grab a lot of ingredients from the shelves, put them in a pot and stir, and see what happens." Her action is rarely so mellow. . . .

Sara Paretsky comes closer than any other novelist to writing a feminist private-eye novel; although her success certainly involves the intersection of historical time, a moment in the genre, and a feminist author, it requires more. What has worked for Paretsky is the simultaneous rejection or minimization of typical features of the formula and the explicit introduction of some essential elements of feminism. These changes are apparent in characterization, plot development, and ambiance. Unlike the preferred male hero, V. I. Warshawski is neither a loner nor a cynic. She forms strong emotional bonds, makes friends, worries about people toward whom she has no professional obligations. In her sexual relationships, she persistently treats men as individuals even when they display sexually stereotypical behavior, not demeaning them as either romantic ideals or available sex objects. Finally, she displays a wide range of emotional behavior: notably, introspection, guilt, self-awareness, and uncertainty. In plotting, Paretsky chooses her crimes and villains carefully: all are associated with corruptible institutions or systems which have traditionally excluded or oppressed women. The criminal underworld and organized labor in *Indemnity Only,* a capitalistic empire in *Deadlock,* the Roman Catholic Church in *Killing Orders,* and the medical establishment in *Bitter Medicine* stand behind the individual killers, offering not only motives and rewards but also fostering arrogance which grows from the long-time assumption of undeserved superiority. Concluding the plots, Paretsky downplays the protagonist's role as judge of the criminals; instead, Warshawski's important task is to share information with those who have been kept systematically uninformed. In this, Paretsky shows her detective breaking down the system; however, this attack is not undertaken in a heroic manner which elevates the protagonist individually (as is true when he bases his judgment of criminals on a private and personal code of morality). Instead, Paretsky's detective expands the collective base of power; her style is inclusive rather than exclusive. Certainly, in this so-called age of information, nothing could be more valuable to the powerless, the unwillingly ignorant, or the disadvantaged than knowledge. Further, the atmosphere of these novels explicitly rejects the masculinist glorification of violence. Certainly, violence itself cannot be avoided in novels centered around murder; however, Paretsky limits the violence initiated or inflicted by her detective, making Warshawski react in these episodes. Finally, Paretsky's novels provide an explicit and persuasive awareness of the gender inequality which pervades American life, persisting despite the hopeful promise of a competent woman doing what is still often called men's work. The tensions between the demands of the detective novel and the feminist ideology require a careful balancing act; Paretsky's is not the only way, but it is virtually the only example.

Kathleen Gregory Klein. *The Woman Detective:*
Gender and Genre (Urbana and Chicago:
University of Illinois Press, 1988), pp. 212–16

It seems that all the female private investigators had midlife identity crises simultaneously in 1988. Muller's McCone, Grafton's Millhone, Muller's Stark, and finally the toughest kid on the block—V. I. Warshawski. In *Blood Shot,* Sara Paretsky's fifth outing with V. I., battles are waged with demons from her past, as well as the present. And, in her typical tough-kid fashion, reconciliations are made only after some soul-searching which is even harder than the battling. . . .

While the mystery is a strong and compelling one, the greater story is V. I.'s personal struggles to come to terms with her past. Her violent reactions to old friends seem to come out of nowhere, and more than once I found myself warily eyeing the pages, muttering something along the lines of, "Lighten up, already—give it a rest." Paretsky, however, accurately gauges both the capacity of her character and the tolerance of her audience: just when the tension became unbearable, just when this reader was ready to stop muttering and start screaming, an insight into V. I.'s character was revealed, helping to make some sense of all the fighting. V. I. never wimps out on us, though. The battles continue, where appropriate, right down to the final sentence of the book.

Blood Shot is Paretsky's best effort to date in an already fine series.

Sue Feder. *The Armchair Detective.* Spring 1989,
pp. 198–99

V. I., your skill counts for plenty—with your fans. Not since the early, great years of Nancy Drew has a female detective so perfectly suited her readers' zeitgeist, from a fixation on good olive oil to a passion for good causes. Here V. I. tackles corruption and murder in Chicago's construction industry, but Paretsky also probes her heroine's stubborn independence. Family allegiances cling to her heart though she longs to jettison them, and she can't help rankling the friends to whom she often owes her life. As she shows at the end of *Burn Marks,* however, her deepest loyalties will survive assaults and indignities.

Perhaps the biggest shock in *Burn Marks* is the unprecedented failure of V. I.'s famous appetite. Eventually cabbage soup and roast chicken bring her back to normal, but by then she's too stuffed to scramble over rooftops as planned. All she can do is fume: "Peter Wimsey and Philip Marlowe never had this kind of problem."

Laura Shapiro. Newsweek. May 14, 1990, p. 67

Although I served on the Mystery Writers of America's committee to choose the Edgar for the best novel in 1989, I was unable even to get Sara Paretsky onto the short list, but Paretsky's doing just fine. So is Sue Grafton, who according to the publicity for her latest novel, sells around 100,000 copies in hard cover. Both Grafton and Paretsky first published in 1982, and both had new novels out last year—*"G" Is for Gumshoe* for Grafton and *Burn Marks* for Paretsky—so it is barely possible that the MWA may come to its senses. Both have won many awards from other crime organizations. The year I failed with the MWA, Paretsky got a Silver Dagger from the Brits.

Any aficionado reading this may be ready to ask: are they both feminist detective writers? The answer is yes, though differently. Paretsky, who founded Sisters in Crime and who, unlike Grafton, calls herself a feminist, writes rather more daring books than Grafton (who isn't a member of Sisters in Crime), but they are so often mentioned together that the distinction becomes dim. Both have women private eyes who are tough and honorable, but Paretsky's V. I. Warshawski—unlike Grafton's also androgynously named Kinsey Millhone—calls *herself* a feminist from time to time, has close women friends, and takes on such adversaries as the medical establishment, toxic waste, and the Catholic church. Both detectives like men, and sleep with them intermittently, but stay free. Both are excellent models of a woman deciding on the life that suits her and living it. Their success bodes well for the nineties, when it's hard to think of much else that does.

Carolyn G. Heilbrun. Ms. March/April 1991, p. 62

With each novel Sara Paretsky lets intrepid detective V. I. Warshawski (a.k.a. "Vic") take a few more physical lumps, though the more interesting dings are emotional ones. In *Guardian Angel,* Paretsky constructs and maintains one monster of a plot. Things move fairly briskly, from the old lady with a dirty house and several dogs to greedy Yuppies across the road who kill off a few of the canines and offload some dodgy bonds on local senior citizens. Meanwhile, Vic's downstairs pal's old buddy is bitching about the factory he once worked for and bragging about a secret that will apparently make his golden years comfy. The factory has ties to a bigger steel/salvage company, itself linked to a suburban bank, itself represented by a prestigious city law firm (with Vic's pompous old hubby, Dick, pretty high up the corporate masthead). Paretsky spends less time portraying Warshawski in full whine and a lot more time having her gun the Trans Am (and a few much-needed loaners when things get nasty) all over Chicago. The author's gift for finding the precise urban setting and crafting her narrative jigsaw puzzle with unerring accuracy remains intact.

Peter Robertson. *Booklist*. December 1, 1991,

p. 660

PARKER, ROBERT B. (1925–   )

It should come as no surprise to a reader of *The Godwulf Manuscript* (1974) to discover striking similarities between it and the novels of Dashiell Hammett, Raymond Chandler, and Ross Macdonald, particularly when he remembers that Parker wrote his doctoral dissertation on the novels of those three writers. What is surprising, however, is the extent to which he has managed to stake out for himself an original claim to the territory already overrun by would-be successors to the three earlier masters of the hardboiled detective novel. Parker manages the tricky task of evoking echoes of all three writers while at the same time creating a character and developing a style that are uniquely his. . . .

Like Sam Spade, Spenser—no given name—is tough and often cynical. Like Philip Marlowe, he has a quick wit, an insolent tongue, and an observant eye for the pompous and absurd. Like Lew Archer, he frequently finds himself drawn into the personal lives of his clients. Like all three, especially Marlowe and Archer, he has a profound sympathy for life's victims and a particular fondness for the young. He has a romantic's belief in the possibility of a better world, but a realist's awareness of the concrete problems of it as it is. He is a loner, preferring to follow his own private code of personal justice. . . .

A close examination of the opening chapter of *The Godwulf Manuscript* illustrates Parker's skill in characterizing his hero. The first sentence of the novel, for example, establishes not only the setting for the action to follow but also reveals the narrator's attitude: "The office of the university president looked like the front parlor of a successful Victorian whorehouse." We learn immediately that the speaker has an eye for pretentious detail and an irreverent sense of humor.

The Godwulf Manuscript is not without its flaws. The resolution of the plot is too pat. The source of evil in the book turns out to be a crackpot whose misguided political idealism gets mixed up with a naïve and dangerous view of drugs as liberators of social consciousness. Parker fails to locate the evil in a larger context, neither placing it in a social frame, as Chandler does, nor in a familial one, as Macdonald does. Parker appears to be less interested in the *why* of crime than many of his predecessors were.

In his second Spenser novel, *God Save the Child* (1974), Parker manages to avoid the problems of the follow-up performance, and takes a confident step forward in his development as a mystery writer. All of the qualities that distinguished *The Godwulf Manuscript* are here—clever dialogue, vivid characters, a witty narrative style, and, as compelling as ever, the character of Spenser. Furthermore, the rough edges and uncertainties of Parker's first novel have been eliminated. The plot, for example, is much more skillfully handled, more logically developed; the characters are more interesting; the excesses of Spenser's narrative have been reduced. . . .

One aspect of Spenser's character more fully developed in this novel is his private life, especially his relationship with women, or more accurately with one woman, Susan Silverman. The wooing of Susan is handled with sensitivity and wit.

Such themes as the alienation of the young, the hostility between parent and child, the search for a substitute family structure, which were implied in *The Godwulf Manuscript,* are treated much more explicitly in *God Save the Child*. Here Parker is much more careful to locate the root of the problem in a familial and a social context, and then to draw an interrelationship between the two. For example, although Spenser initially believes he is working to solve a kidnapping case, and then discovers he has a murder to solve as well, the real crime in the novel is both simpler and more complex: the failure of the American family. . . .

In *Mortal Stakes,* the third Spenser, Parker shows Spenser's compassion through his defense of the Rabbs, but he also reveals Spenser's vulnerability, a quality that proclaims not his weakness but his humanness. The pervasive influence of Hemingway can be seen in all of Parker's writing; one can detect it in *Mortal Stakes* in the conception of Spenser's character, and in the picture of the world that the novel presents. Spenser's actions in *Mortal Stakes* demonstrate that he shares Hemingway's perception that we live in a world characterized by disorder and uncertainty, but that it can be faced honorably and confidently with a coded pattern of behavior. . . .

Although each of Parker's first three Spenser novels was critically well received, it was his fourth, *Promised Land* (1976), that brought him widespread recognition—it received an Edgar Award as the best mystery novel of 1976. Nevertheless, the novel is something of a disappointment, and its failures are in areas that, ironically, were responsible for the success of the first three novels. Parker's strength has never been in his plotting, and the shaky plot of *Promised Land* confirms this. His strongest features are characterization and dialogue, yet there is an overemphasis on character analysis and an excessive talkiness that upsets the novelistic balance in *Promised Land* and results in an often lifeless work that lacks the sparkle and vitality of the first three Spenser books. . . .

The Judas Goat (1978) is a novel with enough action, adventure, and suspense to suggest that Parker was aware of the flaws that weakened *Promised Land*. He sought to avoid them in his new novel by emphasizing what the earlier novel lacked—action—and by returning to those elements with which he had demonstrated his greatest skill—vivid characterization and witty dialogue.

The Judas Goat is an important novel for Parker not only because it shows his willingness to attempt new departures—placing Spenser in a foreign setting, for example; but also because in it he takes measures—more action, sharper characterizations, increased dosages of ironic humor—to correct the drift that marred *Promised Land*. The ironic humor, for example, prevents Spenser from taking himself too seriously (which he tended to do in *Promised Land*). Instances of self-deprecating humor, coupled with Spenser's quick-witted jests with Hawk and typically good-natured sexual banter with Susan, give the novel a liveliness that was notably lacking in *Promised Land*. Moreover, the whole narrative style is as crisp and invigorating as anything Parker has written. He even makes those scenes where Spenser stands around waiting for something to happen interesting to read.

With each novel Parker has exhibited growing independence from his predecessors, confidently developing his own themes, characters, and stylistic idiom. Although one can still detect similarities between Spenser and Philip Marlowe, Lew Archer, and even Rex Stout's Archie Goodwin, Parker has successfully managed to establish Spenser's own separate identity as a private detective. However, despite his innovative efforts, he has remained faithful to the conventions of the genre, so effectively laid down by his predecessors. He has thus earned for himself the right to be designated *the* legitimate heir to the Hammett-Chandler-Macdonald tradition, which, thanks to the efforts of writers like Parker, shows no sign of diminishing.

David Geherin. *Sons of Sam Spade* (New York:
Ungar, 1980), pp. 9–82

Robert B. Parker, whose series figure, Spenser, . . . thinks he is a gourmet, though [Nero Wolfe's] Fritz would not have let him into the kitchen in his brownstone, for he uses catsup and makes his own omelets, badly if one is to believe the recipes (like Wolfe, he likes his beer); he also thinks he is tough, which he is. He is well-read and hides it, and he respects women for themselves and not for how he will use them or what he wants them to be. Starting in *The Godwulf Manuscript* in 1973, through *Mortal Stakes* (1975), the best detective story ever written with a baseball setting, to *Promised Land* (1976), which belongs with *Gaudy Night* on the shelf of women's liberationist literature, to *Early Autumn* (1981), which is about forms of maturity, Parker has grown in stature to the point that he has set in train his own imitators.

Robin W. Winks. *Modus Operandi: An Excursion into Detective Fiction* (Boston: David R. Godine, 1982), p. 101

Last year in *Early Autumn,* Spenser made a man of a fifteen-year-old boy vicitimized by his affectless parents. *Ceremony* seems an alternative version of that novel. This time the child with the destructive parents is a girl, a high-school dropout who volunteers for a life of prostitution, then finds herself a prisoner of it: finally, when freed by Spenser, she finds she has no other talent, no other aim in life. Spenser is faced with an interesting moral decision: what is best for this homeless child? Unpaid, saddled with a job he never wanted but now cannot let go, he's a modern paladin. "It's a way to live," he says. "Anything else is confusion." "How did you ever get to be so big without growing up?" Susan asks. It's lines like that, puncturing the private-eye ethic without leaving lasting damage, which make the Spenser novels so engaging.

The contrast between Spenser and Susan's loving sexiness and the calculated sexual exploitation of children works very nicely here. Another asset is Spenser's sidekick, an improbable, everloyal, brutally efficient black man named Hawk. Parker is treading on thin ice with him—his black man does the dirty work the white man really shouldn't do (in *Early Autumn* Hawk shot the mobster, who needed shooting, when Spenser couldn't)—but he slides over it with good humor. And in *Ceremony* he brings off with good taste a story about an appalling subject.

Peter S. Prescott. *Newsweek.* June 7, 1982, pp. 71–72

The problem I have had with [Robert B. Parker's] Spenser novels is with Spenser himself. It is not that I hate the character—it is just that he can easily get on my nerves. I have no problems with a character with a code of honor. It is just that when a character is portrayed as being the only good man left, one who makes no mistakes, and the whole thing is presented as if the reader should not disagree, it gets hard to take. The code is not just being good and pure of heart, but includes such touchy subjects as who are you allowed to kill, and that being a hooker is the best someone can hope for. At times, it seems like the code is just a justification for such things. It is a human device for coping with things we cannot change (such as prostitution) or things we want to do (like killing someone)—things that make us feel less than human. But, with the code, we can say that prostitution is the best someone can hope for and turn our backs on it. We can say that killing someone is okay if you do it to survive and then put it out of our minds. By using the "code of honor," you can cop out and feel good about it.

Parker seems to have lightened up Spenser's character a bit. Perhaps he is unconsciously being influenced by actor Robert Urich's more human portrayal. There is a funny scene with spray paint used as hair spray but, like the dramatic ones, they underline Spenser's superiority to average folks such as you and I. If that's your cup of tea, then *Taming a Sea-Horse* may be for you.

John Kovaleski. The Armchair Detective. Spring
1987, p. 208

Almost half a century of fictional private eyes lies between Sam Spade and Robert B. Parker's Spenser, yet both are carved in the same image and both march to the same beat. Yet Spenser is careful to correct the unwary's spelling of his name, reminding that it is spelled with an "s" just like the poet Edmund Spenser. Would *Black Mask* have allowed a private detective to talk about Edmund Spenser? Would Hammett have let Spade quote "Musée des Beaux Arts," a W. H. Auden poem, on viewing a young girl's dead body, as Robert B. Parker, Spenser's creator, does? Or would Chandler, Marlowe?

The Hammett and Chandler plots and the Robert B. Parker plots are similar, of course. It is the *treatment* that is different. Spenser himself, paradoxically, is the same as Spade and Marlowe and Archer—yet *different*. His very persona presents a curious composite of conflicted elements. . . .

Parker learned a great deal from his masters. And the result in *The Godwulf Manuscript* is a thoroughly readable and diverting exercise in private-eye country. The hatred is there, the violence is there, the diverting characters are there, the suspense and the fear are there. It is all done in a literary way that is pleasing and stylistically acceptable.

There have now [1988] been almost a dozen novels, each one growing a bit more independent from the early style of Hammett, Chandler, Spillane, and the two Macdonalds. There are still some signs of Marlowe, Archer, Spade, and others, but Spenser is becoming his own man.

Parker has remained faithful to the precepts of the game and keeps to the conventions of the genre—rules laid down by the men he has aspired to follow. He is—along with Spenser, his protagonist—the legitimate heir to the Hammett-Chandler-Macdonald tradition.

But times have changed in many ways since the early 1900s. The mores have altered considerably; the demarcation between right and wrong is blurred. Traditional morality has been all but abandoned for practical considerations. Whatever works is okay; the existentialism that began surfacing during the time of Spillane in the postwar 1950s has in the 1980s become almost a way of life.

Spenser *feels* his way between the rocks and cliffs of right and wrong. Tightrope walking was not necessary for Spade or Marlowe. The way was clear then, the code of knight errantry was secure and in place. Spenser *senses* the way to act; in fact, note how close his name "Spenser" resembles the key word "senser." It is his sensibility and his ability to establish simpatico with others that makes him a 1980s hero.

Fighter he may be, good with his fists, better with a gun. Fearless and brave he may be, able to wade into a fight with all odds against him. But it is the *direction* he takes and the way he treats clients, enemies, and associates that so clearly delineates his character lines.

Adrift on a sea without a compass, Spenser is a composite of the rest of us, trying desperately to find the way to go amidst all manner of dangers and perils. What is right? What is wrong? What is good? What is evil? There are no pat answers anymore. People, Spenser *feels,* are more important than statutes. Therefore, when it comes to judging a person, Spenser uses his own value system, evolved painstakingly through the years by trial and error in reading the politically correct signals sent out by society.

Like his creator Parker, Spenser is essentially a teacher with lessons to be dealt to those he comes in contact with. Forget that Susan Silverman is the counselor; Spenser has an urge to reform. In *The Judas Goat* (1978), when he finally catches one of the terrorists who is bombing innocent citizens in London, Spenser decides to let the young woman go because he feels she is redeemable. Hawk almost goes berserk, calling Spenser a fool and, worse than that, a naive, an innocent.

One critic believes Spenser and Hawk to be both sides of one coin, with Hawk's set of values those of the earlier Spade and Marlowe, and Spenser's the makeshift values of today's everyman.

Again, when Spenser in *Promised Land* (1976) finds a runaway wife who has been helping out a pair of bank-robbing political activists, his instinct is to shield her and give counsel.

It is interesting to contrast this compassionate attitude—obviously an attitude that reflects the American public's ever-changing tastes—with the already mentioned attitude expressed many years before by Sam Spade after he has unmasked Bridgid O'Shaughnessy as the murderer of Miles Archer and listened to her plea to run away with her:

"Well, if I send you over I'll be sorry as hell," he says in that voice eternalized onscreen by Humphrey Bogart. "I'll have some rotten nights— but that'll pass."

Or, even earlier, as he tells a killer:

"What difference does it make which killing we can prove first-degree murder on? They can only hang you once." Followed by that patented "pleasant" smile of Spade's, the punch line: "And they will."

Waltraud Woeller and Bruce Cassiday. *The Literature of Crime and Detection* (New York: Ungar, 1988), pp. 145–47

Why Raymond Chandler decided to marry off his world-famous private eye, Philip Marlowe, is only one of the manifold mysteries of *Poodle Springs,* the novel he left unfinished at his death in 1959. Another mystery is why he chose Linda Loring, one of his least successful and appealing female characters, as the woman who would not only bed but actually wed the lonely bachelor whose undisputed turf was the glamorous and sleazy city of Los Angeles.

The spoiled, beautiful daughter of a very wealthy man (Chandler referred to her in a letter as "the eight million dollar girl from *The Long Goodbye*"), Linda made her first appearance in that novel, which Chandler was writing while his beloved wife Cissy was dying of fibrosis of the lungs. In a letter to Edward Weeks, editor of *The Atlantic Monthly,* three years after Cissy's death in 1954, Chandler said, "While she was dying, and I knew she was dying, I wrote my best book. I wrote it in agony, but I wrote it."

At this time, desolated and distraught, he was struggling with the writing of what would become his *worst* book, *Playback,* which had begun its life as an original screenplay for Universal some ten years earlier. In the last chapter of that book, Linda calls from Paris to propose marriage. In referring to his choice of her as the best mate for Marlowe, Chandler wrote to a friend, "I hope I picked the right woman."

He picked the wrong woman.

It is difficult to believe that the first four chapters of *Poodle Springs* were intended by Chandler to be finished work. Consisting of a mere thirty-one pages (but Chandler's chapters often were very short), they sketch in a Linda Loring who bears only nominal resemblance to the woman we met in her debut appearance and later in her brief phone-in. Floating about in diaphanous lingerie, dropping "darlings" like rose petals, she seems to be doing a bad imitation of Tallulah Bankhead. Marlowe himself, however, is the major disappointment. Enormously uncomfortable in Palm Springs ("Poodle Springs, I call it," Chandler wrote in 1958, "because every third elegant creature you see has at least one poodle"), he cracks wise less humorously and with obvious strain, protests too loudly and unconvincingly about having married rich, and seems overly impressed by his own fame as a private investigator. This is not the Marlowe we know and love.

What Chandler had envisioned as only "a good sub-plot"—Marlowe's marriage to a girl "whose ideas about how to live were completely antagonistic to his"—entirely overwhelms the opening chapters of the novel. A mere hint of a case appears: a man is in trouble. Marlowe mysteriously brushes him off because he himself is looking for an office, presumably out of which he can conduct business. But a man in trouble *is* business, isn't he? In any case, the man sends two hoods to bring in Marlowe. Marlowe dusts them off handily and tells them he'll go see their boss later, at his own convenience.

Enter Robert B. Parker.

In 1988, Knopf published a centennial celebration volume, in which twenty-three writers of crime fiction wrote stories about Marlowe in more-or-less successful pastiches of Chandler's style. Oddly, Robert B. Parker was not one of the writers who contributed to that book. The book was dedicated to Ed Victor, the agent who represents the Chandler estate. It was Victor's idea to ask Mr. Parker to complete *Poodle Springs,* "because he is the closest living writer to Mr. Chandler."

Indeed, it is impossible to think of any other writer in the world better qualified for the task [of finishing Raymond Chandler's unfinished manuscript, *Poodle Springs,* than Robert B. Parker]. Not only had Robert Parker devoted part of his doctoral dissertation to Chandler, but he is himself the creator of the literate, witty, and tremendously readable novels about Spenser, a private detective who has proved his staying power over the course of some seventeen books and a long-running television series. That Mr. Parker pulls off the stunt is a tribute to his enormous skill. In fact, one of the true delights in *Poodle Springs* is to watch this engaging writer as first he tests the impossible shackles fastened to his wrists and his ankles, then breaks free of them to charge exultantly down a road Chandler himself might have chosen in his prime. . . .

At his very best, Mr. Parker sounds more like Chandler than Chandler himself—but with an edge the master had begun to lose in the waning days of his life. Here he is describing Marlowe's favorite mixed drink:

"I sipped some of the gimlet. It was clean and cold and slid down through the desert parch like a fresh rain."

And here he is, throwing away a simile many other writers would kill for:

"The office was as blank as a waiter's stare."

Or describing the Los Angeles Chandler mirrored so accurately in all of his best work:

"I sometimes think that Southern California looks better in the rain than any other time. The rain washes away the dust and glazes the cheapness and poverty and pretense, and freshens the trees and flowers and grass that the sun has blasted. Bel Air under the wet sky was all emerald and scarlet and gold with the rain making the streets glisten."

Nice.

He is good, too, at reconstructing Marlowe's endless battle with the police. It would not be Marlowe (or Chandler) without the telephone call to the "cop house" after discovering a body. Nor could anyone imagine Marlowe *not* becoming a prime suspect, *not* getting batted around by at least one blackjack-wielding cop, or *not* being locked up overnight in the local hoosegow—all the obligatory conventions of the private-eye novel before Miranda. One of the problems with *Poodle Springs,* in fact, is its lack of a consistent time frame. Mr. Parker talks of electric vibrators and Canon 35-millimeter cameras, instant coffee, and newsstand magazines with dirty pictures in them, loafers with gold chains across the tongues, all of which seem to be accoutrements of the here-and-now. But the style and the tone, the very sequence of events—Linda proposing to Marlowe in the 1958 novel, Linda married to Marlowe for only three weeks and four days at the beginning of *this* novel—condition the reader to expect a time thirty years ago, which is when Chandler was writing the opening chapters, and so the anachronisms become jarring.

But this is quibbling.

The book works—even if at one point the insufferable Linda [Loring] says, "This isn't working. . . . I'm not saying it's your fault . . . but it isn't working." This easily could have been Robert B. Parker himself, complaining out loud about Chandler's legacy: four short, unpolished chapters featuring an unrecognizable Marlowe married to an all-but-impossible woman.

At another point in the novel, however, Mr. Parker has Marlowe thinking, "They knew something out here. You could make anything look good with the right lighting."

If *Poodle Springs* looks good, it's because Mr. Parker knew what to do with the right lighting.

Ed McBain. *The New York Times Book Review.*
October 15, 1989, pp. 35–45

POE, EDGAR ALLAN (1809–1849)

Mr. Poe's tales need no aid of newspaper comment to give them popularity; they have secured it. We are glad to see them given to the public in this neat form [*Tales, by Edgar A. Poe*], so that thousands more may be entertained by them without injury to their eyesight.

No form of literary activity has so terribly degenerated among us as the tale. Now that everybody who wants a new hat or bonnet takes this way to earn one from the magazines or annuals, we are inundated with the very flimsiest fabrics ever spun by mortal brain. Almost every person of feeling or fancy could supply a few agreeable and natural narratives, but when instead of using their materials spontaneously they set to work with geography in hand to find unexplored nooks of wild scenery in which to locate their Indians or interesting farmers' daughters, or with some abridgment of history to hunt monarchs or heroes yet unused to become the subjects of their crude coloring, the sale-work produced is a sad affair indeed and "gluts the market" to the sorrow both of buyers and lookers-on.

In such a state of things the writings of Mr. Poe are a refreshment, for they are the fruit of genuine observations and experience, combined with an invention which is not "making up," as children call their way of contriving stories, but a penetration into the causes of things which leads to original but credible results. His narrative proceeds with vigor, his colors are applied with discrimination, and where the effects are fantastic they are not unmeaningly so.

The "Murders in the Rue Morgue" especially made a great impression upon those who did not know its author, and were not familiar with his mode of treatment. Several of his stories make us wish he would enter the higher walk of the metaphysical novel and, taking a mind of the self-possessed and deeply marked sort that suits him, give us a deeper and longer acquaintance with its life and the springs of its life than is possible in the compass of these tales.

As Mr. Poe is a professed critic and of all the band the most unsparing to others, we are surprised to find some inaccuracies in the use of words, such as these: "he had with him many books, but rarely *employed* them."— "His results have, in truth, the *whole air* of intuition."

The degree of skill shown in the management of revolting or terrible circumstances makes the pieces that have such subjects more interesting than the others. Even the failures are those of an intellect of strong fiber and well-chosen aim.

Margaret Fuller. *The Writings of Margaret Fuller*
(New York: Viking, 1941), pp. 396–97

Two or three stories by Edgar Poe have already been translated and published in Russian magazines. Here we present to our readers three more [The Tell-Tale Heart," "The Black Cat," and "The Devil in the Belfry"]. What a strange, though enormously talented writer, that Edgar Poe! His work can hardly be labeled as purely fantastic, and insofar as it falls into this category, its fantasticalness is a merely external one, if one may say so. He admits, for instance, that an Egyptian mummy that had lain five thousand years in a pyramid, was recalled into life with the help of galvanism. Or he presumes that a dead man, again by means of galvanism, tells the state of his mind, and so on, and so on. Yet such an assumption alone does not make a story really fantastic. Poe merely supposes the outward possibility of an unnatural event, though he always demonstrates logically that possibility and does it sometimes even with astounding skill; and this premise once granted, he in all the rest proceeds quite realistically. In this he differs essentially from the fantastic as used for example by E. T. A. Hoffmann. The latter personifies the forces of Nature in images, introduces in his tales sorceresses and specters, and seeks his ideals in a far-off utterly unearthly world, and not only assumes this mysterious magical world as superior but seems to believe in its real existence. Not so Edgar Poe. Not fantastic should he be called but capricious. And how odd are the vagaries of his fancy and at the same time how audacious! He chooses as a rule the most extravagant reality, places his hero in a most extraordinary outward or psychological situation, and, then, describes the inner state of that person with marvelous acumen and amazing realism. Moreover, there exists one characteristic that is singularly peculiar to Poe and which distinguishes him from every other writer, and that is the vigor of his imagination. Not that his fancy exceeds that of all other poets, but his imagination is endowed with a quality which in such magnitude we have not met anywhere else, namely the power of details. Try, for instance, yourselves to realize in your mind anything that is very unusual or has never before occurred, and is only conceived as possible, and you will experience how vague and shadowy an image will appear before your inner eye. You will either grasp more or less general traits of the inward image or you will concentrate upon the one or the other particular, fragmentary feature. Yet Edgar Poe presents the whole fancied picture or events in all its details with such stupendous plasticity that you cannot but believe in the reality or possibility of a fact which actually never has occurred and even never could happen. Thus he describes in one of his stories a voyage to the moon, and his narrative is so full and particular, hour by hour following the imagined travel, that you involuntarily succumb to the illusion of its reality. In the same way he once told in an American newspaper the story of a balloon that crossed the ocean from Europe to the New World, and his tale was so circumstantial, so accurate, so filled with unexpected, accidental happenings, in short was so realistic and truthful that at least for a couple of hours everybody was convinced of the reported fact and only later investigation proved it to be entirely invented. The same power of imagination, or rather combining power, characterizes his stories of the Purloined Letter, of the murder committed by an orangutan, of the discovered treasure, and so on.

Poe has often been compared with Hoffmann. As we have said before, we believe such a comparison to be false. Hoffmann is a much greater poet. For he possesses an ideal, however wrong sometimes, yet an ideal full of purity and of inherent human beauty. You find this ideal embodied even oftener in Hoffmann's nonfantastic creations, such as "Meister Martin" or the charming and delightful "Salvator Rosa," to say nothing of his masterpiece, "Kater Murr." In Hoffmann, true and ripe humor, powerful realism as well as malice, are welded with a strong craving for beauty and with the shining light of the ideal. Poe's fantasticalness, as compared with that, seems strangely "material," if such expression may be allowed. Even his most unbounded imagination betrays the true American.

Feodor M. Dostoevsky. In Eric W. Carlson, ed.,
*The Recognition of Edgar Allan Poe: Selected
Criticism Since 1829* (Ann Arbor: University of
Michigan Press, 1966), pp. 60–62

In his last stories Poe seems to have lost respect for himself, for his art, and for his audience. When he dealt before with horrible images, he dealt with them for some definite enough creative purpose, and with a certain measure and gravity suitable to the occasion; but he scatters them abroad in his last tales with an indescribable and sickening levity, with something of the ghoul or the furious lunatic that surpasses what one had imagined to oneself of Hell. There is a duty to the living more important than any charity to the dead; and it would be criminal in the reviewer to spare one harsh word in the expression of his own loathing and horror, lest, by its absence, another victim should be permitted to soil himself with the perusal of the infamous "King Pest." He who could write "King Pest" had ceased to be a human being. For his own sake, and out of an infinite compassion for so lost a spirit, one is glad to think of him as dead.

It is not the fashion of Poe's earlier tales to be pointless, however it may be with these sorry ones of the end. Pointlessness is, indeed, the very last charge that could be brought reasonably against them. He has the true story-teller's instinct. He knows the little nothings that make stories, or mar them. He knows how to enhance the significance of any situation, and give color and life with seemingly irrelevant particulars. Thus, the whole spirit of "The Cask of Amontillado" depends on Fortunato's carnival costume of cap and bells and motley. When Poe had once hit upon this device of dressing the victim grotesquely, he had found the key of the story; and so he sends him with uneven steps along the catacombs of the Montresors, and the last sound we hear out of the walled-up recess is the jingling of the bells upon his cap. Admirable, also, is the use he makes of the striking clock at Prince Prospero's feast, in "The Mask of the Red Death." Each time the clock struck (the reader will remember), it struck so loudly that the music and the dancing must cease perforce until it had made an end; as the hours ran on towards midnight, these pauses grew naturally longer; the maskers had the more time to think and look at one another, and their thoughts were none the more pleasant. Thus, as each hour struck, there went a jar about the assemblage; until, as the reader will remember, the end comes suddenly. Now, this is quite legitimate; no one need be ashamed of being frightened or excited by such means; the rules of the game have been respected; only, by the true instinct of the story-teller he has told his story to the best advantage, and got full value for his imaginations. This is not so always, however; for sometimes he will take a high note falsetto; sometimes, by a sort of conjuring trick, get more out of his story than he has been able to put into it; and, while the whole garrison is really parading past us on the esplanade, continue to terrify us from the battlements with sham cannon and many fierce-looking shakos upon broom-sticks. For example, in "The Pit and the Pendulum," after having exhausted his bedeviled imagination in the conception of the pendulum and the red-hot collapsing walls, he finds he can figure forth nothing more horrible for the pit; and yet the pit was to be the crowning horror.

He knows no more about the pit than you or I do. It is a pure imposture, a piece of audacious, impudent thimble-rigging; and yet, even with such bugs as these he does manage to frighten us. You will find the same artifice repeated in "Hans Pfaal," about the mysteries of the moon; and again, though with a difference, in the abrupt conclusion of "Arthur Gordon Pym." His imagination is a willing horse; but three times, as you see, he has killed it under him by over-riding, and come limping to the post on foot. With what a good grace does he not turn these failures to advantage, and make capital out of each imaginative bankruptcy! Even on a critical retrospect, it is hard to condemn him as he deserves; for he cheats with gusto.

After this knowledge of the stage, this cleverness at turning a story out, perhaps the most striking of Poe's peculiarities is an almost incredible insight into the debatable region between sanity and madness. The ''Imp of the Perverse,'' for example, is an important contribution to morbid psychology; so, perhaps, is ''The Man of the Crowd;'' ''Berenice,'' too, for as horrible as it is, touches a chord in one's own breast, though perhaps it is a chord that had better be left alone; and the same idea recurs in ''The Tell-Tale Heart.'' Sometimes we can go with him the whole way with a good conscience; sometimes—instead of saying, yes, this is how I should be if I were just a little more mad than ever I was—we can say frankly, this is what I am. . . . [Though] it is delightful enough in the C. Auguste Dupin trilogy—it was Baudelaire who called it a trilogy—yet one wearies in the long run of this strain of ingenuity; one begins to marvel at the absence of the good homespun motives and sentiments that do the business of the everyday world; although the demonstrator is clever, and the cases instructive and probably unique, one begins to weary of going round this madhouse, and long for the society of some plain harmless person, with business habits and a frock coat, and nerves not much more shattered than the majority of his plain and harmless contemporaries. Nor did this exaggerated insight make him wearisome only; it did worse than that—it sometimes led him astray.

It is Poe's merit to carry people away, and it is his besetting sin that he wants altogether such scrupulous honesty as guides and restrains the finished artist. He was, let us say it with all sorrow, not conscientious. Hunger was ever at his door, and he had too imperious a desire for what we call nowadays the sensational in literature. And thus the critic (if he be more conscientious than the man he is criticizing) dare not greatly praise lest he should be thought to condone all that is unscrupulous and tinsel in these wonderful stories. They are to be praised by him in one way only—by recommending those that are least objectionable. If anyone wishes to be excited, let him read, under favorable circumstances, ''The Gold Bug,'' ''The Descent into the Maelström,'' ''The Cask of Amontillado,'' ''The Oval Portrait,'' and the three stories about C. Auguste Dupin, the philosophical detective. If he should then desire to read more, he may go on, but warily; there are trap-doors and spring-guns in these volumes, there are gins and pitfalls; and the precipitate reader may stumble unawares upon some nightmare not easily to be forgotten.

Robert Louis Stevenson. *The Academy.* January 2, 1879, pp. 1–2

The best of Edgar Allan Poe's tales all have the same burden. Hate is as inordinate as love, and as slowly consuming, as secret, as underground, as subtle. All this underground vault business in Poe only symbolizes that which takes place *beneath* the consciousness. On top, all is fair-spoken. Beneath, there is awful murderous extremity of burying alive. Fortunato, in "The Cask of Amontillado," is buried alive out of perfect hatred, as the lady Madeline of "The Fall of the House of Usher" is buried alive out of love. The lust of hate is the inordinate desire to consume and unspeakably possess the soul of the hated one, just as the lust of love is the desire to possess, or to be possessed by, the beloved, utterly. But in either case the result is the dissolution of both souls, each losing itself in transgressing its own bounds.

In "William Wilson" we are given a rather unsubtle account of the attempt of a man to kill his own soul. William Wilson the mechanical, lustful ego succeeds in killing William Wilson the living self. The lustful ego lives on, gradually reducing itself towards the dust of the infinite.

In the "Murders in the Rue Morgue" and "The Gold Bug" we have those mechanical tales where the interest lies in the following out of a subtle chain of cause and effect. The interest is scientific rather than artistic, a study in psychologic reactions.

Poe knew only love, love, love, intense vibrations and heightened consciousness. Drugs, women, self-destruction, but anyhow the prismatic ecstasy of heightened consciousness and sense of love, of flow. The human soul in him was beside itself. But it was not lost. He told us plainly how it was, so that we should know.

He was an adventurer into vaults and cellars and horrible underground passages of the human soul. He sounded the horror and the warning of his own doom.

Doomed he was. He died wanting more love, and love killed him. A ghastly disease, love. Poe telling us of his disease: trying even to make his disease fair and attractive. Even succeeding.

Which is the inevitable falseness, duplicity of art, American art in particular.

D. H. Lawrence. *Studies in Classic American
Literature* (New York: Viking, 1964), pp. 70–88

In the eighteen-thirties occurred a literary dawn directly affecting not only the history of the weird tale, but that of short fiction as a whole; and indirectly molding the trends and fortunes of a great European aesthetic school. It is our good fortune as Americans to be able to claim that dawn as our own, for it came in the person of our most illustrious and unfortunate fellow countryman Edgar Allan Poe. Poe's fame has been subject to curious undulations, and it is now a fashion amongst the "advanced intelligentsia" to minimize his importance both as an artist and as an influence; but it would be hard for any mature and reflective critic to deny the tremendous value of his work and the persuasive potency of his mind as an opener of artistic vistas.

Poe perceived the essential impersonality of the real artist; and knew that the function of creative fiction is merely to express and interpret events and sensations as they are, regardless of how they tend or what they prove—good or evil, attractive or repulsive, stimulating or depressing, with the author always acting as a vivid and detached chronicler rather than as a teacher, sympathizer, or vendor of opinion.

Poe's specters thus acquired a convincing malignity possessed by none of their predecessors, and established a new standard of realism in the annals of literary horror. The impersonal and artistic intent, moreover, was aided by a scientific attitude not often found before; whereby Poe studied the human mind rather than the usages of Gothic fiction, and worked with an analytical knowledge of terror's true sources which doubled the force of his narratives and emancipated him from all the absurdities inherent in merely conventional shudder-coining. Poe, too, set a fashion in consummate craftsmanship; and although today some of his own work seems slightly melodramatic and unsophisticated, we can constantly trace his influence in such things as the maintenance of a single mood and achievement of a single impression in a tale, and the rigorous paring down of incidents to such as have a direct bearing on the plot and will figure prominently in the climax. Truly may it be said that Poe invented the short story in its present form. His elevation of disease, perversity, and decay to the level of artistically expressible themes was likewise infinitely far-reaching in effect; for avidly seized, sponsored, and intensified by his eminent French admirer Charles Pierre Baudelaire, it became the nucleus of the principal aesthetic movements in France, thus making Poe in a sense the father of the Decadents and the Symbolists. . . .

Poe possessed a master's vision of the terror that stalks about and within us, and the worm that writhes and slavers in the hideously close abyss. Penetrating to every festering horror in the gaily painted mockery called existence, and in the solemn masquerade called human thought and feeling, that vision had power to project itself in blackly magical crystallizations and transmutations; till there bloomed in the sterile America of the thirties and forties such a moon-nourished garden of gorgeous poison fungi as not even the nether slopes of Saturn might boast. . . .

Poe's tales, of course, fall into several classes; some of which contain a purer essence of spiritual horror than others. The tales of logic and ratiocination, forerunners of the modern detective story, are not to be included at all in weird literature; whilst certain others, probably influenced considerably by Hoffmann, possess an extravagance which relegates them to the borderline of the grotesque. Still a third group deal with abnormal psychology and monomania in such a way as to express terror but not weirdness. A substantial residuum, however, represent the literature of supernatural horror in its acutest form; and give their author a permanent and unassailable place as deity and fountainhead of all modern diabolic fiction. . . .

Certain of Poe's tales possess an almost absolute perfection of artistic form which makes them veritable beacon lights in the province of the short story. Poe could, when he wished, give to his prose a richly poetic cast;

employing that archaic and Orientalized style with jeweled phrase, quasi-Biblical repetition, and recurrent burthen so successfully used by later writers like Oscar Wilde and Lord Dunsany; and in the cases where he has done this we have an effect of lyrical phantasy almost narcotic in essence—an opium pageant of dream in the language of dream, with every unnatural color and grotesque image bodied forth in a symphony of corresponding sound. "The Masque of the Red Death," "Silence, a Fable," and "Shadow, a Parable," are assuredly poems in every sense of the word save the metrical one, and owe as much of their power to aural cadence as to visual imagery. But it is in two of the less openly poetic tales, "Ligeia" and "The Fall of the House of Usher"—especially the latter—that one finds those very summits of artistry whereby Poe takes his place at the head of fictional miniaturists. Simple and straightforward in plot, both of these tales owe their supreme magic to the cunning development which appears in the selection and collocation of every least incident.

The bizarre conceptions evidenced in these two tales, so awkward in unskillful hands, become under Poe's spell living and convincing terrors to haunt our nights; and all because the author understood so perfectly the very mechanics and physiology of fear and strangeness—the essential details to emphasize, the precise incongruities and conceits to select as preliminaries or concomitants to horror, the exact incidents and allusions to throw out innocently in advance as symbols or prefigurings of each major step toward the hideous denouement to come, the nice adjustments of cumulative force, and the unerring accuracy in linkage of parts, which make for faultless unity throughout, and thunderous effectiveness at the climactic moment, the delicate nuances of scenic and landscape value to select in establishing and sustaining the desired mood and vitalizing the desired illusion—principles of this kind, and dozens of obscurer ones too elusive to be described or even fully comprehended by any ordinary commentator.

H. P. Lovecraft. *Supernatural Horror in Literature*
(Sauk City, Wisconsin: Arkham House, 1965), pp.
347–413

The problem of Edgar Allan Poe's achievement is summarized neatly in the contradictory opinions of two celebrated men of letters, both highly gifted practitioners of their art, both knowledgeable in the history of literature, both professional literary critics. Henry James remarks: "An enthusiasm for Poe is the mark of a decidedly primitive stage of reflection." Edmund Wilson states: "Poe is not, as he is with the French and as he ought to be with us, a vital part of our intellectual equipment."

Let it be said at once that Wilson is demonstrably right and James demonstrably wrong. Complicating the issue, James appears later to have changed his mind about Poe, at least to the extent of developing an enthusiasm for (astonishingly) "Arthur Gordon Pym." Some derogatory pronouncements are sound enough to be accepted by those who admire him.

He *is* sometimes too melodramatic, banal, subjective. The fallacy in this kind of criticism is that it can make any writer look foolish if judiciously applied to his shortcomings. Poe had his faults, but they are not, or ought not to be, the decisive factor in estimating him. He is too good too often to be so circumscribed.

He has the writer's primary virtue of readability, for he writes prose that moves vigorously and is almost never dull. His art is based on an economy of means, the ability to say in a few words what another writer would say in many. He is a master of the great line. He writes with power, producing in his finest works the effect that follows from an understanding of what to say and how best to say it. He is original in that he invented one type of literature, perfected others, and pointed the way in which still others ought to be pursued. He is versatile: poet, storyteller, critic; artist in humor and horror and beauty and fantasy; genius of the Gothic tale, and of satire on the Gothic tale; romanticist, realist, symbolist, surrealist. . . .

In general, it is possible to dislike the type of thing Poe did, even apart from the question of how well he did it. If critics do not like romanticism, surrealism, Gothic horror, detective stories, or verse that appeals primarily to the ear—they will not enjoy Poe. . . .

Poe has been damned as well as praised at every turn; but when wrangling over a writer's achievement has continued for so long and been sustained by critics so conflicting in their premises, it is safe to assume that his defenders are more nearly right than his disparagers. . . .

At this point, half the case for Poe has been established, the half concerning his achievement. The other half concerns his influence. In American literature, his influence affected writers from H. P. Lovecraft to Robert Frost; in English literature, writers from Tennyson to Graham Greene. Foreign writers, certainly in all the major languages of the West and probably in most of those around the world, have submitted to Poe's influence. The most noteworthy examples are Frenchmen. . . .

Poe's literary achievement, great as it is, does not surpass his influence. No other of his fellow countrymen, in any field, subject, discipline, or department of thought, has been so masterly in producing fruitful ideas for other men to cultivate. None has been so perceptive in so multifarious a way of the paths to the future that writers might tread. Even his personal prose was effective. It helped to form the attitude of the typical romantic poet, and it pointed forward to Oscar Wilde the aesthete, to Rossetti the Pre-Raphaelite, to Whistler, and his fierce defense of ''art for art's sake.''

Poe's comprehensive influence ought now to be pursued and documented in a survey covering at least Europe and America. This project would be one of the most worthwhile that any scholar could undertake. It would also be one of the most exacting, for the author would have to range from Canada to Russia, from Argentina to Scandinavia; he would have to branch from literature into art, music, and science; and he would have to explain how submission to Poe's theory or practice, or both, unites such strange allies as the symbolists and the naturalists, the decadents and the new critics, Maeterlinck and Conan Doyle, Jules Verne and Whistler, Swinburne and Dostoevsky.

A survey of this type would leave, not Poe's reputation, but wonderment at it, looking meretricious. Poe would be revealed for what he is— America's greatest writer, and the American writer of greatest significance in world literature.

Vincent Buranelli. Edgar Allan Poe (Boston:
Twayne, 1977), pp. 129–36

Poe is a phenomenon unique in literature. Delving into questions that preoccupied his contemporaries, he tantalizes us still today. His tales and detective stories, the worlds of the occult and parapsychological which he conjures up before us, the domain of psychogenic and psychosomatic illness— that whole pathological dimension—come to life under his aegis. Poe also encapsulates in his works those polarities which hounded him: the empirical and spiritual worlds. These seemingly incompatible domains are meticulously structured in his tales: each is wrought in great detail, and each searches through the rubble of the lives he brings to his readers for insights, for ways to right a wrong, to balance the warped, harmonize conflict, and discover truth. That Poe is drawn to horror and the morbid and was also fascinated by scientific and metaphysical problems, indicates his deep need to break out of the constricting environment in which he found himself, the social structure, and the limited, pragmatic outlook of his times. Yet there was an equally powerful drive within him, based on psychological and emotional needs, to remain in a circumscribed and closed world. The need for love and companionship was primal in Poe, as was his sense of severance from a public that never understood his work, and which rejected him and turned its back on his great literary achievements. Poe's uncontrollable tension perhaps catalyzed his creative urge. Loneliness forced him to speak out, and to disclose the macabre depths raging within him. He was a man of solitude; yet he could not be silenced.

Whatever the area Poe chose to explore in his tales, each was presented with finesse, artistry, and great sensitivity, often also with deep emotion. His poems, particularly those focusing on youthful lost love, sing out their music from the heart and are indeed timeless. They answer a longing in everyone to know or to remember how to love and be loved. They strike a responsive note in all those who listen to these marvelous lyrical creations. Poe's tales, revolving around turbulent storms and maelstroms, are descents into the personal and collective unconscious; they are rites of passage which open up vast areas within the subliminal realm. His feminine characters emerge from the same depths as skeletal anima figures—wraithlike females, sometimes listless, ill phantasmagorias, at other times active presences intent on acquiring more and more knowledge, the better to dominate the unsuspecting male. It is from these regions also that Poe's frightening destructive shadow beings come. The mystical tales take us out of our own limited existence into a world of fantasy and wonderment. Poe's powers of imagination seem virtually limitless in his revelations of extraterrestrial worlds: subterranean and supergalactic domains within and without the limits of the earth proper, immobilizing the reader as Poe recounts with verve—but always with extreme control—the lot of those living in silent spatial spheres, quiescent, astounded, and perplexed by that glowing mystery which is life itself.

Applicable to Poe is the statement made by Thomas Mann in *Death in Venice:* "Solitude gives birth to the original in us, to beauty unfamiliar and perilous—to poetry. But also, it gives birth to the opposite: to the perverse, the illicit, the absurd."

Poe deeply immersed himself in his own interior world, and it is from those depths that he speaks to us today and holds us in his spell as artist and seer.

Bettina L. Knapp. *Edgar Allan Poe* (New York:
Ungar, 1984), pp. 205–7

Edgar Allan Poe, an admirer of the English Gothic novel as well as the works of E. T. A. Hoffmann, tried his hand in 1841 at a new type of short-story writing. The publication of "The Murders in the Rue Morgue" in *Graham's Magazine* ushered in a new literary genre: the detective story. Poe called it a story of "ratiocination," or logical reasoning. Elements of detection had occurred in Hoffmann's *Das Fräulein von Scuderi,* but these deductive principles were the main ingredient in this new genre, while the descriptions of persons and places were relegated to secondary importance, introduced only when absolutely necessary to the solution of the problems posed.

Although careful analysis of apparently unimportant details is the main feature of "The Murders in the Rue Morgue," the most important feature of the story is the appearance of Chevalier C. Auguste Dupin, the prototype of the later Sherlock Holmes. It is he who explains all the ramifications of the investigation to the reader. Thus the reader becomes a member of an exclusive circle—the initiated, those in the know—and feels privileged at being on the inside.

Dupin's motivation is interesting. He solves strange puzzles for the sheer love of testing his powers of reason. A few striking character elements serve to sketch in his personality. For example, he turns night into day, reading and working by candle light; so will his successor, Sherlock Holmes. As Dupin's model Poe used a true historical personage, the ex-rogue and ex-chief of the Sûreté, Eugène Vidocq. It is for this reason that the author set the tale in Paris.

Facts that appear paradoxical are the very ones that lead Dupin to the solution of a crime. He explains this over and over again in the story, maintaining that circumstances that *seem* mysterious often offer up the precise clue that leads to a puzzle's solution. First he listens carefully to everything the witnesses in the Rue Morgue have to say; for example he notes that while some assume the shouts heard were exclamations in Spanish, German, or Russian, others believe them to be the screams of an orangutan! In the end the crime proves to be less horrible than was at first believed. For Dupin the case is closed once he has found the solution. To the public and the police, however, some mystery may still remain. The selection of the word *morgue* (mortuary) in the street name—which happens to be an actual street in the St. Roche quarter in Paris—lends a touch of intrigue to the title, giving the story a tone of romantic horror.

Another long-established mystery motif, "the locked room"—familiar in ancient folklore—was introduced into the new detective story genre by Poe. Careful investigation by Dupin reveals that the locked room in which the crime was committed does indeed possess an alternative means of entry—namely the window!

In November 1842 *Graham's Magazine* published "The Mystery of Marie Rôget," mentioning its connection with "The Murders in the Rue Morgue." The analysis, if not the final solution, is again left to Dupin. While the setting is Paris, the scene of the actual events on which the story is based was the Hudson River, and Weehawken, New Jersey, just across the River. The murder itself was that of a young woman named Mary Rogers. Poe, who did not live in New York at the time, relied largely on press reports for this information. He provided no solution, but did throw suspicion on a naval officer as the possible murderer.

Poe's love of deduction found full satisfaction in "The Purloined Letter" (1845). Here there is no detailed investigation. Instead Dupin discovers the compromising letter of the title by studying closely the mind of the suspect. It has not been cunningly hidden but left—almost carelessly—in a letter rack on a desk, along with other unimportant papers, a triumph of psychology. Later crime writers frequently took up the parallel idea of hiding one particular murder away within a series of crimes.

Poe's "The Gold Bug" (1843) deals with the discovery of a pirate's buried treasure, which brings to light a long forgotten crime—the murder of the accomplices of Captain Kidd. Its great interest, however, lies in the painstaking deciphering of a code that leads to the discovery of the treasure.

"Thou Art the Man" (1844) is almost a parody of the detective story. A seemingly good and honest citizen, aptly called Goodfellow, turns out to be the murderer. He tries to throw suspicion on his victim's heir by collecting false evidence against him. Intuition, not deduction, then leads an honest citizen to conduct his own investigation, in which he manages to trick the culprit into a confession. A cask of wine mysteriously bursts open and the decaying body of the victim rises to accuse Goodfellow with the ominous words: "Thou art the man." Though essentially a parody, the story contains two most important elements of detective fiction: the investigation of false leads and finally the unexpected and spectacular confrontation of the murderer by his victim.

Waltraud Woeller. *The Literature of Crime and Detection* (New York: Ungar, 1988), pp. 55–58

Apart from his genius as a poet of great imagination and sensitivity and a writer of mystery and horror stories, Edgar Allan Poe was at one and the same time the father of the detective story and the spy tale. Purists may repudiate his entitlement to be included in this volume [*Spy Fiction: A Connoisseur's Guide*], yet the facts remain that he undoubtedly influenced many subsequent writers of stories of espionage and that his supreme detective, C. Auguste Dupin, was in some respects more spy, or unofficial secret agent, than detective. In no work is this shown so clearly as in ''The Purloined Letter,'' for the tale contains all the ingredients of the classic spy story. A top-secret document is stolen from the royal departments, and the authorities strongly suspect that the culprit is a Minister, too important and influential to be arrested without positive proof. The secret police search the hotel apartment in which the Minister lives but without success. It is then that Dupin is called in to investigate the whole affair and discreetly locate the missing document.

In another direction, and in an oblique way, Poe also gave some impetus to the future shape of some spy stories by his interest in cryptography. In an article in a Philadelphia weekly magazine in 1840 Poe, who had then been studying cryptography for some time, opined that there was no such thing as an unsolvable cipher and offered to solve any such message sent to him. He received about 100 ciphers and solved all but one—and that one he denounced as a fake intended to deceive him. Out of his interest in this subject came *The Gold Bug* which, though not a spy story, is still one of the best stories yet written about ciphers and codes.

Thus, with Poe, real life inspired fiction and some of his fiction inspired real-life developments in Intelligence. For from 1850 onwards the intelligence game became very much the war of the cryptographers, a period when each major military power included courses in cryptography in its training program.

Donald McCormick and Katy Fletcher. *Spy Fiction: A Connoisseur's Guide* (New York: Facts on File, 1990), pp. 214–215

PRONZINI, BILL (1943–   )

The Nameless novels have a strong sense of continuity. Pronzini achieves a serial effect by aging Nameless accurately across the years and by ending several of the books with a major event still in limbo; will Nameless die of cancer, will he lose his private investigator's license, will he get married? For the answers you must buy the next one.

The Nameless novels are admirably versatile. Some combine the best elements of the Hammett-Chandler tradition with the puzzle plots of the classic detective story; hard-boiled but with a locked room problem (e.g., *Hoodwink, Scattershot*). Others bear faint resemblance to classic detective story plotting (e.g., *Dragonfire*).

More often than we might care to admit, an author's important discoveries may be the benefits of good luck. Pronzini's creation of a detective *sans nom* was serendipitous. He and his editor "could not decide on a name they liked for an overweight, middle-aged Italian private investigator—Tony Rome was already taken." Regardless of the impetus, Pronzini's final decision to leave the detective nameless was a very wise choice.

The anonymity of the hero is no mere gimmick. The novels assume a pronounced autobiographical tone. . . . Leaving the detective unnamed allows Pronzini to use him as a prototype of what a good detective should be—"just a cop," "doing a job, helping people in trouble." He is the Everyman of private investigator fiction: honest, committed, compassionate and tough. Inspired by the nameless Continental Op but patterned after Thomas B. Dewey's "Mac," he is *the* hardworking professional.

Robert A. Baker and Michael T. Nietzel. *Private Eyes: One Hundred and One Knights* (Bowling Green, Ohio: Popular Press, 1985), pp. 256–57

Only once identified by name (in *Twospot* [1978], a novel Bill Pronzini coauthored with Collin Wilcox in which his detective is paired with Wilcox's Lieutenant Frank Hastings, he is called Bill), Pronzini's series private eye has come to be known simply as Nameless. His decision to leave his private eye unnamed has led to much speculation, though Pronzini himself offers a simple explanation for the matter. "The damn detective doesn't have a name because when I began the series in 1968 I couldn't think of one that suited him." When a few years later he decided to move his private eye from short stories to novels, he tried again to come up with an appropriate name, but once he realized that his hero so closely resembled himself ("He was me; I was him"), he decided not to give him one.

In many ways Nameless resembles another famous unnamed private eye, Hammett's Continental Op. Both live and work in San Francisco. Both can be described as no longer young (Nameless is fifty-three in his most recent cases) and no longer thin. A self-styled slob, Nameless admits to a beer belly and "a gray plodding shaggy look." But there the similarities end, for unlike the Op, whose character was defined almost exclusively in terms of his work, and whose private side was seldom glimpsed, Nameless has one of the most fully developed personal lives of all private eyes.

One of the oldest fictional private eyes in the business, Nameless was born and raised in San Francisco. He began his investigative career in Military Intelligence during the war. Following his discharge from the army, he joined the San Francisco Police Department, where he served for fifteen years, until one day a case he was investigating in which a man had hacked his wife and two young children to death with an ax drove him from the force. He opened an office as a private detective near the Tenderloin district, where he remained until recently relocating to more modern quarters near the Hyatt Regency Hotel. He lives in a cluttered flat in Pacific Heights, filled with dirty dishes and dustballs under the furniture, evidence of his sloppy personal habits.

The most important item in his apartment, however, is his collection of pulp magazines, which increases over the course of the series from 5,000 to 6,500 copies and which is the only thing he keeps neat and orderly. His fascination for the pulps began when he was a young man and has resulted not just in his impressive collection but also in his career choices, first as a policeman and then a private detective, for he freely admits to being driven by a desire to emulate the great pulp heroes of the past. His fantasy of being a pulp detective once cost him the love of a woman who finally tired of what she called his adolescent obsession with dead heroes. Stung initially by her charge, he finally concluded there was nothing wrong with trying to follow the example of men who were true champions of justice.

Now he proudly displays a blown-up reproduction of a *Black Mask* cover on his office wall, carries copies of pulps with him to read on the job whenever he has the chance, and even has dreams at night in which he goes after prohibition rumrunners with Jo Gar and Steve McBride and plays poker with Race Williams and Max Latin. The pulps even occasionally assist him in his work. The cover of a *Detective Fiction Weekly* magazine he sees in a bookstore window gives him the clue he needs to solve the crime in *The Snatch* (1971), and a paperback mystery by a pulp veteran provides the key to the solution in *Undercurrent* (1973). In *Hoodwink* (1981) he even gets to attend a convention of pulp writers, where he solves the murder of one of the guests and meets and falls in love with Kerry Wade, the daughter of two veteran pulp writers.

There is one important difference between Nameless and the Op, Race Williams, Max Latin, and the rest of the tough-guy heroes. Instead of the rugged hard-boiled attitude that his pulp forebears adopted toward the world, Nameless wears his heart on his sleeve, the icy reserve that characterized their outlook replaced in his case by a free and open display of emotion. Unlike the pulp tough guy who masked his hurt behind a cynical wisecrack, Nameless is a brooding, hand-wringing worrier who freely bares his soul to the reader. Unlike Philip Marlowe, whose frequent bouts with despair could be traced to disappointment at the failure of the world to measure up to his idealistic expectations, Nameless's disappointments are largely personal. Unlike Lew Archer, who is deeply moved by the troubles of the people he meets,

Nameless worries about his own problems. He is unable to offer the kind of personal commitment to his clients that many of his colleagues do simply because he is so absorbed in his own miseries.

What gives the Nameless series its consistency, despite the awkward shifts in focus, is the very human figure of its main character. Nameless is less fervently the idealistic crusader and less inclined to the swaggering postures and tough heroics that characterize many of his younger colleagues. His intensity usually comes out only in the display of his emotions as he faces one personal crisis after another—disappointment at the several failures in his relationships with women, distress over the suspension of his license. Unafraid to express his feelings and to admit his worries, Nameless emerges as a less-than-perfect man with whom the reader comes to share a deep rapport, rather than a superhero whose dazzling exploits one is expected to admire. . . .

Although neither a brilliant stylist nor an innovative writer, Pronzini is a solid professional who turns out a steady stream of dependable work. Like Nameless, his work isn't flashy, but it is always reliable and honest.

David Geherin. *The American Private Eye: The Image in Fiction* (New York: Ungar, 1985), pp. 166–72

PYNCHON, THOMAS (1937–   )

The book [*V.*] reads like a literary hoax, a parody of the quest romance and tale of international intrigue. We are made to witness violent happenings in Cairo, Florence, and Malta, explorations of the Antarctic, and crocodile hunts in the sewers of New York. The fantastic web of events spans three generations, moving back and forth through space and time at will. The characters, as the author puts it, are mostly yo-yos. The style is elliptic and cockeyed, studded with zany names and improbable locutions. The whole novel gives an impression of studied confusion, a mood that expresses both the futility and vitality of human life.

Ihab Hassan. *Saturday Review.* March 23, 1963, p. 44

As readers of his first novel *V.* (1963) can attest, Pynchon is an enormously well informed man. *Gravity's Rainbow* is a 760-page affidavit that he knows his Freud, he knows his Pavlov, he knows his comparative religions, he knows his rocket technology. He can write a gloss on Abraham and Isaac or a program note on forties jazz. He is equally up on mandalas and Deanna Durbin movies. He is perhaps the only novelist alive who would use a sine curve as a metaphor for life, complete with the appropriate formula.

Pynchon appears almost too resourceful. His prose is gusty, propulsive, sputtering as a last resort into Brechtian verse or the shorthand of one-act playlets. It is as if he were trying to say everything at once, on every page. One has the impression that inside his head is a movie screen on which an endless series of very funny, and very ghastly, one-reelers is being projected: *Pynchon Presents World War II,* with radioactive custard pies for a cast of thousands, and the Four Horsemen of the Apocalypse chased by Keystone Kops.

Pynchon, for all his antics, is a theologian, laying out the road to damnation. *Gravity's Rainbow* serves as Pynchon's occasionally nauseous measure of twentieth-century degradation. (One passage of virtuosic scatology might be described as the Great Toilet Flush: five pages long.) For Pynchon, as presumably for Slothrop [the protagonist], the supreme obscenity is that ordinary people are "willing to have life defined for them by men whose only talent is for death."

What Pynchon is staging is the tragicomedy of modern man engineering himself into a thing, damned to become one with his own machinery, only "in love with his, and his race's, death."

At his worst, Pynchon is the scat singer of Apocalypse, making one-line jokes about the *I Ching,* indulging himself in whimsy on the First International Runcible Spoon Fight. But at its best, *Gravity's Rainbow* is a kind of American *Dog Years.* Like Günter Grass, like Hieronymus Bosch, Pynchon has the power to make death seem as vital as life itself. As "fantasist-surrogate," he assumes the reader's case of the cosmic horrors and manages them for him. Is this called "therapy" or "moral vision"? No matter—it is a frightening and extraordinary talent.

Melvin Maddocks. *The Atlantic Monthly.* March 1973, pp. 98–100

The fantastically variegated and multi-structured *V.,* which made Thomas Pynchon famous in 1963 and the wonder ever since of anyone who has tried to meet or photograph or interview him, is the most masterful first novel in the history of literature, the only one of its decade with the proportions and stylistic resources of a classic. Three years later came *The Crying of Lot 49,* more accessible only because very much shorter than the first, and like some particularly dazzling section left over from it. And now *Gravity's Rainbow.* More ambitious than *V.,* more topical (in that its central mystery is not a cryptogram but a supersonic rocket), and more nuanced, *Gravity's Rainbow* is even less easy to assimilate into those interpretive schematizations of "apocalypse" and "entropy" by which Pynchon's work has, up to now, been rigidified by his admirers.

At thirty-six, Pynchon has established himself as a novelist of major historical importance. More than any other living writer, including Norman Mailer, he has caught the inward movements of our time in outward manifestations of art and technology so that in being historical he must also be marvelously exorbitant. It is probable that he would not like being called "historical." In *Gravity's Rainbow,* even more than in his previous work, history—as Norman O. Brown proposed in *Life against Death*—is seen as a form of neurosis, a record of the progressive attempt to impose the human will upon the movements of time.

The ultimate whip in *Gravity's Rainbow,* the end product of the system, is the supersonic rocket, the German V-2 of the Second World War. It is Moby Dick and the *Pequod* all in one, both the Virgin and the Dynamo of Pynchon's magnificent book.

If in the structure of his books Pynchon duplicates the intricate networking of contemporary technological, political, and cultural systems, then in the style and its rapid transitions he tries to match the dizzying tempos, the accelerated shifts from one mode of experience to another, which characterize contemporary media and movement.

In Pynchon we "return" to ourselves, come back to the remembered earth of our primal being, reified by the objects to which we have joined our passions, our energies, and our needs.

In *Gravity's Rainbow* there are some 400 characters all bearing Pynchonesque names (Old Bloody Chiclitz is back, by the way, from *The Crying of Lot 49*), along with a fair number of people who, if you bother, can be found in reference books (e.g., such pioneers in organic chemistry as Kekulé, von Liebig, and Clerk Maxwell).

No one, for example, will want to keep track of the hundreds of alphabetical agencies from World War II and the international cartels that are mentioned in the book, nor is anyone expected to. The confusion is the point, and CIA is not what you think it is, but Chemical Instrumentality for the Abnormal. The book is full of disguises, of changes and fusions of identity.

Aside from the main plot, which deals with a competitive effort to see who can first put together a facsimile of Rocket 00000, there are at least four other major plots, one of which would alone make or enhance the reputation of anyone now writing fiction.

There are also dozens of wondrous ancillary plots featuring characters whose motives and activities are essential to the movement of all the major ones.

The central character is the Rocket itself, and all the other characters, for one reason or another, are involved in a quest for it, especially for a secret component, the so-called *Schwarzgerät,* which was wrapped in Imipolex G. Because the multiple search gradually exposes the interlocking relationships among the cultural, economic, and scientific aspects of contemporary life, and its historical antecedents, Pynchon can properly refer to it as "the terrible politics of the Grail."

It can and will be said that such a book as this would have no audience except one prepared by the kind of analytic study of literature that has been in vogue for some thirty years. It's been said already of *V.* and of the works of other related contemporary novelists like William Burroughs, who shares, by the way, Pynchon's marvelous sensitivity to the metaphysical implications of technology, especially film technology, and the way the mind can schizophrenically work like a film projector. But the argument that writers like Pynchon and Burroughs are a by-product of contemporary literary criticism is trivial, since, for one reason, the two books—*Moby-Dick* and *Ulysses*—that come to mind most often as one reads *Gravity's Rainbow* indulged in the same kind of complexity, not because criticism had made it fashionable to do so, but because the internal nature of culture made it necessary. And it is further beside the point because *Gravity's Rainbow* marks an advance beyond either book in its treatment of cultural inheritances, an advance that a merely literary education and taste will either distort or find uncongenial.

What distinguishes Pynchon in *Gravity's Rainbow*, especially from such writers as John Barth and Borges, is that he does not, like them, make use of technology or popular culture or literary convention in an essentially parodistic spirit, though he tended to do so in *V.* He is not so literary as to think it odd, an in joke, that literary techniques are perhaps less powerfully revealing about human nature and history than are scientific ones.

Readers who get impatient with this book will most likely be too exclusively literary in their responses rather than not literary enough. They'll stare at designs without listening to voices, wonder about characters when they should be laughing at grotesques, and generally miss the experience in a search for the meaning. Above all, they'll be discomfited by a novelist who posits a world in which experience is often most meaningfully assembled in ways considered alternative, often antithetical to literature, like science, or inferior to literature, like film and comic books. It is not possible dogmatically to feel this way about literature and enjoy *Gravity's Rainbow,* or, I would suppose, read the times with much comprehension.

This is a terribly haunted book. It is written by a man who has totally isolated himself from the literary world of New York or anywhere else. This remoteness is what has freed him from the provincial self-importance about literary modes and manners.

Pynchon is almost unbearably vulnerable to every aspect of contemporary experience, open to every form of sight and sound, democratically receptive to the most common and the most recondite signatures of things.

Richard Poirier. *Saturday Review.* March 1973, pp.
59–64

Gravity's Rainbow will be compared with *Ulysses; Gravity's Rainbow* will be compared with *Duck Soup.* It is at once a farce and an extended, most extended, meditation on the ache left behind when They amputated free will. Pynchon's first book was also a farce of epic reach, a quest novel concerning the search for the mysterious and elusive V. *Gravity's Rainbow,* Pynchon's third, takes up the hunt again. This time the quarry is the elusive and deadly V-2. The first was a female spy, the second is a rocket. Nothing connects them save a letter of the alphabet, what we may call a "character." Yet Pynchon is so prodigal with his talents that it would not be beneath him to deliver a novel from so casual a conception as the symmetry between V and V-2.

Let's get one thing straight now: you won't learn from this review what really happens in *Gravity's Rainbow*. It isn't that I want to keep suspense alive. It's that I don't always know what's going on. Nor does anyone else, except Pynchon. He knows, believe me. He's got his work under control, and the reader can sense rather than articulate the system that connects its contrary qualities and rowdy disarray. Any plot outline of *Gravity's Rainbow* (or of *V.*, for the matter of that) sounds like a Lenny Bruce routine, or a parody of a Lenny Bruce routine.

It is Pynchon's peculiar grace that between the mess of this world and the terror of space he has located all the atoms. Any student of Heisenberg will tell you the sad fact that we can't know an atom's location *and* its velocity—one or the other. Pynchon's novel is so difficult (and so wonderful) because he won't give up trying to bring us the word that gets us the fix on both at once, location and velocity. Sanity and paranoia. Freedom and the social contract. Metaphor and truth.

Geoffrey Wolff. *Washington Post Book World.*
March 11, 1973, pp. 1–2

The world of *V.* is pluralistic, one of unlimited points of view, with reality presumably emergent out of the reconciliation of these diverse perceptions. Thus chancelleries all over the world piece together their picture of an ever-threatening but unknown enemy. And thus both the Stencils—father and son, British Foreign Office agent and amateur historian in search of his past—grope to connect their scraps of information into a coherent design, Stencil *père* on the scene, so to speak, at first hand and Stencil *fils* at second hand from the tantalizing memento mori of his father. This patchwork quilt approach to reality is brilliantly dramatized by Pynchon in the eight versions of the narrative action (more accurately the eight points of view imagined by Herbert Stencil) that comprise all we learn of the intrigues of British spies in Egypt on the eve of the Fashoda incident. The irony is that the eyewitnesses are all peripheral to the action. From the casual observation and incidental eavesdropping of a cafe waiter, a hotel factotum, an English confidence man (who is incidentally a blatant parody of [Nabokov's] Humbert Humbert), a train conductor, a garry driver, a burglar, and a beerhall waitress, only a fragmentary conception of what is happening can be constructed. It is as if the Fashoda incident were rendered on seven picture postcards and mailed by foreign correspondents unable to find transportation to the front or wire service to the home office. Nor in the culmination of the action are we helped to any understanding of what the spies were about. Narrated omnisciently in the elliptical manner of stage directions for a melodrama, the situation is left, as [Robert] Sklar has complained, "deliberately shrouded in mystery." But is not that Pynchon's point about what men call history? that it is an omnia gathering of irrelevancies from which sense is manufactured.

Max F. Schulz. *Black Humor Fiction of the Sixties*
(Athens, Ohio: Ohio University Press), 1973, pp.
79–80

I find it admirable that of the nonacademics Pynchon did not follow the usual lazy course of going for tenure as did so many writers—no, "writers"—of his generation. . . . The fact that he has got out into the world (somewhere) is to his credit. Certainly he has not, it would seem, missed a trick; and he never whines.

Pynchon's first novel, *V.*, was published in 1963. Cute names abound. Benny Profane, Dewey Gland, Rachel Owlglass. Booze flows through scene after scene involving members of a gang known as The Whole Sick Crew. The writing is standard American.

From various references to Henry Adams and to physics in Pynchon's work, I take it that he has been influenced by Henry Adams's theory of history as set forth in *The Education of Henry Adams* and in the posthumously published "The Rule of Phase Applied to History." For Adams, a given human society in time was an organism like any other in the universe and he favored Clausius's speculation that "the entropy of the universe tends to a maximum" (an early Pynchon short story is called "Entropy").

Pynchon's use of physics is exhilarating and as an artist he appears to be gaining more energy than he is losing. Unlike the zero writers, he is usually at the boil. From Adams he has not only appropriated the image of history as Dynamo but the attractive image of the Virgin. Now armed with these concepts he embarks in *V.* on a quest, a classic form of narrative, and the result is mixed, to say the least. . . .

The first section of *Gravity's Rainbow* is called "Beyond the Zero." Plainly a challenge not only to *l'écriture blanche* but to proud entropy itself. Pynchon has now aimed himself at anti-matter, at what takes place beyond, beneath the zero of freezing, and death. This is superbly ambitious and throughout the text energy hums like a . . . well, dynamo.

The narrative begins during the Second War, in London. Although Pynchon works hard for verisimilitude and fills his pages with period jabber, anachronisms occasionally jar (there were no "Skinnerites" in that happy time of mass death). The controlling image is that of the V-2, a guided missile developed by the Germans and used toward the end of the war (has Pynchon finally found V.? and is she a bomb?).

England. Germany. Past. Present. War. Science. Telltale images of approaching . . . deity? Two characters with hangovers "are wasted gods urging on a tardy glacier." Of sandbags at a door, "provisional pyramids erected to gratify curious gods' offspring." And "slicks of nighttime vomit, pale yellow, clear as the fluids of gods.'' Under deity, sex is central to this work of transformation.

Eventually, the text exhausts patience and energy. In fact, I suspect that the energy expended in reading *Gravity's Rainbow* is, for anyone, rather greater than that expended by Pynchon in the actual writing. This is entropy with a vengeance. The writer's text is ablaze with the heat/energy that his readers have lost to him. Yet the result of this exchange is neither a readerly nor a writerly text but an uneasy combination of both. Energy and intelligence are not in balance, and the writer fails in his ambition to be a god of creation. Yet his ambition and his failure are very much in the cranky, solipsistic American vein.

Gore Vidal. *New York Review of Books.*
July 15, 1974, pp. 120–24

Pynchon's stylistic virtuosity has been both praised as awesome and damned as tedious. Unquestionably, he has exploited, with brilliance and originality, the entire range of the novelistic tradition, drawing inspiration from Sterne and Voltaire, from Melville and Mark Twain, and from twentieth-century masters like Conrad, Joyce, Nabokov, and Borges.

He changes modes and moods with disconcerting speed—shifting from romance to satire, from burlesque and slapstick to poignant lyricism. He seems to have overlooked no literary precedent—Anatole France's missionary to the penguins, for example, is matched by Father Fairing and his parish of rats in the sewers of Manhattan in *V*. His pages abound with mandalas, carbon rings, limericks, and notes on art history and musicology. With a wildness of tone and taste, he applies the tricks of cinematography, comic books, and other forms of pop culture. His most powerful and subversive weapon is parody.

Pynchon's work bears evidence of his substantial knowledge of Egyptian and classical myth, the thought of Max Weber, Henry Adams, and Ludwig Wittgenstein and the poetry of Rilke and Eliot. His offbeat erudition enables him to utilize history and anthropology in startling ways (the 1898 Fashoda Crisis in the Sudan, the death of the composer Anton von Webern, Ojibwa customs, the Kirgiz language), although readers must remain on guard against invented peoples, persons and places, and institutions.

Perhaps Pynchon's most stunning achievement is the use he makes of science and technology in the creation of his metaphors. An early short story, ''Entropy'' (1960), revealed his fascination with the Second Law of Thermodynamics. The entropy concept, in its dual application in physics and in information theory, pervades all three novels—iterating a theme of the general breakdown of the contemporary sociocultural order.

Pynchon's prose is strewn with scientific and mathematical allusions—Gödel's Theorem, Maxwell's Demon, Poisson's Distribution. Such concepts, together with discourses on cybernetics, chemistry, and rocketry, are implanted in the very tissue of the fiction, and they grow into symbolic significance that sets him apart from practitioners of science fiction and fantasy. Equipped as he is with the latest and most specialized scientific and technical lore and the most innovative literary techniques, Pynchon seems fitted to provide his readers with a complete Baedeker's guide through the twentieth century.

Carl D. Bennett. *Encyclopedia of World Literature in the 20th Century* (New York: Frederick Ungar, volume 3, 1983), p. 611

QUEEN, ELLERY [FREDERIC DANNAY (1905–1982) and MANFRED B. LEE (1905–1971)] [also known as BARNABY ROSS]

Ellery Queen is the son of a New York police inspector, Richard Queen. His hobby is solving murder mysteries. He is also the author of the Ellery Queen books. In fact, the author Ellery Queen is two cousins, Frederic Dannay and Manfred B. Lee, who invented the technique of using the detective's name as the author. In further fact, Frederic Dannay was born Daniel Nathan, and Manfred B. Lee, Manford Lepofsky. "Frederic" is a tribute to Frederick Chopin; "Manfred" is a tribute to the name itself which means "man of peace."

The success of the Ellery Queen books lies in the complexity of the mystery plots, with Ellery Queen a look-alike for Lord Peter Wimsey or his Americanized version Philo Vance. The stories take place in the skyscrapers and elegant old homes of a rapidly vanishing Old New York. Another feature of the Queen novels is a "Challenge to the Reader" just before the explication of the plot—a point at which author Queen notes that detective Queen has all the facts in hand and has solved the mystery; can the reader?

After the first dozen or so cases, the Queen novels changed style and became more modern, with the plots scaled down in complexity and the format of psychological suspense replacing the earlier scheme of intellectual gamesmanship. The first of the series are still considered prototypes of logical deduction.

Waltraud Woeller and Bruce Cassiday. *The Literature of Crime and Detection* (New York: Ungar, 1988), p. 126

Asked to state what they believe to be the cardinal quality that has brought the Ellery Queen stories their wide reputation and success, the authors modestly speak of the "absolutely logical" fair-play method of deduction, which, indeed, has been the sign-mark of their work from the beginning. But there is more than this. Although the Messrs. "Queen" frankly and necessarily regard their output as a means of livelihood, they had brought to the detective story a respect and integrity which—combined with their unflagging zest—accounts largely for the high level they have consistently maintained. Unlike other writers who have wearied of the game and too often endeavor to substitute mere cleverness or sensationalism for hard work, the "Queens" have never failed to give their multitude of followers honest merchandise.

If the stories have a flaw it is the occasional tendency to too-great intricacy, but even this occurs so rarely as to be negligible.

For the great part, the Queen tales are as adroit a blending of the intellectual and dramatic aspects of the genre, of meticulous plot work, lively narration, easy, unforced humor, and entertaining personae, as can be found in the modern detective novel. They represent the deductive romance at its present-day skillful best.

Howard Haycraft. *Murder for Pleasure: The Life and Times of the Detective Story* (New York: Biblo and Tannen, 1968), pp. 176–77

No major mystery writer anywhere was more influenced by S. S. Van Dine than was Ellery Queen. But in several significant respects Queen altered the Van Dine structure for the better. First of all, even in his earliest novels Queen proved himself far more skillful at drawing character, writing vividly, and plotting with finesse. Second, Queen dropped the first-person narrative employed by Van Dine and thereby gained the flexibility of being able to write scenes at which no official is present. But most important of all was Queen's innovation of fair play, of providing the reader with all the information needed to solve the case along with or ahead of the detective. Fair play was not a ground rule of the game as Van Dine played it, and in fact most of Vance's solutions depend on intricate, and often debatable, psychological analyses of the suspects. Ellery's solutions on the other hand are based on rigorous logical deductions from empirical evidence, which, unlike the mental data from which Vance proceeded, was as accessible to the reader as to the detective, a point emphasized by Queen's famous "Challenge to the Reader" device.

In *The Roman Hat Mystery* (1929), a romantic gangster melodrama entitled *Gunplay* is playing to a well-filled house at the Roman Theater, on 47th Street west of Broadway. Near the end of the second act a scream tears through the audience and the lights snap on. The occupant of LL32, the leftmost seat in the rear aisle, has been found poisoned in his seat. The police are summoned. . . .

The body is identified as that of Monte Field, an unsavory criminal lawyer. The seven seats nearest to the dead man are all strangely vacant, although box-office records show all had been paid for. Field is wearing evening clothes but his top hat is missing. There is a woman's evening bag in his pocket and a half-empty ginger ale bottle under his seat. An usher has been standing at each exit since the beginning of the play and the ticket seller swears no one left by the front door, so the murderer must still be in the theater. Unfortunately the theater seems to be filled with people who might have had reason to want Monte Field dead, including a former underworld client, a former law partner, and a society girl engaged to one of the actors in the play. When the investigators leave the theater and turn to Field's apartment and office, the plot grows murkier still with the addition of an angry mistress, a suspicious valet, a set of books on handwriting analysis, intimations of mass blackmail, several more missing toppers, and a succession of lies in which various suspects are caught.

The solution, when it comes, is distinctively Queenian: fair to the reader, utterly surprising, and so complex as to consume roughly 9 percent of the book's wordage. The debut of Ellery Queen, author and detective, is a wondrous specimen of sustained technique, as readable today as it was almost forty-five years ago.

Francis M. Nevins, Jr. *Royal Bloodline: Ellery Queen, Author and Detective* (Bowling Green, Ohio: Popular Press, 1974), pp. 18–20

The Tragedy of X must be ranked among the supreme untouchable masterpieces of the Golden Age. The plot is staggering in its complexity, stunning in its ingenuity, and dazzling in its complete fairness, employing for the first time in Queen's career two devices of which one became the hallmark of the author's first period and the other was to become his distinctive province during the Fifties and Sixties. A specific description of the first device might spoil several novels for those who haven't read all of Queen's early works; suffice it to say that it rests on the same murderer-murderee relationship that Holmes once unearthed at Birlstone Manor, from which we hereby dub this device the Birlstone Gambit. The second device is, of course, the classic Queenian situation of the Dying Message. While riding in the Weehawken local during the small hours of the morning, Lane and several others, one of whom will die within minutes, discuss the last moments of life—a conversation as central to Queen's work as is the famous locked-room lecture in *The Three Coffins* to the understanding of John Dickson Carr. . . .

The Tragedy of Y (1932) is the equal of *X* in the dazzling perfection of its structure and technique, and in addition is an attempt more sustained and organic than in *X* to integrate the deductive problem with ''serious'' literary intent. The book's central themes can be traced back to the plays of Eugene O'Neill and through him to Greek tragedy, and apparently exerted marked influence on such later works as Raymond Chandler's ''The Curtain,'' William March's *The Bad Seed,* and Hitchcock's *Psycho* which itself influenced Queen when in 1963 he reshaped some elements from *Y* into *The Player on the Other Side.* . . .

The Tragedy of Y is one of the most stunningly brilliant formal deductive problems ever written, easily ranking among the ten finest flowers of the Golden Age. In its deeper aspects, it has had a long and fruitful influence; its black design may well have helped to shape the nightmare stories of Cornell Woolrich (the vision of the dark power), and Hitchcock's *Vertigo* (the interweavings of fiction/illusion and reality) and *Psycho* (the stance at once of compassion and loathing towards the murderer, the horrific shock at the revelation of the truth, the matriarch as a metaphysically evil being, the relation between the mother's and the descendant's perversions). Rooted in a form that has traditionally been oriented to order, reason, and optimism, *Y* evokes depths of tragic despair, and a sense of meaninglessness, that are virtually unparalleled in the deductive genre and to which Queen would return, in a different vein, in his great novels of the late forties.

Francis M. Nevins, Jr. *The Queen Canon Bibliophile.* January 1969, n.p.

The much more than excellent *The Sound of Detection: Ellery Queen's Adventures in Radio* by Francis M. Nevins, Jr., and Ray Stanich, is a "must" trade paperback for the reference shelf. It's a slim book, but it's packed with so much information and detail about the legendary Queen radio series that it must represent thousands of hours of research on the part of its authors.

Fortunately, this volume is unpretentious, well written, and extremely readable too. Of particular interest is a complete log of the Queen series, with details of rebroadcasts, tape availability, performers, guest stars, and publication data. Information about subsequent reworkings into short-story form, with full publication details, is also cited. In addition to all this, there is also much valuable material on the Queen collaborators which was not included in Nevins's magnificent *Royal Bloodline.*

(NOTE: *The Sound of Detection* is the full treatment of a subject barely touched upon in *Royal Bloodline,* and it serves as a welcome addition to, and extension of, its illustrious predecessor.)

Charles Shibuk. *The Armchair Detective.* Winter 1984, p. 91

See also under S. S. VAN DINE: Jon L. Breen, *Bookman's Weekly,* April 16, 1984.

RENDELL, RUTH (1930–)

Using ironic juxtaposition to relate a psychotic killer to ordinary people, Ruth Rendell exposes the thin barrier between madness and sanity. Her murderers are often simple people, pathetically incomplete and isolated from normal life rhythms. Trapped by fears and shames they cannot define, they in turn trap and destroy others. For her readers terror grows from two sources: waiting for an inevitable convergence of killer and victim, and recognizing how closely the two are linked to each other—and to ourselves.

To balance the nightmare world of the suspense stories, Rendell offers a comforting father figure in Wexford (her son suggests that he is actually based on Rendell's own father), who brings to the investigation of murder: intelligence, empathy, tolerance, and a dogged determination to discover the truth. Tensions between members of families—between husband and wife, parent and child—are often the source of violence. Wexford's own happy marriage and amicable relations with his grown daughters create a sense of order that contrasts with the disordered lives he explores professionally. Like Simenon's Maigret, whom he resembles in many ways, Wexford would like to be a "mender of destinies," but too often lives are irreversibly distorted. To justice, Rendell adds understanding; to the practice of analytic detection, a recognition of the dark regions of the human psyche.

Frances Arndt. In Janet Todd, ed., *British Women Writers* (New York: Continuum, 1989), p. 560

A "favorite" crime or thriller writer is, to me, one the whole corpus of whose work I sit down and reread every now and again. Next in line to the favorites—or, as I would call them, the classics—are the writers the whole oeuvre of whom I can imagine myself rereading in five or ten years' time. The essence of the character of a near-favorite is, of course, that one cannot be certain of that future pleasure: one can only hope for it.

In Ruth Rendell's *Shake Hands for Ever* the dyspeptic Inspector Wexford is called to a curious murder scene. A much loved, but sluttish second wife is found murdered in an immaculately clean house by her implacably hostile mother-in-law. Wexford knows that the husband is the killer (I am betraying no secrets that Mrs. Rendell does not give away, and there is a twist I have not revealed) but is hauled off the investigation after over-eagerness, and pursues it privately for more than a year with the aid of his superior copper son-in-law, with whom he came to terms in the last adventure.

The book is not vintage, but it is gripping. Mrs. Rendell's special gift is for tying the stubborn and intuitive personality of Wexford into the fascinating detail of the best *romans policier*. In the new Rendell, Wexford is not quite deep enough a personality for the obsessiveness of the Simenon novels—which is needed—to come across; but to Simenon she must now be compared.

Patrick Cosgrave. *The Spectator*. June 14, 1975,

p. 717

Ruth Rendell is hailed by her publishers as "The New First Lady of Mystery." The fact is that, publishers' enthusiasm aside, Rendell is worth serious critical attention because she has not only created a series of ingenious and clever plots, but has, above all, explored human nature effectively and with genuine insight.

The appeal of the Rendell novels is diversified and full; she uses such interest-generating devices as social criticism, brief comments upon the detective story, and short but striking glimpses of setting (the base of operations is a town called Kingsmarkham in Sussex) to lend depth and strength to her stories. Other elements of style—foreshadowing, simile, metaphor, dialogue, and irony, for instance—are equally well handled, lifting the works above the level of much detective fiction.

Perhaps her most useful device is her treatment of the characterizations of Chief Detective Inspector Reg Wexford and his aide, Detective Inspector Mike Burden. The friendship between the two men is a workable device for maintaining continuity, and the character of Wexford, himself, is developed in such a way as to provide a sane and solid framework of understanding and compassion for her real center of interest: a varied and compelling examination of friendship and love—and their too frequent companion, selfishness. These explorations of two of the most powerful of human relationships are readily perceivable in *From Doon with Death*, 1964; *The Best Man to Die*, 1969; *A Guilty Thing Surprised*, 1970; *No More Dying Then*, 1971; *Murder Being Once Done*, 1972; and *Some Lie and Some Die*, 1973.

Close examination of Ruth Rendell's fiction reveals that her concern with character and its development is perhaps the greatest of her many strengths as a writer. Each personality is clearly drawn; each is believable because each is honestly motivated. From this careful development, plot sources and complications arise; subplots employing comparable or contrasting characters and situations unfold, often generating irony or humor.

The process seems entirely natural because it is so thoroughly thought out and so carefully rendered, and thus the crimes at the center of each plot become the logical, though horrible, results of the interactions of the people involved. Rendell's mastery of her craft, and command of her chief interest, fuse entertainment and thoughtful examination of the human personality. She succeeds in this study of the human condition by refusing to compromise the integrity of the characterizations she depicts, and that integrity holds for the long term in the steadily developing portraits of Wexford and his circle, as well as in the memorable single appearances of other characters.

Just as sound characterization is the unifying quality between Rendell's series and non series works, it is also the factor which combines with careful plotting, fair clue-planting, and sensitive use of irony and humor to produce serious, thoughtful works which help to narrow the gap between crime/suspense writing and "mainstream" fiction. This is indeed a major achievement, enriching to the genre and gratifying to the reader. It places Rendell well forward among current practitioners of the art of fiction.

> Jane S. Bakerman. In Earl F. Bargainnier, ed., *10 Women of Mystery* (Bowling Green, Ohio: Popular Press, 1981), pp. 147–48

Ruth Rendell's first book, the ingenious *From Doon with Death* (1964), introduced Detective Chief Inspector Reginald Wexford who, she has said, was "born at the age of fifty-two" and was "a man because like most women I am very much still caught up in the web that one writes about men because men are the people and we are the others." The Wexford books are orthodox crime stories, set in a mid-Sussex town, and the Inspector is equipped with a wife, daughters who provide occasional problems, friends, and a puritanical sidekick named Inspector Burden, who is inclined to distrust modern youth. Some of the stories have stunning surprise endings, but it is the subjects that divide them from the work of the Golden Age. One book involves transvestism, another is based on the hatred members of a family feel for each other—and the hatred is based on personality, not on the problems of an inheritance. Her subjects justify the remark of a wit who said that in a Rendell novel a couple is not a happy thing to be. Some of the books are about sexual frustration, which is powerfully conveyed without use of a single sexual word, and little in the way of sexual description.

The Wexford books have inevitable similarities of approach, and it is little more than personal preference to pick out *Murder Being Once Done* (1972), *Some Lie and Some Die* (1973), and *Shake Hands for Ever* (1975) as particularly good, although the choice does emphasize that the most accomplished Wexfords are found in the seventies. In her chosen area, which seems always something like suburbia, and among her chosen characters, middle-class or a little lower, Rendell's ear and eye are unerring. The conversations between these people are real, and they convince also when Wexford talks to them. If one wanted to introduce a foreigner to the flavor of British urban life, Ruth Rendell's novels would serve as well as any of those by writers more highly regarded, in part because they don't write crime stories.

Rendell herself prefers the other books she writes, which offer studies in abnormal psychology leading on to violence. In an interview she said that she read Freud, Jung, and Adler, but little criminology, and remarked also that she often felt personal disaster to be imminent. "Some kind of disgrace, humiliation, suffering, pain, disaster, poverty, famine. . . . It is a neurotic state. I wish I didn't have it. I have it.'' She added that many of her characters have it too, and it appears in her books as a flaw in the personality that leads to violence when put under some kind of emotional stress. Again the basis of the flaw is often sexual, like that of Arthur Johnson in *A Demon in My View* (1976), who keeps a dummy woman in his cellar, and finds ecstatic pleasure in strangling her every few days. This book, and *A Judgement in Stone* (1977), are the best of the stories concerned with the psychology of a murderer. Anybody who experiments as freely as Rendell is taking considerable risks, and there are books which fail (*The Face of Trespass* and *Master of the Moor* are two) because the central figure simply does not carry conviction. Taking them all together, Wexford and grueling chillers, humdrum police work made interesting and criminal psychology mostly made plausible, Rendell's work blossomed magnificently in the seventies.

Julian Symons. *Bloody Murder: From the Detective Story to the Crime Novel* (New York: Viking, 1985), pp. 179–80

We still have a Queen of Crime. For nearly twenty years Ruth Rendell has been hailed as the successor to Sayers, Christie, Marsh, and Allingham, perpetuating the old question of why it is that there should be a particularly feminine talent for detective fiction. Her Chief Inspector, Wexford by name, has joined the ranks of legendary police heroes, and although he is Sussex-based he can occasionally, via a nephew, call upon the resources of Scotland Yard.

As Hercule Poirot had waxed mustaches, Lord Peter Wimsey collected first editions and Nero Wolfe wore yellow pajamas, so Wexford is the sort of man who is always badly dressed and is never certain of having a clean handkerchief. Like Appleby, he has a tendency to quote from literature, but the detective whom he most resembles is Maigret: an aging Maigret, worried about his health. We are repeatedly told what Wexford eats and drinks. There is a Mrs. Wexford who, like Madame Maigret, is silent and submissive and to whom Wexford is attached with undemonstrative sentimentality. Just as Maigret, on meeting a widower, reflects on his own good fortune in marriage (see *Maigret et l'Indicateur*), so Wexford, on meeting someone whose wife has been murdered, considers his own happier position (see *Shake Hands with Death*). At times one wonders whether Ruth Rendell has consciously taken Simenon as a model—for example, when Wexford encounters the pompous solicitors and bank managers of the small towns where crimes have been committed or explores specific areas of London in search of a murderer, or when he contemplates the weather with studied idleness.

Ruth Rendell has not, however, remained faithful to her successful creation. To the irritation of Wexford's followers, she has written several ''thrillers'' that have nothing to do with detection but are concerned with the abnormalities of human behavior, with madness, delusions, hatreds, and obsession. If the ideal detective novel presents us with a world which has been thrown into confusion by a crime, usually a murder, the role of the detective in discovering the author of this act is to end the confusion and restore normality. There is often a final scene where the detective explains all, where the ends are tied together, and where the intermezzo of the unusual is declared over. Although Ruth Rendell does not always go in for this studiously coherent ending, she is conscious of the need to keep a normal society going within the upheaval of a story which has begun with the discovery of a corpse. A thriller, however, can have neither beginning nor ending, neither design nor pattern. Its horrors are everlasting, its evils are everywhere. . . .

Ruth Rendell's switch from the classical detective story (even with those darker strains of mystery) to the thriller may illustrate some significant developments in the real world that fiction supposedly reflects. What we all wish to know is how Myra Hindley lived her life, surrounded by relatives, friends and colleagues who never suspected anything, or how Peter Sutcliffe went off to work and came home at night, without someone discerning the violence within him. The readers of detective fiction have never cared about morality, and they have rarely been moved by the characters presented to them. Like Wexford's assistant, Burden, who once said that he had never interrogated a single person whom he had liked, they are curious rather than involved. Why not then cut out all the stuff about Wexford and his daughters and his grandchildren and his remorse when he has spoken sharply to an underling? We no longer want to see dedicated policemen or eccentric amateur sleuths defending society. We want to be presented with the violence that lurks within the mundane, we want paranoia to be made plausible, we want to see those who are nourished on hatred, lives that are so suffused with boredom, pain, and futility that they become unbearable. This is what Ruth Rendell has written about in her last two novels. It will be interesting to see whether she will return to the detective novel or whether she thinks it a genre that has now become moribund.

Douglas Johnson. London Review of Books. March
7, 1985, p. 23

Ruth Rendell, writing as Barbara Vine, begins her latest novel, A Fatal Inversion, with the discovery of a body on the gunroom floor. Contrary to expectation, it isn't that of a well-heeled aristo, but of an old dog—this is a sly wink at the rigid tradition of country house murders which is so important to British crime fiction, but which Rendell leaves far behind.

Both Barbara Vine novels concern crimes committed long ago; the phrase "in the far" resonates throughout the first, A Dark-Adapted Eye. Rendell recreates the past so fastidiously that the present becomes a dying echo of "the far." Hairstyles, dress lengths, perfumes, flowers: every tiny detail permeates the fabric of memory.

What sets both novels in motion is a guilt born of violence, bending present lives out of shape. There are numerous asides on the state of grace from which the characters have fallen: two are named Adam and Eden; *A Fatal Inversion* makes specific reference to the Garden of Eden, *A Dark-Adapted Eye* to the reappearance of the Mark of Cain. But these aren't so much precise allegorical motifs as fleetingly glimpsed signs. Rendell's concerns are entirely secular. *A Dark-Adapted Eye* establishes that the central villainy lies, not with individual characters, but in the tangled structure of family life. "The terrible pressure of love" leads people to desperation, but those pressures have little place in *A Fatal Inversion,* where people are barely able to establish links with each other—love and affection are turned inwards. Therein lies the novel's only weakness: there's little of the compassion so important for a humanist like Rendell.

Her worldview may be humanist, but it's hardly optimistic. A dark-adapted eye is one which has adjusted to darkness—like Rendell's own, so focused on gloom that she sees little else. That's no condemnation: crime fiction demands such morbidity. This country has no novelist better than Rendell at suggesting the unpleasantnesses just below civilized surfaces.

Nick Kimberley. *New Statesman.* April 17, 1987,
p. 31

In subject matter, Ruth Rendell is light-years removed from Dorothy L. Sayers and even P. D. James, with her plots treating of sexual repression and its fatal consequences, transvestism, lesbianism, and all manner of the modern psychological ills familiar to readers of Krafft-Ebbing. Rendell sees the world with modern eyes and treats her characters in like fashion. She is particularly interested in looking just under the surface of a personality to scrutinize the psychological irregularities that make the individual tick.

The Wexford novels recreate suburbia as it exists today in the modern English countryside, with a fine ear for dialogue, and with a fine eye for picking up the nuances of modern living.

The best of these conventionals? Probably *Shake Hands for Ever* (1975) and *A Sleeping Life* (1978). Of course there are others. Rendell proves in these novels that she can handle the traditional, structured, classic detective novel effectively and competently.

It is in her non-series novels—those that do not feature Wexford—that many readers and critics believe she excels. It is in them that she explores the quirks in psychological behavior that make human beings into monstrous creatures, into forces of evil propelled to disrupt, destroy, and ruin those about them.

These novels are described by some as chillers, and they do certainly chill the reader. They do not adhere to any of the rules of the mystery genre as it was practiced by the Golden Age writers. Indeed the very first words of *A Judgement in Stone* (1977) reveal the murderer and the plot line: "Eunice Parchman killed the Coverdale family because she could not read or write.'' Despite this infraction of the rules of the Detection Club of London observed faithfully by the mentors of the Golden Age, the book itself is as suspenseful and as gripping as any story in which the killer's identity is deliberately withheld until the end.

In effect, Rendell probes into the *meaning* of the psychology of murder in these chillers. With the quirks of the mind in plain view, she then watches the maimed personalities wander through their wastelands much like Frankenstein's monster wandered about the countryside unable to realize the impending tragedy of which he was the central force.

Waltraud Woeller and Bruce Cassiday. *The Literature of Crime and Detection* (New York: Ungar, 1988), pp. 154–55

Inspector Wexford is back in *The Veiled One*—and Ruth Rendell can once again challenge P. D. James's role as the queen of the British mystery writers. *The Veiled One* is her fourteenth in the Wexford series among over thirty books of mystery. It may not be the most suspenseful of the series, but it is certainly crafted with the skill and precision of a fine-tuned engine.

Rendell does not need to shock her readers with gratuitous violence or frighten them with shallow psychopaths. Her reputation firmly established, she is free to write as a novelist who happens to focus on crime. Thus Chief Inspector Reginald Wexford continues to grow as a character. His sidekick, Inspector Mike Burden, also has expanded as a person—and he plays his largest role in this novel.

The psychopathic personality is obviously Rendell's chief focus at this time, as her last three novels, different as they are, all provide significant insights to characters with deranged minds. In *Live Flesh,* Victor Jenner is the central character, whose agonizing decline is painfully presented by Rendell; the story has its fascination, but it is not a book with which most readers can be very comfortable. *Talking to Strange Men,* Rendell's last novel, is truly unique—with its bright schoolboys engaged in espionage—and a psychopathic pederast, though a secondary character, brings the novel to its climax. In *The Veiled One,* Clifford Sanders is Burden's chief suspect in the killing of a woman in a shopping-center parking garage. The scenes with Burden trying to elicit a confession as Clifford undergoes transference from his analyst to Burden ultimately seem to detract from the novel's otherwise taut story line.

Besides Clifford, suspects include his mother, the victim's daughter, and three Kingsmarkham neighbors. Wexford explores these possibilities while Burden tries to wait out Clifford's confession. Eventually forced to drop Clifford as a suspect, Burden feels responsible when his rejection of Clifford leads the young man to violent behavior.

A subplot involves Wexford's near death when a bomb in his daughter's car explodes, he instinctively leaping out in the nick of time. His actress-daughter Sheila, in trouble for a civil protest, is apparently the target of a terrorist, a situation which draws the Wexfords and their two daughters together until circumstances are sorted out.

The title refers to the killer, whose identity is not unveiled until the last few pages. Rendell has Inspector Wexford provide several possible murder scenarios until the true one is fully evident. The next Rendell novel is eagerly awaited.

Doug Simpson. *The Armchair Detective*. Summer
1989, pp. 313–14

Ruth Rendell . . . seems to be the most highly praised crime writer of our time. I don't happen to care for novels set in small towns where evil lurks behind every countenance, and didn't read her until 1985 when her new novel, *An Unkindness of Ravens* (Pantheon), was sent to me. It was the most virulent antifeminist diatribe I had read in years, and I suspected that Ruth Rendell was a pen name for Midge Decter or Phyllis Schlafly. I have just reread it, and still stand amazed. The novel concerns a group of women who hate men and stab them indiscriminately, eventually achieving murder. What particularly struck home more than the plot and the nasty cracks about the women's movement is that the murderers, young women believed to be the victims of incest, turned out only to have fantasized it. In 1964, when I published my first mystery, scarcely feminist but as much as I dared, I reiterated Freud's theory that his patients' memories of sexual abuse were fantasies. I now regret having done so, but that's where too many of us were in those days. Yet here is Ruth Rendell saying the same thing in 1985. And very likely she is the most decorated of women detective novelists, standing in, as "honorary men" ever do, for all the women the men can't bring themselves to honor. I haven't read any more of Ruth Rendell, and she may have reformed, but her continuing acclaim makes me doubt it.

Carolyn G. Heilbrun. *Ms.*
March/April 1991, p. 62

RINEHART, MARY ROBERTS (1876–1958)

Mary Roberts Rinehart wrote a number of mainstream novels and stories, but found her forte and gained her literary reputation in the composition of detective stories, which she wrote for fifty years corresponding roughly to the first half of the twentieth century.

Her career began with stories that hewed closely to the conventional formula of the day—the closed milieu of a country house, a "detective" searching out clues and hidden facts, and the revelation of the murderer in the last scene. For all its haste of composition, *The Circular Staircase* (1908), has remained a classic of the genre. Twelve years later this story was adapted for the Broadway stage as *The Bat,* where it became a long-running hit.

Rinehart's literary career blossomed in the 1930s with the development of her own Americanized version of the typically English country-house detective story. Setting her stories in a mansion or country house of the well-to-do, she simply moved the English "cozy" formula to the United States and put her own stamp on it by her thematic material and her astonishing ability to work up complex and baffling plots.

Structurally, she spends as much time on the "inner" story of her novel— what has happened in the past to cause the present conflicts—as she does on the "surface" story. To prevent the typical confusion of the end-of-book "revelation," she allows parts of the inner story to appear piece by piece during the narration, until only the salient elements are left to clear up at the end.

Thematically, she builds her plots on complex social and personal conflicts. A favorite is mésalliance, the crossing of class barriers in marriage— the female "nobody" who pretends to be a "somebody" and marries an unsuspecting upper-class male—as in *The Wall* (1938). Repressed emotion, sexual passion, and jealousy frequently serve as building blocks for her plots, as in *The Album* (1933). In that novel she even plays with the theme of amnesia, later a workhorse of the soap opera genre; she hints at incest in that same book years before it became literarily fashionable. The problem of identity—concealed by amnesia or by deliberation—always fascinated Rinehart.

The Great Mistake (1940) has a monumentally complex plot whose murders hinge on past relationships rather than present ones, thus providing a smokescreen to hide the killer's motivation. Once again, the real relationships, revealed at the end, contain a hint of the incestuous. *The Yellow Room* (1945) is a story of a government agency, a mésalliant marriage, and amnesia, plus a soupçon of incest.

Her reputation as the "had I but known" mystery author, while deserved, is essentially unfair. Writing primarily for magazine serialization, she would create suspense by remarking, "Had I but known then what I know now, I would have. . . ." She did not invent the style, but it seems to cling to her in retrospect. The other cliché of the mystery—"The butler did it"—could just as easily have been applied to her. Ah, but for which book?

> Bruce Cassiday. *Encyclopedia of American*
> *Literature* (New York: Continuum, in preparation)

Virtually all Mary Roberts Rinehart's crime novels have detectives of a sort. Most of them have two: an official detective of more or less astuteness; and the first-person narrator, usually a woman, most often a romantic spinster engaged in protecting young love from unjust suspicion, who alternately complicates the plot and aids detection in unpremeditated fashion—a combination of participating (usually interfering!) Watson, and detective-by-accident.

This is the readily recognizable "Rinehart formula," still delightful when practiced by its originator, but becoming increasingly tedious in the hands of her far-too-numerous imitators among American women writers. It is, in fact, only Mrs. Rinehart's superlative talent as one of the great story-tellers of the age (and the intensely human quality of her writing) that induces us to overlook in her own tales breaches of detective etiquette we could excuse in nobody else: what Waldo Frank calls her "carpentry." Foremost in any catalogue of these flaws must be the manner in which romantic complications are allowed to obstruct the orderly process of puzzle-and-solution. Similarly, the plots are always being prolonged by accidents and "happenstances"—not honest mistakes of deductive judgment by the investigator, which would be a legitimate part of the game, but unmotivated interferences and lapses on the part of the characters, who are forever blundering into carefully laid traps and springing them prematurely, or "forgetting" to tell the official detective of important clues. ("Four lives might have been spared if I had only remembered. . . .") Only too frequently, it must be confessed, these clues turn out at the dénouement to have had no bearing on the puzzle anyway!

We can excuse, perhaps, the interminable "had-I-but-knowns" as a harmless but irritating species of auctorial mannerism. Much more serious is the writer's tendency to abuse the least-likely-person theme, to pin the crimes on psychologically (and sometimes physically) impossible characters. A final and vital flaw is the painful stretching of the long arm of coincidence which would have us believe, in utter defiance of the laws of probability, that fate will obligingly and repeatedly bring together without other cause whole groups of persons who, usually unknown to themselves, are intimately related through some complex pattern of antecedent events.

Unfortunately, it is too often these weaknesses that Mrs. Rinehart's imitators are prone to mimic, rather than her points of strength—of which there are many. For the "formula" she devised possesses immense technical advantages, quite apart from its inventor's personal narrative skill. Chief among them are the reader's participation in the adventure by self-identification with the narrator; and the "forward action" of the plot, the direct antithesis of the over-intellectualized puzzle story. In a Rinehart murder novel the initial crime is never the be-all and end-all but only the opening incident in a progressive conflict between the narrator and the criminal. Sometimes this dramatic approach goes too far and carries the story past the borderline of detection and into the realm of mere mystery-adventure; but kept within bounds it is a technique that practitioners of the cut-and-dried Static School might profitably study. In Mrs. Rinehart's own skilled hands it results in a mood of sustained excitement and suspense that renders the reader virtually powerless to lay her books down, despite their logical shortcomings.

Whether mystery or detection, Mary Roberts Rinehart's works have played an incalculable role in introducing women, both readers and writers, to puzzle fiction. She represents the quintessence of the romantic mood in the literature. She is the unquestioned dean of crime writing by and for women.

Howard Haycraft. *Murder for Pleasure: The Life and Times of the Detective Story* (New York: Biblo and Tannen, 1968), pp. 89–91

In *The Man in Lower 10,* (1907) Lawrence Blakely, hero and narrator, travels from Washington to Pittsburgh to take a deposition from steel-magnate West about a forgery case. Returning to Washington on the train, his papers are stolen and, the numbers on the berths in the sleeping car having been altered during the night, his assigned berth is discovered to contain a dead body. A train wreck follows and Blakely finds himself sitting on an embankment, sooty and shaken, with Alison West, the steel man's granddaughter and his own partner's fiancée.

Although the mystery opens with the problem of forgery compounded with the theft of some bonds from Blakely's briefcase, a second criminal conspiracy soon appears. Alison West is the prize in this network of villainy: a particularly wicked woman forces her weak-willed brother Sullivan to woo Alison. Although Alison is already engaged (and Sullivan married!), he manages to press his suit to the point where he compromises her—unfairly of course—and, her reputation apparently ruined, she elopes with him.

Blakely confronts a mass of difficulties. He must recover the bonds, prosecute the forger, release Alison from her false (bigamous) marriage, and persuade her to break her engagement to his partner. These tasks are undertaken in an atmosphere of considerable creepiness: a hand appears mysteriously out of a trap door; a carriage ride to a deserted country mansion brings Blakely into the darkness of an old and unfamiliar house to be terrorized by enemies both human and feline.

Sometimes Rinehart develops comedy in *The Man in Lower 10* by deliberately deflating the horror of the creeps, as she does with the black cat who terrorizes Blakely in that dark mansion. But there is another source of humor as well and it probably had its origin in Rinehart's self-consciousness about writing thrillers. Just as she had burlesqued the mystery genre in her early poem, ''The Detective Story,'' so she parodies the detective himself in the character of Wilson Budd Hotchkiss. Hotchkiss is an altogether disinterested person; he involves himself in the murder in Lower 10 for intellectual reasons alone. As he tells Blakely, ''I use the inductive method originated by Poe and followed since with such success by Conan Doyle.'' Armed with enthusiasm and a small notebook, he collects clues and tails suspects, finally announcing his discovery of the murderer. Unfortunately, he sends the police off to arrest Blakely's own confidential clerk, the most innocuous of men.

Jan Cohn. In Earl F. Bargainnier, ed., *10 Women of Mystery* (Bowling Green, Ohio: Popular Press, 1981), pp. 184–85

Cited by Howard Haycraft for his "cornerstone" list, this 1908 novel—*The Circular Staircase,* by Mary Roberts Rinehart—undoubtedly has historical importance, and its milestone status is acknowledged by most critics. Unfortunately, it's not really a major work in terms of quality.

The Circular Staircase appears at times to be hastily, almost carelessly written (probably due to the exigencies of magazine publication), and its narrative line often lacks fluid continuity, although it was carefully revised for its hardcover publication.

But this novel is an excellent memento of an era long past and forgotten. It is leisurely, civilized, and deals with the problems of robbery and murder among the upper classes. Its chief appeal is mainly to a feminine audience, but it doesn't offend masculine sensibilities with any foolishness or the excesses of the HIBK [had-I-but-known] school in which it is a pioneering effort.

Miss Rinehart's skill as a storyteller has been noted by many historians of the genre, and *Staircase,* written with some degree of skill and charm, has been knowingly designed to appeal to a specific audience. Its moments of action and suspense are nicely underplayed, and, fortunately, its middle-aged heroine-narrator doesn't take herself too seriously, and is graced (like her creator) with a good sense of humor.

Charles Shibuk. *The Armchair Detective.* Fall 1977, pp. 311–12

It is Rachel Innes's voice that more than any other element has made *The Circular Staircase* a perennial delight—and a classic. A perfect lady, a responsible guardian to her orphaned niece and nephew, she finds in the course of her adventures altogether new aspects to her character: "somehow, somewhere, from perhaps a half-civilized ancestor who wore a sheepskin garment and tailed his food or his prey, I have in me the instincts of the chase." She becomes certain that she would enjoy a life of trapping criminals and regrets that her sex closes this career to her: "with the handicap of my sex, my first acquaintance with crime will probably be my last." The reviewers of *The Circular Staircase* did not want to believe this; they hoped for another Rachel Innes mystery. That never happened. Instead, Rinehart's comic spinster was transformed into Tish Carberry whose zany adventures appeared in *The Saturday Evening Post* for twenty-five years. . . .

Rinehart's characteristic blend of the puzzling and the chilling marks *The Circular Staircase.* Terror comes largely from eerie shadows and sounds, usually enhanced by midnight darkness through which her characters show a remarkable penchant for wandering. Similarly, her villains suffer an insatiable need to break into houses and Sunnyside is often as busy after midnight as a good-sized bus terminal. Puzzles, meanwhile, develop with curious clues and bizarre events. As the plot of *The Circular Staircase* unravels at the close, it turns out that a good number of the oddest clues and events are by no means to be laid to the criminal. For all kinds of reasons from self-protection to selfless loyalty, the characters defend themselves and one another by withholding information, destroying evidence, and planting false clues. The police must work their way through this welter of red herrings, for Rinehart's characters are not intimidated by the law. If they don't want to talk, they announce, with no little sense of social superiority, that they will not talk. And if they don't want to tell the truth, then they lie—even the best of them. . . .

One of the finest elements in the plotting of *The Circular Staircase* is the rush of events that makes up the climax. Since all of these involve Rachel Innes, there is not only terror and excitement but also the comic delight of watching her cope with them. She joins in a midnight excursion to the cemetery to dig up a grave and she really has quite a lovely time, grateful to be part of things.

Soon after, Rachel's sleuthing leads her to the roof of the house. Though she has some fear of heights, "I climbed out on to the Sunnyside roof without a second's hesitation. Like a dog on the scent . . . to me now there was the lust of the chase, the frenzy of pursuit, the dust of battle." And finally, she finds the device that opens the secret room—and ends up locked inside. Worse, a figure joins her in the darkness and at the consummately creepy moment, Rachel feels his hand, "cold, clammy, death-like." Rescue and resolution follow rapidly and Rachel's adventure, to her great discontent, is over.

When *The Circular Staircase* was published by Bobbs-Merrill in the spring of 1908, Mary Roberts Rinehart had no notion of what she had created. In fact, embarrassment at publishing a thriller and anxiety over the reviews combined to send her into hiding out of town, where she rented rooms at a farmer's house for herself and her three sons. Almost fifty years later she found that she had altogether altered the form of the mystery novel by adding flesh and muscle to the skeleton of plot.

Jan Cohn. In Earl F. Bargainnier, ed., *10 Women of Mystery* (Bowling Green, Ohio: Popular Press, 1981), pp. 186–88

The books of Mary Roberts Rinehart deal with crime, and the crime is almost always murder. There is a detective, but his activities are often less important than those of the staunch middle-aged spinster, plucky young widow, or marriageable girl who finds herself hearing strange noises in the night, being shut up in cupboards, overhearing odd and apparently sinister conversations, and eventually stumbling upon some clue that solves the mystery.

Much of what happens in these stories occurs by chance, and the mystery is prolonged only by the obstinate refusal of the characters to reveal essential facts. . . .

These are the first crime stories which have the air of being written specifically for maiden aunts, and they exploited a market which, with the spread of library borrowing, proved very profitable. From Rinehart's second book and first success, *The Circular Staircase* (1908), at the climax of which spinster Rachel Innes finds herself shut up with the murderer in a small secret room behind the great old chimney piece ("I knew he was creeping on me, inch by inch"), the formula of needless confusion and mock terror did not change. The settings became more varied, yet also more enclosed. As one commentator has said, "It does not really matter much to the world view which emerges whether the backdrop is New York City or Connecticut, a town or a country house, the stability and balance most usually associated, sentimentally at least, with an agrarian order are assumed." People in the books die, but this is not important, because in relation to the real world none of them was ever alive. Nobody is ever doing any work, although suspects may be labeled solicitor, doctor, chauffeur.

Sometimes the confinement of the society in which violence takes place is carried to fantastic lengths. Rinehart went on writing until a year or two before her death, and *The Album* (1933) is typical of her later novels. It deals with five families living in Crescent Place, "a collection of fine old semi-country houses, each set in its own grounds," insulated from the city outside by an entrance gate marked *Private*, "so that we resemble nothing so much as five green-embattled fortresses." The action literally never moves outside the Crescent. Reporters and photographers cause no trouble after an initial visit, and make no attempt to gain access to the houses, although four murders are committed, the first with an axe and the last involving a headless trunk. Within this totally closed circle, none of the characters works, although one apparently did, since we are told that "he had given up even the pretense of business since the depression, and spent a good bit of time tinkering with his car in the garage." Even such tinkering is unusual, for there are cooks, a gardener, a chauffeur, various helpers. These people really have nothing to do, apart from being suspected of murder. The murderer, naturally, is one of them. Her actions, when her identity is revealed, are outrageously unlikely.

Julian Symons. *Mortal Consequences: A History—
From the Detective Story to the Crime Novel* (New
York: Harper & Row, 1972), pp. 96–98

Nurse Hilda Adams is Mary Roberts Rinehart's sole series character and appears in only three books written between 1932 and 1942. Romantic terror is the central theme of all of Rinehart's stories. Murder does occur to be sure, but is almost incidental to the plot in which a young, beautiful heroine is terrorized and thwarted in achieving her heart's desire. Called to cases by

Inspector Patton (in the first book, Fuller in the third), this attractive, thirty-eight-year-old is all that a good nurse should be. From *Miss Pinkerton:*

> And then I had made that alliance with Inspector Patton and the Homicide Squad. By accident, but they had found me useful from the start. There is one thing about a trained nurse in a household: she can move about day and night and not be questioned. The fact is that the people in a house are inclined pretty much to forget that she is there. She has only one job ostensibly, and that is her patient. Outside of that job she is more or less a machine to them. They see that she is fed, and if she is firm that she gets her hours off-duty. But they never think of her as a reasoning human being, seeing a great deal more than they imagine, and sometimes using what she sees, as I did.

Nurse Adams has a gun, a snub-nosed little automatic which the inspector gave her for protection. At home, she keeps it in the jardiniere with the Boston fern which her housekeeper never remembers to water. A canary named Dicky lives in a cage in the living room, which is—in all books—newly done in chintz. "Miss Pinkerton" doesn't get to spend much time at home, though. The inspector does not hesitate to call upon her at all hours in her professional capacity to tend a patient, and, unofficially, to assist him with behind-the-scenes investigation.

Danger, bordering on the supernatural, lurks in the houses Nurse Adams attends. The stories are veiled with an eerie quality designed to build suspense for the reader.

> It was midnight when he went away. Miss Juliet had wakened by that time, and so I went down at half-past twelve and heated a glass of milk for her. But I must admit I was not comfortable down there. A wind was blowing outside, and the kitchen wing seemed to be even more out of repair than the rest of the house. It creaked and groaned, and once I would have sworn that the tea-kettle moved right across the stove! If it had been possible to gallop upstairs with a glass of hot milk in my hand I would have done it! As it was, I went up with my head turned over my shoulder, until I got almost to the top of the stairs. Then I fixed my eyes on the landing, and if Miss Juliet had appeared there at that minute in her white nightgown I dare say I would have died of heart failure.

The Nurse Adams stories are not up to Rinehart's classic standard of terror and foreboding. They have a lighter, more humorous touch than many of this author's other works. The device of the nurse as the central character is clever. She is a respected professional, upon whom the inspector relies. The suspense is well done, if a bit melodramatic and follows a tried and true formula. Fans of Rinehart are urged to seek out these books.

Victoria Nichols and Susan Thompson. *Silk Stalkings: When Women Write of Murder* (Berkeley: Black Lizard Books, 1988), pp. 112–14

SAYERS, DOROTHY L. (1893–1957)

I set out to read *The Nine Tailors* in the hope of tasting some novel excitement, and I declare that it seems to me one of the dullest books I have ever encountered in any field. The first part of it is all about bell-ringing as it is practiced in English churches and contains a lot of information of the kind that you might expect to find in an encyclopedia article on campanology. I skipped a good deal of this, and found myself skipping, also, a large section of the conversations between conventional English village characters: "Oh, here's Hinkins with the aspidistras. People may say what they like about aspidistras, but they do go on all the year round and make a background," etc. There was also a dreadful stock English nobleman of the casual and debonair kind, with the embarrassing name of Lord Peter Wimsey, and, although he was the focal character in the novel, being Miss Dorothy Sayers's version of the inevitable Sherlock Holmes detective, I had to skip a good deal of him, too. In the meantime, I was losing the story, which had not got a firm grip on my attention, but I went back and picked it up and steadfastly pushed through to the end, and there I discovered that the whole point was that if a man was shut up in a belfry while a heavy peal of chimes was being rung, the vibrations of the bells might kill him. Not a bad idea for a murder, and Conan Doyle would have known how to dramatize it in an entertaining tale of thirty pages, but Miss Sayers had not hesitated to pad it out to a book of three hundred and thirty, contriving one of those hackneyed cock-and-bull stories about a woman who commits bigamy without knowing it, and larding the whole thing with details of church architecture, bits of quaint lore from books about bell-ringing, and the awful whimsical patter of Lord Peter.

I had often heard people say that Dorothy Sayers wrote well, and I felt that my correspondents had been playing her as their literary ace. But, really, she does not write very well: it is simply that she is more consciously literary than most of the other detective-story writers and that she thus attracts attention in a field which is mostly on a sub-literary level. In any serious department of fiction, her writing would not appear to have any distinction at all.

Edmund Wilson. "Who Cares Who Killed Roger Ackroyd?" *Classics and Commercials: A Literary Chronicle of the Forties* (New York: Farrar, Straus & Giroux, 1950), pp. 258–59

Sayers represents the farthest point yet reached in the development of detective stories towards complete sophistication.

From the first, Dorothy Sayers insisted upon being humorously informative. She had that inconvenient readiness of comment which flows from a mind lively and in good order. She knew a great many things which ordinarily would not find a place in the tale of crime and its detection; she had a number of opinions, also, which no respect for the wooden tradition of Dick Donovan and his peers led her to repress.

From her mental encyclopedia, accordingly, came richly spiced thoughts and views; and all were stirred into the mystery, or mysteries, until one really felt as if Aldous Huxley himself had taken to lethal weapons. Dorothy Sayers decorated the corpse with jovial detail; she then produced quite a dozen persons whom, as it is shown with Socratic cunning, one must suspect of committing the crime. These persons were all exceedingly tortuous in character and movement upon essential days; and they had peculiar occupations or hobbies which needed to be explored and dilated upon. She was a mistress of complications, a perfect fisherwoman of red herrings; and complications and herrings are of Brobdingnagian size and detail. When, as sometimes happened, Lord Peter Wimsey viewed the body and illustrated his love of incunabula, wines, and haberdashery, everything assumed so facetious and fantastic a turn that from being a light diversion the detective mystery novel became what has been described to me as "deep." It became, that is, very intricate, and for adult intellects only.

This is because the scholastic or scholarly mind is never content with the simple. For Dorothy Sayers, the plots of Doyle were thin; she knew all about Aristotle and his unities and E. M. Forster and his dislike of "story." And as she found the Aristotelian unities well observable in the modern detective story it is clear that in spite of her admission that the detective story may never hope to rise to the extremist heights of art she could approve as well as write tales in which form is of more significance than emotion. On the subject of the detective story she was a scholar *facile princeps*. Her preface to the collection she first made of *Great Short Stories of Detection, Mystery, and Horror* is the best and most authoritative survey of the whole ground yet written. And her novels became increasingly and impressively the work of a scholar to whom every formula and every possible deviation from formula was already a sentence in single syllables. Could one who had passed the sixth standard be content with child's play?

If I dwell for a moment longer, as I fear I must, upon the weakness of too much scholarship in the arts, it is because I think scholarship is nowadays excessively valued as a necessary preliminary to creative writing. Much as I admire Dorothy Sayers, it is my suspicion that she led the detective story into dust. She wrote with distinction; she invented with ingenuity. But in the same way that modern composers consciously and deliberately serve out music representing the acme of musical scholarship and little else, she, it seems to me (like equally accomplished workers in other literary fields), by her very virtuosity began to kill the thing she loved.

Frank Swinnerton. *The Georgian Literary Scene 1910–1935* (London: Hutchinson, 1935), pp. 333–35

Gaudy Night as a romance is cloudy and longwinded; as a novel it has moments of atmospheric interest; but as a detective story it is a thorough-going, dismal flop. This tale of the terrorization of an Oxford woman's college commits at least three unforgivable detective-story sins. In the first place, there is no murder; and while some detective-story readers like few murders and some like many, all detective-story readers like *one* murder. In the second place, there is no action: almost 275 pages of the conversation of female dons must be leafed through before the Shrewsbury College Menace becomes anything more than mildly annoying. In the third place, there is no problem, and therefore, really, no mystery. It is true that the identity of the culprit is shielded until the last few pages of the novel, but more than this is needed to make a mystery story truly mysterious. The essence of the pure detective story is that it should present a central problem, or problems, which seems, on the face of it, impossible of solution: the mystery of the locked room and the mystery of the perfect alibi are the problems most frequently used and therefore most familiar to detective-story readers. In the perfect mystery the murderer avoids detection, not because the detective cannot physically lay his hand on him, but because the criminal has so cleverly distorted and thereby camouflaged his crime that it is impossible for the detective even to grasp its nature and meaning, let alone its perpetrator. Dorothy Sayers has, in the past, produced excellent examples of the pure detective story, but in the hybrid *Gaudy Night* she has given us a primer mystery in which the criminal escapes her pursuers only by being slightly fleeter of foot.

Mary McCarthy. *The Nation.* April 8, 1936, pp. 458–59

No single trend in the English detective story of the 1920s was more significant than its approach to the literary standards of the legitimate novel. And no author illustrates the trend better than Dorothy Sayers, who has been called by some critics the greatest of living writers in the form. Whether or not the reader agrees with this verdict, he can not, unless he is both obtuse and ungrateful, dispute her preëminence as one of the most brilliant and prescient artists the genre has yet produced.

In the Introduction to the *Second Omnibus,* she devoted considerable attention to the rather tentative experiments which had been made up to that date toward the amalgamation of the detective story with the legitimate novel, particularly the novel of psychology and character; and concluded by prophesying just such a transfusion as the ultimate salvation of a form fast approaching its limits. This commentary is significant not only as an egregiously accurate forecast of what has actually occurred in the intervening years, but also as an explanation of the later Sayers works.

Even in her early novels strong hints of experimental technique had been observable. (This iconoclasm supplies an interesting paradox in itself, for in all her other views Miss Sayers is a cheerfully unapologetic Tory and traditionalist.) But with *Gaudy Night,* she definitely attempted to achieve a new form. Really the story of Lord Peter's intensive and finally successful wooing of his Harriet, it introduced a psychological and (mirabile dictu!) murderless mystery, but as a counter-theme rather than as a principal plot. Again, in *Busman's Honeymoon,* frankly sub-titled "a love story with detective interruptions," she told the story of the Vane-Wimsey nuptials, injecting a considerably inferior (for Sayers) murder problem as complication, in place of the usual domestic contretemps of the honeymoon novel.

These two experiments must, in all fairness, be termed less than completely successful. Some critics, in fact, have been much more outspoken. In the opinion of the present writer (who, incidentally, considers *Gaudy Night* the truer detective story of the two, for all its excess of erudition and lack of a corpse), would be that the author in her frank and laudable experimentation intruded unwittingly on the dangerous no-man's-land which is neither good detection nor good legitimate fiction. . . .

Despite the presence of some casual similarities, and Miss Sayers's well-known penchant for utilizing real-life material in her fiction, one can not quite credit the belief, held in some quarters, of an autobiographical basis for the Harriet-Lord Peter romance. Of the depth, however, of the author's literary devotion to her titled sleuth—monocle, aristocratic lineaments, esoteric erudition, and all—there is ample documentary proof. Her hero-worship, it is true, frequently borders on preciosity. In the words of more than one reader, she is sometimes too WIMSEYCAL for comfort. But taken all in all her admiration is not misplaced. For only a few of all of fiction's detectives have so brilliantly demonstrated their right to immortality as Lord Peter in his prime. . . .

If these criticisms seem too numerous and minute, let it be said that only a really great writer could deserve or receive them. Dorothy Sayers is one of the fructifying and distinguished names in the form for all time. Her very errors do her honor.

Howard Haycraft. Murder for Pleasure: The Life
and Times of the Detective Story (New York:
Appleton-Century, 1941), pp. 135–40

In her introduction to the first *Omnibus of Crime,* Dorothy Sayers wrote: "It [the detective story] does not, and by hypothesis never can, attain the loftiest level of literary achievement." And the reason, as she suggested somewhere else, is that it is a "literature of escape" and not "a literature of expression." I do not know what the loftiest level of literary achievement is: neither did Aeschylus or Shakespeare; neither does Miss Sayers. Other things being equal, which they never are, a more powerful theme will provoke a more powerful performance. Yet some very dull books have been written about God, and some very fine ones about how to make a living and stay fairly honest. It is always a matter of who writes the stuff, and what he has in him to write it with.

As for "literature of expression" and "literature of escape"—this is critics' jargon, a use of abstract words as if they had absolute meanings. Everything written with vitality expresses that vitality: there are no dull subjects, only dull writers. All men who read escape from something else.

I think what was really gnawing at Miss Sayers's mind was the slow realization that her kind of detective story was an arid formula which could not even satisfy its own implications. It was second-grade literature because it was not about the things that could make first-grade literature. If it started out to be about real people (and she could write about them—her minor characters show that), they must very soon do unreal things in order to form the artificial pattern required by the plot. When they did unreal things, they ceased to be real themselves. They became puppets and cardboard lovers and papier-mâché villains and detectives of exquisite and impossible gentility.

The only kind of writer who could be happy with these properties was the one who did not know what reality was. Dorothy Sayers's own stories show that she was annoyed by this triteness; the weakest element in them is the part that makes them detective stories, the strongest the part which could be removed without touching the "problem of logic and deduction." Yet she could not or would not give her characters their heads and let them make their own mystery. It took a much simpler and more direct mind than hers to do that.

Raymond Chandler. *The Atlantic Monthly.*
December 1944, pp. 53–59

One must begin by saying that Miss Sayers wrote superbly well. She was never guilty of sloppy syntax, careless grammar or weak vocabulary: if her erudition was flamboyant, her command of the language was, in this age, dangerously near to deserving the epithet unique. . . . Her presentation . . . of the art and craft of campanology (bell ringing) in *The Nine Tailors* was so expert that she was reputedly invited to become vice-president of the Campanological Society of Great Britain, despite the fact that until her book was finished she had never even seen bells rung. . . .

Most importantly, perhaps, the conversation of Lord Peter and his associates is in the best tradition of the comedy of manners—which may explain why, when she had tired of writing detective novels about him, Miss Sayers determined to put him on the stage. Kingsley Amis, in a clever book on James Bond, has observed, with perfect veracity, that readers want to be Bond. But Lord Peter's audience, if they engage in any fantasy at all about that sprig of the peerage, dream of having him to tea. They don't want to *be* Lord Peter, only to know him, for the sake of hearing him talk.

Of course, Miss Sayers's plots were absolutely sound, fair to the reader, and put together with an eye for detail and knowledge of construction that made her the Mies van der Rohe of the detective story. Josephine Tey, Sayers's only rival in the creation of detective novels that are also masterly novels of manners, had great difficulty with plots, borrowing them, getting friends to help, and leaving them, in the end, full of holes and excessive coincidence. Her detective novels are superb nonetheless, but the achievement of Sayers in combining murder and manners must, in the comparison, awaken special admiration. . . .

I had always supposed, when I began reading the exploits of Lord Peter Wimsey, that only women could appreciate him—particularly after he had got himself involved with Harriet Vane. But a quick survey of my acquaintance indicates that this is oddly wrong. Lord Peter may be every woman's idea of the perfect man—his lack of height, indeed, is his only drawback, if one does not prefer strong, silent men on principle—and all women may secretly concede that they know of no man who could really love Harriet Vane. Nevertheless, men read the books too, and while, according to James Sandoe, "the Vane," as he calls her, makes many readers howl with rage, they don't stop reading on that account. Jacques Barzun, infuriated by how much of the contemporary detective's private life he is forced to imbibe along with his mystery plots, recently cast a nostalgic glance backward to *Busman's Honeymoon,* despite the fact that the interesting revelations of the marriage bed play no small part in that novel. For the sake of Miss Sayers's writing, he was apparently prepared to put up with them. . . .

That Lord Peter should be outlasting, in the memories of Miss Sayers's readers, her comments on the creations of God is an irony that one feels she might, under the aspect of eternity, learn to understand, even to appreciate. No longer merely a detective, rich nobleman, purveyor of wit and charm, he is now cherished also as a survivor from an important moment in our past, a symbol of the last age in which we had produced comedies of manners, those works of art refined by the extraordinary attention their characters pay to conversation and the subtleties of personal relationships; their energies are not expended on social revolution.

Carolyn Heilbrun. The American Scholar. Spring
1968, pp. 324–34

The most austerely intelligent, the wittiest, liveliest practitioner of the tidy art of detective fiction was—although her irritably individualistic nature led her to reject the label—a feminist. Generally acknowledged to be one of the greatest mystery writers of the century, Dorothy L. Sayers—who wrote more than a score of short stories, more than a dozen full-length mysteries—is best known for her stunning Lord Peter Wimsey trilogy: [*Strong Poison, Gaudy Night,* and *Busman's Honeymoon.*]

Ingeniously plotted, meticulously crafted, these novels are deliciously happy-ending romances starring a feminist hero—Wimsey—as well as a feminist heroine—Harriet Vane. For anyone with a taste for comedies of manners, the eminently rereadable Wimsey trio is a perfect wallow in bliss. But here is substance as well as glitter: these novels reflect their author's serious concerns.

Sayers the theologian and Sayers the feminist are present in her detective fiction; all her work was of a piece. . . .

Sayers's reputation as an artist is secure. But she has continued to infuriate critics whose resentment of class structure finds a focal point in rich Lord Peter. Sayers's feminism was as radical as it was individualistic; yet she confessed herself unmoved by the vision of social revolution. She wrote between two world wars; like all of her generation, she was a permanently misplaced person. The terrible upheavals of the First World War, which destroyed the rigid stratifications of an ordered society, may have inspired her with a misguided longing for the rooted comfort of tradition, for the security of a structured society in which everyone knew her or his place. But the pleasure she took in a mythical England in which people of all classes moved "like chessmen upon their alloted squares" was the pleasure of a hungry girl whose nose is pressed against the bakery window; she may have been an elitist, but she was not a snob—she had not a condescending, or a patronizing, bone in her body.

From a novelist's point of view, Peter's enormous wealth is a stroke of genius: accountable to no man, he may follow the path of righteousness with divine single-mindedness. From a feminist point of view, however, Lord Peter's wealth may be interpreted as a copout: Vera Brittain tells us that the central feminist problem of her time was "how a married woman without being inordinately rich can have children and yet maintain her intellectual and spiritual independence as well as having . . . time for the pursuit of her own career." It must be admitted that Sayers funked the question.

Sayers managed to solve the problem in her own life; perhaps she is to be forgiven for obviating the struggle in the Wimsey-Vane never-never land. Because of her frequently reiterated belief that "what we ask is to be human individuals, however peculiar and unexpected," she had a great distrust of mass movements, which she equated with forced unanimity. Devoted to the idea of individual excellence, she resisted the idea that she was a member of a class.

She rested her hopes, not on concerted political activity, but on the power of the enlightened individual to effect change; the brain, she said, was the "great and true, sole androgyne."

It is easy to charge her with arrogance. But it is difficult, while recognizing her limitations, not to love her. The world she created in her superlative fiction is a world of passion and order; she wrote beautiful fairy tales, fairy tales which were also morality fables. She was determined to find truth and beauty in the same place. Toward the end of her life she put away the

Wimsey-Vane fable and devoted herself almost entirely to theology. For her, finally, the most profoundly exciting and terrifying mystery drama of all was God-made-human. Her God-Jesus was a feminist who "took women seriously, rebuked without querulousness, never patronized, condescended, nagged, flattered, coaxed, never urged them to be feminine or jeered at them for being female." (He sounds, as a matter of fact, not at all unlike Lord Peter.)

Barbara Grizzuti Harrison. Ms. November 1974,
pp. 66–67, 69, 84–86, 89

Have His Carcase

This novel with the Pickwickean title is fully fifty pages longer than any of Dorothy L. Sayers's previous detective books; it is the most complex detective story that she wrote. In it we find few excursions into personal, social, or moral problems—. . . the focus is almost entirely on solving the detective problem. Sayers put into this novel most of her most baffling and complicated detective story ideas. A list shows this best:

1. There is a criminal who uses disguise and establishes a double identity as in *Unnatural Death*.
2. There is an alibi puzzle which turns on a disabled automobile and which is solved in part through the use of lists and time-tables as in *Five Red Herrings*.
3. There is a complex problem concerning the time of death as in *Unpleasantness at the Bellona Club*.
4. There is an unusual medical fact with diagnosable symptoms at the heart of the mystery as in *Strong Poison*.
5. There is the fact that the circumstances of the body and the evidence which they present have been scrambled as in most of the novels—only here the false appearances are caused by natural instead of human agencies.
6. The identity of the murderer is clear long before the end of the novel as in *Unnatural Death,* etc.

To these devices, in order to make things more complicated still, Sayers adds a new one (for her), cryptography: this novel, like the two succeeding books, *Murder Must Advertise* and *The Nine Tailors,* depends in part for its solution on the cracking of a code. As if this were not enough, Sayers fortifies the plot by using the thriller devices of disguised accomplices . . . and international intrigue of the most exotic, Ruritanian sort. In short, the book is a complex construct in which discoveries and hypotheses need to be constantly reevaluated.

But why make it so complex, especially when she must go to the lengths of introducing thriller elements which by the thirties had been marked off as taboo by most serious writers of detective fiction? . . . She realized that the main weakness of detective writers lay in their tendency to use the same basic plot over and over, so that readers could read the writer instead of the story and predict pretty accurately what would happen at the end without reference to the text. Sayers simply did not want her plots to be predictable . . . so she mixed up elements which she had already used and added a few new ones to knock her readers off stride and to keep them interested and guessing.

The thriller comes into *Have His Carcase* on two levels: Sayers uses the thriller readers' desire for romance . . . by introducing certain plot elements like the accomplices. At the same time Sayers has her characters self-consciously allude to thriller heroes and devices, thereby implying certain critical concepts.

After *Have His Carcase,* Sayers's novels change substantially, moving away from the puzzle story which had dominated her attention for the past few years and toward the novel of manners. In some respects this novel can be seen as a summation of the previous puzzle books; one which she wrote in order to clear the way for a new kind of novel. It is, moreover, something else; it is a dismissal. This becomes apparent at the end of the novel. The earlier Wimsey books usually ended with the hero's distress or depression caused by the human outcome of the detective story. Here, however, the story ends with a rejection:

> "Well," said Wimsey, "isn't that a damned, awful, bitter, bloody farce? The old fool who wanted a lover and the young fool who wanted an empire . . . God! What a jape! King Death has asses' ears with a vengeance."
>
> "Let's clear out of this," he said. "Get your things packed and leave your address with the police and come up to town. I'm fed to the back teeth. . . ."

This is what Sayers felt about the detective story in this form, and she went up to town for the next novel, which is different indeed. The detective story for her was becoming less of a romp and less of a game. Human life began to once again move into the foreground of Sayers's attention.

LeRoy Lad Panek. *Watteau's Shepherds: The Detective Novel in Britain 1914–1940* (Bowling Green, Ohio: Popular Press, 1979) pp. 96–99

The fame and popularity of Dorothy Sayers's detective fiction are incontrovertible; in the Golden Age of the genre, her works provide perfect examples of what this kind of story ought to be. Well plotted and well written, they satisfy both the imaginative and the ratiocinative impulses of their readers; never merely novels of detection, they also respond to literary and moral expectations.

In style, the series and the individual books are considerably diverse, showing a pattern of change and development. Sayers tries intellectual games, timetable puzzles, epistolary form and the interweaving of detection with serious material or a love interest. The thirteen novels and several dozen short stories do not fall predictably into the same pattern in each case. However, they are dependable for a careful, almost scholarly concern for language; word choice and sentence patterns in both narration and dialogue are believable and entertaining (if not altogether realistic). The stories' most witty passages arise not from Lord Peter Wimsey's idle and piffling remarks but through the author's aware use of language.

The novels, in particular, could be read by someone uninterested in detection simply for the rich and full description of the period. The atmosphere of privilege and wealth is luxuriously drawn; Peter's flat, his stuffy gentleman's club, and his sequence of elegant cars are carefully detailed, then contrasted with Charles Parker's middle-class upbringing or Mr. Rumm's fireside revival meeting. A Scottish village with its eccentric collection of painters and fishermen, an advertising agency with its witty writers, a woman's college with its two hundred students, dons, and staff can be visualized through Sayers's explicit descriptions, even if change ringing never really is comprehended. Never satisfied with the staple country house or body in the library, Sayers fits her murders to each new setting, building a complete world for the investigation.

The characters who people these worlds may sometimes be stereotyped: the predictable servants, the slow-thinking locals, the flighty and the tedious duchesses with the beefy duke, or the absentminded vicar. Nevertheless there are individually developed minor characters and some memorable episodes involving the stereotypes in unexpected behavior. A gleefully drunk Inspector Parker, the Dowager Duchess at an exhumation, or Marjorie Phelps declining cocoa and fizzy lemonade on Peter's behalf expand their personalities beyond conventional limitations. Peter is never bound by traditional expectations in his roles either as wealthy aristocrat or talented detective; new facets of his character are regularly developed throughout the series. He grows from a conventional puzzle solver into a feeling, responsible human being.

Clearly then, Sayers is not just writing detective fiction; she presents more than the usual respect for the value of life and the return of society to its ordered ways. Instead she chooses also to define social order and society's future in terms of work. Neither individuals nor segments of society which disdain or betray work are respected in the fiction. Through successful completion of his own work, the detective restores respect to the criminal's dishonored profession or craft; this, in turn, keeps the social order functioning. In meshing these two distinct elements, Sayers leaves her own unique stamp on the genre she helped create.

Kathleen Gregory Klein. In Earl F. Bargainnier, ed., *10 Women of Mystery* (Bowling Green, Ohio: Popular Press, 1981), pp. 36–37

Murder Must Advertise tells a story about people who are either bored, rootless, and wealthy, or who are trapped in dull work, both of whom seek a life of material enrichment. The plot juxtaposes cocaine and advertising. The sling shot that murders Victor Dean and begins the action fires into the midst of British society.

When Dean, a copywriter at Pym's Publicity, falls down a dangerous iron staircase, the coroner's inquest ends with the verdict of accidental death. Pamela Dean, the sister of the deceased, sends Mr. Pym the fragment of a letter that she found in her brother's desk. The letter warns that something odd is going on in the conservative advertising agency. Mr. Pym hires Mr. Death Bredon to investigate (he does not know at first that he has actually hired Lord Peter Wimsey). Peter replaces Victor Dean as a copywriter, and he and the reader deduce early on that Dean was dead before he fell.

In this novel, How did he die? is answered soon; Who did it? next; and Why? last. By chapter 5, we know (1) that Dean was murdered; (2) that the weapon was ironically Dean's good-luck charm, an onyx scarab; (3) that because people constantly move around in an advertising agency, alibi will have little to do with this case; and (4) that an important clue will be the wild and wealthy crowd with whom Dean associated. Our curiosity about how Dean was murdered disappears and is replaced by our interest in Lord Peter's investigation to find out who and why. His search for the answers to those questions takes us to the center of the novel's social concerns. . . .

At the end of the novel, the murderer, whose spirit has been killed long before his actual death by the dope mob, tells Lord Peter why he got involved with the drug ring and then murdered Dean to protect himself. In trying to find the good life—marriage, house, furniture—he found instead a trap; our verdict about this murderer: he is neither devil nor "Freke." He tells Peter, "You've got to keep going, and it breaks your heart and takes all the stuffing out of you." But these are not dolls, although the advertising images that the believers try to emulate are pitiful ghosts. As Mr. Bredon, Lord Peter learns that advertising is a drug not for the wealthy, but for "the comparatively poor . . . aching for luxury beyond their reach and for a leisure for ever denied them," a will-o'-the-wisp created by those who know how to arrange dreams in language. . . .

Because it is ever present, the Pied Piper's spell of advertising and mindless popular entertainment may seem as harmless as the murder weapon in *Murder Must Advertise*. Like the purloined letter in Poe's story, the scarab lay undetected for what it was. By advertising, murder almost succeeded. Only Wimsey was perceptive enough to really see the object. In this world of things-that-are-more-than-what-they-seem, Sayers suggests, one must be as observant as a detective. One must watch for the significance in the everyday and the familiar, which may camouflage an instrument of death, as in *Murder Must Advertise*.

Dawson Gaillard. *Dorothy L. Sayers* (New York:
Ungar, 1981), pp. 61–63

SIMENON, GEORGES (1903–1989)

Georges Simenon, perhaps one of the most internationally known of crime writers, created Inspector Jules Maigret of the Sûreté in the early 1930s, portraying him and his colleagues in his own unique style. Though most of Simenon's work is connected with crime, he is equally concerned with the study of character, and is remarkably successful in the way he presents *real* men and women. Maigret is the head of a murder squad, although in the end it is the collaboration of all branches involved that solves the crime—a fact true to reality. Maigret is an amiable, understanding man who loves his pipe, his comfortable home, and his wife's excellent cooking. Equally he loves his office at 36 Quai des Orfèvres with the inspectors Lucas, Lapointe, Janvier, and Torrence. Of course, his inspectors make mistakes sometimes, and Maigret acts as something of a father figure to his colleagues. His many cases have made him a friend of reader and filmgoer alike. Simenon's novels have the special attraction of taking the reader into the heart of Paris to experience its day-to-day life, as well as into France's provincial towns and countryside. Only now and again does Simenon choose far-off regions for his plots: Arizona in *Maigret at the Coroner's* (1949), for example. Maigret is not interested in the mere facts of each case as such. He considers the whole human condition; in that sense he might well be linked to Balzac. From 1932 on, Maigret novels appeared in quick succession. In *Maigret and the Enigmatic Letter*, a.k.a. *The Story of Peter the Lett* (1933), Simenon described Maigret as experienced, slightly graying, and thoroughly professional. And he has remained that way, not aging at all, even though from time to time he is sent into retirement. His inspectors and Madame do not get any older either as everything in the world around them changes, with the exception, of course, of the Quai des Orfèvres.

Maigret is always ready to understand the criminal, yet he does not tolerate crime or ever seek to excuse it. He investigates the environment in order to discover a criminal motive or sometimes the criminal himself. This environment is largely a family circle. In that way Simenon's work is closely related to the French "family novel," continuing a literary tradition dating back to before Gaboriau. Some critics accuse Simenon of churning out too many books. Certainly he wrote at times under financial pressure—not just the Maigret novels but other crime fiction, stories, literary essays, and even "penny dreadfuls."

However, in his letters to André Gide and in some of his essays he makes it abundantly clear that he has literary ambitions although he never set out to write a "great" novel. He is a first-class storyteller who wants to entertain his public without pretentious moralizing.

Waltraud Woeller. *The Literature of Crime and Detection* (New York: Ungar, 1988), pp. 173–76

In the Maigret novels, Simenon approaches the professional detective as a phenomenon. He holds no brief for or against, and refuses to judge, just as Maigret refuses to judge others until his later years, when he becomes occasionally fractious. The point of view is biological, a study of someone who decides to join the police force, who discovers powers of intuition that make him famous, then gradually feels the pressures of his chosen life. The novels hinge on the fact that Maigret finds himself up against a contradiction. Since he can only solve a case when he "understands" the criminal, which means imagining how he feels, he has a natural sympathy for the man whom society pays him to capture. A deductive virtuoso like Holmes exercises his genius by analyzing facts, but in the early *A Battle of Nerves* (1931), Maigret declares his principle of "moral proof." The final evidence lies in character, revealed by a sudden act of empathy. Yet to understand is not to forgive but to arrest.

The murderer's identity may be disclosed halfway through a Maigret story without loss of suspense, because his psyche is more important. The real element of surprise is the human shock. After the motive has been decoded or the moment of self-betrayal engineered, Maigret confronts Simenon's "naked man."

Since he sees the world outside his novels as an artificial creation of politics, Simenon never dates his fiction. Only a few scattered internal clues locate the action in the 1930s or later. Only a light handful of his 214 books acknowledges the Second World War. A private theater of fear and greed and anger exists within its own time continuum, and history is what happens in people's minds every day. But Maigret himself can be dated specifically, since Simenon tells us when he was born (in 1877) and when he was promoted to his first case (in 1913). He must have reached the retirement age around 1942, although Simenon continues to write about him until the early seventies. As Simenon has admitted, Maigret could never have functioned in contemporary Paris. Born thirty years later, he would certainly have resigned in protest against corruption and the new methods. Towards the end of his career he already feels the climate changing, and doesn't like it.

Yet if Maigret himself belongs to the past, his criminal arena remains undated. A different kind of detective in Paris today would encounter many of the same murderers. Many of them could also be the protagonist of a non-Maigret novel, and sometimes you feel a direct emotional overlap. *Maigret Has Scruples* (1951) begins with a man telling the inspector that his wife is trying to poison him. It is immediately followed by *Sunday,* a non-Maigret about a man who decides to poison his wife. Both tales share a climate of sexual duplicity and domestic hatred, at its most intensely concentrated in *Sunday.* Simenon has pointed out that a Maigret often resembles a sketch for the painting to follow. The detective himself also seems like a first sketch for a self-portrait—or, put another way, like a transitional device for Simenon the detective of life when he feels ready to move from potboilers to reality.

Like his creator, Maigret changes his life after his father dies unexpectedly, abandoning his medical studies to join the Paris police. He comes from a family that has to struggle against poverty—his father managed several farms on a country estate—and marries in his early twenties. He lives an outwardly conventional middle-class life in a suburban apartment. He rises from the ranks of street and vice squad duty as Simenon rose from the apprenticeship of pulp fiction. Even before he becomes famous his professional methods are unorthodox, and he seems driven by a private intensity. During his first case he develops an ability to escape into the lives of others, "to put himself inside everybody's mind." Like Simenon writing a novel he works against time, absorbing a new atmosphere and unfamiliar set of characters and yet reaching a solution as quickly as possible. Simenon begins a novel with a series of routines, card-indexing characters, making street maps, and outlining events on the back of a manila envelope. Maigret begins a case by taking statements, consulting reports, making notes. Then he waits for the key moment, the start of an imaginative process by which the abstract turns into something human and complex. Like Simenon he is irritated by theorists. Examining magistrates oppress him with their middle-class attitudes and sermonizing, psychiatrists lack "physical intimacy with the criminal world." Alcohol and withdrawal into oneself are much more stimulating. Maigret constantly nips on the job, white wine at one café and calvados at another. And as Simenon becomes a total recluse during his ten days' stretch on a novel, ignoring the telephone and hanging a "Do Not Disturb" sign outside his study door, Maigret takes to his bed to sweat out a problem alone.

His private evolution is a vital part of the cycle. Between 1931 and 1934 Simenon wrote about twenty Maigrets. Their plots are notably complicated and Maigret himself seems a relatively simple character, a big slow man in a bowler hat who plays his hunches and a few unorthodox tricks. Between 1935 and 1949 only nine Maigrets appear, low-profile and rather perfunctory. Simenon is preoccupied with other work. Since 1949 he's produced another fifty, and the later Maigret reveals more of himself as he becomes more emotionally involved with his cases. His view of the world darkens. He feels the exhaustion of prolonged contact with criminal life. He is famous but suspects younger colleagues of secretly dismissing him as old hat. He looks back nostalgically to childhood and looks forward to the dreaded release of retirement.

Gavin Lambert. The Dangerous Edge (New York:
Grossman, 1976), pp. 177–79

This son of a bailiff [Jules Maigret] is never at ease with aristocrats, or for that matter with politicians, as he is with children, criminals, and bourgeois of the lower class, and with professional men like doctors and solicitors. There are certain kinds of people about whom his understanding is limited—artists, scientists, eccentrics generally. He has instinctive respect for but also distrust of the rich. If he solves the cases in which such people are mixed up, it is through his gift of empathy combined with the sudden moments of instinctive understanding that come to him. The personage created by Simenon, through stroke after stroke in book after book, has a plodding energy and endless patience. He is not of great intellectual stature, but has flashes of what can only be called artistic penetration, through which he understands ways of life alien to his own. We do not know how he votes, but are sure that it will always be for stability rather than for change. We do not know his sexual habits, but they will certainly not be markedly unusual. Maigret is a typical bourgeois, but with a breadth of sympathy that most bourgeois lack. He is one of the most completely realized characters in all modern fiction.

Julian Symons. *Mortal Consequences: A History—*
From the Detective Story to the Crime Novel
(New York: Harper & Row, 1972),
p. 149

Georges Simenon has probably done as much for the common cold as the aspirin and more for travel than the overnight suitcase. Limp, semi-recumbent people all over the world wanly open his latest tale set in a bracingly seamy café or a stifling provincial salon alive with intrigue and somehow, no matter what the outcome, close it with a feeling of inexplicable pleasure. His works have appeared with awesome regularity for more than five decades, but no one seems able to say with certainty how many books Simenon has written; his American publishers—Harcourt Brace Jovanovich—place the figure at more than two hundred and fifty. No wonder one takes him so much for granted, unique though his writing is. . . .

Most writers of mysteries assume that they must elicit at least a passing interest in the deceased for form's sake. Not Georges Simenon. The passions and plots of the living are his subject. One rarely is permitted to see or sympathize with his victims before they attain literary immortality; they are erased before the story begins. In *Maigret in Exile,* [a nineteen-forties book about a mysterious corpse that turns up in the attic of a distinguished judge] the murder even brings about a kind of holiday spirit. The strongest emotion Maigret feels when he hears about the case is gratitude, since it provides a bit of excitement in the dull provincial life to which he has been banished for somehow offending the higher-ups at the Quai des Orfèvres. . . . In an elegant country house the chief murder suspect, the judge, pours him Armagnac from a cut-glass decanter on a silver tray. The judge, we perceive *at once,* is *not* the murderer. Simenon's world is unequivocally divided between decent folk (hard workers, passionate lovers, loyal friends, tidy homebodies, salt-of-the-earthers, devoted elderly couples, dutiful children, eccentric but tame loners) and bad ones (the newly rich, narcissistic promiscuous women, petty snobs, sleazy businessmen, inveterate crooks, greedy relatives, lazy louts). The judge exudes blue-ribbon decency. No matter that he has indeed murdered a man, a long time ago. He had his reasons (a narcissistic promiscuous woman).

Maigret enjoys making a great show of his deductive powers when he wraps matters up, but at heart he is really a *flâneur*. While ostensibly ferreting out clues, he pauses at every pleasure, like a dog on an early-morning walk. There is rarely any sense of urgency about finding the murderer in these stories. Eventually, we will see the dagger glinting in the sun beneath the currant bushes. Eventually, someone will blab and give himself or someone else away. Meanwhile, diversions are everywhere; in the present volume there is the sea air to enjoy, the lives of half a dozen diversely odd suspects to poke into, the fishermen's brightly painted shacks to admire, the sun-dappled town-council chambers overlooking a lime tree to conduct the more official phases of the investigation in, and the locals' gruff accents and tureens of mussel stew to savor at the hotel café. . . .

Many, if not most, of the places that Simenon loves to describe, especially in these books from the forties, will be gone in the not too distant future. Simenon's descriptions have taken on a distinctly quaint, almost operetta-ish aura. No cultural anthropologist could have better preserved such scenes for posterity.

Lis Harris. The New Yorker. April 2, 1979, pp.
122–24

[Georges] Simenon, like Graham Greene, consciously divided his work into entertainments—the conventional Maigret stories—and into psychological novels. The gap between these is, I think, less self-conscious and also less successful than in Greene's work, for both types of books are concerned with a single set of questions: Who does society appoint to ask its questions for it? How does society deal with the answers when they are unpleasant? . . .

Simenon . . . produced well over two hundred books, some in three or four days; such productivity led many critics to dismiss him as an autodidact. In general it is true that his Maigret stories are less compelling than the psychological novels that won him great praise from Andrew Gide and others, though there is no firm evidence that he took longer to write the psychological novels. One suspects, rather, that as an author takes on a different persona, his perception of the intended audience rightly changes, with substantially different results.

Robin W. Winks. Modus Operandi: An Excursion
into Detective Fiction (Boston: David R. Godine,
1982), pp. 41–43

In a Georges Simenon novel, *Maigret and the Burglar's Wife,* originally published in France in 1951 and appearing in English for the first time, Sad Freddie, Paris's most accomplished safecracker, is hard at work in a house in Neuilly, a suburb of Paris, when the rays of his flashlight suddenly reveal a dead woman, chest covered with blood, lying on the floor by the safe. Freddie flees, going underground immediately. His wife, an ex-prostitute, contacts Maigret, who once arrested her but was kind to her, to set the record straight and to get Sad Freddie off the hook. Maigret searches the house, but there is no sign of the body, although the wife of the man of the house has vanished. Maigret's men ransack the premises, but turn up no corpse. He must settle for intensive—and extensive—Q. & A.s with the usual suspects—interrogation duels that resemble Porfiry's pursuit of Raskalnikov, or a Parisian version of Sergeant Columbo at his slo-mo best. In the end pursuer and pursued have a psychological meeting of the minds and the case is closed. Much of the nostalgic magic of a Simenon lies in his marvelous word pictures of Paris as she should have been. Storywise, no one quite combines psychological suspense with the Golden Age detective story in the way the author does with his dependable and unforgettable Maigrets. The up-to-date translation has been artfully managed by J. Maclaren-Ross; most of all he has discarded the constant ellipses that used to clutter some early renditions of Simenon's work and drive the American reader half mad. There are apparently other early Maigrets that have never been translated into English; *encore, s'il vous plaît!*

Bruce Cassiday. *Border Patrol*. Summer 1991,

pp. 5–6

SJÖWALL, MAJ (1935–   ) and WAHLÖÖ, PER (1926–1975)

In a 1966 essay Per Wahlöö stated the basis for the Martin Beck series he and Maj Sjöwall had started a year earlier. The series would consist of only ten novels. They chose the crime novel as a form because of its strong connection between people and society: it is impossible to be a lawbreaker—or a law enforcer—without a law, laid down and maintained by a society based upon certain political and economic realities and opinions. They wrote together, each writing alternate chapters after long research and detailed synopses. They were both communists, and the outspoken aim of their series was to "use the crime novel as a scalpel cutting open the belly of an ideologically pauperized and morally debatable so-called welfare state of the bourgeois type." The first two or three books would be almost totally apolitical; later ones would put down the mask and speak loud and clear.

Bo Lundin. In John M. Reilly, ed., *Twentieth-Century Crime and Mystery Writers: Second Edition* (New York: St. Martin's Press, 1985),

p. 947

The work of the Swedish writer Peter Wahlöö is of two different kinds. He has written at least two novels which combine the moral symbolism of Dürrenmatt with a flavor of Orwellian fantasy. *Murder on the Thirty-First Floor* (1966) and *The Steel Spring* (1970) make their points about dictatorship and paternalism through the medium of crime, and Chief Inspector Jensen, who appears in both books, is trying to discover the nature of society in terms of what is called criminal activity. The books that Wahlöö (now Per and not Peter) has written in collaboration with Maj Sjöwall are less ambitious and more successful. They are police investigations carried out by Inspector Beck, a gloomy version of Freeling's Van der Valk, and they might come under the heading of "Police Novels" except that the authors are still more interested in the philosophic implications of crime than in straightforward police routine. *The Man on the Balcony* (1968), *The Man Who Went up in Smoke* (1969), and *The Laughing Policeman* (1970) are markedly individual and very good.

> Julian Symons. *Mortal Consequences: A History—*
> *From the Detective Story to the Crime Novel* (New
> York: Harper & Row, 1972), pp. 197–98

The serious moral, in so far as Mr. Wahlöö is concerned with one, seems to be that boredom with a complacently well-ordered society can have disastrous consequences if people try to puncture it with far-fetched libertarian alternatives: the banner of revolution, however modest, is inevitably raised by incipient authoritarians. It might be well to have this said for the democratic society Mr. Wahlöö is implicitly defending [in *The Generals*], just as *Animal Farm* made the point about bloody revolution against an autocratic regime. Yet to invoke Orwell shows just how far *The Generals* falls short.

> *The Times Literary Supplement.* April 19, 1974,
> p. 409

In their Martin Beck Series the Wahlöös wanted to trace a decade in the life of Inspector Beck, an intelligent, conscientious policeman trying to do his job in what they regarded as a high-handed, soulless, Kafkalike bureaucracy. For the Wahlöös, little remains of the early promise of what Marquis Childs once called the Swedish "middle way." Their disillusionment is filtered through the personality of Beck, their policeman.

Beck's sour stomach provides a barometer to both his unhappy marriage and the state of Swedish life.

Each book can stand by itself, but to be savored fully, it should be read as part of a running saga. Beck changes and so do his views of himself as well as society. Characters drop out and reappear. The murderer in the first novel, *Roseanna*, a sad man driven to an insane frenzy by sexual prudishness when he is teased by an oversexed coquette, returns in *Cop Killer*, the ninth, as a victim when police and neighbors rush to judgment because of his past. In *The Locked Room,* Beck is recovering, both in body and spirit, from a near-fatal wound suffered in *The Abominable Man.* In that case, a retired police inspector, allowed to practice sadism under the cloak of his official uniform, is killed by another policeman whose wife was left to lie and die in a drunk cell while in a diabetic coma. In *Murder at the Savoy,* Beck, an honest, dogged investigator, doesn't hide his disgust for the victim, Viktor Palmgren, an industrialist who had made a fortune by ignoring the welfare of his employees and by running guns to Angola and South Africa. Some of the other books have titles that sound like those children's tales—*The Fire Engine That Disappeared* and *The Man Who Went up in Smoke.* The best of the lot may be the first, *Roseanna,* and *The Laughing Policeman.*

Lately, Beck has allowed his gloomy philosophizing to interfere with the dispatch of his police work. And he can become a trifle querulous and tiresome in his unabated attacks on the Swedish establishment. I'm very fond of Beck, but I can't help thinking that it would be pleasanter if he just weren't so sour and could laugh without much cause (a trait that Beck himself envies in a colleague). Now that he has found Rhea, a younger woman with a relaxed life style and philosophy, perhaps Beck can find a measure of personal contentment and get back to his ship models despite the stultifying atmosphere that he feels within the Swedish welfare state.

Jean M. White. *The New Republic.* July 31, 1976,

pp. 28–29

Maj Sjöwall and Per Wahlöö . . . are writers who set about showing us how to lose our innocence in ways that arise from society more than from human character, and to this extent they share the vaguely deterministic views of the anti-individualist school, while they are also clear that, because . . . a prostitute named Teresa (in . . . *Laughing Policeman*) had limits, individual acts still count. . . . By creating a series figure . . . they show how . . . Martin Beck is slowly worn down by the role of grand inquisitor, diminished, made tired of society itself. When the protagonist is a series figure, he is able to grow, to develop from book to book, and provided the author is concerned with life and not pasteboard . . ., age brings exhaustion, boredom, the loss of illusions. In this way, series figures actually grow as they diminish, for they become more real for becoming less heroic. . . . Martin Beck's stomach problems, decaying marriage, and blandly unattractive daughter do not grow on one from book to book. . . . A sharper, ultimately angrier statement about how government must corrupt, Swedish style, provide [a] valuable and sustained critique of modern life as lived in the West, by writers who would not, their critical views to the contrary, care to live in Dostoevsky's Russia.

Robin W. Winks. *Modus Operandi: An Excursion*

into Detective Fiction (Boston: David R. Godine,

1982), pp. 41–42

STOUT, REX (1886–1975)

In the movement toward what may be loosely termed the "liberalization" of the straightaway or routine American detective story, Rex Stout stands in the forefront. Indiana-born, he was educated in Kansas, joined the navy, and had a dozen different "careers" before he "retired" in 1927, at the age of forty, and went to Paris to write a psychological novel. This novel and three later ones in similar vein were respectfully received by the critics but did not by any means approach the best-seller lists. The "economic disillusionment" of the 1930s was, Stout says, the underlying cause of his turn to detective fiction.

His first work in this field, *Fer-de-Lance,* was published in 1934, introducing crabbed, elephantine Nero Wolfe, whose two great loves are beer and orchids, and his paint-fresh assistant, the narrator of the stories, Archie Goodwin—the one example in history (in this writer's opinion) of a Watson who steals the play from his Holmes, and a first-rate Holmes to boot. Rex Stout brought to the detective story not only its keenest wit, but also exceptional literary talent, a fact sometimes missed by readers who overlook the bland art that gives Archie's picturesque slang and breezy narration their appeal. It is this skill, rather than any technical innovation, which has given him his high station in the form.

Whether or not he succeeds in his declared ambition to write "one of the two or three best mystery stories in the world," Rex Stout has already produced several of the most intelligent and entertaining works of his time. His plots, detection, and narration, are of the highest order. He has created several detective characters, all told, but none to rival seriously the popularity of Wolfe and his Archie.

Howard Haycraft. Murder for Pleasure: The Life
and Times of the Detective Story (New York: Biblo
and Tannen, 1968), pp. 208–9

The name of Rex Stout and the universe he created are familiar in some degree even to casual readers of mystery fiction. At the hub of this universe, behind his desk in the study of the old brownstone on West 35th Street between Tenth and Eleventh Avenues that serves as his office and home, sits an irascible, gargantuan genius of a consulting detective named Nero Wolfe—the only sleuth extant who cries out to be portrayed by Orson Welles. Wolfe is a lover of orchids, good books, and good food, and keeps himself supplied therewith through the fees he earns by sweeping away murder problems from the doorsteps of the very rich. Inspector Cramer of the Homicide Squad grudgingly tolerates Wolfe's interferences because he has learned from bitter experience the efficacy of Wolfe's massive intellect against those statistically inevitable murderers who are beyond the power of official routine to unmask. Wolfe's campaigns are recorded in magnificently brash and breezy manner by private detective Archie Goodwin, at once Wolfe's Watson, his errand boy, and his gadfly.

Stout's shortcomings include his herculean labors to keep from putting in his novels a plot that is adequate to book length; his incessant use of that laziest of denouement devices from the old Charlie Chan movies, the trap to make the murderer (whose identity is unknown to the detective) betray himself; and his refusal in almost all of his stories to "play fair" with his readers. But, just as the grievous defects in the Sherlock Holmes stories did not destroy our delight in the living universe Conan Doyle created, it is most probable that our great-grandchildren will find the world of Rex Stout and Nero Wolfe, despite its weak spots, almost equally enthralling.

Francis M. Nevins, Jr. Journal of Popular Culture.
Summer 1969, pp. 170–72

It looked at one time as though the work of Rex Stout . . . might . . . represent a peak . . . in the creation of the most original and plausible Holmes-and-Watson pair. He began to write crime stories late in life, after the production of some interesting but commercially unsuccessful novels, and *Fer-de-Lance* (1934) introduced his puffing, grunting Montenegrin-born heavyweight detective Nero Wolfe, and Wolfe's tough, sometimes aggressive assistant Archie Goodwin. Stout may have begun with the intention of guying a little, in the gentlest way, the whole detective form. Wolfe sits in his oversize chair, unable to cross his legs because they are so fat, taking trips in the elevator up to his collection of ten thousand orchids in the plant room on the roof, and solving crimes without moving from the house. Goodwin, a barbarian man of action ("I do read books, but I never yet got any real satisfaction out of one"), is Wolfe's eyes and legs for anything that takes place outside the old brownstone on West Thirty-fifth Street.

Plotting was not Stout's strong suit, and Wolfe's solutions were sometimes arbitrary or instinctive, but in *Fer-de-Lance, The League of Frightened Men* (1935), and other early books, notably *The Red Box* (1937), the dialogue crackles, Archie dashes around and almost falls in love, and Wolfe is built up into a slightly comic but always impressive figure. But as time went on and the books piled up, Wolfe had sometimes to be taken away from home, and the problems involved in all series characters who appear in a lot of stories became evident. These are, of course, all the greater when the characters are built up from a few superficial attributes, like love of beer and orchids and a gourmet's appreciation of food. Slowly, slowly, the Wolfe stories have declined. The decline became steep after the end of the forties, which still contain some books very near to Stout's best work, like *The Silent Speaker* (1946) and *The Second Confession* (1949). Stout himself is the Grand Old Man of American crime fiction.

Julian Symons. Mortal Consequences: A History—
From the Detective Story to the Crime Novel (New
York: Harper & Row, 1972), pp. 123–24

Nobody who claims to be a competent critic can say that Rex Stout does not write well. His narrative and dialogue could not be improved, and he passes the supreme test of being rereadable. I don't know how many times I have reread the Nero Wolfe stories, but plenty. I know exactly what is coming and how it is all going to end, but it doesn't matter. That's *writing*.

Does the ordinary reader realize how exactly right those Nero Wolfe stories are? There are no loose ends. One could wonder why Sherlock Holmes, fawned on by kings and prime ministers, was not able to afford rooms in Baker Street—price at the turn of the century thirty bob a week including breakfast—unless he got Doctor Watson to put up half the money, but in Nero Wolfe, a professional detective charging huge fees, you can believe. Those orchids, perfectly understandable. He liked orchids and was in a financial position to collect them. He liked food, too. Again perfectly understandable. He refused to leave his house on business, and very sensible of him if his wealth and reputation were such that he could get away with it. In other words, there was nothing contrived about his eccentricities, purely because Stout knew his job.

But Stout's supreme triumph was the creation of Archie Goodwin.

Telling a mystery story in the third person is seldom satisfactory. To play fair you have to let the reader see into the detective's thoughts, and that gives the game away. The alternative is to have him pick up small objects from the floor and put them carefully in an envelope without revealing their significance, which is the lowest form of literary skulduggery. A Watson of some sort to tell the story is unavoidable, and the hundreds of Watsons who have appeared in print since Holmes's simply won't do. I decline to believe that when the prime minister sends for the detective to cry on his shoulder about some bounder having swiped the naval treaty and finds that he has brought a friend along, he just accepts the detective's statement that "This is Augustus So-and-So, who has been associated with me in many of my cases." What he would really do would be to ring the bell for the secretary of state and tell him to throw Mr. So-and-So out on his ear. "And I want to hear him bounce," he would add. Stout has avoided this trap. Archie is a Watson in the sense that he tells the story, but in no other way is there anything Watsonian about him. And he brings excellent comedy into the type of narrative where comedy seldom bats better than .100.

Summing up, I would say that there is only one Rex Stout, and if you think I am going to say "That's plenty," you are wrong, witty though it would be. I could do with a dozen.

P. G. Wodehouse. Foreword to John McAleer, *Rex Stout: A Biography* (Boston: Little, Brown, 1977), pp. xv–xvi

The formal detective story is an allotropic form of the novel of manners. The novel of manners was designed to show that society is at its most secure and men happiest when they can find their identity in a stable order. During its first eighty years, the detective story concentrated on instances in which the polite world repudiated behavior which went against the rules it subscribed to. Detectives themselves were gentlemen.

Then, in the early 1920s, an American author, Carroll John Daly, originated the hard-boiled detective story and murder forsook the vicar's rose garden for the mean streets which Dashiell Hammett and Raymond Chandler would celebrate in the years ahead. With this development the detective story jumped the banks of the novel of manners to run in the rapids of naturalism.

The hard-boiled detective is nomadic, seedy, hard-drinking, promiscuous, tough-talking, and tough-acting. He has little formal education. Culturally he is illiterate. He mistrusts established institutions. Yet he is likely to be sincere, downright, just, and truthful.

To a genre which hitherto had justified its existence by justifying society, the hard-boiled detective proved a near fatal addition. In the nick of time, Rex Stout stepped in and saved it by creating a fiction which fused the best elements of both traditions.

Nero Wolfe is a "Great Detective" in the classic mold. Archie Goodwin is hard-boiled. The reconciliation was managed with care. Rex Stout had been irritated by the simpering mannerisms of the orthodox detective story as it had come to be written by the early thirties. He drew on the strengths of hard-boiled detective fiction—its honesty, directness, social awareness, and idealism—to generate reforms, but, holding firm to the tradition of the novel of manners, he worked for peaceful change within the existing social order, rather than opting for that order's violent overthrow. The detective story was, for him, an advanced base from which he could promote realizable reforms. As he worked to save the genre, he was engaged in the larger labor of saving the existing social order which that genre shadowed forth. . . .

For the fusion he effected, Rex exacted a price from both rebels and conservatives. His hard-boiled detective adheres to basic standards of decency. Archie Goodwin lives under Wolfe's roof and accepts Wolfe's values. Wolfe does not champion the establishment as a matter of course. Even as he entertains us with a detective story, Rex Stout attacks a wide assortment of social evils: fascism, communism, McCarthyism, racism, censorship, Madison Avenue, commercial radio; abuses in the law profession, the FBI, labor unions, the National Association of Manufacturers, and the publishing industry; exploitation of displaced persons; the Nixon government; and social pretense wherever found.

Within his brownstone, Wolfe maintains a comic system of order that is overlaid on the heroic social order civilization depends on. Even as it entertains us, this comic order reaffirms the integrity of that heroic order. . . . Wolfe and Archie actually are extensions of their creator, and both relate intimately to his intrapsychic life.

The day after his wife returned home from the hospital with a daughter, Rex created Nero Wolfe and Archie Goodwin. In Wolfe, Rex created a surrogate father. To him he assigned many of [his own father's] characteristics: brown eyes, dark coloring, discipline, earnestness, idealism, and a fine sense of indignation. On this figure he superimposed two substitute authority figures whom he had turned to earlier when normal gravitation toward his father was blocked—his mother's mother, plump and lazy in her special chair, addicted to flowers, dictionaries, and atlases, . . . and Alvey Augustus Adee, scholar, sleuth, gourmet, bachelor, a model of efficiency, a master of the English language, the Second Under Secretary of State of the United States for thirty-six years, with whom Rex was thrust into intimate association during the time he served in the navy.

In Archie Goodwin, Rex created a persona through whom he could approach Wolfe to continue his probing of the father-son relationship. In many particulars Archie duplicated Rex Stout's self-image at that time. To Archie, Rex assigned the salient Todhunter characteristics: gray eyes, fair complexion, enthusiasm, curiosity, restiveness, and a spirit of fun.

The dialogue between Wolfe and Archie is, in essence, a father-son dialogue. What is more remarkable, while the flow of Rex's traits into Archie gradually subsides, Nero Wolfe and Rex Stout come increasingly to share characteristics in common. Through Wolfe and Archie, Rex at last found a satisfactory self-image and slipped (though certainly not sheepishly) into Wolfe's clothing.

Nero Wolfe, then, is an amalgam of ideals brought together by Rex Stout in his search for an acceptable self-image. Understanding himself was the greatest challenge Rex Stout ever faced, and, ultimately, he did attain a satisfactory self-image. For Rex this was essential. To offer himself as an advocate of a stable social order, while retaining no more than an obscure sense of his own identity, would have been to Rex fraudulent.

John McAleer. *Rex Stout: A Biography* (Boston: Little, Brown, 1977), pp. 5–9

Rex Stout did more than write very fine mystery novels; he permanently altered the course of crime fiction by showing how it was possible to combine the two separate traditions—those of the hard-boiled op and the Great Detective—which had comprised the genre before him. At the same time he helped advance the place of the mystery novel among the genres of fiction by bringing it closer to the novel of manners. He showed how the crime novel could broaden its scope and its pretensions. He helped bring it into the mainstream of fiction. . . .

The hard-boiled detective, exemplified in American fiction by Spade and Marlowe and alive today in Robert B. Parker's Spenser, spends his time on the streets, solving crimes by interrogating, chasing, often brawling; as often as not he ends up wounded himself. His arena is the city, especially Los Angeles or New York. His weaknesses are women and alcohol.

The Great Detective, descended from Poe's Dupin and typified by Sherlock Holmes, is a different sort. His kingdom is his study and his weapons are intellectual—logic, memory, concentration. He traps criminals in the corridors of his own mind rather than in a back alley at midnight. He is a cultivated gentleman, whose recreation is the library, whose background is often European.

Archie, even with all his glib sophistication, is at heart a hard-boiled type. He chases, punches, shoots, breaks and enters. He knows locksmiths, cabbies, doormen. Wolfe occupies the other extreme. . . .

But Rex Stout put them both in an office on West Thirty-Fifth Street. Such a combination opened vast possibilities for the development of plot, character, and theme in the crime novel. Take plot, for example. The hard-boiled novel is fast-paced and lean; the classical crime novel, on the other hand, is contemplative, intricate, sophisticated. The partnership between Wolfe and Archie allowed for novels which were both fast-paced and contemplative, both lean and sophisticated. . . .

This partnership also had advantages for characterization. The partnership of the two detectives is like a marriage between two strong-willed people: the two kinds are bound to rub against each other. But the resulting tensions, far from rocking the novels, contribute to the richness of texture that Rex Stout contributed to the mystery novel. . . .

Important changes within a genre prompt corresponding changes in the relations between that genre and other forms of writing. As crime fiction became richer and more complex with Rex Stout, its place among the other genres altered too. It moved further in the direction towards which, since its inception, it had inevitably tended—towards the mainstream of fiction. Stout's contribution to this process deserves emphasis: he helped to attach the crime novel to mainstream fiction at a particular point—the novel of manners.

No one has done more with character in crime fiction than Rex Stout. This holds not only for the main characters but for the minor ones as well. Rex Stout's world was populated not only by Wolfe and Archie but also by Cramer, Saul Panzer, Fred and Orrie, Fritz and Theodore, and Lily Rowan, as well as the gallery of memorable characters who appear in individual novels, from Paul Chapin to Julie Jaquette. The criminals one meets in the Wolfe saga offer portraits of bombast, greed, trickery, obsession, seduction, and betrayal. The minor characters of the Wolfe circle act as foils for Wolfe and Archie, highlighting their personalities and their values.

Few crime fiction writers have been as amusing as Rex Stout. His humor also marks his affinity with the novel of manners, for that genre characteristically portrays human behavior with a lightness of tone. That lightness Rex Stout brought into the crime novel. Other narrators before Archie Goodwin had been funny, but their humor was sardonic, mordant, acid. Archie is whimsical. Instead of a grim surface of hard-boiled dialogue that pounds in to the reader the action of the crime novel, Rex Stout offers a surface compounded largely of the inventive and optimistic wit, which distances the grim misdeeds committed in the book.

The Wolfe novels minimize violence, sex, and melodrama, the hallmarks of cheap crime fiction. As one would expect from a writer who helped move the whole genre away from the whodunit, Rex Stout deemphasized the shoot-out, the vulnerable and pliant female, the tough interrogations in dimly lit rooms. He was a novelist with something more sturdy upon which to base his work—dialogue, character, and setting—and his treatment of the conventions of the genre amply demonstrated that fact.

In evaluating Rex Stout's achievement there is one other fact to keep in mind: he sustained it over forty years. Few writers, and even fewer crime writers, can lay claim to the sustained excellence of Rex Stout's Nero Wolfe novels. To write one book, excellent in its kind, is a difficult achievement. Having done so marks Stout as a writer with a significant enough vision and supple enough mind to please readers over a period of time marked by great political, social, and cultural change. He could discuss World War II or Watergate, civil rights or women's rights, and do so as cogently in his eighty-ninth year as in middle age.

Stout owed his success over forty years not to mercenary reliance on a formula or to callow exploitation of novelty. He simply created a variation of the crime novel that suited him and then elaborated on it.

Ultimately this must be the greatest praise of a writer—that he was capable of imagining a world complex enough and yet real enough to interest readers, to supply him with events and characters and themes, and to bear variation and elaboration over so long a period of time. Such sustained achievement is of course a tribute to persistence and to technical skill. Most of all though it must be a tribute to imagination, and it is on the score of his imagination that finally Rex Stout merits our praise and admiration.

David R. Anderson. Rex Stout (New York; Ungar,
1984), pp. 112–20

Rex Stout created his detective, formidable both in bulk and in intellect, at a time when the conventional detective story involved a closed milieu of suspects and a traditional revelation of the killer to that group at its conclusion; he kept to that format throughout the Nero Wolfe series. But he heeded the American rebellion against the closed milieu and added a street-wise urban loner to his basic format by creating a second detective, Archie Goodwin to act as narrator *and* investigator, thus Americanizing his format.

Thematically, Stout concocts his plots out of tensions and conflicts arising in family situations; his killers are rarely loners or rootless individuals. The plot complications in the first Wolfe novel *Fer-de-Lance* (1934) involve a father-mother-son triangle that is responsible for five deaths. In *The Red Box* (1937) a daughter's search for her true father and her true mother initiates murder. In *Some Buried Caesar* (1939) there are father-son tensions in two separate families, and brother-sister conflicts as well. Stout hewed to the family formula in his detective and assistants as well: Wolfe's family was composed of Archie, his cook, his gardener, and other legmen.

A secondary theme that informs Stout's fiction is politics—cold-war in some instances and domestic in others. Stout became tangled up politically at times: outside his writings he supported the Vietnam War, but attacked the head of the FBI as a villain in *The Doorbell Rang* (1965). In political as well as sociological considerations, Wolfe is the romantic idealist, Goodwin the pragmatist. Together they form a total persona and compleat detective.

In technique, Stout achieved a smooth, effortless writing style larded with humor, some overt, some covert. Wolfe, admittedly a genius, thinks and *talks* like a genius. Goodwin narrates the stories with a wise-cracking bonhomie that intrigues and impels one to read on. If the solutions sometimes appear too pat, with Wolfe "discovering" the murderer in a roundup of suspects, it must be noted that deduction is not the author's forte—it is the Q. & A.s and the Goodwin-Wolfe byplay that carry the day.

One of the founders of the Mystery Writers of America, Stout was awarded the association's highest honors in 1958, that of Grand Master. Edward Arnold played Nero Wolfe in a motion picture version of *Fer-de-Lance* titled *Meet Nero Wolfe* (1936); later a television series appeared starring William Conrad as Wolfe (1981).

Bruce Cassiday. *Encyclopedia of American
Literature* (New York: Continuum, in preparation)

STRUGATSKY, ARKADI (1925–   ) and BORIS (1933–   )

The work of the brothers Strugatsky has become so well known over the last twenty-five years outside the Soviet Union that it has almost become a symbol of what the rest of the world understands by Soviet science fiction.

Arkadi Natanovich Strugatsky was born in 1925. He took part in World War II and was wounded. After 1945, he enrolled for English studies and Japanese studies in Moscow, after which he worked as foreign language assistant in a publishing house, translating books from English and Japanese into Russian. Since 1957 the brothers have collaborated on science fiction literature. The list of their work consists of some fifteen novels or long tales, two collections of shorter texts, and, very characteristic of their work as a whole, a cycle of stories under the general title *Polden', XXII Vek* (Noon: twenty-second century) with its many associations. They view the novel and the novella as the best forms in which to realize their literary aims.

It is particularly striking that the Strugatskys published no short prose pieces during the 1970s. Actually, they favor the characteristic Russian length of the *povest'*, which, while called "novella" for lack of a better word, in reality falls between the length of the novel, the novella, and the short story. It has, as a rule, "just one main focus, and in most cases [concentrates] on the presentation of the character of one literary figure, or [places] the spotlight on very particular circumstances."

In *The Time Wanderers* (1987), the Strugatskys once again turn to the theme of the incomprehensible alien, as they did in the short novel *Roadside Picnic. Wanderers* concerns scientific experiments about unusual human responses to new techniques of brain-and-body-strengthening and the artificial construction of living organisms. Why, for example, do some, *but not all,* inhabitants of a resort village react with panic when confronted by ugly, menacing, alien monsters? The novel is in the form of a series of excerpts from official documents selected by Maxim Kammerer, head of the "Department of Unusual Events of the Commission on Control." The action focuses on Toivo Glumov, one of his team, whose intuitive reactions initiate most of the action as the Strugatskys delve deeply into the mysteries of human cultural and physical evolution.

Nearly all the work of the brothers Strugatsky avoids the neat solutions, and for the most part they equally avoid repetition of the cliché situations of early science fiction. "Not only the Strugatskys' heroes but the authors themselves are tireless in their never-ending searchings. In each new book they reveal new facets of their great talent."

Dieter Wuckel. *The Illustrated History of Science Fiction* (New York: Ungar, 1989) pp. 165–70

In several ways *Hard to Be a God* falls straight into an identifiable American science fiction subgenre: the feudal planet on which agents of the advanced civilization of Earth have the job of leading the natives anonymously to progress. Just like Poul Anderson or Lloyd Biggle or a dozen others, the Strugatskys make straight for a set of connected themes—the difficulty of changing belief systems, the way in which innovations are misunderstood, the obstinate habit slaves have of understanding their masters better than their liberators, the danger that revolutions can turn out to be cyclic rather than spiral. Is this derivation, or parallel evolution? The question hardly matters, for in spite of the similarities of narrative convention the Russian novel remains wholly different both in tone and ideology from its American analogues.

Probably the main non-English feature is the implied theory of history. The protagonist Anton (or Don Rumata) in fact opposes his superiors of the Institute of Experimental History in wanting to become involved, to intervene in the processes of class warfare and the decline of feudalism; but even he believes in the inevitability of those processes and wants only to speed them up. His situation, then, is that of an Orwell, unable to reconcile what he knows about the front line with what he is told back at base, and right at the end, indeed, he expresses a philosophy close to that of *Animal Farm.* But however sympathetic he is on a human level, we never really know whether Anton is right in his compassion, or wrong in his weakness. At the end his involvement in the fighting, however antifascist it may be, is seen as a disgrace to his profession; and the stain on his fingers in the pastoral "frame" may be strawberries, but looks like blood.

The genuineness of his dilemma is the strength of *Hard to Be a God*. There is no neat, technological finish as in its American counterparts. Instead the change has to be gained by blood; but the blood must be shed by natives, not outsiders. So the end is in a way depressing, and in a way majestic, just like *Dr. Zhivago*.

As we expect from Russian novels, also, the sweep of characterization is astonishingly wide. And as we might *not* expect, the feudal scenes have a certain Gogol coarseness about them which could hardly be matched by the most inventive of Westerners. "Water won't wash away your sins," the peasants mutter cheerfully, "so why, noble don, should I wash myself?" The forests are full of slave-raiding monks, the cities of bourgeois Sturmo-viks with butcher's cleavers, the roads are crowded with fleeing "book-worms," and everyone from king to beggar joins in worship of the myste-rious Holy Mickey. Again, the rationalism of the genre seems to go down before something older and deeper. And yet, one must say, something closer to modern experience. In the center of the palace revolution one is forced to think of Ekaterinburg; and Anton's private symbol for resistance to the laws of history is the skeleton he finds (or pretends to find) of a German soldier chained to his machine gun. Echoes like these involve the Strugatskys with their science fiction in a way that is hard for us to match.

T. A. Shippey. New Statesman. January 18, 1974,
p. 81

Roadside Picnic is a "first contact" story with a difference. Aliens have visited the earth and gone away again, leaving behind them several landing areas (now called The Zones) littered with their refuse. The picnickers have gone; the packrats, wary but curious, approach the crumpled bits of cello-phane, the glittering fliptops from beercans, and try to carry them home to their holes. . . .

Some of the mystifying and dangerous debris proves useful—eternal batteries which power automobiles—but the scientists never know if they are using the devices for their proper purpose, or employing (as it were) Geiger counters as hand axes and electronic components as nose rings. They cannot figure out the principles of the artifacts, the science behind them. An international Foundation sponsors research. A black market flourishes; "stalkers" enter the forbidden Zones and, at risk of various kinds of terrible and painful death, steal bits of Visitors' litter, bring the stuff out, and sell it, sometimes to the Foundation.

The implied picture of humanity is not flattering. In the traditional first contact story, communication is achieved by courageous and dedicated spacemen, and an exchange of knowledge, or a military triumph, or a big-business deal ensues. Here the aliens were utterly indifferent to us if they noticed our existence at all; there has been no communication, there can be no understanding; we are scarcely even savages or packrats—we are just garbage. And garbage pollutes, ferments. Corruption and crime attend the exploration of the Zones; disasters seem to pursue fugitives from them. A superintendent of the Institute thinks, "My God, we won't be able to do a thing! We don't have the power to contain this blight. Not because we don't work well. . . . It's just that that's the way the world is. And that's the way man is in this world. If there had never been the Visitation, there would have been something else. Pigs always find mud."

The book built on this dark foundation, is lively, racy, and likable. It is set in North America—Canada, I assumed, I am not sure on what evidence—which may have some relevance to the economics of exploitation shown at work, but very little otherwise; the people are just ordinary people. But vivid, alive. The slimiest old stalker-profiteer has a revolting and endearing vitality. Human relations ring true. And there is courage and selflessness (though not symbolized by power, wealth, or a Star-Fleet uniform) in the protagonist, Red, a stalker, a rough and ordinary man. Humanity is not flattered, but it isn't cheapened. Most of the characters are tough people leading degrading or discouraging lives, but they are presented without sentimentality, and without cynicism; the authors' touch is tender, aware of vulnerability.

Judging from *Hard to Be a God, The Final Circle of Paradise,* and this book, the Strugatsky brothers are immensely versatile writers; the traits common to all three books are rather subtle: a quality of good humor; of compassion; of emotional honesty. The "premise" of this one, the picnic-litter idea, could have lent itself to easy sarcasm, or to wishful thinking, or to sensationalism. There is irony, yearning, and adventure in the book, but it does not stick in any one vein; it is a novel. Complex in event, imaginative in detail, ethically and intellectually sophisticated, it is, in the last analysis, the story of a particular person, an individual destiny. Red is not an interchangeable part, as the protagonists of idea-stories are. It's his book. His salvation is at stake. The landscape has changed greatly, but see, there, that's Mt. Dostoyevsky, and there's the Tolstoy Range. . . .

The end, the very end, leaves me brooding. Is it a spiritual victory, or a raising of the irony to the next power? Perhaps both; for Red, epiphany and spiritual liberation; for humanity—what? "HAPPINESS FOR EVERYBODY, FREE, AND NO ONE WILL GO AWAY UNSATISFIED."

Ursula K. Le Guin. *Science-Fiction Studies.* July
1977, pp. 157–59

The Strugatskys are among the most Westernized sources of Eastern European science fiction, and normally their work thus rings familiarly upon the ears of the American aficionado. But competitive pressure from Poland's Stanislaw Lem has apparently sent them back in search of their roots. The result in the case of *Definitely Maybe* is a story that combines the gloomy desperation of Yevgeny Zamyatin's seminal *We* with a Lemlike satirical strain expressed as slapstick humor.

The proposition is that the universe can sense attempted reversals of entropy—the grand thanatopsical running down of all energy to the state of matter at Absolute Zero. The Strugatskys postulate that the universe wants it that way. Accordingly, whenever intelligent life begins making fundamental discoveries about how the universe works—discoveries which might have antientropic practical applications—the universe frustrates them. So far, so good, but by faking liquor orders at the grocery, sending nubile "cousins" to overwrought savants whose wives are on vacation, and causing mature trees to appear overnight in barren courtyards?

Zamyatin—a contemporary of H. G. Wells and, oddly enough, a spiritual father of Ayn Rand—finds his best Western reflection in George Orwell. What was passable in the early chaotic days of the twentieth century in Russia, however, is not likely now. Nobody who lives there is going to publish a version of *1984* these days. Lem, a cantankerous and very self-aware personality, writes satires on human folly carefully out of context. So it is perhaps inevitable that the Strugatskys' self-conscious universe is made frivolous rather than impressive, and that the principal satiric scenes feature drunken comic scientists declaiming at each other like dialecticians rather than like even broadly cartooned investigators of real things.

Algis Budrys. *Washington Post Book World.*
September 3, 1978, p. E3

The Strugatskys and I both started with a tone of "happy futuristic optimism" and gradually arrived at a darker vision of things. My pessimism (which, by the way, is far from absolute) originated with my despair in the lack of perfection to be found in human nature; the Strugatskys' on the other hand was a rather social type of despair. The Strugatskys have tried very hard to turn their books into a kind of instrument of righteousness. I can even perceive a positive correlation between the very weakness of some of their titles and their stated intention of socially improving the "state of affairs" (*The Ugly Swans*, seen by them as an act of defiance and rehabilitation, attempts to present in a favorable manner the situation of the Jews in the Diaspora and is among their weakest novels). When the Strugatskys plan something, they do so within a narrower range than I am myself accustomed to, and appear to be more interested in emotional interactions than in providing a rational diagnosis; they function nearer to a pole of social criticism while I am more attracted to philosophical reflections. Their books are generally more ethnocentric than mine, and this very ethnocentricity means that it must be difficult to understand them fully without having a personal knowledge of the social conditions in which their books were conceived (*Tale of the Troika* is, despite its farcical nature, far more realistic than a lot of readers might think, not having experienced certain local realities at first hand). It is precisely this aspect of the Strugatskys' output, which I would describe as using of science fiction for sociopolitical criticism, which must explain why they enjoy such a difficult reception outside Russia, as it too often implies a necessary knowledge of the things criticized therein.

I am certainly not claiming that the above kind of criticism should not be practiced in literature, but I don't think the Strugatskys' way is the right way to do it. If you are dealing in allegories and metaphors for a critical purpose, then it becomes necessary to achieve a comprehensive form of universality, just as in a scientific theory, capable of widespread application. (*Tale of the Troika* does not hit any specific targets of American life; on the other hand, *Memoirs Found in a Bathtub* does succeed in reaching targets in the American Establishment.) I would rather not take sides as to what is good and bad, but I feel that the Strugatskys have not managed to break out of the great sociocritical tradition of Russian literature, while I on the other hand have not allowed myself to surrender to the ethnocentricities of the traditions of Polish literature. It might appear something of a paradox that the Strugatskys, who put much more faith into the belief that literature could good-naturedly influence reality than I did, have experienced greater disappointment, and have sunk into a deep form of misanthropy; a perfect example of this is their novel *Roadside Picnic*. Never in science fiction have I ever come across such an extreme example of contempt for humanity as in this book, where "visitors" treat humankind like parasites or noxious insects. I would also add that some of the Strugatskys' books (*Hard to Be a God, Roadside Picnic*) are partly polemical answers to my own books (respectively *Eden* and *Solaris*). This could easily be documented by a direct comparison of the problems evoked in the novels. I think this all simply describes the differences between the Strugatskys' attitudes and mine; however, I cannot state in a categorical manner that these differences explain why our books are received differently.

Stanislaw Lem. *Foundation.* January 1979, pp.
48–50

STURGEON, THEODORE (1918–   )

Authors had created monsters before, many whose names became synonyms for terror, but none of them had been treated with such objectivity or presented with such incredible mastery of style as Theodore Sturgeon's monster in "It."

"Styles" would have been the better term, for the author was a virtuoso, possessing an absolute pitch for the cadence of words, altering the mood and beat of his phraseology with the deliberateness of background music in a moving picture.

"The Ether Breather" was a clever spoof of the television industry, in a year when there was virtually no such industry, involving "etheric" intelligences that humorously altered television transmission. Lightly, almost frothily written, it invited examination of the style to no greater a degree than would a theatrical bedroom farce.

The same slick, lightweight prose, and superficially bubbling good humor dominated *A God in the Garden,* a fantasy in which a prehistoric "god" grants a man the handy attribute of having every word he utters come factually true, even if it were not so before he opened his mouth; "Derm Fool" is built about the plight of several people who shed their skin every twenty-four hours as the result of a poisonous snake bite; and *He Shuttles* is a variation of the old tale of a man granted three wishes which ends up with the wishes in such contradiction that the man must back up in time and perpetually repeat his actions.

Sturgeon's first four stories had entertained but made no permanent impact. They were written, apparently by a lighthearted, pleasing young man with a facile style who intended to do no more than entertain. "It," however, displayed that an extraordinary talent was at work, capable of producing serious work of a lasting nature. . . .

Admittedly, with a writer as superbly gifted as Sturgeon, who strives in *every* story to be as differently and bizarrely off-trail as he is able, whose adroitness at altering the rhythm of his writing to conform to the subject, gives him as many styles as stories (an artistic facility that has cost him the accruing audience that familiarity brings), it is necessary to poise near to presumption in relating the subject matter of *More Than Human* to the personality of its author. Yet, the Gerard hero of *More Than Human* bears strong resemblance to his creator. The feeling in the story that individuals in the Gestalt relationship may be replaced without destroying the entity fits the pattern of Sturgeon's early marital changes; just as does the final decision of Gerard to keep the unity intact, supplementing his abilities with responsibility.

All the children who make up the symbiotic power relationship in *More Than Human* have been sorely abused in their formative years, particularly the hero, who serves as the "ganglion" of the talented group. Though their lives are frequently far from comfortable, they gain courage from their mutuality. The dramatic finale arrives when, with the passing of years, the nerve center of the group learns the meaning of morality and the desirability of channeling his powers into constructive channels.

The literary production of Sturgeon ever since the appearance of *More Than Human,* with his obvious striving for achievement, lends strong credibility to the theory that Sturgeon finally has established a "Gestalt" arrangement that is emotionally harmonious without sacrificing that naive inquiry.

Sam Moskowitz. *Seekers of Tomorrow: Masters of Modern Science Fiction* (New York: Harper & Row, 1966), pp. 229–48

There seems to be a certain incredulity in the title and in the author's preface of *Sturgeon Is Alive and Well,* so perhaps it's not surprising that one of the most powerful stories in it is that of a man trying to fight his way out of a bungled suicide attempt. Appropriately, it is the last story.

There are twelve stories all told, of which three may be familiar to you. The others all appeared in men's magazines, and sometimes show it—by the time I finished the book I was a little tired of the heroine who lies down for the hero a few hours after they've met.

Of the nine probably unfamiliar tales, five, including "Suicide," are straight mainstream stories and very good ones; it's well past high time that editors allowed Sturgeon to show his potentials in this field. Another, "Crate," is a shipwreck-and-survival story to which the science-fiction trappings are nearly superfluous (and it's also very good). "Uncle Fremmis," about a man who can thump people's worn-out thinking patterns back into alignment as he would thump a misbehaving old radio, is on the borderline between fantasy and science fiction, as is the marvelous prime mover of "Brown-shoes"; only "The Patterns of Dorne" is pure-quill science fiction, as seen through the unique Sturgeon eye. "To Here and the Easel," which is about a stuck painter whose blockage takes the form of identification with a character in Ariosto's *Orlando Furioso,* is a fine, free-wheeling tour de force of what can be either pure fantasy or abnormal psychology, as you will.

There is not a dud in the lot. My favorite, by a whisker, is "It Was Nothing—Really!", but possibly my preference for it may be because it is outright comic, whereas all the other stories are either intense or grim. It is also uncharacteristic in another way: of all the stories, it is the one which least exploits the Sturgeon Eye, which sees better than any other writer's eye in our field that people become truly themselves (or fail to) primarily through their relationships with other people; the recluse, the conformist, or the man self-trapped in an obsession or an ideal image of himself, is living a pseudolife, which is, whether he knows it or not, a private hell.

Almost all the stories in this volume dramatize one facet or another of this observation, which greatly broadens Sturgeon's earlier preoccupation with the various forms of love; he has grown a great deal during his six years of silence. Of them all, the one which makes the point most openly is "The Girl Who Knew What They Meant," but it is almost omnipresent.

I see that I have made the book look blatantly moralistic, and it is; but I seriously doubt that that will bother any grown-up reader. The stories are almost all good as tales told for their own sakes, they are without exception technically adroit, and the fact that they are also About Something is the rarest and most treasurable of fictional qualities.

James Blish. The Magazine of Fantasy and Science
Fiction. December 1971, pp. 22–26

In *Venus Plus X,* Sturgeon makes subtle use of various conventions of the science-fiction genre and of social conventions, particularly sexual conventions. The well-nigh-perfect society of the Ledom, a new form of "humanity,'' is explained as a consequence of their hermaphroditic sexuality. Everybody is equipped with both male and female sexual organs. Impregnation is a mutual affair. With the lack of sexual differentiation goes, it is assumed, a corresponding lack of other dichotomies. In a series of alternating chapters devoted to the conventionalized sexual responses of a pair of contemporary American families, Sturgeon presents, as an effective satiric contrast, our alternative and divisive situation. This arrangement serves to disguise the fact that *Venus Plus X* is really a short story skillfully padded out. The utopia theme simply does not allow for very much in the way of narrative elaboration. . . .

The finished utopia is now seen, with conviction, as a scattered motif in a novel that is, in fact, concerned almost entirely with the transition to utopia. But Sturgeon has succeeded in suggesting, as a science fictional motif, a utopia when man, having attained a new plane of existence as a result of natural evolution, will inhabit a pastoral Arcadia. While other conventions in this novel are exposed as forms of imposture, this convention is allowed hopefully to stand.

David Ketterer. *New Worlds for Old: The Apocalyptic Imagination, Science Fiction, and American Literature* (New York: 1974), pp. 96–122

Sturgeon is enough of a craftsman, stylist, and rhetor for us to know that he must have something important to say. The major thing he has to say (at least in his two longer fictions of the fifties) concerns not just loneliness and love—his well-known stated themes—but rather the nature of change and newness itself. And like the best of stylists, *what* he has to say (some comment on the origins of newness) is integrated amazingly well with the considerations of style, or *how* he says it that has drawn so much attention to his career. In other words, wherever we look at Sturgeon's work—either at the protean-form changing of his craft or at his ideas, which he chooses to belittle for the sake of art—we see related images. And these images have to do with the nature of change itself, and with the origin of new images themselves.

A question that might be asked and one that Sturgeon does ask in his fiction is whether or not such a description of a continually growing universe is sufficient.

When Sturgeon puzzles over this conundrum, he aligns himself with at least a two-century-old tradition in Western thought of worrying about what causes things to become what they become. *More Than Human* and *The Cosmic Rape* treat this problem in detail and suggest unexplored possibilities. . . .

Sturgeon's protean sense of play, that is his style, can perhaps be more fully understood now after seeing that playfulness can be a very serious idea indeed—an idea that allows some balance between the longing for anthropocentrism, and perhaps even the cessation of change, on the one hand, and the realizations of an open universe on the other. Sturgeon's style, in short, allows him the flexibility not to have to dwell for long at either pole of that opposition. He writes about people and love and loneliness; but he lets us know that there are many more things in heaven and earth as well. And his style is the way both to convey and to endure this complexity. Finally, then, the style of proliferation and the content of love and concern are blended in Sturgeon's work. It is a truism in literary studies that style and content are related, but with Sturgeon the relationship goes beyond the truism and becomes intriguingly almost incestuous. His changes and his virtuosity are both his way of loving and his way of avoiding loneliness.

Obviously, Sturgeon the stylist and literary form changer is the same Sturgeon who is the lover. Form and content in the overall effects of his work are one, and his continual interest in the nature of change and newness is closely related to his interest in style. And yet, whether or not he actually does it consistently, a high ideal for Sturgeon as a writer is that he works "assiduously," not at ideas, but at writing images. The result is a richly proliferating aping of nature that conveys finally the most valuable idea *from* nature: its complexity and continually changing newness. The commonplace of at least a major portion of Sturgeon's literary life is that style and loving concern are counterparts of one another, because it is the comprehension of all the complexity, done through style, that allows the most genuine love. Perhaps in a simpler, more anthropocentric universe, love could be more single minded; and we might prefer that. But the comic tension of our complex universe arms us to love things as they are, and Sturgeon's complex literary fabrications contribute to the expression of this comic tension.

In another sense, the question raised [in this article], because it is a question raised again and again by Sturgeon himself, is what is the final end of development. What is the definition of "maturity"? Significantly, his story by that title, first published in 1947, is also a love story. But the human love, which is deeply developed in the story, can neither explain nor control the tendency toward unlimited growth and fecundity. The young genius in the story, who is also a clever and protean stylist, in spite of, or because of, his initial hormone imbalance, grows in wisdom to the point where the reader thinks that "maturity" or the final purpose in development, might be defined. But Robin's answer is finally only that *"Enough is maturity."* Growth simply goes on and on until it is "enough," and then it stops. Such an ethos necessitates both continual protean form changing to portray it, as well as comic defense to endure it.

Donald M. Hassler. *Extrapolation.* Summer 1979,
pp. 176–88

Throughout his writing career, Theodore Sturgeon has shown two faces in his fiction. First and foremost, he is a stimulator of thought. Sometimes as side effect, and sometimes with deliberate intent, he has teased and enticed and shocked his readers, herding them as best a writer can in the general direction of independent thought and open mind.

Second, Sturgeon is an artist. In the words of James Blish, he is a "conscious artist," one who loves his art and works at it. Speculative fiction has not been the most fertile milieu for the development of Sturgeon's art, however. Its low pay militates against careful writing and, moreover, this genre nurtures ideation far better than it does artistry. Had Sturgeon concentrated his talents in a different field of fiction . . . who knows?

Be that as it may, Sturgeon's work deserves a wider audience than it has gained. The major bar to its greater popularity seems to be that Sturgeon *is* a writer of speculative fiction. Speculative fiction is primarily a literature of ideas, rather than of emotion, and such a literature is simply not everybody's dish. In fact, judging from the relative popularity of this genre versus other genres (the detective story, gothic tales, romances, etc.) or mainstream fiction, speculative fiction's appeal is to a relatively small, though increasing, minority of readers. This being the case, a writer of speculative fiction, no matter how talented, has generally been doomed to an audience of comparatively modest size.

And what of Sturgeon's portrait stories and his few other nonspeculative works that would appeal to a broader audience? Unfortunately, these stories, too, have almost invariably appeared in genre magazines or in anthologies of speculative fiction, effectively rendering them invisible to readers who do not care for genre writing.

Nevertheless, for over forty years Sturgeon's fiction has amazed and delighted many readers. No better proof of the durability and worth of his writing could be found than the amount of it in print today. Many of his early books, anthologies and novels both, are still available. Moreover, despite the numerous capable writers now in the speculative field, several new collections of his stories have recently been published. Others will probably appear. There may yet be fine *new* fiction bearing the respected legend, "by Theodore Sturgeon."

Lucy Menger. *Theodore Sturgeon* (New York: Ungar, 1981), pp. 118–19

TEY, JOSEPHINE [ELIZABETH MACKINTOSH] [also known as GORDON DAVIOT] (1897–1952)

Daughter of Time is equal in graces and interest to *The Franchise Affair* and by that measure more satisfying than any of the rest of that still very welcome company which includes *Miss Pym Disposes, Brat Farrar,* and *To Love and Be Wise.*

Truth is the daughter of time and it is Detective Inspector Grant, flat on his back in a hospital bed and very bored indeed, who sets out to discover the truth about the bloody hunchback King of England, Richard III. This may sound like unpromising stuff, but I think you'll discover the search as effective an erasure of boredom as Grant did. Mild curiosity turns to livelier doubts and then to fierce conjecture and deduction. Grant is aided by the charming actress he was squiring in an earlier chronicle, by the stalwart Sergeant Williams and by a rather unconvincing young American scholar.

This is the sort of especially satisfying book we have been led to expect from Miss Tey (whose interest in history has been observable in the books and plays she has written as "Gordon Daviot") and it gains its delight principally in the warmth and discernment of her observation of people and things. It is a rather special gift and if a more enchanting book comes my way this year I shall be surprised.

James Sandoe. *New York Herald Tribune Book
Review.* February 24, 1952, p. 10

The detective story has existed now for 111 years; and at least as long ago as 1905 critics were asserting that all conceivable changes had been rung, and the form was doomed to sterile repetition. But every year brings new evidence that true creative talent can freshen any form, however hackneyed may be the run-of-the-mill products; and 1952's entry has an astonishingly different kind of detective story in Josephine Tey's *The Daughter of Time.*

There have been other attempts by mystery novelists to solve historical puzzles by detectival methods; the classic specimens are John Dickson Carr's *The Murder of Sir Edmund Godfrey* and Lillian de la Torre's *Elizabeth Is Missing* (the latter on the same theme which Miss Tey handled so beautifully in *The Franchise Affair*). But Tey goes further: she not only reconstructs the probable historical truth, she re-creates the intense dramatic excitement of the scholarly research necessary to unveil it.

Her unique formula is this: Inspector Alan Grant (of *To Love and Be Wise*), convalescent and bored by inactivity, becomes fascinated by a portrait of Richard III, which in no way jibes with the monstrous Wicked Uncle of "history." With the help of the British Museum and a young American scholar, he sets to work to find out what really happened in the late fifteenth century, what kind of man Richard actually was—and who, in fact, murdered the two young Princes in the Tower.

The result is a total bouleversement of schoolbook and encyclopedia "history," treated with compelling logic, precise scholarship, and a cumulative intensity which makes the fictional, and even the factual, crimes of 1952 seem drab affairs indeed. It is also an exceedingly healthy demonstration, with many allusions to other instances, of the fact that the history which "everybody knows" is a body of legend bearing only the faintest relationship to demonstrable fact. The relative lack of contemporary action may put a few readers off this book; but most will, I trust, like this reviewer, clasp it to their hearts as one of the permanent classics in the detective field.

Anthony Boucher. *The New York Times Book Review*. February 24, 1952,

p. 31

It has been said that Hammett took the mystery out of the vicar's garden and put it in the hands of those who knew what murder was about. Allowing the too apparent truth of where the pseudo-Hammetts dragged this body of fiction, I wonder if it cannot be said that Josephine Tey spirited it back to the vicar's garden. And there, I submit, it is neither more nor less seemly, and possibly a bit more newsworthy.

The vicar's garden may seem to imply a small world. It is small only if the vicar is small minded, and of course my allusion is meant only to imply the pleasantness of the company of the late Josephine Tey. She knew her share of vicars: it is quite as impossible to ignore the vicar in England as it is to miss teatime. And as foolish. There was practically no stratum of English society with which she was not conversant, and if any one characteristic most distinguished Miss Tey's work it was her power to evoke character, atmosphere, mores by conversation. Her people talk as though speech comes natural to them. It is good talk as well as story propelling. Indeed it makes one nostalgic for the art of conversation.

"Josephine Tey" was one of two pseudonyms of Elizabeth Mackintosh. It is not surprising to learn that under the other, "Gordon Daviot," she wrote chiefly plays, the best-remembered of which was *Richard of Bordeaux*. Her talent was not changed with a name. The dramatist's evocation runs through all of Tey. As James Sandoe says, choosing a favorite from among the eight mysteries Miss Tey wrote is like trying to select a favorite Alec Guinness film. Something particularly endearing leaps to mind out of one after another of them. I am partial to *The Daughter of Time* which is not in this trio, but having said that I am immediately tempted to say: no, rather I think *The Franchise Affair,* which is. . . .

I know that upon reading *The Daughter of Time* I promised myself that if ever I got to London I should search the National Portrait Gallery for Richard III. I did just that. For this I was indebted to the provocativeness of Josephine Tey, and I thought how she herself would have enjoyed such an encounter. What more can be asked of books than that they provoke laughter, more reading, discussion, a pilgrimage? Much of the praise of Miss Tey has been written since her death, no uncommon occurence surely, but it does make one sad that after all "truth is the daughter of time."

Dorothy Salisbury Davis. *The New Republic.*
September 20, 1954, pp. 17–18

The most important qualities any writer can bring to the production of formula fiction are a personal view—a philosophy— and a fund of special experience or interest. The "lore," often derided by theorists of the form, to which the reader of detective fiction is introduced may be one of the chief delights new versions of old formulas offer, whether it consists of campanology, or a tour of Greece, or the world of horse racing. Josephine Tey's utilization of the "lore" of the theater and the matter of history, combined with a felicitous realization of a set of nonmarried women, supplies in her works a final, necessary ingredient.

The world of Josephine Tey's mysteries is shaped by a special vision. It also obeys most of the rules which were never written down for members of its exclusive club. Proper language and dress are mandatory. Corrupt police and detectives are not allowed. There is a proper place for everyone, and the social order must not be overturned. Force will not prevail over reason. The id will not triumph over the superego. Progress and the superiority of western culture over primitive or eastern cultures are assumed. These rules are seldom questioned in the classic detective novel, and the possibility of alternative views seldom intrudes. But in the works of Tey, some innocent people do suffer, some of the guilty do escape justice, and some may not live happily ever after. There is a network of fine cracks in the restored world to which the characters are returned at the end of her novels.

She is most heterodox in her ambiguous conclusions to *Miss Pym Disposes* (where justice does not prevail), *The Man in the Queue* (where the case perfectly constructed by the typical detective method is wrong), and *The Franchise Affair* (where the beam that falls into the lives of the Sharpes in the person of Betty Kane narrowly misses them but leaves them with an altered view of the ultimate triumph of good). Grant's attitudes toward women are perfectly orthodox, but characters like Marion Sharpe, Lee Searle, and Marta Hallard provide for a different perception.

While the readability of Tey's novels derives partly from her improvisations on the standard traditions of mystery fiction, it is primarily her exploration of the sufferings of the innocent and the reflections of her personal experience and views of the theater, history, and women, which raise her works well above the level of the average detective novel. She produces a sense of quiet drama in her novels, in splendidly realized scene after scene. The characters come alive, not as deep and complex creations, or always as very clever figures in drawing room comedy, but as human figures observantly drawn, caught momentarily up in small crisis. There are many slight turns in Tey's best novels, and she has an ability to maintain pace and momentum without the more artificial aids such as a body to end each chapter. Moreover, throughout every work is the humorously ironic observation of all that occurs. There is, in fact, more variety and originality in her eight novels than in many longer shelves of her contemporaries' works, and her place in detctive fiction is secure.

Nancy Ellen Talburt. In Earl F. Bargainnier, ed.,
10 Women of Mystery (Bowling Green, Ohio:
Popular Press, 1981), pp. 74–76

TOLKIEN, J. R. R. (1892–1973)

The Lord of the Rings is spun out in a masterly way. It is plotted with an astonishing prodigality of invention that never fails in the approximate 600,000 words of the whole. Tolkien can evoke hideousness, terror, horror, and dreadful suspense, as well as beauty, laughter, nobility, and joy. The style is always graceful, often highly eloquent, occasionally lyrical with descriptive passages of much loveliness and color. Tolkien is an adept painter of scenes and evoker of images, who can orchestrate his narrative and descriptive effects with flexibility and variety, from pianissimo to forte, while keeping his themes or motifs tightly interwoven and steadily developing. Also he is a poet of much skill in the special veins appropriate to the work. He creates runic rhymes and bardic songs in a wide range of moods and meters, from comic to heroic to elegiac, in the modes of those that characterize Anglo-Saxon and Scandinavian literature.

   I think it safe to say that whatever anyone might hold to be the flaws, idiosyncrasies, or excesses of the hobbit story, this extraordinary imaginative feat in the making of an Other-world, meaningfully related to our own, is likely to be one of the most tenacious works of fiction in this present age of Middle-earth. It gives joy, excitement, a lift of spirits, and it contains the kind of wisdom and insight which, if applied to the world we inhabit, might help our sore-beset race to hang on through the present shadows of modern Mordor into yet another age.

Edmund Fuller. *Books with Men behind Them*
(New York: Random House, 1962), pp. 174–75,
196

The Lord of the Rings is a twentieth century *Beowulf.* It too "glimpses the cosmic and moves with the thought of all men concerning the fate of human life and efforts.'' But the epic tradition was no longer open to Tolkien. The epic, for all its magnitude, moves within realms of the possible and expected. We sense that even Grendel and the Dragon have for the Beowulf poet and his audience a certain inherent probability. (If this judgment is unacceptable, the reader may follow Tolkien's lead and exclude *Beowulf* from the epic canon.) For precisely the same reason, and for others as well, the chronicle was not suited to Tolkien's purposes. The chronicle depends on a substantial core of historically probable events which then enable it to absorb a host of improbabilities, both real and fictitious. However, Tolkien's pretense that *The Lord of the Rings* is based on ancient chronicles is not entirely unfounded. As the Appendices which round out Volume III show, Tolkien himself has written the chronicles of Middle Earth, and *The Lord of the Rings* is an elaborate exposition of certain events in the chronicles relating to the end of the Third Age.

The substantiality and magnitude of Tolkien's book is sufficient proof that epic and chronicle were within the reach of his technical and creative ability; but they were not suited to his purposes. Only the romance tradition, with its radical displacement of probable reality, could accommodate the many wonders of Tolkien's imagined world and so allow us to glimpse the cosmic and the thought of all men.

> George H. Thomson. *Wisconsin Studies in*
> *Contemporary Literature: Vol. 8, No. 1.* 1967, pp.
> 43–59

Although Tolkien must be believed when he denies that the book is in any sense allegorical, *The Lord of the Rings* definitely presents an ethos which is as significant for the contemporary world as it would be for any other. It is not simply an attenuated sequel to *The Hobbit*. Perhaps the issues explicit in *The Lord of the Rings* are not original, but the vehicle used to present these issues is. This vehicle is the product of a powerful imagination; it deserves critical attention and imaginative readers, Edmund Wilson to the contrary notwithstanding. Moreover, few really important issues are altogether new. Have we never as a species experienced anything similar or even analogous? Few of those writers read today outside of scholarly work, trade in topical subjects, and we may be forgiven for presuming to say that the same will be true of our contemporaries. Although each age and each writer may say something different about them, the same problems seem to arise in different forms.

> Noreen Hayes and Robert Renshaw. *Critique:*
> *Studies in Modern Fiction*, Vol. 9, No. 2, 1967,
> pp. 58–66

I take it that one of the main things Tolkien wants to say is that the real life of men is of a mythical and heroic quality. One can see the principle at work in his characterization. Much that in a realistic work would be done

by "character delineation" is here done simply by making the character an
elf, a dwarf, or a hobbit. The imagined beings have their insides on the
outside; they are visible souls. And Man as a whole, Man pitted against the
universe, have we seen him at all till we see that he is like a hero in a fairy-
tale? . . .

   The Lord of the Rings is too original and too opulent for any final
judgment on a first reading. But we know at once that it has done things to
us. We are not quite the same men. And though we must ration ourselves
in our rereadings, I have little doubt that the book will soon take its place
among the indispensables.

C. S. Lewis. In Neil D. Isaacs and Rose A.
Zimbardo, eds., *Tolkien and the Critics* (South
Bend, Indiana: University of Notre Dame Press,
1968), pp. 12–16

Tolkien sets his story neither in a dream world nor in the actual world but
in an imaginary world. An imaginary world can be so constructed as to
make credible any landscape, inhabitants, and events which its maker wishes
to introduce, and since he himself has invented its history, there can be only
one correct interpretation of events, his own. What takes place and why is,
necessarily, what he says it is. . . .

   "And so they lived happily ever after" is a conventional formula for
concluding a fairy tale. Alas, it is false and we know it, for it suggests that,
once Good has triumphed over Evil, man is translated out of his historical
existence into eternity. Tolkien is much too honest to end with such a pious
fiction. Good has triumphed over Evil so far as the Third Age of Middle-
earth is concerned, but there is no certainty that this triumph is final. . . .
Victory does not mean the restoration of the Earthly Paradise or the advent
of the New Jerusalem. In our historical existence even the best solution
involves loss as well as gain. . . .

   If there is any Quest Tale which, while primarily concerned with the
subjective life of the individual person as all such stories must be, manages
to do more justice to our experience of social-historical realities than *The
Lord of the Rings,* I should be glad to hear of it.

W. H. Auden. In Neil D. Isaacs and Rose A.
Zimbardo, eds., *Tolkien and the Critics* (South
Bend, Indiana: University of Notre Dame Press,
1968), pp. 40–61

When J. R. R. Tolkien's trilogy, *The Lord of the Rings,* appeared some
seven years ago, it accomplished on a modest scale the sort of critical controversy which *The Waste Land* and *Ulysses* had occasioned a generation
earlier. Like them, it could not be easily reviewed; it was anomalous; it
forced examination of critical principles; it demanded a judgment that necessarily became a position to be defended. Before the quarrel subsided, the
trilogy had been compared to the *Iliad, Beowulf, Le Morte d'Arthur,* and

the work of Ariosto and James Branch Cabell. Critics reexamined the genres of epic, romance, novel, defended their views of such techniques as symbolism and allegory, went beyond the techniques and found themselves talking of fate and free will, essential human nature, natural law. But when the dust had settled, the trilogy remained an anomaly heartily liked or disliked not so much on literary grounds as on fundamental religious or ideological ones. It demanded extraliterary value judgments, and it got them. . . .

The trilogy is at least partly an attempt to restore the hero to modern fiction. . . .

Now *The Lord of the Rings* is certainly not a realistic novel, not a symbolic novel, perhaps not a novel at all as we usually understand the term. It would seem closest to "myth," except that we generally think of myth as some sort of adumbration of what was once either fact, or felt to be fact, or desired to be fact. But here there is no question of fact at all. It is clearly sheer invention, and that is the sharp edge of the razor which both friendly and hostile estimators have had to get over. The trilogy poses the question of the value of invention in our time. It follows, of course, that to ask the value of invention is to assume a knowledge of, and a judgment of, "reality," and to ask how far, and in what way, and for what reason this invention departs from reality—and whether this invention is justifiable. Most of the essential criticisms of the work resolve themselves to this question.

Robert J. Reilly. In Neil D. Isaacs and Rose A. Zimbardo, eds., *Tolkien and the Critics* (South Bend, Indiana: University of Notre Dame Press, 1968), pp. 128–50

My position is this: *The Lord of the Rings* is a magnificent performance, full of charm, excitement, and affection, but it is not—at least as I am here using the term—literature. Tolkien's three volumes tell an entrancing "good and evil story" and tell it with power and wisdom; he has succeeded in constructing a self-contained world of extraordinary reality—and grace. . . . Yet I contend that making stories, even wonderful stories, is not the same thing as making literature. . . .

The Lord of the Rings is a genuine epic, with all the vast sweep and complex dovetailing necessary to sustain a large and powerful tale. Narrative art is . . . Tolkien's primary concern; it is also and quite obviously his forte. The trilogy almost never flags.

Tolkien's inventiveness carries off variation after variation; his storytelling virtuosity is wonderful, and I do not want to deny this talent its worth. All the same, there is a certain amount of what comes close to the trickery, the mechanical plot manipulation of the lesser tale-teller.

Burton Raffel. In Neil D. Isaacs and Rose A. Zimbardo, eds., *Tolkien and the Critics* (South Bend, Indiana: University of Notre Dame Press, 1968), pp. 218–46

Generously Tolkien wishes to preserve old myths and literary forms, magic swords and battle cries, for the hapless present. A kindly man, he also makes himself accessible to anyone without real knowledge of his sources and allusions. Ironically; many may safely wander through Tolkien in blissful, sleepy ignorance of all he so conscientiously is trying to transmit. It is also unfortunate for Tolkien that wonderful, but outworn, sources fail to ensure excellence. A writer's energy alone forges borrowed elements together to make his work transcendent. James Joyce had such energy. Tolkien, despite erratic originality and perpetual persistence, does not. As a result, his earnest vision seems syncretic, his structure a collage, and his feeling antiquarian. Properly he praises the mythical mode of the imagination: the ability to feel the prophetic meaning of material, including the supernatural. Yet Tolkien's exercise of the imagination has brought forth a hollow, inscribed monument, with many, many echoes. . . .

Many find Tolkien's moral vision serious and impeccable. Surely men ought to be both courageous and charitable. Surely men ought not to be haughty and selfish. Of course, the good is creative. Of course, evil is corroding, then corrupting, and finally canceling. However, Tolkien seems rigid. He admits that men, elves, and dwarfs are a collection of good, bad, and indifferent beings, but he more consistently divides the ambiguous world into two unambiguous halves: good and evil, nice and nasty. Any writer has the right to dramatize, not to argue, his morality. However, Tolkien's dialogue, plot, and symbols are terribly simplistic. Readily explicable, they also seem to conceal intellectual fuzziness and opaque axioms. Moreover, Tolkien gives way to a lust for miracles. Wizards, weapons, and thaumaturges, leaping in and out of the action at Tolkien's will, are as sophisticated as last-minute cavalry charges in the more old-fashioned Westerns. . . .

Tolkien generally ignores the rich medieval theme of the conflict between love and duty. Nor is it startling that the most delicate and tender feelings in Tolkien's writing exist between men, the members of holy fellowships and companies. Fathers and sons, or their surrogate figures, also receive attentive notice. When Tolkien does sidle up to genuine romantic love, sensuality, or sexuality, his style becomes coy and infantile, or else it burgeons into a mass of irrelevant, surface, descriptive detail. . . .

He writes, not for children, but for adults. He concentrates, not on character, but on narrative. (Tolkien never regrets his thin, neo-Aristotelian sacrifice of person to action. His own fiction, of course, suffers accordingly.)

Tolkien vows that the purpose of his Perilous Realm is to amuse, to delight, to evoke emotion. Both he and his friends vow that he despises simple allegory, in which characters and plot signify one thing other than themselves. Bluntly, *The Lord of the Rings* is not about the hydrogen bomb. Tolkien sets his readers free to find what they want and to take him as seriously as they need. Yet even genuine mythologies, which have the shape of art and the endless resonance of truth, embody themes. Tolkien's pastiche, wittingly or unwittingly, also makes explicit statements. Condemning selfishness and greed, it praises sacrifice and generosity. Ridiculing complacency, it magnifies sensitivity. Fearing evil, it exalts good. Most obviously, Tolkien, eloquently, rightly, lambasts power. Yet his attack is oddly flawed. Both more and less than a symbol, the ring itself becomes a transferable band of active ill will. Tolkien's prose takes on a rollicking glee when the home team wins, surely an exercise of power. . . .

Tolkien is bogus: bogus, prolix, and sentimental. His popularization of the past is a comic strip for grown-ups. *The Lord of the Rings* is almost as colorful and easy as *Captain Marvel*. That easiness is perhaps the source of Tolkien's appeal. His intellectual, emotional, and imaginative energies are timid and jejune. Yet to those who have puzzled over the ambiguous texts of twentieth-century literature in the classroom, he offers a digest of modern despair: *The Waste Land*, with notes, without tears. To those who pride themselves on cynicism, an adolescent failure, he spews forth a reductive, yet redemptive, allegory of the human urge to fail. For those who actually long for security, he previews a solid moral and emotional structure. His authoritarianism is small price for the comfort of the commands: Love thy Aragorn; fear the Nâzgul. . . .

Oddly, though Tolkien, Hermann Hesse, and William Golding are three very different writers, they have two suggestive common denominators. First, they caused student literary fads, which the adult world then acclaimed. Next, they offered the seductive charm of moral didacticism, cloaked in remote and exotic settings.

Tolkien ought to be what he wants to be. His audience is free to be what it wants to be. Yet readers might cultivate some critical awareness. If they do, they might find, not only midnight rides and unfurled banners, but weak prose and pernicious thought. They might begin by asking just one simple question. What does it mean that Tolkien so blandly, so complacently, so consistently, uses the symbol of light and of white to signify the good and the symbol of dark and of black to signify evil? He is, of course, following an enormously complex literary tradition. No arbitrary decision, but the physical heritage of Northern and Western Europe has shaped that tradition. Like all alchemists, he appeals to us. His very ambition is attractive. Like all alchemists, he has his deceptive triumphs. But history has made alchemy remote. Science has fulfilled its more marvelous predictions. One might wish that history will make much of Tolkien remote. We need genuine myth and rich fantasy to minister to the profound needs he now is thought to gratify.

Catharine R. Stimpson. *J. R. R. Tolkien* (New
York: Columbia University Press, 1969), pp. 9–45

The Lord of the Rings has most often, I would say, been compared to Spenser. That is, to Spenser's masterpiece, a very long poem called *The Faerie Queene*, which is both a poetic romance and an allegory. But the trilogy is not in any way either a satire or an allegory, but a romance pure and simple. Equating Tolkien with the great masters of allegorical romance is an easy and logical notion because there are certain points of similarity in depth and richness and complexity of style and background detail; but these are superficial. Tolkien is merely telling a story, and it has no overtones of symbolic meaning at all. *The Lord of the Rings* is, quite simply, a fantasy novel.

How well, then, does his own trilogy match Tolkien's stated requirements for a successful fantasy? For one thing, keeping in mind his thesis that a fantasy "must be presented as *true*," we can see how he has lived up to this criterion. *The Lord of the Rings* is presented as a true history, and the author has buttressed his contention by surrounding the tale with an elaborate machinery of appendices, containing factual data on his world not given in the narrative. His Middle-earth languages are equipped with copious vocabularies and alphabets. He has worked out a chronology of the previous ages which gives a historical summary, complete with dates, for many centuries. Lists of kings and genealogies support the major characters of his story and supply background history. This, of course, is completely in line with his belief that the subcreator of a Secondary World must make his fabricated cosmos complete, realistic, and self-consistent in every detail. What about his final contention—that the vital quality he calls "joy" should be present through sudden glimpses of underlying truth? It is a little difficult to make out quite what he means, but I have arrived at a satisfactory interpretation—at least for myself. By underlying realities he probably alludes to the eternal verities of human nature. While the trilogy is, on the surface at least, an entertaining narrative of fantastic adventure, the moral element is plainly obvious. The jealous, the greedy, the proud, the power-hungry, all receive commensurate punishments. The humble, the unselfish, the hardworking, the honest, and the noble are rewarded beyond their own estimates of their due.

The trilogy is most obviously cognate with epic poetry. It is truly Homeric in size, in concept, in the sweep and grandeur of the narrative, in the fact that the heroes are painted larger than life. Thus it would be no misnomer to class *The Lord of the Rings* as "epic fantasy." But this definition is not quite sufficient. Tolkien draws from other bodies of literature as well as the tradition of the classical epic. He has absorbed much of the tradition and form of the Norse saga, much from Germanic folktale and legend, much from medieval romance, Grail quest, and heroic tale, and to a certain extent from other fantasy novelists.

Lin Carter. *Tolkien: A Look behind "The Lord of the Rings"* (New York: Ballantine, 1969), pp. 80–95

J. R. R. Tolkien seems to want to make his art serve the cause of religion. Forty years after the fin de siecle decadents in England, the tide had turned sufficiently for a group of new Christian humanists to emerge. Among scholars, the poets Eliot and Auden are possibly the best known of this group, though the reputations of C. S. Lewis, Charles Williams, and J. R. R. Tolkien are rising. Not until the latter part of the 1950s and the early 1960s did Tolkien's reputation as a creative writer (as distinct from that as an Anglo-Saxon scholar) become established. Yet it was in the latter part of the 1930s that his imaginative world and aesthetic theories took shape, just when the excitement of the new movement was running strongest. Tolkien's ideas are generally unfamiliar to scholars, but for the generation that has grown up on Eliot and Auden, a plunge into Tolkien is akin to the happy shock of recognition that would come if one found a new manuscript by a much-loved and familiar author—the same ideas, but seen from a wholly fresh perspective.

Tolkien tells us that even as a child he had an almost compulsive desire to recreate Norse and Greek myths in his own words. Later his serious scholarly work convinced him that many of these legends were sketchy, had gaps, and (as in the poem of *Beowulf*) were weak in details though strong in structure. So Tolkien set out to improve on mythology by making it "credible." His name for his imaginary world of Middle-earth is, as he explained, "only an old-fashioned word for world," it being the *middangeard* of Anglo-Saxon myths. Tolkien has populated Middle-earth with men, hobbits, elves, trolls, Orcs, dwarves, Ents, and spirits, drawn from European folklore, medieval literature, and his own imagination.

In Tolkien's imaginative world, all nature is animate, helping or hindering human (or nonhuman) will for good or ill. Eagles and birds can talk, forests crowd travelers with fell intent. Only where evil dwells—in the dragon's mountain or in Mordor—is nature sterile, for evil is in its very being noncreative. Utilizing in *The Hobbit* a variation of the fisher-king legend, Tolkien describes the land of the King Under the Mountain as having a curse upon it—the dragon. Or to be more specific, the curse on the land is actually the "dragon sickness," the immoderate greed for material property. As in T. S. Eliot's *Waste Land*, so here in *The Hobbit* we have a story about the lifting of the curse from a stricken land and the new life which enters in.

One might be tempted to say that because Tolkien's use of symbols is so complex he, like Joyce, is a Symbolist, his aim being to produce an epiphany through concentrated meditation on symbols which do not symbolize any exact thing, but rather are meant to produce such moments of insight. There is a similarity: the question of just precisely what Tolkien's ring symbolizes, for example, will always elude simple definition; indeed, to ask such a question at all betrays a certain naïveté.

But Tolkien's Introduction, although warning us against allegory, also puts us on our guard against seeing *The Lord of the Rings* as a Symbolist work. His emphasis upon "history, true or feigned," together with his insistence in *Beowulf* that myth must be incarnated in history, points toward an emphasis upon the temporal process which is alien to the thought of Symbolism.

Tolkien's affirmation of primary reality came at a crucial moment in the history of British culture. The industrial cities of Birmingham and Sheffield, which in the nineteenth century turned not only the face but also the soul of England black, gave way in the twentieth to a World War which completed the desacralization and fragmentation of natural and spiritual reality. The way of aestheticists and Symbolists was to flee to the subjectivity of a vision of beauty alien to this cultural wasteland. Unlike them, however, Tolkien, in company with the Christian humanists of his generation, chose to affirm the images of this world, seeing the rich thicket of nature as a potent reality in itself. As a Christian he could do little else, for the Incarnation had redeemed the temporal process, bestowing value on even the humblest objects. But although the original curse on the wasteland has already been lifted, the healing of the schism between fact and fantasy has not yet been wholly worked out in time. The quest, the web of story, will go on until all histories, true and feigned, will exist as an eternally complete whole.

Gerald Monsman. South Atlantic Quarterly. Spring
1970, pp. 264–78

By presenting the situation mainly from the limited perspective of the characters in the story Tolkien makes the forces of evil appear at first glance equal to or even greater than the forces of good; but this is only from a limited perspective. The world of Tolkien is not a dualistic world; it is the Biblical world of the good creation. Evil is presented as a corruption of the good. Even Sauron, the preeminently evil figure in the novel, we are told, had once been good.

Tolkien also reveals, and this, too, pervades the book, that the proper response to the good creation is to enjoy it. From the hobbits and their beer to the wonders of Lothlorien, this is a major factor in the novel's charm.

Tolkien's tale may be read as a parable of the need to adapt means to ends, and of the difficulty of abiding by this when the end seems of very great importance. The end must justify the means if the means are to be justified at all; but one is aware in Tolkien's story that there is a meaning and a plot transcending and including the struggle in which we may be immediately involved, and that action is not defensible which contradicts the overarching purpose in which our own historical setting is but an episode. We are aware of such a purpose, but it remains a mystery: we do not know explicitly the future or the ultimate goal; we know the larger purpose primarily as a certain moral quality which is authoritative and regulative.

The Christian intellectual tradition, which is reflected to so considerable a degree in Tolkien's novel, is a tradition of remarkable richness and power. To think of Western culture without its influence is simply to imagine some basically different culture. The contradictions and malaise of our contemporary age must be, in part at least, due to a loss of the integrating function it performed when it was the expression of a commonly shared faith. It follows that a better understanding of this tradition might be expected to shed significant light on our present cultural situation. *The Lord of the Rings* may help us to such an understanding; but it is not a treatise, and readers of it ought not to fret themselves unduly with meanings and interpretations. Although the novel is well worth our analysis and serious criticism, its excellence as literature is seen in the fact that it speaks for itself without burdening us with explanations or the need of them. Many find the Ring books to be very effective escape literature, and there is nothing wrong with reading them for that purpose. But the reader may find himself escaping, not from reality to illusion, but from the illusions generated by our current confusions to the realities revealed by Tolkien's art.

Willis B. Glover. Criticism. Winter 1971,
pp. 39–54

That a three-volume novel by a distinguished medievalist should be as popular as J. R. R. Tolkien's *The Lord of the Rings* may be a little odd. That it should be popular with people who paint "Frodo lives!" on walls and wear pins that say "Go! Go! Gandalf" in elf script; with people who have never seen an English pub or walked more than two miles consecutively; with artists of the stature of W. H. Auden; and with respected critics who compare it to Malory, Spenser, and Ariosto; and that it should achieve this with six appendixes and no sex is an event Aristotle would banish from any plot as an "improbable possible." That the trilogy should be a novel at least in being "a piece of prose fiction of a certain length" and yet show itself so different in kind from the literature on which our current tools for understanding and evaluating aesthetic experiences work best, makes the riddle one of real concern to the critic of fiction.

What Tolkien has done is to attempt a story concerned with language in the communal sense, yet which is as different from epic as it is from the novel. *The Lord of the Rings* enacts the nature of language. Tolkien has created an entire world in its spatial and chronological dimensions, peopling it with languages which have, in a necessarily stylized and simplified version, all the basic features of language, from writing systems and sound changes, through diction and syntax to style. By playing them against one another, he has created a "model" (in the scientific sense of the term) for the relationship of language to action, to values and to civilization.

Elizabeth D. Kirk. Novel. Fall 1971, pp. 5–18

Defending the integrity of the literature he called "fairy-stories" against proponents of those varieties of literature that seek to represent "real life," J. R. R. Tolkien wrote, "Why should a man be scorned if, finding himself in prison, he tries to get out and go home? Or if, when he cannot do so, he thinks and talks about topics other than jailers and prison-walls?'' Had he wished to write of "jailers and prison-walls," Tolkien could have found abundant material in his own life to provide plots and incidents for novels in the mold of *Oliver Twist,* or, in a more modern vein, for ironic little stories of men who lead lives of quiet desperation. Orphaned at an early age, dependent for his education on scholarships and the support of a benefactor, kept for several years from association with the woman he loved by the wishes of that same benefactor, and graduated from university just in time to participate in the Battle of the Somme, one of the bloodiest tragedies of World War I, Tolkien had opportunities early and often to observe and to experience the depressing, frustrating, and limiting possibilities of modern life as well as the joyous, fulfilling, and liberating. But Tolkien's imaginative faculty was not inclined toward the careful recreation of the world around him or the slow building up of detail that creates recognizably real characters or settings. Rather, his was a mythopoetic imagination, one that created a mythology as it worked, and Middle-earth, the subject matter and inspiration of the mythology he created, became the home to which the prisoner longed to return.

As is true of mythologies of much greater antiquity, Tolkien's tales of Middle-earth take place years and miles away from the modern reader; but as is true also of other mythologies, the tales are psychologically as close to us as we can wish or as we can bear. His tales of elves, dwarves, hobbits, and men, are not about our world in the sense that they are about Europe or Africa, or shortages of natural resources, or the threat of nuclear disaster; they are about us in the sense that they are about good and evil, sorrow, pain, injustice, and sometimes heroism, and even joy. They are, that is, not so much about what is real as they are about what is true. The difference between the two is a difference that Tolkien's life, from his earliest years, taught him to appreciate. . . .

Finally, Tolkien felt strongly the importance of the human past in defining and permitting that most human and yet most divine activity, artistic creation. Every story, every poem, every language, and etymolology was for him demonstration of humanity's origins in a greater creator. "Fantasy remains a human right," he wrote in "On Fairy-Stories," "we make in our measure and in our derivative mode, because we are made: and not only made, but made in the image and likeness of a Maker."

Katharyn W. Crabbe. *J. R. R. Tolkien* (New York: Continuum, 1988), pp. 1–2, 214

TWAIN, MARK [SAMUEL L. CLEMENS] (1835–1910)

Mark Twain's ironic little novel, *Pudd'nhead Wilson,* is laid on the banks of the Mississippi in the first half of the 1800s. It concerns itself with, among other things, the use of fingerprinting to solve the mystery of a murder. But *Pudd'nhead Wilson* is not a mystery novel. The reader knows from the beginning who committed the murder and has more than an inkling of how it will be solved.

Although introduced early, it is not until near the end of the book that Wilson becomes a major figure in the tale. The novel is rather the story of another young man's mistaken identity—a young man who thinks he is white but is in reality colored; who is heir to wealth without knowing his claim is false; who lives as a free man, but is legally a slave; and who, when he learns the true facts about himself, comes to ruin not through the temporarily shattering knowledge of his physical status, but because of weaknesses common to white or colored, slave or free.

Puddn'head Wilson is the man, who, in the end, sets things to rights. But for whom? Seemingly for the spectators only, not for the principals involved, for by that time to them right is wrong, wrong is right, and happiness has gone by the board. The slave system has taken its toll of all three concerned—mother, mammy, ward, and child—for the mother and mammy, Roxana, matriarch and slave, are one. Roxy is a puppet whose at first successful deceits cause her to think herself a free agent. She is undone at the climax by the former laughing stock of the town, Pudd'nhead Wilson. . . .

In this book the basic theme is slavery, seriously treated, and its main thread concerns the absurdity of man-made differentials, whether of caste or "race." The word *race* might properly be placed in quotes for both of Mark Twain's central Negroes are largely white in blood and physiognomy, slaves only by circumstance, and each only "by a fiction of law and custom, a Negro." The white boy who is mistakenly raised as a slave in the end finds himself "rich and free, but in a most embarrassing situation. He could neither read nor write, and his speech was the basest dialect of Negro quarter. His gait, his attitudes, his gestures, his bearing, his laugh—all were vulgar and uncouth; his manners were the manners of a slave. Money and fine clothes could not mend these defeats or cover them up, they only made them the more glaring and pathetic."

On the other hand, the young dandy who thought his name was Thomas à Becket, studied at Yale. He then came home to Dawson's Landing bedecked in Eastern finery to lord it over black and white alike. . . . It took a foreigner with no regard for frontier aristocracy of Old Virginia lineage to kick Thomas à Becket right square in his sit-downer at a public meeting. In the ensuing free-for-all that breaks out, the hall is set afire. . . . The members of the nearby fire department donned their uniforms to drench the hall with enough water to "annihilate forty times as much fire as there was there; for a village fire company does not often get a chance to show off." Twain wryly concludes, "Citizens of that village . . . did not insure against fire; they insured against the fire-company."

Against fire and water in the slave states there was insurance, but none against the devious dangers of slavery itself. Not even a fine old gentleman like Judge Driscoll "of the best blood of the Old Dominion" could find insurance against the self-protective schemes of his brother's bond servant, Roxy, who did not like being a slave, but was willing to be one for her son's sake. Roxy was also willing to commit a grievous sin for her son's sake, palliating her conscience a little by saying, "white folks has done it." With "an unfair show in the battle of life," as Twain puts it, Roxy, as an "heir of two centuries of unatoned insult and outrage," is yet not of an evil nature. Her crimes grow out of the greater crimes of the slave system. . . . .

Curiously enough, as modern as *Pudd'nhead Wilson* is, its format is that of an old-fashioned melodrama, as if its structure were borrowed from the plays performed on the riverboat theaters of that period. Perhaps deliberately, Twain selected this popular formula in which to tell a very serious story. Moving from climax to climax, every chapter ends with a teaser that makes the reader wonder what is coming next while, as in Greek tragedy, the fates keep closing in on the central protagonists. And here the fates have no regard whatsoever for color lines. It is this treatment of race that makes *Pudd'nhead Wilson* as contemporary as Little Rock, and Mark Twain as modern as Faulkner, although Twain died when Faulkner was in knee pants.

Langston Hughes. Introduction to Pudd'nhead
Wilson, by Mark Twain (New York: Bantam
Books, 1981), pp. vii–xiii

A Connecticut Yankee in King Arthur's Court has been called Mark Twain's finest possibility, combining satire, the tall tale, humor, democracy, religion, and the damned human race. Loosely picaresque and brightly anecdotal, it was an attempt, Clemens explained, "to imagine and after a fashion set forth, the hard condition of life for the laboring and defenseless poor in bygone times in England, and incidentally contrast those conditions with those under which civil and ecclesiastical pets of privilege and high fortune lived in those times." But what finally emerges from beneath the contrast between Yankee ingenuity and medieval superstition is the portrait of an American. He is unlearned; with "neither the refinement nor the weakness of a college education," but quick-witted and completely, even devastatingly successful. Consciously created or not, it is the image of Samuel Clemens and of many of his friends. And it explains something of the nature of the literature which he and his fellows produced.

The Tragedy of Pudd'nhead Wilson is filled with familiar failings, false starts, and rambling excursions. The title makes us wonder why it is Pudd'nhead's tragedy. But it contains excellencies also, of a kind which Sherwood Anderson was to use in writing about village people, and which have earned for it a reputation as "the most extraordinary book in American literature," filled with intolerable insights into evil. Even distorted by drollery, it penetrates toward recognition of social ills not unlike those which William Faulkner was later to probe. Beneath the burlesque which peoples the sleeply village of Dawson's Landing with representatives of decayed gentry bearing such exuberant names as Percy Northumberland Driscoll and Cecil Burleigh Essex runs a vein of satire which allows recognition of these people as ancestors of the Sartorises and Compsons.

Its failure is literary, the failure of words, not of ideas. Mark Twain is telling a story according to a familiar pattern, incident strung on incident as if they might go on forever. Humor, pathos, sentiment, anger, and burlesque, rub shoulders with intimacy bred of long acquaintance. *Pudd'nhead Wilson* is serious in intention, for all its belly-laughs and tears. It faces up to problems made by the venality of man. Seldom is it plainly evident that Mark Twain's eyes rarely twinkle when he laughs. A social conscience here is plainly showing. Scorn looks boldly out from behind the burlesque. But the words do not come true, as Huck's words did or as Clemens's did when he remembered apprentice days on the river. He is saying what he wants to say, but in accents which ring false because they speak now as people expected him to speak.

Lewis Leary. Mark Twain (Minneapolis,
Minnesota: University of Minnesota Press, 1960),
pp. 32–36

The medieval values that Hank Morgan confronts in *A Connecticut Yankee in King Arthur's Court* were not confined to Arthurian Britain. For one thing, there was also present-day England, for whatever remnants had remained of an Anglophilia once cherished by Twain were now totally demolished by Matthew Arnold who, after a visit to America, had declared, in "Civilization in the United States," that the idea of "distinction" in this country could not survive the "glorification of 'the average man' and the addiction to the 'funny man.'" In his outraged patriotism and outraged *amour propre,* Twain, a "funny man," tended to merge the England of Arthur with that of Victoria. . . .

If the anachronistically slave-holding society of Britain is an image of the Old South and if Hank's military masterpiece, the Battle of the Sand Belt, in which, after the explosion of Hank's mines, the air is filled with the ghastly drizzle of the atomized remains of men and horses, is an image of the Civil War (the first "modern" war), then Hank's programs for Britain is a fable of the Reconstruction of the South and the pacification of that undeveloped country. Furthermore, in being a fable of that colonial project, this is also a fable of colonialism in general and of the great modern period of colonialism in particular, which was now well under way from the Ganges to the Congo; thus to Hank, Britain is simply something to develop in economic terms—with, of course, as a paternalistic benefit to the natives, the by-product of a rational modern society. In this context *A Connecticut Yankee* is to be set alongside Conrad's *Nostromo* and *The Heart of Darkness* and the works of Kipling.

There is, however, another and more inclusive context in which to regard it. More and more in our century we have seen a special variety of millennialism—the variety in which bliss (in the form of a "rational" society) is distributed at gunpoint or inculcated in concentration camps. So in this context, *A Connecticut Yankee* is to be set alongside historical accounts of Fascist Italy, Nazi Germany, or Communist Russia. This novel was prophetic.

The body of the work has to do with Hank's operations from the moment when he decides that he is "just another Robinson Crusoe," and has to "invent, contrive, create, reorganize things." The narrative proceeds in a two-edged fashion: there is the satirical exposure of the inhuman and stultifying life in Arthur's kingdom, with the mission for modernization and humanitarian improvement, but there is also the development of Hank's scheme for his economic and political aggrandizement, his way of becoming the "Boss." By and large, it seems that the humanitarian and selfish interests coincide; what is good for Hank is good for the people of Britain, and this would imply a simple fable of progress, with the reading that technology in a laissez faire order automatically confers the good life on all. There is no hint, certainly, that Twain is writing in a period of titanic struggle between labor and capital, a struggle consequent upon the advent of big technology. In the new order in Britain there are no labor problems. The boys whom Hank had secretly recruited and instructed in technology are completely loyal to him, and as his Janissaries, will fight for him in the great Armageddon to come, enraptured by their own godlike proficiency; if they represent "labor" they have no parallel in the nineteenth-century America of the Homestead strike and the Haymarket riot. . . .

In the fable there are, indeed, many lags and incoherences that, upon the slightest analysis, are visible. . . . One is fundamental. If the original idea of the book had been a celebration of nineteenth-century technology, something happened to that happy inspiration, and in the end progress appears a delusion, Hank's modernization winds up in a bloody farce, and Hank himself can think of the people whom he had undertaken to liberate as merely "human muck." In the end Hank hates life, and all he can do is to look nostalgically back on the beauty of premodern Britain as what he calls his "Lost World," and on the love of his lost wife Sandy, just as Twain could look back on his vision of boyhood Hannibal. . . .

When the book was finished, Twain wrote to Howells: "Well, my book is written—let it go. But if it were only to write over again there wouldn't be so many things left out. They burn in me. . . . They would require a library—and a pen warmed up in hell." But the pen had already been warmed enough to declare that dark forces were afoot in history and in the human soul to betray all aspiration, and with this we find, at the visceral level of fable, the same view of history later to be learnedly, abstractly, and pitilessly proclaimed by Henry Adams and dramatized in (to date) two world wars.

Robert Penn Warren. *The Southern Review.*
Summer 1972, pp. 459–92

Although he was raised in what has been called the country's "Bible Belt," Twain found church services, especially the praying, to be downright comical. Why? Because, in an age of steam engines and dynamos and the telegraph and so on, praying seemed so *impractical*, I think.

Twain himself had had tremendously satisfying adventures with the most glamorous conglomerations of machinery imaginable, which were riverboats. So praying, as opposed to inventing and engineering, was bound to seem to him, and to so many like him, as the silliest possible way to get things done.

He was what would later be called "a technocrat."

He wished to sweep away superstitions and romantic illusions with laughter—because they were so *useless*. Connecticut Yankees should run the world, because they kept up with scientific discoveries and they had no illusions. They knew what would *really* work. They knew what was *really* going on.

I have heard it said that the ending of *A Connecticut Yankee* was a prophecy of the World Wars Twain did not live to see. Superstitious knights fight technocrats, and both armies become parts of a pestilential mulch of corpses. This seems to me a better description of the war between the Confederacy and the Union than of the World Wars, which pitted technocrats against technocrats, and in which no one could have any illusions any more.

It is my belief that Twain was less interested in prophecy than ending his tale some way—almost any *which* way. So he did what Herman Melville did in *Moby-Dick*. He killed everybody, except for one survivor to tell the tale.

It is such a clumsy ending, in my opinion, that it destroys the balance of the author himself. It causes him to suggest some things about himself which he would have preferred not to see the light of day.

For instance: Merlin, the personification of contemptible superstitions, is present at the end. All through the book, Merlin has been a transparent fraud. But then he casts a spell which is more astonishing than anything the Connecticut Yankee has done. Merlin puts the Yankee to sleep for thirteen centuries. He can work miracles after all.

Not only that, but Merlin comes on his wicked errand *disguised as a woman*.

Imagine that.

Is it possible that Twain, the clear-eyed technocrat, could not help believing in magic after all? I think maybe so.

Is it possible that he suspected that women and their praying, from whom Huck Finn fled in such a frenzy, had mysterious powers superior to those of scientists and engineers? I think maybe so.

I do not mean to raise Freudian questions about Twain. I am not particularly respectful of the sorts of answers they can bring.

Sigmund Freud himself *did* write about Twain, incidentally—after Twain was dead. He set a refreshingly un-Freudian example by saying little about

Twain's relationships to women, or any of that. He did what we should do,
too, which was to celebrate how cunningly Twain's best jokes were made.

Kurt Vonnegut, Jr. Opening Remarks, in *The
Unabridged Mark Twain* (n.p.: Running Press,
1976), pp. xi–xv

Mark Twain took up the subject of crime in his novels *Tom Sawyer* (1876)
and *Huckleberry Finn* (1884). *Tom Sawyer, Detective,* a novella published
in 1896, is possibly the first detective story written for children. In it Tom
appears for the defense in a murder case against Tom's Uncle Silas, proves
his innocence, exposes the real murderer, and at the same time unmasks
false witnesses and traces two stolen diamonds. Tom and his devoted help-
meet, Huck Finn, earn much praise, although Tom modestly explains to a
surprised judge and public in court that all he has done is to look at the facts
and draw his own conclusions. It is merely a piece of detective work in
which he has carefully watched the unconscious gestures the murderer makes
at the trial, thus revealing his true identity, rather than the one he has assumed.

Twain later turned to the subject of fingerprints at a time when the use
of such evidence was not yet officially accepted. Only in 1901 did Scotland
Yard start a special department of dactyloscopy and abandon the Bertillon
system used worldwide at that time to identify criminals by complicated
body measurements. By then Twain had used the subject of fingerprints
twice, in *Life on the Mississippi* (1883) and *The Tragedy of Pudd'nhead
Wilson* (1894). In 1892 Sir Francis Galton had published *Finger Prints,* the
first book on the subject. Twain got a copy from his London publisher. He
later said that Galton changed the whole plot of *Pudd'nhead Wilson,* in
which he had planned to use footprints as a means of nailing the murderer.
Twain's story goes as follows:

A lawyer, David "Pudd'nhead" Wilson, settles in an idyllic small town
on the Mississippi, collecting fingerprints as a hobby. A baby who is only
one-thirty-second black is maliciously substituted for a white baby, the only
son in the town's best family. When eventually the ne'er-do-well (surrogate)
heir kills his uncle and guardian, an innocent suspect is tried, with Wilson
appearing for the defense. He not only unmasks the real murderer, but also
helps the true heir to obtain his birthright—all through the proof in the fingerprint file he has kept since coming to the town. The novel's conclusion
is laden with typical Twain irony. The true heir, brought up servile and
cringing, is illiterate as well, and unable to take his proper place in society;
he sinks back into slavery with the people he knows best. Besides, the estate
has been so badly managed it is in debt to creditors. The governor of the
state grants the murderer a pardon, and sells him as a slave to help pay off
the estate's debts—proving that a working slave is worth more to society
than an imprisoned murderer! Even though critical undertones pervade Twain's

writing, he is first and foremost a humorist, and his ''crime'' stories often show signs of the near-grotesque.

Waltraud Woeller and Bruce Cassiday. *The Literature of Crime and Detection* (New York: Ungar, 1988), pp. 94–95

VAN DINE, S. S. [WILLARD HUNTINGTON WRIGHT] (1888–1939)

Mr. Van Dine's first attempt at detective fiction introduces a new detective, Mr. Philo Vance, and we are promised other adventures of this crime debutante, who is introduced on the jacket in these fulsome words: "Philo Vance, we believe, will inevitably find a literary niche alongside of that triumvirate of immortal sleuths, Monsieur Le Coq, Auguste Dupin, and Sherlock Holmes."

We can only say that if Philo ever finds such a niche it will prove most uncomfortably large for him. Also he would be rather embarrassed, for we are certain that Messrs. Le Coq, Dupin, and Holmes, could never tolerate for a moment such a complacent ass.

Carty Ranck. *New York Herald Tribune Books.*
November 21, 1926, p. 16

Alvin Benson is found sitting in a wicker chair in his living room, a book still in his hand, his legs crossed, and his body comfortably relaxed in a life-like position. He is dead. A bullet from an Army model Colt .45 automatic pistol, held some six feet away when the trigger was pulled, has passed completely through his head. That his position should have been so slightly disturbed by the impact of such a bullet at such a range is preposterous, but the phenomenon hasn't anything to do with the plot, so don't, as I did, waste time trying to figure it out. The murderer's identity becomes obvious quite early in the story. The authorities, no matter how stupid the author chose to make them, would have cleared up the mystery promptly if they had been allowed to follow the most rudimentary police routine. But then what would there have been for the gifted Vance to do?

This Philo Vance is in the Sherlock Holmes tradition and his conversational manner is that of a high-school girl who has been studying the foreign words and phrases in the back of her dictionary. He is a bore when he discusses art and philosophy, but when he switches to criminal psychology he is delightful. There is a theory that anyone who talks enough on any subject must, if only by chance, finally say something not altogether incorrect. Vance disproves this theory: he manages always, and usually ridiculously, to be wrong. His exposition of the technique employed by a gentleman shooting another gentleman who sits six feet in front of him deserves a place in a *How to be a detective by mail* course.

To supply this genius with a field for his operations the author has to treat his policemen abominably. He doesn't let them ask any questions that aren't wholly irrelevant. They can't make inquiries of anyone who might know anything. They aren't permitted to take any steps toward learning whether the dead man was robbed. Their fingerprint experts are excluded from the scene of the crime. When information concerning a mysterious box of jewelry accidentally bobs up, everybody resolutely ignores it, since it would have led to a solution before the three-hundredth page.

Mr. Van Dine doesn't deprive his officials of every liberty, however: he generously lets them compete with Vance now and then in the expression of idiocies. Thus Heath, a police detective-sergeant, says that any pistol of less than .44 calibre is too small to stop a man, and the district attorney, Markham, displays an amazed disinclination to admit that a confession could actually be false. This Markham is an outrageously naïve person: the most credible statement in the tale is to the effect that Markham served only one term in this office. The book is written in the little-did-he-realize style.

Dashiell Hammett. *Saturday Review.* January 15, 1927, n.p.

The amazing success of S. S. Van Dine about four years ago has given new life to detective fiction.

The singular thing about this success is that it was achieved in spite of the author, who created a disagreeable pedant for his detective and treated him as if he were the most admirable and amiable of men. Crotchety detectives are no novelty; Cuff, in *The Moonstone,* anticipates them as he does nearly everything interesting. Van Dine's Philo Vance, with his implausible English accent, his unparalleled erudition, and his swank, would be enough to turn anyone away from the stories after five pages were it not that the stories, by that time, are more interesting than the detective.

Van Dine is in the good tradition of the detective novel because his interest is in deduction. In his early stories his detective insisted that every murder was, in a sense, a work of art, and the murderer, like the artist, left his imprint on his handiwork. In the latest book he returns to more ordinary reasoning, suggesting that the murderer commits his crimes in the way he does because of his character—in this case, because he is an adept of interstellar mathematics and holds finite life in contempt. But what he now omits is the entirely human interest of motive. The first two cases were fairly motivated; but as Van Dine grew more and more anxious to conceal his criminal, he gradually deprived him of any plausible motive, so that in the latest version we have a man putting seven or eight of his nearest friends to death in order to cast suspicion on someone else. It is true that he is professionally jealous of this last person.

What constitutes fair dealing with the reader in this type of story has never been well defined. It is, however, considered desirable that the actual criminal should be more or less in plain sight while the detection is going on—the fact that in actual murders he usually manages not to be, is put aside—and nothing is more irritating, or bad form, than the introduction of an unknown at the end to shoulder the blame. The excellent *Bellamy Trial* by Frances Noyes Hart gave each character exactly its due because each appeared before the jury, the criminal included, and each received just the importance the trial would give him. It would also be fair dealing to make the motive adequate. To complicate mysteries, authors have assigned adequate motive to three or four characters, and it is almost obligatory that several of them should have opportunity as well. Van Dine has built up motive for each of a series of characters, killing them off just as the motivation becomes convincing, and then has had nothing left for his murderer.

The general intelligence, the superior style, the careful construction of the Philo Vance series have, without doubt, brought thousands of readers to a formerly despised type of fiction, and they, in turn, will bring more intelligence and care to the detective story itself. I share Mr. Alexander Woollcott's weakness, which he confessed recently in a violent and reasonable attack on Van Dine: I would rather read a poor detective story than none at all. But I hope that the followers of Van Dine—and he himself before he makes good his threat to stop writing—will profit by his excellences and avoid his mistakes. For the detective story ought to keep its purity, approaching the serenity and the perfection of the mathematical formula; and it ought to be written in complete and honest respect for the reader. With that respect, pedantry is always at war.

Gilbert Seldes. *The New Republic*. June 19, 1929,
pp. 125–26

The new Philo Vance story suffers by comparison with many of its predecessors. I do not think *The Garden Murder Case* will gain Mr. Van Dine new admirers, although it may very well not lose him any of his old brigade. It is disappointing to have to say this, as I had been counting on Mr. Van Dine to provide detective readers with a merry Christmas. But, presumably, as *The Purple Murder Case* will not be forthcoming for the usual six months or so, we must take this—and like it. So to begin with the book's merits: Mr. Van Dine's work is always cast in a classical mold; he never relaxes his grip on the detective unities, a single criminal, a single motive, and a singular solution. In *The Garden Murder Case* the crime is committed in one of those New York penthouses which seem to have been built to the plans of intending murderers. The victim is one of a betting set, who are listening in to the broadcast of a race in which all are financially interested: and naturally he meets his fate during the broadcast. The technical background, which always bulks large in Mr. Van Dine's cases, will have little appeal for English readers, seeing it consists of American horse-racing jargon, which may be genuine or spurious for all I know. There are two complaints to be lodged against the book. The first is technical, and therefore very unusual in a Van Dine; the criminal is highly conspicuous from the very outset. Anyone who likes spotting the villain as they go along will find this one almost too easy. The second objection is aesthetic; that admirable

mental automaton, Philo Vance, is credited with an emotion. Until I saw
The Dragon Murder Case in the films I never realized what an absolute
neuter that man was bound to be for the purposes of Mr. Van Dine's plots.
The only human features an actor could evolve out of him were dropping
his "g"s and smoking *Régie* cigarettes; otherwise he had to play the difficult
rôle of a superhuman needle of intelligence. The consequence is that I can't
even remember who acted the part. Naturally, therefore, one asks oneself
what on earth has come over old Philo in *The Garden Murder Case*—can it
be Love? Oh, no, it is only a new idea of Mr. Van Dine's to round off his
story elegantly, and a shocking one, as in fact it ruins the plot by indecent
exposure.

Ralph Partridge. *New Statesman & Nation.*
December 14, 1935, pp. 941–42

Overnight, with the publication in 1926 of *The Benson Murder Case,* by
"S. S. Van Dine" (Willard Huntington Wright), American crime fiction
came of age. Forbidden by his doctors to do any "serious" reading during
a serious illness from 1923 to the middle of 1926, Wright spent his long
convalescence assembling a library of nearly two thousand volumes of detective fiction and criminology. Convinced from his studies that the highly
individual technique of the detective story had suffered from poor execution
in America, thereby limiting its field of appeal, he determined to write tales
aimed at a higher stratum of the public than had previously been accustomed
to read them. . . .

He began by preparing three thirty-thousand-word synopses and sub-
mitting them to Scribner's, under a pledge of secrecy. They were immediately accepted, and were published in successive years. *The Benson Murder
Case,* presumably suggested by the murder of Joseph Bowne Elwell, the
New York bridge expert, was for the first few weeks principally a succès
d'estime among the chosen few. One must remember that in 1926 in America the pastime of the detective novel was still regarded a little apologeti-
cally and cautiously. But gradually the word spread that something unusual
had happened in the detective story, and sales began to pick up. The second
Vance investigation, *The "Canary" Murder Case* (another roman à clef,
based this time on the "Dot" King murder), magnificently smashed the old
tabus into fine smithereens for all time. Serialized in *Scribner's Magazine*
prior to book publication, it became a sort of national *cause,* rivaling Floyd
Collins, Mah Jong, and King Tut as a popular fad.

The book, published in 1927, broke all modern publishing records for
detective fiction and was translated into seven languages. Hollywood's interest was engaged, and each succeeding story was filmed shortly after it
appeared in print, with a sizable list of silent and talking screen heroes
making Vance, for a few years, the best known fictional sleuth on the globe.
Needless to say, each novel earned Wright more money than all his serious
books together, and the picture rights brought him a fortune. In all, he wrote

twelve; nearly all critics have agreed in pronouncing the last six inferior to the first.

Aside from the brilliant plot work of the initial novels, two factors contributed principally to the success of the Van Dine books: the great literacy with which they were written, matching the hero's—at first—impressive learning; and a high degree of verisimilitude, so carefully worked out in every detail that in the early years numerous uncritical readers thought the cases had really occurred, while Vance, District Attorney Markham, Sergeant Heath, and the Watsonian chronicler, became the household familiars of thousands of their countrymen. To these attributes of popularity, certain unkind critics have added another: the undeniable aura of pictured ostentation which (say these scoffers) destined the stories for sure success in a decade which measured its own success in terms of yachts or silk shirts, as the case might be.

Whether or not this was the case, it is unfortunately true that the many superlative qualities of the novels were accompanied by a heavy pretentiousness and lack of humor which became increasingly obtrusive as tastes changed. Much of Vance's popularity had evaporated, rather unjustly on the whole, before Wright died of thrombosis in 1939, at the age of fifty-one.

But whatever he thought on the matter, "S. S. Van Dine" should have died content. In a few short years he had become the best known American writer of the detective story since Poe; he had rejuvenated and reestablished the genre in his native land; and his name and that of his sleuth will endure—for all their joint pretentious faults—among the immortals of the literature.

Howard Haycraft. *Murder for Pleasure: The Life and Times of the Detective Story* (New York: Biblo and Tannen, 1968), pp. 163–68

S. S. Van Dine is of no "importance" whatsoever to the history and development of the detective novel. I know that this is a startlingly heretical statement, but it is high time that somebody said the Emperor has no clothes on. The tremendous vogue of Van Dine in the twenties (*The Bishop Murder Case* is said to have had an advance sale of 70,000 copies!) is a fascinating phenomenon, but quite irrelevant to the history and development of the detective story.

Stranger even than the popular reception of Van Dine's first stories was the aesthetic exaltation of the critics. Anyone trying to reread Van Dine now, as I have recently done, will find not only that Philo Vance is insufferable and fully worthy of the treatment which Ogden Nash prescribed for him ("a kick in the pance"), but that the characters are wooden, the plots unfair, the technique ragged, and the prose compounded of the damnedest pretentious jargon of erudition (on the part of all the characters) that ever tried to pass itself off as the English language.

But British and American critics joined in Hallelujahs proclaiming that at last the detective story had become Literature, capital L and all. Those who had scorned whodunits, according to the Chicago *Post,* "may be willing to admit that the writing of such a novel can be raised to a high art." Van Dine, said Harry Hansen, "belongs to the aristocracy of detective fiction." And those are typical of the major reviews.

This overflowing joy might be understandable if Van Dine had come earlier in detective fiction. But when the first Van Dine appeared, Dorothy Sayers, Anthony Berkeley, Philip MacDonald, Father Knox, Freeman Wills Crofts, and Agatha Christie were all practicing mystery novelists. Milne's *Red House Mystery* was four years old and *Trent's Last Case* thirteen. Hanaud had been detecting for sixteen years and Dr. Thorndyke for almost twenty.

One can only surmise that Van Dine's outrageous pretensions ensnared that horrible species, *Snobbus americanus,* and where *Snobbus* leads, *Boobus* follows. It was a curious phenomenon, but where is its "importance"? Many of the writers mentioned above as preceding Van Dine are still practicing; all are still influential. But where is Van Dine's influence? In the twenties he did exert an influence, but it vanished with merciful rapidity. The only important writer to show markedly Van Dinian affects was Ellery Queen himself, and he shook the shackles off speedily. Nothing could be less Vance-like than *Calamity Town.*

For a long time I clung to memories and said, "To be sure, Van Dine fell off badly, and *The Dragon Murder Case* may well be the worst whodunit ever written; but still *The Greene* and *The Bishop* were something wonderful." If you feel that way, try to reread them. Go ahead, I dare you.

Anthony Boucher. *San Francisco Chronicle.* June 25, 1944, n.p.

Van Dine's great feat with Vance is that we are not permitted to like him. Chandler and Hammett, for all their self-conscious hard-boiledness, made their detectives lovable; they kicked them in the mud to win our hearts. "Down these mean streets a man must go who is not himself mean," said Chandler in "The Simple Art of Murder," an essay propelled by sentimentality. Van Dine on the other hand, who manufactured the "fragrant world" which Chandler condemned, where only the rich bump each other off, came much closer than Chandler to creating a truly hard-boiled egg. In *The Benson Murder Case* Vance ridicules the D.A., Markham, his close friend, in front of a suspect. Neither Sam Spade, Phillip Marlowe, or even the shady Ned Beaumont would have done that.

Nobody loves a man who wears a monocle. Vance is not despicable; it is merely impossible to like him actively. Unlike Holmes or Nero Wolfe he has no interesting assistant to warm the narrative. Van Dine, the family lawyer, is too pompous and corny to make Vance attractive in any sense deeper than the Abercrombie and Fitch catalogue. Vance's aloneness conveys no feeling of underlying melancholy, precisely because Van Dine is always, and deliberately, pushing the possibility too hard. Vance's elaborate independence from the world is in fact reassuring; we don't worry for his mental health between cases. Even the love touch of *The Garden Murder Case* is just a touch.

His solitariness is essential to these stories, nevertheless, because over half the murders occur in families: brothers knife brothers; children poison parents. Like the Greeks, Van Dine knew that families are dangerous. Vance stands outside both the story and the institution of the family, which he implicitly criticizes. He is the most important person in the story—he puts it in order by solving the crime—but he is also free of the participants, free of connections. By ending the mystery, he restores his bachelorhood.

Like other detectives, Vance imposes order on disorganized events. His loneliness is also like a god's, whose sense of order is higher than and hidden from that of ordinary people. Vance is rich but no conservative; he creates his own systems. As the only one on the case with the power to make his system work, he is relied upon by others. Yet he does not give his sense of order to anyone for future use, certainly not to the police who must start from scratch at every murder.

He stands outside the law as well, openly contemptuous and covertly supportive, in the American way. He does not think the law is evil or unnecessary, merely beside most points: "No. Legal technicalities quite useless in such an emergency. Deeper issues involved. Human issues, d'ye see." He is so confident in his knowledge of human issues that he refers to these murders as "unnatural" and "grotesque" because they jostle his theories of behavior. Vance's idea of justice is purely poetic. More often than not he allows the culprit to cheat the State.

Of course it is not his capability for organization that we seek in these stories, but the assurance, in the distance, that that capability exists. What we wish for and indulge in, here and in all mysteries, is the thrill of unknowing, unknowing who the murderer is, and particularly who is going to get it next. By using devices which keep Vance unlikable, Van Dine extended this thrill to fine lengths, without stalling. Vance's knowledge of fish or rare coins is always pertinent to the crimes. His foppish presentation of information makes us as impatient as Markham, but like Markham we hear him out on the suspicion that the information will be valuable, and allow us to beat both Markham and Vance to the killer.

This is a set up, in fact, because Van Dine's killers are not detectable by information alone: "The material indications of the crime don't enter into my calculations. . . . I have other, and surer, ways of reaching conclusions." The detective tells us outright in every story that he will expose the guilty person by determining temperament and likely action in given circumstances. From then on, however, he piles on motives and clues, non irrelevant, and gulls us into using deduction as a method; in effect, he turns us into Markhams. He meanwhile remains psychological, which is what any logician in his right mind would prefer to be. While we struggle with chess moves (the *Bishop*) and lines of trajectory (the *Benson*), he announces (usually with a third of the novel to go) that he already knows who the murderer is—indeed that he has known for some time—but needs to slum in facts in order to prove it. Thus at the end we concentrate almost totally on Vance, which allows the suspects to dwindle down to a precious few (two in the *Greene*) without our being certain about the murderer.

Roger Rosenblatt. *The New Republic*. July 26,

1975, pp. 32–34

According to conventional detective fiction history, the twenties and thirties in Great Britain belong to the classicists—writers like Agatha Christie, Dorothy L. Sayers, and Ngaio Marsh—while the between-wars period in the United States belongs to the hard-boiled *Black Mask* school, pioneered by Dashiell Hammett and Carroll John Daly and brought to its highest fruition by Raymond Chandler. But America also had an intriguing group of formal detective story writers, some of whom still loom as important figures.

American classicists differ from their British brethren in the same way general novelists of the two English-speaking countries are commonly claimed to differ. American writers (says the stereotype) always go for the homerun rather than the base hit, to try for the Great American Novel every time out rather than to attempt the well-wrought but less ambitious minor novel. British mystery writers generally wrote in a sedate, low-key style and relied on sound, painstaking, but comparatively unspectacular detective work to undergird their novels. Their method delights many readers still, but leads others to brand British Golden Age writers as plodding and dull.

The most famous American detective novelists of the classical school, S. S. Van Dine and Ellery Queen, always strove for the big effects, increasingly more elaborate and spectacular plot edifices, perhaps harder to believe than British plots but infinitely fancier and showier, the more so for being described in flamboyant and dramatic prose. Though Christie also aimed to dazzle (and certainly succeeded), she can be called a "cozy" writer in a way that Van Dine and Queen cannot.

In a sense, Van Dine is the key figure in the American detective story between the wars, though some of his followers (notably the Queen team) would ultimately surpass him in both quality and popularity. In his Philo Vance novels, Van Dine (the pseudonym of art critic Willard Huntington Wright) included many elements that others would copy: the great detective's boundless erudition on a wide variety of subjects; the list of characters at the beginning of the book; and a whole cornucopia of devices intended to give the illusion of a true-crime case rather than a work of pure imagination: dates and times of day at each chapter heading; maps, floor plans, and scholarly footnotes; pretentious publisher's notes and introductions.

Overrated in his own time, Van Dine has probably been excessively disparaged by commentators since. In a form that constantly runs the risk of mid-novel sag, he had a sense of pace that many of his imitators lacked.

His creation of elaborate detective problems and of a brooding, ominous atmosphere can be compared to those of Queen and John Dickson Carr, though he did not have the whole-hearted commitment to fair play of those writers. The errors Van Dine makes in police procedure and legal medicine, noted in a famous *Saturday Review* piece by Dashiell Hammett, were probably no worse than those of most Golden Age detective novelists. Van Dine's frequently reprinted "Twenty Rules for Writing Detective Stories" are indeed unreasonably rigid, but fortunately Van Dine did not always follow them himself. And Vance's overwhelming intellectual shtick is more amusing than irritating if approached in the right frame of mind. While some critics have charged Van Dine with humorlessness, I choose to believe the outpouring of erudition is intentionally tongue-in-cheek.

Van Dine's novels were all published by Scribner's, under the aegis of the famed editor Maxwell Perkins. The first two titles in the series, *The Benson Murder Case* (1926) and *The "Canary" Murder Case* (1927), both loosely based on real-life murders of the period, have a surprisingly light tone, especially in the repartee of Vance and his official collaborators, District Attorney Markham and Sergeant Heath. In the next two novels, the mood darkens somewhat, and the breezy byplay of the first two books is never completely recaptured. But *The Greene Murder Case* (1928), a compelling account of a series of murders in a wealthy and poisonous family, and *The Bishop Murder Case* (1929), with its nursery-rhyme serial killer, represent Van Dine at the height of his powers.

It has become a truism that the second six of the dozen Vance novels are markedly inferior to the first, and when Van Dine is reprinted today (most recently by Scribner's in paperback and Gregg Press in hardcover), efforts are invariably confined to those first six. The drop-off in quality is more gradual than sudden, however. *The Garden Murder Case* (1935) was the first Vance novel to receive generally unfavorable reviews but, with its very accurate use of horse racing lore, is a better book than reputed. Only *The Kidnap Murder Case* (1936) and *The Gracie Allen Murder Case* (1938) are out-and-out embarrassments. The novelette *The Winter Murder Case* (1939), left at Van Dine's death before the final laying on of detail and learned talk could be added, is a good enough mystery for the reader to forget it began life as a screen treatment for Sonja Henie. *Winter* is also the hardest Van Dine title to find. The Philo Vance novels were kept in print for years, and copies of the first six are fairly plentiful, though first editions are relatively elusive.

The Ellery Queen team (Frederic Dannay and Manfred B. Lee) followed the Van Dine formula rather closely in their early novels, producing in the young Ellery an amateur detective nearly as erudite and exasperating as Philo Vance. They constructed plots as outre and convoluted as Van Dine's but added a much more abiding loyalty to the concept of fair play to the reader. As the years went by, detective Ellery would become a more fully developed and likeable character. The team would experiment as much in theme and approach as any writer in the genre, but the fairly-clued detective plot would continue to be their hallmark.

Queen's contribution to the accompanying apparatus of thirties detective fiction was the "Challenge to the Reader." They would stop the story at a point near the end to give assurance all the clues Ellery needed to solve the case are now on the table for the alert reader to reason it out as well. The alert reader would have to be a genius, of course, but indeed all the clues were there. In later books, the overt challenge would be omitted, but it was still there implicitly.

Queen also had fun with chapter titles, and this would continue to some extent in later years. For example, in *The Dutch Shoe Mystery* (Stokes, 1931), the thirty chapters all are titled with "tion" words, e.g., Operation, Agitation, Visitation, Revelation, Strangulation, etc., finishing of course with Termination and Explanation. In *The Greek Coffin Mystery* (1932), the first letters of the chapter titles spell out the title of the book and the author's name. The chapters of the first two Drury Lane novels, *The Tragedy of X* and *The Tragedy of Y* (both Viking, 1932), published by Barnaby Ross, are divided into acts and scenes, appropriate to the detective's theatrical background.

All the Queen and Ross novels of the thirties are notable for their brilliance of plotting and clue-planting, but among the best of them are those first two Drury Lanes, *The Egyptian Cross Mystery* (Stokes, 1932), *The Chinese Orange Mystery* (Stokes, 1934), and *Halfway House* (Stokes, 1936). Deserving special nods are the first Queen novel, *The Roman Hat Mystery* (Stokes, 1929), which makes excellent use of the sure-fire theatrical setting, and the final Ross, *Drury Lane's Last Case* (Viking, 1933), which rivals Agatha Christie's *The Murder of Roger Ackroyd* for its extreme example of Least Suspected Personage.

Jon L. Breen. *Bookman's Weekly.* April 16, 1984,
pp. 2879–82

The naming of [Willard Huntington Wright's] sleuth required great care. In its etymology, "Philo" implied, of course, the love of language in the protagonist he was shaping, whereas "Vance" was a suitably plain and euphonious match to an otherwise odd first name. Yet there was another, very minor detective writer in the business—Louis Joseph Vance—and a character, Philo Gubb, by Joseph Ellis Butler, whose pairing would serve to remind book buyers, consciously or otherwise, of other novelists they might know. . . .

If the name "Philo Vance" harked to the future and the new world he was entering, the name of Willard's author-narrator looked to his past. Of the "S.S.," Willard commented that the steamship abbreviation would be easy for readers (and booksellers) to remember; of the "Van Dine," that it was an old family name on his mother's side. The first point is true, but the second is not. There are no Van Dines evident in the family tree [although his mother's maiden name was Van Vraken]. At another time Willard remarked that he selected the word "dine" with some ironic thought to his years of living on less food than he had cared to, and there is probably more seriousness than not in that tidbit of humor. It is also the case that "S.S." was the common abbreviation for *The Smart Set*—echoes of Willard's happiest days [he was its editor in 1913–14]—and that Van Dine is very close to Van Dyck, Rubens's peer, with all the associations with painting, aristocratic living, and accomplishment that that great name reverberates. . . .

Ultimately as famous in his day as Sherlock Holmes or Hercule Poirot, [Philo] Vance was an original. Embodying so many of his creator's interests, quirks, and frustrations, Philo Vance could only have been a character of Willard Huntington Wright's design. An art student and connoisseur, Vance is a man with the intellectual skill to solve brilliantly devised crimes and serve the law better than the police but who does so only on his own terms. His terms involve firm control of the interrogations, emotional detachment from the plight of the victims, more-than-occasional bending of the letter of the law, and a healthy skepticism for circumstantial evidence and mere facts. Needless to add, despite the aggressively flippant manner of Willard's character, the murderer never escapes detection, nor are the police ever of the slightest help in solving the case.

Philo Vance leads the intellectual's ultimate fantasy life. A bachelor, untroubled by women, he lives in quiet luxury, impressing everyone with his formidable vocabulary and occupying his time with whatever scholarly pursuits interest him at the moment. Yet the world-at-large needs him. The men of practical affairs come knocking at his door. The expert help he offers the police with their toughest cases is given largely for the satisfaction of his own curiosity, for the joy of wrestling with a complicated challenge, or as a favor to [District Attorney] Markham. So divorced is Vance from the ordinary motives of detectives and police officers that, when the criminal is particularly clever, Vance is apt to unmask him with reluctance, regretfully ending a well-suited match. His respect is often with his adversary. Only grudgingly does Vance admit the necessity of serving something as abstract and unpleasant as "the good of society." Were it not for the involvement of the authorities in each case, Vance is perfectly capable of solving the crime as he would a difficult puzzle—and then letting the guilty one go free, if he had reason to believe that the murderer would resist any further temptations to homicide. His highest regard is reserved for the murderer who commits suicide in preference to a trial and imprisonment, an act he will even tacitly assist in.

Between and during cases, Vance buys Cézanne watercolors at preview exhibitions, reads Freud and Spengler, attends afternoon concerts at Carnegie Hall, and works sporadically on his translations (never completed, as far as we know) of Delacroix's journals and lost Menander plays. Attended to by his friend and assistant S. S. Van Dine, the narrator of all the books, and by his butler, Currie, Vance makes his home in Manhattan in a town house between Park and Madison Avenues on 38th Street—an address, by the end of the twenties, as recognizable as Holmes's Baker Street flat. The surroundings include Renoir bathers, Picasso still-lifes, Chinese ceramics, and a vast, esoteric library. An inheritance from an ''Aunt Agatha'' has made this charmed life possible (Agatha Christie paving the way for Willard Wright?), but Philo Vance makes no apologies for his privileged life-style. In the Jazz Age none was needed, as Willard had rightly concluded. A man who knew how to spend his money, a know-it-all with style, had automatic appeal.

John Loughery. Alias S. S. Van Dine (New York:
Scribner's, 1992), pp. 176–77, 186–88

VERNE, JULES (1828–1905)

The year 1963 should not be allowed to pass without some salute to Jules Verne who, a century ago, brought out *Five Weeks in a Balloon,* a novel that initiated a new literary form. It was Jules Verne who set science fiction going.

The physical context and the scale of gadgetry were to be widely varied in his later books, but in other respects *Five Weeks in a Balloon* shows Verne's method already firmly settled. He introduces his favorite trio of intrepid adventure types. In this instance they are Dr. Fergusson, the eccentric, obstinate, absurdly omniscient, and resourceful scientist who designs, builds, and skippers the dirigible; Kennedy, the honorable but hot-tempered man of action with his rifles and pistols; and Joe, the brave, loyal servant who is allowed to provide some comic relief, though never of a sort that might threaten Fergusson's dignity (or raise much more than an indulgent smile). Girls are soppy and don't come into it: this is a boy's world: To say so is not to denigrate it, for an adult's world that was not also a boy's world here and there, now and then, would be a chilly place.

The airborne voyage across Africa with which the story mainly deals is preceded by a short scene at a London Geographical Society meeting. Kenneth Allott, in his excellent biography, suggests that this mundane opening, a favorite device of Verne's, was aimed at reassuring Parisian sophisticates who might have balked at unleavened romance.

However this may be, anything so ambitious is dropped with the balloon's first load of ballast, and all the way across the Dark Continent enthusiastic earnestness flourishes unchecked. In the intervals between Fergusson's lectures on history, geography, and science the travelers incur adventures, described with innocent energy, see remarkable sights, decked out in profuse but largely unevocative detail, and deliver volubly wooden harangues. It is hard to imagine any sort of equivalent to these verbal postures in mid-twentieth-century idiom, nor should we feel happy with them, I think, if they could be devised. Verne's flavor is of the later nineteenth century and, to a great degree, of his original Victorian translators.

One settles down to read or reread Verne with an eagerness based on ruminating about him, rather than on any notion of what he is actually like to read. He displays that curious property—shared perhaps with Dickens?—of making his effect not so much when the book is open as after it is shut and put away, so that each novel starts to improve in retrospect the moment one starts to forget it. At any rate, he arouses an expectation that is never properly fulfilled. It is not that the style and narrative method are a barrier; they are part of the fun. And although Verne had no interest in character, his people always endear themselves, so much so as to cast doubt on the first clause of this sentence. The trouble is partly that the adventures, which sound all right in summary and feel all right in memory—a typhoon, an attack on the gas envelope by gyrfalcons, the rescue of a French missionary from the sacrificial stake—are never brought to the pitch of real suspense. We know much too certainly that if Fergusson hasn't got the answer, Kennedy or Joe will come up with it rather too soon.

The most obvious chances of drama and excitement are missed. When Joe, imprisoned by tribesmen in a town on an island in Lake Chad, wakes up to find that a cataclysm has submerged tribesmen, town, and island, he might have been pardoned a momentary sense of puzzlement, even alarm. *Mais non!* In a trice the worthy fellow has taken his courage in his hands and seized a sort of boat, roughly hewn out of a tree trunk, that chances to be drifting past!

This kind of insensitivity is connected with a rather deadening scrupulousness about probability and fact. The Africa seen by the Fergusson expedition is altogether too much the Africa of reliable contemporary report, of Livingstone and Burton and Speke.

Again, Verne's balloon traveled four thousand miles, but a real one had gone eight hundred miles four years earlier, and a straight multiplication factor of five is hardly enough for a tale of wonder. (The immediate source of the novel, Poe's *Balloon-Hoax* of 1844, featured a nonstop flip from North Wales to South Carolina.) A similar conservatism saw to it that that supposed marvel, Captain Nemo's *Nautilus,* was behind the submarine technology of its era in every respect but its electrical power supply; and a voyage to the Moon that omits a landing on the Moon is a dud, never mind the author's excuses about the impracticability of returning to Earth.

All this might matter less if Verne's science were consistently real science. But it is not. The account of the cruise of the *Nautilus* is riddled with errors and contradictions of fact and principle, all of which could have been put right by a session with an encyclopedia of the day or even half an hour's chat with a reasonably informed schoolmaster. The Moon projectile was fired from a gun at an initial acceleration that would have instantly killed its occupants.

Verne got his fingertips on to some of the great myths of our time—the wonderful submarine, the ship so huge that it becomes a floating island, the moon voyage, the monstrous explosion—without ever showing the ability to grasp them. And yet, in more than one sense, this inability hardly matters. Up to a point a myth works without the intervention of style and treatment and is more durable than these in the memory.

But only up to a point. An author who cannot be read without continuous disappointment is only half an author, however much the larger that half may be. It is tempting to urge of Verne, as others have urged of Dickens, that he should be swallowed whole; but how do you do that?

Kingsley Amis. *What Became of Jane Austen? and Other Questions* (New York: Harcourt Brace Jovanovich, 1971), pp. 33–37

My object has been to depict the earth, and not the earth alone, but the universe, for I have sometimes taken my readers away from the earth, in the novel. And I have tried at the same time to realize a very high ideal of beauty of style. It is said that there can't be any style in a novel of adventure, but that isn't true; though I admit that it is very much more difficult to write such a novel in a good literary form than the studies of character which are so in vogue today.

Dumas used to say to me, when I complained that my place in French literature was not recognized, "You ought to have been an American or an English author. Then your books, translated into French, would have gained you enormous popularity in France, and you would have been considered by your countrymen as one of the greatest masters of fiction. But as it is, I am considered of no account in French literature."

I am not and never have been a money-getting man. I am a man of letters and an artist, living in the pursuit of the ideal, running wild over an idea, and glowing with enthusiasm over my work.

Jules Verne. Interview by R. H. Sherard, *McClure's Magazine*. January 1894, pp. 115–24

My scientific romances have been compared with the work of Jules Verne and there was a disposition on the part of literary journalists at one time to call me the English Jules Verne. As a matter of fact there is no literary resemblance whatever between the anticipatory inventions of the great Frenchman and my science fantasies. His work dealt almost always with actual possibilities of invention and discovery, and he made some remarkable forecasts. The interest he invoked was a practical one; he wrote and believed and told that this thing or that thing could be done, which was not at that time done. He helped his reader to imagine it done and to realize what fun, excitement, or mischief would ensue. Many of his inventions have "come true." But my stories do not pretend to deal with possible things; they are exercises of the imagination in a quite different field.

H. G. Wells. Introduction to *The Scientific Romances of H. G. Wells* (London: Gollancz, 1933), n.p.

Although later he was to have misgivings—he was not altogether easy about the theory of evolution, for instance—Verne belongs to the early scientific period, the period of the Great Eastern and the Hyde Park Exhibition of 1851, when the key phrase was "Command over Nature" rather than, as now, "Mysterious Universe." The mechanical sciences were advancing at tremendous speed and their sinister possibilities were seldom foreseen. The modern wars of extermination had not only not started, but, no doubt, would have been difficult to imagine. Later, however, Verne watched with disgust the rise of modern imperialism and the scramble for Africa. One result of this was the disappearance from his books of the sympathetic Englishman. In his earlier work this character appears over and over again—a queer figure, as in most nineteenth-century French novels, given to wearing check suits and breaking long silences with cries of "Hip, hip, hurrah!" but symbolizing the pragmatism and inventiveness which Verne admired in the English-speaking races.

It is difficult not to couple Verne's name with that of H. G. Wells. Wells, even more than Verne, has made himself the apostle of Science, but he belongs to a less confident period in which the smallness of man against the background of the spiral nebulae is more obvious than his mastery over Nature. Wells's early romances are less scientific than Verne's—that is, less close to the established knowledge of the time—but there is far more feeling of *wonder* in them. If one compares *A Journey to the Moon* with *The First Men in the Moon,* one sees the advantage, at any rate from a purely literary point of view, of a less anthropocentric standpoint. Verne's story is scientific, or very nearly so. Granted that one could fire a projectile out of the earth's gravitational pull, and that the human beings inside it could survive the shock, the thing might have happened as it is recorded. Wells's story is pure speculation, based on nothing except a predilection for thinking that the moon and the planets are inhabited. But it creates a universe of its own, which one remembers in detail years after reading it. The most memorable incident in Verne's book is the time when the oxygen cylinder sprang a leak and produced symptoms of drunkenness in the explorers—precisely the incident that tethers the story to the earth. It seems doubtful whether Verne will be read much longer, except by schoolchildren "doing" *A Journey to the Center of the Earth* as an alternative to *Tartarin of Tarascon.* He set out to combine instruction with entertainment, and he succeeded, but only so long as his scientific theories were more or less up to date. He does, however, enjoy a sort of anonymous immortality because of a controversy that has sprung out of one of his books. In *Around the World in Eighty Days*—

itself based on a short story of Poe's—he makes play with the fact that if one travels round the world eastward one gains a day in the passage. And this has given rise to the question, "What will happen when an aeroplane can fly round the world in twenty-four hours?", which is much debated by imaginative boys, readers of the *Wizard* and the *Hotspur,* who have probably never heard Verne's name.

George Orwell. *The New Statesman & Nation.*
January 18, 1941, p. 64

During our last fifty years, scientific progress has been so enormous that one might think that any work of science fiction written during the nineteenth century would be hopelessly out of date. But Verne's stories do not depend on their science alone to make them interesting; if they did, they would have been forgotten except by a few specialists and collectors. The reason Verne is still read by millions today is simply that he was one of the best story-tellers who have ever lived; and *A Journey to the Center of the Earth* is a particularly flawless specimen of his art.

The leading character, Professor Hardwigg (Lidenbrock in the original French version) is one of Verne's most memorable creations, in the same tradition as Captain Nemo of the *Nautilus* [in *Twenty Thousand Leagues under the Sea*], and Michael Arden of *From the Earth to the Moon,* or Phileas Fogg of *Around the World in Eighty Days.* All these Verne heroes are implacably (one might even say demoniacally) determined individuals who will let nothing—and nobody—stand in the way of their ambition, whether it is to race round the world for a wager or to uncover some new secret of science. They usually lack a sense of humor, but the author more than makes up for this with his sly asides. Verne derived a great deal of amusement in his books by poking good-natured fun at national characteristics. In this volume, the contrast between the erudite German professor, the imperturbable Icelandic guide, and the easygoing English narrator provides all the variation of characters that is needed. It is something of a feat to write an entire book about three people; Verne brings it off perfectly.

But perhaps his greatest achievement is the absolute plausibility he maintains; it looks simple, but few later writers of scientific romances have been able to manage it. How did Verne succeed? Chiefly by a strict attention to detail. Every book involved an enormous amount of research—probably quite as much as would be required to write a serious factual work on the same subject. Not that Verne always avoided errors; in chapter 2 he refers to Galileo when he should have said Huygens, and in the dream sequence in chapter 40, he repeats the old fallacy that a shark has to turn on its back to bite. Yet such slips are trivial, and do little to detract from the merit of the book.

Verne was not a great writer by the standards of such literary giants as Melville, Dickens, Poe, Scott, Dumas, and the other titans of the nineteenth century. But he was one of the most influential writers who ever lived, for he inspired literally hundreds of inventors and explorers.

He was the first writer to welcome change and to proclaim that scientific discovery could be the most wonderful of all adventures. For this reason he will never grow out of date; though he died in 1905 his spirit was never more alive than it is at this moment, when his greatest dream—that of space travel—is about to become reality.

Arthur C. Clarke. Introduction to *A Journey to the Center of the Earth,* by Jules Verne (New York: Dodd Mead, 1959), pp. v–viii

A child's ignorant eye can make a Western out of a Dumas tapestry.

If we revisit our childhood's reading, we are likely to discover that we missed the satire of *Gulliver,* the evangelism of *Pilgrim's Progress,* and the loneliness of *Robinson Crusoe.*

But when we revisit some books in this way, we find that the iridescent film has burst, to leave nothing behind but a wet mark. Henty, Ballantyne, Burroughs, require an innocence of approach which, while it is natural enough to a child, would be a mark of puerility in an adult. I declare this with some feeling, since during the last week or so I have undertaken a long course of Jules Verne, and suffer at the moment, not from indigestion so much as hunger.

Yet once his books satisfied me. They held me rapt, I dived with the *Nautilus,* was shot round the moon, drifted in the South Atlantic, dying of thirst, and tasted—oh rapture! It always sent me indoors for a drink—the fresh waters of the Amazon. And now?

Of course the books have not vanished wholly. They have the saving grace of gusto. Verne had his generation's appetite for facts, and he serves them up in *grande cuisine:* "How amazing . . . were the microscopical jellyfish observed by Scoresby in the Greenland seas, which he estimated at 23,898,000,000,000,000,000 in area of two square miles!" But a diet of such creatures palls, for Verne's verbal surface lacks the slickness of the professional; it is turgid and slack by turns. Only the brio of his enthusiasm carries us forward from one adventure to another. What is left for the adult is offbeat; something so specialized that to enjoy it is about as eccentric as collecting the vocal chords of prima donnas. For Verne attracts today, not so much by his adventures as by the charm of his nineteenth-century interiors. . . .

What the child misses most in [Verne's] books—if I am anything to go by—is the fact that Verne was a heavy-handed satirist. The organization which fires its shot at the moon is the Gun Club of Baltimore. These were the savants who engaged in the arms race of the American Civil War.

Their military weapons attained colossal proportions, and their projectiles, exceeding the prescribed limits, unfortunately occasionally cut in two some unoffending bystanders. These inventions, in fact, left far in the rear the timid instruments of European artillery.

Throughout the seventeen books there is an almost total absence of women. Verne was honester here than some of his science fiction descendants who lug in a blonde for the look of the thing. His male world was probably all he could manage. You cannot hack out a woman's face with an axe; he could not, or would not, write about women. He remains the only French writer who could get his hero right round the world without meeting more than one woman while he was doing it.

Verne's talent was not spurred by a love of what we should now call pure science, but by technology. His books are the imaginative counterpart of the Great Eastern, the Tay Bridge, or the Great Steam Flying Machine. It is this which accounts for his continued appeal to subadolescent boyhood. For the science sides of our schools are crammed to bursting with boys who have confused a genial enjoyment in watching wheels go round with the pursuit of knowledge. His heroes, too, are a pattern of what the twelve-year-old boy considers a proper adult pattern—they are tough, sexless, casually brave, resourceful, and *making something big*. Compared with the Sheriff of Dumb Valley, or the Private Eye, they constitute no mean ideal; to the adult, their appeal is wholly nostalgic. Apart from the odd touch that convinces—the pleasures of Professor Aronnax when, after years of groping for fish, he observes them through the windows of *Nautilus;* the willingness of the Frenchman to go to the moon with no prospect of coming back— apart from this they are a dead loss.

William Golding. *The Spectator*. June 9, 1961,

n.p.

Science fiction can be understood in the context of nineteenth- and twentieth-century spiritual loneliness as a manifestation of our culture's longing to escape the prison house of the merely human. It might be considered as an attempt to reestablish, in some way that will sustain conviction even in our technological and post-Christian culture, the channels of communication with the nonhuman world.

The *voyages extraordinaires* explore worlds known and unknown: the interior of Africa, the interior of the Earth, the deeps of the sea, the deeps of space. Characteristically, Verne's voyagers travel in vehicles that are themselves closed worlds—his imagination projects itself in terms of "inside" and "outside"—from which the immensity of nature can be appreciated in upholstered comfort. The *Nautilus* is the most familiar of these comfortable, mobile worlds; inside all is cozy elegance, the epitome of the civilized and human, while outside the oceans gleam or rage in inhuman beauty or mystery.

The basic activity in Verne is the construction of closed and safe spaces, the enslavement and appropriation of nature to make a place for man to live in comfort.

Journey to the Center of the Earth is just such an exploration of "insideness," except that here the interior world is the nonhuman world, a realm of subterranean galleries, caverns, and seas, and here rather than being the place of enclosed safety the interior world becomes an immensity, a fearful abyss. Abysses dominate the novel. Even before Professor Lidenbrock and his nephew, Axel, begin their journey into the interior, Axel, the story's narrator, has nightmares in which he finds himself "hurtling into bottomless abysses with the increasing velocity of bodies dropping through space." The idea of the abyss is continually kept before us, and always the danger is as much psychic as physical. Standing on the edge of the first real chasm, Axel speaks of the "fascination of the void" taking hold of him: "I felt my center of gravity moving, and vertigo rising to my head like intoxication. There is nothing more overwhelming than this attraction of the abyss." The danger, evidently, is of losing one's sense of self and of disappearing, intoxicated, into the infinite void.

The abyss in this novel is a version of the cosmic void, but the geometry of the earthly chasm differs from that of the astronomical infinity, for the Earth is round and therefore has both poles and a center. Poles and center are magical loci, the three still places on the turning globe. To reach and explore the poles is to achieve the completion of the human sphere by defining the Earth in its entirety. (This is the meaning that seems to generate the nineteenth- and early twentieth-century obsession with polar exploration.) To reach the center of the globe also means to achieve completion, except that now the Earth itself has become the imagined immensity, and the attainment of the center means the penetration of the essence, the achievement of the heart of the mystery. The liminal poles are frigid; the mystical center is generally imagined as hot, as the fluid, living core of the globe. The earthly chasm thus opens onto a different kind of imaginative space from the astronomical void; at the bottom of the bottomless abyss is the region not of transcendence but of immanence, the locus in which all knowledge, all being, all power are immediately present. To attain the center of the Earth, then, means to penetrate the heart of nature, to possess nature absolutely. This is the object of Professor Lidenbrock and his nephew Axel's quest.

Mark Rose. *Alien Encounters: Anatomy of Science Fiction* (Cambridge, Massachusetts: Harvard University Press, 1981), pp. 50–59

Motion and transport are important themes in Verne's books. He uses all kinds of agencies: animals, carts, railways, rowboats, big ships, carriers, even tightrope walkers—and, of course, balloons. But he also made many forecasts in this field: the most famous after the launch of the rocket must be the secret submarine *Nautilus* by Captain Nemo. And in *Robur the Conqueror* he introduces a primitive kind of helicopter.

Verne can describe the battle between the ichthyosaur and the plesio-saur (*Journey to the Center of the Earth*) with as much excitement and imagination as he can the quasi-military attack of the ice bears (*Hatteras*).

Rogues figure often in Verne's dramatis personae, as do pirates, kid-nappers, and gangs of thieves. These all contribute to the danger through which the hero moves, appearing to put the outcome in doubt, and delaying the successful return home as well as constituting a threat to life itself. The most abominable of these villains are those who exploit their private inven-tions or discoveries or sudden acquisition of wealth for their own ends or who attempt to conquer the world (*Face to the Flag; The Begum's Fortune*). But the good and fair in Verne will always triumph—though usually only in the nick of time! The villain is routed—balance is restored.

The novels of Jules Verne's last ten years testify to their author's in-creasing sense of sympathy with oppressed peoples (*Mathias Sandorf, A Drama in Livland, The Danube Pilot*), which he manages to incorporate in his tried and tested formula.

All his novels have neat endings: the main plot is resolved, what is sought is found, the outcast is rescued, suspicion is lifted from the innocent, humanity rescued from terror and—most of all—the race is won, the journey is brought to a successful conclusion. In these closing sections of his books, Verne often uses an effect made popular in the theater, when the tension is wound so tight the whole structure seems in danger of snapping.

The story reaches a climax where failure is imminent and appears in-evitable, the destination of the travelers is lost from sight, the villains are poised on the very point of total triumph. But then at the very last moment the tables are turned and the moral world is once more established.

Since Jules Verne was so extraordinarily successful with this basic structure, it is really not to be wondered at that many writers sought to borrow his formula, and that they were promoted by various publishers as "the German Verne," "the Hungarian Verne," and so on. But none of these achieved the high quality of the original. Elements of Verne's concepts were common in adventure fiction up through the middle years of our own century, especially in the realms of popular literature.

Dieter Wuckel. *The Illustrated History of Science Fiction* (New York: Ungar, 1989), pp. 45–51

VONNEGUT, KURT, JR. (1922–   )

Kurt Vonnegut, Jr., born in Indianapolis, Indiana, in 1922, is a mainstream writer whose works were categorized and marketed as science fiction at the beginning of his career. It was obvious early on that he had an antic sense of fantasy and allegory, but it was hardly typical science fiction.

His first novel, *Player Piano* (1952), is an ironic commentary on automation, on technological breakthroughs, and on the evils of American big business: hardly the kind of thing to excite a science fiction fan. However, his second book, *The Sirens of Titan* (1959), is almost pure science fiction—conventional, at least, in structure and insight. By the time *Cat's Cradle* (1963) was published, it was obvious that Vonnegut was being erroneously categorized. *Cat's Cradle* has an invented religion, acceptable to the science fiction genre, but its unconventional structure and its ending—complete catastrophe with irreversible results—is scarcely in the conventional genre. Of course, *Cat's* interesting concept of "foma"—the telling of lies to make for human happiness—certainly fits into the satiric science fiction vein, but the book was a bit surrealistic for proper science fiction fantasy. As science fiction, these Vonnegut books were received by the fraternity with somewhat lukewarm acclaim.

When *Slaughterhouse-Five; or, the Children's Crusade* appeared in 1969, it was obvious that Vonnegut was actually a mainstream author. Nevertheless, many of the science fiction genre's favorite elements continued to appear in his works—time warps, doppelgängers, utopian and dystopian worlds, space travel, and so on. After 1969, Vonnegut's early works suddenly appeared in reprintings—this time being reviewed by the publishing establishment in New York. It had taken *Cat's Cradle* ten years to be "received." After his breakthrough into the mainstream, Vonnegut continued to write the same kind of books he had always written, but now they were reviewed by mainstream reviewers and Vonnegut was suddenly an *in* figure. *Breakfast of Champions* appeared in 1973, and *Slapstick* in 1976—both featuring characters created earlier but now involved in the irony of the future. Vonnegut's novels are all basically pessimistic, although he does not necessarily *admit* that they are. He came into science by the back door, working for General Electric as a publicist in his early years. His brother is a full-fledged scientist, hard-core. "It's just superstitious, to believe that science can save us all," Vonnegut once said. "We're starting to back down on a lot of our technology now." Generally, his attitude toward humanity is the same as that depicted in *The Sirens of Titan*—a blind mob pursuing high aspirations secretly manipulated by "higher forces" to satisfy trivial whims. "I get curious about—what if there was a God who *really did care,* and had things He *wanted done.* How inconvenient that would be!"

Dieter Wuckel and Bruce Cassiday. *The Illustrated
History of Science Fiction* (New York: Ungar,
1989), pp. 203–4

Vonnegut belongs with the desperate humorists, of whom Joseph Heller, author of *Catch-22,* is the best known. Donald Barthelme, Bruce J. Friedman, and Richard Stern are of that company. John Hawkes can also be funny in the same way, though he has other virtues that are more important. Vonnegut's particular asset is the wildness of his imagination: there is nothing so ridiculous that he cannot make use of it. And, though one doesn't have to regard him as an infallible prophet, he has put his finger on an essential problem of our times.

Granville Hicks. Saturday Review. April 3, 1965,
n.p.

Readers who remember Kurt Vonnegut's *Player Piano* with wistful pleasure are in for a surprise: Vonnegut's second science fiction novel, *The Sirens of Titan,* is nothing like that at all. *Player Piano* was subtle, ironic, and cool, with a surface smooth as gelatin, and all the jags buried deep under. *The Sirens of Titan* is jazzy, impudent, sarcastic, and about as smooth as gravel pudding; in a style like Harvey Kurtzman trying to imitate Doc Savage and Alfred Bester simultaneously, it piles one deadpan extravagance on another: superlatives, shock-for-shock's-sake, epigrams, parodies, boyish vulgarity. The plot concerns a Groton type named Wilson Niles Rumfoord, who "had run his private space ship right into the heart of an uncharted chrono-syn-clastic infundibulum." Vonnegut explains it:

"Chrono (kroh-no) means time. Synclastic (sin-class-tick) means curved toward the same side in all directions, like the skin of an orange. Infundi-bulum (in-fun-dib-u-lum) is what the ancient Romans like Julius Caesar and Nero called a funnel. If you don't know what a funnel is, get Mommy to show you one."

What this adds up to is that (a) Rumfoord (and his dog Kazak, who was also in the private space ship) is scattered in time and space along a helix with one end in the sun and the other in Betelgeuse; and (b) Rumfoord, who materializes on Earth and other solar bodies whenever they intercept his helix, can see all aspects of truth at once and has accordingly become a sort of highly refined (but nasty) demigod.

Some of this is funny as hell, some is grotesquely moving, some awful by any imaginable standards. ("But Fate spared him that awful knowledge for many years.")

Whereas most writers use the same story pieces, and only try to put them together in mildly novel ways, Vonnegut's pieces are all different—e.g., (1) diamond-shaped, music-eating, paper-thin cave creatures on Mercury (they form harmonious patterns on the walls, and "reproduce by flaking. The young, when shed by a parent, are indistinguishable from dandruff"); (2) a financier who corners practically everything by interpreting the Book of Genesis as a coded series of buy & sell orders; (3) Schliemann Breathing (i.e., inhaling through the lower intestine when in airless places), and so on, and on.

You may not like all of it; you may not even be able to decide whether you like it or not; but read it.

Damon Knight. In Search of Wonder (Chicago:
Advent, 1967), pp. 236–37

We are best cheered by untruths, so the bigger the whopper, the better—says Vonnegut. In his masterpiece, *Cat's Cradle,* the founder of a new religion insisted at every step that his own doctrines were lies. Solace, apparently, came immediately.

In the preface to *Welcome to the Monkey House* he announces that one of the themes of his novels is "No pain." Kurt Vonnegut, Jr., probably our finest Black Humorist, is offering us comfort.

He is the little Dutch boy stopping the hole in the dike: while he conscientiously aids us, he reminds us that we live in the shadow of deep waters. Or, to use the idea that appears frequently in his work as a main character, a minor figure, part of the background, or the tail of a metaphor, he is the volunteer fireman, unselfishly and innocently rushing to put out the random blazes of civilization. His comforts frighten us with their inadequacy, and we laugh in self-defense.

Vonnegut's special enemies are science, morality, free enterprise, socialism, fascism, Communism, all government—any force in our lives which regards human beings as ciphers. His villains are simple egotists, indifferent to other people, his protagonists men who adapt events to their own discontent with the system, rolling with the times to create change, which is rarely, in Vonnegut's world, an improvement. His third group of characters, his saints, his volunteer firemen, are content to aid others in their own small world, unaware of the larger actions that swirl around them. Failing to participate in events, they nevertheless become the focus of all activity, their relevance being the undeniable fact that they exist.

Charles Nicol. The Atlantic Monthly. September
1968, pp. 123–24

Vonnegut is a sardonic humorist and satirist in the vein of Mark Twain and Jonathan Swift. In earlier works, such as *Player Piano, Cat's Cradle,* and *God Bless You, Mr. Rosewater,* he has made fun of the worship of science and technology. Now we can see that his quarrel with contemporary society began with his experiences in World War II, about which he has at last managed to write a book *Slaughterhouse-Five.*

Vonnegut never does get around to describing the raid on Dresden, and that shows the wisdom of the strategy he was finally led to adopt. When the planes came over, Billy and a few other prisoners, together with four of their guards, took refuge in a meat locker. . . . In trying to tell what he and his fellow survivors saw the next morning when they emerged from the locker, about all Billy can say is, "It was like the moon." It is by this and other kinds of indirection that Vonnegut makes his impression.

Vonnegut's satire sweeps widely, touching on education, religion, advertising, and many other subjects.

But the central target is the institution of war. . . . The terrible destruction of Dresden is, as Vonnegut sees it, an example of the way the military mind operates. (He quotes a military historian to the effect that the raid served no essential purpose.) He shows that in great matters as in small war is brutal and stupid.

Like Mark Twain, Vonnegut feels sadness as well as indignation when he looks at the damned human race. Billy Pilgrim is a compassionate man, and meditates a good deal on the life and teachings of Jesus and on institutionalized Christianity. . . . Partly as a result of what he has learned on Tralfamadore, Billy is to some extent reconciled to life as it is lived on Earth. But Vonnegut is not, and in this book he has expressed his terrible outrage.

As I read it, I could hear Vonnegut's mild voice, see his dead pan as he told a ludicrous story, and gasp as I grasped the terrifying implications of some calm remark. Even though he is not to be identified with Billy Pilgrim, he lives and breathes in the book, and that is one reason why it is the best he has written.

Granville Hicks. Saturday Review. March 29,
1969, p. 25

Slaughterhouse-Five; or, The Children's Crusade is a book that hasn't yet been written. Vonnegut is so obsessed, so horrified by his subject that he quite literally cannot approach it, can only hint at it, surrounding it with semicomic non sequiturs, a kind of toned-down *Catch-22*. The subject is the firebombing of Dresden. But this subject is not the content of this novel. The novel is about any number of other things, and it is also about Vonnegut's failure to write the novel, his sense of despair, his conviction that it is a lousy novel, and so forth. Rarely has the failure of a piece of fiction been so obviously tied up with the author's intense desire to write about it. Vonnegut says in his introductory chapter that he has been writing or trying to write the story of the firebombing of Dresden for years, this is his "famous" unwritten novel, and yet what he has finally turned out is a highly artificial, glib, picaresque tale of someone named "Billy Pilgrim." Billy is captured by a flying saucer from the planet Tralfamadore on his daughter's wedding night and, gifted with a peculiar talent for timelessness, he can see past, present, and future, and relive or live these various times, but without the power to alter anything. This gives Vonnegut the chance to jump maniacally back and forth and ahead in time, creating a jumble of events and nonevents, since he is anxious not to write about his alleged subject, which is apparently the firebombing of Dresden. Of course, a writer writes about what he wants to write about, and it is quite possible that Vonnegut has been deluding himself for decades—what he really wants to write about is the nonsense of Billy Pilgrim, and not the seriousness of Dresden. It would have been kind of someone to tell him that he couldn't write about it anyway, since fiction is not written about events but about people: Vonnegut has not created any people here, only bizarre cutouts mouthing lines that are

sometimes funny and sometimes not. His grotesque scenes are unfelt because they are unimagined.

Joyce Carol Oates. *The Hudson Review.* Autumn
1969, pp. 535–36

Vonnegut's novels have something of Swift in them—not merely in the canny
pokes he takes at human weakness and the status quo, but a kind of fantasy
that allows him, as it allowed Swift, to isolate the objects of his attack and
praise. What Vonnegut praises is the human being—at least the human being
as Vonnegut defines the phrase. The human being is most human—and most
praiseworthy—when he lives wholeheartedly in his natural condition, working in the open, doing joyfully and spontaneously for his own support, loving other life, and being loved. Human worth—and hence significance—
resides in the *being* of the human. The self is its own reason for being; its
being is its own guarantee of its value. The more conscious one is of his
being, the more individual he is and the firmer is his guarantee.

For Vonnegut, one of the defining characteristics of authentic human
life is physical labor. The significance or worth of such Thoreauvian values
is not in the end of labor—profit—but in the act of labor itself, which is a
confirmation of the individual experience.

The act of loving also confers high value, both upon the lover and the
loved. Such love is the basis of Vonnegut's conception of morality, and it
rises from the metaphysical assumption that there can be no individual identity or satisfaction without ties with others, without a relationship with other
actual entities. In relativity, for example, there can be no motion—or entity—without other bodies. For Vonnegut, as for Fromm and Jaspers and
others, love is the foundation of satisfaction.

Love and work are the bases of human satisfaction; they are what the
human being is uniquely capable of. His moral relationship to others—to
society—is founded upon those attributes. They are virtues because they
intensify the reality of the highest good—the individual. Yet, noble as man
might be—and sometimes is—through love and work, he has his other side,
his "lack." Human satisfaction must always fall short of its conception, and
Vonnegut consistently undercuts the admirableness of human values and actions, introducing into his picture of experience moderation and ambiguity.
It is not this inherent "lack," however, that Vonnegut attacks with his bit-
terest satire. It is the institutions that men have built which turn men aside
from their proper activities to pursue the dehumanizing goals of empty material wealth and technological success. It is also the ignorance and the hate-
fulness of men that Vonnegut attacks, and he deals with these characteristics
in their social aspect, for they are evil mainly as they thwart the valuable
satisfactions of others. What excites his ire also is the impediments men set
in their own way toward their own satisfaction and meaning, which exist

only in the individual. What inhibits the full play of the individual must be attacked and pulled down.

Man for Vonnegut is a complex combination of nobility and meanness, knowledge and ignorance, grandeur and ignominy. Thus, for all its tone of despair, *Cat's Cradle* is probably Vonnegut's most "mature" book. It expresses man's tremendous need to make myths in explanation of his condition, and it shows as that need's companion the inescapable recognition that our explanations are only myths. This is the definition and the frustration of being human.

Jerry H. Bryant. *The Open Decision* (New York: The Free Press, 1970), pp. 303–5

Kurt Vonnegut, Jr., who has always considered himself of the mainstream and rejects the claim to being a science fiction writer, is reviewed with respect and enthusiasm by the literary pundits of America, and, by God, he deserves every word of it and is, in my opinion, one of the most originally brilliant science fiction writers going.

Of Vonnegut's seven hardcover books, four are distinctly in the science fiction genre and the other three are spectacular in their own way. What makes him, then, a mainstream writer rather than a science fiction writer?

The answer is because he says so, because he never wrote for the pulps or the category magazines and because he gets the highest rates for his writings—much higher than the sums paid by the standard science fiction publishers. Vonnegut is unique in that he apparently caters to nobody in his storytelling, that he has a positively scintillating cynicism the like of which cannot be found elsewhere, that he packs his books with razor-edged social comments, that he apparently does not seem to take his science fiction elements with that often deadly seriousness that so many of the regulars do.

Donald A. Wolheim. *The Universe Makers* (New York: Harper & Row, 1971), pp. 70–71

Kurt Vonnegut, Jr., through his novels and stories, has crafted for his readers an exceedingly mad world. Grouped perhaps rashly with the Black Humorists, Vonnegut holds his own, matching Yossarians with Howard Campbells, Guy Grands with Eliot Rosewaters, and Sebastian Dangerfields with Malachi Constants. But unlike Joseph Heller, Vonnegut is prolific, tracing his vision through many different human contexts. He surpasses Terry Southern by striking all limits from human absurdity: destruction by nuclear fission is for Vonnegut the most passe of apocalypses. Moreover, he teases us with a Mod Yoknapatawpha County; "Frank Wirtanen" and "Bernard B. O'Hare" (originally characters in his third novel, *Mother Night*) and others appear again and again, always (as befits the modern county) in a maddening metamorphosis of roles. Favorite cities such as "Rosewater, Indiana" and "Ilium, New York" are storehouses for the paraphernalia of middle-class life which so delight Vonnegut, whose region is one of cultural value rather than geographical place. But unlike Southern and Bruce Jay Friedman, who mock such culture in the sociosatiric mode of Evelyn Waugh, Vonnegut uses his roots more like John Barth uses Maryland: interest lies beneath the surface and the surface itself is constantly changing. Vonnegut, in short, demands independent investigation. One finds at the end of Vonnegut's vision a "fine madness" indeed, but a madness at the same time more clinical and more comic than found elsewhere.

Perhaps a reason for the long critical neglect of Kurt Vonnegut is that his vision is superficially akin to that of Orwell, Huxley, and others who have written dolefully of the mechanical millennium to come. His first novel, *Player Piano,* warns of the familiar *Brave New World* future, while the much praised title story of *Welcome to the Monkey House,* with its Ethical Suicide Parlors and waning sentimental Romanticism, recalls Evelyn Waugh's alternatives of "Love Among the Ruins."

Jerome Klinkowitz. *Critique: Studies in Modern Fiction, Vol. 12, No. 3.* 1971, pp. 38–53

Vonnegut is moral in an old-fashioned way. He does take the full weight of responsibility, while more and more people are shrugging off the *we should have* and *we ought to have* and *we can if we want* and coming to see history as a puppet show and our—humanity's—slide into chaos as beyond our prevention, our will, our choice. The strength of Kurt Vonnegut, Jr., this deliberate and self-conscious heir, derives from his refusal to succumb to this new and general feeling of helplessness.

Precisely because in all his work he has made nonsense of the little categories, the unnatural divisions into "real" literature and the rest, because he is comic and sad at once, because his painful seriousness is never solemn, Vonnegut is unique among us; and these same qualities account for the way a few academics still try to patronize him: they cling to the categories. Of course they do: they invented them. But so it has ever gone.

Ordinary people, with whole imaginations, reading the newspapers, the comic strips, and Jane Austen, or watching the world reel by on television, keep an eye out for Ice 9 while hoping that we are indeed recognizing the members of our *karasses* when they come near, try to make sure that we don't pay more than what is due to the false *karasses,* and dare to believe that while there is life, there is still life—such readers know that Vonnegut is one of the writers who map our landscapes for us, who give names to the places we know best.

Doris Lessing. *The New York Times Book Review.* February 4, 1973, p. 35

In Vonnegut's seventh novel, *Breakfast of Champions,* which he refers to as his fiftieth birthday present to himself, is Vonnegut's own parody of Vonnegut. The absurd, insignificant details he has used to highlight his earlier novels becomes the major fictional technique of this work, as Vonnegut deliberately overemphasizes his view of man's obscenely inflated opinion of himself. Science fiction writer Tagore Trout, a minor figure in previous novels, is the major character in this one. Trout's market for his futuristic writings is a hard-core pornography publisher, World Classics Library, which uses his texts to provide the socially redeeming excuse for completely unrelated graphic illustrations. Within the covers of one of these volumes, *Now It Can Be Told,* Trout presents a story which causes Pontiac Thaler Dwayne Hoover to go mad. In the story, the one sane man in the universe is surrounded by human robots created for the pleasure of the Creator of the universe, who wants to see how the only man with free will chooses to act toward them.

"I am cleansing and reviewing myself for the very different sorts of years to come," says Vonnegut. To accomplish this, he says, he is freeing his literary slaves, the characters who have served him in earlier works. A must for Vonnegut aficionados, *Breakfast of Champions* will be a bewildering first reading for those unfamiliar with the iconoclastic views of this country's best unreconstructed science fiction writer.

Robin Ahrold. Library Journal. April 15, 1973,
p. 1311

Kurt Vonnegut, with his new novel, his best so far, has become for me a hero of modernist culture. *Breakfast of Champions* is a minutely ordered representation of cosmic chaos. It endorses the only values that can be endorsed, even the chaos, and it endorses them the only way they can be endorsed (given the chaos), and that is ironically, but they are endorsed just the same. They are endorsed by a plot in the course of which the novel's characters restore its author's health. What they believe and what they do serve equally to reveal the source of his distress and the grounds for health. They are calculated to serve us in the same way, but they will do so only if we will submit ourselves to their reality, as does their author, who is not entirely Kurt Vonnegut.

The awareness of this novel of itself as a novel is part of its assertion of the human against the mindless and mechanical chaos of reality that the novel represents. Another constituent of that assertion is the *how* of the representation, the aesthetic rendering, which stands against the *what* that is represented. The relations of part to part and part to whole are Byzantine and beautiful. Every part of the representation is linked to every other part to form an ordered world of fiction, one in opposition to a real world without end that has been whirled without aim. "It is hard to adapt to chaos, but it can be done. I am living proof of that: It can be done."

Given the fidelity with which this fictional order represents real chaos, all I can say to any fellow bands of light about to read this novel, people about to go Trout fishing in America, is what one character in *Breakfast of Champions* says to another: "Welcome to the real world, Brother."

George Stade. *Harper's*. May 1973, pp. 87–90

To many, Kurt Vonnegut remains more of a phenomenon than a writer to be taken seriously, his success more of an accidental product of the 1960s than anything else. But even though there is some validity in this view, it is neither fair nor complete. . . .

Vonnegut establishes what seems to be an essential and unusual bond between himself and his audience. He is the kindly uncle of American fiction, and this is a good thing for him to be. Like so many of his readers in the 1960s, Vonnegut argues for the existence of multiple realities and multiple life-styles, expresses a general disbelief in history and religion, tends to see himself as a victim of forces beyond his control, and despairs about any lasting hope for the human condition. But through his willingness to suggest internalized solutions involving imagination and rationalizing fantasies, Vonnegut expresses what are essentially moral-uplift messages.

Nonetheless, Vonnegut masterfully uses his technique to present a view of self-destructive humanity working at full speed to destroy the world through global war, manic rates of reproduction, automation, pollution, political chauvinism, drugs, and good old greed. As pessimistic as this vision is, Vonnegut employs it for essentially comic purposes—and this is where the uplift comes in. He adopts the viewpoint of cosmic irony, which allows him to ridicule hilariously the comical absurdity of human attempts at alleviating chaos through self-contradicting philosophies and programs for living.

At one point or another, Vonnegut parodies human faith in the efficacy of technology, in the soundness of capitalism, in the benefits of philanthropy, in the saving grace of religious systems, and in the social and intellectual values to be found in the traditional novel. His jibes are not always easy to take, and his manner often seems discouragingly stoical. But behind all of his novels is the voice of someone who is himself the victim of some too dimly apprehended, too late understood, cosmically ironic joke. And Vonnegut puts himself into several of his books as a character, just to make certain that he is seen taking his licks along with the rest of us.

Vonnegut's method does sometimes seem to go against his admittedly sentimental and even homely themes. Vonnegut does hold throughout to a pervasive and often dismaying skepticism or cool, but he does it with a mitigating earnestness that takes some of the hard edges off. Similarly, his forthright, self-effacing, unadorned language is an implied rebuke of the double-speak that has assailed America from Joe McCarthy to Richard Nixon.

Vonnegut does deserve to be taken seriously, both as a moralist and an artist. "His basic views," as Richard Bodtke points out, "are not profound or complex, but they are relevant, deeply felt, and (most important) transmuted into first-rate comic art.'' He offers more than levity; he gives us an honest perception of the quality of twentieth-century life, and he creates a gnomic style that imposes a visionary end on his sense of discontinuity— even if it is summed up in his most famous aphorism, ''So it goes.''

James Lundquist. *Kurt Vonnegut* (New York:

Ungar, 1977), pp. 101–4

WAUGH, HILLARY (1920–   )

If a single book had to be chosen to show the possibilities in the police novel which are outside most crime fiction, no better example could be found than *Last Seen Wearing* (1952), by Hillary (Baldwin) Waugh. This brilliant, realistic novel opens with the disappearance of Marilyn Lowell Mitchell, a pretty eighteen-year-old freshman at Parker College, Bristol, Massachusetts. We see the wheels move slowly as her friends become alarmed, the house mother rings the girl's father in Philadelphia, her address book is examined, a telephone call is reluctantly made to the Bristol police. Thereafter we follow the investigation as Chief Frank W. Ford and Detective Sergeant Burton K. Cameron conduct it, with all its false trails, fending off of newsmen, consultation with parents, teachers, friends. Perhaps Creasey should have ignored that advice not to put in the dull part of police work, for it is "the dull part," the painstaking checking and the following of every thread until it breaks in the hand, that Waugh makes most interesting. By treating seriously the anguish of the parents and their certainty that their daughter would never have done anything they did not approve of, he produces some fine character studies. And the ending has the neatest possible twist, with one of the chief characters never appearing on stage at all.

Like other writers of the police novel—and he preceded both McBain and Marric—Waugh was confronted with the problem of writing similar books sufficiently varied to keep the reader's interest. He solved it by replacing Ford and Cameron with Fred C. Fellows, Chief of a small-town police force, and his right-hand man, Detective Sergeant Sidney Wilks. Fellows and Wilks have more humanity than the earlier detectives—indeed, Fellows is a little too folksy for some tastes—and the small-town atmosphere gives their activities a personal flavor. *Last Seen Wearing* remains Waugh's best book, but almost all the later ones manage to be reasonably realistic without dullness. *That Night It Rained* (1961) and *Pure Poison* (1967) are particularly good.

Julian Symons. *Mortal Consequences: A History—
from the Detective Story to the Crime Novel* (New
York: Harper & Row, 1972), p. 207

Hillary Waugh was one of the first writers of police procedurals. An early police routine novel with a good twist ending, *Last Seen Wearing* (1952), details an investigation into the disappearance of a Massachusetts college girl. At the time he wrote it, Waugh lived in New Haven, and his future bride, Diana M. Taylor, was a freshman at Smith College. The Waughs have two daughters and a son.

The policemen in *Last Seen Wearing* never became series characters, but Waugh did create two series detectives. One is Fred Fellows of "Stockford," Connecticut, a patient and thorough rural policeman who is capable of great compassion. In *Prisoner's Plea* (1963), Fellows, acting on his own, reopens a murder case because he believes the personal appeal made by a convicted murderer.

Harsher and more brutal is Waugh's series about New York detective Frank Sessions of Homicide North, introduced in *"30" Manhattan East* (1968). In *The Young Prey* (1969) Sessions investigates the brutal killing of a teen-age girl in Harlem.

Waugh has also written mysteries under the pseudonyms Harry Walker and H. Baldwin Taylor. As Taylor, he wrote *The Triumvirate* (1966), in which the detective is the editor of a New England newspaper.

Chris Steinbrunner and Otto Penzler. *Encyclopedia of Mystery and Detection* (New York: McGraw-Hill, 1976), pp. 413–14

If Hillary Waugh had done nothing else than create the character of Chief Fred Fellows, he would hold an enviable place in the annals of detective fiction. Waugh has, however, another distinguished credit on his record: he wrote *Last Seen Wearing. . .* , widely recognized as one of the master-pieces of mystery-suspense fiction.

Unlike most writers of police fiction who set their stories in places like New York or Los Angeles, Waugh chose the small town of "Stockford," Connecticut, as the setting of the Fred Fellows series. Stockford is a rather ordinary town inhabited by conventional people, though it does have a de-lightfully high homicide rate.

Chief Fellows, a tobacco-chewing, story-telling folksy type who has problems with keeping his chest measurement greater than his waist mea-surement, may give a first impression of being the stereotyped rube cop, but that he most decidedly is not. Fellows knows his police work, and although his methods are usually informal, they are well organized and consistent with forensic science. In *Road Block,* for example, he can get an approxi-mate fix on the robbers' hangout by figuring the mileage on a car that has been driven to that point, and in *The Con Game* he uses publicity to deter-mine the whereabouts of a fugitive. Fellows also has the abilities of the police expert, however, as in *The Late Mrs. D.,* where he identifies some typing on the basis of very competent analysis of the idiosyncrasies of the type face used.

Fellows is a strict chief (he chews out a patrolman for showing up with an unpolished button and chases a group of card-playing reporters out of headquarters), but he is a considerate officer who allows his men as much latitude as he can, and he is interested in justice to the extent that he once spent his vacation (in *Prisoner's Plea*) investigating the case of a condemned criminal who had appealed to him for help.

In some ways Fellows is closer to the Great Policeman tradition of Inspector Maigret than to that of the police procedural. He is a believer in police teamwork, but more often than not the solutions to his mysteries come from the workings of Fellows's intelligence rather than lucky breaks or the legwork of his subordinates. On more than one occasion Fellows has solved the case only two-thirds of the way into the story and spends the rest of the time searching for confirmatory proof.

Before he began the Fred Fellows series, Waugh wrote *Last Seen Wearing . . .*, which Julian Symons selected for his list of the hundred greatest crime novels. Aspiring writers of mystery fiction could profitably study the structure of this fine story, which is a model of sustained suspense. The tight form of *Last Seen Wearing . . .* is shaped by a pure, uncluttered storyline, with no sub-plots and no spinoffs, no distraction of attention from the consuming problem presented at the beginning, repeatedly analyzed, and finally resolved without having been diluted or distorted. The most remarkable feature of the novel, as far as its structure is concerned, is that all the relevant facts (including a reasonably accurate speculation regarding the solution) are presented in the original definition of the problem, which occupies the first fourth of the book. From there on, the suspense is sustained by means of re-examination of the mystery from different points of view, and by the growing intensity of excitement as various explanations are tested. False leads and false clues are not allowed to stand for more than two or three pages, and periods of confusion are of short duration. One indication of the tight plotting of the story is that the first real break in the case does not come until halfway through the book.

Waugh is a practitioner of the well-made novel. Unlike many other writers of police procedurals, he avoids multiple plots, and the mystery presented at the beginning of a story is the one solved at the conclusion. The typical Waugh story fits the classic pattern of detective fiction: the Problem, the Initial Solution, the Complication, the Period of Confusion, the Dawning Light, the Solution, and the Explanation.

Waugh's other series policeman is Detective Second Grade Frank Sessions of Homicide, Manhattan North. Although his sphere of operation is quite different from Fred Fellows's Stockford, Sessions shares with Fellows the mold of the Genteel Policeman, in that he is more like Ngaio Marsh's Roderick Alleyn than most of the other roughnecks of police fiction: dining with a young woman at a good French restaurant, Sessions is annoyed by her apparent impression that a policeman is out of his depth anywhere else than at a lunch counter. He is, also like Fellows, a real professional who deplores the lack of pride and enthusiasm among young cops and who feels frustrated when a rapist-murderer gets off free. Society is all wrong. Sessions believes, but the police have to keep on trying.

Waugh has also written mysteries involving Sheridan Wesley and Philip Macadam, both standard private-eye types that might have come from the pages of Raymond Chandler, and he has produced a considerable body of non-series suspense stories, including ghostly tales and women's gothics.

Hillary Waugh has been a pioneer in the development of the police procedural story, along with Lawrence Treat in the United States and Maurice Procter in England. His main contribution to the craft has been his refusal to follow the formula adopted by most other writers with the result that his police stories are less conventional and harder to imitate, depending more on sharp definition than on multiplicity of involvements in the development of mystery and suspense.

George N. Dove. In John M. Reilly, ed.,
Twentieth-Century Crime and Mystery Writers:
Second Edition (New York: St. Martin's Press,
1985), p. 884

WELLS, H. G. (1866–1946)

In *The Time Machine* a speculative mechanician is supposed to have discovered that the "fourth dimension," concerning which mathematicians have speculated, is Time, and that with a little ingenuity a man may travel in Time as well as in Space. Mr. Wells supposes his Time Traveller to travel forward from A.D. 1895 to A.D. 802,701, and to make acquaintance with the people inhabiting the valley of the Thames. He finds that the gentle, pleasure-loving race of the surface of the earth has improved away all its dangers and embarrassments while the race of the underworld—the race which has originally sprung from the mining population—has developed a great dread of light, and a power of vision which can work and carry on all its great engineering operations with a minimum of light. At the same time, by inheriting a state of servitude it has also inherited a cruel contempt for its former masters, who can now resist its attacks only by congregating in crowds during the hours of darkness, for in the daylight, or even in the bright moonlight, they are safe from the attacks of their former serfs. This is, we take it, the warning which Mr. Wells intends to give: "Above all things avoid sinking into a condition of satisfied ease; avoid a soft and languid serenity; even evil passions which involve continuous effort, are not so absolutely deadly as the temperament of languid and harmless playfulness." We have no doubt that, so far as Mr. Wells goes, his warning is wise. But we have little fear that the languid, ease-loving, and serene temperament will ever paralyze the human race after the manner he supposes, even though there may be at present some temporary signs of the growth of the appetite for mere amusement.

In the first place, Mr. Wells assumes, what is well-nigh impossible, that the growth of the pleasure-loving temperament would not itself prevent that victory over physical obstacles to enjoyment on which he founds his dream.

In the next place Mr. Wells's fancy ignores the conspicuous fact that man's nature needs a great deal of hard work to keep it in order at all, and that no class of men or women are so dissatisfied with their own internal condition as those who are least disciplined by the necessity for industry. There would be no tranquillity or serenity at all in any population for which there were not hard tasks and great duties. Yet Mr. Wells's fanciful and lively dream is well worth reading, if only because it will draw attention to the great moral and religious factors in human nature which he appears to ignore.

Richard Holt Hutton. *The Spectator*. July 13,
1895, pp. 41–43

Frankly—*The Invisible Man* is uncommonly fine. One can always *see* a lot in your work—there is always a "beyond" to your books—but into this (with due regard to theme and length) you've managed to put an amazing quantity of effects. If it just misses being tremendous, it is because you didn't make it so—and if you didn't, there isn't a man in England who could. As to b— furriners they ain't in it at all.

I suppose you'll have the common decency to believe me when I tell you I am always powerfully impressed by your work. And if you want to know what impresses me it is to see how you contrive to give over humanity into the clutches of the Impossible and yet manage to keep it down (or up) to its humanity, to its flesh, blood, sorrow, folly. *That* is the achievement! In this little book you do it with an appalling completeness. I'll not insist on the felicity of incident. This must be obvious even to yourself. Three of us have been reading the book and we have been tracking with delight the cunning method of your logic. It is masterly—it is ironic—it is very relentless—and it is very true. We all three (the two others are no fools) place the *I.M.* above the *War of the Worlds*. Whether we are right—and if so why— I am not sure, and cannot tell. I fancy the book is more strictly human, and thus your diabolical psychology plants its points right into a man's bowels. To me the *W. of the W.* has less of that sinister air of truth that arrests the reader in reflection at the turn of the page so often in the *I.M.* In reading this last, one is touched by the anguish of it as by something that any day may happen to oneself. It is a great triumph for you.

Joseph Conrad. In G. Jean-Aubry, ed., *Joseph
Conrad: Life and Letters* (New York: Doubleday,
1927), pp. 259–60

The world having survived the attack of the Martians [in *The War of the Worlds*], Mr. Wells carries on its history a stage further [in *When the Sleeper*

Wakes], and shows us what it will be two hundred years hence. The blasphemer will say, after reading Mr. Wells's prognostications, that it is a great pity that the Martians did not clear the whole place out, for a duller and more disreputable world than it becomes, always according to Mr. Wells, it would be difficult to conceive.

The chief innovation to be introduced is flying machines, which are of two kinds—aeropiles, a sort of flying private hansom, and aeroplanes, a volatile omnibus of huge capacity. For the rest, London and other cities will be entirely roofed in, sweating will be a worse abuse than ever, and phonographs will take the place of books and newspapers. The Salvation Army will be interested to hear that its match factories are the germ of a vast system of slave labor, or something very like it; and as for the morals of our great-granddaughters the less said about them the better.

The method by which Mr. Wells leads up to all this arid prophecy is by giving a man of this age a cataleptic trance for two hundred years, when he wakes up to find that his wealth, increasing at compound interest, has made him virtually master of the world. At the end of the book he has an exciting fight from an aeropile; but on the whole he is a sorry, incoherent creature, who does not make the most of his opportunities. Mr. Wells cannot be congratulated on his latest effort; it is not very ingenious, and it is distinctly dull.

The Athenaeum. June 3, 1899,
n.p.

There is an author whose work has appealed to me very strongly from an imaginative standpoint, and whose books I have followed with considerable interest. I allude to Mr. H. G. Wells. Some of my friends have suggested to me that his work is on somewhat similar lines to my own, but here, I think, they err. I consider him, as a purely imaginative writer, to be deserving of very high praise, but our methods are entirely different. I have always made a point in my romances of basing my so-called inventions upon a groundwork of actual fact, and of using in their construction methods and materials which are not entirely without the pale of contemporary engineering skill and knowledge.

Take, for instance, the case of the *Nautilus*. This, when carefully considered, is a submarine mechanism about which there is nothing wholly extraordinary, nor beyond the bounds of actual scientific knowledge.

The creations of Mr. Wells, on the other hand, belong unreservedly to an age and degree of scientific knowledge far removed from the present, though I will not say entirely beyond the limits of the possible. Not only does he evolve his constructions entirely from the realm of imagination, but he also evolves the materials of which he builds them. See, for example, his story *The First Men in the Moon.* You will remember that here he introduces an entirely new antigravitational substance, to whose mode of preparation or actual chemical composition we are not given the slightest clue, nor does a reference to our present scientific knowledge enable us for a moment to predict a method by which such a result might be achieved. In *The War of the Worlds,* again, a work for which I confess I have a great admiration, one is left entirely in the dark as to what kind of creatures the Martians really are, or in what manner they produce the wonderful heat ray with which they work such terrible havoc on their assailants.

In saying this, I am casting no disparagement on Mr. Wells's methods; on the contrary, I have the highest respect for his imaginative genius. I am merely contrasting our two styles and pointing out the fundamental difference which exists between them, and I wish you clearly to understand that I express no opinion on the superiority of either the one or the other.

Jules Verne. Temple Bar. June 1904, pp. 664–71

Frank Harris relates that when Oscar Wilde was asked about Wells, he called him "a scientific Jules Verne." That was in 1899; it appears that Wilde thought less of defining Wells, or of annihilating him, than of changing the subject. Now the names H. G. Wells and Jules Verne have come to be incompatible. We all feel that this is true, but still it may be well to examine the intricate reasons on which our feeling is based.

The most obvious reason is a technical one. Before Wells resigned himself to the role of a sociological spectator, he was an admirable storyteller, an heir to the concise style of Swift and Edgar Allan Poe. Verne was a pleasant and industrious journeyman. Verne wrote for adolescents; Wells, for all ages. There is another difference, which Wells himself once indicated: Verne's stories deal with probable things (a submarine, a ship larger than those existing in 1872, the discovery of the South Pole, the talking picture, the crossing of Africa in a balloon, the craters of an extinguished volcano that lead to the center of the earth); the short stories Wells wrote concern mere possibilities, if not impossible things (an invisible man, a flower that devours a man, a crystal egg that reflects the events on Mars, a man who returns from the future with a flower of the future, a man who returns from the other life with his heart on the right side, because he has been completely inverted, as in a mirror). I have read that Verne, scandalized by the license permitted by *The First Men in the Moon,* exclaimed indignantly, *"Il invente!"*

The reasons I have given seem valid enough, but they do not explain why Wells is infinitely superior to the author of *Hector Servadac,* and also to Rosny, Lytton, Robert Paltock, Cyrano, or any other precursor of his methods. Even his best plots do not adequately solve the problem. In long books the plot can be only a pretext, or a point of departure. It is important for the composition of the work, but not for the reader's enjoyment of it. That is true of all genres; the best detective stories are not those with the best plots. (If plots were everything, the *Quixote* would not exist and Shaw would be inferior to O'Neill.) In my opinion, the excellence of Wells's first

novels—*The Island of Doctor Moreau,* for example, or *The Invisible Man*—
has a deeper origin. Not only do they tell an ingenious story; but they tell a
story symbolic of processes that are somehow inherent in all human destinies. The harassed invisible man who has to sleep as though his eyes were
wide open because his eyelids do not exclude light is our solitude and our
terror; the conventicle of seated monsters who mouth a servile creed in their
night is the Vatican and is Lhasa. Work that endures is always capable of
an infinite and plastic ambiguity; it is all things for all men, like the Apostle;
it is a mirror that reflects the reader's own traits and it is also a map of the
world. And it must be ambiguous in an evanescent and modest way, almost
in spite of the author; he must appear to be ignorant of all symbolism. Wells
displayed that lucid innocence in his first fantastic exercises, which are to
me the most admirable part of his admirable work.

Those who say that art should not propagate doctrines usually refer to
doctrines that are opposed to their own. Naturally this is not my own case;
I gratefully profess almost all the doctrines of Wells, but I deplore his in-
serting them into his narratives. An heir of the British nominalists, Wells
condemns our custom of speaking of the "tenacity of England" or the "intrigues of Prussia." The arguments against that harmful mythology seem to
be irreproachable, but not the fact of interpolating them into the story of
Mr. Parham's dream. As long as an author merely relates events or traces
the slight deviations of a conscience, we can suppose him to be omniscient,
we can confuse him with the universe or with God; but when he descends
to the level of pure reason, we know he is fallible. Reality is inferred from
events, not reasonings; we permit God to affirm *I am that I am* (Exodus
3:14), not to declare and analyze, like Hegel or Anselm, the *argumentum
ontologicum.* God must not theologize; the writer must not invalidate with
human arguments the momentary faith that art demands of us. There is another
consideration: the author who shows aversion to a character seems not to
understand him completely, seems to confess that the character is not inevitable for him. We distrust his intelligence, as we would distrust the intelligence of a God who maintained heavens and hells. God, Spinoza has written, does not hate anyone and does not love anyone.

Like Quevedo, like Voltaire, like Goethe, like some others, Wells is
less a man of letters than a literature. He wrote garrulous books in which
the gigantic felicity of Charles Dickens somehow reappears; he bestowed
sociological parables with a lavish hand; he constructed encyclopedias, enlarged the possibilities of the novel, rewrote the Book of Job—"that great
Hebrew imitation of the Platonic dialogue"; for our time, he wrote a very
delightful autobiography without pride and without humility; he combated
Communism, Nazism, and Christianity; he debated (politely and mortally)
with Belloc; he chronicled the past, chronicled the future, recorded real and
imaginary lives. Of the vast and diversified library he left us, nothing has
pleased me more than his narration of some atrocious miracles: *The Time*

Machine, The Island of Doctor Moreau, The Plattner Story, The First Men in the Moon. They are the first books I read; perhaps they will be the last. I think they will be incorporated, like the fables of Theseus or Ahasuerus, into the general memory of the species and even transcend the fame of their creator or the extinction of the language in which they were written.

Jorge Luis Borges. In Patrick Parrinder, ed., H. G.
Wells: The Critical Heritage (London: Routledge &
Kegan Paul, 1972), pp. 330–32

I have lately read all H. G. Wells's scientific books from *The Time Machine* to *The War in the Air* and it has been a refreshing experience. There was a time, one realizes, when science was fun. For the food of the gods is more entertaining than the prosaic efficacy of vitamins; the tripods of the Martians are more engaging than tanks. And then, here you have Wells at his best, eagerly displaying the inventive imagination, first with the news and at play, with an artist's innocence. Here you see his intoxicated response— a response that was lacking in his contemporaries—to the front-page situation of his time, and here you meet his mastery of the art of storytelling, the bounce and resource of it. Above all, in these early books, you catch Wells in the act, his very characteristic act, of breaking down mean barriers and setting you free. He has burst out himself and he wants everyone else to do the same. . . .

I cannot include *The War in the Air* among his best; it is an astonishing piece of short-term prophecy and judgment. One remembers the bombing of battleships and the note on the untroubled minds of those who bomb one another's cities; but the book is below Wells's highest level. So, too, is *The Invisible Man*, which is a good thriller, but it develops jerkily and is held up by horseplay and low comedy. Without question *The Time Machine* is the best piece of writing. It will take its place among the great stories of our language. Like all excellent works it has meanings within its meaning and no one who has read the story will forget the dramatic effect of the change of scene in the middle of the book, when the story alters its key, and the Time Traveller reveals the foundation of slime and horror on which the pretty life of his Arcadians is precariously and fearfully resting. I think it is fair to accuse the later Wells of escaping into a dream world of plans, of using science as a magic staircase out of essential social problems. I think the best Wells is the destructive, ruthless, black-eye-dealing and house-burning Wells who foresaw the violence and not the order of our time. Where *The Time Machine* relieves us by its poetic social allegory, *The Island of Dr. Moreau* takes us into an abyss of human nature. This book is a superb piece of storytelling from our first sight of the unpleasant ship and its stinking, mangy menagerie, to the last malign episode where the narrator is left alone on the island with the Beast-Men. The description of the gradual break in the morale of the Beast-Men is a wonderful piece of documented guesswork. It is easy enough to be sensational. It is quite another matter to do-mesticate the sensational. One notices, too, how Wells's idea comes full circle in his best thrillers. There is the optimistic outward journey, there is the chastened return.

It would be interesting to know more about the origins of *The Island of Dr. Moreau,* for they must instruct us on the pessimism and the anarchy which lie at the heart of Wells's ebullient nature. This is the book of a wounded man who has had a sight of sadism and death. The novelist who believes in the cheerful necessity of evolution is halted by the thought of its disasters and losses. Perhaps man is unteachable. It is exciting and emanci-pating to believe we are one of nature's latest experiments, but what if the experiment is unsuccessful? The price of progress may be perversion and horror, and Wells is honest enough to accept that. . . .

Wells's achievement was that he installed the paraphernalia of our new environment in our imagination; and life does not become visible or tolera-ble to us until artists have assimilated it. We do not need to read beyond these early scientific works of his to realize what he left out. He did not reckon with the nature, the moral resources, the habits of civilized man. Irresponsible himself, he did not attribute anything but an obstructive value to human responsibility. That is a serious deficiency, for it indicates an ignorance of the rooted, inner life of men and women, a jejune belief that we live by events and programs; but how, in the heyday of a great enlarge-ment of the human environment, could he believe otherwise? We turn back to our Swift and there we see a mad world also; but it is a mad world dominated by the sober figure of the great Gulliver, that plain, humane fig-ure. Not a man of exquisite nor adventurous spirituality; not a great soul; not a man straining all his higher faculties to produce some new mutation; not a man trying to blow himself out like the frog of the fable to the impor-tunate dimensions of his program; but, quite simply, a man. Endowed with curiosity, indeed, but empowered by reserve. Anarchists like Wells, Kip-ling, Shaw, and the pseudo-orthodox Chesterton, had no conception of such a creature. They were too fascinated by their own bombs.

V. S. Pritchett. *The Living Novel* (New York:
Random House, 1947), pp. 32–38

Wells's importance was primarily as a liberator of thought and imagination. He was able to construct pictures of possible societies, both attractive and unattractive, of a sort that encouraged the young to envisage possibilities which otherwise they would not have thought of. Sometimes he does this in a very illuminating way. His "Country of the Blind" is a somewhat pessi-mistic restatement in modern language of Plato's allegory of the cave. His various utopias, though perhaps not in themselves very solid, are calculated to start trains of thought which may prove fruitful. He is always rational, and avoids various forms of superstition to which modern minds are prone. . . . In spite of some reservations, I think one should regard Wells as having been an important force toward sane and constructive thinking, both as regards social systems and as regards personal relations. I hope he may have successors, though I do not at the moment know who they will be.

Bertrand Russell. *The Listener*. September 10, 1953, n.p.

Wells's pessimistic last writings and utterances were, and still are, being represented as an abandonment of a superficial optimism in the face of those realities of which his coming death was a part. The suggestion is made that they were some kind of final admission that he had been wrong about the nature of things for the greater part of his life. I cannot now agree that his final phase of scolding and complaining at human folly represented any essential change in his views at all.

It is impossible to believe in progress if you believe in a universe in which mind figures as a local accident, and which by its nature cannot support any permanent moral order or indeed any permanent thing. That Wells was deeply committed to this view is evident from his first novel, *The Time Machine*, which has its climactic scene at a point some thirty million years in the future. A cosmic catastrophe is impending which will finally obliterate the material context in which such concepts as mind, consciousness, and value, can possess any meaning. The possibility of such a situation is irreconcilable with the idea of progress, and Wells states his disbelief in it in this book without ambiguity. . . .

One of the difficulties of writing about Wells is that his mind was undisciplined, and that on any given point he can be found either to contradict himself, or to appear to do so. *The Time Machine* was immediately followed by *The Island of Dr. Moreau*, which Wells discussed much later, in the twenties, as if he had accepted a dualistic picture of human nature while he was writing it.

This would give innate virtue a refuge in the intellect, and would allow for optimism as a possibility. But what happens in *The Island of Dr. Moreau* is a disaster, the liberated intellect in the person of a Darwinian humanitarian arrives on the island and disintegrates its theocratic moral order by making an appeal to reason which assumes that Dr. Moreau's victims are moral creatures with better natures. When they are set free from the Hobbesian régime of terror under which they have been living it is revealed that they are, beneath Dr. Moreau's scar tissue, brutes interested only in the satisfaction of their appetites. So far as a conflict between instinct and injunction goes, it is no contest; order and law are imposed on the brutish inhabitants of the island by an exterior force, and as soon as that is removed the system collapses. What the book in fact expresses is a profound mistrust of human nature, and a doubt about the intellect's ability to contain it. There is even a doubt about the intellect as a possible containing force, since its role in the story is a purely destructive one.

The Island of Dr. Moreau relates closely to two other stories, a short novel and a short story, which deal with the same theme of the liberated intellect as a destructive element. *The Invisible Man* is a parable about the amoral aspects of the scientific outlook, and invisibility figures in it as a symbol of intellectual isolation. "The Country of the Blind" is a much more mature version of the same parable. The theme is carried further in *The War of the Worlds* and in *The First Men in the Moon.* The Martians, like the ruling class on the moon, are brain cases with the merest of vestigial bodies, symbols of the intellect triumphant over the animal. The point that techno-logical mastery has given the Martians a sense that they are free from moral responsibility is obscured by the surface action in *The War of the Worlds.* Most readers do not see beyond the fact that the Martians arrive, and treat Europeans as Europeans had been treating native populations and animals in the hey-day of colonialism, to the deeper argument. But there is no possi-bility of misunderstanding the description of lunar society which appears towards the end of *The First Men in the Moon.* The unfettered intellect rules, and respect for efficiency stands in the place of morality. What has come into being is the worst kind of slave state. In the end, what Wells is saying in *The First Men in the Moon,* is that the basis of operations which Huxley recommended in his famous Romanes lecture, and which he had himself adopted and stated in the concluding paragraphs of *The Time Machine,* is not viable. Because if a mechanistic view of the universe is con-structed by the right hand, the left will inevitably loose its grip on any ethical system it may have decided to grasp.

It may seem that this is reading something into *The First Men in the Moon* which is not there, but Wells went out of his way to state it in a mundane context in *When the Sleeper Wakes.* It stands as the optimistic and naïvely uncritical forerunner of Aldous Huxley's *Brave New World,* and Orwell's *1984.* The difference between Wells's horrors and those described by Huxley and Orwell reside mainly in points of detail. Wells was writing before the two great wars and the dictatorships had made the State as dan-gerous an engine as it now seems. For Wells the enemy was monopoly capitalism as it presented itself in the form of the great corporations. But his business State is just as monstrous as the police State of Orwell's imagina-tion, and is perhaps worse in that it does not bother to persecute individuals as individuals, but simply treats people in terms of social categories and utility.

Anthony West. *Principles and Persuasions: The
Literary Essays of Anthony West* (New York:
Harcourt, 1957), pp. 10–23

H. G. Wells has been called the father, the one authentic genius, even the Shakespeare of science fiction. All these judgments can be called into question. But even today, when science fiction is attracting more first-rate writers than ever and is taken more seriously by "official" literary critics than ever, the burden of proof is still on the person who wants to question such judgments, not the one who affirms them. Wells's first novel, *The Time Machine* (1895), was an immediate success. Between 1895 and 1914 he produced, among many other works, a series of "scientific romances" that, by the outbreak of the First World War, had helped to make him one of the best-selling and most controversial writers of his time. And the influence of those novels and stories on what came to be called "science fiction" continues to be nothing less than gigantic.

If science fiction is, as some defenders argue, mainly important as technological prophecy, Wells's record is impressive. *The Time Machine* can be read . . . as a prophecy of the effects of rampant industrialization on that class conflict which was already, in the nineteenth century, a social powder keg. Disraeli had warned—and Marx had demonstrated—that the industrialized state was in danger of becoming two nations, the rich and the poor; but the real horror, Wells warns, is that they might become two races, mutually uncomprehending and murderously divided. In *The War of the Worlds* (1898) he hinted at, and in later stories fully anticipated, the disastrous innovations the discovery of flight could bring to the business of warfare. In *When the Sleeper Wakes* (1899) he predicted a future society in which devices very like video cassettes have replaced printed books, and an ignorant populace is force-fed censored news through things he calls "Babble Machines." And in *The World Set Free* (1914)—perhaps his most celebrated anticipation—he invented the phrase "atomic bomb," and detailed with some accuracy the apocalyptic power of chain reaction weapons or, in his phrase, "continuing explosives." . . .

H. G. Wells gave us a series of novels of more and more homiletic, more and more strenuous and urgent social analysis and prophecy whose explicit aim was to change the course of history, bringing human science into congruity with human moral development, and thereby saving the world from a second, total, perhaps final world war.

Frank McConnell. *The Science Fiction of H. G.
Wells* (New York: Oxford University Press, 1981),
pp. 3–5

Despite the remarkable range of his work in fiction, philosophy, and social criticism, H. G. Wells is undoubtedly best known to most readers as a writer— indeed the inventor—of "science fiction," the man who built a time machine, created an invisible man, put men on the moon, and described the destruction of much of England by hideous creatures from Mars. But of course well before Wells, writers in various times and places had already written of daring journeys to far-flung locales; Cyrano de Bergerac, for one, wrote of rocket ships and extraterrestrial life in *The History of the States and Empires of the World of the Moon,* published in 1656. In the early nineteenth century, Mary Shelley (in *Frankenstein*) and Nathaniel Hawthorne (in such stories as "The Birthmark" and "Rappacini's Daughter") evoked the eerie atmosphere of the Gothic romance as they pointed to the kind of horrific consequences that can accompany scientific experimentation—a theme that continues to recur in the science fiction of today. *Five Weeks in a Balloon,* the first of Jules Verne's highly popular novels of scientific adventuring, appeared in 1863, three years before Wells was born. With such similar novels as *Journey to the Center of the Earth* (1864) and *From the Earth to the Moon* (1865), Verne built the foundation of modern science fiction. . . .

Wells did squander much of his enormous talent. Despite calling repeatedly for selflessness and the transcendence of ego, Wells was thoroughly self-absorbed; he could find few human beings as fully fascinating as himself—obviously a major shortcoming in a novelist with serious artistic aspirations. . . .

And of course, as Wells himself admitted, the ability to maintain a steady writing routine is itself no guarantee of consistent quality. In the beginning of his career, as he worked desperately to survive both professionally and economically, Wells produced his very best work. But he was always susceptible to distraction, and once he found himself with ample opportunities to play the part of the famous prophet and sage, he found it increasingly difficult to sustain the kind of intense concentration that is essential for the steady production of first-rate work. Artistically, Wells ceased to stretch and chose to coast. True, there is almost always something to admire in even the least of Wells's fictions; often, there is intellectual power, lively dialogue, stylistic grace. But, as frequently, there is little more than garrulousness and pontification, symptoms of an unusually gifted man operating on automatic pilot, repackaging characters and plots, and justifying this practice by insisting, disingenuously, that he never aspired to artistic greatness anyway. . . .

Still, it remains a fact that nearly one hundred years after their publication such works as *The Time Machine, The War of the Worlds, The Invisible Man* continue to sell well throughout the world, reminding yet another generation of readers of Wells's imaginative powers and narrative skills, his brilliant ability to combine humor with suspense, to bring an air of plausibility to the utterly impossible. . . .

Of course, in other respects, the world that Wells had exhorted and excoriated at the turn of the century remains little changed. There is everywhere fear, violence, illiteracy, poverty, greed. In much of the world, population growth remains dangerously unchecked; cities choke in pollution made possible because of governmental indifference and, too frequently, a total lack of respect for the idea of careful social planning. . . . Without wide and immediate action—without, for example, systematic cuts in the use of those fuels that produce carbon dioxide—it is quite possible that Wells's vision of the apocalypse could materialize. His image of a bleak and barren earth will no longer be merely a chilling image in a haunting fiction. Our world is not likely to made better by squads of Wells's pious airmen leveling buildings and burning books. But that it could still use far more education and anticipation—and far less illusion—would be hard to deny. At his best, Wells stood for the best in humanity: for reason, foresight, courage, cooperation, hope. And it is at his best that he deserves to be remembered and read.

Brian Murray. *H. G. Wells* (New York: Continuum, 1990), pp. 86, 155–58

WESTLAKE, DONALD E. [also known as RICHARD STARK and TUCKER COE] (1933–   )

It was Donald Westlake who broke new ground to make a career out of humor in the mystery genre—humor that was slapstick and outrageous enough to satisfy large groups of people and make him a kind of cult figure in the genre. Writing under different names—Richard Stark and Tucker Coe were two of his most popular pseudonyms—Westlake in the 1950s produced some routine "tough guy" mysteries. After experimenting with several comic mysteries in the 1960s, he found his voice in the early 1970s, with what was to become his own light-hearted "caper" formula. In *The Hot Rock* (1970), Westlake unveiled Dortmunder, a stylized reincarnation of the rogue thief, the picaro, transported to the twentieth from the seventeenth century— but with one crucial difference. Dortmunder is a flake, a nerd, an inept.

Although the picaro tends to tempt the writer to discursive, plotless structure, Westlake eschewed this element and instead perfected the "inside" story of a specific "job"—in effect, he made each Dortmunder story a detailed caper in itself, a *Topkapi* or *Rififi*, but portrayed in a comic vein. Because of the popularity of the anti-hero during the 1960s, Westlake's books featuring Dortmunder were bought up by Hollywood, and were made into popular comic movies.

Westlake's caper novels include *The Fugitive Pigeon* (1962), *The Spy in the Ointment* (1966), *The Hot Rock* (1970), *Bank Shot* (1972), and *Jimmy the Kid* (1972), *Nobody's Perfect* (1977), *Why Me?* (1983), and *Good Behavior* (1986). While the serious caper works—Eric Ambler's *The Light of Day*, for example (the basis for the motion picture *Topkapi*); or, in America, W. R. Burnett's classic *The Asphalt Jungle*—create suspense by the detailed recounting of the planning, practicing, and final execution of a complicated criminal effort, in the typical Westlake story everything goes wrong at the crucial moment. The effect on the reader is one of laughter and hilarity rather than cold perspiration on the brow.

The key element that makes Westlake's anti-hero work is the milieu of the 1960s and 1970s in which his stories take place. The anti-hero is bent on pulling the tail of the lion (read, establishment); he robs because he is getting back at the fat cats whom he dislikes. Besides, the fat cats are, in his mind, just as dishonorable as he is, even though their actions may be within the letter of the law. When things fall apart, it is a big laugh to the reader. No one is going to kill the anti-hero; he is too inept and pitiable to deserve *that* kind of treatment. He is to be laughed off at the end; maybe, in fact, he might even get to keep the loot!

Bruce Cassiday. The Literature of Crime and
Detection (New York: Ungar, 1988), p. 188

Donald E. Westlake is only in his early thirties, very young as crime novelists go these days; but already one can speak of his oeuvre in terms of Periods. In his First Period, 1960–63, Westlake proved himself one of the ablest practitioners of the absolutely tough, hard-nosed novel of crime, with an acute insight into criminal thinking and an enviable ability to shock legitimately, without excess or bad taste. Then, after a one-book interlude (a psychological whodunit in 1964: Period I–A), he entered on his present and glorious Second Period of criminous farce-comedies, as warm and funny as his early books were cold and frightening. The only common element in the two periods is a faultless professional craftsmanship in plotting, dialogue, and characterization.

In earlier comedies Westlake has enjoyed his sport with the Syndicate and with espionage. *God Save the Mark,* the season's most pleasing title, is about con games. Fred Fitch is a born mark—a predestined victim of every shrewd operator. When he inherits $317,000 from his murdered uncle, he also inherits the murderer; someone is now out not to fleece him but to kill him. What results is a splendid action-farce, a delightful comedy of character, and a brief encyclopedia on the art of the con, long and short. I've no idea what skills Mr. Westlake has yet to reveal to us; but I'm sure that his Second Period will go down as one of the most entertaining episodes in suspense novel history.

Anthony Boucher. The New York Times Book
Review. July 23, 1967, p. UK

Donald E. Westlake, the comic novelist of American crime fiction, has written his Profane Comedy, irreverent, impudent, and rakish. If not his choice effort to date, *Brothers Keepers* still has some glorious moments of divine comedy undefiled by any uncharitable act of scorn or blasphemy.

Amid all his comic antics, Westlake never is merely silly. He is a genuine comic novelist, using laughter to expose the incongruities, complacencies, hypocrisies, and pretensions of society. Rarely does Westlake's comedy backslide to the level of gross burlesque. . . .

Westlake's high-spirited humor is somewhat constrained within the bounds of a monastery, and *Brothers Keepers* doesn't attain the mad dash of some of the earlier capers, particularly those with the engaging Dortmunder gang. After all, an innocent lamb can stray only so far, even on monastery business in the outside world. Westlake must strain to reach a happy ending, but all can be forgiven for those hilarious moments of high comedy of character and situation.

> Jean M. White. *The New Republic*. December 13,
> 1975, p. 31

Donald Westlake explains why he decided to end the Tucker Coe series featuring private investigator Mitch Tobin: "The problem for me was that Mitch Tobin wasn't a static character. For him to remain miserable and guilt-ridden forever would have changed him into a self-pitying whiner. My problem was once Mitch reaches that new stability and becomes functional in the world again, he's merely one more private eye with an unhappy past. Not to name names, but don't we have enough slogging private eyes with unhappy pasts?"

> Dilys Winn. *Murder Ink/The Mystery Reader's
> Companion* (New York: Workman, 1977), n.p.

Under the pen name of Richard Stark, Donald Westlake has published a long series of novels featuring the professional thief Parker. Westlake comments about Parker:

"Parker is a Depression character, Dillinger mythologized into a machine. During the affluent days of the sixties he was an interesting fantasy, but now that money's getting tight again, his relationship with banks is suddenly both to the point and old-fashioned. He hasn't yet figured out how to operate in a world where hesitating is one of the more rational responses to the situation."

> Robert A. Baker and Michael T. Nietzel. *Private
> Eyes: One Hundred and One Knights* (Bowling
> Green, Ohio: Popular Press, 1985), p. 175

Donald E. Westlake's *Trust Me on This* is an amusing lampoon of the sort of news reporting represented by supermarket checkout tabloids. And a criminous thread runs through the narrative. Sara Joslyn lost her job with a New England weekly and in some desperation accepted a position with the *Weekly Galaxy,* where no news is unfit to print (as long as passed by the checkers and the lawyers). In fact, *WG* specializes in drivel, pure and unalloyed, triply distilled, and scrupulously guarded against contamination. While driving down the four-lane highway in Florida that leads only to *WG*, Sara passes a parked car containing one bullet-dispatched corpse—an observation in which everyone at *WG* proves supremely disinterested. They are preoccupied with trying to sell their ideas to Bruno DeMassi, owner and editor and publisher, whose office is an elevator. The penalty for subeditors not supplying enough grist to the *WG* mill is being put on the street with the sure knowledge that no one will hire an ex-*WG* employee. This peril hounds editor Jack Ingersol, to whose team Sara is assigned. The corpse in the car recedes a bit in Sara's mind under the pressure of manufacturing stories— such as the hundred-year-old twins' birthday party (but what's to be done when one dies before the magnificent bash that Sara has conjured up?), the wedding of TV star John Michael Mercer (but what famous person in his right mind would talk to a *WG* staffer?), the death of a country singer of renown (but how to get a picture of the body in the box?). And yet, what about the corpse in the car and other strange (including dangerous) things that have been happening to Sara? Joyously entertaining stuff.

Allen J. Hubin. The Armchair Detective. Winter
1990, p. 27

WHITNEY, PHYLLIS A. (1903–   )

Phyllis A. Whitney's books are not classic Gothics, yet she hews persistently to Gothic elements: the isolation of the heroine in a house, residence, or enclosed milieu of some kind; weird, sometimes supernatural, occurrences piling up one on top of another; strange events with no rational explanation, at least on the surface; the placing of the heroine in jeopardy; the atmosphere and mood of the old-fashioned ghost story.

Whitney was born in Yokohama. Perhaps because of this ingrown interest in the exotic, she sets the majority of her romantic suspense novels in foreign locales—or at least locales with a specific glamour and ambience. Setting to her is almost as important as characterization and plot. She thoroughly researches each place she writes about.

The Quicksilver Pool (1955) revolves around a Civil War crisis in New York City. *Skye Cameron* (1957) is a story about New Orleans at the close of the Civil War. *Thunder Heights,* the title of a 1960 novel, is named for a place on the Hudson River in New York State. *Blue Fire* (1961) takes place in South Africa. *Black Amber* (1964) is set in Turkey. Japan is the scene of *The Moonflower* (1958), an English country house of *Hunter's Green* (1968), the Virgin Islands of *Columbella* (1966), and Norway provides the background for *Listen for the Whisperer* (1972).

Her first books were written for young adults. With *Red Is for Murder* (1943), she began writing for an adult audience, and by 1955, with *The Quicksilver Pool,* most of her works were crafted for the adult market.

Most of Whitney's novels concern the members of a specific family; essentially, she writes a "family mystery," and in doing so, favors two basic variations of this formula. One involves the return of the female protagonist to a home she has left many years before. Events occur that upset her. She cannot understand what is happening. A feeling of anxiety and unease is in the air. She begins to fear for her life. And with good reason. In another, a young bride settles into the home of her husband. In this brand new milieu strange, upsetting events occur. She does not understand why these unnerving things are happening, and tries to find out what is causing such obvious anxiety and distress. With dire results.

The typical Whitney offering usually involves an actual unsolved crime— probably murder—that has occurred sometime in the past. The arrival of the protagonist on the scene then sets off complications that place her life in jeopardy.

In many cases, the heroine is searching into her background. Usually she uncovers a criminal plot of some kind, and on its discovery achieves a sense of personal identity. She may be involved in a mother-daughter relationship, possibly one overlaid with competitive antagonism.

The story line rarely delves into detection or deduction, but there is a great deal of poking about, with few real secrets divulged in the course of the narrative action. This unsuccessful probing heightens suspense to an almost unbearable degree, until at the very end the villain is unmasked, the methodology of the crime is revealed, the motive is divulged, and the reward goes to the heroine. Only at this point does everything come clear in a blinding flash.

The evil is usually that of an ambiguous kind; the unease, the angst experienced by the protagonist is overall, pervasive, and amorphous at best. Yet it is nevertheless very real. Real enough to put Whitney's books frequently on the best-seller lists, constantly swelling her legions of faithful fans.

> Waltraud Woeller and Bruce Cassiday. *The*
> *Literature of Crime and Detection* (New York:
> Ungar, 1988), pp. 164–65

Skye Cameron is another story of New Orleans in the 1880s, of lacy ironwork, shadowy courtyards and the heady scent of jasmine.

When Skye Cameron, twenty-two and red-headed, suddenly found herself transported from a small New England town to the home of her aristocratic Uncle Robert, in the Vieux Carré, she realized that the changes in her life had only begun—but would they be for the better or for the worse? To her mother's warnings regarding the character of her uncle she paid little heed—Uncle Robert had received them most graciously. Besides, here was young Courtney, her uncle's law clerk, who was already paying her compliments.

On the other hand, as Skye was soon to discover, customs in New Orleans differed from customs in New England, and the tall quadroon servant, Delphine, was destined to be to her more of a duenna than servant. Then, too, a young lady of twenty-two was highly marriageable, and marriage, to the Creole mind, had much more to do with family fortunes than with romantic love. And it was about this time that Skye got her first glimpse of Justin Law, the man with the shadow over his past.

The author of this tale is a practiced weaver of romances, and the story moves along at a good pace toward an artfully prepared climax. Unfortunately, it seems always to hover on the border line between teenage and adult fiction, as if Miss Whitney, experienced in both fields, could not quite make up her mind which one she was working in. The events too have a familiar ring, as do the characters, and the latter are so superficially realized that they fail to arouse much interest in the reader's mind as to what is going to happen to them.

Jennings Rice. *New York Herald Tribune Book Review*. December 22, 1957, p. 8

Jane Eyre as a prototype has been successfully used again by Phyllis Whitney in her latest novel *Columbella*. The governess-cum-mystery is set in St. Thomas, Virgin Islands, and has all the necessary ingredients of interesting characters, exotic setting, and fast-paced story.

When Jessica Abbott accepted Maude Hampden's request to be a tutor for her granddaughter, she had a twofold purpose: the one was to detach herself from a past spent caring for her invalid mother, now deceased; the other to help Leila Drew, (the granddaughter of Mrs. Hampden), whose mother was using her as a pawn against her father. Jessica entered the beautiful Hampden mansion, a seething environment that led to violence; but her persistence also led to a satisfactory denouement which must not be divulged here.

The characterization is secondary to the story, which keeps the reader suspensefully alert. The portrait of Catherine Drew, (Leila's mother), as an embodiment of evil is unconvincing; she is a spoiled willful woman who makes life miserable for her family, but she is too shallow to be more than a pest. Jessica is her antithesis in quiet efficiency and stability. Leila is a typical fourteen-year-old. Kingdon Drew, the father of Leila, has strength but his weaknesses seem more apparent.

Columbella may be recommended to anyone who likes a romantic mystery. It is almost certain to become a best-seller. Phyllis Whitney fans will not be disappointed and Mary Stewart readers will like her American counterpart. *Columbella* is a most pleasant diversion.

Lucille G. Crane. *Best Sellers*. May 1, 1966, pp. 55, 60

Phyllis Whitney has been hailed as the American counterpart of Mary Stewart and Virginia Holt. *Hunter's Green* is another gothic story with all the details of the required ingredients: an ancient and history-crammed English estate; a gruff, dedicated, and misunderstood owner; an elderly woman; a few characters that may or may not lead the reader to guess which one is the villain; and of course, a newcomer, an outsider, innocent and victim of intrigue.

Yet one must admit that though the pattern is in general as unvarying as the rules for a sonnet or the recipe for a cake, there are always fresh approaches and the reader's attention is held. The story is very much up to date: there is a "Twiggy" sort of model, Cockney and assured; there are modern conveniences even though the house is cold; and that gruff hero has dedicated his obstacle-crammed activity to producing a fireproof fluid which will propel a crash-and-collision proof car—noiselessly.

There is one good thing about a narrative in the first person. One knows that the heroine isn't going to be killed, even though only four pages from the end of the book she is being driven at a murderous rate for a drop into a lethal quarry. She certainly has to live to tell the tale!

The conversation is good, distinguishing as it does the American from the Bahamian from the Cockney model from the aristocratic English. I would object somewhat to the title of the book: it does not do justice to the very clever scheme of the topiary with its yew tree carvings of chess pieces.

Miss Whitney's smiling promise has been satisfactorily fulfilled.

Sister M. Marguerite, RSM. Best Sellers. May 1,
1968, p. 61

The latest novels of Victoria Holt and Phyllis A. Whitney, two established authors in the romantic suspense field, illustrate some disappointing changes in this genre brought about by the onslaughts of current permissive attitudes toward sex and drugs, and by competition from the currently popular romance genre.

The modern world, with its pervasive social problems, is intruding on this genre and destroying its magic. This is disappointing because romantic suspense novels are read purely for entertainment and escapism. . . .

Whitney's *Rainsong* has a contemporary setting. The contemporary aspects of the plot and some of the characters' involvement in the music industry, in drug use, and in illicit sexual relationships, are superimposed over the traditional elements—assumed identities, a past tragedy, a brooding mansion, and a heroine in distress. The effect is jarring, and *Rainsong* simply doesn't work. The contemporary aspects rob the story of any possible fairy-tale qualities the traditional elements might provide. To top it off, the heroine, Hollis Sands, a songwriter and widow of a famous singer, is so incredibly naive, unwise, and unperceptive that she fails to elicit the necessary sympathy in the reader.

Names such as Victoria Holt and Phyllis A. Whitney were once synonymous with good quality romantic suspense fiction. That, unfortunately, seems to be changing.

Jane Stewart Spitzer. *The Christian Science Monitor.* April 6, 1984, p. B5

Every story has a setting. When setting is integrated into plot it becomes background. When setting affects actions and emotions of the characters, it becomes atmosphere. When setting becomes more important than characters, however, what you are left with is a diminution of story, because nothing is quite so interesting as people. . . .

What you have in Whitney's books, then, is an agreeable story interwoven with a travelogue, or an architectural exploration, and the psychological profile of an interesting "place," peopled with rather two-dimensional characters, and a puzzle that Whitney hopes is unsolvable until the last page.

"I'm not very blood-thirsty," Whitney says. "I like to tantalize. I love intrigue and I love to fool my readers."

Readers so tantalized, intrigued, and fooled, then, number in the millions; they have made Whitney an extremely wealthy woman. Her books, both hardcover and paperback, satisfy a large audience of faithful addicts.

Some critics of the author's chosen genre—romantic suspense—insist that it is formula writing without serious literary value. To which Whitney replies: "I don't care about critics. My goal is to write a better book each time. I simply try to tell a good story about interesting people." Usually she does that. To wish that she would go a little farther, dig a little deeper, is perhaps pointless.

Elaine Budd. *13 Mistresses of Murder.* (New York: Ungar, 1986), pp. 134–35

Phyllis A. Whitney has just published another book, *Flaming Tree*—her sixty-seventh. Nearly all her adult fiction works have been best-sellers and all were major book club selections. Since 1941, when her first hardcover publication appeared, she has been hard at work producing the kind of mainstream mystery suspense novels which have earned her a wide following, with over thirty million copies of her books in print.

Devoted fans know what to expect in a Phyllis A. Whitney novel, and I can think of at least eight things they can count on without fear of disappointment:

• A well-constructed story and a twisty plot, with an ending which almost always takes you by surprise.

• Plenty of mystery, suspense, and a heartfelt romance which is an integral part of the story.

• Characters who are motivated. You may not figure out why some of them do what they do until after the slam-bang climax, but you don't come away from one of her novels with that low-level irritation one feels with major characters whose behavior starts out—and remains—inexplicable.

• That necessary ingredient to a good plot: personal conflict.

• Heroines who are gutsy, intelligent, and resourceful, pitting their strength and savvy against intriguing heroes who are often troubled but, in the end, irresistible.

• An indelibly wrought sense of place. Each novel explores an exotic or appealing new locale, rendered in such living color and loving enthusiasm that Palm Springs and Newport and Key West—and now Carmel—should consider making her an honorary member of their Chambers of Commerce. (I, for one, come away from every Phyllis A. Whitney novel determined to put her latest discovery on some future itinerary.)

• An insider's look at some interesting or unusual human activity, expertly woven into the fabric of the story—and ranging imaginatively from orchid growing and scuba diving for treasure (*Dream of Orchids*) to songwriting and the pop music scene (*Rainsong*).

• A writing style laced with vivid imagery and a keen sense of drama.

In *Flaming Tree,* Whitney delivers all of the above—and something more. She has written a mystery with a core-theme of compassion.

You experience compassion almost from the first dramatic page. You sense its presence—or absence—in every character, and it is the leitmotif of the novel's heroine, Kelsey Stewart. . . . At the heart of the story is a small boy who struggles with much more than the secret locked in his damaged brain. Nine-year-old Jody Hammond . . . has fallen from the rocky cliff of Point Lobos, an accident which has put him in a coma and his mother Ruth, who fell with him, in a wheelchair. Kelsey Stewart is a skilled and sensitive physical therapist who must fight her own way back from a personal tragedy even as it spurs her on to greater efforts on behalf of the little boy.

The backdrop for the story's events is California's contribution to fairy-tale land: Carmel. "With its rocky seacoast, white sand beaches, and wind-shaped cypress and pine," it is a place of breathtaking, almost haunting beauty on the Monterey Peninsula. It is also a place with a pervasive sense of an age-old clash: good and evil. . . .

Flaming Tree, like its author, holds out a message of hope. In the words of the heroine: "One certainty that no one had taught her in any classroom, but which she had learned painfully through trial and error, was that unless one could *believe* in a return to the normal, the impossible could never be accomplished." In the words of the author: "We must never stop seeking for alternative and supplemental help, no matter how grave the problem. New answers are always coming in.''

Phyllis A. Whitney has written a novel that is highly entertaining even as it enlightens and uplifts.

Erika Holzer. *The Armchair Detective.* Summer 1986, pp. 310–11

WORKS MENTIONED

All genre novels mentioned in the reviews and critical studies are listed here. The titles are predominantly fiction. Collections of short stories are marked with the letter (s). Other special identifications are listed below. If no identification appears, the book is a genre novel.

The publication date refers to first American publication. When a British title differs from the American, it follows in brackets. If the British publication date differs, it is so noted. Translated titles appear in English only, with publication date first American publication. Occasionally, publication dates in the excerpts may differ from Works Mentioned. The editor has tried to include accurate bibliographical references in the Works Mentioned, according to the publications themselves, or other authoritative bibliographies.

Identifications include:

b	biography
c	critical study
d	drama
e	essay, essays
f	film, screen play
l	letters
r	review, reviews
s	short stories
t	travel

DOUGLAS ADAMS
(1952 –   )

The Hitchhiker's Guide to the Galaxy, 1979; *The Restaurant at the End of the Universe*, 1980; *Life, the Universe, and Everything*, 1982.

ERIC AMBLER
(1909 –   )

The Dark Frontier, 1936; *Background to Danger*, 1937 [*Uncommon Danger*]; *Cause for Alarm*, 1939; *A Coffin for Dimitrios*, 1939 [*The Mask of Dimitrios*]; *Epitaph for a Spy*, 1952; *State of Siege*, 1956 [*The Night-Comers*]; *The Light of Day*, 1962; *To Catch a Spy*, 1964; *Dirty Story*, 1967; *The Levanter*, 1972; *Doctor Frigo*, 1974; *The Care of Time*, 1981.

POUL ANDERSON
(1926 –   )

Brain Wave, 1954; *Virgin Planet*, 1959; *Trader to the Stars*, 1964; *Tau Zero*, 1970; *The Dancer from Atlantis*, 1971; *Operation Chaos*, 1971; *The Enemy Stars*, 1972; *The Winter of the World*, 1975; *The Avatar*, 1978.

PIERS ANTHONY
(1934 –   )

Chaining the Lady, 1978; *Cluster*, 1978; *Kirlian Quest*, 1978; *Thousandstar*, 1980; *Blue Adept*, 1981; *Juxtaposition*, 1982; *Viscous Circle*, 1982; *Dragon on a Pedestal*, 1983; *On a Pale Horse*, 1983; *Refugee*, 1983; *Bio of a Space Tyrant*, 1984; *Prostho Plus*, n.d.

ISAAC ASIMOV (a.k.a. PAUL FRENCH)
(1920–1992)

I, Robot, 1950 (s); *Pebble in the Sky*, 1950; *C-Chute*, 1951; *Foundation*, 1951; *The Stars, Like Dust*, 1951; *The Currents of Space*, 1952; *Foundation and Empire*, 1952; *Second Foundation*, 1953; *The Caves of Steel*, 1954; *The End of Eternity*, 1955; *The Martian Way and Other Stories*, 1955 (s); *The Naked Sun*, 1957; *The Silly Asses*, 1957; *Asimov's Mysteries*, 1968; *The Early Asimov; or Eleven Years of Trying*, 1972 (s); *The Gods Themselves*, 1972; *Foundation's Edge*, 1982.

MARGARET ATWOOD
(1939 –   )

The Circle Game, 1966; *The Edible Woman*, 1969; *Power Politics*, 1971; *Lady Oracle*, 1976; *Bodily Harm*, 1982; *The Handmaid's Tale*, 1985.

J. G. BALLARD
(1930 –   )

The Drowned World, 1962; *Four Dimensional Nightmare*, 1963 (s); *Terminal Beach*, 1964 (s); *The Crystal World*, 1966; *Love & Napalm*, 1972 [*Atrocity Exhibition*, 1970] (s); *Vermilion Sands*, 1973 (s); *Crash*, 1973; *Concrete Island*, 1974; *High-Rise*, 1975; *The Best Science Fiction of J. G. Ballard*, 1977; *The Unlimited Dream Company*, 1979; *Hello America*, 1981; *Empire of the Sun*, 1984.

ROBERT BARNARD
(1936 –   )

Death of an Old Goat, 1977; *Blood Brotherhood*, 1978; *Death on the High C's*, 1978; *Death of a Mystery Writer*, 1979 [*Unruly Son*, 1978]; *Death of a Literary Widow*, 1980 [*Post-humous Papers*, 1979]; *A Talent to Deceive: An Appreciation of Agatha Christie*, 1980 (b); *Death in a Cold Climate*, 1981; *Death of a Perfect Mother*, 1981 [*Mother's Boys*]; *Death and the Princess*, 1982; *Death by Sheer Torture*, 1982 [*Sheer Torture*, 1981]; *The Case of the Missing Brontë*, 1983 [*The Missing Brontë*]; *A Little Local Murder*, 1983; *School for Murder*, 1984 [*Little Victims*, 1983].

E. C. BENTLEY
(1875–1956)

Trent's Last Case, 1929.

LAWRENCE BLOCK
(1938 –   )

In the Midst of Death, 1976; *The Sins of the Father*, 1977; *Time to Murder and Create*, 1977; *A Stab in the Dark*, 1981; *Eight Million Ways to Die*, 1982.

RAY BRADBURY
(1920 –   )

The Martian Chronicles, 1950 (s); *Fahrenheit 451*, 1953; *Dandelion Wine*, 1957; *A Medicine for Melancholy*, 1959 (s); *Something Wicked This Way Comes*, 1962 (s); *S Is for Space*, 1966 (s); *I Sing the Body Electric!* 1969 (s); *The Veldt*, 1972 (in *The Wonderful Ice Cream Suit and Other Plays*) (d); *Long after Midnight*, 1976 (s); *The World of Ray Bradbury*, 1980 (d).

SIMON BRETT
(1945 –   )

Cast, in Order of Disappearance, 1976; *An Amateur Corpse*, 1978; *The Dead Side of the Mike*, 1980; *Not Dead, Only Resting*, 1984; *A Shock to the System*, 1984; *A Nice Class of Corpse*, 1987; *What Bloody Man Is That?* 1988.

ANTHONY BURGESS
(1917 –   )

A Clockwork Orange, 1962; *The Wanting Seed*, 1962; *A Vision of Battlements*, 1965; *1985*, 1978.

JAMES M. CAIN
(1892–1977)

The Postman Always Rings Twice, 1934; *Serenade*, 1937; *Mildred Pierce*, 1941; *Double Indemnity*, 1944; *The Butterfly*, 1947.

KAREL ČAPEK
(1890–1938)

R.U.R., 1923; *The Insect Play*, 1923; *Krakatit*, 1925; *The Makropulos Secret*, 1925 (d); *War with the Newts*, 1936; *The Absolute at Large*, 1927.

JOHN DICKSON CARR (a.k.a. CARTER DICKSON and CARR DICKSON)
(1906–1977)

It Walks by Night, 1930; *The Blind Barber*, 1934; [as Carter Dickson] *The Plague Court Murders*, 1934; *The Three Coffins*, 1935 [*The Hollow Man*]; *The Arabian Nights Murder*, 1936; *The Burning Court*, 1937; [as Carter Dickson] *The Peacock Feather Murders*, 1937 [*The Ten Teacups*]; [as Carter Dickson] *The Judas Window*, 1938; *The Problem of the Green Capsule*, 1939 [*The Black Spectacles*]; *The Problem of the Wire Cage*, 1939; [as Carter Dickson] *The Reader Is Warned*, 1939; *The Case of The Constant Suicides*, 1941; *The Emperor's Snuff Box*, 1942; *The Life of Sir Arthur Conan Doyle*, 1949 (b); *The Bride of Newgate*, 1950; *The Devil in Velvet*, 1951; (with Adrian Conan Doyle) *The Exploits of Sherlock Holmes*, 1954 (s); *Fire Burn!* 1957.

RAYMOND CHANDLER
(1888–1959)

The Big Sleep, 1939; *Farewell, My Lovely*, 1940; *The High Window*, 1942; *The Lady in the Lake*, 1943; *The Little Sister*, 1949; *The Long Goodbye*, 1954; *Playback*, 1958; *Raymond Chandler Speaking*, 1962 (l); *Poodle Springs* (unfinished) [in *Raymond Chandler Speaking*] (finished by Robert B. Parker); *Killer in the Rain*, 1964 (s); *The Smell of Fear*, 1965 (s).

G. K. CHESTERTON
(1874–1936)

The Napoleon of Notting Hill, 1904; *The Man Who Was Thursday: A Nightmare*, 1908; *The Ball and the Cross*, 1909; *The Innocence of Father Brown*, 1911 (s); *Manalive*, 1912; *The Man Who Knew Too Much and Other Stories*, 1922 (s); *Tales of the Long Bow*, 1925; *Collected Poems*, 1933 (p); *The Father Brown Omnibus*, 1947 (s); *The Return of Don Quixote*, 1927; *The Poet and the Lunatic: Episodes in the Life of Gabriel Gale*, 1929 (s); *The Paradoxes of Mr. Pond*, 1937 (s).

AGATHA CHRISTIE
(1891–1976)

The Man in the Brown Suit, 1924; *The Murder of Roger Ackroyd*, 1926; *The Big Four*, 1927; *The Mysterious Affair at Styles*, 1927; *Peril at End House*, 1932; *Thirteen at Dinner*, 1933 [*Lord Edgware Dies*]; *The Boomerang Clue*, 1934 [*Why Didn't They Ask Evans?*]; *Murder in the Calais Coach*, 1934 [*Murder on the Orient Express*]; *The A.B.C. Murders*, 1936; *Cards on the Table*, 1937; *Death on the Nile*, 1938; *Easy to Kill*, 1939 [*Murder Is Easy*]; *And Then There Were None*, 1940 [*Ten Little Niggers*, 1939]; *Evil under the Sun*, 1941; *Death Comes as the End*, 1944; *The Hollow*, 1946; *Come, Tell Me How You Live*, 1946 (t); *Crooked House*, 1949; *Mrs. McGinty's Dead*, 1952; *The Mousetrap*, 1954 (d); *Witness for the Prosecution*, 1954 (d); *What Mrs. McGillicuddy Saw!* 1957 [*4.50 from Paddington*]; *Towards Zero*, 1957; *A Caribbean Mystery*, 1965; *At Bertram's Hotel*, 1966; *Passenger to Frankfurt*, 1970; *Nemesis*, 1971; *Curtain*, 1975.

MARY HIGGINS CLARK
(1929 –   )

Where Are the Children? 1975; *A Stranger Is Watching*, 1977; *The Cradle Will Fall*, 1980.

ARTHUR C. CLARKE
(1917 –   )

Childhood's End, 1951; *The City and the Stars*, 1956; *2001: A Space Odyssey*, 1968; *Rendezvous with Rama*, 1973; *The Fountains of Par-*

adise, 1979; *2010: Odyssey Two*, 1982; *Profiles of the Future*, 1973.

WILKIE COLLINS
(1824–1889)

Antonina, 1850; *Basil*, 1852; *The Dead Secret*, 1857; *The Woman in White*, 1860; *No Name*, 1862; *Armadale*, 1866; *The Moonstone*, 1868; *The New Magdalen*, 1873; *The Law and the Lady*, 1875; *The Fallen Leaves*, 1879.

MICHAEL CRICHTON [a.k.a. JOHN LANGE, JEFFREY HUDSON, and MICHAEL DOUGLAS]
(1942 –)

[as Jeffrey Hudson] *A Case of Need*, 1968; *The Andromeda Strain*, 1969; [as Michael Douglas] (with Douglas Crichton) *Dealing, or The Berkeley-to-Boston Forty-Brick Lost-Bag Blues*, 1971; [as John Lange] *Binary*, 1972; *The Terminal Man*, 1972; *The Great Train Robbery*, 1975.

AMANDA CROSS [CAROLYN G. HEILBRUN]
(1926 –)

In the Last Analysis, 1964; *The James Joyce Murder*, 1967; *Poetic Justice*, 1970; *The Theban Mysteries*, 1971; *The Question of Max*, 1976; *Death in a Tenured Position*, 1981; *Sweet Death, Kind Death*, 1984; *No Word from Winifred*, 1986; *The Players Come Again*, 1990.

DOROTHY SALISBURY DAVIS
(1916 –)

The Judas Cat, 1949; *The Clay Hand*, 1950; *A Gentle Murderer*, 1951; *A Town of Masks*, 1952; *Men of No Property*, 1956; *Death of an Old Sinner*, 1957; *Old Sinners Never Die*, 1959; *The Evening of the Good Samaritan*, 1961; *The Pale Betrayer*, 1965; *Enemy and Brother*, 1966; (with Jerome Ross) *God Speed the Night*, 1968; *Where the Dark Streets Go*, 1969; *Shock Wave*, 1972; *The Little Brothers*, 1973; *A Death in the Life*, 1976; *Scarlet Night*, 1980; *Lullaby of Murder*, 1984.

LEN DEIGHTON
(1929 –)

The Ipcress File, 1963; *Funeral in Berlin*, 1965; *Billion-Dollar Brain*, 1966; *Horse under Water*, 1968; *Bomber*, 1970; *Eleven Declarations of War*, 1975 [*Declarations of War*, 1971 (s)]; *Yesterday's Spy*, 1975; *Fighter*, 1978; *XPD*, 1981; *Berlin Game*, 1984; *Mexico Set*, 1985; *London Match*, 1985.

SAMUEL R. DELANY
(1942 –)

Babel-17, 1966; *The Einstein Intersection*, 1967; *Nova*, 1968; *Fall of the Towers*, 1970 (incl. *Captives of the Flame, The Towers of Toron*, and *City of a Thousand Suns*); *Dhalgren*, 1975; *Triton*, 1976; *The Jewel-Hinged Jaw: Notes on the Language of Science Fiction*, 1977 (c); *Stars in My Pocket Like Grains of Sand*, 1984.

ARTHUR CONAN DOYLE
(1859–1930)

Micah Clarke, 1889; *A Study in Scarlet*, 1890; *The White Company*, 1891; *The Adventures of Sherlock Holmes*, 1892 (s); *The Sign of Four*, 1893; *Round the Red Lamp, Being Facts and Fancies of Medical Life*, 1894 (s); *The Stark Monro Letters*, 1895; *Rodney Stone*, 1896; *The Hound of the Baskervilles*, 1902; *The Lost World*, 1912.

DAPHNE DU MAURIER
(1907 –)

The Loving Spirit, 1931; *The Progress of Julius*, 1933; *Jamaica Inn*, 1936; *Rebecca*, 1938; *Frenchman's Creek*, 1942; *My Cousin Rachel*, 1952; *The Parasites*, 1958; *Not after Midnight and Other Stories*, 1971 (s); *The Winding Stair: Francis Bacon, His Rise and Fall*, 1977.

FRIEDRICH DÜRRENMATT
(1921 –)

The Judge and His Hangman, 1954; *The Visit*, 1958 (d); *The Pledge: Requiem for the Detective Novel*, 1958; *Traps*, 1960; *The Quarry*,

1962; *Once a Greek . . .* , 1965; *The Execution of Justice*, 1990.

DICK FRANCIS
(1920 –   )

Dead Cert, 1962; *Nerve*, 1964; *For Kicks*, 1965; *Knock-Down*, 1975; *Whip Hand*, 1980; *Reflex*, 1981; *Twice Shy*, 1982; *Banker*, 1983; *Longshot*, 1990.

ERLE STANLEY GARDNER [a.k.a.
A. A. FAIR]
(1889–1969)

The Case of the Dangerous Dowager, 1937; *The D.A. Calls It Murder*, 1937; [as A. A. Fair] *The Bigger They Come*, 1939; *The Case of the Empty Tin*, 1941; [as A. A. Fair] *Double or Quits*, 1941; [as A. A. Fair] *Spill the Jackpot*, 1941; [as A. A. Fair] *Bats Fly at Dusk*, 1942; [as A. A. Fair] *Owls Don't Blink*, 1942; [as A. A. Fair] *Cats Prowl at Night*, 1943; [as A. A. Fair] *Give 'em the Ax*, 1944; *The D.A. Breaks an Egg*, 1949; *The Case of the Murderer's Bride and Other Stories*, 1969 (s); [as A. A. Fair] *All Grass Isn't Green*, 1970.

MICHAEL GILBERT
(1912 –   )

They Never Looked Inside, 1949; *Smallbone Deceased*, 1950; *Death in Captivity*, 1952; *Fear to Tread*, 1953; *The Country-House Burglar*, 1955 [*Sky High*]; *The Claimant*, 1957; *The Doors Open*, 1962; *After the Fine Weather*, 1963; *Close Quarters*, 1963; *The Crack in the Teacup*, 1966; *Game without Rules*, 1967 (s); *Overdrive*, 1968 [*The Dust and the Heat*, 1967]; *The Family Tomb*, 1969 [*The Etruscan Net*]; *The Body of a Girl*, 1972; *The Night of the Twelfth*, 1976; *Petrella at Q*, 1977 (s).

SUE GRAFTON
(1940 –   )

"A" Is for Alibi, 1982; *"B" Is for Burglar*, 1985; *"C" Is for Corpse*, 1986; *"D" Is for Deadbeat*, 1987; *"E" Is for Evidence*, 1988; *"G" Is for Gumshoe*, 1990; *"H" Is for Homicide*, 1991.

GRAHAM GREENE
(1904–1991)

The Man Within, 1929; *This Gun for Hire*, 1936 [*A Gun for Sale*]; *Brighton Rock*, 1938; *The Confidential Agent*, 1939; *The Labyrinthine Ways*, 1940 [*The Power and the Glory*]; *The Ministry of Fear*, 1943; *The Heart of the Matter*, 1948; *Nineteen Stories*, 1949 (s); *The Third Man*, 1950; *The End of the Affair*, 1951; *The Quiet American*, 1956; *Our Man in Havana*, 1958; *A Burnt-Out Case*, 1961; *The Honorary Consul*, 1973; *The Return of A. J. Raffles*, 1975; *The Human Factor*, 1978; *The Tenth Man*, 1985.

DASHIELL HAMMETT
(1894–1961)

The Dain Curse, 1929; *Red Harvest*, 1929; *The Maltese Falcon*, 1930; *The Glass Key*, 1931; *The Thin Man*, 1934.

ROBERT A. HEINLEIN
(1907–1988)

Beyond This Horizon, 1948; *The Puppet Masters*, 1951; *Double Star*, 1956; *The Door into Summer*, 1957; *Starship Troopers*, 1959; *Stranger in a Strange Land*, 1961; *The Moon Is a Harsh Mistress*, 1966; *Time Enough for Love: The Thieves of Lazarus Long*, 1973; *The Number of the Beast*, 1980; *Friday*, 1982.

FRANK HERBERT
(1920–1986)

Under Pressure, 1955 [a.k.a. *Dragon in the Sea* and *21st Century Sub*]; *Dune*, 1965; *Destination: Void*, 1966; *The Heaven Makers*, 1968; *Dune Messiah*, 1969; *Whipping Star*, 1970; *Hellstrom's Hive*, 1973; *Children of Dune*, 1976; *Santaroga Barrier*, 1976; *Dune Trilogy*, 1979 [including *Dune*, *Dune Messiah*, and *Children of Dune*]; *The Jesus Incident*, 1979; *The Lazarus Effect*, 1983.

HERMANN HESSE
(1877–1962)

Siddhartha, 1922; *The Steppenwolf*, 1929; *Magister Ludi*, 1949; *The Journey to the East*,

1957; *Demian*, 1965; *The Glass Bead Game*, new translation 1969.

PATRICIA HIGHSMITH
(1921 –   )

Strangers on a Train, 1950; *The Blunderer*, 1954; *This Sweet Sickness*, 1960; *The Two Faces of January*, 1964; *Those Who Walk Away*, 1967; *The Tremor of Forgery*, 1969; *A Dog's Ransom*, 1972; *Ripley's Game*, 1974; *Slowly, Slowly in the Wind*, 1979 (s); *Found in the Street*, 1987.

TONY HILLERMAN
(1925 –   )

The Blessing Way, 1970; *The Dark Wind*, 1982; *A Thief of Time*, 1988.

CHESTER HIMES
(1909–1984)

If He Hollers Let Him Go, 1945; *Lonely Crusade*, 1947; *Cast the First Stone* 1952; *The Third Generation*, 1954; *The Primitive*, 1955; *The Crazy Kill*, 1959; *The Big Gold Dream*, 1960; *The Real Cool Killers*, 1959; *All Shot Up*, 1960; *Cotton Comes to Harlem*, 1965; *Pinktoes*, 1965; *Blind Man with a Pistol*, 1969; *For Love of Imabelle*, 1957 [a.k.a. *A Rage in Harlem*, 1965]; *Black on Black: Baby Sister and Selected Writings*, 1973 (s).

EDWARD D. HOCH
(1930 –   )

The Judge of Hades and Other Simon Ark Stories, 1971; *City of Brass and Other Simon Ark Stories*, 1971; *The Thefts of Nick Velvet*, 1978; *The Quests of Simon Ark*, 1984; *Leopold's Way*, 1985.

ALDOUS HUXLEY
(1894–1963)

Crome Yellow, 1921; *Mortal Coils*, 1922; *Antic Hay*, 1923; *Those Barren Leaves*, 1925; *Point Counter Point*, 1928; *Brave New World*, 1932; *Eyeless in Gaza*, 1936; *After Many a Summer Dies the Swan*, 1939; *Grey Eminence: A Study in Religion and Politics*, 1941 (e); *Time Must Have a Stop*, 1944; *The Perennial Philosophy*, 1945 (e); *Ape and Essence*, 1948; *Brave New World Revisited*, 1960; *Island*, 1962; *Literature and Science*, 1963.

MICHAEL INNES [J. I. M. STEWART]
(1906 –   )

Seven Suspects, 1937 [*Death at the President's Lodging*, 1936]; *Hamlet, Revenge!* 1937; *Lament for a Maker*, 1938; *The Spider Strikes*, 1939 [*Stop Press*]; *The Daffodil Affair*, 1942; *A Night of Errors*, 1947; *The Long Farewell*, 1958; *The Man Who Wrote Detective Stories and Other Stories*, 1959 (s); *Sheiks and Adders*, 1982; *Appleby and Honeybath*, 1983.

P. D. JAMES
(1920 –   )

Cover Her Face, 1966; *A Mind to Murder*, 1967; *Unnatural Causes*, 1967; *Shroud for a Nightingale*. 1971; *An Unsuitable Job for a Woman*, 1973; *The Black Tower*, 1975; *Death of an Expert Witness*, 1977; *Innocent Blood*, 1980.

FRANZ KAFKA
(1883–1924)

The Trial, 1925; *The Castle*, 1926.

STEPHEN KING
(1947 –   )

Night Shift, 1970 (s); *Carrie*, 1974; *Salem's Lot*, 1975; *The Shining*, 1977; *The Stand*, 1978; *The Dead Zone*, 1979; *Firestarter*, 1980; *Creepshow*, 1981 (f); *Danse Macabre*, 1986.

JOHN LE CARRÉ [DAVID JOHN MOORE CORNWELL]
(1931 –   )

Call for the Dead, 1962; *A Murder of Quality*, 1963; *The Spy Who Came in from the Cold*, 1964; *The Looking Glass War*, 1965; *A Small Town in Germany*, 1968; *The Naive and Sentimental Lover*, 1972; *Tinker, Tailor, Soldier, Spy*, 1974; *The Honourable Schoolboy*, 1977; *Smiley's People*, 1980; *The Little Drummer Girl*, 1983; *The Perfect Spy*, 1986; *The Russia House*, 1989.

URSULA K. LE GUIN
(1929 –   )

Planet of Exile, 1966; *Rocannon's World*, 1966; *City of Illusions*, 1967; *A Wizard of Earthsea*, 1968; *The Left Hand of Darkness*, 1969; *The Lathe of Heaven*, 1971; *The Tombs of Atuan*, 1971; *The Farthest Shore*, 1972; *The Ones Who Walk Away from Omelas*, 1972; *The Dispossessed*, 1974; *The New Atlantis*, 1975; *The Wind's Twelve Quarters*, 1975 (s); *Orsinian Tales*, 1976 (s); *The Word for World Is Forest*, 1972, 1976 (s); *Very Far Away from Anywhere Else*, 1976.

FRITZ LEIBER
(1910–1992)

Gather, Darkness! 1950; *Conjure Wife*, 1953; *The Green Millennium*, 1953; *Destiny Times Three*, 1957; *The Big Time*, 1961; *The Silver Eggheads*, 1962; *The Wanderer*, 1964; *Night of the Wolf*, 1966 (s); *A Specter Is Haunting Texas*, 1969; "Coming Attraction," 1974 (in *The Best of Fritz Leiber*); *The Worlds of Fritz Leiber*, 1976 (s); *Our Lady of Darkness*, 1977; *The Change War*, 1978 (s); "Adept's Gambit," n.d.

STANISLAW LEM
(1921 –   )

Solaris, 1961; *The Invincible*, 1973; *The Cyberiad: Fables of the Cybernetic Age*, 1974 (s); *The Futurological Congress*, 1974; *The Star Diaries*, 1976 (s); *Mortal Engines*, 1977; *A Perfect Vacuum*, 1979; *Tales of Pirx the Pilot*, 1979 (s); *Return from the Stars*, 1980; *Memoirs of a Space Traveler*, 1981; *The Cosmic Carnival of Stanislaw Lem*, 1981; *Microworlds: Writings on Science Fiction and Fantasy*, 1985 (c); *The New Cosmogony*, n.d.

ELMORE LEONARD
(1925 –   )

Hombre, 1961; *The Big Bounce*, 1969; *Valdez Is Coming*, 1970; *Fifty-two Pickup*, 1974; *Mr. Majestyk*, 1974; *Swag*, 1976; *The Hunted*, 1977; *Unknown Man No. 89*, 1977; *The Switch*,
1978; *City Primeval*, 1980; *Split Images*, 1981; *Cat Chaser*, 1982; *LaBrava*, 1983; *Stick*, 1983; *Glitz*, 1985; *Bandits*, 1987; *Freaky Deaky*, *Killshot*, 1988; *Get Shorty*, 1990.

DORIS LESSING
(1919 –   )

The Four-Gated City, 1969; *Memoirs*, 1974; *Canopus in Argos*, 1979; *Shikasta*, 1979; *The Marriages between Zones Three, Four, and Five*, 1980; *The Sirian Experiments*, 1981; *The Making of the Representative for Planet 8*, 1982; *The Sentimental Agents*, 1983.

C. S. LEWIS
(1898–1963)

The Pilgrim's Regress: An Allegorical Apology for Christianity, Reason, and Romanticism, 1933; *The Allegory of Love: A Study in Medieval Tradition*, 1936; *Out of the Silent Planet*, 1938; *The Screwtape Letters*, 1942; *Perelandra: A Novel*, 1943; *The Great Divorce: A Dream*, 1945; *That Hideous Strength: A Modern Fairy-Tale for Grownups*, 1945; *The Problem of Pain*, 1948; *English Literature in the Sixteenth Century, Excluding Drama*, 1954; *Till We Have Faces: A Myth Retold*, 1956; *The Last Battle*, 1959; *The Four Loves*, 1960; *The Discarded Image: An Introduction to Medieval and Renaissance Literature*, 1964; *The Letters to Malcolm: Chiefly on Prayer*, 1964.

H. P. LOVECRAFT
(1890–1937)

Supernatural Horror in Literature, 1925–27 (c); *The Dream-Quest of Unknown Kadath*, 1926–27; *The Case of Charles Dexter Ward*, 1927; *The Shuttered Room and Other Pieces*, n.d. (s); *Fen River*, n.d. (d).

ED McBAIN [SALVATORE A. LOMBINO] (a.k.a. EVAN HUNTER and RICHARD MARSTEN)
(1926 –   )

Cop Hater, 1956; *McBain's Ladies*, 1988; *Kiss*, 1992.

ANNE McCAFFREY
(1926–   )

Dragonflight, 1967; *Dragonquest*, 1971; *Dragonsong*, 1976; *Get off the Unicorn*, 1977 (s); *Dinosaur Planet*, 1978; *White Dragon*, 1978; *Dragondrums*, 1979.

JOHN D. MacDONALD
(1916–1986)

The Brass Cupcake, 1950; *Slam the Big Door*, 1960; *The Deep Blue Goodbye*, 1964; *Bright Orange for the Shroud*, 1965; *The Dreadful Lemon Sky*, 1975; *Condominium*, 1977; *One More Sunday*, 1984; *Barrier Island*, 1986.

ROSS MACDONALD [KENNETH MILLAR] (a.k.a. JOHN ROSS MACDONALD)
(1915–1983)

[as Kenneth Millar] *Blue City*, 1947; *The Way Some People Die*, 1951; *The Galton Case*, 1959; *The Wycherly Woman*, 1961; *The Zebra-Striped Hearse*, 1962; *The Far Side of the Dollar*, 1965; *Black Money*, 1966; *The Instant Enemy*, 1968; *The Goodbye Look*, 1969; *The Underground Man*, 1971.

NGAIO MARSH
(1895–1982)

Artists in Crime, 1938; *Death of a Peer*, 1940 [*Surfeit of Lampreys*, 1941]; *Vintage Murder*, 1940; *Death in Ecstasy*, 1941; *Enter a Murderer*, 1942; *A Man Lay Dead*, 1942; *Color Scheme*, 1943; *Tied up in Tinsel*, 1972; *Light Thickens*, 1982.

MARGARET MILLAR
(1915 –   )

The Invisible Worm, 1941; *The Devil Loves Me*, 1942; *Wall of Eyes*, 1943; *The Iron Gates*, 1945; *Beast in View*, 1955; *The Air That Kills*, 1957 [*The Soft Talkers*]; *The Listening Walls*, 1959; *A Stranger in My Grave*, 1960; *How Like an Angel*, 1962; *Beyond This Point Are Monsters*, 1970; *Ask for Me Tomorrow*, 1976; *Banshee*, 1983; *Spider Webs*, 1986.

MARCIA MULLER
(1944 –   )

Edward of The Iron Shoes, 1977; *Ask The Cards a Question*, 1982; *The Cheshire Cat's Eyes*, 1983; *The Tree of Death*, 1983; (with Bill Pronzini) *Double*, 1984; *Games to Keep the Dark Away*, 1984; *Leave a Message for Willie*, 1984; *The Legend of the Slain Soldiers*, 1985; *There's Nothing to Be Afraid Of*, 1985; (with Bill Pronzini) *Beyond the Grave*, 1986.

GEORGE ORWELL [ERIC ARTHUR BLAIR]
(1903–1950)

Down and Out in Paris and London, 1933; *Coming up for Air*, 1939; *The Lion and the Unicorn*, 1941; *Animal Farm*, 1945; *1984*, 1948.

SARA PARETSKY
(1947 –   )

Indemnity Only, 1982; *Deadlock*, 1984; *Killing Orders*, 1985; *Bitter Medicine*, 1987; *Blood Shot*, 1989; *Burn Marks*, 1990; *Guardian Angel*, 1991.

ROBERT B. PARKER
(1925 –   )

The Godwulf Manuscript, 1973; *God Save the Child*, 1974; *Mortal Stakes*, 1975; *Promised Land*, 1976; *The Judas Goat*, 1978; *Early Autumn*, 1981; *Ceremony*, 1982; *Taming a Sea-Horse*, 1986; (with Raymond Chandler) *Poodle Springs*, 1989.

EDGAR ALLAN POE
(1809–1849)

Tales, by Edgar A. Poe, 1845.

BILL PRONZINI
(1943 –   )

The Snatch, 1971; *Undercurrent*, 1973; *Twospot*, 1978; *Hoodwink*, 1981; *Dragonfire*, 1982; *Scattershot*, 1982; (with Marcia Muller) *Double*, 1984 and *Beyond The Grave*, 1986.

**THOMAS PYNCHON
(1937 –   )**

V., 1963; *The Crying of Lot 49*, 1966; *Gravity's Rainbow*, 1973.

**ELLERY QUEEN [FREDERICK
DANNAY (1905–1982) and MANFRED
B. LEE] (a.k.a. BARNABY ROSS)
(1905–1971)**

The Roman Hat Mystery, 1929; [as Barnaby Ross] *The Tragedy of X*, 1932; [as Barnaby Ross] *The Tragedy of Y*, 1932, *The Player on The Other Side*, 1963. [And see under S. S. Van Dine, p. 587] *The Dutch Shoe Mystery*, 1931; *The Egyptian Cross Mystery*, 1932; *The Greek Coffin Mystery*, 1932; [as Barnaby Ross] *Drury Lane's Last Case*, 1933; *The Chinese Orange Mystery*, 1934; *Halfway House*, 1936.

**RUTH RENDELL (a.k.a. BARBARA
VINE)
(1930 –   )**

From Doon with Death, 1965; *The Best Man to Die*, 1970; *A Guilty Thing Surprised*, 1970; *Murder Being Once Done*, 1972; *No More Dying Then*, 1972; *Some Lie and Some Die*, 1973; *The Face of Trespass*, 1974; *Shake Hands for Ever*, 1975; *A Demon in My View*, 1976; *A Judgement in Stone*, 1978; *A Sleeping Life*, 1978; *Master of the Moor*, 1982; *An Unkindness of Ravens*, 1985; [as Barbara Vine] *A Dark-Adapted Eye*, 1986; *Live Flesh*, 1986; [as Barbara Vine] *A Fatal Inversion*, 1987; *Talking to Strange Men*, 1987; *The Veiled One*, 1989.

**MARY ROBERTS RINEHART
(1876–1958)**

The Circular Staircase, 1908; *The Man in Lower 10*, 1909; *The Wall*, 1928; *Miss Pinkerton*, 1932; *The Album*, 1933; *The Great Mistake*, 1940; *The Yellow Room*, 1945.

**DOROTHY L. SAYERS
(1893–1957)**

Strong Poison, 1930; *Have His Carcase*, 1932; *Murder Must Advertise*, 1933; *The Nine Tai-*

lors, 1934; *Gaudy Night*, 1936; *Busman's Honeymoon*, 1937.

**GEORGES SIMENON
(1903–1989)**

A Battle of Nerves, 1931; *Maigret and the Enigmatic Letter*, 1933 [*The Story of Peter the Lett*]; *Maigret at the Coroner's*, 1949; *Maigret Has Scruples*, 1951; *Sunday*, 1960; *Maigret in Exile*, 1982; *Maigret and the Burglar's Wife*, 1991.

**MAJ SJÖWALL
(1935 –   )
and PER WAHLÖÖ
(1926–1975)**

(by Wahlöö only) *Murder on The Thirty-First Floor*, 1966; *Roseanna*, 1967; *The Man on the Balcony*, 1968; *The Man Who Went up in Smoke*, 1969; *The Laughing Policeman*, 1970; (by Wahlöö only) *The Steel Spring*, 1970; *The Fire Engine That Disappeared*, 1971; *Murder at the Savoy*, 1971; *The Abominable Man*, 1972; *The Locked Room*, 1973; *The Generals*, 1974; *Cop Killer*, 1975.

**REX STOUT
(1886–1975)**

Fer-de-Lance, 1934; *The League of Frightened Men*, 1935; *The Red Box*, 1937; *Some Buried Caesar*, 1939; *The Silent Speaker*, 1946; *The Second Confession*, 1949; *The Doorbell Rang*, 1965.

**ARKADI
(1925 –   )
and BORIS STRUGATSKY
(1933 –   )**

Hard to Be a God, 1973; *The Final Circle of Paradise*, 1976; *Definitely Maybe: A Manuscript Discovered under Unusual Circumstances*, 1977; *Roadside Picnic; Tale of the Troika*, 1977; *The Ugly Swans*, 1979; *The Time Wanderers*, 1987; *Memoirs Found in a Bathtub*, n.d.

THEODORE STURGEON
(1918 –   )

"The Ether Breather," 1939, "It," 1940 (in *Not without Sorcery*, 1940 [s]); "Derm Fool," 1940 (in *Starshine[s]*); "He Shuttles," April 1940 (in *Unknown*); *More Than Human*, 1953; *The Cosmic Rape*, 1958; *Venus Plus X*, 1960; *Sturgeon Is Alive and Well*, 1971 (s); *A God in the Garden*, n.d.

JOSEPHINE TEY [ELIZABETH MACKINTOSH] (a.k.a. GORDON DAVIOT)
(1897–1952)

The Man in the Queue, 1929; *Richard of Bordeaux*, 1933 (d); *Miss Pym Disposes*, 1948; *The Franchise Affair*, 1949; *Come and Kill Me*, 1950 [*Brat Farrar*, 1949]; *To Love and Be Wise*, 1951; *The Daughter of Time*, 1952.

J. R. R. TOLKIEN
(1892–1973)

The Hobbit, 1937; *The Lord of the Rings*, 1954–55.

MARK TWAIN [SAMUEL L. CLEMENS]
(1835–1910)

Tom Sawyer, 1876; *Life on the Mississippi*, 1883; *Huckleberry Finn*, 1884; *A Connecticut Yankee in King Arthur's Court*, 1889; *The Tragedy of Pudd'nhead Wilson*, 1894; *Tom Sawyer, Detective*, 1896.

S. S. VAN DINE [WILLARD HUNTINGTON WRIGHT]
(1888–1939)

The Benson Murder Case, 1926; *The "Canary" Murder Case*, 1927; *The Greene Murder Case*, 1928; *The Bishop Murder Case*, 1929; *The Dragon Murder Case*, 1933; *The Garden Murder Case*, 1935; *The Kidnap Murder Case*, 1936; *The Gracie Allen Murder Case*, 1938; *The Winter Murder Case*, 1939.

JULES VERNE
(1828–1905)

[EDITOR'S NOTE: Jules Verne was such a prolific and popular writer that it is difficult to determine accurate titles and publishing dates not only because some of his novels were published under several different titles but because nineteenth-century books did not always include publication dates. In addition, some American translations were pirated from European editions using deliberately altered titles. In the following list only the most popular of Verne's works mentioned are verified; dateless titles are included in alphabetical order.] *A Journey to the Center of the Earth*, 1864; *From the Earth to the Moon*, 1865; *Five Weeks in a Balloon*, 1869; *Around the World in Eighty Days*, 1873; *Twenty Thousand Leagues under the Sea*, 1873; *The Adventures of Captain Hatteras*, 1876; *The Begum's Fortune*, 1880; *For the Flag*, 1897; *The Danube Pilot*; *A Drama in Livland*; *A Journey to the Moon*; *Sandorf*; *Robur the Conqueror*.

KURT VONNEGUT, JR.
(1922 –   )

Player Piano, 1952; *The Sirens of Titan*, 1959; *Cat's Cradle*, 1963; *God Bless You, Mr. Rosewater*, 1965; *Welcome to the Monkey House*, 1968 (s); *Slaughterhouse-Five, or the Children's Crusade*, 1969; *Breakfast of Champions*, 1973; *Slapstick*, 1976; *Mother Night*, 1988.

HILLARY WAUGH
(1920 –   )

Last Seen Wearing, 1952; *Road Block*, 1960; *The Night It Rained*, 1961; *The Late Mrs. D.*, 1962; *Prisoner's Plea*, 1963; *The Triumvirate*, 1966; *Pure Poison*, 1967; *The Con Game*, 1968; *"30" Manhattan East*, 1968; *The Young Prey*, 1969.

H. G. WELLS
(1866–1946)

The Time Machine, The Stolen Bacillus and Other Incidents, 1895; *The Island of Dr. Mo-*

reau, 1896; *The Invisible Man*, 1897; *The Plattner Story and Others*, 1897 (s); *The War of the Worlds*, 1898; *When the Sleeper Wakes*, 1899; *The First Men in the Moon*, 1901; *The War in the Air*, 1908; *The World Set Free*, 1914.

**DONALD E. WESTLAKE (a.k.a.
RICHARD STARK and TUCKER COE)
(1933 –   )**

The Fugitive Pigeon, 1965; *The Spy in the Ointment*, 1966; *God Save The Mark*, 1967; *The Hot Rock*, 1970; *Bank Shot*, 1972; *Jimmy the Kid*, 1974; *Brothers Keepers*, 1975; *Nobody's Perfect*, 1977; *Why Me?* 1983; *Good Behavior*, 1986; *Trust Me on This*, 1990.

**PHYLLIS A. WHITNEY
(1903 –   )**

Red Is for Murder, 1943; *The Quicksilver Pool*, 1955; *Skye Cameron*, 1957; *The Moonflower*, 1958; *Thunder Heights*, 1960; *Blue Fire*, 1961; *Black Amber*, 1964; *Columbella*, 1966; *Hunter's Green*, 1968; *Listen for the Whisperer*, 1972; *Rainsong*, 1984; *Dream of Orchids*, 1985; *Flaming Tree*, 1986.

COPYRIGHT ACKNOWLEDGMENTS

reau, 1896; *The Invisible Man*, 1897; *The Plattner Story and Others*, 1897 (s); *The War of the Worlds*, 1898; *When the Sleeper Wakes*, 1899; *The First Men in the Moon*, 1901; *The War in the Air*, 1908; *The World Set Free*, 1914.

DONALD E. WESTLAKE (a.k.a. RICHARD STARK and TUCKER COE) (1933 –   )

The Fugitive Pigeon, 1965; *The Spy in the Ointment*, 1966; *God Save The Mark*, 1967; *The Hot Rock*, 1970; *Bank Shot*, 1972; *Jimmy the Kid*, 1974; *Brothers Keepers*, 1975; *Nobody's Perfect*, 1977; *Why Me?* 1983; *Good Behavior*, 1986; *Trust Me on This*, 1990.

PHYLLIS A. WHITNEY (1903 –   )

Red Is for Murder, 1943; *The Quicksilver Pool*, 1955; *Skye Cameron*, 1957; *The Moon-flower*, 1958; *Thunder Heights*, 1960; *Blue Fire*, 1961; *Black Amber*, 1964; *Columbella*, 1966; *Hunter's Green*, 1968; *Listen for the Whisperer*, 1972; *Rainsong*, 1984; *Dream of Orchids*, 1985; *Flaming Tree*, 1986.

COPYRIGHT ACKNOWLEDGMENTS

The editor and publisher are grateful to individuals, literary agencies, periodicals, newspapers, and publishers for permission to include copyrighted material. Every effort has been made to trace and acknowledge all copyright owners. If an acknowledgment has been inadvertently omitted, the necessary correction will be made in the next printing.

AMERICA PRESS. For excerpt from article on Frank Herbert, "Children of Dune" in *America*. Reprinted with permission of America Press, Inc. 106 West 56th Street, NY, NY 10019 © 1976 All Rights Reserved.

ARIZONA QUARTERLY. For excerpt from article on Anthony Burgess. Copyright © 1963 by Arizona Board of Regents.

ARKHAM HOUSE PUBLISHERS. For excerpts from essay by H. P. Lovecraft on Edgar Allan Poe in *Supernatural Horror in Literature*. Reprinted by permission of Arkham House Publishers, Inc., Sauk City, WI.

THE ARMCHAIR DETECTIVE. For excerpts from articles by William White on Robert Barnard; Mattie Gustafson on Robert Barnard; John Kovaleski on Simon Brett; Carl A. Melton on Simon Brett; Donald A. Yates on John Dickson Carr; J. M. Purcell on Amanda Cross; Marvin Lachman on Erle Stanley Gardner; Allen J. Hubin on Michael Gilbert; Robert Randisi on Elmore Leonard; Bernard A. Drew on Ed McBain; Charles Shibuk on Ross Macdonald; Jacques Barzun and Wendell Hertig Taylor on Margaret Millar; Bernard A. Drew on Marcia Muller; Jacques Barzun and W. H. Taylor on Sara Paretsky; John Kovaleski on Robert B. Parker; Charles Shibuk on Ellery Queen; Jane S. Bakerman on Ruth Rendell; Doug Simpson on Ruth Rendell; Charles Shibuk on Mary Roberts Rinehart; Allen J. Hubin on Donald E. Westlake; Erika Holzer on Phyllis A. Whitney. Reprinted by permission of *The Armchair Detective*, 129 West 56th Street, New York, NY 10019.

ASSOCIATED UNIVERSITY PRESSES. For excerpts from *ALDOUS HUXLEY: A Critical Study* by Lawrence Brander; published by Bucknell University Press.

THE ATLANTIC. For excerpts from article by D. C. Russell on Raymond Chandler, as originally published in *The Atlantic*, March, 1945, © 1945 by the author; Oscar Handlin on Dashiell Hammett in *The Atlantic*, July, 1966, © 1966 by the author; Melvin Maddockson on Thomas Pynchon in *The Atlantic*, March 1973, © 1973 by the author; Raymond Chandler on Dorothy L. Sayers in *The Atlantic*, December, 1944, © 1944 by the author; Charles Nicol on Kurt Vonnegut, Jr. in *The Atlantic*, September 1968, © 1968 by the author. Reprinted with permission of *The Atlantic*.

from an essay by Roger Sale. Reprinted by permission from *The Hudson Review,* vol. XIX, no. 1 (Spring 1986). Copyright © 1966 by The Hudson Review, Inc. For an excerpt from "Fiction Chronicle" by Joyce Carol Oates. Reprinted by permission from *The Hudson Review,* vol. XXII, no. 3 (Autumn 1969). Copyright © 1969 by The Hudson Review, Inc.

INDIANA UNIVERSITY PRESS. For permission to reprint an excerpt from Charles M. Holmes, *Aldous Huxley and the Way to Reality.* Copyright ©1970. Reprinted by permission of the publisher.

JOURNAL OF AMERICAN STUDIES. For excerpt by John S. Whitley on Dashiell Hammett in *Journal of American Studies,* December 1980. Reprinted by permission of Cambridge University Press.

JOURNAL OF POPULAR CULTURE. For excerpts by Stephen Dimeo on Ray Bradbury, Spring 1972; Ronald Lee Consler on Robert A. Heinlein, Spring 1972; Francis M. Nevins, Jr., on Rex Stout, Summer 1969. Reprinted by permission of the *Journal of Popular Culture.*

KENT STATE UNIVERSITY PRESS. For permission to reprint excerpts from the following articles in *Extrapolition:* Diane Speer on Robert A. Heinlein, December 1970; Dennis E. Showalter on Robert A. Heinlein, May 1975; Elizabeth Ann Hull on Robert A. Heinlein, Spring 1979; Leon E. Stover on Frank Herbert, May 1976; Dena C. Bain on Ursula K. Le Guin, Fall 1980; and Donald M. Hassler on Theodore Sturgeon, Summer 1979. Reprinted by permission of The Kent State University Press.

KLIATT YOUNG ADULT PAPERBACK GUIDE. For permission to reprint excerpts from articles by H. Sue Hurwitz on Piers Anthony, September 1980 and Sister Avila Lamb on Piers Anthony, September 1982. Reprinted by permission.

ALFRED A. KNOPF, INC. For permission to reprint an excerpt from the Introduction by Dorothy L. Sayers to *Trent's Last Case* by E. C. Bentley. Copyright © 1930 by Alfred A. Knopf, Inc. and renewed 1958 by Nicolas Bentley. Reprinted by permission of Alfred A. Knopf, Inc.

LONDON REVIEW OF BOOKS. For permission to reprint excerpts from articles by John Sutherland on Len Deighton, April 1, 1981, pp. 21–22, and Douglas Johnson on Ruth Rendell, March 3, 1985, p. 23. Reprinted by permission.

JOHN McALEER. For permission to reprint excerpts from *REX STOUT: A Biography,* pp. xv–xvi and pp. 5–9 (Boston, Little Brown, 1977). Reprinted by permission of John McAleer.

MACLEAN'S. For permission to reprint an excerpt from an article by Anne Collins on Stephen King, *Maclean's,* December 18, 1978, p. 51. Reprinted by permission.

MACMILLAN PUBLISHING COMPANY. For excerpts from *STEPHEN KING: The First Decade, "Carrie" to "Pet Sematary"* by Joseph Reino. Copyright © 1988 by G. K. Hall & Co. Reprinted with permission of Twayne Publishers, an imprint of Macmillan Publishing Company. For excerpts from *DAPHNE DE MAURIER* by Richard Kelly. Copyright © 1987 by G. K. Hall & Co. Reprinted with permission of Twayne Publishers, an imprint of Macmillan Publishing Company. For excerpts from *EDGAR ALLAN POE,* Second

9/15/54. Copyright © 1950/51/52/54/63/65/73/74/90/91/92 by The New York Times Company. Reprinted by permission.

VICTORIA NICHOLS & SUSAN THOMPSON. For excerpts from *SILK STALKINGS: When Women Write of Murder* by Victoria Nichols and Susan Thompson. Copyright © 1988 Creative Arts Book Co./Black Lizard Books. Reprinted by permission of Victoria Nichols and Susan Thompson.

OHIO UNIVERSITY PRESS. For excerpt from an essay by T. O. Mabbott in S. T. Joshi, ed., *H. P. LOVECRAFT: Four Decades of Criticism* (Athens, Ohio, 1980). Reprinted by permission of the publisher.

PENGUIN USA. For excerpt from *THE LIFE OF RAYMOND CHANDLER* by Frank MacShane. Copyright © 1976 by Frank MacShane. Used by permission of the publisher, Dutton, an imprint of New American Library, a division of Penguin Books USA Inc.

PETERS FRASER & DUNLOP. For excerpt from essay on Dorothy Salisbury Davis by J. R. F. Keating in *WHODUNIT?: A Guide to Crime, Suspense, and Spy Fiction* (New York: Van Nostrand Reinhold, 1982). Reprinted by permission of Peters Fraser & Dunlop.

POPULAR PRESS. For excerpts from articles by Steven R. Carter on Amanda Cross, Nancy Joiner on P. D. James, Earl F. Bargainner on Ngaio Marsh, John M. Reilly on Margaret Millar, Jane S. Bakerman on Ruth Rendell, Jan Cohn on Mary Roberts Rinehart, Nancy Ellen Talburt on Josephine Tey, and Kathleen Gregory Klein on Dorothy L. Sayers in *10 WOMEN OF MYSTERY* edited by Earl F. Bargainner (Bowling Green: Popular Press, 1981). Excerpt from an article by Nancy Joiner on P. D. James, pp. 154–56, in *VOICES FOR THE FUTURE: Essays on Major S. F. Writers* edited by Thomas D. Clareson (Bowling Green: Popular Press, 1979). Excerpts from articles by Brian Aldiss on J. G. Ballard, Rudolf B. Schmerl on Aldous Huxley, and Patrick Callahan on C. S. Lewis in *SCIENCE FICTION: The Other Side of Realism—Essays on Modern Fantasy and Science Fiction* edited by Thomas D. Clareson (Bowling Green: Popular Press, 1971). Excerpts from articles by Earl F. Bargainner on Simon Brett and George N. Dove on Michael Gilbert in *TWELVE ENGLISHMEN OF MYSTERY* edited by Earl F. Bargainner (Bowling Green: Popular Press, 1984). Excerpts from *WATTEAU'S SHEPHERDS: The Detective Novel in Britain 1914–1940* by LeRoy Lad Panek, (Bowling Green, Popular Press, 1979). Excerpts from *BEAMS FALLING: The Art of Dashiell Hammett* by Peter Wolfe (Bowling Green: Popular Press, 1980). Excerpts from *SCIENCE FICTION AND THE NEW DARK AGE* by Harold L. Berger (Bowling Green, Popular Press, 1976). Excerpts from *PRIVATE EYES: One Hundred and One Knights* by Robert A. Baker and Michael T. Nietzel (Bowling Green: Popular Press, 1985). Excerpts from *ROYAL BLOODLINES: Ellery Queen, Author and Detective* by Francis M. Nevins, Jr. (Bowling Green, Popular Press, 1973). All reprinted by permission of Popular Press.

PRINCETON UNIVERSITY PRESS. For excerpt from *THE NOVELS OF HERMANN HESSE* by Theodore Ziolkowski, pp. 341–60. Copyright © 1965 Princeton University Press. Reprinted by permission of Princeton University Press.

SOUTHERN ILLINOIS UNIVERSITY PRESS. For excerpts from articles by Joyce Carol Oates on James M. Cain (pp. 110–28), Herbert Ruhm on Raymond Chandler (pp. 171–85), and Robert I. Edenbaum on Dashiell Hammett (p. 81) in *TOUGH GUY WRITERS OF THE THIRTIES* edited by David Madden. Copyright © 1968 Southern Illinois University Press. Reprinted with permission.

THE SPECTATOR. For excerpts from articles by Anthony Lejeune on Agatha Christie, 9/19/70, p. 294; Pat Rogers on Daphne Du Maurier, 7/31/76, p. 20; on Patricia Highsmith, 3/23/74, p. 366; John Welcome on P. D. James, 12/23/72, p. 1011; Norman St. John Stevas on C. S. Lewis, 7/20/74, p. 85; David Hare on Ngaio Marsh, 12/12/70, pp. 772–73; on Ngaio Marsh 5/4/74, p. 550; W. H. Auden on George Orwell, 1/16/71, pp. 86–87; and William Golding on Jules Verne, 6/9/61, of *The Spectator*. Published with permission of *The Spectator*.

JANE SPITZER. For excerpt from her article on Phyllis A. Whitney in the 4/6/84 issue of *The Christian Science Monitor*. Reprinted with permission of Jane Spitzer.

STERLING LORD LITERISTIC, INC. For excerpt on H. G. Wells from *The Living Novel* by V. S. Pritchett. Copyright © 1947 by V. S. Pritchett. Reprinted by permission of Sterling Lord Literistic, Inc.

STUDIES IN SHORT FICTION. For excerpt from an article by William Peden on Chester Himes, "The Black Explosion" (pp. 234–35) in *Studies in Short Fiction 12* (1975). Copyright © 1975 by Newberry College. Reprinted with permission.

TIME INC. For excerpt from the article "Dame Agatha: Queen of the Maze," p. 75 in the January 26,1976, issue of *TIME* magazine. Copyright © 1976 by Time Inc. For excerpt from the article "Future Grok," pp. 86–87 in the March 29, 1971, issue of *TIME* magazine. Copyright © 1971 Time Inc. Reprinted with permission.

TIMES NEWSPAPERS LIMITED. For excerpt on Per Wahlöö and Maj Sjöwall by Alan Brownjohn, *Times Literary Supplement,* 19 April 1974. Copyright © Times Supplements Ltd. 1974. For excerpt from review on Douglas Adams by Philip Howard, *The Times,* July 2, 1981. Copyright © The Times, 1981. For excerpt from review on Douglas Adams by Tom Hutchinson, *The Times,* September 9, 1982. Copyright © The Times, 1982.

UNIVERSITY OF CHICAGO PRESS. For excerpts from essay on Eric Ambler, pp. 123–24, in *THE SPY STORY* by John C. Cawelti and Bruce A. Rosenberg. Copyright © 1987 The University of Chicago Press. Reprinted by permission.

UNIVERSITY OF ILLINOIS PRESS. For excerpts from essays on Erle Stanley Gardner, pp. 191–93, on Sue Grafton, pp. 203–5, and on Marcia Muller, pp. 206–9 in *WOMAN DETECTIVE* by Kathleen Klein. Copyright © 1989 The University of Illinois Press. Reprinted by permission.

UNIVERSITY OF MICHICAN PRESS. For excerpt from *A RAGE FOR ORDER* by Austin Warren. Copyright © by the University of Michigan. Renewed 1975 by Austin Warren. Published by the University of Michigan Press. Reprinted by permission.

INDEX TO CRITICS

Names of critics are cited on the pages given.